Frank Bates

The Trace of Burning Stars

Law, Poetry and Rhetoric

LAP LAMBERT Academic Publishing

Impressum / Imprint
Bibliografische Information der Deutschen Nationalbibliothek: Die Deutsche Nationalbibliothek verzeichnet diese Publikation in der Deutschen Nationalbibliografie; detaillierte bibliografische Daten sind im Internet über http://dnb.d-nb.de abrufbar.
Alle in diesem Buch genannten Marken und Produktnamen unterliegen warenzeichen-, marken- oder patentrechtlichem Schutz bzw. sind Warenzeichen oder eingetragene Warenzeichen der jeweiligen Inhaber. Die Wiedergabe von Marken, Produktnamen, Gebrauchsnamen, Handelsnamen, Warenbezeichnungen u.s.w. in diesem Werk berechtigt auch ohne besondere Kennzeichnung nicht zu der Annahme, dass solche Namen im Sinne der Warenzeichen- und Markenschutzgesetzgebung als frei zu betrachten wären und daher von jedermann benutzt werden dürften.

Bibliographic information published by the Deutsche Nationalbibliothek: The Deutsche Nationalbibliothek lists this publication in the Deutsche Nationalbibliografie; detailed bibliographic data are available in the Internet at http://dnb.d-nb.de.
Any brand names and product names mentioned in this book are subject to trademark, brand or patent protection and are trademarks or registered trademarks of their respective holders. The use of brand names, product names, common names, trade names, product descriptions etc. even without a particular marking in this works is in no way to be construed to mean that such names may be regarded as unrestricted in respect of trademark and brand protection legislation and could thus be used by anyone.

Coverbild / Cover image: www.ingimage.com

Verlag / Publisher:
LAP LAMBERT Academic Publishing
ist ein Imprint der / is a trademark of
OmniScriptum GmbH & Co. KG
Heinrich-Böcking-Str. 6-8, 66121 Saarbrücken, Deutschland / Germany
Email: info@lap-publishing.com

Herstellung: siehe letzte Seite /
Printed at: see last page
ISBN: 978-3-659-41740-5

Copyright © 2013 OmniScriptum GmbH & Co. KG
Alle Rechte vorbehalten. / All rights reserved. Saarbrücken 2013

**To the
Eternal Memory
of
Margaret Daphne Scott
(1934-2005)**

Here were fond climates and sweet singers suddenly
Come in the morning where I wandered and listened
To the rain wringing
Wind blow cold
In the wood faraway under me.

Dylan Thomas "Poem in October"

The sombre pages bore no print
Except the trace of burning stars
In the frosty heaven.

Wallace Stevens, "The Reader" in *Ideas of Order* (1936).

Perhaps the most worthwhile lessons I have learned are the scholarly ones. First, that disciplinary divisions are not barriers. If they are, they are not well guarded. They are doors which cannot withstand the temptation to open them, as full of wonder though perhaps as potentially lethal, as those to Bluebeard's castle. Secondly, that the joys and treasures of comparison are endless. Thirdly, that one can never have enough tools, whether of languages or other professional skills, to do the job as thoroughly as one would like. But, fourthly, one must get stuck in. Even if you know you are going to be out of your depth, that is no excuse for not having a go and doing your best. It would be insufferable arrogance not to have faith in others to see your errors and make something of your failures. You just have to try to make it worth their while.

Derek Roebuck, *Disputes and Differences: Comparisons in Law, Language and History* (2010)

Table of Contents

Table of Contents iii
Preface and Acknowledgements 1
Chapter I Law and Literature: A Self-Justification 5
Chapter II Poetry, Rhetoric & Law: The Sound and the Fury 86
   1. Introductory Comments 86
   2. Poetic Images 91
   3. The Nature Of Rhetoric 103
   4. Poems In Court 113
Chapter III Aspects of Rhetoric 143
   1. The Rhetoric of War 143
      a) The Anticipation of War 143
      b) The Conduct of War 166
      c) The Aftermath of War 176
   2. Rhetoric in Other Contexts 203
      a) Generally 203
      b) Animals and their Welfare 207
      c) The Rhetoric of Religion 227
Chapter IV The Writer in the Law and the Law in the Writer 248
   1. Introductory 248
   2. The Writer in the Law: The Case of D H Lawrence 253
      a) Lawrence and the Literary/Censorship Laws 253
      b. Lawrence in the Public Law Area 268
   3. The Law in the Writer: The Strange Case of A C Swinburne 281
   4. Some Concluding Thoughts 296
Chapter V Crime and Retribution 308
   1. Introductory : Divine Retribution...? 308
   2. Aspects of Formal Retribution 335
   3. Crime and Consequence 348
   4. Other Consequences 362
   5. A Concluding Reflection 385
Chapter VI Love, Pain, Marriage and the Whole... 396
   1. An Overview 396
   2. An Intriguing and Illustrative Case 410
   3. Love's Aftermath 444
Chapter VII Accidents, Neighbours and other Nuisances 478

1.	Accidents	478
2.	Disputes Between Neighbours	518
3.	Privacy, Rights and Relationships	530

Chapter VIII Concluding Reflections 575
Bibliography 601
Table of Cases 615
Index 622

Preface and Acknowledgements

The genesis of this book lay in a collection of teaching materials which I prepared for use in a course on *Law and Literature* which I taught in the Fall Semester 2008 at the Law School of St Mary's University in San Antonio, Texas. I must, accordingly, thank Associate Dean Michael Ariens for suggesting that I teach that course. I am also happy to thank Dean Charles E Cantu and other faculty members of that Law School for making my time there so productive and pleasant.

Throughout this book, I endeavour, as I did in the original course, to bring attention to the original sources and texts, both in Law and Poetry, and to draw attention to the Rhetoric which brings the two areas together. This, inevitably, has meant that, in addition to my own thoughts and comments on the poems and cases, other critical and explicatory writings are themselves analysed, contextualised and related to one another and their subjects. Although, at first glance, Law and Poetry may appear to be a strange combination on which to write a monograph, it is derived from my deeply and seriously held belief that both are major objects of humane study. It is to fall into most serious error, I suggest, to regard the study of law, at whatever level, as simply a training for a particular occupation, particularly as practiced in suburbia. Its context - either social or, more broadly, humane - is invariably and permanently with us. Similarly, it is equally as wrong to dismiss poetry as ephemeral or dilettante: one must always bear the comments of the United States poet Josephine Jacobson (1908-2003) in mind. Poetry, she says, is like walking along, "...a narrow ridge up on a precipice. You never know the next step, whether there's going to be a plunge. I think poetry is dangerous, there's nothing mild and predictable about poetry." As the text will, I hope, show much the same can legitimately be said of many areas of legal activity. In other words, although certainty and predictability are desirable qualities for the law to possess, they are not invariably achieved and may, indeed, not be achievable. In essence, throughout this book, I have sought to examine the responses of both the law and poetry to various aspects of the human condition: war, relationships (of one kind or another), anti-social activities and societal response and so on. In addition, I have attempted to examine the moral and societal issues which emerge from the relationship between law and poetry.

This is, of course, a significant undertaking and I could not have attempted it without assistance from a variety of people. My major debt is, particularly, due to D Ronan McGinty whose influence on, especially, the first part of Chapter IV is notably apparent. Dr McGinty is a scholar of D H Lawrence, particularly of his poetic works. In addition to Chapter IV, where his influence can be found in various ways throughout the discussion of Lawrence's dealings with various aspects of the law at difficult times, Dr McGinty provided considerable help in the preparation of the original course materials. In so doing, Dr McGinty proved remarkably helpful in planning what was to be the framework of the course at St Mary's Law School.

Inevitably, though, despite Ronan's major contributions, other people have provided help of various kinds. First, an extremely experienced legal practitioner, both in New Zealand and Australia, Laurie O'Brien, has, over a period of some years, passed the benefit of his wide experience and knowledge in the law, music and humanities to me for which I am most grateful. There is much of his deep thought and analytical skills to be found in this book. The same can be said of Ross Morgan, a wise and experienced teacher of English in New South Wales. Ross has made a very substantial contribution to the many informal discussions which are part of the creation of an interdisciplinary book of this nature.

Over the years which I have spent in academic life there have, of course, been many people – some living, though others, sadly not – who have made numerous indirect contributions to *The Trace of Burning Stars*. In Newcastle, apart from Ronan, Laurie and Ross, three stand out: Professors Barry Gordon, Norman Talbot and Godfrey Tanner. I could learn more that was valuable in an hour in their company than in ten times that time in more formal meetings. In Tasmania, Derek Roebuck and Norman Palmer provided , and so continue to provide, wit and inspiration. But, there, I owe a particular debt to the late Michael and Margaret Scott, whose joint and several learning, experience and generosity of spirit represented much worth remembering and appreciating from my time there. This book is dedicated to the memory of an exceptional person: poet, writer, teacher and scholar – Margaret Daphne Scott (1934 – 2005).

Before my own career as a University teacher and researcher, there was one major influence on my attitude to literature and its relationship with the human (or legal) condition. He was Larry Watson, English teacher at the Royal Grammar School, Newcastle upon Tyne. He genuinely created my interest in poetry by his inspirational teaching, in 1960. His role in my creative life is ongoing.

Closer to my present home, Deb Willett typed the manuscript. Michael Guihot provided invaluable assistance at the proof stage. Other colleagues helped in various ways, by suggesting poems and cases for discussion. My wife, Mary Howard,and to Anthea Sims who prepared the book for publication as well as the various tables. After all of that, the major responsibility is mine alone, though I should also thank Ted Wright, Dean of the Newcastle Law School, and Stephen Nicholas, former Pro Vice Chancellor for Business and Law at the University of Newcastle, for encouragement and assistance.

Frank Bates

Newcastle (NSW)

September 2012.

Chapter I
Law and Literature: A Self-Justification.

On various levels, there is little doubt that Law and Literature are mutually involved: many well known works of literature are concerned with legal matters – such, for example, as *Bleak House* and *Little Dorritt* by Charles Dickens are concerned with the operation of the machinery of the Court of Chancery during the Nineteenth Century in England. *To Kill a Mockingbird* by Harper Lee deals directly with the operation of the criminal justice system in the Southern States of the United States of America in the Twentieth Century. Inevitably, rather than incidentally, these novels raise important and central issues relating to morality, of one sort or another, and personal and financial relationships of various kinds.

On the other hand, the factual situations which have given rise to legal involvement are often of such a nature that they could very well provide the basis for works of literature and some of these cases will be discussed at various points later in this book.[1] Of course, they may coincidentally come to be entangled. Thus, a late friend of the author obtained his first academic position at a university in a southern United States jurisdiction and was having not a little difficulty in finding accommodation. Finally, he persuaded a lady to let him accommodation, which she did not a little grudgingly. "All right Professor," she said, "I will rent you a room on the sole condition that you bring no alcohol nor novels by William Faulkner into this house."

However, coincidence, however risible, should not be used as a justification for suggesting that the study of law and literature is of intrinsic value and is worthwhile. This issue has been explored by the English writer Ward[2] who has drawn, in so doing, on United States writing in the area. Ward's view, as well as the thoughts from which he has partly derived inspiration, are of significance in both philosophical and pedagogical terms.

In particular, Cook has agreed[3] that better methods of teaching law might be found than the traditional North American Law School methods created, initially, by Dean Christopher Columbus Langdell of the Harvard Law School. As the eminent International Private Law scholar,[4] Cavers described[5] the situation, "Dean Langdell rebelled against the doctrinaire lecturing that was typical of the law schools of the day. He insisted that the decisions of the courts were the true materials of legal science in a common law system. Accordingly, he decided to focus legal instruction upon judicial opinions. For his course in the law of contracts, he brought together in one volume a selection of leading opinions of English and American courts in contract cases, presenting these in a logical sequence that was to be followed in the classroom." Cavers continues by suggesting that students, in consequence of the teaching methodology derived from this approach,[6] must grow adept in analysing, composing, evaluating and projecting, "… the lines of judicial decisions and legislation which have been developed in those fifty social laboratories, the states." Note will already have been taken of the phrases "legal *science*" and "social *laboratories*" as noted by Cavers, and Cook urges that legal study has become too *scientific* and too prescribed by the methodology described by Cavers.

Although such a view may have much immediately to commend it – and Cavers himself admitted that, because of that very methodology, a student can scarcely gain a precise knowledge of a single body of legal doctrine – the role of literature as a counterbalance must be examined. Cook suggests that legal training itself required the skills which literature itself provides: thus, she argues[7] that literature can provide the student with a real-life situation and so assist in concentrating the student's attention on the realities of case-resolution. At the same time, proponents if the Langdell system, and its variants, would argue that study of a judicial decision could achieve that.[8]

Thus, for example, to derive examples from the area of Equity and Trusts law: in *Nelson v Nelson*,[9] a mother of two children bought, and paid for, a property. However, she transferred it into the names of the children so as to ensure that she would qualify for a defence service loan on a further property which she was purchasing. Such a loan would not have been available had she already held property in her name.[10] It was found as a fact that the mother had no intention of conferring any beneficial interest in the property to the children and had transferred it into their names solely for the purposes of obtaining the subsidy. It was also held that, owing to the closeness of their relationship, the presumption of advancement[11] arose. In order for the mother to be able successfully to claim her equitable right to the property under a resulting trust,[12] she had to be able to rebut the presumption. However, in order to be so able, the only cause of action open to her was to reveal her illegal purpose, a course which was precluded by the Rule in *Bowmakers Ltd.* v *Barnet Instruments*.[13] Accordingly, the New South Wales Court of Appeal refused to condone the mother's using an illegal purpose for the purpose of rebutting the presumption of advancement. The mother successfully appealed to the High Court of Australia.

First of all, in a joint judgment, Deene and Gummow JJ raised two central factors: first, they pointed[14] out that where the illegality was the creature of statute, but was not directly proscribed, courts must examine the Act's underlying policy. Hence, courts were required to consider whether the particular illegality genuinely contravened that policy. If so, they were required to consider whether that purpose or policy was adequately served through the imposition of any internal penalties. If such were the case, then equitable relief rebutting the presumption of advancement should not be denied, because the intention of the legislature to do so had not manifested itself.

The second factor which was considered by Deane and Gummow JJ related to the nature of the equitable jurisdiction which was involved. In so doing, the judges regarded[15] it as contrary to the range and flexibility of equitable relief to impose absolute principles concerning the assessment of illegal transactions. "[E]quity has not," they stated, "subscribed to any absolute proposition that the consequence of any illegality, particularly where what is involved is contravention of public policy manifested by statute, is that neither side may obtain any relief, so that the matter lies where it falls. Rather, in various instances, equity has taken the view that it may intervene, albeit with the attachment of conditions, lest there be no redress against the fraud nor anybody to ask it."[16]

In essence, the approach adopted by Deane and Gummow JJ was that, as the purpose of the legislation was the provision of public money for selected people, who did not already own property, to buy their own houses, the policy of the Act had been contravened.[17] However, they found that the penalties specified in the Act dealt adequately with the situation which existed in *Nelson*. To put the matter another way, there was nothing to be gained by denying the mother the right to enforce the resulting trust in terms of furthering the aims of the legislation. In addition, Deane and

Gummow JJ regarded the possibility as restricting equitable jurisdiction unnecessarily.

Two other judges in the High Court of Australia, Toohey and McHugh JJ adopted similar approaches. The former emphasised [18] the policy which underpinned the Act and noted that there was no rule either derived from the Act or public policy which would deny relief to the mother in *Nelson*. At the same time, Toohey J suggested [19] that once the realm of public policy was entered, the court came into a *shadowy world*.[20] It was the more shadowy, the judge commented, in the instant situation because, "... Mrs Nelson is not asking the court to enforce a contract but rather to give effect to a resulting trust which would ordinarily arise once the presumption of advancement has been rebutted."

McHugh J laid very considerable emphasis on the scheme of the legislation[21] and commented[22] that, "Federal Parliament saw the legislative sanctions and remedies as being sufficient to deal with unlawful conduct of similar to that which has occurred in the present case. That being so, I can see no justification for the courts imposing a further sanction by refusing to enforce the legal or equitable rights of applicants under the Act, particularly when such a refusal may often result, as it does in this case, in a penalty out of all proportion to the seriousness of an applicant's conduct." At the same time, McHugh J pointed out that equity could not, of course, condone or encourage the mother's unlawful purpose; so far as it was possible, rights associated with, or arising out of, unlawful conduct should only be enforced on the condition that the wrongdoer takes all lawful steps to overcome the consequences of the conduct. "It will," McHugh J continued, "not always be possible for the claimant to do so or for the courts to impose terms designed to remedy the wrongdoing." It may, one might think, not be easy to maintain all of these attitudes simultaneously and satisfactorily. McHugh J sought to do so by his initial emphasis on the scheme of the legislation.

It is, however, with the judgment of Dawson J in *Nelson* that the prior decision of the House of Lords in *Tinsley v Milligan*[23] is thrown into stark relief. In that earlier case, the parties, who were female lovers, jointly purchased a house which was registered in the name of the appellant as the sole owner, even though both had contributed to the purchase. The house was used as a lodging house which was run as a joint business venture which provided most of the parties' income. However, the real purpose of the arrangement was to enable the respondent, with the full knowledge and acquiescence of the appellant, to claim social security benefits. That money was shared, although it did not form a substantial part of the parties' income. Eventually, the respondent confessed her fraud to the Department and, afterwards, continued to draw benefits without prosecution. Subsequently, the parties quarrelled and the appellant moved out, leaving the respondent in occupation. The appellant brought an action for possession of the house and claiming ownership of it. The respondent counterclaimed for an order for sale and a declaration that the house was held by the appellant on trust for the parties in equal shares. In respect of that counterclaim, first, that applying the maxim *ex turpi causa non oritur actio*, the respondent was precluded from denying the appellant's ownership of the house because the 'aim' of the arrangement has been the facilitation of the fraud on the Department of Social Security and, therefore, her claim to joint ownership had been tainted by illegality. Second, that, applying the equitable principle that [s]he who comes to equity must come with clean hands, the court ought to leave the estate to lie where it fell. As the property had been conveyed into the name of one party in those circumstances, the court ought not to enforce a trust in favour of the other party.

The trial judge dismissed the appellant's claim and gave judgment in favour of the respondent on her counterclaim. The appellant appealed to the Court of Appeal which dismissed the appeal on the grounds that, when confronted with the defence of illegality, courts should adopt a flexible and pragmatic approach in applying the *ex turpi causa* and the *clean hands* maxims. They should then determine whether enforcement of the claim, with its attendant illegality, would be an *affront to the public conscience*[24] and that, since both parties had collaborated in the fraud, both their claims being tainted with illegality, it would be a disproportionate penalty to deprive the respondent of her share of the house, it would be such an affront not to grant her relief. The appellant then unsuccessfully appealed to the House of Lords.

Although the House of Lords did dismiss the appeal, they also unanimously rejected the *public conscience* test which had been enunciated in the Court of Appeal. The majority of the House of Lords[25] reverted to the strict principle as found in the *ex turpi causa* maxim and the *Bowmaker* rule.[26] Thus, an illegal transaction might be enforced, but only if the plaintiff could establish title without relying on any illegality. Further, it was immaterial whether the transaction involved was at common law or in equity: in the words of Lord Browne-Wilkinson,[27] "More than 100 years has passed since the administration of law and equity became fused. The reality of the matter is that, in 1993, English law has one single law of property made up of legal and equitable interests. Although, for historical reasons, legal and equitable estates have differing incidents, the person owning either type of estate has a right of property, a right *in rem*, not merely a right *in personam*. If the law is that a party is entitled to enforce property right acquired under an illegal transaction, in my judgment the same rule ought to apply to any property right so acquired."

The test applied by Lord Browne-Wilkinson was strict and traditional and was a rejection of the *public conscience* test espoused by the Court of Appeal. "A party to illegality can recover," his Lordship stated,[28] "by virtue of a legal or equitable property interest if, but only if, he can establish his title without relying on his own illegality. In cases where the presumption of advancement applies, the plaintiff is faced with the presumption of gift and therefore cannot claim under a resulting trust unless and until he has rebutted the presumption of gift; for those purposes the plaintiff does have to rely on the underlying illegality and therefore fails." Lord Browne-Wilkinson then sought[29] to apply the principle to the facts of *Tinsley v Milligan:* the respondent, he noted, had established a resulting trust by showing she had contributed to the purchase of the house and that there was a common understanding between the appellant and her that they owned the house equally. She had no need to prove or allege *why*[30] the house was conveyed into the appellant's name alone, because that fact was irrelevant to any claim because it was sufficient to show that the house was vested, in the appellant alone. The illegality only emerged at all because the appellant had sought to raise it. Having proved those facts, the respondent had raised the presumption of a resulting trust, and there being no evidence to rebut it, the respondent should succeed.[31]

Lord Goff agreed with the remainder of the House in rejecting the Court of Appeal's formulation, but he disagreed with the other members of the Court in applying the traditional test to cases involving an equitable interest. Lord Goff's view, essentially, was that the approach should be based on an assessment as to whether the plaintiff came to equity with clean hands. It seems, he said,[32] "... particularly harsh not to assist the respondent to establish her equitable intent in the house where not only was the appellant implicated in precisely the same fraud on the Department of Social Security, but the fraud in question can be regarded as relatively minor and indeed all too prevalent, and the respondent has readily confessed her wrongdoing to the department and has made amends to them. Furthermore, it is probable that, if the appeal should be allowed, the effect will be that she will lose all her capital. But it is not to be forgotten that other cases in this category will not evoke the same sympathy on the part of the court." Lord Goff then went on to postulate instances of such cases: thus, he noted the situation where the fraud had been much more substantial than in the present case and where its discovery was not the result of a voluntary admission but the product of a lengthy investigation and a prolonged criminal trial. Second, there might be instances where a group of, say, terrorists or armed robbers secure a base for their activities by buying a house in the name of a third party who is not directly implicated in those activities. In cases of that kind, no presumption of advancement would arise. "Is it really to be said," Lord Goff asked,[33] "that criminals such as these, or their personal representatives, are entitled to invoke the assistance of a court of equity in order to establish an equitable interest in property? It may be said that these are extreme cases: but I find it difficult to see how, in this context at least, it is possible to distinguish between degrees of iniquity. At all events, I cannot think that the harsh consequences which will arise from the application of the established principle in a case such as the present provide a satisfactory basis for developing the law in a manner which will open the door to far more unmeritorious cases, especially as the proposed development in the law appears to be contrary to the established principle underlying the authorities."

Of course, in the light of the facts of *Tinsley v Milligan* and, indeed, *Nelson*, Lord Goff's remark regarding distinguishing between degrees of iniquity seems to beg the question which he has posed. Both in legal and dramatic terms, if the methodology urged by Lord Goff, as opposed to that offered by Lord Brown-Wilkinson, were to be adopted, then such a distinction must necessarily be made.

A similar point has been made by Lord Millett writing, extra-judicially, commenting on Shakespeare's play *The Merchant of Venice*.[34] Lord Millett chooses[35] to begin his study with the character of Bassanio, who, it seems safe to say, is generally regarded as, at least, one of the heroic characters in one of Shakespeare's most directly orientated plays.[36] "Bassanio" writes Lord Millett, "... is a scoundrel and a wastrel. Having run through his fortune by being (in his own words) 'something too prodigal', he tells his friend, the merchant Antonio, who is also his biggest creditor that he has a scheme which will enable him to 'get clear of all the debts I owe'." The scheme, of course is his suit of the lady Portia, whom he describes as, "a lady richly left." As Lord Millett notes,[37] "What matters to [Bassanio] is her money. She is a prize, not a lover. Everyone's motivation is mercenary." Likewise, Antonio does not come out of Lord Millett's analysis well. As he states,[38] "Antonio despises Shylock because he lends money at interest, a practice which Antonio considers to be usury and contemptible in a gentleman. This is rank hypocrisy. Antonio is in trade himself. He is in the import and export business. He carries on his business for gain, and openly boasts about the large profits which he hopes to make."

In addition to that, less than desirable, pair, Lord Millett's attitude to Portia is instructive because he is at pains, at the beginning of his essay, to emphasise that he was seeking to look at *The Merchant of Venice* from his standpoint as a lawyer and a judge, rather than as a Shakespearean scholar or producer. Lord Millett notes[39] that Portia's cross-examination of Shylock is. "... a superb example of the art. All students of advocacy should study it and note the way in which she cross-examines Shylock. She never descends into the arena or argues with Shylock in the manner of a bad trial lawyer in an American film. She keeps her distance and remains aloof. She remains fully in control throughout, the better to manipulate Shylock. She sets out to win his confidence, while carefully getting him to close off all avenues of escape before springing the trap shut." Those comments are borne out by advice given by Wells, a former judge of the Supreme Court of South Australia, who wrote[40] that, "the right to cross examine gives you opportunities to test opposing witnesses and to supplement or confirm the case made, or to be made, through your own. You will fail to take advantage of these opportunities if you do not, at every stage, bear in mind the immediate aim of the questions you are then asking, and the place you have given them in the strategy of cross-examining the witness then in the box and other witnesses to be called. Moreover, the cross-examinations of previously called witnesses sometimes have a bearing on that strategy. In short, you must know what you are doing; you may do your case irreparable harm if you ask questions at random." Wells goes on to emphasise that, "... most effective work in cross-examination is achieved through an orderly, patient and thorough inquiry, undertaken according to a prepared plan, with definite aims, and by using one or more proven techniques."

Thus, Portia/Balthasar's cross-examination of Shylock would seem to be in accord with traditional practice. However, as Lord Millett properly points out[41], a careful reading of the text, "... yields a darker tale. For Portia is not an advocate. She has no business to be cross-examining Shylock at all. She is not, as the audience might assume, counsel for Antonio. She is the judge; and far from seeking to give a just and impartial verdict, she deliberately sets out to ruin Shylock and makes fraudulent use of the justice system to achieve her purpose." Lord Millett's interpretation is clearly correct for, although the Duke presides over the trial, he does not adjudicate the matter. In order for that to be done, the Duke has sent for Bellario, to do that,[42] but Bellario never appears. Who does appear is Portia, by the time of the trial, married to the adventurer Bassanio, disguised, and with a forged letter, as one Balthasar, a Doctor of Laws.

Lord Millett notes[43] that the Duke's practice was common in Italy at about the time the play was first produced. Italy is, of course, and was, a civil law based jurisdiction[44] with the judge having a role different from that perceived in common law jurisdictions. However, as the great comparatist John Henry Merryman had pointed out in his notable work, *The Civil Law Tradition*[45] the differences may be more apparent than real. Merryman writes that, "Foreign observers are sometimes confused by the fact that, in some civil law nations, questions are put to the witnesses by judges rather than by counsel for the parties. This leads some to the conclusion that the civil law judge determines what questions to ask and, unlike the common law system, in effect determines the scope and extent of the inquiry. People talk about an 'inquisitorial' system of proof-taking as contrasted with the 'adversary' system of the common law. In fact, the prevailing system in both the civil law and the common law world is the 'dispositive' system, according to which the determination of what issues to raise, what evidence to introduce and what argument to make is left almost entirely to the parties. Judges in both traditions have some power to undertake inquiries on their own, but civil law judges rarely exercise this power." That statement by a leading commentator makes the trial scene in *The Merchant of Venice* all the more bizarre and Lord Millett's comments on it all the more apposite. Lord Millett concludes his commentary on that scene in terms which invert traditional perceptions which, as we have seen from Merryman's commentary of judicial roles,[46] are frequently in error. "The villain," states Lord Millett, "is Portia. She is cruel, relentless, cunning, deceitful and (despite her eloquence on the subject) merciless. It is obvious that her judgment cannot possibly stand. She is not an impartial or independent judge, but the wife of the principal debtor. That alone would be enough for any appellate court to set aside her judgment and order a new trial. But it goes much further than that. Portia's conduct is not only partial but fraudulent."

On the question of the relevance of civil law notions and concepts, Merryman notes[47] that, "… a litigant in a civil law jurisdiction has somewhat broader powers of direct attack on a judgment than does a litigant in the common law jurisdictions: he is entitles to an appeal in which he may introduce new evidence in support of his case and in which he is entitled to a new consideration of the facts as well as the law. He may also be entitled to recourse in cassation [France] or revision [Germany] on questions of law." Portia's decision does not look as though it will stand up well before an appellate court with such powers and, even, with Lord Millett as a member!

There is, inevitably, more to *The Merchant of Venice* than the profiteering and deceptions of the gentile bourgeoisie: Shylock's own conduct whereby he delivers himself into the hands of these people cannot be described as generally magnanimous. As Lord Millett himself has pointed out,[48] although Shylock, initially at least, may very well not to have sought to exact the bond of a pound of Antonio's flesh, he was determined to humiliate him by obtaining a public judgment against him and, generously, refrain from enforcing it would prove to be a humiliation of the kind which Antonio would find unbearable as it would put him permanently in Shylock's debt.[49]

At this stage it might legitimately be asked what an apparently eccentric interpretation of a well-known Shakespeare play by someone which does not profess to be a literary scholar has to do with two obliquely connected decisions in equity or with the study of the relationship between the law and literature. The key to all of this lies in Lord Goff's comment regarding degrees of iniquity[50] - unless rigid tests are to be adopted, as Lord Browne-Wilkinson sought to do in *Tinsley v Milligan*,[51] then the evaluation of the nature of conduct (or calculation of degrees of iniquity) is a necessary process if fair and equitable results are to be achieved in situations such as pertained in *Tinsley v Milligan* and *Nelson*. In literary study, the text must be studied appropriately to examine the conduct involved and evaluate it. Lord Millett's acute study of *The Merchant of Venice* shows that perception of conduct and textual reality may not always be congruent. Hence, some readers may, for whatever reason, be unwilling to agree with Lord Millett's evaluative conclusion, derived from Miss Prism's comment in the *Importance of Being Ernest* by Oscar Wilde[52] who states that, "The good ended happily, the bad unhappily. That is what fiction means."

"But", asks Lord Millett after his incisive discussion, "who are the good and who are the bad? If Antonio and his friends are 'the good' and Shylock is 'the bad', then 'the good' are worthless and contemptible and 'the bad' is the one serious character who deserves not merely our pity but our respect. He is the only character with any moral stature."

But, at the same time, in *Tinsley v Milligan*, Lord Goff tells us[53] that the fraud on the Department of Social Security, which was the reason for much of the difficulty and expense which ensued, was relatively minor, if all too prevalent. Yet it is apparent that there are other perceptions of that particular kind of fraud: thus, Cooke discusses[54] the differences in response to frauds committed in relation to taxation and to supplementary benefit in the United Kingdom and she considers that attitudes towards what she describes as the *myth of redistribution*[55] justify different perceptions of the types of fraud she has investigated. "For example," she writes,[56] "it has been argued that the fraudsters may successfully justify their actions in terms of excessive state regulation and penal rates of personal tax. Their 'need' to be economically successful remains unquestioned, their accumulation motive taken for granted." Conversely, those who defraud the Department of Social Security are unable to invoke their main, and real, motivation which is poverty, because, they are perceived as committing their fraud by reason of *greed* rather than *need*. "The attribution of this motive," she states, "derives from concepts of the undeserving poor, coupled with the invocation of Robin Hood myths which present benefit claimants as prime recipients of the 'gift' of state support, enabled by the selfless redistribution of the *taxpayer's* money."

Hence, Cooke continues, the vocabularies offered in justification of tax fraud are predicated on ideas of resistance to pay over money due to[57] the state, whilst the benefit defrauder attempts to justify taking money illegally *from*[58] the state. Thus, Cooke suggests, "... differential attribution of motive essentially derives from the historical and ideological construction of the relationship between taxpayer and state, and supplementary benefit claimant and the state; the vocabulary of 'givers' and 'takers' thus helps to explain why tax fraudsters may gain popular acceptance (and even muted praise) in defrauding both the state and the honest taxpayer; yet it is benefit fraudsters who are attributed the motives of greed, selfishness and immoral lack of public spirit." Cooke also suggests[59] that benefit offenders are more severely sentenced.

Perceptions of law, perhaps unlike literature, can have practical effects: thus, to return to illegality in equitable transactions, in *Nelson v Nelson*, Dawson J expressed[60] strong disapproval of the decision in *Tinsley v Millligan*. First, whilst accepting that disconformity was undesirable in the rules relating to illegality in both law and equity, he found difficulty in accepting the distinction, which had been made in *Tinsley v Milligan*, between a resulting trust established without the need to rebut the presumption of advancement and a resulting trust that can only be established by rebutting that presumption. "In the former case, according to the decision," he stated[61], "an illegal purpose does not preclude relief because the resulting trust will be presumed upon proof that the purchase price was paid by the party asserting the trust without any need for that party to place reliance upon the illegal purpose. In the latter case, however, where the presumption of advancement cannot be rebutted without revealing the illegal purpose, there can be no assertion of a resulting trust."

That difference, Dawson J regarded[62] as being entirely fortuitous, being based on the relationship between the parties and is wholly unjustifiable on any policy grounds. Thus, "... the transfer of property by a husband to his wife for an illegal purpose and not intended as a gift should not give rise to a resulting trust whereas a similar transfer of property by a man to his de facto wife should do so, because in the former instance the husband is required to rebut the presumption of advancement and cannot do so merely because he would reveal the illegal purpose, cannot, in my view, have any basis in principle." The only way in which a presumption of advancement should be rebuttable was its being established that no gift was intended. "Intention," he said, "is something different from a reason or motive. The illegal purpose may thus be evidentiary, but it is not the foundation of a claim to rebut the presumption of advancement. Both the presumption of a resulting trust and the presumption of advancement may be rebutted by showing the actual intention of the parties. Each presumption dictates where the evidentiary burden of doing so lies. But that affords no basis for drawing a distinction between the effects of an illegal purpose where the presumption of advancement applies and where it does not. Reliance is placed in each case upon the intention of the parties, whether aided by a presumption or not, and not upon the illegality."

Although Dawson J agreed that the mother's appeal should succeed, his approach is clearly different from that of his brother judges and that, when taken together with the differing approaches in *Tinsley v Milligan*, suggests that resolution of the question of the effect of illegality in equitable transaction is far from complete. In literature, the text will normally be complete in itself and any resolution, howsoever unsatisfactory it might seem to be to the reader – as the ritual humiliation of Shylock in *The Merchant of Venice* is to Lord Millett[63] - must, necessarily, remain as it was written. In law, change is always a possibility at the hands of various agencies: thus, for example in *Tinsley v Milligan*,[64] Lord Goff made reference to s6 of the New Zealand *Illegal Contracts Act* 1970 which provided that, "... every illegal contract shall be of no effect and no person shall become entitled to any property under a disposition made by or pursuant to such contract ..." The Act goes on, in S7, to confer power on courts to provide relief, "... by way of restitution, compensation, variation of the contract, validation of the contract in whole or part or for any particular purpose, or otherwise howsoever as the court in its discretion thinks just." As Lord Goff pointed out,[65] the terms of the legislation are such as demonstrate the New Zealand legislature's enthusiasm for developing a system of discretionary relief, rather than the rigid approach as demonstrated by the arguments advanced by Lord Browne-Wilkinson in *Tinsley v Milligan*. Even so, he noted, *prima facie*, at least, the Act is limited to contracts and his Lordship had no way of knowing how successful the legislation had been in practice or, more particularly, whether its operation might be extended to include other forms of illegality.

"The real criticism of the present rules," he concluded, "is not that they are unprincipled, but rather that they are indiscriminate in their effect, and are capable therefore of injustice... I would be more than happy if a new system could be evolved which was both satisfactory in its effect and capable of avoiding the kind of result which flows from the established principles in cases such as the present."

Indeed, the English Law Commission, as Pearce and Stevens have pointed out,[66] did make that recommendation. In *Illegal Transactions: The Effect of Illegality on Contract and Trusts,*[67] the Commission recommended the replacement of the established position taken by the majority in *Tinsley v Milligan* by the system whereby courts would be granted a discretion to declare a contract or a trust invalid. However, as Enanchong has emphasised[68], the discretion would be structured so as to ensure that five factors would be taken into account. These factors are: first, the seriousness of the illegality. Second, the knowledge and intention of the illegal trust beneficiary. Third, whether invalidity would tend to deter the illegality. Fourth, whether invalidity would further the purpose of the rule which renders the trust illegal and, last, whether invalidity would be a proportionate response to the claimant's participation in the illegality.

The point of this discussion in the context of law and literature is that both *Nelson v Nelson* and *Tinsley v Milligan* could have provided a legal backdrop for a literary work – as did the evidentiary presumption of death in Tennyson's poem "Enoch Arden" or, for that matter, Antonio's bond in *The Merchant of Venice* and, as a most distinguished equity lawyer and scholar, Lord Millett has been especially critical[69] of Portia's treatment of that central issue. In other words, the cases discussed in the preceding pages can provide the kind of scenario which Cooke regards as providing insights.[70]

Ward then seeks to address[71] the concerns raised by Getman,[72] whose essential thesis is that in the United States, at any rate, law school teaching methods there employed,[73] have resulted in something of a schizoid personality manifestation generated by those methods – thus, Getman sought to identify two voices there generated: the *professional* and the *human*. This linguistic dichotomy, Getman argues, does neither the law nor the lawyer good as it removes them from the concerns of ordinary life. From an educational perspective, in Getman's own words,[74] "... [such a] myopic focus on the professional voice does a major pedagogical disservice by preparing students for only a part of what students do ... successful lawering frequently requires human understanding far more than it does intellectual rigour." Another writer referred to by Ward[75] who shares Getman's concerns is Hodges[76] who contends that, when they are compared to other students, law students seem to attempt to remove signs of non-professional discourse from their language. That is so even though their language, "... fails to reflect the unavoidable fact of their membership in a larger community from which they derive their fundamental linguistic abilities and to which as mediators from the world of law, they must communicate." It should be said that, from my own experience of teaching *Law and Literature* in the United States, law students are, indeed aware of their own tendency to withdraw into their own professional discourse, although most did not seem particularly concerned by the fact!

Probably, though, the situation has been put most graphically by Getman who writes[77] that, "...the need to address reality in words understandable to most of humanity is particularly great for those of us who seek to influence social policy in a more liberal direction ... I do not deny that the conveyance of complex ideas sometimes requires a special vocabulary, but such special circumstances occur far less frequently than many would like to pretend. In most cases, when we present our ideas in a form designed to separate us from the great mass of humanity, we are almost certain to obscure their meaning, limit their reach, and reduce their significance." Although there clearly is much to that view, it very well may not be the whole of the story.

Contrary to the views expressed by these commentators, Brown[78] suggests that the ultra-careful who discuss thoroughly the meaning of clauses in their leases or hire purchase agreements with their lawyers will still be likely to spend money on that expert guidance when the document is written in *Plain-English*. Indeed, he goes on, "... it will probably cost him more for the additional demands that such language will make on the lawyer's time. To the great majority, who do not seriously address themselves to what they sign and consult 'the expert' only when ambulance is essential, the kind of English in which the document is expressed will malk little or no difference. And the do-it-yourself conveyancer will quickly learn both the ordinary and legal meanings of *volenti non fit injuria*." Further, Brown continues by suggesting[79] that most, in his experience, advocates of *Plain-English* are highly literate and socially responsible who, like Brown himself, aim to mobilise directly the politically potent middle and upper echelons, which would include lawyers and legislators, of the societies. "None would deny," he states, "...that the Greater Goal is to make law and its procedures and its documentation accessible (or as nearly accessible as it can realistically be made) to the general public. Until the vast *lumpen* constituencies can be persuaded their stake in much greater legal comprehensibility is vital to their everyday interests, the 'unspannable gulf-perception will persist and deepen." Brown considers that the most which activists and critics can reasonably hope for is a trickle-down effect. "If" he writes, "that continues to gather strength and range, the legal-societies will get a notable bonus. Swift attainment of the 'the Goal' might be possible only by the replacement of existing law arrangements with a *Tsao-fan* – or a Castro-style 'revolutionary legality" – and the far reaching societal changes that would occasion."

Brown, wisely perhaps, confines himself largely in the remainder of his essay to the realities and what is realisable in the mid-term. It is, suggested, important to bear continually in mind what actually is capable of achievement. In 1993, the Full Court of the Federal Court of Australia[80] decided the rather extraordinary case of *Re Blunn v Cleaver: Re Section 48 of the Administrative Appeals Tribunal Act 1975 (Cth).*[81] In that case, a determination had been made in the previous year that the respondent was entitled to the payment of weekly amounts of compensation in respect of particular periods in 1989 and 1990 when he was incapacitated for work.[82] Before that entitlement was received by the respondent in a single payment, a deduction was made which represented sickness and unemployment benefits which he had received in relation to the relevant periods. Part 3.14 of the *Social Security Act* 1991 dealt with the payment of social security benefits to persons who are entitled to, or who receive, certain forms of compensation. Sections 1165 and 1166 were expressed to apply, where a person, "... receives compensation in the form of a lump sum." Section 1165 disentitled that person from receiving social security benefits for a period, whilst s 1166 dealt with the recovery of benefits which a person had already received. Sections 1168 and 1170 were expressed as operating where a person received, "...a series of periodic compensation payments. The first provision reduced the rate at which social security benefits were payable for a period whilst the latter dealt with the recovery of excess benefits which a person has received in these circumstances. In addition, s1174, which the Court considered[83] to be crucial so far as the instant proceedings were concerned provided that, under s 1174, if a compensation payer is liable to pay compensation to a person in respect of the person's lost earnings or lost capacity to earn[84] and the person received or claims social security benefits for the periodic payments period or the lump sum payment period,[85] the Secretary of the Department of Social Security may give written notice to the compensation payer that the Secretary proposes to recover the amount specified in the notice from the compensation payer. If a compensation payer is given such notice, the compensation payer is liable to pay to the Commonwealth the amount specified in the notice.[86] The section then goes on to specify the amounts recoverable and the methods for calculating them. [87] By reason of s 1175, payment to the Commonwealth of an amount that a compensation payer was liable to pay under s 1174 operated, to the extent of the payment, as a discharge of the compensation payer's liability to pay compensation to the person in question.

A question of law had been referred to the Federal Court by the Administrative Appeals Tribunal.[88] The question, as the Court put the matter,[89] was expressed in the following terms: "Whether the compensation payment is properly characterised as 'periodic compensation payments' under Part 3.14 of the Act or whether it was 'compensation in the form of a lump sum' under that Part." After a detailed analysis of the relevant statutory provisions and their historical development, the Court pointed out[90] that, "The essential issue as formulated by the parties in the course of argument is whether, for the purposes of the relevant legislative provisions, a compensating payment is to be characterised by reference to its nature and the circumstances in which the person's entitlement to it arose or by reference to the manner in which the liability to make the compensation payment has, as events turned out, been discharged.

In holding that the compensation was properly characterised as being, at least for the purposes of the *Social Security Act* 1991, a series of periodic compensation payments or, more accurately, bearing in mind that the amount related to a continuous period but to a number of separate periods, a number of series of periodic compensation payments, the court made various subordinate, though necessary decisions.

First, it was determined[91] that the intention of the legislature was, in so far as it was possible , to eliminate instances of what was described as "double dipping" in cases where there was a prescribed correlation between an entitlement to certain social security payments and a claim to compensation. "To achieve that end," the court stated, "the legislation has sought to deal with a variety of situations and it would not be surprising given the context, to find that the language used is not entirely apposite in some of the situations with which the legislation intends to deal." That *dictum* was to presage some quite remarkable developments, and additional comments, in relation to the case at large,

Next, relying on the earlier decision of the High Court of Australia in *Cooper Brookes (Wollongong) Pty Ltd v FCT*,[92] the Court held[93] that s 1174 operated by reference to the entitlement to compensation rather than be reference to the manner in which the liability to make the compensation payment has been actually discharged. Further, again relying on the *Cooper Brookes* case, the Court held that[94] the legislative intention required that all of the provisions of the relevant Part of the *Social Security Act* should operate according to the nature of the entitlement to the compensation payment rather that the manner in which the payment, in fact, was made.

In addition, and more significantly for the purposes of this chapter, the Court held[95] that the context and purpose served by ss 1065, 1066, 1068 and 1070 were better guides to their meaning than a bare appeal to the literal sense of the words used. In that context, the Court went on to state[96] that they saw, "…nothing incongruous in treating a person who receives a single payment which is made up of weekly amounts of compensation in respect of a number of consecutive weeks as being the recipient of a series of periodic compensation payments. Nor is the reference in s 1174(4)(b) to, 'the sum of the amounts of the periodic payments' inapt to refer to the sum of the weekly amounts of compensation which are 'payable' to a person or to which the person is entitled. There being two constructions open, we prefer that for which the applicant contended, being a construction which will avoid what seems to us to be the arbitrary or capricious result which would ensue if the alternative construction were adopted."

Although the utilisation of *ex post facto* reasoning (or rationalisation) is far from unknown in other areas of legal activity,[97] one must ask why it was so obviously and readily employed in *Re Blunn v Cleaver*. There is no doubt that *Blunn* is a complex and difficult case involving complex and difficult legislation. However, it is fortunate that the Court itself set out to seek to explain why the rationative processes were as they were. At the outset of this part of their judgment, the Full Court of the Federal Court of Australia commented[98] that, "Before concluding this judgment, we feel constrained to make a general reference to the Act in which the legislation in question is contained, the *Social Security Act* 1991. The Act in its current form contains more than 1364 sections. We have not counted the precise number. To do so would involve taking account of a number of sections which are identified by letters as well as numbers. These have been added to the Act in the short period of two years in which it has been in force. The Act, including the notes to it, occupies 1471 pages of the Commonwealth Statutes."

The Court then turned its attention to a further factor which is altogether more germane to the discussion in this chapter. The Court continued by noting that the professed aim of the drafting of the Act was to make it *more accessible*[99] to people without legal training. The Court was at pains to emphasise that "less inaccessible" would be more appropriate because[100] no one, "... seriously believes the layman can master the Act unaided. This case shows its authors did not – for if they had, they would not have left it so ambiguous. But their aim was to assist the inexpert."

The Court's comments then become both more direct and pungent: "Clear statement proceeds," the judges said, "from clear thinking. If the substance of the intended rule is analysed by a lawyer trained to understand the implications of various kinds of rules, the appropriate expression is a consequence of the analysis. 'Plain English' alternatives may really be less precise, and a self-conscious search for them will certainly be a distraction. In the present case, undistracted attention to the substance of the nature of the obligations involved, and the circumstances in which the rule might be expected to have been applied, would have obviated much perplexity. It is not as if the problem was new – it has been known to workers' compensation lawyers for years."

The Court then noted[101] a government document[102] which urged that, in an increasingly complex society, new laws be drafted in Plain English, easy to understand and regularly consolidated. The document had expressed the view that those standards were not met sufficiently often. The Court in *Re Blunn* were frankly sceptical and said[103] the comments which they had made earlier were not intended to undervalue simplicity, but, "... the pursuit of simplicity without due regard for the subject matter may be foolishness. And one Act that is two or three times as long is not necessarily easier to read because some technical expressions (which once understood were succinct) have been replaced by wordier ones."

The Court also pointed out that that problem was not confined to Australia and referred to the decision of Millett J, as he then was in *Arab Bank plc v Mercantile Holdings Ltd*.[104] That case, Millett J stated, "...illustrated the danger inherent in any attempt to recast statutory language in more modern and direct form for no better reason than to make it shorter, simpler and more easily intelligible." Although those were desirable qualities, the Court in *Re Blunn* thought,[105] they should not have priority over the first requirement of legislation which was the clear expression of what parliament intended.

Finally on that issue, the Court refused to apologise for the complexity and detail to be found in their judgment: "Indeed," they said, "without a copy of the Act within one's hand and a reference to a succession of provisions, one can make no sense of it. It is difficult to know what can be done about this problem. As the Senate Committee remarked, the increasingly complex society in which we all live very often demands that legislation be expressed in a complex form. That is the factor which will so often operate to prevent simplicity in legislative drafting."

Having made that general point, the court continued [106] by referring more specifically to social security legislation which they regarded as especially complex, as represented by earlier legislation and the decisions based on it. The present legislation, with which the Court in *Re Blunn* was concerned, could well, the Court considered, have represented a response to that situation. However, the Court considered that the *Social Security Act* 1991, regrettably consisted of, "... a maze of provisions made the more complex by prolix definitions, provisos and exceptions. Both those who claim entitlements under it and those responsible for its administration will not always find it easy to discover whether or not a benefit is payable. It may be expected that the Administrative Appeals Tribunal and the courts will continue to be troubled by difficult problems of construction which will be thrown up by a variety of factual circumstances which, in an increasingly complex world will not be few."

Thus, it may very well be that, quite apart from any difficulties which arise from Plain-English drafting, the area of social security is especially fraught (and there is some evidence from an area where compassion ought to be manifest – that of benefits payable in respect of children with disabilities – to suggest that that is the case).[107] An alternative explanation might simply be that, rather than any attempt at (over) simplification, the culprit may simply be poor drafting – and there have been criticisms of legislative drafting made long before the ideas of Plain-English drafting began to be felt. Thus, in 1974, Pearce wrote[108] that, "Draftsmen of legislation can assist in easing the difficulties of statutory interpretation by a greater familiarity with the rules of interpretation and by consistent use of those rules. The approach that one also frequently detects of drafting in general terms and 'letting the courts work it out' might be acceptable if the courts were better informed as to the purpose of legislation ... Finally the legislature itself must realise that it has a responsibility to produce intelligible legislation."

In that context, Ward points[109] to the work of James Boyd White[110] who has latterly urged that lawyers be educated to realise the importance of language and, hence, of literature and, especially, the *integration* of law and literature rather, perhaps, than as two different notions which are occasionally contiguous. Ward, and the writers he cites in support, and who have been considered here, concludes that part of his discussion[111] by suggesting, in spite of some intellectual obstacles, which will later be considered,[112] that, "... there is much to be said in favour of the 'renaissance' of law and literature and, moreover, regardless of its political potential, the greatest and least disputed virtue lies in its educative potential. It must be stressed, once more, that the two kinds of law and literature – law *in* and law *as* - are in no way exclusive. Indeed, both facets are indistinguishable in text use... the educative ambition of law and literature, it is suggested, is both a credible and a creditable. Moreover, it is one which teachers of law should not seek to dispute, if they do indeed cherish the ambition of educating lawyers to be more than simply lawyers."

There is a great deal to be comprehended in that crucial passage: first, the word *educative* as used by Ward cannot, and, certainly, should not, be used solely to refer to a pedagogical device to simplify, or sweeten, the study of law. Reference has already been made to the crevasse between legal discourse and more colloquial discourse.[113] There are, as I hope this book as a whole will suggest, good reasons for thinking that literature may very well be able – if carefully used – to provide a bridge which will span that crevasse.

At the same time as he was drawing attention to the educative value of law and literature, Ward was conscious of various obstacles which may exist. The first to which he makes reference is the approach represented by the writings of the United States commentator, Posner. That writer begins[114] his major work on the area with the following comment: "Law is so common a subject of literature that one is tempted to infer a deep affinity between the two fields, giving the law privileged access if not to the whole body of literature then at least to those works that are explicitly about law. But I shall argue that the frequency of legal subjects in literature is partly a statistical artefact and that law figures in literature more often as a metaphor than as an object of interest in itself, even where the context is a lawyer (like Kafka) or a law 'buff' (like Melville). This is in general, however, and not in every case. Moreover, the validity of the generalization depends on the precise sense in which the word 'law' is used – and also the word 'literature'."

This short passage contains much that is of interest: first, later in his book, Posner comments[115] on the dissent of Holmes J in the United States Supreme ourt's decision in *Lochner v New York*.[116] In the course of a very short judicial opinion, Holmes J stated[117] that, "This case is decided upon an economic theory which a large part of the country does not entertain... the liberty of the citizen to do as he likes so long as he does not interfere with the liberty of others to do the same, which has been a shibboleth of some well-known writers, is interfered with by school laws, by the Post Office, by every state or municipal institution which takes money for purposes thought desirable, whether he likes it or not. The Fourteenth Amendment does not enact Mr Herbert Spencer's Social Statics."

Posner comments[118] that Holmes J has made Spencer's book a metaphor for *laissez-faire*. For the purposes of this book, which is largely concerned with poetry,[119] Posner's next statement is especially germane: "And metaphors," he writes, "because of the concreteness, their vividness, and when they are fresh, their unexpectedness, are more memorable than their paraphrases." Thus, Holmes J's reference to, "...a book with a weird title written by an Englishman..." lends emotional force, Posner considers, to the sentence. Thus, it would seem that parallels exist between prosody and some kinds of judicial writing.

In the initial passage from Posner's book on law and literature, earlier quoted,[120] he refers to Herman Melville, the Nineteenth Century

American writer as a "law buff". This is unduly dismissive it is suggested. Melville had, indirect, although close, contact with some of the greatest legal and moral dilemmas faced by his generation. The person who was responsible for this contact was his father-in-law, Lemuel Shaw,[121] Chief Justice of the Supreme Judicial Court of Massachusetts. Schwarz, who argues[122] that Shaw was the greatest American judge not to sit on the Supreme Court of the United States, states that, "although largely forgotten today, Lemuel Shaw (1781-1861) was one of the giants of American Law. Indeed, according to Justice Oliver Wendell Holmes, Shaw was 'the greatest magistrate which this country has produced'. As Chief Justice of the most prestigious state court during the pre-civil War period, Shaw played a primary role in recasting the common law into an American mould."

However, as Schwarz himself admits[123] there was one area of the law which Shaw failed to move forward. "Like other judges at the time," Schwarz accepts with reluctance, "Shaw felt compelled to follow the positive law in cases involving slavery, particularly those under the Fugitive Slave Act. The ultimate picture becomes a poignant one – with the judge refusing to adapt the law to the moral imperative in which he firmly believed." The literary parallel is, as Schwarz himself notes, inescapable: those judges found themselves in the dilemma which confronted, and which he sought to escape, Captain Vere in Herman Melville's novella *Billy Budd*[124] and Schwarz, with some plausibility suggests[125] that it may have been written to illustrate that very dilemma faced by judges such as Shaw, to whom he was related and, doubtless, admired.

Like Captain Vere, perhaps, Lemuel Shaw's approach to slavery and related issues was bivalent: thus, on the one hand, in *Commonwealth v Aves*[126] it was held that slaves became free at the moment they were brought into the North because freedom was the only natural state for humanity. Hence, slavery could only exist as the product of positive law. In consequence, in the absence of any positive law establishing slavery in the Commonwealth of Massachusetts, any slave brought there would be automatically freed. The effect of that decision was, however, as Finkelman states[127] that Southern states began to arrest free Blacks who entered their jurisdictions. "Before the 1830s," he suggests, "about half the slave states did recognize the freedom of slaves who had lived in the North, but by 1860 only a few Southern states did so." Conversely, in *Roberts v City of*

Boston,[128] Shaw permitted the city to establish segregated schools, a decision which paved the way for the decision in *Plessy v Ferguson*.[129] *Plessy v Ferguson* represented the United States Supreme Court's *imprimatur* of institutionalised segregation in the South. Only Haslan J rejected the direction in which the decision would take American law in some of its jurisdictions.

Posner's criticisms in relation to methodology may have more substance. "Scholars", he claims,[130] "who believe that legal texts can be analogized to literary texts rarely specify which literary genre provides the best analogy to law." However, he does admit of one exception, the legal philosopher Dworkin. Here, too, though, the whole process becomes rather fraught as Dworkin himself admits[131] that a more fruitful comparison between law and literature may be found by, " ... constructing an artificial genre of literature that we might call the chain novel." Dworkin then goes on to describe how this enterprise would operate : "... a group of novelists writes a novel *seriatim*; each novelist in the chain interprets the chapters he has been given in order to write a new chapter, which is then added to what the next novelist receives and so on." Each, Dworkin comments, has the job of writing his chapter so as to make the novel being constructed the best it can be and the complexity of this task *models the complexity of deciding a hard case under law as integrity.*[132] Dworkin goes on to set out the processes by which the aims can be achieved and notes[133] that, judgments about textual coherence and integrity, reflecting different formal literary values are interwoven with more substantive aesthetic judgments that themselves assume different literary aims."

Dworkin has referred to *hard cases* as involving a parallel methodology in relation to the chain novel. What does Dworkin specifically mean by a *hard case*? An example used by Dworkin[134] is the decision of the English Court of Appeal in *Spartan Steel and Alloys Ltd v Martin & Co (Contractors) Ltd.*[135] In that case, the defendant, whilst excavating with a mechanical shovel, carelessly damaged a cable which interrupted the supply of electricity to the plaintiff's factory, which was some 400 metres away. In order to prevent damage to a furnace, the plaintiffs had to damage its contents, on which they would have made a profit. They were also prevented by the absence of electricity from processing four further "melts" from which they would have made £1,767. The court of Appeal, with Edmund Davies LJ dissenting, held that the plaintiff could recover in respect of the initial melt[136] and the profit which they would have made from its sale as an ingot. However, they could not recover for the loss of the four additional melts which could have been processed before the electricity was restored.

That decision meant that the defendants owed the plaintiff a duty of care in respect of damage to their property but did not owe a duty in respect of loss of profits which were unconnected to that property damage. The problem which is immediately apparent is that the property damage was, in fact, the cause of the whole problem suffered by the plaintiff. However, the property damage was not damage to the plaintiff's property, even though it was more damaging to the plaintiff than the electricity authority who had suffered damage only to the extent of having to repair the cable, or, conceivably, for loss in income during the period of the interruption. Dworkin comments [137] that the court could have proceeded by asking whether a firm in the position of the plaintiff had a *right* to recovery which represented a matter of *principle* or whether it would be economically wise to distribute liability for accidents in the manner sought by the plaintiff, which would be a matter of *policy*. As regards that distribution, Dworkin describes[138] a *principle* as being, "... a standard that is to the observed, not because it will advance or secure an economic, political or social situation deemed to be desirable, but because it is a requirement of justice or fairness or some other dimension of morality." Whereas, a *policy* is, "... that kind of standard that sets out a goal to be reached, generally an improvement in some economic, political or social feature of the community (though some goals are negative, in that they stipulate that some present feature is to be protected from adverse change)." Thus, in Dworkin's view, the standard that automobile accidents are to be decreased is a *policy* and the standard that no man may profit from his own wrong is a *principle*.[139]

To return to his specific discussion of *hard cases*, and *Spartan Steel* (which he assumes to be a hard case) in particular, Dworkin considers[140] that both *principles* and *policies* should be followed. "That," he writes, "is, I suppose, what is meant by the popular idea that a court must be free to decide a novel case like *Spartan Steel* on policy grounds." In *Spartan Steel* itself, of course, Lord Denning MR expressed himself in strongly policy oriented terms when he said[141] that, "At bottom I think the question of recovering economic loss is one of policy. Whenever the Courts draw a line to mark out the bounds of *duty*, they do it as a matter of policy so as to limit the responsibility of the defendant. Whenever the courts set bounds to the *damages* recoverable – saying that they are, or are not, too remote – they do it as a matter of policy so as to limit the liability of the defendant." It should also be said, and Dworkin did not refer to this – and his failure to do so could well weaken his argument – and Edmund Davies LJ, in dissent, specifically rejected[142] the use of policy considerations as determinants of legal principle in the way in which Lord Denning had done. In making that comment, Edmund Davies LJ stated that it had been accepted in England[143] that compensation was recoverable for both types of damage. It follows that this must be regardless of whether the injury – physical, economic or a mixture of both – is large or small or diffused over a large area or locally confined, provided only that the requirements as to foreseeability and directness are fulfilled. Edmund Davies LJ could not see why the loss of the £400 profit should be sustained and not the claim for the £1,767. "It is common ground," he said,[144] "that both types of loss were equally foreseeable and equally direct consequences of the defendant's admitted negligence and the only distinction drawn is that the former figure represents the profit lost as a result of the physical damage done to the material in the furnace at the time when the power was cut off. But what has that purely fortuitous fact to do with legal principle? In my judgment, nothing…"

It will have been apparent, if not wholly surprising – given the structure and emphasis of his opinion – that Edmund Davies LJ used the word *principle*, although not, perhaps, in the strictly Dworkinian sense.[145] However, he did go on[146] to say that, "Having considered the intrinsic nature of the problem presented by this appeal and having consulted the relevant authorities, my conclusion, as already indicated, is that an action lies in negligence in respect of purely economic loss, provided that it was a reasonably foreseeable and direct consequence of failure in a duty of care." Tellingly, he continued by saying that the application of such a rule could undoubtedly give rise to problems in particular situations, but so can a rule that economic loss could be recovered *provided*[147] that it was directly consequential on physical damage. The judge also noted that many, "… alarming situations were conjured up in the course of counsel's arguments before us. In their way they were reminiscent of those formerly advanced against awarding damages for nervous shock; for example, the risk of fictitious claims and expensive litigation, the difficulty of proving the alleged cause and effect, and the impossibility of expressing such a claim in financial terms. But I suspect that they would ... for the most part be resolved either on the grounds that no duty of care was owed to the injured party or that the damages sued for were irrecoverable *not* because they were simply financial but because they were too remote..."

Lawton LJ agreed with Lord Denning MR when he stated[148] that the differences which, "... undoubtedly exist between what damage can be recovered in one type of case and what in another cannot properly be reconciled on any logical basis. I agree with Lord Denning MR that such differences have arisen because of the policy of the law. Maybe there should be one policy for all cases; the enunciation of such a policy is not, in my judgment, a task for this court...."

If there was any doubt, given the nature of the judgment in *Spartan Steel*, that the facts which gave rise to it produced a difficult case, then the policy, espoused by Lord Denning MR and Lawton LJ, and the principle, espoused by Edmund Davies LJ, dichotomy should remove it! It may be that there might be situations which could give rise to harder cases: thus, suppose[149] that a large articulated truck jack-knifes on a motorway in poor weather, though elements of negligent driving or faulty maintenance may also be present. A car, which is following the truck, collides with it and the driver of the car is seriously injured. No one else, though, is physically hurt. However, the motorway is closed for some hours and many people miss important appointments including job interviews and urgent medical consultations and treatments. Any court would find it hard to attempt to distinguish between the kinds of harm caused by, apparently, a single incident. In the light of this, albeit hypothetical, situation Dworkin's suggestion that devising a chapter in a chain novel is as difficult as adjudicating a *hard case* does not, one feels, stand up well.

Posner is, thus, necessarily at pains to point out the fault in Dworkin's analogy between the legal process and the chain novel. First of all, he points out[150] that, in the chain novel (at least as Dworkin depicts it) there are no constraints on the authors of subsequent chapters. "Each author," Posner writes, "can in the first sentence of his chapter kill off the existing characters and start anew. Of course this would not be seen as cricket, but that just means that the writing of a chain novel is a more complex practice than Dworkin's description of it. It is thus unclear to what he is analogizing the legal interpretive process."[151]

Perhaps, in that regard at least, Posner does something of a disservice to Dworkin's argument. Earlier [152], reference was made to Dworkin's comments about weaving the succeeding chapter into the aesthetic fabric of the novel as a whole, Dworkin then goes on to say[153] that, "Yet the various kinds of judgments, of each general kind, remain distinct enough to check one another in an overall assessment, and it is that possibility of contest between textual and substantive judgments that distinguishes a novelist's assignment from more independent creative writing." Put another way, the various demands are likely very much to diminish the risk of the course adverted to by Posner: killing off all the characters and reinvigorating the plot by that subterfuge undermines the integrity of the enterprise at large – assuming the enterprise to have any integrity in the first place.

Next, and with rather more substance, Posner suggests [154] that Dworkin's analogy is flawed on a hierarchical level by placing, say, the judges who interpret the Constitution on the same level as the original framers of that very Constitution. Even if the author of the first chapter of a chain novel could exclude some possible sequels, all of the remainder would be equally authoritative. Conversely, decisions which interpret an authoritative legal document, such as a Constitution or a Statute, stand at a lower level than the text as it is only the text which is authoritative. Dworkin's analogy, Posner claims, equates the judges who interpret the Constitution with the framers of the Constitution. Yet the Constitution (presumably of the United States) is only one of many legal documents adverted to be Posner: the situation may, on occasion, be a little difficult with regard to statutes where some effective equation may be made.

Thus, in the decision of the Full Court of the Family Court of Australia in *K v Z*[155], the wife had appealed against orders made at first instance that the two children of the marriage reside with the husband. The parties had begun living together in 1989, married in 1991 and separated in 1993. After the separation, the parties shared the care of the children, alternating their care every few days each. In early 1995, the wife moved to another Australian State to pursue her studies. She left the children with her husband, returning in the middle of that year. The parents then shared the care of the children over alternate weeks until late 1996, when the wife once again relocated, this time to another city in the same State, for the purposes of completing her studies. The wife sought orders that the children reside with her.

The trial judge found that both parents were capable of caring for their children, but also found that the wife's personal relocations were more concerned with her own needs than those of the children. He also found that, though the children's wishes were important, those had been influenced by the wife and her feelings of negativity towards the husband. The trial judge found, further, that the husband had a better attitude towards the children and towards parenthood than did the wife and, so, made orders that the children reside with the husband. On the other hand, there was evidence from several witnesses, including a court counsellor that the children pined for their mother and wanted to live with her.

The Full Court[156] allowed the appeal and, in doing so, noted[157] that the relevant statutory provision[158] (as the law then stood) specified matters which the judge must consider. That provision is only exhaustive, the Court considered, because it contained a "catch-all clause". [159] The Court, centrally, then went on to point out that, "Some most significant factors which are not spelt out significantly ... include the child's happiness and contentment. If both parents offer reasonable homes for a child with comparable standards of excellent child care, then the child's level of contentment and happiness in one household as compared with that in the other must become a significant, and almost determinative factor in deciding with which parent the child should live. The court should avoid the spectre of placing or leaving a child in a situation of unhappiness where it is able to do so consistently with otherwise meeting the 'best interests' criteria." Even allowing for the last sentence – the *best interests* criterion is not, after all, a notably precise notion[160] - this is, *in toto*, a very strong *dictum*. There is no *imprimatur* in the legislation, catch-all clause apart, for permitting the Court in *K v Z* to make the interpolation which they did and, indeed, they could probably have justified their decision to overturn the judge at first instance on other grounds: for example, on the basis of the children's wishes, for which there was a statutory *imprimatur*.[161] It may be that such interpolations are not unknown in the broad field of family law so that, in relation to the operation of Art 13(b) of the *Hague Convention on Civil Aspects of International Child Abduction*, Boggs J of the United States Court of Appeals for the Sixth Circuit in the case of *Friedrich v Friedrich*[162] added, without any real justification from the body of the Convention itself, a *zone of war* to that article. His view was adopted by the majority of the Full Court of the Family Court of Australia in *Genish-Grant v Director General, Department of Community Services*.[163]

However, the issue which makes the decision of the appellate court in *K v Z* of interest was that, they acknowledged[164] that, ordinarily, a reversal of a trial judge's decision in a case such as the present, would lead to an order for a retrial they did not do so. The reasons for that view, the Court considered to be obvious: first, a reversal did not, of itself mean that the opposite orders should have been made. Further, an appellate court may not usually be in a position to form final views regarding the parties themselves and their proposals. "However," they stated, "this court has on previous occasions intervened to reverse the order where the welfare of the child dictates that course and this appears to be a compelling case to do so. It would in our view be ritualistic to return the matter for retrial." The Court continued by saying that, owing to the fact that the children had articulated that they were missing their mother, a retrial would add nothing to that situation. It was not, the Court continued, suggested that the essential facts would be changed on a retrial but, in the court's view, the best interests of the children would best be advanced by a reversal of the trial judge's decision. Hence, in the instances quoted, notably *K v Z*, it may be that, depending on the nature of the originating document, Dworkin's view may not be as simplistically incorrect as Posner has suggested.

Posner then moves on from originating documents such as Constitutions or Statutes to the processes of common law reasoning and, in that context, Posner considers[165] that the *chain novel* analogy is misleading. First, he states that the initial case – the equivalent of the first chapter in the chain novel, is likely to be highly tentative, more closely analogous to an introduction or to a preface. Second, he writes[166] that the perpetrators of the next case/chapter are not bound to adhere to the direction set by the originating author. That means that if the accumulated experience of the succeeding courts/authors suggests or demonstrates that the originating text took a wrong turn, the judges, especially, can discard it. "Third," Posner comments, "the common law is merely the set of legal concepts created by judicial decisions and, as with any concept, the precise articulation is mutable, can be refined, reformulated. The concept is inferred from the decision (more often from a sequence of decisions) but exists apart from it. The common law judge is not engaged in the exegesis of fixed authoritative texts. The literary critic, the biblical exegete, and the judge engaged in statutory and constitutional interpretation all have the difficult task of interpreting a fixed text.

However, we have seen from the analysis of *K v Z*[167] that the fixed text may very well not be as fixed as Posner seems to suggest or, possibly, as it ought to be. In the processes of the common law, it may be that the initial chapter/introduction/originating case may be more fixed than might ordinarily be expected, but, even so, subsequent developments may be continually more surprising. Where the common law processes and the hypothetical[168] chain novel do part company is that the writers of the successive chapters only have to respond to the efforts of their predecessors, judges in the common law have to respond to the context in which the originating cases and its successors operate.

As regards the fixed text in the common law context, in the Conflict of Laws, the *dictum* of Willes J in *Phillips v Eyre*[169] that, "As a general rule, in order to found a suit in England for a wrong alleged to have been committed abroad, two conditions must be satisfied. First, the wrong must be of such a character that it would have been actionable if committed in England ... Secondly, it must not have been justifiable by the law of the place where it was done" has been treated as a fixed text. Thus, as one leading commentator has stated,[170] they, "... have sometimes been treated as if they were contained in a statute..." Though that, indeed, may once have been the case, the history of Choice of Law in torts has been the history, to a degree, of attempts to circumvent the dual actionability principle, which has no analogue elsewhere in Private International Law, which was created by Willes J in *Phillips v Eyre*.[171]

As regards the response to context, an instance from the law relating to vitiating factors in the law of Contract may suffice. First, in *Phillips v Brooks, Ltd*[172], in April 1918, a man entered the plaintiff's jewellery shop and asked to see some pearls and some rings. He selected pearls to the value of £2,550 and a ring priced at £450. He produced a cheque book and wrote out a cheque for £3000. When he was signing it, he said, "You see who I am, I am Sir George Bullough" and gave an address in St James Square. The plaintiff was aware that there was such a person as Sir George Bullough, and, finding in a directory that Sir George Bullough did live at the given address inquired as to whether he would like to take the articles with him. The man replied, "You had better have the cheque cashed first, but I should like to take the ring with me as it is my wife's birthday tomorrow." The plaintiff allowed him to take the ring. The cheque was dishonoured. The person who gave it was, in fact, a swindler named North, who was, afterwards convicted of obtaining the ring by false pretences. Meanwhile, the following day, North had pledged the ring with the defendants, using the name Firth. The defendants, who were pawnbrokers, *bona fide* and without notice advanced North £350 upon the ring. The issue before Horridge J was whether the plaintiff, clearly a society jeweller, or the defendants, pawnbrokers, should bear the loss caused by North's activities. Horridge J gave judgment in the defendants' favour.

    The judge commented[173], regardless of an extract from Pothier,[174] that, "... the seller intended to contract with the person present, and there was no error as to the person with whom he contracted, although the plaintiff would not have made the contract if there had not been a fraudulent misrepresentation ... In this case, I think, there was a passing of the property and the purchaser had a good title..." Inevitably, there was comment on the outcome of that case much of which involved manipulation of the facts so as to achieve a different result: thus, one commentator[175] inquires, "What if A wearing a false nose and beard, had represented to B that he was Lord Rotschild or Mr Bernard Shaw? It could hardly be said that in such a case B would not be 'in error' with regard to the person with whom he was contracting. And it is difficult to believe that the element of a false nose and beard makes the difference between a good title and no title." Goodhart, in a well known article[176] asked himself "Did the shopkeeper believe that he was entering into a contract with Sir George Bullough and did North know this? If both the answers are in the affirmative then it is submitted there was no contract. If a blind man makes an offer to A, who is present, in the mistaken belief that he is B, can A, who is aware of the mistake, accept the offer? Again, Wade asks[177] why should a seller who relies on a written representation be protected?[178] Whereas, "... the shopkeeper, who has in the interests of his business often to decide on the spur of the moment, runs the risk of being unable to have the contract set aside after the pretender had parted with his acquisitions to a purchaser or pawnbroker; this, of course, he invariably hastens to do." After having notes that Scots Law avoids such transactions *ab initio*,[179] Wade then reorganised the facts of *Phillips v Brooks, Ltd* into a differently perceived factual sequence:

    "(1) A sale of pearls for £2550 and a ring for £450 by B to A, whereupon

(2) by virtue of s 18 of the *Sale of Goods Act* 1893, the property passed from

B to A;

(3) a fraudulent misrepresentation by A as to his identity which

(4) successfully induced voluntary delivery of the ring on the part of B to

A".[180]

Wade considered that that view of the facts was a possible one and would support Horridge J's decision that the swindler had obtained a voidable title to the ring and was able to pass a good title to the pawnbroker. It could be assumed that the fraud had been practised to induce the plaintiff to hand over the ring after the contract of sale had been completed.

Of course, the manipulation of facts either to confirm a dubious ruling (as in *Phillips v Brooks, Ltd*) or to suggest why an apparently suitable decision was wrong is not unknown in the law (or certain types of literature), but in the instance under discussion, the confusion was not increased by hypothetical issues such as were raised by the writers who have been noted, but by new factual situations. These may very well modify the existing situation.

Thus, in 1961, the English Court of Appeal was faced with the case of *Ingram and Others v Little*.[181] There, the three plaintiffs (Hilda Ingram, Elsie Ingram and Mrs Badger) were the joint owners of a motor car, which they advertised for sale. A rogue, who introduced himself as Mr Hutchinson, offered to buy it. He was taken for a run in the car during the course of which he talked about his family and said that they were presently on holiday but that his home was at a particular address in Caterham. Later, the rogue offered Elsie Ingram, who was conducting the negotiations on the part of the plaintiffs, £700, which she refused. He then offered £717 which she was prepared to accept. The rogue then produced a cheque book, at which point Elsie said that she would not accept a cheque under any circumstances and that the proposed deal was at an end. The rogue then said that he was P. G. M. Hutchinson, with business interests in Guildford and living at Stanstead House, Stanstead Road, Caterham. Hilda Ingram then checked in the telephone directory that there was a person of that name at that address. The plaintiffs then permitted the rogue to have the car in exchange for the cheque.

Inevitably, it transpired that the rogue was not P. G. M. Hutchinson, who had nothing to do with the transaction. The cheque was dishonoured. The rogue sold the car to the defendant and then disappeared and remained untraced. The plaintiffs sued the defendant for the return of the car or for damages for its conversion. At first instance, judgment was given for the plaintiffs and the defendant appealed unsuccessfully to the Court of Appeal.

Pearce LJ noted,[182] first, as had Wade[183] that an apparent contract, "... made orally *inter praesentes* raises particular difficulties. The offer is apparently addressed to the physical person present. Prima facie, he, by whatever name he is called, is the person to whom the offer is made. His physical presence identified by sight and hearing preponderates over vagaries of nomenclature... Yet clearly, though difficult it is not impossible to rebut the prima facie presumption that the offer can be accepted by the person to whom it is physically addressed." Pearce LJ then turned his attention to hypothetical instances: "If a man," he continued,[184] "orally commissions a portrait from some unknown artist who had deliberately passed himself off whether by disguise or merely by verbal cosmetics, as a famous painter, the imposter could not accept the offer. For although the offer is made to him physically, it is obviously, as he knows, addressed to the famous painter." At the other end of Pearce LJ's extreme instances, in his own words, where a shopkeeper sells goods in a normal cash transaction to man who misrepresents himself as being a well-known figure, the transaction will normally, be valid because, "... the shopkeeper was ready to sell goods for cash to the world at large, and the particular identity of the purchaser in such a contract is not sufficient importance to override the physical presence identified by sight and hearing."

On the facts of *Ingram*, Pearce LJ noted[185] that they lay in the debatable area between the two extremes. At the beginning of the negotiations, which were always an important part of the transaction, Pearce LJ regarded the name or personality of the false P. G. M. Hutchinson were of no importance and there was no other identity competing with his physical presence. "The plaintiffs," Pearce LJ stated,[186] "were content to sell their car for cash to any purchaser. The contractual conversation was orally addressed to the physical identity of the false Hutchinson. The identity was the man present, and his name was merely one of his attributes. Had matters continued thus, there would clearly have been a valid but voidable contract."

Unfortunately, matters did not go on in that way; the false Hutchinson attempted to persuade Elsie Ingram to take a cheque which she refused to do. At that point, the focus of the transaction changed. As Pearce LJ put the matter:[187] "He did not demur but set himself to reconstruct the negotiations. For the moment had come, which he must all along have anticipated, as the crux of the negotiations, the vital crisis of the swindle… thereafter the negotiations were of a different kind from what the vendor had mistakenly believed them to be hitherto. The parties were no longer concerned with a cash sale of goods where the identity of the purchaser was prima facie unimportant. They were concerned with a credit sale in which both parties knew that the identity of the purchaser was of the utmost importance."

That was the fulcrum of the entire situation, Elsie Ingram had made it clear that she was not going to sell to the man physically present *on credit*.[188] Pearce LJ, after having considered various *dicta* of the trial judge and the relevance of *Phillips v Brooks, Ltd*[189] noted that *Ingram* was a borderline case concerned with ascertaining the intention of the parties and, as such, the views of the trial judge ought not to be lightly displaced. However, he then emphasised[190] that each case must be decided on its own facts but the question to be resolved in each case was whether it had, "...been sufficiently shown in the particular circumstances that, contrary to the prima facie presumption, a party was not contracting with the physical person to whom he uttered the offer, but with another individual whom (to the other party's knowledge) he believed to be the physical person present. The answer to that question is a finding of fact."

Pearce LJ, by way of conclusion, noted[191] that it had been argued that such a finding could legitimately have been reached, had the rogue pretended to be, "… some great man or someone known already to the sellers either by prior dealing or by reputation." However, in the instant that could not be so because the vendors had never previously heard of P.G.M. Hutchinson. Indeed, in *Phillips v Brooks, Ltd*, the jeweller had, in fact, heard of Sir George Bullough. Had Hilda Ingram not taken the short walk to the Post Office to check the telephone directory, then that might well have continued to be the case. The entry in the telephone directory did seem, as Pearce LJ suggested,[192] to represent, "… an individual of apparent standing and stability, a person whom the vendor was ready to trust with her car against his cheque. His individuality was less demanding than that of a famous man would be, but that is a question of degree. It does not, I think, preclude the judge from finding that it was with him that the vendor was intending to deal."

Since Sellers LJ also delivered a judgment to like effect and the appeal was dismissed. The feeling which we presently are likely to have is one of disquiet – an immediate student reaction is, very often, that the vendors in the latter case were successful because they were three vulnerable and elderly ladies, who were likely to excite judicial sympathy. Whereas, the society jeweller in *Phillips v Brooks, Ltd* was not. From the point of view of the present discussion regarding Posner's response to Dworkin's *chain-novel* thesis, the situation is, at present, rather more confused, if not scattered, than one might expect in a novel, perhaps even in a chain-novel. However, there are further complexities ahead.

In *Ingram and Others v Little*, there was, in addition, a dissenting judgment by Devlin LJ who began[193] his discussion by stating that a court could not come to a satisfactory solution of a case such as *Ingram* except by formulating a presumption and by taking that presumption as, at least, a starting point. The presumption that a person intends to contract with the other person whom he is actually addressing seemed to Devlin LJ to be simple and sensible, and supported by appropriate authority. On the facts of the case at hand, Devlin LJ considered[194] that that presumption could not be rebutted, "… by piling up the evidence to show that Miss Ingram would never have contracted with H unless she had thought him to be P.G.M. Hutchinson. That fact is conceded and, whether it is proved *simpliciter* or proved to the hilt, it does not go any further than to show that she was the victim of fraud." Accordingly, Devlin LJ took the view that there was offer and acceptance in form.

It followed that the next stage was to consider whether there had been a mistake which vitiated the contract: Devlin LJ was, almost inevitably, of the view that there was not.[195] In doing so, he assumed, in his *ipsissima verba*, "… without argument, what I take to be the widest view of mistake that is to be found in the authorities; and that is that a mistake avoids the contract if at the time it is made there exists some state of fact which, as assumed, is the basis of the contract and as it is in truth, frustrates its object." In the present case, the fact that Elsie Ingram refused the enter into a contract with the rogue until his supposed name and address had been checked demonstrated that she regarded his identity as crucial. In that, Devlin LJ suggested, she was misguided. What was important was his creditworthiness, rather than his identity *per se*. The judge then expressed [196] the same idea, more directly, when he said that, "... the consent is vitiated by non-agreement about essentials. It is for the court to determine what in the light of all the circumstances is to be deemed essential. In my judgment, H's identity was immaterial. His creditworthiness was not, but creditworthiness in relation to contract is not a basic fact; it is only a way of expressing the belief that each party normally holds that the other will honour his promise."

After having said that he would prefer to follow *Phillips v Brooks, Ltd*,[197] Devlin LJ then threw a further link into the chain-novel on *Mistaken Identity as a Vitiating Factor in Contract*, even though it was not of the same pattern as the initial link. "The great virtue of the common law," he stated,[198] "is that it sets out to solve legal problems by the application of principles which the ordinary man is expected to recognise as sensible and just: their application in any particular case may produce what seems to him a hard result, but as principles should be within his understanding and merit his approval. But here, contrary to its habit, the common law, instead of looking for a principle that is simple and just, rests on theoretical distinctions... The true spirit of common law is to override theoretical distinctions when they stand in the way of doing practical justice. For the doing of justice, the relevant question in this sort of case is not whether the contact was void or voidable, but which of two innocent parties shall suffer for the fraud of a third. The plain answer is that the loss should be divided in such a proportion as is just in all the circumstances. If it be pure misfortune, the loss should be borne equally; if the fault or imprudence of either party has caused or contributed to the loss, it should be borne by that party in the whole or in the greater part."

All in all, a confused enough story line is emerging from the cases. At least, one is waiting for what the next chapter, in what is not dissimilar to a chain-novel, because the authors are, after all, different, will bring. The next case to be decided on the area, which, if Pearce LJ had said *Ingram* fell between the extremes,[199] *Lewis v Avery*[200] is a still more graphic instance. The facts in that case were that the plaintiff (later the respondent before the Court of Appeal in England), who was a postgraduate student of

Chemistry, advertised his car for sale. He was approached by a rogue, who introduced himself as Richard Greene, the well known actor and star of the *Robin Hood* television series. He added verisimilitude to his bold, and, perhaps, unconvincing narrative by producing a special admission pass to Pinewood Television Studies. The plaintiff accepted that as evidence of the rogue's identity and accepted a cheque as payment for the car. Inevitably, the cheque proved worthless. When the defendant, who was a music student bought the car from the rogue, he had no knowledge of the rogue's fraudulent conduct towards the plaintiff.

The plaintiff sued the defendant claiming ownership of the car. However, the County Court Judge awarded damages in tort for conversion. In order to retain this judgment for the defendant's subsequent appeal to the English Court of Appeal, it was necessary for the Court to be convinced that no title had been passed to the rogue. That would only come about if the contract between the plaintiff and the rogue was void by reason of the former's mistake as to the rogue's identity. The Court of Appeal held that the plaintiff intended to contract with the person who was actually present before him. Therefore, the contract was merely voidable for fraud and, consequently, the defendant acquired the property in the car as against the plaintiff.

After considering *Phillips v Brooks, Ltd* and *Ingram v Little*, Lord Denning MR raised[201] the inevitable question as to what was the effect of a mistake by one party as to the identity of the other. "It has," he went on, "sometimes been said that if a party makes a mistake as to the identity of a person with whom he is contracting there is no contract or, if there is a contract, it is a nullity and void, so that no property can pass under it." Lord Denning referred to Pothiers,[202] but emphasised that his statement was no part of English law. Further, Lord Denning MR continued, "… it has been suggested that a mistake as to the identity of a person is one thing: and a mistake as to his attributes another. But this is a distinction without a difference. A man's name is one of his attributes. It is also a key to his identity. If, them he gives a false name, is it a mistake as to his identity? Or a mistake as to his attributes? These fine distinctions do no good to the law."

Lord Denning MR continued[203] by saying that he felt it wrong that an innocent purchaser (the defendant), who knew nothing of what had passed between the plaintiff and the rogue, should have his title depend on such refinements. After all, the Master of the Rolls went on, the purchaser has acted in complete circumspection and wholly in good faith. On the other hand, it was the seller who allowed the rogue to have the goods and, thus, enabled him to commit the fraud. It followed that Lord Denning could not accept the theory that a mistake as to identity renders a contract void. He regarded the true situation as being that, "Where two parties have come to a contract – or rather what appears, on the face of it, to be a contract – the fact that one party is mistaken as to the identity of the other does not mean that there is no contract, or that the contract is a nullity and void from the beginning. It only means that the contract is voidable, that is, liable to be set aside at the instance of the mistaken person, so long as he does before third parties have in good faith acquired rights under it." On the facts of *Lewis v Avery*, therefore, Lord Denning MR, though he regretted that either of the "good and estimable gentlemen"[204] should suffer, he believed that the plaintiff should bear the loss.

Phillimore LJ was of the view[205] that there was nothing in the present case which could displace the *prima facie* presumption that the plaintiff was dealing with the person present in the fact – that is, the rogue. It seemed to Phillimore LJ that, at the conclusion of the transaction, when the car and the logbook were handed over, the cheque was accepted and the receipts were given, it was impossible to say that a contract had not been made. Phillimore LJ concluded by saying that *Lewis v Avery* was really on all fours with *Phillips v Brooks, Ltd*, which had been good law for over fifty years.

Megaw LJ began[206] his judgment by stating that he found it difficult to understand the basis, either in logic or practical considerations, of the test laid down by the majority of the Court of Appeal in *Ingram v Little*.[207] He commented that, given that the promisee in that rules as formulated, was the rogue, the rule was, "… made to depend upon the view which some rogue should have formed, presumably knowing that he is a rogue, as to the state of mind of the opposite party to the negotiation, who does not know that he is dealing with a rogue." In addition, Megaw LJ found[208] that the plaintiff's mistake went no further than a mistake as to the rogue's attributes, namely, the rogue's creditworthiness. Consequently, there was no evidence that the plaintiff regarded the rogue's identity as being of vital importance.

Prima facie, it is not easy to draw convincing distinctions between the cases themselves and it is, at least, questionable whether some statements of principle, even from within the same decision can appropriately be reconciled. Thus, in *Lewis v Avery*, Lord Denning MR stated[209] that there was no real difference between a mistake as to identity and a mistake as to attribute, whilst Megaw LJ seemed to regard it as being sufficiently crucial for its warranting the rejection of the plaintiff's case.[210] On one level, *Ingram v Little* may be explained (or explained away) on the basis of the, "… very special and unusual facts of the case", as one Government instrumentality described it.[211]

However, there might very well be a further chapter in the chain novel, but how are we to effectively guess at the direction in which it will take us? It is, accordingly, necessary to hypothesise[212]: hence, let us suppose that *X, knowing that Y will almost certainly refuse to contract with him, disguises himself so as to conceal his identity and so brings about a sale of goods from Y*. An immediate reaction might be that this is a situation which is not so different from that which occurred in cases earlier discussed. In reality, though, there is a considerable difference: in the newly posited situation, there is no third party to whom the offer is really addressed. It is addressed to *X*, even though *Y* believes, mistakenly, that *X* is not really *X*. *X* is not precluded, thereby, from accepting the offer, which has, of course, been addressed to him. The contract will, thus, be valid.

Depending on the actual nature of the facts themselves, any offer made by *Y* may contain a stipulation which excludes *X*. An obvious instance being the case of a football supporter who has been excluded from a particular stadium on the grounds of misbehaviour. Such a person could not conclude a contract by going to the ticket box in disguise. In those circumstances, it is difficult to know when such a term might be implied into a contract. The answer appears to be that it is only, rarely, that such a term could be implied, if, indeed, ever. Thus in *King's Norton Metal Co Ltd v Eldridge, Merrett W Co Ltd*[213], the plaintiffs, who were metal manufacturers, received a letter, apparently emanating from a firm called *Hallam & Co*, asking for quotations for metal wire. On the letterhead was a picture of a large factory and a list of European depots. The plaintiffs replied and Hallam & Co, who were apparently based in Sheffield, ordered a quantity of wire which was dispatched to them by the plaintiffs. In reality, *Hallam & Co* consisted solely of a man called Wallis, who fraudulently obtained goods by the means he had used in respect of the plaintiff. Wallis sold the goods to the defendants, who bought them in good faith. The plaintiff then sued the defendants arguing that their contract with the fictitious company was void and that the wire, hence, remained their property.

The trial judge non-suited the plaintiffs on the grounds that the property in the goods had passed to Wallis, who sold them to the defendants before the plaintiffs had disaffirmed the contract. That view was affirmed by the Court of Appeal. A. L. Smith J stated[214] that, "The question was, with whom upon this evidence, which was all one way, did the plaintiff contract to sell the goods? Clearly with the writer of the letters. If it could have been shown that there was a separate entity called Hallam & Co and another entity called Wallis then the case might have [been different]... There was only one entity, trading it might be under an alias, and there was a contract by which the property passed to him."

Contrary authority, albeit dubious, does exist in the shape of the decision of Tucker J in *Sowler v Potter*[215] where the defendant had, at an earlier date and under another name (Ann Robinson), been convicted of permitting disorderly conduct in a café. She later assumed the name of Ann Potter and had been granted, by the plaintiff, lease of certain premises under that name. The plaintiff's agent gave evidence to the effect that, at the time the contract was entered into, he knew of Ann Robinson's record and would never have granted the defendant a lease had he known that they were the same person. The plaintiff argued, therefore, that the lease was void for mistake and that the defendant was a trespasser. Tucker J accepted that argument. "This case," the judge said,[216] "of landlord and tenant is clearly a case where the consideration of the person with whom the contract was made was a vital element in the contract and that, therefore, if there was any mistake on the part of the plaintiff with regard to the identity of the person with whom he was contracting, the contract is void *ab initio*."

However, there are some features of *Sowler v Potter* that are of some interest. The first is that Tucker J relied on the passage from Pothier, to which reference has earlier been made[217] and which was rejected by Horridge J in *Phillips v Brooks, Ltd.* Second, there was no mention of the *Kings Norton Metal* case in Tucker J's judgment in *Sowler v Potter*. Third,

Sowler v Potter appears to have been generally disapproved in subsequent decisions.[218]

What conclusions can be drawn, in the context of the discussion of the Dworkin/Posner debate? It is suggested that both Dworkin and Posner are mistaken at any rate in their ultimate conclusions. The cases on mistaken identity as a vitiating factor in contract do not present anywhere near as tidy a picture as would a piece of creative writing – even a chain novel. In that sense, Posner may be more nearly correct when he states[219] that, "...the common law is merely the set if legal concepts created by judicial decisions, and, as with any concept, the precise articulation is mutable, can be refined, reformulated. The concept is inferred from the decision (more often from a sequence of decisions) but exists apart from it." Given the source of these concepts and, perhaps, because they do exist apart from the original sources, they may actually be difficult to identify and, more especially, specify. Thus, what legal concepts can readily be identified from *Phillips v Brooks, Ltd* and the cases which actually, or hypothetically, surround it? It may be that the most we can say is that there is a presumption that a person who makes an offer to sell to a person who is physically present when the offer is made intends to sell to that person, regardless of any representations which have been made by that person regarding his/her identity. Though that presumption may, in some circumstances, be rebutted. That does not tell us a very great deal. Especially as it may be that its factual application may be strictly circumscribed.

Thus, in the earlier case of *Cundy v Lindsay*,[220] the respondents had received an order for goods from Blenkarn (the rogue), who gave his address as 37 Wood Street, Cheapside. He imitated the signature of a respectable firm, Blenkiron & Co, who carried on business in the same area. That firm were known to the respondents by reputation. Hence, the respondents had been fraudulently induced to send the goods to the rogue's address and the rogue then sold the goods to the innocent purchasers, who became the appellants. The respondents sued the appellants for the return of the goods. The House of Lords held that the respondents should succeed. Lord Cairns LC stated[221] that the respondents knew nothing of Blenkarn and never considered his existence. "With him," the Lord Chancellor went on, "they never intended to deal. Their minds never even for an instant of time rested upon him, and as between him and them there was no *consensus* of minds which could lead to any agreement or any contract whatever. As between him and them there was merely the one side to the contract, where, in order to produce a contract, two sides would be required."

That, or course, is surely the situation in the other cases which we have considered: Lord Cairns was of the view that once the rogue's offer was accepted, the rogue knew that the respondents thought that they were entering into a contract with Blenkiron & Co. Hence, the contract was void *ab initio*. But what, in truth, is the difference between *Cundy v Lindsay* and, say, *Phillips v Brooks, Ltd.* and *Lewis v Avery*, apart from the result? The only distinction which can be found is that the transaction was not conducted on a personal basis. One would not have thought there was much difference between a rogue, who gave a false name, and a rogue who, in effect, forged a signature on a letter. The distinctions begin to bear an almost metaphysical quality.

Indeed, it is suggested that these cases represent more fantasy than fact. Suppose that we were to collapse all the rogues into one (excluding the potential lessee in *Sowler* v *Potter*,[222] as the transaction there was rather different in kind), then genuinely phantastical scenarios can be devised. The stories of the various frauds and the judicial responses are, of themselves, strange enough – even from the standpoint of strict law – but the possibilities, when one seeks to flesh out the personalities involved and the results which might come about are seemingly endless. Thus, for instance, Devlin LJ's suggestion in *Ingram* v *Little*[223] that the loss be borne by parties according to their contribution to the deception might lead to reform, as in New Zealand,[224] but it could well produce a fictionalised account of the socio-political processes leading to those reforms. Indeed, the socio-political forces surrounding the Australian *Family Law (Shared Parenting Responsibility) Act* 2006[225] could be similarly treated. In fact, in addition to the educative (or didactic) function referred to by Ward,[226] the reality is that law and literature are concerned with the same issues and, therefore, are able to illuminate one another. This, of course, is inevitably connected to the educative process mentioned by Ward and which is apparent throughout his entire book.[227] In an earlier article,[228] I had made that very point, but was cautious in urging its implementation because the cultural and literary background of many law students was not strong and, owing to the pressures of legal education itself, were unlikely to develop.

Nevertheless, that may not either demonstrate any deficiencies in seeking to develop the Law and Literature connection, or, indeed the students from whom the information was obtained themselves, but in the orientation of legal education.[229]

All of this is relevant to the Dworkin Posner debate where Posner, after having written[230] that the sceptical vein in literary criticism and the hermeneutic theories (and I will return to the issue of hermeneutics later in this Chapter)[231] which, he considered nourish it, demonstrate how difficult the interpretation of texts can be. That, in turn, he suggests should make lawyers, judges and legal scholars more cautious, self-conscious, more tentative about the process of interpreting legal texts. Indeed, from the standpoint of this discussion, there are sufficient instances from the mundane operation of the law to have made that readily apparent the discussion of *Re Blunn*[232] should be a sufficient illustration of that, What all of that means, I would venture to suggest, is that this factor which might seem to separate the disciplines does, in reality, bring them closer together.

Posner continues by saying that the burden of his argument, at least in that part of the book, that no specific techniques or discoveries of literary criticism, or literary analogies (like that of the chain novel) were transferable to the law. However, Posner goes on to make a point which is central to the development of the theses to be found in this book. "Like law", he writes,[233] "literary criticism lacks a formalizable method or theory – a lack that all the theoretical endeavours since Aristotle show no signs of closing. A good literary critic is a careful, thorough, scrupulous, informed logical and practical reader of literary texts, and a good lawyer is a careful, thorough, scrupulous, informed, logical and practical reader of legal texts. They are both close readers, but of different materials. Their strength as close readers comes from immersion in a voluminous, diverse, but particular body rather than from mastery of a theory."

It is not proposed to depart from that view in this book: there are many situations where theory, of whatever kind, can obfuscate, rather than illuminate, texts. An aim of this book is to relate factual, or emotional or spiritual situations or ideas with the approach to the law and to literature. Very often as, I hope, we have already seen, and will see more clearly, law and literature deal, perforce in one case and largely voluntary in the other, with the same subject matters. Of course they approach them through different media by way of different conventions, and may often arrive at different conclusions, but that should not, and I hope this book will show, may not preclude analysis or commentary on that relationship.

This does not mean that all consideration of sociolegal or literary theory can wholly be avoided – even if it obfuscates the relationship between the legal and literary texts. Thus, in the first chapter of his book,[234] Ward refers to the *Critical Legal Studies Movement* (CLS), a school of thought which is important particularly in relation to the educative function which has been earlier noted. In general terms, Critical Legal Studies Movement perceives itself, in the words of a formative statement[235] that, "The central focus of the critical legal approach is to explore the manner in which legal doctrine and legal education and the practices of legal institutions work to buttress and support a pervasive system of oppressive, inegalitarian relations. Critical theory works to develop radical alternatives and to explore and debate the role of the law in the creation of social, economic and political relations that will advance human emancipation." However, Fitzpatrick and Hunt note[236] that the movement, so-called, may have more than one manifestation: thus, in the early days of critical legal studies in the United States, it appeared that it was characterised by the key note played by a relatively small number of individuals. That resulted in an apparent uniformity in language and style of presentation. Conversely, in Britain, there was no such unifying individuals or groups of individuals. Further, participants in the United States, Fitzpatrick and Hunt suggest, have been more prepared to borrow from a range of intellectual traditions so as to generate a *mélange* of influences. In Britain, they suggest that the influences on the movement have been less eclectic with the key traditions which have informed the debate being Marxism, feminism and critical social theory of the Frankfurt variety.

As regards their attitude towards the educative function, Thomas has written[237] that, "Like the emergence of most movements, what we can retrospectively now call the critical legal movement arose in Britain out of dissatisfaction with, and opposition to, the existing order of things. That order of things in legal education was the equation of legal education with 'learning the law.' In this expository or dogmatic tradition, legal education is confined to the exposition of the currently existing rules. This exposition is pursued through the reading of legal texts to disclose what 'the law' in the singular is (an activity which this tradition assumes to be possible) and through seeking 'correct' legal answers to hypothetical problems." A new generation of law teachers grew up from the 1960s onward,[238] sought to establish themselves as academics, rather than as legal practitioners *manqués* and, to them, "…the expository approach appeared not only intellectually barren but to occupy a peculiar middle ground between the genuinely academic and the truly practical: an inadequate way of relating theory and practice. What…motivated those teachers to seek a way of vacating that territory was a sense of the unreality of law as it appeared through the legal texts. Thus, the gap between legal appearance and reality became… [and] remains a central theme of the critical legal movement in its attempt to establish a new relationship between theory and practice."

None of those comments, of themselves at least, would seem to be cause for major alarm. However, that does seem to have been what has resulted. As regards to two leading writers whose work we have been considering in the context of Law and Literature, Posner does not seek to take the critical legal studies movement head on, but, at the same time, is especially severe on what he calls *Narrative Legal Scholarship*,[239] into which he subsumes *Judicial Biography*. In Posner's *ipsissima verba*: "…others write stories that purport to be autobiographical and as so are offered as literally true, yet not only are the stories unverifiable, but the story mode, and sometimes specific details, undermine their veracity. Autobiographical legal scholarship shades into biographical legal scholarship…"

Posner is notably critical of one book[240] – W N Eskridge's book urging the recognition of same-sex marriage – which is based on a reported decision.[241] His criticism is the author's attribution of personal characteristics to the protagonists,[242] which Posner finds unconvincing. It may be, but, surely, at worst these apparent attributes neither subtract from, nor add to, the strength of Eskridge's argument in strictly intellectual terms. Posner continues[243] in polemic turn of phrase: "There is enough fiction in law already. I refer not to legal fictions, but the self-serving and often phony stories, told by litigants and witnesses and faithfully transcribed, that find their way into appellate decisions because accepted by credulous jurors or, for procedural or tactical reasons, simply not challenged." That statement is redolent of the distinction between appearance and reality as described by Thomson.[244] In the context of *Baehr* v *Lewin*, Posner goes on to say that the real art of Eskridge's book on the decision and its implications is the, "...patient, measured, rational, unemotional tone in which he states the case for legalizing homosexual marriage. The implied author that the book creates is a more effective refutation of the homosexual stereotypes that stand athwart Eskridge's goal than the ice-cream – parlour normality of his model lesbian couple."

There is, though, as Douzinas and Warrington[245] have appropriately pointed out, a relationship between critical legal studies and the theory of literary criticism through the agency of *deconstruction*.[246] This, they propose, is a reading of texts, especially philosophical texts, drawing on literary criticism. "It claims," they state, "that the old distinction between philosophy and literature, that the former gives a scientific insight into truth which the latter obscures in the play of language is simply untenable. Philosophic texts are linguistic constructs inevitably subject to the figurality of language... The argument then is that all philosophical text involve linguistic play... In particular, the metaphors of texts are scrutinised to show how the means claimed to contain meaning are, at the same time, those that ground the opposites of the apparent claims." Given the nature of the passage itself, it would have been surprising had Posner not had something to say regarding he applications.

Posner writes[247] that literature interests the proponents of deconstructionism because literature is not attempting to convey concepts in the most economical manner possible.[248] "The use of figurative language," Posner exposits, "rhyme, assonance, meter, fiction, parable, punning the arrangements of words on a page (as in poetry), and other devices that call attention to the signifiers and thus decrease the transparency of the medium of communication fits the deconstructionists' program of placing the properties of language that impede forthright communication on a par with the properties that enable it... Literary deconstruction...presents literature as being self-referential. In so doing it closes the loop with philosophical deconstruction by directing attention to the medium of communication and indeed making the problematics of meaning."

The next theoretical/critical notion, to which reference has already been made in relation to Posner's writing[249] is *"hermeneutic.* The word itself, Goodrich suggests,[250] is ultimately derived from the name Hermes, son of Zeus, who in Greek mythology, acted as messenger (or herald) of the gods. "In its broadest and most ancient meaning," he states, hermeneutics thus refers to a form of communication which takes place across the gulf that separates the mortal, the immortal, the human from the divine. What is involved is essentially an act of translation in which an original, foreign or alien language and meaning is unlocked and communicated: the signs and symbols of the gods are rendered intelligible and familiar by the interpreter Hermes." Put another way, Goodrich argues that the task of the earliest hermeneutics was that of translating the foreign and strange into the familiar and recognisable, or the distant and written into the present and spoken. Goodrich then notes the words of Gadamer,[251] "...the word hermeneutics points back to the task of the interpreter, which is that of interpreting and communicating something that is unintelligible because it is spoken in a foreign language. Gadamer goes on to, rather cryptically, add that, "...everything that is set down in print is to some extent foreign and strange and hence it poses the same task of understanding as what is spoken in a foreign language."

Of course, most legal discourse, be it Constitution, Statute or case law is necessarily set down in print and we have seen from the previous analyses of illegality in trusts law,[252] mistaken identity[253] as a vitiating factor in contracts law, as well as the search for plain English drafting,[254] it is clear that, despite the rather overblown prose of both Gadamer and Goodrich, elements of translation vary from the simple to the, at least, arcane. Although it must be emphasised that Goodrich interpreted the notion of hermeneutics in a narrow way:[255] "In talking of hermeneutics and hermeneutic techniques of interpretation," he states, "we are referring specifically to that branch of textual criticism that developed, primarily in the European Universities, in the Eighteenth and Nineteenth Centuries and is associated with post-medieval humanism and the development of scientific methodologies for the reconstruction and interpretation of classical Greek and Roman literature."

As regards *legal hermeneutics,* Goodrich makes clear the relationship both with *deconstructionism* and the *critical legal studies* movement. "Innovations in ideology," he writes,[256] "changes in the manner in which the legal community represents and justifies its social and political roles, should not blind the student of legal texts to the fact that the claim (declarative) that there is a strict logic of legal interpretation or the belief that 'legal reason' can alone provide 'correct' answers to legal problems are no more than exaggerated (dogmatic) assertions of the hermeneutic requirement that law be respected and obeyed (imperative)". He then notes, like Thomson,[257] that the claim to a logic of law and of law-application is found frequently within law teaching and within the textbook tradition of jurisprudence (presumably, Goodrich is not referring to *jurisprudence* as theory of law, but as forming an important part of the media representation of law).

For that reason, Goodrich continues by examining the relationship between *law and tradition*: "In a very general sense," he suggests, "reading law as a tradition is a mechanism for creating a sense of legal identity: legal meanings develop over time, they are handed down in carefully preserved and reported formulations and most important of all, the legally transmitted meaning is part of a tradition of interrelated legal meanings... The great antiquity of the law is matched only by the slow boring logic of its adaptation to contemporary circumstances. The law goes back before memory; 'time immemorial' has elapsed since the law was made and it is thereby recognised that legal change always lags behind social change – the law is a force for conservation. It is measured and majestic in its attitude to change and the legal tradition has always to some extent maintained an image of distance and seriousness which separates legal problems from the interests and conflicts of everyday life."

That, again, is very much the rhetoric[258] of the critical legal studies movement, although perhaps, writ large. *Time immemorial* is almost wholly figurative and there are numerous instances of statutes being perceived as being too far advanced and being intended to have a didactic effect. One such is the Australian *Family Law Act* 1975.[259] Further, Goodrich comments[260] that common law texts emphasise, "...the tradition and the age of legal meanings and the sources of law. To some extent this stress upon history as the antiquity and continuity of legal rules is simply a way of justifying legal judgments which might otherwise be seen to raise contemporary issues of a political and ideological character: because the legal issue has been decided before, it can be answered without reference to any factors other than those of legal history."

The example chosen by Goodrich is, though, not a little misleading. It is the decision of Lynskey J in *R* v *Miller*,[261] where the wife had presented a petition for divorce, but after the presentation but before the decree had been granted, the husband had sexual intercourse with the wife without consent. After a detailed examination of the authorities, the judge held that the husband, who had been charged with rape, had no case to answer. Goodrich emphasises Lynskey J's reliance on Sir Matthew Hale's *Pleas of the Crown*, written in 1736, where it was stated[262] that, "The husband cannot be guilty of rape committed by himself upon his lawful wife, for by their mutual matrimonial consent and contract the wife hath given herself in this kind unto her husband which she cannot retract."

In 1949, in *R v Clarke*,[263] Byrne J seemed to have accepted that statement of Hale represented in the general thrust of the present law but on the facts of *Clarke* decided that an indictment would lie. The reason being that justices had made an order that the wife should no longer be bound to live with the husband. As Byrne J put the matter:[264] "The position, therefore, was that the wife, by process of law, namely, by marriage, had given consent to the husband to exercise the marital right during such time as the ordinary relations created by the marriage contract subsisted between them, but by further process of law, namely the justices' order, her consent to marital intercourse was revoked." In *Miller,* Lynskey J, rather predictably, distinguished *Clarke* on the grounds that the presentation of the petition was an irrelevance. However, he did say *obiter* that if there had been a non-molestation order, or an agreement to separate, then the wife's consent would have been revoked. It seems safe to extrapolate from that dictum and state that consent would likewise be revoked by a decree *nisi* of divorce or nullity.

However, it must also be said that *Clarke* was not the only instance of inroads having been made into the formulation by Hale, Thus, as early as 1888, some judges, in *R v Clarence*,[265] in the Court for Crown Cases Reserved, expressed doubt on its applicability even then. Wills J expressed the view that he was not prepared to accept that rape in marriage was impossible. Field and Charles JJ were doubtful. The other judges – A L Smith, Hawkins and Stephen JJ – appeared to accept the Hale formulation, but did so with scant enthusiasm.

But there were some established exceptions: thus, Hale himself[266] recognised that there was no reason why a husband should not be convicted as a principal in the second degree in respect of a rape committed on his wife by another party. As Hale himself described the matter: "tho in marriage she hath given up her body to her husband, she is not to be by him prostituted to another." In addition, in *Miller* itself it was held that, though the husband might have a right to sexual intercourse, he was not entitled to use force or violence in exercising that right. As Lynskey J himself[267] put the matter: "If he does so, he may make himself liable to the criminal law, not for the offence of rape but for whatever other offence the facts of the particular case warrant. If he should wound her, he might be charged with wounding or causing actual bodily harm, or he may be liable to be convicted of common assault."

The issue has been resolved, at any rate in its country of origin, by a combination of case and statute, although the statutory part of the process has been not a little confused. In *R v R*,[268] the wife had left the husband having informed him that she intended to petition for divorce. Three weeks later he broke into her parent's house, where she was living, and attempted to have sexual intercourse with her against her will. At first instance, it was held that the immunity was lost, whereupon the husband pleaded guilty to attempted rape. He appealed, successively, to the Court of Appeal and, to the House of Lords. Lord Keith, with whom the other members of the House of Lords agreed, took the view that the common law was capable of evolving in the light of changing economic, social and cultural developments. If followed, he went on,[269] that marriage was, "…in modern times regarded as a partnership of equals and no longer one in which the wife must be the subservient chattel of the husband. In consequence, any reasonable person must regard the Hale formulation as being unacceptable.

However, there was one statutory obstacle to the removal of the formulation: for the first time in the history of the criminal law in England, s 1 of the *Sexual Offences (Amendment) Act* 1976, had introduced a statutory definition of rape into the law. The definition included the phrase "*unlawful* sexual intercourse."[270] Traditionally, that phrase has connoted sexual intercourse outside the marriage relationship and it was, accordingly, agreed by the appellant that that definition had reintroduced the Hale formulation, had there been any prior doubt. Lord Keith rejected that argument on the grounds that it was inconceivable that the legislature had any such intention and, hence, that use of the word *unlawful* could not import that interpretation. It was, thus, concluded that the word should merely be regarded[271] as surplusage and that, "…in modern times the supposed marital exception in rape forms no part of the law of England."

However, that was not to be the end of the process. The husband thereupon argued before the European Court of Human Rights that the decision of the House of Lords was in breach of Art 7 of the *European Convention on Human Rights* on the grounds that it retrospectively criminalised his actions. The Court, not wholly surprisingly, rejected[272] his complaint, with the Court stating[273] that, "...the abandonment of the unacceptable idea of a husband being immune against prosecution for rape of his wife was in conformity not only with a civilised concept of marriage but also, and above all, with the fundamental objectives of the Convention, the very essence of which is respect for human dignity and human freedom." The Court had also noted that earlier decisions, which have been earlier commented upon[274] had already eroded, to a degree, the marital immunity rule and, hence, the ultimate decision of the House of Lords in *R v R*[275] was reasonably foreseeable.

That, however correct, is not the end of the story by any means. As two distinguished English writers[276] have pointed out that the situation may well be less certain in cases which do not involve formal marriage. A particular difficulty, as I have elsewhere pointed out[277] relates to the determination of when the relationship begins and ends. As a consequence of the decision of the New Zealand Court of Appeal in *Ruka v Department of Social Welfare*,[278] I asked, especially as there is more legal cognisance being given to a variety of family forms,[279] whether some note[280] should be made of dissolution of family forms which have never been formalised. In some respects that might already be being done indirectly; thus, in the *Ruka* case itself, the Department had recognised that the applicant's unformalised relationship had ceased to exist by its reinstatement of her social security payments. The instant problem is, though, that, to the parties themselves, it is clear that their relationship has broken down, that may not be apparent to third parties. Those third parties might be courts, government instrumentalities or, more often perhaps, caring observers. In *Ruka* itself, on any objective appraisal, the relationship had been dead for some years, but, nonetheless, it required an appellate decision on an ancillary matter officially to say so.

Thus, it is respectfully submitted – for Goodrich does, across the board, have much to tell us – that he has not selected an especially pertinent example to illustrate the valuable point that he makes. Much the same can be said of the example which he has selected to illustrate his next major point.[281] Goodrich's next major point is that, "One moment in the process of reading the case law can thus be designated as the search for traditional or historical sources and meanings. As much as anything else, the technique involved is one of memory, that of ability to recall and presumably repeat ancient and highly technical usages… the legal meanings remembered are always related to other legal meanings and to the principles and reasoning of the law as a whole. It remains the case, however, that past authority or precedent is generally required in the justification of a decision – reason alone is insufficient – and that if the judge believes that there is no authority for deciding a case then the plaintiff must be non-suited or a verdict of no case to answer must be entered." Given that apparent process, one must be put in mind of that described by the poet Swinburne (of whom more later),[282] who wrote[283] that:

> "For winter's rains and ruins are over,
> And all the season of snows and sins;
> The days dividing lover and lover,
> The light that loses, the night that wins;
> And time remembered is grief forgotten,
> And frosts are slain and flowers begotten,
> And in green underwood and cover
> Blossom by blossom, the spring begins."

Various questions will be asked, and issues raised regarding the poem at large and that stanza in particular in the following chapter. However, in order to justify his views, Goodrich needs to produce example or examples. He seeks to do so by means of the judgment of Lord Dilhorne in *Home Office* v *Dorset Yacht Co.*[284] In that case, that Home Office had appealed, from decisions at first instance and in the Court of Appeal, to the House of Lords. The facts were that seven boys,[285] who were detailed in a Borstal institution for young offenders, escaped when they were on a training exercise on an island. They did so when the three officers in charge of them were, contrary to instructions, in bed. They boarded one of the many vessels in the harbour, started it, and collided with the plaintiff's yacht, which they boarded and further damaged. The preliminary question of law – whether, on the facts as pleaded, any duty of care capable of giving rise to liability in damages was owed by the Home Office, its servants or agents – was answered in the affirmative at first instance, by the Court of Appeal and, ultimately, by the House of Lords.

Goodrich however, concentrates on the dissenting judgment of Viscount Dilhorne, who was of the opinion that the point in issue had never previously been decided and that[286] therefore, there was, "…no authority for claiming a duty of care exists with respect of custodians of persons lawfully in custody to anyone suffering damage consequent on their escape. We are therefore being asked to create a *novel* duty… no doubt very powerful arguments can be advanced that there should be such a duty." Yet that, to Viscount Dilhorne, was insufficient as, "…the facts of a particular case may be a wholly inadequate basis for a far reaching change of the law. We have not to decide what the law should be and then to alter the law. That is the function of Parliament." Goodrich's reaction[287] to that judicial dictum is to say that, in brief, the law always exists and that it is, "…the constitutional function of the judge to declare that law. The principal tool or technique for aiding in such declarations is clarity…, that of memory or textual technique and nothing more."

But in a case like *Dorset Yacht Co.* that, surely, cannot be correct. Indeed, it is not a wholly accurate account of the processes of memory, in one sense, at least: the reason for there not being any prior authority on the subject may very well largely be coincidental. Thus, the reasons why prisoners had not previously escaped and done damage whilst at large may have been because prison regimes might have been such as to preclude escapes, at any rate in circumstances such as occurred in the *Dorset Yacht Co.* case. It may also have been that victims might not have been enthusiastic about pursuing litigation against Government instrumentalities.[288]

As regard the first objection which I have just raised to the memory based thesis of Viscount Dilhorne – and it must be remembered that he was in effective lone dissent – it was taken up by Lord Diplock in *Dorset Yacht Co*,[289] who believed that an appropriate approach was the utilisation of the public law doctrine of *ultra vires*. "According to this concept," he stated, "Parliament has entrusted the department or authority charged with the administration of the statute the exclusive right to determine the particular means within the limits laid down by the statute by which its purpose can best be fulfilled. It is not the function of the court, for which it would be ill-suited, to substitute its own view of the appropriate means for that of the department or authority by granting a remedy by way of a civil action at law to a private citizen adversely affected by the way in which the discretion has been exercised. Its function is confined in the first instance to deciding whether the act or omission complained of fell within the statutory limits imposed upon the department's or authority's discretion." That is just one instance of an approach which can legitimately be taken to the facts of what was a multifaceted case.

If a historical approach is regarded as being necessary, then one might return to the fundamental decision of the House of Lords in *Donoghue v Stevenson*,[290] where Lord Atkin made the famous statement, which must be quoted *in extenso* (not confining it to its latter part): "In English law there must be, and is, some general conception of relations giving rise to a duty of care, of which the particular cases found in the books are instances. The liability for negligence, whether you style it such or treat it as in other systems as a species of 'culpa' is no doubt based upon a general public sentiment of moral wrong doing for which the offender must pay. But acts or omissions which any moral code would censure cannot in a practical world be treated so as to give a right to every person injured by them to demand relief. In this way rules of law arise which limit the range of complainants and the extent of their remedy. The rule that you are to love your neighbour becomes, in law, you must not injure your neighbour, and the lawyer's question. Who is your neighbour? Receives a restricted reply. You must take reasonable care to avoid acts or omissions which you can reasonably foresee would be likely to injure your neighbour. Who, then, in law is my neighbour? The answer seems to be – persons who are so closely and directly affected by my act that I ought reasonably to have them in contemplation as being so directly affected when I am directing my mind to the acts or omissions which are called in question." In *Home Office v Dorset Yacht Co*, Lord Reed had suggested[291] that the time had arrived when that principle – the latter part especially – should be applied in all cases where there was no justification or valid explanation for its exclusion. Although that represents a reliance on a famous precedent rather than a reliance on what one might derivatively,[292] describe as *tricks of memory*. Although, too, Lord Reid's view was adopted by Lord Wilberforce in the later, and controversial, decision of the House of Lords in *Anns v Merton London Borough*.[293]

Of course, Goodrich does not confine himself to law and tradition: in addition, he considers *law and community*,[294] before moving on[295] to formulate some of the layers of legal meaning to be found in legal texts and to seek to outline relevant techniques of relevant interpretation. On those issues, Goodrich concludes[296] that, "Precedent and our reading of precedent as the expression of legal community is at its most basic and explanation of institutional bases of legal decision. Hermeneutics teaches that an adequate reading of legal texts will pay less attention to the self-conscious formulation of method and rules to be found in the text itself than to the methods of interpretation, to the traditions and values of which the text is evidence. That tradition and values change is indisputable and Parliament itself will frequently intervene to remove the more obviously archaic elements of the common law. Nonetheless, the point remains that the interpretation of legal categories is an exercise in moral judgment and that lawyers can predict the outcome of that enterprise not by means of mathematically precise rules but rather by virtue of knowledge of legal values and legal community in which rules play only a general and really very limited role."

There is a very considerable truth in that statement, but the true situation may be rather more complex in that more than one attitude may be perceptible from particular appellate cases. Thus, in one dissentient judgment in a House of Lords case – *Gillick* v *West Norfolk and Wisbech Area Health Authority*[297] – Lord Templeman stated[298] in emphatic terms that "...any decision on the part of a girl to practice sex and contraception requires not only knowledge of the facts of life and of the dangers of pregnancy and disease but also an understanding of the emotional and other consequences to her family, her male partner and to herself. I doubt whether a girl under the age of 16 is capable of a balanced judgment to embark on regular, frequent or casual sexual intercourse fortified by the illusion that medical science can protect her in mind and body and ignoring the danger of leaping from childhood to adulthood without the difficult formative transitional experiences of adolescence. There are many things which a girl under 16 needs to practise but sex is not one of them."

The facts of the *Gillick* case, which is, by now, almost notorious, were that, in December 1980, the British Department of Health and Social Security issued a circular to area health authorities containing, inter alia, advice to the effect that medical practitioners consulted at family planning clinics by girls under the age of sixteen would not be acting unlawfully were they to prescribe contraceptives for the girls so long as they were acting in good faith to protect the girls from the harmful effects of sexual intercourse. The circular further stated that, though they should proceed on the basis that such advice and treatment should not be given to a girl under sixteen without parental consent, nonetheless the principle of confidentiality between doctor and patient applied to girls under sixteen seeking contraceptives. Therefore, in exceptional cases, doctors could prescribe contraceptives without consulting the girl's parents or obtaining their consent if, in the medical practitioner's clinical judgment, it was desirable to prescribe contraceptives.

The plaintiff, who had five daughters under the age of sixteen, sought an assurance from her local area health authority that her daughters would not be given advice or treatment on contraception without her prior knowledge or consent when they were under the age of sixteen. The authority refused to give the assurance and the plaintiff brought an action against the authority and the Department, seeking, first, a declaration that the advice contained in the circular was unlawful.[299] Second, as against the local health authority, she sought a declaration that a doctor or other professional person employed by the authority in a professional capacity by it in its family planning service could not give advice or treatment on contraception to any child of the plaintiff below the age of sixteen without the plaintiff's consent. To do otherwise, she argued, was inconsistent with the plaintiff's parental rights.[300]

The plaintiff failed at first instance, but succeeded before the Court of Appeal. The defendants appealed to the House of Lords regarding the Court of Appeal's grant of the first declaration.[301] The House of Lords, by a majority, overturned the decision of the Court of Appeal. It should be said, both generally and for the particular purposes of this discussion, that *Gillick* is not an especially easy case to evaluate because of the differently orientated judgments which are to be found in the House of Lords decision.

Reference has already been made to the judgment of Lord Templeman,[302] which would seem, to a degree at least, to bear out the thesis which had been advanced by Goodrich[303] and that is probably the more so when later comments of Lord Templeman are taken into account. "A parent", he said[304] "is the natural and legal guardian of an infant under the age of 18 and is responsible for the upbringing of an infant who is in the custody of that parent. The practical exercise of parental powers varies from control and supervision to guidance and advice depending on the discipline enforced by the parent and the age and temperament of the infant…[S]ubject to the discretion of the court to differ from the views of the parent, the court will, in my opinion uphold the right of the parent having custody of the infant to decide on behalf of the infant all matters which the infant is not competent to decide." Inevitably, there is much prior authority to support Lord Templeman's view,[305] the reality of the situation is that he was in a genuine minority.[306]

In addition, the judgment of Lord Scarman, which unquestionably attracted the most legal and popular attention, was orientated wholly differently. "The law relating to parent and child," he said,[307] "is concerned with the problem of the growth and maturity of the human personality. If law should impose on the process of 'growing up' fixed limits where nature knows only a continuous process, the price would be artificiality and a lack of realism in an area where the law must be sensitive to human development and social change." It followed that the test for determining whether a particular decision could be made by a child was one of fact: namely, whether the child had a sufficient intelligence and understanding of what is involved to make a proper decision – that test became known later as *Gillick Competence*. It is possible, to a small degree, to find earlier authority, though by no means as established and, perhaps, from a rather more mercurial source: thus, in *Hewer v Bryant*,[308] Lord Denning had said that a parent's right to custody ended when the child reached eighteen and, "…even up till then it is a dwindling right which the courts will hesitate to enforce against the wishes of the child. It starts with a right of control and ends with little more than advice."

The fact, of course is that Lord Scarman's approach was truly radical and not dependent on precedent (or memory). The distinguished English legal commentator, Eekelaar, has emphasised[309] that it is impossible to overrate Lord Scarman's view of the autonomy interests of children. The reason for that is that once, regardless of chronological age, the child has attained *Gillick Competence*, a parent will not be permitted to impose a contrary view even if that view accords more with the child's best interests.[310] The issue of predictability[311] – including self-predictability – makes the process a fraught one. So, once again, we see that, although a place may be found for the antiquity-based reasoning described by

Goodrich, it does not, by any means, account for the whole story. Indeed, it is likely that Lord Scarman, and the judges who adopted a like approach, was consciously seeking to point the law in a new direction.

It may also be that an outcomes approach may be resorted to by courts, to avoid necessarily a particular course. *Characterisation* in the Conflict of Laws is a topic often regarded as being too difficult for detailed scrutiny.[312] In a series of Australian cases, which I have elsewhere canvassed,[313] there is a dispute as to whether direct claims against motor vehicle insurers should be regarded as arising out of contract or tort. Despite the fact that this commentator considers[314] that there can be little doubt that *tort* is the appropriate characterisation, the reason for attempting to characterise it as arising out of *quasi-contract* may not be far to seek. If a transaction can be so characterised, it would avoid the double actionability rule enunciated in *Phillips* v *Eyre*, which has no analogue elsewhere in the Conflict of Laws.[315] If a combination of circumstances can be characterised as something other than tort, then the *Phillips* v *Eyre* rule, which requires that actionability be shown in both the *lex loci delicti* and the *lex fori*, can be avoided, together with the other inconveniences which attract to it. Thus, although antiquity may be involved, the process of characterisation does not necessarily involved the adherence to it that Goodrich suggests: the process is concerned with circumscription and restriction.

Although Goodrich's discussion does not, it is suggested, stand up to close analysis and examination, it is not nearly the totality of the *critical legal studies* movement. Hunt depicts[316] that movement as being, "...the *enfant terrible* of contemporary legal studies. It delights in showing what it takes to be the legal establishment. Its roots lie in a deep sense of dissatisfaction with the existing state of modern legal scholarship. These dissatisfactions and grievances are many and varied: some are more concerned with the state of legal education, others with the political conservatism of legal education, whilst others experience frustration at the failure of orthodoxy to grapple with what they see as the real problems of the role of law in the contemporary world. Advocates of critical legal studies may not all share the same rank ordering of dissatisfactions but all are reacting against features of the prevailing orthodoxies in legal scholarship, against the conservatism of the law schools and against many features of the role taken by law and legal institutions in modern society."

Hunt goes on in his essay[317] to seek to develop what he describes as *relational theory of law*. That theory, he suggests, "...proposes an analysis which posits the existence of a number of different forms of legal relations which interact in varying ways with other forms of social relations. Its project is one which takes 'law' as its object of inquiry but which pursues it by means of the exploration of the interaction between legal relations and other forms of social relations rather than treating it as an autonomous field of inquiry linked only be external relations to the rest of society." Hunt goes on[318] to re-emphasise that the area of legal relations is not, in fact, autonomous and is characterised by the penetration of extra-legal relations. Hunt considers that, for too long, the study of judicial decision making has been, preoccupied by a search for distinctive and exclusive forms of *legal*[319] reasoning. A relational approach, he continues, would examine both the presence and the source of other discursive and rhetorical forms. It is in that context, that the interaction and interrelationship of law and literature clearly becomes both a relevant, and attainable, object of inquiry. Analysis of the discursive and rhetorical forms which are to be found in both law and literature (especially poetry) becomes realisable.

Yet, although there are aspects of critical legal studies which immediately make it attractive in the context of law and literature – and can certainly help in devising a self-justification – it would be quite wrong wholly to ignore other views of the movement and its influences. Thus, Dworkin argues[320] that the name (Critical Legal Studies) is, "...so far defined by subscription: it acolytes assemble in conferences whose purposes include deciding what the movement is." However, Dworkin does state that the movement does share important attitudes about legal education. This is, of course, important because of the educative function of Law and Literature as referred to by Ward and others, commented on earlier in this Chapter.[321]

Further, Dworkin continues[322] that, apart from the movement's generally perceived left wing political orientation (at least by United Stated standards) and its choice of other disciplines to be studied, the movement closely resembles the earlier movement of American *Legal Realism*.[323] Dworkin is scarcely flattering of that movement when he writes that it was too early to say whether critical legal studies, "...represented more than an anachronistic attempt to make that dated movement reflower." Dworkin regards the movement's major contribution as realising that legal culture can only be grasped through the metric of contradiction. Critical legal studies reflects two antagonistic ideologies at odds within the law. "One drawn, perhaps," Dworkin states, "from communitarian impulses of altruism and mutual concern and the other from the contradictory ideas of egoism, self-sufficiency and judgmental moralism."

Dworkin, although seeming to find the idea of interest, is critical[324] of the movement's writings on the grounds that they merely announce, rather than interpret, the contradiction. "Critical legal historians," he argues, "describe law genetically by tracing different pieces of legal doctrine back to the interests and ideologies that originally placed each in the law or moulded or retained it." Goodrich clearly allies himself[325] with that movement and the discussion of the case law which he sought to use to illustrate his fundamental points about law and antiquity[326] would seem to bear out Dworkins view. As will have been apparent, I find Goodrich's historical approach less than pellucid and, in parts, not a little misleading.

A more general attack on the movement has been launched by Harris,[327] who notes that its members, "…are disenchanted with the institutions of modern western democracies. They deplore the hierarchical structures of social power and the differentiation of social roles fostered in the work-place, the class room, the family and in the process of political decision-making." Harris further considers that had its members reserved their comments for extra-curricular activities (presumably, such as political meetings) no one would have been much troubled. However, Harris states, they have brought them into the Law School , where they seek[328] to *deconstruct*[329] the law by showing how relevant materials might be manipulated, that coherent expression is illusory, that there are no purposes, principles or polices without dispositive bite and, hence, that all outcomes are arbitrary. That is what, Harris claims, adherents of the critical studies, want law students to be taught and that it is acceptance of that message which ought, it was considered by the movement's adherents, to be represented in Law School appointments and promotions!

Although Harris is clearly very unsympathetic to Critical Legal Studies, his major point is not its educationally subversive influence, but that it has been a conspicuous failure! "There is no evidence," Harris writes,[330] "that students who have sat at the feet of the critical scholars and then accepted posts in firms handling corporation or tax law have taken with them any special attitude towards their clients' affairs. What of that!

The radical scholar is revolted by the notion of playing poodle to the demands of legal practice, it is for him to spill the beans about the spurious nature of legal reasoning and the horrible legitimising effects of legal discourse."

I am not as hostile to the essential ideas of the critical legal studies movement as is Harris, and the idea that there is no such distinct conceptual entity as *legal reasoning*, may well assist in bringing together structures and methodologies which are found in law and other disciplines, including literature.

In that context, we should return to the Posner/Dworkin debate regarding the chain novel and its relationship with legal processes. Lindquist and Cross have sought[331] empirically to test the Dworkin chain novel and have produced some interesting conclusions. After noting that the practical significance of precedent, which is *ex hypothesi* a question of considerable legal significance, has been little studied, these writers comment that their own study has shed light on one important feature of precedent. That is, the degree to which, and the circumstances under which, precedent binds subsequent decisions and, in consequence, overrides the policy preferences of the subsequent judge. That, they consider, is the basis of Dworkin's chain novel hypothesis, for which they could only find limited support.

From their study of decisions at first instance, Lindquist and Cross observed that precedent did have some consequentialist effect on decisions. They found that judges exercised relatively more ideological decision making freedom in cases at first instance, which meant that judges could exercise less ideological freedom in other cases which were already governed by relevant precedent. Their results also tended to show that, in all cases, judges tended to exercise some ideological discretion, but the presence of existing precedent did circumscribe that discretion to a significant degree. However, Lindquist and Cross were at pains to point out that their study also called into question the extent to which legal outcomes were driven by precedent. The fact judicial discretion appeared to expand with the growth of additional precedent suggests that the chain novel analogy/hypothesis does not fully describe the operation of law, in the United States at any rate.

Lindquist and Cross's work, thus, suggests that precedent does have some constraining effect on judicial decisions, but that it is not the overriding determinant. In other words, precedent appears to have a moderate constraining effect on judicial freedom. The associations of ideology and outcome in the cases which those writers studied provide measured support for *realist*[332] hypotheses, but the study of cases at first instance refute that school's most extreme claims. Judicial decision making is influenced by precedent, of course, but it is also influenced by ideology and other factors. Hence, the growth of precedent in an area does not appear to restrict judicial discretion – if anything, the development of the law may actually increase such discretion. Lindquist and Cross, therefore, suggest that, whilst the United States system of precedent may create some path dependency, it is a relatively weak path dependency. This, in turn, means that there is ample opportunity for judges to abandon a given path of the law, should it appear, in the clearer light of hindsight, wise.

Though it may be that the light of hindsight may be more dubious than clear, because it may generate an intellectual climate where *ex post facto* rationalisation is acceptable,[333] there are instances discussed in the Chapter which would tend to bear out the point made by Lindquist and Cross. Thus the development of the case law surrounding the so-called marital immunity in rape would seem to bear out the conclusions of those scholars.[334] Likewise matters of ideology or fairness may motivate the finding or creation of distinction where none might immediately be apparent (as in the case law regarding mistaken identity as a vitiating factor in contract.)[335]

It has already been suggested that the chain novel metaphor does not stand up well[336] at least when compared to adjudicating a *hard case* in the sense in which Dworkin himself uses that phrase; once again it does not seem to stand up well against Lindquist and Cross's empirical work; but there may be another and more genuinely literary reason why Dworkin and, hence, Posner are tilting at (possibly non-existent) windmills. The reality is that chain novels are very *rarae aves*. Indeed, it is fair to say that, in terms of serious writing, the chain novel is a very rare creature indeed. It may be that as the Internet develops in a more creative way, then the chain novel will become less unusual phenomenon. It may be that some novels such as *Tristram Shandy* by Tobias Smollett and other novels written in an epistolary or journal form may read as though they were such (and were probably intended to be). But that is precisely not the point that Dworkin was seeking to make.

Before leaving Posner's contribution to the consideration of some of the less specific issues involved in the relationship of law and literature, one other point which he raises should be examined. Posner states unequivocally[337] that legal and literary interpretation have nothing *useful*[338] in common. Consistent, he claims, with that thesis, he takes notable exception to Fried's attempt[339] to infer the intelligibility of the United States Constitution from that of Shakespeare's Sonnet LXV. Sonnet LXV reads as follows:

> Since brass, nor stone, nor earth, nor boundless sea,
> But sad mortality o'ersways their power,
> How with this rage shall beauty hold a plea,
> Whose action is no stronger than a flower?
> O, how shall summer's honey breath hold out
> Against the wrackful siege of battering days,
> When rocks impregnable are not so stout,
> Nor gates of steel so strong, but Time decays?
> O fearful meditation! Where, alack,
> Shall Time's best jewel from Time's chest lie hid?
> Or what strong hand can hold his swift foot back?
> Or who his spoil of beauty can forbid?
> O, none, unless this miracle have might,
> That in black ink my love may still shine bright.

Fried's argument, in essence, is that the sonnet's premise is the intelligibility of writing and that that premise is justified by the poem's being over four hundred years old and still presents no problems of interpretation for the modern reader. Posner disagrees and considers that Fried has (deliberately...?) overlooked such problems as there might be – thus, he argues, for instance, that Fried has ignored the note of dubiety which is sounded in the concluding couplet:[340] thus, he has overlooked *unless* and *may* as well has having overlooked the possible pun in the word *might* there. In other words, Posner suggests, Shakespeare may have been less confident than Fried argues that *black ink* could survive the ravages of mortality. Further, Posner continues by referring to Wilson Knight, who has argued[341] that the reference to *black ink* is contemptuous and that Shakespeare, not caring about publication, sought the *miracle* elsewhere.[342]

Nonetheless, despite what he calls *quibbles,* Posner concedes that Fried has shown that a great work of literature can, because of its theme's timelessness, be universal and unambiguous. However, Posner baulks, as do I, at Fried's rather sudden transference of this theme to the interpretation of the United States Constitution. Although, he continues, some of Shakespeare's works do not pose problems of interpretation, others do. As do works of literature of mere recent origin.

Thus, by way of example, there are serious problems of interpretation arising out of the, so-called, Holy Sonnets of the 20th Century poet Dylan Thomas. Although these problems of interpretation are apparent both from the poem(s) themselves and critical commentary, it would be a writer more courageous than am I who would seek to transfer their interpretation to a legal context. Thus, the first stanza/sonnet is well known and begins the sequence strikingly and starkly:

> Altarwise by owl-light in the halfway-house
> The gentleman lay graveward with his furies;
> Abaddon in the hang-nail cracked from Adam,
> And, from his fork, a dog among the fairies,
> The atlas-eater with a jaw for news,
> Bit out the mandrake with tomorrow's scream.
> Then penny-eyed, that gentleman of wounds,
> Old cock from nowheres and the heaven's egg,
> With bones unbuttoned to the halfway winds,
> Hatched from the windy salvage on one leg,
> Scraped at my cradle in a walking word
> That night of time under the Christward shelter,
> I am the long world's gentleman, he said
> And share my bed with Capricorn and Cancer.

Considerable claims have been made for the *Altarwise* sonnets, as they also sometimes known: thus, Moynihan[343] states that they are, "…Thomas's most complex depiction of the fallen world, the world of exodus or wilderness, the world of the lost wanderer, the outcast voyager. The sonnets are also the epitome of Thomas's obscurity. The whole sequence, and every word within it, is intended to be meaningful on so many different levels that it may almost be said that the ambiguity itself is an image of the fallen world which it depicts" Moynihan perceives the sequence as representing a loose chronological framework based on reference to various periods in the process from birth to maturity and, ultimately, through death to the day of judgment.

But there are other interpretations, although an autobiographical slant is one which tends to recur amongst commentators. Tindall has written[344] that the poet himself so regarded the sonnets and that Thomas himself was the constant subject of his prose and verse. Tindall takes issue with another critic, Olsen, who regards[345] the poem as corresponding to an astrological source, whereby the poem's narrator refers to the movements of the heavenly bodies, especially the Sun and the constellations of Hercules and Cygnus so as to articulate his thoughts about sin and redemption. Hence, the *half-way-house* in the first sonnet/stanza is the autumn equinox and the *gentleman* is the Sun who moves south towards Ara (*altarwise*). Tindall comments that, "Thomas who knew a little about the zodiac, knew himself entirely."

It is, despite Moynihan's claim for the poem,[346] hard to engraft the *Altarwise* sonnets on to any legal document or structure onto the poem, the more so as it is hard to identify the narrator or, indeed, ascertain accurately how many narrators there actually are. The fact that a literary work appears to deal with timeless issues cannot necessarily mean that it can provide a guide to the interpretation of a document such as the Constitution of the United States. At the same time, though, that does not mean that Dylan Thomas is wholly irrelevant to matters relating to law.[347]

Thus far, it has been sought to relate works of literature to legal issues and interpretations or the subject matter of legal activity to literary processes. However, there is another approach to which reference ought to be made: that is the attempt to categorise legal documents, notably judgments, as literature. A particular exponent of this approach is Harris, who has written[348] that, "Litigation is seldom exciting to anyone without a direct interest in it. Even when grappling with the most profound issues lawyers, like philosophers and theologians, manage all too often to strip them of every vestige of human interest. But when a penetrating legal intellect is combined with outstanding felicity of expression the results can be electrifying, even to the non-lawyer." Harris was writing an introduction to an anthology of judgments which he considers to be worthy of characterisation as literature.

This, one supposes, is a characterisation which is not to hard make, provided that *literature* is a term sufficiently widely defined. "Literature", Posner tell us,[349] "is a label that we give to texts, of whatever character or provenance, that are meaningful for readers who are not in the writer's contemplation." He goes on to say that College courses with titles such as *The Bible as Literature* tell the whole story: the authors of the Bible did not aim to write for future readers of literature. It may also be that Shakespeare, "Even Shakespeare", he continues,[350] "may not have thought so, at least when writing plays, as he made no effort to revise them for publication or to get them published. He may have thought of them as strictly quotidian productions, a way of making money." The same is *generally*[351] true of judges who, although they may consciously be writing for posterity, are merely seeking a statement of the law for posterity, rather than anything more. However, some statements of the law appear to have taken on a creative life of their own. An obvious instance is the *neighbour principle* enunciated by Lord Atkin in the landmark decision in *Donoghue v Stevenson*, and noted earlier.[352] A variety of judgments will be discussed in the remainder of this book and it will become apparent that some judgments, rather than others, may be more likely to be categorised as *literature*. Much is likely to be determined by the subject matter with which the court is concerned, the more so as Posner suggests[353] that literature is characteristically dramatic and, consequently, deals in conflict. In further consequence, law provides, as a method of managing conflict, a rich stock of metaphors for authors to use – since the metaphor is very much the stock-in-trade of the poet. In the words of Dylan Thomas,[354] once again:

> And what's the rub? Death's feather on the nerve?
> Your mouth, my love, the thistle in the kiss?
> My Jack of Christ born thorny on the tree?
> The words of death are dryer than his stiff,
> My wordy wounds are printed with your hair.
> I would be tickled by the rub that is:
> Man be my metaphor.

Posner is suspicious of the use of the metaphor in the writing of judgments[355] and he states that, "The danger, when judges try to be literary, is not that they will make pompous fools of themselves, though often they will, or make the worse appear to better cause. It is that they will muddy the law." Yet, at the same time, Posner seizes upon a sentence from the judgment of Cardozo J, an internationally regarded judge,[356] in the case of *People* v *Defoe*.[357] That case involved the rule that, in the State of New York, evidence which had illegally been obtained by the police remained admissible in a criminal trial.[358] In *Defoe*, Cardozo J encapsulated[359] the case against an exclusionary rule in eleven words: "the criminal is to go free because the constable has blundered." Posner states, first, that compassion was not that sentence's only virtue. He goes on to comment that the use of the slightly archaic word *constable* for *policeman* was *inspired* because it not only improved the sentence's rhythm, but makes it more memorable. More memorable because it puts the reader/listener in mind of, "...the unarmed British policeman, so different (in legend anyway) from his rough American counterpart. And Cardozo's constable is not a uniformed thing but a blunderer – a Gilbert and Sullivan constable whose pratfalls are unlikely to strike anyone as a menace to personal liberty." Of course, Posner could well have added to W S Gilbert's comical police/constables, Constable Dogberry in Shakespeare's *Much Ado About Nothing*. Given the context of his discussion at large, Posner seems to regard Cardozo J's metaphor and aphorism as actually accentuating compression and, more particularly, vividness.[360] However, not all judicial metaphor has that effect.

The issue of *metaphor* has been taken further by Goodrich,[361] who, like Aristotle, regarded it as a figure of *substitution*, in the sense that it states a resemblance either explicitly – by way of analogy or simile, usually denoted by the word *like* – or implicitly, by direct reference. The figure of *analogy*, Goodrich goes on,[362] explicitly states a likeness or similarity between two acts, situations or things. "The figure of analogy does not," he writes, "however, of itself explain or prove the basis of the similarity predicted: if we accept that each situation before a court of law is in principle unique, analogies are always evaluative or interpretative." More specifically when an appellate court states, as such courts frequently do, that case X is "on all fours" with case Y, Goodrich considers that simply a vivid, or metaphoric, way of asserting an interpretive choice as to the features of the two cases which render them similar. The process though, may not be all that simple: thus, by way of example already raised, the court in *Lewis v Avery*[363] were required to decide whether that case was more similar to *Phillips v Brooks Ltd*[364] or to *Ingram v Little*.[365] Goodrich seems aware of that particular responsibility when he writes that *any* [366] metaphoric figure suggests *comparability* [367] and it does so most appropriately when it can be associated with its subject matter and audience.

This is important for law and literature studies, not least because of the self-image that lawyers, in whatever sphere they operate, have of themselves. Thus, Goodrich states[368] that, "For the legal audience, in the conventional view at least, the proportional metaphor is most likely to be effective because it retains the appearance of logic, whereas the political and literary genres are more frequently or explicitly concerned with vivid or dramatic metaphors that will increase the audience's sense of presence…or of belonging…"

That issue is also of genuine concern to Posner who asks[369] whether a judicial writing style, which might be adopted for reasons independent of one's jurisprudential stance, could affect content. There are reasons, Posner suggests which might account for such a situation: judges may not be able to write in any other way, they may have particular aesthetic principles or a particular mode of expression may be in fashion. To add to Posner's list of explanations one might add a judicial urge to be dramatic, and being dramatic for its own sake at that. Thus, for instance, in one decision of the Court of Appeal in England, one famous judge began his judgment in these[370] terms: "It happened on April 19, 1964. It was bluebell time in Kent. Mr and Mrs Hinz had been married some 10 years, and they had four children, all aged nine and under. The youngest was one. Mrs Hinz was a remarkable woman. In addition to her own four, she was foster mother to four other children. To add to it, she was two months pregnant with her fifth child." From the point of view of the facts of the case as well as from that of the direct legal issue involved that rather overblown beginning adds very little to what was to eventuate later in the judgments. The case involved a shocking motor accident which had traumatic consequences for the plaintiff. However, all of that emerged without the initial floral symbolism.

Where, Posner suggests, it is possible to formulate a proposition for oneself in pragmatic terms and then wrap it up in formalism, there is a danger that the wrapping will make it more difficult for the writer, as well as the readers, to come to terms with the essential questions. "We believe that words enable thought," continues the author, "But words can also substitute for thought. The pure style is an anodyne for thought. The impure style forces – well invites the writer to dig below the verbal surface of the doctrines that he is interpreting and applying. There he may find merely his own emotions, but if he is lucky, he may find the deep springs of the law."

Further, Posner argues[371] that, in thinking about a case, a judge may come to an initial conclusion and yet may find that conclusion to be untenable when he comes to write an opinion justifying it. It is at this point in his argument that Posner seems to realise how entwined the creative processes of law and literature genuinely are: "We do not think entirely in words," he stated, " and certainly not in sentences and paragraphs. Inarticulable or even unconscious feelings and impressions fill in around the sentence fragments that form in our minds as we think about a problem." Posner urges that language is not only a medium of communication but is also an aid to thought and, hence, writing can be an aid to critical detachment. Similarly, it may even be necessary to bring deep intuitions to the surface. "Many writers", Posner states, "have the experience of not knowing except in a general sense what they are going to write until they start writing. A link is sometimes forged between the unconscious and the pen. The link is lost to the judge who does not write. It is not only poets who write better than they know."

Throughout this chapter and, indeed, throughout the remainder of the book are examples of lawyers/judges and poets who write better than they know (or sometimes worse). We have seen how legal and literary notions are intertwined and debated. It is suggested that the very fact that these issues are being debated in the terms discussed in this chapter demonstrate that the study of Law and Literature is worthwhile for its own sake as well as for the light which the one may be able to cast on the other. Thus, the operation of the doctrine of precedent has been noted by way of various examples, as has the use of language in both law and literature. It should also be reiterated[372] that the aim of this book is not to view the relationship between legal and literary study through the glass (darkly?) of theory –

even though some of those theories required discussion – but to do so by direct reference to the texts in question. By so doing, it is hoped to be able to examine the approaches taken by writers in the law and by more traditionally literary writers to the same events and situations.

In fine, and by way of introduction to the next chapter, an example of the way in which literature can, in some respects, imitate law. A graphic instance is provided by two poems – one written in extreme circumstances quite some time ago and another written very recently – one derived from the other, though they are not saying the same things, but have a common metaphor attached to objects which are, and yet are not, the same. The first is well known: "Anthem for Doomed Youth" by Wilfred Owen, written in 1917. The key phrase is *passing-bells* in the first line of the sonnet.[373]

> What passing-bells for these who die as cattle?
> - Only the monstrous anger of the guns.
> Only the stuttering rifles' rapid rattle
> Can patter out their hasty orisons.
> No mockeries now for them; no prayers nor bells;
> Nor any voice of mourning save the choirs, -
> The shrill, demented choirs of wailing shells;
> And bugles calling for them from sad shires.
>
> What candles may be held to speed them all?
> Not in the hands of boys but in their eyes
> Shall shine the holy glimmers of goodbyes.
> The pallor of girls' brows shall be their pall;
> Their flowers the tenderness of patient minds,
> And each slow dusk a drawing-down of blinds.

The theme has been very much more recently taken up by the present Poet Laureate, Carol Ann Duffy, in her own poem, "Passing Bells"[374]

> That moment when the soldier's soul
> slipped through his wounds, seeped
> through the staunching fingers of his friend
> then, like a shadow, slid across a field
> to vanish, vanish, into textless air…

Having begun the poem wiwth those dramatic five lines which link the later porem directly with the earlier, Duffy then changes the direction of her thoughts, and of her poem from *passing*, in the sense of the soldier's death itself, to *bells*, in the sense of the various, traditional or non-traditional, responses of bells to it. She details by, initially, location; the kinds of bell which provide a response to the initiating event. The response is depicted, paradoxically, as both causally and, yet coincidental. Interspered with the locations which are scattered thrugout, apparently at random, England, Scotland and Wales are the various bells, coupled with their sounds. Often the kinds of bell are placed in delicate counterpose: in the eighth line, there is abell, "…rung be a landlord in a sweating, singing pub…", next, in the ninth, a bell rung by an altar boy. The sight and sound of mortality is, inevitably present in the, "… songbird fluttering from a tinkling cat…" That last instance apart, the majority of instances which have been selected by Duffy represent very traditional values of the places which she names and the activities of people who had bells and who are ineviatbly, by tthat aural contact linked to the death of the soldier who, thereby, is as one with communities and people Duffy describes in the remainder of the poem. However mundane they may all be : "the crowded late night bus; a child's bicycle, the old familiar clanking cow bells of the cattle"

The themes and the responses are similar but the ways in which those responses are reached are wholly different. How various themes are treated in law and in literature will take up much of the remainder of this book.

---

[1] See, for example, *Louth v Diprose* (1992) 175 CLR 162, see below Ch VI; *The Church of the New Faith v Commissioner for Payroll Tax, Victoria* (1983) 154 CLR 120; see below Ch III; *Alcock v Chief Constable of South Yorkshire* [1992] 1 AC 310, see below Ch VII.
[2] I. Ward, *Law and Literature: Possibilities and Perspectives* (1995) at 24 *ff*.
[3] N. Cook, "Shakespeare Comes to the Law School" (1988) 68 *Denver ULR* 387.
[4] For a commentary on the contribution of Cavers to United States Conflicts of Laws theories, see E.F. Scoles, P. Hay, P. Borchers, S.C. Symeonides, *Conflict of Laws* (4th Ed, 2000) at 22 *ff*.
[5] D.F. Cavers, "Legal Education in the United States" in *Talks on American Law* (Rev. Ed., 1971. Ed. Berman) 273.
[6] In Cavers's own words, "… the law teacher seldom delivers formal lectures, even though he may have 150 or 200 students in his class. Instead, by asking probing questions and by posing a succession of problems, he directs his students in a close analysis of the judicial opinions assigned for the day's class. The teacher tries to stimulate a lively discussion amongst the students. The student taking part must have a firm grasp of each case and not only know the court's reasoning but be prepared to criticize it. He cannot accept the court's reasoning as

necessarily authoritative, for the very next case he reads may be drawn from the law reports of another state which takes a squarely contradictory position."

[7] Above n3 at 411.
[8] See R.S. Redmount, "A Conceptual View of the Legal Education Process" (1972) 24 *J Legal Ed* 129.
[9] (1995) 184 CLR 538.
[10] See *Defence Services Homes Act* 1918. For comment, see R.P. Meagher and W.M.C. Gummow, *Jacobs' Law of Trusts in Australia* (6th ed 1997) at 139.
[11] For comment on the presumption of advancement, see ibid at 294 *ff*.
[12] For comment on the operation of the notion of the resulting trust, see ibid at 285 *ff*.
[13] [1945] 1 KB 65. The so-called *Bowmaker Rule* operates as an exception to the contextual operation of the equitable maxim *ex turpi causa non ortur actio* which means that the courts cannot permit a plaintiff to bring an action to enforce a transaction involving an illegal purpose. The *Bowmaker Rule* permits property interests under illegal transactions to pass if the plaintiff could establish title without relying on the illegality. For comment, see B. Coote, "Another Look at *Bowmakers v Barnet Instruments*" (1972) 35 *MLR* 38.
[14] (1995) 184 CLR 538 at 570.
[15] Ibid at 559.
[16] They also noted, ibid at 560, that earlier cases such as *Cottington v Fletcher* (1740) 2 Atk 155 and *Minckleston v Brown* (1801) 6 Ves 53 were instances of individual responses to particular statutory provisions rather than representing more general statements of principle.
[17] (1995) 184 CLR 538 at 595.
[18] Ibid at 593.
[19] Ibid at 595.
[20] Author's emphasis. See generally N. Enonchong, "Illegality : The Fading Flame of Public Policy" (1994) 14 *Oxford J Legal Studies* 295.
[21] (1995) 184 CLR 538 at 615.
[22] Ibid at 617.
[23] [1994] AC 340. For comment, see H. Stowe, "The Unruly Horse Has Bolted: *Tinsley v Milligan*" (1994) 57 *MLR* 441.
[24] A view adopted by Toohey J in *Nelson v Nelson* (1995) 184 CLR 538 at 597.
[25] Lords Browne-Wilkinson, Lowry and Jauncey.
[26] Above n13.
[27] [1994] AC 340 at 371.
[28] Ibid at 371.
[29] Ibid at 375.
[30] Lord Browne-Wilkinson's emphasis.
[31] For an analogous proceeding, see the decision of the Ontario Court of Appeal in *Gorog v Kiss* (1977) 78 DLR (3d) 690.
[32] [1994] AC 340 at 362.
[33] Ibid at 362.
[34] P. Millett, "Villainy In Venice" in *On Villainy* (2007) at 3.
[35] Ibid at 5.
[36] It does, after all, as Lord Millett points out, ibid at 3, include a trial scene which, in Lord Millett's own words, "… helps to resolve the main problem that the play poses: is Shylock a villain or a victim? It may also help to resolve a subsidiary question: did Shylock always intend to exact his pound of flesh? Or did he change his mind later, and if so when?" The other, though for different reasons, is *Measure for Measure*.
[37] Above n 34 at 5.
[38] Ibid at 8.
[39] Ibid at 4.
[40] W.A.N. Wells, *Evidence and Advocacy* (1988) at 167.
[41] Above n 34 at 4.
[42] *The Merchant of Venice* Act IV, Sc 1.

[43] Above n 34 at 12.
[44] See, for example, O.F. Robinson, T.D. Ferguson and W.M. Gordon, *European Legal History* (2nd Ed., 1994) at 109 *ff*.
[45] J.H. Merryman, *The Civil Law Tradition* (1969) at 123.
[46] Above text at n45.
[47] Above n 45 at 129.
[48] Above n 34 at 11.
[49] Ibid at 12.
[50] Above text at n 33.
[51] Above text at n 28.
[52] Act II.
[53] Above text at n 32.
[54] D. Cooke, *Rich Law, Poor Law: Different Responses to Tax and Supplementary Benefit Fraud* (1989).
[55] Ibid at 172.
[56] Ibid at 173.
[57] Cooke's emphasis.
[58] Cooke's emphasis.
[59] Above n 54 at 162 *ff*.
[60] (1995) 184 CLR 538 at 579.
[61] Ibid at 579.
[62] Ibid at 580.
[63] Above text at n 51*ff*.
[64] [1994] AC 340 at 363.
[65] Ibid at 364.
[66] R.A. Pearce and J. Stevens, *The Law of Trusts and Equitable Obligations* (4th Ed, 2006) at 262.
[67] Law Com CP No 154 (1999)
[68] M. Enonchong, "Illegal Transactions: the Future" [2000] *Restitution LR* 82.
[69] Above n 34 at 16 *ff*
[70] Above text at n 7.
[71] Above n 2 at 24.
[72] J. Getman, "Voices" (1988) 66 *Texas LR* 577.
[73] Above text at n 5.
[74] Above n 72 at 579.
[75] Above n 2 at 25.
[76] E.P. Hodges, "Writing in a Different Voice" (1988) 66 *Texas LR* 629.
[77] Above n72 at 588.
[78] B.J. Brown, *Shibboleths of Law: Reification, Plain-English and Popular Legal Symbolism* (1987) at 22.
[79] Ibid at 23.
[80] Sheppard, Neaves and Burchett JJ.
[81] (1993) 119 ALR 65.
[82] See *Commonwealth Employees' Rehabilitation and Compensation Act* 1988 s19.
[83] (1993) 119 ALR 65 at 71.
[84] *Social Security Act* 1991 s1174(1)(a).
[85] Ibid s1174(1)(b)(ii).
[86] Ibid s1174(2).
[87] Ibid s1174(4)
[88] See *Federal Court Rules* O 50, r1.
[89] (1993) 119 ALR 65 at 67.
[90] Ibid at 77.
[91] Ibid at 80. Indeed, that was conceded by counsel for the respondent, ibid at 77.
[92] (1981) 147 CLR 297.

[93] (1993) 119 ALR 65 at 81.
[94] Ibid at 81.
[95] Ibid at 81, See also *Busby v Chief Manager, Human Resources Department, Australian Telecommunications Commission* (1988) 183 ALR 67.
[96] Ibid at 81.
[97] For a particular instance, see F. Bates, *The Reality of Conflicts Reasoning: Choice of Law in Torts* (2010) at 254 ff.
[98] (1993) 119 ALR 65 at 81.
[99] Author's emphasis.
[100] (1993) 119 ALR 65 at 82.
[101] Ibid at 82.
[102] Senate Standing Committee on Legal and Constitutional Affairs, *The Cost of Justice* (1993).
[103] (1993) 119 ALR 65 at 82.
[104] *The Times* (Law Reports) October 10th 1993.
[105] (1993) 119 ALR 65 at 83.
[106] Ibid at 83.
[107] See F. Bates, "Benefits for Handicapped Children in Australian Family Law: A Disaster in Statutory Interpretation and Reform" (1991) 11 *Statute LR* 108, "Social Security Law and Children with Disabilities: Change and Decay in Australian Statute Law" (1997) *Statute LR* 215, "Benefits for Children with Disabilities: A Light at the End of the Tunnel" (1999) 20 *Statute LR* 154.
[108] D.C. Pearce, *Statutory Interpretation in Australia* (1974) at 151.
[109] Above n 2 at 26.
[110] J.B. White, *Justice as Translation: An Essay in Cultural and Legal Criticism* (1990).
[111] Above n2 at 26.
[112] Below text at n 155.
[113] Above text at n 7, 78, for instance.
[114] R.A. Posner, *Law and Literature* (1998, Revised and Enlarged Ed.) at 11.
[115] Ibid at 266 ff.
[116] 198 US 45 (1905).
[117] Ibid at ???.
[118] Above n 114 at 270.
[119] Below text at 373 ff
[120] Above text at n 114.
[121] For a detailed discussion of Shaw's contribution see L.W. Levy, *The Law of the Commonwealth and Chief Justice Shaw: The Evolution of American Law* (1957).
[122] B. Schwarz, *A Book of Legal Lists : The Best and Worst of American Law* (1997) at 131.
[123] Ibid at 132.
[124] For an interesting discussion of *Billy Budd*, see above n 114 at 165 ff.
[125] Above n 122 at 133.
[126] 18 Pick, (35 Mass) 193 (1839).
[127] P. Finkelman, "Law of Slavery" in *The Oxford Guide to American Law* (2002, Ed. Hall) 744 at 746.
[128] 5 Cush. (Mass) 198 (1849).
[129] 163 US 537 (1896). See generally, C.A. Lofgren, *The Plessy Case : A Legal Historical Interpretation* (1987).
[130] Above n 112 at 246.
[131] R. Dworkin, *Law's Empire* (1986) at 229.
[132] Author's emphasis.
[133] Above n 131 at 231.
[134] R. Dworkin, *Taking Rights Seriously* (1977) at 83.
[135] [1973] QB 27.
[136] Which had solidified as a result of a chemical change caused by the partial processing.
[137] Above n 134 at 84.

[138] Above n 134 at 22.
[139] Dworkin notes, ibid, that his distinction may be collapsed through construing principles as social goals (*e.g.* the goal of creating a society in which people do not seek to profit from their own wrongs) or by expressing social goals as principles. Dworkin, ibid at 23, considers that, in some contexts, the distinction has uses which are lost if it is so collapsed.
[140] [1973] QB 27 at 36.
[141] Ibid at 36.
[142] Ibid at 40.
[143] See *S.C.M. (United Kingdom) Ltd v W.J. Whittall and Sons Ltd* [1971] 1 QB 337.
[144] [1973] QB 27 at 40.
[145] Above text at n 138.
[146] [1973] QB 27 at 41.
[147] Edmund Davies LJ's emphasis.
[148] [1973] QB 27 at 49
[149] Derived from T. Weir, *A Casebook on Tort* (5th Ed. 1983) at 48.
[150] Above n 114 at 246.
[151] Note should be made of the *cricket* analogy which is continued in Chapter II of the book in connection with the discussion of the English Court of Appeal's decision in *Miller v Jackson* [1977] QB 966.
[152] Above text at n133.
[153] Above n 114 at 231.
[154] Above n 114 at 246.
[155] (1997) FLC 92-783.
[156] Fogarty, Kay and Morgan JJ.
[157] (1997) FLC 92-783 at 84, 656.
[158] *Family Law Act* 1975 s 68F(2).
[159] Ibid s 68F(2)(l).
[160] See, for example, F. Bates, "Children's Best Interests in Australia: Camouflage, Persiflage or What?" [2005] *International Fam. L.* 138.
[161] *Family Law Act* 1975 s 68F(2)(a) For comment, see F. Bates, " *'Completing the Charm' – the Relevance of Children's Wishes in Contested Cases"* (2004) 5(2) *Newcastle LR* 97.
[162] 78 F 3d 1060 (1996, 6th Cir) For comments, see F. Bates, "War and Disorder: The Hague Child Abduction Convention – Australian Law in Context" (2010) 13 *Asia Pacific LR* 133 at 140. For comment on the relevance of such considerations on the operation of the Convention at large, see F. Bates, *International Disorder and the Hague Child Abduction Convention: A Discursive Commentary* (2009).
[163] (2002) 29 Fam LR 51.
[164] (1997) FLC 92-783 at 84, 657.
[165] Above n114 at 246.
[166] Ibid at 247.
[167] Above text at n 155 *ff.*
[168] Below text at 226 *ff.*.
[169] (1870) 6 LR QB 1 at 28.
[170] J. G. Collier, *Conflict of Laws* (3rd Ed, 2001) at 222.
[171] See generally, F. Bates, *The Reality of Conflicts Reasoning: Choice of Law in Torts* (2010)
[172] [1919] 2 KB 243.
[173] Ibid at 248
[174] R.J. Pothier, *Traité des Obligations* (1761) para 19 (Evans, trs), "Whenever the consideration of the person with whom I am willing to contract enters as an element into the contract which am willing to make, error with regard to the person destroys my consent and consequently annuls the contract."
[175] (1919) 35 LQR 289.
[176] A. L. Goodhart, "Mistake as to Identity in Contract" (1941) 57 *L.Q.R.* 228 at 240.
[177] E. C. S . Wade, "Mistaken Identity in the Law of Contract" (1922) 38 *LQR* 201 at 204.

[178] See *Cundy v Lindsay* (1878) App Cas 459.
[179] *Morrison v Robertson* 1908 S.C. 332.
[180] Section 18 of the *Sale of Goods Act* 1893 provides that, unless a different intention appears, "Where there is an unconditional contract for the sale of specific goods in a deliverable state, the property in the goods passes to the buyer when the contract is made, and it is immaterial whether the time of payment or the time of delivery or both be postponed."
[181] [1961] 1 QB 31.
[182] Ibid at 57.
[183] Above n177.
[184] [1961] 1 QB 31 at 57.
[185] Ibid at 58.
[186] Ibid at 58.
[187] Ibid at 58.
[188] Author's emphasis.
[189] Above text at n 172 *ff*.
[190] [1961] 1 QB 31 at 61.
[191] Ibid at 62.
[192] Ibid at 62.
[193] Ibid at 66.
[194] Ibid at 67.
[195] Ibid at 67.
[196] Ibid at 68.
[197] Above text at n 172 *ff*.
[198] [1961] 1 QB 31 at 73.
[199] Above text at n 185.
[200] [1972] 1 QB 189.
[201] Ibid at 206.
[202] Above n 174.
[203] [1972] 1 QB 189 at 207.
[204] Lord Denning MR's expression.
[205] [1972] 1 QB 189 at 208.
[206] Ibid at 208.
[207] Which he took to be correctly stated in the headnote to the authorized report, *viz*, "Where a person physically present and negotiating to buy a chattel fraudulently assumed the identity of an existing third person, the test to determine to whom the offer was addressed was how ought the promisee to have interpreted the offer." The previous discussion, text at 184*ff*, must surely suggest that that is an oversimplification of what the case actually said.
[208] [1972] 1 QB 189 at 209.
[209] Above text at n 202.
[210] Above text at n 208.
[211] *Twelfth Report of the Law Reform Committee* (1969) Cmnd. 2958 para 15.
[212] This is not truly a hypothetical, more of a derivation as much of what follows is derived from A. L. Goodhart, above n 176.
[213] (1897) 14 TLR 98.
[214] Ibid at 99.
[215] [1940] 1 KB 271.
[216] Ibid at 275.
[217] Above text at n174.
[218] *Solle v Butcher* [1950] 1 KB 671; *Gallie v Lee* [1969] 2 Ch 17; *Lewis v Avery* [1972] 1 QB 198.
[219] Above n 114 at 247.
[220] (1878) 3 App Cas 459.
[221] Ibid at 465.
[222] Above text at 215.

[223] Above text at n 198
[224] *Contractual Mistakes Act* 1977.
[225] For comment on this item of legislation, see F Bates, "Blunting the Sword of Solomon – Australian Family Law in 2006" in *The International Survey of Family Law* (2008, Ed Atkin) 21.
[226] Above text at n 112.
[227] Above n 2
[228] F Bates, "A Reflection upon Law and Literature" (1981) 28 *Chitty's LJ* 13
[229] See above text at n 3 *ff*. See also, F Bates, "The Responsibility of the Law School" (1982) 15 *The Law Teacher* 172, " 'Like an Unwelcome Guest': The Moral Crisis in Modern Legal Education" (1985) 18 *The Law Teacher* 181. See also, F Bates, "The Perils of the Small Law School *Or* A Lesson from *Captain Carpenter* (1984) 5 *Otago LR* 458.
[230] Above n 113 at 247.
[231] Below text a n 249.
[232] Above text at n 80 *ff*.
[233] Above n 113 at 247.
[234] Above n 2.
[235] Quoted in P Fitzpatrick and A Hunt, "Critical Legal Studies: An Introduction" in *Critical Legal Studies* (1987, Eds Fitzpatrick and Hunt) at 1.
[236] Ibid at 2.
[237] A Thomson, "Critical Legal Education in Britain" in above n 234, 183 at 184.
[238] Ibid at 185.
[239] Above n 113 at 345 *ff*.
[240] W N Eskridge, *The Case for Same-Sex Marriage From Sexual Liberty to Civilized Commitment* (1996).
[241] *Baehr* v *Lewin* 852 P 2d 44 (1993).
[242] Thus, Ninia Baehr, the plaintiff is "fawnlike" and possessed of, "…brown eyes that engulf you with understanding and alert sympathy." The other party's, "…broad, dimpled smile and friendly easy going disposition belie her serious work ethic." *Baehr* v *Lewin* is an important decision; for comment, see F Bates, "Same Sex Marriages, Conflict of Laws and Public Policy – A Modern Commentary (1999) 21 *Liverpool LR* 49.
[243] Above n 113 at 352.
[244] Above text at n 236.
[245] E Douzinas and R Warrington, "On the Deconstruction of Jurisprudence" above n 234 33 at 33.
[246] See, for example, C Norris, *Deconstruction: Theory and Practice* (1982); J Culler, *On Deconstruction* (1983). Posner, above n 113 at 211 *ff*.
[247] Above n 113 at 214.
[248] In contrast to, for instance, an *executive summary*.
[249] Above text at n 229.
[250] P Goodrich, *Reading the Law: A Critical Introduction to Legal Method and Techniques* (1986) at 132.
[251] H Gadamer, *Truth and Method* (1979) at 487.
[252] Above text at n 9 *ff*.
[253] Above text at n 171 *ff*.
[254] Above text at n 80 *ff*.
[255] Above n 249 at 133.
[256] Ibid at 141.
[257] Above n 237.
[258] See below Chapter III.
[259] For a rehearsal of the various arguments relating to this ground breaking legislation, see H A Finlay, *To Have But Not To Hold: A History of Attitudes To Marriage and Divorce in Australian 1858-1975* (2005) at 362 *ff*.
[260] Above n 249 at 142.

[261] [1954] 2 QB 282.
[262] *Plautae Coronae* (1736) 620.
[263] [1949] 2 All ER 448.
[264] Ibid at 449.
[265] (1888) 22 QBD 23.
[266] Above n 261.
[267] [1954] 2 QB 282 at 292.
[268] [1992] 1 AC 599.
[269] Ibid at 616.
[270] Author's emphasis.
[271] Section of the *Sexual Offences (Amendment) Act* 1976 was amended by the *Criminal Justice and Public Order Act* 1994 s 142 by deleting the word *unlawful*. The statutory definition is now found in s 1 of the *Sexual Offences Act* 2003.
[272] *CR v United Kingdom; SW v United Kingdom* [1966] 1 FLR 434.
[273] Ibid at 448
[274] Above text at n 260 *ff*.
[275] Above text at n 267 *ff*.
[276] N Lowe and G Douglas, *Bromley's Family Law* (10th Ed, 2006) at 113.
[277] F Bates, "Violence, Money and Informal Families in Australia and New Zealand" (1999) 7 *Asia Pacific Law Review* 1.
[278] [1996] NZFLR 913.
[279] See, for example, Nicholson CJ, "The Changing Nature of Families" (1997) 11 *Aust J Fam L* 13.
[280] Above n 276 at 18.
[281] Above n 249 at 143.
[282] See below Chs II and IV.
[283] A C Swinburne, "Chorus" from *Atalanta in Calydon* (1865) st 4.
[284] [1970] AC 1004.
[285] Three of whom had previously escaped.
[286] [1970] AC 1004 at 1051.
[287] Above n 249 at 144
[288] There had, as J Bell, *Policy Arguments in Judicial Decisions* (1983) at 44, notes, been an earlier County Court decision in *Greenwell v Prison Commissioners* (1951) 101 LJ 486, which had been of scant effect.
[289] [1970] AC 1004 at 1067.
[290] [1932] AC 562 at 580.
[291] [1970] AC 1004 at 1027.
[292] The title of a book of poems by the distinguished Australian writer Margaret Scott.
[293] [1978] AC 728 at 751. For comment, see P Craig, "Negligence in the Exercise of a Statutory Power" (1978) 94 *LQR* 428; J Bell, above n 287 at 48. For reaction to *Anns,* see *Murphy v Brentwood District Council* [1991] 1 AC 398. For comment, see Cooke, R. "An Impossible Distinction" (1991) 107 *LQR* 46.
[294] Above n 249 at 144.
[295] Ibid at 148.
[296] Ibid at 153.
[297] [1986] AC 112. For comment, see J M Eekelaar, "The Emergence of Children's Rights" (1986) 6 *Oxf J Legal Studies* 161.
[298] [1986] AC 112 at 201.
[299] In the sense that it amounted to advice to medical practitioners to commit the offence of causing or encouraging unlawful sexual intercourse with a girl under the age of sixteen (contrary to s 28 (1) of the *Sexual Offences Act* 1956) or the offence of being an accessory to unlawful sexual intercourse with a girl under the age of sixteen (contrary to s 6 (1) of the same Act).

[300] For the purpose of the present discussion, it is the latter argument which is of the greater importance.
[301] The authority did not appeal against the grant of the second.
[302] Above text at n 297.
[303] Above text at n 295.
[304] [1986] AC 112 at 300.
[305] See, for example, *Re Agar-Ellis* (1883) 24 Ch D 317 From the Australian State of Queensland, see *Re Ewing and Ewing* (1881) 1 QLJ 15; *Teppa* v *Teppa* 8 QLJ (N.C.) 109.
[306] Lord Brandon, who agreed with Lord Templeman as to the ultimate result, confined himself to the statutory issue. See above n 298.
[307] [1986] AC 112 at 186.
[308] [1970] 1 QB 357 at 369.
[309] Above n 296.
[310] For iconoclastic comment on that notion, see F Bates, "Children's Best Interests in Australia: Camouflage, Persiflage or What?" [2005] *International Family Law* 138.
[311] See, A Freud, "Child Observation and Prediction of Development: A Lecture in Honour of Ernst Kris" (1958) 13 *The Psychoanalytical Study of the Child* 97.
[312] The last monographic treatment of the topic was that by A H Robertson, *Characterisation in the Conflict of Laws* (1940).
[313] Above n 96 at 65 *ff*.
[314] Ibid at 83.
[315] Ibid at 28.
[316] A Hunt, "The Critique of Law: What is 'Critical About Critical' Legal Studies?" in above n 234 5 at 5.
[317] Ibid at 16.
[318] Ibid at 17.
[319] Author's emphasis.
[320] Above n 133 at 271.
[321] Above text at n 70 *ff*.
[322] Above n 133 at 272.
[323] For comment, see J W Harris, *Legal Philosophies* (2nd Ed 1997) at 99 *ff*.
[324] Above n 133 at 273.
[325] Above n 249 at 209.
[326] Above text at n 259 *ff*.
[327] Above n 312 at 108 *ff*.
[328] Ibid at 109.
[329] See above text at n 244 *ff*. Or *trash*, as Harris, ibid, has it.
[330] Ibid at 113.
[331] S Lindquist and F B Cross, "Empirically testing Dworkin's Chain Novel" (2005) *New York ULR*.
[332] Author's emphasis. Above n 316.
[333] See above n 96 at 259.
[334] Above text at n 261 *ff*.
[335] Above text at n 171 *ff*.
[336] Above text at n 148.
[337] Above n 113 at 250.
[338] Posner's emphasis.
[339] C Fried, "Sonnet LXV and the 'Black Ink' of the Framers Intention" (1987) 100 *Harvard LR* 761.
[340] Posner also suggests, above n 326, that Fried has obviated some of those problems by *Sub Silentio* modernising the spelling and punctuation.
[341] Above n 113 at 251.
[342] G Wilson Knight, *The Mutual Flame: On Shakespeare's Sonnets and The Phoenix and the Turtle* (2nd Ed 1982) at 86. In Wilson Knight's own words, ibid: "The poet knows that through

his poetry, or the poetic consciousness he establishes, or focuses, a supernal reality, or truth, what we might call a 'poetic dimension', that cannot otherwise be attained: and of this the written poetry ('black ink'), though it be necessary, is really subsidiary, the carrot to the donkey, but not the journey's purpose."

[343] W T Moynihan, *The Craft and Art of Dylan Thomas* (1966) at 254.
[344] W Y Tindall, *Reader's Guide to Dylan Thomas* (1962) at 137 *ff*.
[345] E Olsen, *The Poetry of Dylan Thomas* (1954) at 87 *ff*.
[346] Above text at n 332.
[347] See, especially, his late poem, "Over Sir John's Hill." For comment, see F Bates, "Dylan Thomas and the Idea of Law" (2007) VIII (3) *Down Under Milk Wood* 13.
[348] B Harris, *The Literature of the Law* (1998) at xi.
[349] Above n 113 at 20.
[350] See also above text at n 34 and n 331.
[351] Author's emphasis. See below Chapter II.
[352] Above text at n 289.
[353] Above n 113 at 22.
[354] From, "If I Were Tickled by the Rub of Love" in *18 Poems* (1934).
[355] Above n 113 at 279.
[356] In the words of S R Gottlieb, "Cardozo, Benjamin Nathan" in *The Oxford Guide to the Supreme Court* (2nd Ed 2005 Ed Hall) 148 at 149, "Cardozo's opinions, like those of Holmes and Brandeis, are cited for the authority of the author and the clarity of his pen." See also B Schwarz, *A Book of Legal Lists: The Best and Worst in American Law* (1997) at 134 *ff*.
[357] 150 NE 585 (1926).
[358] For a more modern commentary on Anglo-Australian law, see F Bates, "Improperly Obtained Evidence and Public Policy: An Australian Perspective" (1994) 43 *ICLQ* 379.
[359] Above n 346 at 587.
[360] Above n 113 at 280. He disagrees with a frequently expressed view that Cardozo's style is ornate. An *ornate* style, he considers, is, "…one rich in subordinate clauses, parentheses, digressions redundancies and other curlicues."
[361] Above n 249 at 184. The explicit example used by Goodrich is, "The Moon was like a bloodstain in the sky" and the implicit, "The bloodstained moon."
[362] Ibid at 185.
[363] Above text at n 199.
[364] Above text at n 171.
[365] Above text at n 180.
[366] Author's emphasis.
[367] Goodrich's emphasis.
[368] Above n 249 at 185.
[369] Above n 113 at 294
[370] *Hinz v Berry* [1970] 2 QB 40 at 42 *per* Lord Denning MR
[371] Above n 113 at 294.
[372] See above text at 232 *ff*.
[373] J Stallworthy, in a note to the poem in *The Poems of Wilfred Owen* (Ed Stallworthy, 1985) at 76 comments that Owen was probably referring to an anonymous preparatory note to *Poems of Today: An Anthology* (1916) which states that, "…there is not arbitrary isolation of one theme from another; they mingle and interpenetrate throughout to the music of Pan's flute, and of Love's viol, and the bugle call of Endeavour, and the passing-bells of Death."
[374] *New Statesman*, 11th October 2010 at 55.

Chapter II
Poetry, Rhetoric & Law: The Sound and the Fury

1. Introductory Comments

It will have been apparent from, *inter alia,* the discussion of *hermeneutics*[1] that detailed and careful reading of texts is important both in the reading of a legal documents and literary texts. However, it is also apparent that this is not necessarily, and of itself, sufficient. It is important that, at this point, we seek to be more specific and concentrate on the relationship between poetry and rhetoric and the law – which, after all, is the major thrust of this book.

Boyd White seeks to compare[2] lawyers with poets (and historians) and argues[3] that the activities which make up the professional lives of lawyers and judges constitute an enterprise of the *imagination*[4] and, further, an enterprise the central performance of which is the claim of meaning against the odds, by which he means the translation of the imagination into reality by the power of language. "Its art," he goes on, "is accordingly a literary one, most obviously perhaps in the demand that one masters the forces and the limits of...the legal language system – speaking, as it does, in a set of official voices, reducing people to institutional identities, insisting on the repetition of inherited patterns of thought and speech (most frustratingly in the use of the rule) and reposing an impossible confidence in its fictional pretences." The Lawyer's art is, first of all, the literary art which controls that language. That means, in Boyd White's view, that the lawyer is, essentially a writer, who lives by the power of his imagination. Boyd White admits that that is not a usual cultural definition of the law, which is frequently regarded as a *subject* rather than an *activity*, let alone an imaginative and literary one.

The notion of the magical power of words is, of course, nothing new: the Swedish jurist Olivecrona[5] noted that the Romans were extremely careful in phrasing their legal *formulae* and went on[6] to say that, "It is of quite subordinate significance that I have characterised as mystical and magical the supersensible powers with regard to things or persons that the Romans understood [by certain concepts and ideas]; or that I have characterised these ideas, as well as the belief in the gods being astringed by external ceremonies as superstitious. I have called the power in question magical because it is an ability to control things or persons – though this ability has no foundation in empirical reality – I have called it magical, because in magic one handles such mysterious powers: and I have labelled the whole outlook superstitious because I hold that belief in such powers – or goods as having powers of such nature – can have no basis in reality." Nonetheless, Olivecrona believed that Hägerström's approach to Roman notions and *formulae* could be applied to contemporary law.[7]

Boyd White suggests to his readers that they should imagine that they are arguing a case and must continually imagine, ahead of time, what a judge or another lawyer might say in relation to an objection to evidence or in refutation of one's proposition and be prepared, in turn, to meet it. "To argue well, " Boyd White suggests,[8] "you must imagine another mind and have some sense of how someone else might look at your client and his case. How can you put your case in his terms or get him to see it in yours? Likewise, as a legislator or rule maker, the heart of your task is making a just assessment of what your audience, the judges and lawyers, are likely to do with what you have written. The lawyer must be able to tell himself imaginary stories about the future."[9]

Further, Boyd White considers that the lawyer's imagination is more than a capacity for pretending or perceiving - additionally, it is also a power which *organises* what is seen and claims a meaning for it. In Boyd White's own words: "The lawyer must be constantly ready to express things in an original way, to make an imaginatively organised statement, to speak in a way that meets the occasion and says what it calls for. When he rises in the courtroom to make a closing argument to the jury or to argue on appeal, or when he speaks in a letter or orally to his client, the demand is a literary one; he must organise what he knows about the case, the individuals and the law, and do so not only for himself but for others, in such a way that his statement, his version of this can stand the test of comparison with another version, so that is will be taken as the right one." All of this, hitherto, is inexorably connected the very idea of *rhetoric,* which will be discussed later in this Chapter.[10]

Boyd White then posits [11] another imaginative facet of the lawyer's existence, which is represented as a *self-imaginative* process. By this he means that, as lawyers work through their professional life, and as they choose what to say, lawyers work out an identity for themselves. In other words, the lawyer defines a mind and a character, much as a historian, poet or novelist might be said to do. Thus, in Boyd White's own words, "At the end of thirty years, you will be able to look at shelves of briefs, think back on negotiations and arguments and interviews and say 'Here is what I have found it possible to say.' "

Boyd White then seeks to conclude that part of his argument by suggesting[12] that his initial premise – that law can be regarded as an imaginative activity and its art as a literary one – should be regarded as a metaphor rather than, say, as a proposal for a solution or a programme for a way to face the writer's situation.

Boyd White justifies that approach by suggesting that the judge is like the poet – or the historian or the mathematician – which seems to be more promising than using the more mechanical metaphors of the mind and arguing that a judge is like a person using a pair of scales or a tape measure or a mathematical formula. Once then, inevitability, has to ask, in that context, what does a poet seek to attempt to achieve?

Much of Boyd White's view is derived from other much earlier sources. Thus, for example, Sir Philip Sidney, writing in 1595[13] examined the roles of the philosopher, the historian and the poet. Sidney is critical of the first two. The knowledge of the philosopher, he writes, "...standeth so upon the abstract and general, that happy is the man who may understand him, and more happy that can apply what he doth understand." Conversely, the historian, claims Sidney, "...is so tied not to what should be but to what is, to the particular truth of things and not to the general reason of this, that his example draweth no necessary consequence and therefore a less fruitful doctrine." There can be little doubt that there are many historians whose work would tend, at least, to circumvent Sidney's strictures.[14] However, and this is altogether more central to Boyd White's thesis, Sidney says this of the poet in terms which meld together the virtues of the philosopher and the historian: " Now doth the peerless poet perform both; for whatsoever the philosopher saith should be done, he giveth a perfect picture of it in someone by whom he presupposeth it was done; so as he coupleth the general notion with the particular example. A perfect picture I say, for he yieldeth to the powers of the mind an image of that whereof the philosopher bestoweth but a wordish description; which doth neither strike, pierce, nor possess the sight of the soul so much as that other doth."

Boyd White then seeks [15] to illustrate his theme by reference to Emerson who wrote [16] that, "We are like persons who have come out of a cave or cellar into the open air. This is the effect on us of tropes, fables, oracles and all poetic forms. Poets are thus liberating gods. Men have really got a new sense, and found within their world another world, or nest of worlds; for, the metamorphoses once seen, we devine that it does not stop..." Finally, Boyd White calls Coleridge in aid. Coleridge has stated [17] that the power of the poetic imagination, "...reveals itself in the balance or reconcilement of opposite or discordant qualities: of sameness with difference; of the general with the concrete; the idea with the image; the individual with the representative; the sense of novelty and freshness with old and familiar objects; a more than usual order; judgment ever awake and steady self-possession with enthusiasm and feeling profound or vehement; and while it blends and harmonizes the natural and artificial, still subordinates art to nature; the manner to the matter, and our emanation of the poet to our sympathy with the poet."

These are all well known and established statements regarding the function and effect of the poet on the human conscious, but one is still left with the question as to how these statements may be connected to the role and effect of the judge with whom Boyd White is seeking to relate the poet. He suggests [18] that one way to attempt to do so is to ask the basic question relating to the motive of both – namely, why do you write poems? - In the one case and, why do you write judgments/opinions? – in the other. "Presumably," Boyd White ventures, " the judge could decide his cases and draw his salary without writing opinions if he chose, and in fact it is often a real question for a judge whether to explain a decision or a vote."

Although Boyd White's *redictio ad absurdum* suggestion may appear more absurd than strictly necessary, Schwarz refers [19] to the career of one Alfred Moore, a judge of the United States Supreme Court from 1799 until 1804. Schwarz notes that Moore holds the record, with Justice Thomas Johnson, for having delivered the fewest opinions – one – and Johnson was only on the Court for one year. That was in the case of *Bas* v *Tingy*[20] and it was less than one page in length. Although Moore J. was a member of the court in the important decision in *Marbury* v *Madison*,[21] he took no part in the decision and he also acquiesced in *Stuart* v *Laird*.[22] So, perhaps, Boyd White's example is not so strange after all.

Inevitably, Boyd White makes the analogous point that a poet could proceed adequately without writing poems: after all, it very rarely makes the poet rich and she or he is not coerced into writing them. It may be that there are some poets who write few poems, but there may be sufficient, if not necessarily good, reasons for that. Thus, the English poet Basil Bunting issued[23] various suggestions to potential poet's, including, "Put your poem away till you forget it". He continues by urging, "Cut every word you dare" and then "Do it a week later, and again". Such a process would necessarily reduce a poet's output!

Boyd White then turns to the reaction of the potential readers of poems or of judgments/opinions and asks why they should be read at all. Some might argue that neither has any genuine value. If so, why, then, are they written at all? Boyd White suggests[24] that it might be claimed that the poet has a message to communicate whilst the judge has a rule to enunciate. But, he goes on, if that is all there is to it, why do they not make a simple statement of that message or rule? Further, why do readers, he asks, continue reading once that message or rule has been initially grasped. It is quite clear, of course, from material that has already been considered, from both areas of activity that *message* or *rule* may not be simple concepts. Thus, for example, in the two poems noted[25] towards the conclusion of the previous chapter, the message might be stated as: *The tragedy of war may sometimes be appropriately represented by the sound of bells*. However, that rather self-evident message tells the readers nothing of the kinds of bell which can represent the tragedy of war, or the sounds that those bells can make or, indeed, whether the accoutrements of war, in Owen's poem, can more accurately represent the bells in the *message* than bells themselves! Likewise, it would be easy to state the *rule* to be derived from the cases, once again discussed in the previous chapter,[26] relating to mistaken identity as a vitiating factor in the law of contact as: *There is a presumption that a person selling goods intends to sell those goods to the person seeking to purchase them rather than the person represented.* However, that tells us little about the nature of the representation or of the way in which the presumption may be rebutted. In other words, the continuation of an apparently simple *message* or *rule* may be of greater impact (or importance) than the message or the rule itself may be. That, to answer Boyd White's question, may be why the readers of poems or judgments continue their task.

However, as Boyd White himself points out,[27] the central question is whether the judicial opinion/judgment, like the poem, has a form with its own meaning (by which he seems to mean having its own resources for expression and demands on the reader). If such a form exists, then Boyd White asks how the form may be defined? In his own words: "Can you tell what figure an opinion makes? What are the structured tensions, the permanent questions each writer must address hat give it a life and an interest?" If such a form does exist, does it, Boyd White asks, impose a restraint that makes meaning possible. He also wonders whether there is a paradox present in that the limitations on freedom provide for the expression of an individual mind. It should, at that juncture, be said that the present writer is aware of some of the paradoxes which can exist in particular areas of law.[28] Thus, complaints have been made that the area designated as *Family Law* cannot really, for a variety of reasons, be regarded as *Law*.[29] At the same time, it is effectively paradoxical that the reason given - that the family and its activities are areas which the law should not enter[30] - is clearly at odds with the notion that adjudication in the area represents, "... a falling away from the rigorous discipline of common law reasoning, or a mutation into a discretionary gloop that is beneath serious intellectual endeavour."[31] The fact that some statements or concepts may appear paradoxical does not, for that reason alone, mean that it cannot provide a valuable illustration of both the legal and poetic aspects of Boyd White's literary and imaginative experience.

2. Poetic Images

In 1936, the American poet Wallace Stevens produced a collection, *Ideas of Order,* in which was a central remarkable poem "The Idea of Order at Key West." In that very title, a number of conceits, in the Eighteenth Century sense, are apparent. The first lies in the poet himself. First of all, as the commenter Grey, paradoxically, describes[32] Wallace Stevens "An air of mystery hangs over Steven's working life for most of his readers". Grey states, "we are curious about just what he did at the office, and about its relation to his poetry. The curiosity is not idle or random, but stems from a sense that an inexplicable abyss divides the Stevens who made so respectable a bourgeois living as vice-president of the Hartford Accident and Indemnity Company from the Stevens who wrote the gaudy, exotic, mysterious poetry for which he is remembered." In fact, as Grey later notes,[33] he was the son of a successful lawyer and, himself, attended law school and was a member of the New York Bar. He found himself unable to make a living as a trial lawyer and, in 1908, found a job with an insurance company. He ultimately became very successful in that industry and, as Grey states, "The money he made at his work largely freed him from the financial worries common to most poets." Grey goes on to emphasise[34] the problems which some commentators have had with the two *personae* which Wallace Stevens seemed to present.[35] Their approach towards Stevens's *personae* seemed to be that, in Grey's words, "Capitalists may collect but not produce art. If by any chance they do produce it, they are expected to do so, consumer like, as dilettantes: thus, to stress the business side of Stevens's work feeds into the standard, unflattering portrayal of him as an isolated sensualist, a gourmet of the spirit as well as the body, a finicky connoisseur of fine foods and wines, rare pictures and books, and exotic images, finding his *materia poetica* in bric-a-brac".[36]

Because of the highly specialised nature of Stevens's mundane work, a problem of characterisation[37] (as it is known in Private International Law) arises. In other words, should Stevens be treated as a lawyer or as an insurance practitioner. If the latter, then an element of financial dubiety is certainly implicit.[38] Perhaps the most clear instance is provided by the opening lines of John Berryman's mock/serious elegy:[39]

He lifted up, among the actuaries
a grandee crow. Ah ha & he crowed good.
That funny money-man

Conversely, if Stevens is to be perceived as a lawyer, then it is easier, both professionally (perhaps wrongly...[40]) and intellectually, to imbue him, and his work, with some kind of respectability. Thus, Grey notes[41] that other commentators such as Kermode[42] and Bates[43] have sought to emphasise Stevens's role as an insurance *lawyer*. Grey, in that context, notes that such a perception is quite natural for the reasons which I have suggested but also because he forms a part of the law and literature movement, which was selectively discussed in the previous chapter. Hence, that takes up Boyd White's view[44] concerning law and imagination. In other words, as Grey suggests, law is a part of the humanistic tradition, whereas the insurance industry, important though it must be in modern commercial life, is not.

In the end, Grey, after an analysis of the tasks undertaken by Stevens seems to concede[45] that he was an in-house lawyer who worked for an insurance company, though, at the same time he notes[46] that Stevens had no vocation for his work and, more particularly, did not write about it. Perhaps, then in Stevens *ipsissima verba*:[47]

> But I am, in any case
> A most inappropriate man
> In a most unpropitious place.

Very often (too often...?) the notions of *Law* and *Order* are tied together. *Order* in the sense it is used in this regard is concerned with the continuance of a peacefully structured society brought about by *imposed* regulation which is reinforced by, preferably, brutal *sanctions*. It is not concerned with the kind of order which governed Wallace Stevens occupational life. As Grey describes[48] it: "On a typical working day, Stevens came to the office around nine, read his mail, then turned to the stack of claims requesting review, and worked on them systematically through the day. He was renowned both for his steady diligence at work...and for his meticulous attention to detail, he left a clear desk and did not take work home. As already noted,[49] Stevens poem "The Idea of Order at Key West" raises issues about the nature of *order* and how it came about. At one level, and it is suggested that the poem can be read quite enjoyably at that level, it tells a simple story of the narrator and his friend walking along a beach in Florida and observing a young woman dancing and singing. I am reinforced in that view by Schmidt's comment about Stevens work generally, when he wrote[50] that, "It is possible to read Stevens for years with intense pleasure and never to care what the poems mean because the sense of sense is so strong and the movement of feeling so assured. If we do question his meanings and try to tie the poems in to them, we may displace the poetry itself. The subtlety of thought is less compelling than the magic of its effects on the ear and the eye, his ability to arouse the 'intellectual emotions!'

However, there is very much more to "The Idea of Order at Key West" than simple narrative. Grey, to whom copious reference has already been made, interprets[51] the poem as representing a celebration of the need to impose form, however arbitrary, on the otherwise incomprehensible chaos of the natural world because, in the words of the poem's first line, "She sang beyond the genius of the sea". Because:

The sea was not a mask. No more was she.
The song and water were not medleyed sound
Even if what she sang was what she heard,
Since what she sang was uttered word by word.
It may be that in all her phrases stirred
The grinding water and the gasping wind;
But it was she and not the sea we heard.

For she was the maker of the song she sang.
The ever-hooded, tragic-gestured sea
Was merely a place by which she walked to sing.

When the song was finished and the narrator and his friend turned away from the sea and towards the town, they saw:

...the glassy lights,
The lights in the fishing boats at anchor there,
As the night descended, tilting in the air,
Mastered the night and proportioned out the sea,
Fixing emblazoned zones and fiery poles,
Arranging, deepening, enchanting night.

Oh! Blessed rage for order, pale Ramon,
The maker's rage to order words of the sea,
Words of the fragrant portals, dimly-starred,
And of ourselves and our origins,
In ghostlier demarcations, keener sounds.

In other words, Grey suggests,[52] the poet/narrator has experienced a feeling of grateful relief at the momentary imposition of order on otherwise uncontainable chaos. He then goes so far as to say that, a judge or legal theorist can be moved by the same 'rage for order' to want to impose, policeman style' a sharp edged code of positive law on a turbulent sea of otherwise unintelligible social life." Grey goes on to comment that that legal point does not only operate in one political direction because the oppressed may seek clear rules rather than vague standards as against social violence and official prejudice.

From the point of view of the legal commentator, Grey's view of "The Idea of Order at Key West" may very well be the most satisfying, but we must ask ourselves whether it is necessarily the most satisfactory. After all, as has already been noted,[53] different varieties of order exist and this, in the passages last noted,[54] is acknowledged by Grey. Yet Grey's interpretation must not be thought illegitimate and has, with some variation, been rehearsed by Brown, writing in 1970.[55] Brown considers[56] that the elemental impulse of " The Idea of Order at Key West" which is the "Blessed rage for order" is not to be identified (with what Grey calls "the beach striding woman"[57]), but also with the questioning of Ramon Fernandez. The narrator/poet both in his relationship with Ramon and as narrator of the poem and, through that, to "The ever-hooded tragic-gestured sea" and, last, through the address to Ramon, with which the poem concludes, all lead us to the *leitmotiv* of the poem (the "Blessed rage for order") which, in Brown's words, was. "...the spirit that dominates the poem, and it belongs to all who participate in it."

In the context of all of this, the first question to be asked relates to the relevance and identity of Ramon Fernandez. Moore argues[58] that the book by Fernandez, *Messages: Literary Essays,*[59] is the dominant sense of "The Idea of Order at Key West." Fernandez, it should be said has been described in somewhat different terms by Benamon, who states[60] that Fernandez was the French votary of classicism and that his views are synonymous with a heroic posture. It is, though, perhaps not without significance that Stevens himself denied[61] having consciously had that writer in mind. Brown further argues that the answer to the question in the penultimate stanza which the narrator/poet asked of Fernandez is clearly "Blessed rage for order". However, the rage is, "not simply of the woman singing but also, and even more, of the poet Wallace Stevens ordering the woman's ordering of the sea. The singing, the dominant music we have heard throughout the poem, is not that of the woman but of Stevens. He has been ordering her singing throughout the poem...Stevens seeing the lights master the night is not a carry-over and echo of what the woman was doing, it is rather a continuation of what he, as the living, present poet, has been doing all along with the woman's singing. The central notion is not: as the woman to the sea, so now Stevens to the lights and night. It is: as Stevens was to the woman and sea, so now is Stevens to the lights and night."

At the same time, Brown urges[62] that the rage stirring in one's immediate art is a blessed rage but it seeks to achieve an order which can never be achieved, because so to do would destroy the rage that is one's very self. Although Brown takes a different, more internalised, approach to "The Idea of Order at Key West." than does Grey, there is little which is incompatible between their views of the poem. Although Grey, as a Law Professor, directly draws parallels between the poem and some law processes, he remains strictly within the bounds set by the poem itself.

There are, inevitably other ways of perceiving "The Idea of Order at Key West". Thus, for example, Bevis disagrees[63] with Brown's view of the singer, who, Bevis notes, was not a derivation from Steven's own *personae*, but a creative force in her own being:

> It was her voice that made
> The sky acutest at its vanishing.
> She measured to the hour its solitude.
> She was the single artificer of the world
> In which she sang. And when she sang, the sea,
> Whatever self it had, became the self
> That was her song, for she was the maker.

In Bevis's view, "The artist through an act of imagination writes self and other in a third reality, her song. However, the more surprising move, and the better poetry, occurs in the next stanza when two members of the audience, inspired by the song, are walking back toward town and suddenly see the boats in the harbour in a new way".[64]

Bevis, at this point, externalises the phenomenon in terms other than the poem's and comments[65] that Stevens description of the town and harbour resembles a painting by Paul Klee, who was one of Stevens favourite artists. Bevis writes that, "A work of art by either Klee or the singer arranges self and other in a new constraint, likening a moment of imaginative perception in the life of two members of the audience arranges self and other in a new contract. The active participant lives a life of art: things as they are have become things as they are painted... The passionate self creates a new reality through the secret arrangements, the rage for order present in imaginative perception, and therefore imaginative perception is essentially a work of art." Benamon also takes up the theme of painting[66] though he does not specifically mention Paul Klee until a little later. He suggests that "The Idea of Order in Key West" is a poem about poetic creation and, as illustration, Stevens has an image of a port at nightfall. "The order of the description," Benamon posits, "suggests the brush of a painter arguing his pictorial space. The perspective he defines with sure repetitions becomes a symbol of the victory of art over chaos. The verbs carry the magic of his art: mastering, deepening, enchanting; the nouns and the adjectives are fraught with pictorial vividness: fiery pole, glassy lights, emblazoned stones."

Although it is clear that "The Idea of Order at Key West" is capable of an interpretation which represents Stevens's legal background and techniques,[67] it is not through that poem that Grey seeks to tie Stevens's prosody to law, but the poem "The Motive for Metaphor" which appeared in *Transport to Summer*, in 1947. It should be said that this is not an easy poem and required Grey to comment[68] that regarding the various antitheses which occur throughout the poem that, "The exercise of working through to both sides of the poem's antitheses, with the intelligence resisted and the feelings involved at each step, may better simulate, hence better teach, the exercise of legal judgment in a live dispute than could following any set of arguments in analytic prose. An especially graphic instance of the antithesis noted by Grey can be found in the final stanza:

> The ruddy temper, the hammer
> Of red and blue, the hard sound –
> Steel against intimation – the sharp flash,
> The vital, arrogant, fatal, dominant X.

Grey admits[69] that the metaphor ("steel against intimation") contained in the third line is the most opaque in the entire poem. However, Grey notes[70] that the phrase parenthetically sits amongst figures which suggest a blacksmith's forge. Even so, although the word *steel* suggests a hammer, what countervailing force does *intimation* represent? Grey, considers that the primary jurisprudential interpretation of the poem, "…locates law's powers to inflict pain and death in the hot plate of high noon." However, that reading leaves the phrase "Steel against intimation" incongruous in a forge – related collection of surrounding expressions.

Accordingly, Grey suggests that the *steel* represents the metal to be worked in the forge which provides a metaphor whereby, "…the intimating and metaphorizing imagination heats and softens the steel of an impersonal role of law, so that in the decisive moment of legal judgment the jurist can reshape the rule for the task at hand." From that it follows, Grey considers, that the phrase "steel against intimation" juxtaposes two aspects of law: on the one hand, there is its sharp rigidity,[71] which is able to enforce order (again) and dominance, sometimes fatally. On the other hand lies its flexibility in the face of imagination, which maintains vitality but tempts its servants to arrogant self – assertion. Grey concludes the chapter[72] on the poem "The Motive for Metaphor" by stating that those two aspects, "…correspond to the two relations between poetry and law portrayed in the poem as a whole: they are separate spheres; they are intertwining webs."

From the point of view of this book, though, Grey in the context of "The Motive for Metaphor", notes[73] two significant difference between the genres of case and poem: first of all, the facts of a case, if they are skilfully stated, flow easily and naturally. Poetry, conversely, requires more concentration in reading and can, Grey considers, "thereby intensify and fuse both emotional and intellectual response." Second, he is of the view that a story well told may well sound like whole truth, even though it cannot be so. "Poetry, especially Stevens kind of poetry," he claims, "reminds the reader that the bright obvious is not everything: that something, which may be the most important thing, always remains obscure; that a principle, a moral of the story, always carries its own implicit qualification." In law, facts may not always be skilfully stated (or even coherently stated) and there are relatively few principles of law – if there can, in the common law at any rate, be said truly to be any – to which there are no exceptions. But there can equally be little doubt that Grey has alerted us to the way in which the process of legal decision can operate through the approach of the lawyer-trained poet, Wallace Stevens.

It is now necessary to examine a legal decision which has at least some of the elements mentioned by Stevens in the last line of the final stanza of "The Motive for Metaphor" – "The vital, arrogant fatal, dominant X" – that is the decision of the English Court of Appeal in *Miller* v *Jackson*.[74] At the outset, it must be said that one of the judgments in that case adopted a style which might broadly be described, at any rate in a pejorative sense, as poetic. Though how seriously it can, or ought to be taken is an entirely subjective matter, although an appropriate comparison will be made later in the chapter.[75]

So in *Miller* v *Jackson*, Lord Denning MR began his judgment with his own description[76] of the scene where the events leading up to the action took place. "In summertime," said the judge, "village cricket is the delight of everyone. Nearly every village has its own cricket field where the young men play and old men watch. In the village of Lintz in County Durham they have their own ground where they have played these last 70 years. They tend it well. The cricket area is well rolled and mowed. It has a good clubhouse for the players and seats for the onlookers. The village team play there on Saturdays and Sundays. They belong to a league competing with the neighbouring villages. On evenings after work they practise while the light lasts." Lord Denning MR then noted that the cause of the appeal before him was that a High Court judge had issued an injunction to stop the club from playing cricket on the ground which he had so glowingly described. He then went on to describe the plaintiff in the original action. To revert to Lord Denning's own words: "[The judge] has issued it at the instance of a newcomer who is no lover of cricket. This newcomer has built, or has had built for him, a house on the edge of the cricket ground which four years ago was a field where cattle grazed. The animals did not mind the cricket. But now this adjoining field has been turned into a housing estate. The newcomer bought one of the houses on the edge of the cricket ground. No doubt the open space was a selling point." The Master of the Rolls then turned his attention to the substance of the *newcomer's*[77] reasons for seeking the injunction initially: "Now," said Lord Denning, "he complains that when a batsman hits a six the ball lands in his garden or on or near his house. His wife has got so upset about it that they always go out at the weekends. They do not go into the garden when cricket is being played. They say that this is intolerable. So they asked the judge to stop the cricket being played." Lord Denning further continued by projecting the possible consequences of the injunction's being enforced, the first of which being that he supposed that the cricket club would disappear. In addition, "The cricket ground will be turned to some other use. I expect for more houses or a factory. The young men will turn other things instead of cricket. The whole village will be much the poorer."

The judge then considered the causes of the action when he said that "And all of this because a newcomer who has just bought a house there next to the cricket ground. I must say that I am surprised that the developers of the housing estate were allowed to build houses so close to the cricket ground. No doubt they wanted to make the most of their site and put up as many houses as they could for their own profit. The planning authorities ought not to have allowed it. The houses ought to have been so sited as not to interfere with the cricket. But the houses have been built and we have to reckon with the consequences."

It will readily be apparent where the sympathies of that particular judge lay. Had he been the only appellate judge the fate of the injunction was sealed – on the one hand, was the healthy, traditionally English sport of cricket, which provided a valuable pastime for local youth and, on the other, an emphatic newcomer who was just not interested in that valuable pastime and property developers who seemed only interested in profit. Indeed, as will later be seen,[78] the court was necessarily required to balance the rights of both parties to the action, though not necessarily strictly in the *rhetorical*[79] terms used by Lord Denning MR at the beginning of his judgment in *Miller* v *Jackson*. Lord Denning, of course, was not the only judge in the Court of Appeal and other approaches to the dilemma are possible.

Of course just as other approaches to the dilemma outlined, albeit in a rather fulsome and tendentious way, by Lord Denning exist, so there are different attitudes to sports fields. Thus, the Cumbrian poet Norman Nicholson, in his poem. "The Field" written in 1949, describes the field itself:

> A common sort of field you'll say:
> You'd find a dozen any day
> In any northern town, a sour
> Flat landscape shaped with weed and wire,
> And nettle dump and ragwort thicket -

But then the poet emphasises that this especially ordinary field is, "...put by for cricket..." However, the kind of cricket described by Norman Nicholson is different from that over which Lord Denning effused in *Miller* v *Jackson*. The sport has an altogether harsher edge than that which his Lordship seemed to understand. In Nicholson's words:

But this field is put by for cricket.
Here among the grass and plantains
Molehills matter more than mountains,
And generations watch the score
Closer than toss of peace and war.
Here, in matches won and lost,
The town hoards an heroic past,
And legendary bowlers tie
The child's dream in the father's lie.
This is no Wisden pitch; no place
For classic cuts and Newbolt's verse,
But the luck of the league, stiff and stark
With animosity of dark
In-grown village and mining town
When evening smoke-light drizzles down,
And the fist is tight in the trouser pocket,
And the heart turns black for the want of a wicket...

At this point, the author must declare an experiential interest: for some years, he played cricket in the Leagues[80] to which reference was made in both case and poem, and considers that the poet's account is altogether more accurate. Put another way, art, on this occasion at least, is closer to life than life itself.

One could go one further stage – life and art may be brought together through satire. In 1933, the writer A. E. McDonell published a satirical novel *England, Their England* which contained a description of a cricket match between a village, albeit in a location topographically distant from Lintz, and a team from London organised by Mr Hodge, who is a thinly disguised portrait of Sir John Squire. Squire was described[81] by the humorous writer and anthologist Frank Muir in these terms: Squire was, "...a literary journalist, Georgian poet and critic...[who founded] a magazine called the London Mercury to nurture Georgian poetry and new authors, which managed to do quite well in every respect except financially. He was no businessman but he was a tremendous enthusiast, not only for poetry of the hearty, 'foaming tankard' school, but also for architecture and cricket."[82] McDonell describes the picturesque setting of the ground on which the farcical game is played (It should be said that the description is one of the most concentrated pieces of humorous prose in the English language). "The sight" McDonell writes, "was worth an eager gaze or two. It was a hot summer's afternoon. There was no wind, and smoke from the red-roofed cottages curled slowly up into the golden haze. The clock on the flint tower of the church struck the half hour, and the vibrations spread slowly across the shimmering hedge rows, spangled with white blossom of the convolvulus, and lost themselves tremulously among the orchards. Bees lazily drifted. White butterflies flapped their aimless way among the gardens. Delphiniums, larkspur, tiger-lilies, evening primrose, monk's hood, sweet peas, swaggered brilliantly above the box hedges, the wooden palings and the rickety gates. The cricket field itself was a mass of daisies and buttercups and dandelions, tall grass and purple vetches and thistledown, and great clumps of dark red sorrel, except, of course, for the oblong patch in the centre – mown, rolled, watered – a smooth, shining emerald of grass, the Pride of Fordenden, the Wicket...Blue and green dragonflies played at hide and seek among the thistledown, and a pair of swans flew overhead. An ancient man leaned upon a scythe, his sharpening stone sticking out of a pocket in his velveteen waistcoat. A magpie flapped lazily across the meadows. The parson shook hands with the squire. Doves cooed. The haze flickered. The world stood still".

The description is more obviously satirical of particular attitudes towards an essentially English (or so the English would have us believe, despite its enthusiastic reception on the Indian subcontinent) pastime, as well as of a particular style of writing there are echoes of it in Lord Denning's introduction to his judgment in *Miller* v *Jackson*.[83]

Accordingly, it may be thought that it is difficult to extrapolate from the consideration of the particularly national view of one, not wholly universal activity. However, at risk of sounding self-corroborative,[84] I have elsewhere written[85] that, "...law is as much of a country's culture and its music: a fact which is all too infrequently recognised by the law's framers, practitioners, teachers and those responsible for the appointment of its teachers. It is also part of its history... Thus it was for historical and political reasons that the legal system of Scotland developed along very different lines from its southern neighbour. However, that differentiation is becoming a cause for dissatisfaction amongst some Scots commentators.

Historical considerations also influence the modern day-to-day social and cultural life of any society of which law is an integral part. This applies to all societies, ancient and modern..."[86]

3. The Nature Of Rhetoric

Throughout this chapter, oblique reference has been made to the notion of rhetoric. It, thus, becomes necessary to examine what is, or might be, meant by that expression. Once again, a useful starting point is provided by the work of Posner.[87] The chapter of his book which discusses judicial opinions as literature regards rhetoric as referring to the, "...subset of stylistic devices that is used to persuade readers or listeners to believe or do something." Posner then goes on[88] to note that Aristotle used the term to refer to all persuasive devices, not merely stylistic ones, which are to be found in fields of debate or inquiry in which logical or scientific proof is unavailable. Aristotle, Posner argues,[89] thereby enlarges the scope of rhetoric to the propositional meaning or truth value of a speech or writing, as well as its form he seeks to include authority, anecdote, analogy and all other methods of reasoning used to attempt to establish the probable truth of a proposition when exact demonstration is impossible.[90] It may be that Posner, in attempting to encapsulate Aristotle's view of rhetoric as he has, has rather oversimplified the scope and organisation of Aristotle's conception of the notion. From the point of view of the law, Higgins has appositely described[91] Aristotle in these terms: "Aristotle's contribution to classical learning is of peerless scope and dimension, of his many works, 47 treaties, ranging across ethics, physics and metaphysics survive. Various biographies suggest that he was a balding man with a sardonic expression, who had a taste for elegant clothes, jewellery and dining. His natural appeal to the advocate should be manifest."

Higgins's essay is of especial interest because she emphasises[92] the function of Aristotle's rhetoric as being perception of *the means of persuasion*. In turn, that perception implies exclusionary as well as inclusionary devices and there are two sets of constraints necessarily involved. First, Higgins notes[93] that the Aristotelian pursuit of a *techne* (or art) means that the rhetorician must learn and identify the means of persuading in any case. In consequence, she states that, "...rhetoric has internal values of construction, composition, style and so on. The precepts of the rule of law demonstrate that imposing procedural values on an otherwise value-neutral instrument, ensures – to the extent that the internal values are respected – the instrument is less likely to be put to debasing ends." The same, one can readily suppose, is true of rhetoric. Thus, by way of example Higgins posits, one might fail to persuade but, because one has responded to those precepts, one can succeed as an orator.[94]

Second, she continues, the ethical orator must see the available means of persuasion. That means that the hypothetical orator must, to the greatest possible extent, argue rationally, ethically and emotively within the parameters which are expounded in more detail by Aristotle in *The Art of Rhetoric*. Put another way, in Higgins's own words, "My decision to seek to persuade you implies various things. Negatively, it implies that I have decided not to ignore your interests and that I have decided not to use physical or psychological intimidation or coercion to convert you to my preferred position. Positively, it implies weak egalitarianism: I have extended to you a minimum moral respect by including you within the community of possible and valued interlocutors."

More disturbing, though, than Posner's oversimplification of Aristotelian rhetoric is his comment[95], first, that some law and literature scholars use rhetoric as a term of high approbation and inseparable from morality and signifying humanistic values as opposed to the cold rationality of social science analysis.[96] Posner equates that fusion of ethic and aesthetic with the aspect of the law and literature movement which concerns itself with ethical criticism, an activity with which Posner is not himself much impressed.[97] With that approach Posner contrasts the everyday use of the word *rhetoric* as meaning *empty verbiage*. In so doing, Posner suggests that such a meaning can be found in Plato's *Georgias*. Higgins, however, is less taken[98] with that interpretation of Plato's view of rhetoric, which she regards[99] as "uncharitable" and suggests[100] that, "... a more charitable and coherent. [The character of] Socrates juxtaposes dialectic and rhetoric thus, Dialectic enquires and pursues knowledge. Rhetoric flatters and pursues persuasion. Rhetoric is persuasion without knowledge and hence a parasitic art." Nonetheless mundane observation goes at least some way towards confirming Posner's comment.

Posner, additionally and importantly for the instant context, distinguishes between *rhetoric* and *style*, although, as has already been noted,[101] Posner regards *rhetoric* as a *stylistic device*. Posner's view of *style*[102] is that it refers to the literary properties of judicial opinion or judgment and, hence the *persuasive style and empty verbiage* meanings attached to *rhetoric* are, in reality comprehended in style. As Posner put the matter himself,[103] "...style is the smooth capsule or the flavour additive that makes the medicine easier to swallow and hold down – or that makes some readers want to throw up. But it is also the earmark of 'good' writing (that is not 'just rhetoric'), whether or not the writing has any purpose other than to keep the reader reading to the end." On the issue of style in judicial opinions or judgments, Posner argues that one opinion may be better than another not because the argument was more persuasive but, "... because by candidly discussing the facts and authorities tugging against its result, by being tentative and concessive in tone, even by confessing doubts about the soundness of the result, it was a more credible, a more impressive judicial document, though not a more convincing defence of the outcome."

Indeed, we have already seen this in the discussions of Lord Denning's prefatory remarks in *Miller* v *Jackson*.[104] Although they were by no means the whole of the judgment, it is certainly possible to discuss the thrust of what Lord Denning was likely to say from those comments. Whether Lord Denning's judgment at large will be regarded as *better* than the others delivered in the case remains to be seen.[105] It is surely neither difficult, nor is it unreasonable, to regard Lord Denning's initial remarks in that case as tendentious. Indeed, it may be that very *stylistic tendentiousness* which may well remove it from Posner's category of *impressive judicial document*.

However, it may also be that Posner's description is not by any means a complete analysis of the concept. Goodrich seeks to add a further dimension when he writes[106] that, "To understand speech, according to the rhetoricians, one must understand, first, its context and its purpose. Speech aims to communicate. It is always a dialogue – even inner speech is addressed to oneself – and it should therefore be understood analytically and a social activity or at least as an interaction between socially organised individuals. The speech is a process and the rhetoricians wanted to classify the various stages and contexts of that process. Obviously enough the speech begins with a speaker and it is consequently important to examine that such qualities of the speaker and the effect that such qualities can have upon what is said and upon the influence or effectiveness of the statement."

Much, therefore, depended, Goodrich continues[107] on the nature of the speaker's audience. Thus rhetoric recognises that, "Political society and more particularly the media will automatically provide the properly qualified speaker with an audience and the more strictly controlled access to the audience is, the less the personal qualities of the speaker matter." Hence, by way of example, in strictly scientific contexts, the quality of the speaker is considered to be of very little importance and, therefore, the most rhetorically effective scientific speech will be one which gives the greatest appearance of impersonality and objectivity. The scientific speech should appear to instruct or inform and to prove. However, if it does perform other persuasive functions of rhetoric, that ought to be because of the rational strength of the content, rather than because of the persuasive power of the particular speaker. The point which Goodrich then seeks to draw from that example, "…is a simple and crucial one. *The rhetorical speech must be appropriate to its audience.*"[108]

Goodrich then goes on[109] to seek to apply those essential rhetorical principles so that, "Having ascertained the genre, the type and character of the audience, the speakers must look for (invention) arguments appropriate to that particular context. Each genre and each type of audience is to be analysed in terms of the values, beliefs and attitudes that it is likely to adhere to, that are persuasive to it or are of particular relevance for it." What Goodrich is aiming to show is that any speech must select an argument or premise from which to start and that an orator must select an argument or develop the theme of the speech from such a beginning. Goodrich notes that the classical rhetoricians provided two sets of techniques which related to available arguments which Goodrich considers could best be classified in terms of universal and particular topics or places. The former category, Goodrich considers, might be treated rapidly because they are general truths which are available to all arguments and will appeal to any rational audience or any group of listeners who are concerned with truth or objectivity. In legal terms, Goodrich argues,[110] those arguments will primarily be concerned with ways of asserting justice or with injustice before courts, but more particularly, in his own words, "The rhetorical point, however, is not so much to review the content of the specific topics of a particular field of argument but to observe the general character of the audience as the most important element in a discourse. Literary skill, legal expertise, successful preaching, victory at the political hustings and so on will all depend to a large degree upon making use of the conventions or topics of argument within their special field or discursive domain. The reason for this is simply that recognising the needs of the immediate audience by formulating the speech in terms of arguments that are familiar to the audience, the speaker is far more likely to achieve the broad objective of persuading the audience, of leading it in the direction that the rhetorician wishes to advocate. In brief, speech is always speech in a concrete situation and before a variety of established audiences.

Rhetoric will study the character and beliefs of that concrete audience and will attempt to understand both the structure of the concrete audience and will attempt to understand both the structure of the audience and also its current needs, so as to provide the speech with such situational relevance or topicality as may be likely to ensure a sympathetic reception.

It follows, according to Goodrich,[111] that rhetoric differs from other disciplines in that it does not seek to attach to one particular set of values or conception of truth. In Goodrich's *ipsissima verba*, "For the rhetorician all speech, all discourse is contingent: all discourse belongs to a context and is addressed to a particular audience at a particular time and place. Just because the speech happens to be a legal judgment, a philosophical address, a prime ministerial or presidential broadcast does not make it any less a rhetorically organised statement with its own historical limitations. For the rhetorical analysis, all speeches are the same in that they are all attempts to engage in dialogue and in so far as the discourse has a purpose, they endeavour to persuade to make their point. For the rhetoricians, speech is always a process, action within a context, and it would be wrong to allow any one context a privileged claim to have access to truth or to objectivity; precisely because discourse is situational it is not concerned with truth but with probability and improbability (verisimilitude), with what seems true to a particular audience".

In addition to *rhetoric* as such, we have already seen[112] that Posner has raised the issue of *style*. Posner further comments[113] on that matter by saying that, in relation to poetry, "Rhyme and meter, the most musical features of poetry, have an appeal that, being non-verbal, is not tied to the local culture out of which the poetry emerged. We might have lost interest in a particular legal issue discussed in a judicial opinion yet the style of the opinion may make us want to read it anyway: and then the opinion will have outlived the occasion of its creation… The vivid and therefore memorable opinion is not chained to the immediate context of its creation. It can be pulled out and made to exemplify law's abiding concerns."[114]

Goodrich, however, takes issue[115] with Posner directly on that issue: "Despite," he writes, "popular images of rhetoric as the manipulation of language as a discipline which disregards the truth in favour of the ornate or flowery style or persuasion, rhetoric was classically much more concerned with proof and probability than it was with questions of more style…" In both legal and religious rhetoric, he claims, particularly, argument relating to proof was the appropriate form of speech. More generally, Goodrich contends that, in origin, the virtue of the rhetorical style lay in clarity and perspicuity and it was several centuries later that *literary rhetoric* came to be more – and, indeed, eventually – wholly concerned with matters of *style*.

As regards the particular issue of *literary style*, Goodrich continues[116] that, although it has frequently been argued to the contrary, it was only in relation to literary and poetic genres of *rhetoric* that *style* had become a primary focus of study. Thus, in the cases of the religious and legal varieties of rhetoric a concern with *style* – that is, speaking well or with eloquence – was really no more than representative of a concern with presenting the topics and probabilities of the case to be argued in the best possible light. To put the matter another way: although rhetoric might be value-neutral,[117] it was never consciously immoral. Rather its eloquence was aimed at supporting arguments as to the truth of the case which was being presented.

Finally, Goodrich encapsulates[118] the various roles of *rhetoric* and, in so doing, notes that good *style* is effective and hence, ought not to interfere with the content of a speech. By that Goodrich means that the appropriate style will illuminate rather than obscure the arguments or proofs which are being advanced. This, he suggests, is quite obvious, "…since each rhetorical genre or discipline has different topics and goals of argument, a different style will be required. For the legal audience it is best, for instance, to concentrate on a logical style, upon a style which emphasises proof and the balance of probabilities." Goodrich goes on to comment that a political speech, on the other hand requires a dramatic approach and one which presents the arguments in such a way as to exhort the audience so as to induce the decisions or courses of action which are viewed as beneficial to the community. "Only", he concludes, "the ceremonial or panegyric speech, the speech originally concerned with praise and blame, honour and dishonour, would occasionally concentrate on an ornate style or see embellishment of the arguments as being an end or a purpose itself."

Of course, a major purpose of this book at large is to attempt to bring these theories of rhetoric to bear on instances of law and poetry. However, I intend to do so through exposing readers to text directly rather than through the, sometimes obscurantist, gloss of theory. In the subsequent chapters there will be many instances drawn from activities with which both writers, and especially poets, and the law are required to deal. At the outset however, a simple, instance will suffice by way if illustration.

In 1965, as part of a collection, *Highway 61 Revisited*, Bob Dylan wrote a lyric "Queen Jane Approximately." Its first stanza is as follows:

> When your mother sends back all your invitations
> And your father to your sister he explains
> That you're tired of yourself and all of your creations
> *Won't* you come see me, Queen Jane?
> Won't you come see me, Queen Jane?

There are five stanzas in all, each describing a separate misfortune which has occurred to the protagonist ("Queen Jane") and each stanza ends with the same repeated two lines. It is easily possible by reading the poem and giving emphasis to different words in the repeated concluding lines to give quite different meanings to the poem as a whole. Thus, for instance, an initial reading with the emphasis on the first word ("Won't you come see me, Queen Jane?") is a fairly conventional plea from, say, a rejected suitor changes if the emphasis is placed on the penultimate word ("Won't you come see me, Queen Jane?"). It may carry with it an altogether more pejorative tone, which questions the protagonist's right to the title which she has been given or, more possibly, given herself. Much depends on the tone to which the speaker, or, indeed, the speaker's audience wish to derive from the poem.

As Goodrich has suggested,[119] rhetoric has been utilised in the law since classical times. Thus Crook, in his socio-legal study of ancient Rome, has stated,[120] "In the Greco-Roman world litigation was a public spectacle. Rhetoric (which of course was not only forensic but also political and sometimes just epideictic – for display) and rhetoricians fulfilled in ancient society that role that the stars of entertainment hold today. And these theatrical performances, including the speeches of the great barristers in legal actions took place in public in the stoas and basilicas the remains of which are still to be seen." In order to gauge the atmosphere, a comment by Pliny regarding his performance in one such trial and quoted by Crook,[121] should be noted. Pliny writes[122] that he, "…piled on every canvas – indignation, rage distress – and sailed the sea of that tremendous action like a ship before a gale."

In the context of that self-indulgent remark, two matters raised by Crook are of importance: the first relates to the role of the individual in the legal process in the time studied by Crook.[123] Crook comments[124] that, "…it was a part of the philosophy of the Romans that the duty of a citizen included taking his share of the burdens of the law: acting as a judge, arbitrator or juror and supporting his friends in their legal affairs by coming forward as witness, surety and so on. Many a familiar passage of Latin verse testifies to this…" Thus, Crook notes[125] Horace's description[126] of a *good man* as being, "…the man who keeps the resolutions of the senate, the statutes and the law, before whom many great suits are brought to judgment; when he is surety affairs are safe, when he is witness causes are upheld."

The second matter relates to the training of barristers: in that regard, as Crook emphasises,[127] *praetors*[128] were not necessarily legal experts, nor were the judges. Thus, there was no *Bench* as that term would presently be understood. As regards barristers, their training, Crook states, "…was in the school of rhetoric – simply, indeed, a more protracted and purposeful immersion in the secondary education that everybody had. There was plenty of law in it, and in so far as the rhetoric was forensic (which it came to be more exclusively under the principle when political oratory ceased to be a reality) it dealt with legal situations however fantastic. But the barrister's job was to make a case; he was not *amicus curiae*...". Crook then, perhaps not wholly surprisingly, goes on to inquire[129] how, "…the law ever got done or at least how it ever became so precise, detailed and technical." In other words, who could tell the praetor, the judge, the governor or the advocate what the law was? The answer to Crook's question is that the people who did so were the *juris prudantes* or *juris consulti*, that is, people who were *learned in the law*. However, as Crook points out,[130] initially at least, it would be incorrect to regard these people as representing a *profession* in the modern sense. "Its practitioners," he writes, "were members of the Roman upper class, for whom even public or political office were only incidents in the lives of leisure, and it was therefore an amateur activity just as much as being a historian or an agricultural expert." He also comments[131] that, during the period of which he was writing,[132] the bar was not organised in the structured way which came to characterise the later empire.

The point of all this discussion is that it strongly suggests that the view of *rhetoric* espoused by Goodrich, especially where it relates to its original practices, may not wholly be correct. In other words, the processes of proof and analysis, to which he has alluded,[133] in their original form, techniques of persuasion, of whatever nature, seemed to have predominated. Amongst those, however, - and this is an issue which Goodrich has emphasised [134] - is the response of the speaker to the particular audience and the particular time. In addition, as the instance of the Bob Dylan lyric "Queen Jane Approximately" suggests,[135] rhetorical devices may be used to achieve different meanings for different purposes and, moreover, to raise issues which might not have been readily apparent to an audience. *In fine*, it might properly be said that *rhetoric* is any combination of rhetorical devices, designed according to context and audience, to persuade, or describe, a view or an attitude to that audience. Much of the remainder of this book will be describing and analysing applications contextually of that notion.

Both Posner and Goodrich were writing of the common law and its judiciary and advocates. However, there may be other standpoints from which *rhetoric* and *style* may be viewed. The European commentator and philosopher Perelman has considered *rhetoric* from the point of view of *civil* (i.e. Roman – based) law. At the outset of his discussion[136] he notes that Aristotelian rhetoric is subject to two limitations. First, where an admitted thesis was self-evident there will be no cause for argumentation and, hence, when truth is manifestly clear and that self-evidence means that there is no room for wilful choice, then rhetoric becomes superfluous. Second, when a thesis is shown to be arbitrary and no reason arises to support it, the demand for submission to a constraining power can only come about through force, without any concern for intellectual acceptance. Perelman comments that those two extreme situations are very rare, with the result that the field of rhetoric is necessarily immense.

Perelman next considers that the Aristotelian view of rhetoric – the study of persuasive discourse and its modalities – probably arose, "...at the time when litigations began to take place over properties which had been confiscated during periods of political changes. The old property holders, many years later, claimed restitutions when the former governments returned to power. It is conceivable that these successive political changes, with all the legal complications which occurred in the intervals, caused difficulties which no legalisation could foresee and which the simple application of laws could hardly resolve equitably."   Accordingly, Perelman states, throughout history, from classical times, legal development occurred alongside rhetorical developments. In consequence, general principles of law, together with various particular rules, can be traced to their rhetorical origins: it is due to those rhetorical origins and the introduction of such notion of *good faith* or *equity* that the highly formalistic Roman law was transformed and became a better instrument in the service of justice.

In particular litigation, according to Perelman,[137] it will be normal for disputants to present all of the general forms of argumentation which seek to show what values and interests should prevail and for what reasons. The judge, during the proceedings, will indicate which values and considerations have a bearing in law and in equity and, after having heard the parties' arguments will give the reasons which have determined the decision. "He will seek," suggests Perelman,[138] "to provide the motivation which will allow his final decision to be accepted by the parties to the litigation, by public opinion and by higher judicial tribunals." From that perspective, Perelman continues, the best lawyers' argument is the one which the judge uses in his own deliberations and the best motivated decision will be one which is not contested or is, at least, upheld on appeal. It is important to remember that Perelman was writing on the systems and conventions of continental Europe. One characteristic of such systems is that the writings of jurists are of more direct influence in the development of doctrine and principle than is generally the case in common law systems. Thus, for instance, the noted comparatist Merryman has described[139] the scholar as, "...the great man of the civil law. Legislators, executives, administrators and lawyers all come under his influence. He moulds the civil law tradition and the formal materials of the law into a model of the legal system. He teaches this model to law students and writes about it in books and articles. Legislators and judges accept his idea of what law is, and, when they make or apply law, they use concepts he has developed...it is reasonably accurate to say that the law in a civil law jurisdiction is what the scholars say it is." The result may be that the approach to rhetoric as demonstrated by a leading civilian such as Perelman is amore systemic one than that which exists in common law jurisdictions where, to take up a point made by Merryman,[140] the law is what the judges say it is. Merryman comments that the judge has to characterise a legal problem presented to him, which principles of law to apply to the problem and how to apply them in order to arrive at a result. "Whether the principles he chooses," Merryman continues, "are embodied in legislation or in prior decisions, they achieve substantive meaning only in the context of a specific problem, and the meaning attributed to them in that context is necessarily the meaning supplied by the judge."

4. Poems In Court

Another reason why law and poetry (or verse) maintain a connection is that, on occasion, the latter has been used as a means of communication, or illustration, by members of the judiciary. An extraordinary instance – though, unfortunately not the only one – is provided by the decision of Becker J of the District Court of Pennsylvania in *Mackensworth* v *American Trading Transport Co*[141] where all the accoutrements of the standard United States law report – headnote, annotations, judgment, footnotes and order[142] – were in verse. The headnote will give the flavour of the whole:

> A seaman, with help of legal sages,
> Sued a shipowner for his wages.
> The defendant, In New York City
> (Where served was process without pity)
> Thought the suit should fade away,
> Since it was started in Pa.
> The District Court there (Eastern District)
> Didn't feel itself restricted
> And in some verse by Edward R Becker, J.,
> Let the sailor have his day.

> The owner, once to earn freight fare,
> Sent ship to load on Delaware.
> Since it came to reap in port,
> T'was turnabout to show in court,
> With process so to profit tied.
> Motion to dismiss denied.

"In one respect," Megarry comments,[143] "the report is welcome, for the precedent that it sets is overwhelming. So lame is most of the verse, so forced is most of the rhyming, and so contorted is some of the language that the case is strongly persuasive against any attempt at repetition. Indeed, Becker J seemed to agree with the sentiment expressed by Megarry, when he began his judgment[144] with the following:

> The motion now before us has stirred up a terrible fuss.
> And what is considerably worse, it has spawned some preposterous doggerel verse.
> The plaintiff, a man of the sea,
> After paying his lawyer a fee,
> Filed a complaint of several pages to recover statutory wages.

Inevitably, the issue of a controlling precent arose and the trial judge continued by saying[145]

> And we found one written in '68 by three big wheels
> on the Third Circuit court of Appeals.
> The case, a longshoreman's personal injury suit,
> is Kane v. USSR,
> and it controls the case at bar.
> It's a case with which defendants had not reckoned,
> and may be found at page 131 of 394 F.2d.
> In *Kane*, a ship came but once to pick up stores
> And hired as agents to do its chores a firm of local stevedores.
> Since the Court upheld service on the agents,
> the case is nearly on all fours,
> and to defendant's statutory argument
> *Kane* closes the doors.

After disposing of other arguments in the case, also in execrable verse, the judge made his order:

> Finding that service of process is bona fide,
> the motion to dismiss is hereby denied.
> So that this case can now get about its ways,
> defendant shall file an answer within 21 days.

There had, as with the *Kane* case referred to by Becker J in *Mackensworth*, of course been a precedent for he use of verse as a vehicle for judgment. In *Wheat v Fraker*,[146] a jury had delivered a verdict for the plaintiff [Douglas] in an action for damages arising out of an intersectional collision. The defendant [Judd] moved for a new trial on the sole ground that the wife of the foreman of the jury was first cousin to the defendant's wife. The Georgia Court of Appeals upheld a first instance decision which decided that a juror was not disqualified because his wife was related to the wife of a party to the cause. The judgment of the Court was delivered by Eberhart J, in verse.[147] It is relatively short and may be quoted in its entirety, the move so as it calls on one of the best remembered events in the history of the common law.

> 'Foul, foul play' the defendant cried.
> 'That I by kinsman be not trammelled
> Let the issue again be tried
> Before another jury impanelled.
> Remember how from John at Runnymede
> The Charta was forced and wrested
> That no matter what the issue or the deed
> By my peers it must be tried and tested.
> [1] With juror mine adversary durst
> Try the cause, whose wife is second cousin to my wife
> And to plaintiff's wife at first.
> A new trial, sire, I demand to settle strife.'
> 'No foul play do I find or see,'
> The judge replied. 'Foreman's wife to thine
> And to plaintiff's wife may kinsman be,

But to Doug and thee no kinship do I find.
[2] Thus, it doth not appear
For any cause or reason told
That the juror was not thy peer
The case to try and verdict mold.
[3] Moreover, when kinships we sought to learn
It doth not appear that as best befits
One who would a kinsman spurn
Thou revealed that cousin did on the panel sit.
Thy day in court thou hast had,'
The judge asserted, 'and law commands
That, no error made, whether good or bad,
The issue tried and settled stands.'
Judgment affirmed.

One extraordinary feature of the case was that Felton CJ and Russell J concurred in Eberhart J's judgment. It may be possible to explain the phenomenon on the grounds that the point appeared to have been well settled in Georgia law and, hence, it might have been that the Court were unwilling to take what appeared to be a disastrous action especially seriously. However, the same could not really be said of the *Mackensworth* case, which concerned what might have been a potentially intricate dispute regarding civil procedure and interstate conflict of laws. Further, in *Mackensworth*, it was not merely Becker J who was involved in the versification of the decision, but also all of those who were involved with the preparation of the report.

It might be, as Megarry suggested,[148] highly desirable for these attempts not to be repeated, but it would be expecting too much, after *Mackensworth* and *Fraker*, for that to have happened. A particularly extraordinary instance is provided by the Michigan Court of Appeals in *Fisher* v *Lowe*[149] which contains echoes of both Stephen Foster and Ogden Nash. In that case, the plaintiff began proceedings in tort against the defendant for damage to his *beautiful oak tree* caused when the first (named) defendant struck it whilst operating the second defendant's automobile. The trial court granted summary judgment in favour of the defendants because they were immune from tort damage by reason of

Michigan's no fault statute. The Court of Appeals[150] affirmed the decision at first instance. Gillis J delivered the opinion of the Court:

[1] [2] We though that we would never see
A suit to compensate a tree.
A suit whose claim in tort is prest
Upon a mangled tree's behest;
A tree whose battered trunk was prest
Against a Chevy's crumpled crest;
A tree that faces each new day
With bark and limb in disarray;
A tree that may forever bear
A lasting need for tender care.
Flora lovers though we three,
We must uphold the court's decree.
Affirmed.

Again in *Fraker*, the form of the judgment may be an example of the court seeking to ridicule the plaintiff/appellant for bringing an action which was clearly incompetent[151] under State legislation.

It will have been noted that all the instances hitherto quoted, the medium used by the various judges was the *couplet*. Traditionally, that literary device is associated with satirists – such as, for example, John Dryden and Alexander Pope – or writers who seek to portray mundane matters – such as George Crabbe in *The Borough*.[152] An example, though of another verse form being used, and probably for much the same reason, is to be found in the opinion of Buchmeyer J in *Devine* v Byrd.[153] In that case, a civil rights action seeking good time credit was summarily dismissed because of the plaintiff's death.

First of all the judge began[154] by quoting from the united States Court of Appeals for the Tenth Circuit in *Lane* v *Wallace*[155] that a judge should not talk so much. Buchmeyer J then went on to describe the case and its outcome in what Megarry described[156] as, "...brief free verse." It is, indeed, extremely brief:

This pro se § 1983 suit seeks "good time credit."
But the plaintiff is now dead.
That means this suit is, too.

The first is with prejudice.

It may be that brevity is intended to serve the same purpose as the satirical couplets in the *Fraker* and *Fisher* cases. That view is reinforced by the tone of the footnotes which are attached to the free verse,[157] both of which are couched in a humorous vein and relate to Buchmeyer J's comment regarding judicial verbosity.

However, using verse as a vehicle through which to ridicule apparently pointless actions may not be the whole story, especially given the factual situation in *Mackensworth*.[158] In one case, the decision of the Georgia Court of Appeals in *Brown* v *State*,[159] the reason for Evans J's opinion being delivered in verse is revealed in a footnote.[160] The footnote states that, "This opinion is placed in rhyme because approximately one year ago, in Savannah at a very convivial celebration, the distinguished Judge Dunbar Harrison, Senior Judge of Chatham Superior Courts, arose and addressed those assembled, and demanded that if Judge Randall Evans, Jr. ever again was so presumptuous as to reverse one of his decisions, that the opinion be written in poetry. I readily admit I am unable to comply, because I am not a poet, and the language used, at best, is mere doggerel. I have done my best but my limited ability just did not permit the writing of a great poem. It was no easy task to write opinion in rhyme." In *Brown*, the defendant had appealed against conviction on the grounds that the State had won unfairly because the trial judge, the first named judge in the footnote, had incorrectly refused to grant the defendant a day's delay so that his missing witness was available to appear. The Court of Appeals reversed the decision at first instance.[161] It is worth noting that, in beginning his judgment, Evans J Stated,[162] "The DA was ready. His case was red-hot. Defendant was present, his witness was not," and in a footnote to that line, the judge referred to *Wheat* v *Fraker*[163] as precedent for writing an opinion in rhyme.

It should be said that there was good reason for the appeal against the first instance refusal of delay. As Evans J put the matter:[164]

The jury went out to consider his case And then they returned The defendant to face.
'What verdict, Mr. Foreman?' The learned Judge inquired. 'Guilty, your honor.' On Browns face-no smile.

'Stand up' said the judge, Then quickly announced 'Seven years at hard labor' Thus his sentence pronounced.

A point, too arising from Evans J's judgment was that he was able to obtain, at least, some satisfaction from the trial judge's initial challenge, when he wrote in his opinion, in which Deen PJ and Tolz J concurred:

'This trial was not fair,' The defendant then sobbed. 'With my main witness absent I've simply been robbed.'
'I want a new trial-State has not fairly won.' 'New trial denied,' Said judge Dunbar Harrison.

'If you still say I'm wrong,' The able judge did then say 'Why not appeal to Atlanta? Let those Appeals Judges earn part of their pay.'
"I will appeal, sir'-Which he proceeded to do-'They can't treat me worse Than I've been treated by you.'

Given the initial sentence passed upon the defendant by the trial judge, the behaviour of both judges, in a social situation notwithstanding, must surely be deprecated. The liberty of a person who may very possibly have been innocent should not be trivialised in the manner represented by *Brown* v *State*. The failure to provide an accused person with what, essentially, was a fair trial cannot, surely, be seriously equated with some of the apparently pointless civil actions which were in issue in some of the other cases.

Indeed, the relationship with the criminal law and versification of judgment or opinion is, it is suggested not a little disturbing, as the case of *In re Rome*[165] still more strongly suggests. This decision of the Supreme Court of Kansas involved a discipline proceeding brought against a Judge of the magistrate court of that State. The Supreme Court held that the methods which had been specified in a 1972 constitutional amendment governing the removal of judges was cumulative to any other methods of prescribed statutes which existed at the time of the adoption of the amendment - that a magistrate was subject to discipline by Supreme Court for cause, that acts or omissions committed during a prior term could be considered in determining the propriety of disciplinary measures and that there was no right to jury trial in such disciplinary proceedings. Further, the Court held, that commission on judicial qualifications has the dual functions of investigating matters and making findings and recommendations does not violate due process. Finally, and most important for the purposes of the present discussion, that the Court held that a judge's right to freedom of speech is circumscribed by the code of judicial conduct, so that a judge's use of a particular manner of writing – for example, by holding up a litigant to public ridicule or scorn – cannot be said to be a legitimate exercise of judicial discretion which can only be corrected on appeal and that a judicial utterance which had the effect of holding a litigant out to public ridicule or scorn warrants censure. In the event, the judge in question was censured.

What, then, were the events in question which warranted the censure in question? The facts which led up to the finding were that on a particular date a woman was arrested and charged with agreeing to perform an act of sexual intercourse for a man. Her arrest was brought about through her unwitting solicitation of a police officer. The trial was presided over by the respondent. The defendant was convicted and she was given the maximum sentence which was six months imprisonment and a fine of $1000. The defendant then filed a notice of appeal to the District Court, the appeal was subsequently dismissed with consent and the case was remanded to the magistrate court where the defendant applied for probation. The respondent took the matter under advisement[166] and placed the defendant on probation for two years. In addition to filing an order of probation and making routine notations in his docket, the respondent filed a written instrument entitled *Memorandum Decision*, which was an account, in verse, of the subject matter of the decision albeit with the defendant's name deleted. It began:

> This is the saga of _ _
> Whose ancient profession brings her before us.
> On January 30th 1974,
> The lass agreed to work as a whore. Her great mistake, as was to unfold
> Was the enticing of a cop name Harold.
> Unknown to _ _, this officer, surnamed Harris,
> Was duty-bent on _ _'s lot to embarrass.

It concludes:
The judge showed mercy and _ _ as free,
But back to the street she could not flee.
The fine she'd pay while out on parole,
But not from men she used to cajole.
From her ancient profession she'd been busted,
And to society's rules she must be adjusted.
If from all of this a moral doth unfurl,
It is that Pimps do not protect the working girl!

It will be apparent from these extracts that this judge's verse was of no higher standard than one has come to expect and can be further emphasised by another short extract:

Formally charged by this great State,
With offering to Harris to fornicate.
Her arraignment was formal, then back to jail,
And quick as a flash she was admitted to bail.
On February 26, 1974,
The State of Kansas tried this young whore.
A prosecutor name Brown,
Represented the Crown.
_ _, her freedom in danger,
Was being defended by a chap named Granger.

Subsequent to its filing, the *Memorandum Decision* was widely publicised by quotation in the local news media as well as throughout the State of Kansas at large. That publicity resulted in a complaint against the respondent from a feminist group in the town where the initiating events had taken place. That group wrote a letter to the editor of the local newspaper, with copies to both the Bar Association and to judicial authorities. Publication of the letter in the newspaper caused the respondent to cite its signatories to appear in the magistrate court and show cause of court. The signatories engaged legal representation and appeared as directed. At that hearing, before a substantial crowd, the respondent articulated his views on the prostitution problem in the area in question and dismissed the charges of contempt. The whole matter ultimately reached the commission of Judicial Qualifications and resulted in the instant proceedings. In defending himself before the Supreme Court of Kansas, the respondent raised a variety of issues, not all of which were germane to the present discussion.

The Supreme Court noted[167] in particular that the respondent was not being subjected to disciplinary proceedings because he wrote and filed a *Memorandum Decision* in poetic form, but because the particular manner in which it was written was, allegedly, holding out a litigant to public ridicule or scorn. A particular problem which the respondent faced was canon 3A of the *Canons of Judicial Ethics* which required a judge to be patient, dignified and courteous to litigants with whom he deals in his judicial capacity. It was clear, the Court considered, that canon related to the manner in which a judge conducted his court rather than to rulings or judgments made, about which a contention may arise as to abuse of judicial discretion. Although, the Court went on, the canon did not, in the strictest sense, deal with the exercising of judicial discretion, the Court was still of the view that, in the manner of exercising judicial discretion, a judge was governed by the provisions of canon 3A, no matter what his decision on the merits might be.

The Court then turned[168] to the subject of *judicial humour*, of which Smith, a judge writing extra-judicially had said,[169] "Judicial humour is neither judicial nor humorous. A lawsuit is a serious matter for those concerned in it. For a judge to take advantage of his criticism-insulated, retaliation-proof position to display his wit is contemptible, like hitting a man when he's down". After having quoted Smith's apposite *dictum* the Court, in *Rome*, emphasised that, "judges simply should not 'wisecrack at the expense of anyone connected with a judicial proceeding who is not in a position to reply. When judges do this the stage is set for an imbroglio like that which apparently occurred after the respondent here cited the three objectors for contempt of court, and respect for the administration of justice suffers. Nor should a judge do anything to exalt himself above anyone appearing as a litigant before him." The Court were also of the view that judges, because of their unusual role should be objective in their task and mindful that the damaging effect of any improprieties may be out of proportion to their actual seriousness. Judges are likewise expected to act in a manner inspiring confidence that even-handed treatment will be affected to everyone coming into contact with the judicial process.

As regards the *Memorandum Decision* in the *Rome* case, the Court regarded it as portraying the defendant in the initiating case, "...in a ludicrous or comical situation - someone to be laughed at and her plight found amusing. She was referred to throughout in terms designed to evoke chuckles over her activities. Her own integrity as an individual, convicted of crime though she was, disregarded." The Court further noted[170] that the fact that neither the defendant nor her parents had themselves complained was not to be taken as meaning that the defendant was not being held out as being an object of public ridicule. It might, indeed, have been the case that the respondent did not have the intention to ridicule the defendant nor hold her out to public scorn, though that was the effect of that which was done, the more so as publicity about the memorandum was expected.

Without seeking to exonerate the respondent from the consequences of his own, rather foolish, actions, it may be possible to interpret his behaviour. In the contempt proceedings which he brought against the letter's three signatories, he had raised some general issues relating to prostitution in the areas where the defendant had been arrested and the Court noted[171] that the respondent had testified as to his concern regarding the matter. "Prostitutes or their pimps," he had sworn, "were openly accosting people on the streets or waiting for stoplights; some prosecution cases had been tried in police court; he gave the maximum sentence in the defendant's case; his concern was to jolt the south end and, more particularly, the pimps' and the memorandum decision was used to 'get the point across'." In other words, the respondent was attempting – though, clearly, the Supreme Court of Kansas did not believe that the means which he used were appropriate or desirable – to draw attention to what he clearly considered was a serious problem.

At the same time, the Court seemed at pains to point out[172] the respondent's exemplary record as a lawyer.[173] It is at this point that the picture becomes a little confused: first, the respondent argued that there was no *clear and convincing*[174] evidence that he had violated canon 3A in issuing the *Memorandum Decision*. The Court, in responding to that argument, stated[175] that they agreed that, "...in a proceeding of this kind [the quantum of proof] should be greater than that required in an ordinary civil action i.e., preponderance of the evidence, and further that an appropriate standard is proof by clear and convincing evidence. In so grave a matter as depriving a judge of his office or subjecting him to some form of discipline the burden of proof should be less and we so hold. "Ultimately of course, the Supreme Court found the allegations proved to that degree. However, the Court continued[176] by discussing the alleged quality of the respondent's behaviour. "Our code of judicial conduct," they stated, "and its implementing rules deal with a wide range of problems of varying degrees of seriousness. The particular proceeding does not present one of the greatest magnitude. Neither venality nor criminality is present nor can it be said the memorandum decision was written with deliberate intent to harm anyone. Yet, everything considered, we believe a violation of the canon in question has been shown. A litigant was not afforded the kind treatment mandated." Accordingly, the respondent was censured.[177]

With respect to the Supreme Court in *In re Rome*, the combination of the *clear and convincing* standard of proof and the relatively low level of judicial misconduct seem to sit together rather oddly. It was clearly a foolish way in which to approach what the judge, at least, considered to be quite a serious, if localised, social problem. This would seem particularly to be the case when his initial sentence of the defendant in the originating case is taken into account. Further, despite the Supreme Court's finding regarding the exposure of the defendant to ridicule,[178] a reading of the *Memorandum Decision* as a whole seems, to this commentator at any rate, to be directed at satirising the entire process and, especially in the final couplet, to criticise the role played by pimps in the organisation of what he seemed truly to regard as an anti-social activity.

However, with the respondent's ability apparently to irritate local establishment, it would have been surprising had Judge Rome not found himself involved in further proceedings – though, on this occasion rather more serious from his own point of view. As *State of Kansas ex rel Commission on Judicial Qualifications* v *Richard J. Rome*[179] is not concerned with the thrust of the text, it will be noted in outline only. In that case, an original proceeding in discipline was brought against the respondent who was, by then, an associate district judge. The Supreme Court held that there was clear and convincing evidence to establish that the judge had violated the *Code of Judicial Conduct* by allowing, or appearing to allow, his personal views on the political issue of the selection of judges to influence his judicial conduct or judgment. He had done so by deliberately writing a memorandum which was critical of the actions of a county attorney and a fellow judge by making allegations of fact and stating, as conclusions, factual matters which were being contested in two criminal cases, and by intentionally attempting to gain publicity for those statements by giving copies of those statements to the news media. The Supreme Court of Kansas were of the view[180] that removal from office was warranted and so ordered.

It is not only in State matters that judges resort to verse, nor do they necessarily attempt to reduce the whole of their judgments to verse forms. Thus, in the decision of the United States Court of Appeals for the Fifth Circuit's decision in *US v Ven-Fuel Inc,*[181] Brown CJ began his opinion, in which he summarised the arguments which he was later to canvass. In *Ven-Fuel*, the corporate defendant had been convicted in the United States District Court on seven counts out of a fifteen count indictment that charged violations of a federal law which made it an offence to import merchandise by means of a false statement or practice. The defendant appealed and the Court of Appeals[182] held that, first, though the provision under which the defendant had been convicted did not, on its face, require that the allegedly false or fraudulent statements relating to the entry, or attempted, entry of the merchandise be material, it was necessary that a requirement of materiality be read into the statute. Second, under the circumstances, even though a throughput agreement was required to obtain a licence to import residual fuel oil, alleged misrepresentations relating to the defendant's throughput agreement, made in connection with the defendant's licence application, were immaterial as a matter of law to the proposed importation of residual fuel oil and, hence, did not violate the statute under which the defendant had been indicted. The Court of Appeals thus overturned the conviction.

Brown CJ encapsulated the matter as follows:
> This case presents a vicious duel,
> Between the U.S. of A. and defendant Ven –Fuel.
> Seeking a licence for oil importation,
> Ven-Fuel submitted its application.
> It failed to attach a relevant letter,
> And none can deny, it should have known better.
> Yet the only issue this case is about,
> Is whether a crime was committed beyond reasonable doubt.
> Ven-Fuel was convicted of fraudulent acts,
> By the trials court's finding of adequate facts.

> We think it likely that fraud took place,
> But Materiality was not shown in this case.
> So while the Government will no doubt be annoyed,
> We declare the conviction null and void.

Some seven years later, the Court of Appeals for the Fifth Circuit was once again involved in *U.S. v Batson*.[183] In *Batson*, the factual situation involved was scarcely above mundane interest. The Government sought repayments under the cotton set-aside programme. The District Court had entered judgment in favour of the Government, but ordered interest to run from the date of determination and appeals were lodged. The Court of Appeals[184] held, first, a determination that operators as well as producers had attempted to avoid programme limitations on payments amounted to a determination of *facts constituting the basis* for payments under the cotton set-aside programme and were not reviewable. Second, any legal conclusions were reviewable. Third, the defendants had not, as they claimed, been denied due process but, fourth, the Government was entitled to interest from the date of determination that repayments were required.

Goldberg J, in giving the judgment of the Court, began[185] by setting out the basic facts in the form of two limericks:

> Some farmers from Gaines had a plan
> it amounted to quite a big scam.
> But the payments for cotton
> began to smell rotten.
> Twas a mugging of poor Uncle Sam.
> The ASCS and its crew
> uncovered this fraudulent stew.
> After quite a few hearings,
> the end is now nearing-
> They await our judicial review.

If that was not regarded as sufficient, Goldberg J concluded[186] his opinion with yet another:

> With thought and comment most candid,
> affirmance shall now be commanded.

But the court below missed the prejudgment interest:
The cases are therefore remanded.

These findings had the rather curious effect that the decision of the District Court was affirmed in part, reversed in part and remanded!

Goldberg J. of the United States Court of Appeals for the Fifth Circuit had also taken part in a rather differently versified decision in *Anderson Greenwood and Co* v *NLRB*.[187] In that case, the National Labour Relations Board had appealed from a District Court order which required it to provide an employer with certain statements of witnesses which had been taken during an NLRB investigation of a challenged representation election. The Court of Appeals decided that statements of witnesses taken during the investigation, involving challenged election of union representation, were not subject to disclosure before hearing on objections, but did fall within the purview of FOIA exceptions. Accordingly, the decision of the District Court was reversed.

In delivering the opinion of the Court of Appeals,[188] Goldberg J. referred[189] to the decision of the United States Supreme Court in *NLRB's* v *Robbins Tyre and Rubber Co*[190] which had decided that the particular witness statements which were there sought were exempt from disclosure, because the disclosure would interfere with the NLBR's pending unfair labour practice proceedings. Goldberg J had this to say about that decision:

> Our decision in Robbins Tire,
> Interpreting Congresses' reported desires,
> Exposed workers to their bosses' ire.
> The High Court, avoiding this sticky quagmire,
> And fearing employers would threaten to fire,
> Sent our holding to the funeral pyre.

Goldberg J then turned his attention to the subsequent decision of the United States Court of Appeals for the Fifth Circuit in *Clements Wire and Manufacturing Co. Inc* v *NLRB*[191]. That case extended *Robbins Tire* to representation election hearings. It sought to present the issue in a different procedural context, involving a request for a preliminary injunction preventing the NLRB from proceeding with a representation election case until final resolution of the employer's FOIA action seeking particular information from the NLRB's files. The Court of Appeals vacated the District Court's grant of the preliminary injunction and found it apparent that the employer's Freedom of Information claim would not succeed on the merits. The FOIA issue presented in *Clements Wire* was identical to the claim involved in *Anderson Greenwood*. Goldberg J describe the contribution of *Clements Wire* in verse:

> Then along came Clements Wire,
> Soon after its venerable sire.
> To elections, Wire extended Tire,
> Leaving app'llees arguments higher and drier.
> Now to colors our focus must shift,
> To Green wood and stores that are Red.

That last line referred to the decision of the same Court in *Red Food Stores* v *NLRB*,[192] which was decided on the same day as *Anderson Greenwood* and which involved a very similar issue. Goldberg J concluded his opinion by saying, in verse, that,

> We hope this attempt at a rhyme, perhaps two,
> Has not left this audience feeling too blue.
> Since Clements Wire directly controls our decision here, we reverse.

Again one might wonder at the motivation for Goldberg J's muse - In *Anderson Greenwood*, it might have arisen through the achievement of the Court of Appeals for the Fifth Circuit of having broken away from a strait jacket imposed by the United States Supreme Court! Similarly in *Batson*,[193] the judge may have been similarly moved by the enormity of the farmers' enterprise. In both cases the other judges concurred in the versified decision.

That, however, was not the case in the decision of the Supreme Court of Indiana in *Nelson* v *State*.[194] There, the defendant, who had pleaded guilty, and was sentenced by the Superior Court, petitioned for post-conviction relief. The Supreme Court held, by a majority, that, although the record showed that the trial court had carefully informed the defendant of the constitutional right which he waived by pleading guilty, he was not informed of, "...any possible increased sentence by reason of the fact of a prior conviction or convictions..." as was required in the legislation. The trial court did take prior convictions into account which increased the defendant's sentence. Accordingly, the Supreme Court reversed and remanded the Superior Court's decision.

Hunter J expressed,[195] in verse, the view of the majority[196] was that,

> In petition for post-conviction relief,
> The petitioner herein expounds his grief.
> The record show he does not lie;
> With the Code the court did not comply.
> The problem is, as we herein perceive,
> Petitioner was not told he could receive
> A possible increased sentence by reason
> Of criminal convictions in another season.
> In previous cases this Court has found
> We must remand upon this ground.
> It is the rationale of such decision
> That rights by given with much precision.
> We give the trial court instructions attendant:
> To vacate the guilty plea of this defendant,
> And the not guilty plea to reinstate;
> It is so ordered from this date[197]

There was a dissent by Pivarnik J, though there is no indication from the report, on what grounds the judge based his dissent. Megarry, though, expressed the hope[198] that it was Hunter J's verse which induced the dissent. One's only response can be that such was unlikely because the standard of verse was no lower than much that has been discussed in this section and, perhaps, better than some.

In addition to the judges who seek to fashion (or craft) their own versified opinions, there are others who utilise existing poems to reinforce their own conclusions or attitudes – sometimes in rather unusual circumstances. Thus, for example, in *Mozes* v *Mozes*,[199] the United States Court of Appeals for the Ninth Circuit was concerned and an appeal by a father against an order which had denied his petition seeking to have his three younger children returned to Israel pursuant to the *Hague Convention on Civil Aspects of International Child Abduction*. The Court[200] reversed and remanded the appealed decision and, in so doing, laid down various tests which were applied in later decisions.[201] However, for our purposes, in discussing the meaning of the phrase *habitual residence* Kozinsky J had stated[202] that, "Cutting fact-finding tribunals adrift with only the Bellman's map to guide them does not lead to consistency; it leads only to the absence of any common standard by which inconsistency can be identified." The Bellman's Map, as Kozinsky J pointed out, is a reference to Lewis Carroll's nonsense poem "The Hunting of the Snark"[203] where the Bellman

> ...had bought a large map representing the sea,
> Without the least vestige of land:
> And the crew were much pleased when they found it to be
> A map they could all understand.
> "What's the good of Mercator's North Poles and Equators,
> Tropics, Zones, and Meridian Lines?"
> So the Bellman would cry: and the crew would reply
> "They are merely conventional signs!
> "Other maps are such shapes, with their islands and capes!
> But we've got our brave Captain to thank"
> (So the crew would protest) "that he's bought us the best-
> A perfect and absolute blank!"

All of that, the judge explained[204] meant that, although a judgment as to *habitual residence* may be primarily factual, it has not been comprehended so as to mean that it is left to the unreviewed discretion of the trial court. At the same time, it may be that Kozinsky J by juxtaposing an extract from a poem, written as nonsense by a noted practitioner of that art, with case law and scholarly commentary on the area of the notoriously and increasingly slippery area of *habitual residence,*[205] is offering a commentary on those contributions!

5. "The Vital Arrogant, Fatal, Dominant X"

This line, as has already been noted[206] is the final line of Wallace Stevens's poem "The Motive for Metaphor" and represents the end of the process of curial adjudication. By way of practical introduction to that process, I introduced Lord Denning MR's description of the situation which led up to the decision of English Court of Appeal in *Miller* v

Jackson.²⁰⁷ It is not necessary to attempt to draw these variously knitted and coloured threads together and discuss the processes by which adjudication was ultimately reached.

It is, first of all, necessary to place the adjudicative process in a context which is less *rhetorical* in the sense used by Posner and Goodrich, both jointly and severally. As has already been pointed out,²⁰⁸ the result of any case would have been susceptible of easy prediction from Lord Denning MR's description of the background. Hence, an altogether more neutral description of the factual situation is necessarily required. The facts of *Miller* v *Jackson* may be set out as follows:²⁰⁹ in 1972, houses were built on an empty field next to a cricket ground which had been in use for nearly seventy years. That summer, the plaintiffs bought one of the houses; its garden wall was only 102 feet from the wicket, so cricket balls frequently went over it and the plaintiffs, in consequence, complained. The cricket club erected the highest possible wire fence on top of the wall and instructed players to try to keep the ball low but even so, in 1975, five more balls came over. The plaintiffs refused offers to install unbreakable glass and to cover the garden with a safety net and they then sought an injunction to prevent the defendants from playing cricket in such a manner that cricket balls came into the plaintiffs' garden. At trial, it appeared that cricket could not be played there at all without the occasional ball going over the enhanced wall. The trial judge granted the injunction. The defendants appealed and, in the Court of Appeal, it was held, with Lord Denning dissenting, that the defendants were liable in nuisance, notwithstanding that the plaintiffs were aware of the defendants well-established activity at the time when they purchased the house. However, the defendants' appeal was allowed and the injunction discharged, with Geoffrey Lane LJ dissenting.

Since the discussion of the case began with Lord Denning's rhetorical flourish, it is not unreasonable that he be permitted to explain in a more legalistic manner. Lord Denning noted²¹⁰ that the rule in nuisance cases was based on the maxim *Sic utere tuo ut alienum non laedas,* but regarded it as being misleading and as having been, in his own words, "put in its place" by Lord Wright in *Sedleigh-Denfield* v *O'Callaghan.*²¹¹ Lord Wright had said that "[I]t is not only lacking in definiteness but is also inaccurate. An occupier may make in many ways a use of his land which causes damage to the neighbouring landowners and yet be free from liability...a useful test is perhaps what is reasonable according to the ordinary usages of mankind living in society, or, more correctly, in a particular society."

Accordingly, Lord Denning sought to adopt a derivative test for application to the facts of the case at hand. That test was. "...is the use by the cricket club of this ground for playing cricket a reasonable use of it?" For Lord Denning, it was, indeed, a most reasonable use of it: for over seventy years, he went on, "...the game of cricket has been played on the ground to the greatest benefit of the community and to the injury of none. No one could suggest that it was a nuisance to the neighbouring owners simply because an enthusiastic batsman occasionally hit the ball out of the ground for a six to the approval of the admiring onlookers." He further continued by stating that the building of a house on the very edge of the ground did not convert the playing of cricket into a nuisance when it was not so before.

Lord Denning then once more referred[212] to the judgment of Lord Wright in *Sedleigh-Denfield* v *O'Callaghan*[213] where it had been said that, "A balance has to be maintained between the right of the occupier to do what he likes with his own and the right of his neighbour not to be interfered with." In the instant case, Lord Denning considered, it was the task of the courts to balance the right of the cricket club to continue playing cricket on their cricket ground, as against the right of the householder not to be interfered with. "On taking the balance" Lord Denning said, "I would give priority to the right of the cricket club to continue playing cricket on the ground, as they have done for the last 70 years. It takes precedence over the right of the newcomer to sit in his garden undisturbed. After all, he bought the house four years ago in mid-summer when the cricket season was at its height. He might have guessed that there was a risk that a hit for six might possibly land on his property." Lord Denning then went on[214] to outline the steps which the respondent might take to avoid the consequences of that occurrence. In the Master of the Rolls's own words: "If he finds that he does not like it, he ought when cricket is played, to sit on the other side of the house or in the front garden. Or go out, or take advantage of the offers the club has made to him of fitting unbreakable glass, and so forth. Or if he does not like that, he ought to sell the house and move elsewhere. I expect that there are many who would gladly buy it in order to be near the cricket field and the open space."

Lord Denning MR noted[215] that the case was new and ought to be approached on the basis of principles applicable to modern conditions. In *Miller* v *Jackson*, there was a contest between the interest of the public at large and the interest of a private individual. The *public* interest lay in the protection of the environment through preserving playing fields in the face of mounting development and by enabling young people to enjoy all the benefits of outdoor games, such as cricket and football. The *private* interest lay, his Lordship considered, in securing the privacy of the plaintiff's home and garden without. He then emphasised that the solution could not lie in an award of damages, particularly as the club had already offered to pay for any damage which might be caused. The issue[216] was whether an injunction ought to be granted. Lord Denning had no doubts on that score when he stated that, as between the conflicting interests, the *public* interest should prevail in that, "The cricket club should not be driven out."

Although Geoffrey Lane LJ ultimately disagreed with Lord Denning MR regarding the ultimate adjudication , he also recognised[217] that a balance was required to be maintained between, on the one hand, the right of an individual to enjoy his house and garden without the threat of damage and, on the other, the right of the public in general or a neighbour to engage in lawful pastimes. However, Geoffrey Lane LJ did note that, "Difficult questions may sometimes arise when the defendants' activities are offensive to the senses, for example, by way of noise. Where, as here, the damage, or potential damage is physical the answer is more simple... The danger of injury is obvious and is not slight enough to be disregarded. There is here a real risk of serious injury."

The only point which Geoffrey Lane LJ could find in the defendants' favour was that cricket had been played on the same field for some seventy years. He then posed the relevant issue in the form of a question, "Put briefly, can the defendants take advantage of the fact that the plaintiffs have put themselves in such a position by coming to occupy a house on the edge of a small cricket field with the result that what was not a nuisance in the past now becomes a nuisance?" In answer to that question, Geoffrey Lane LJ responded that, had the matter been *res integra*, he would have been inclined to find in favour of the defendants, because it did not seem to be just that a long-established activity, which was itself harmless, should be brought to an end because someone chooses to build a house nearby and so turn an innocent pastime into an actionable nuisance.

However, the matter did not stand alone. Geoffrey Lane LJ referred to the Nineteenth century decision of the same Court in *Sturges* v *Bridgman*.[218] In that case, the defendant had used noisy machinery on his premises for more than twenty years without complaint from other people living in the neighbourhood. However, the plaintiff, a medical practitioner, who lived in adjoining premises built a consulting room close to the defendant's machinery and, later complained of the noise. The Court of Appeal held that the plaintiff's claim could not be disputed by the argument that he had brought the problem on himself by building the consulting rooms in such close proximity to the machinery.[219] Geoffrey Lane LJ found himself bound[220] by that decision and did not perceive it as being the present Court's function to disturb a ruling which had stood for so long. Like Lord Denning MR,[221] Geoffrey Lane LJ agreed that an injunction was the only available appropriate remedy but, unlike Lord Denning, he upheld the initial grant of the injunction, even though he did suspend its operation so that the cricket club had the opportunity of finding a new ground (A possibility which Lord Denning had regarded as being remote[222]).

The third judge, Cumming Bruce LJ, agreed[223] with Geoffrey Lane LJ that the defendants were liable in negligence and nuisance and that *Sturges* v *Bridgman* was binding. But he agreed with Lord Denning, however, that no injunction should lie. His reason for so doing[224] was that the trial judge did not have sufficient regard to the interests of the inhabitants of the village as a whole. "Had he done so, "Cumming Bruce LJ stated, "he would in my view have been led to the conclusion that the plaintiffs having accepted the benefit of the open space marching with their land should accept the restrictions upon the enjoyment of their garden which they reasonably may think necessary. That is the burden which they have to bear in order that the inhabitants of the village may not be deprived of their facilities for an innocent recreation which they have so long enjoyed on this ground. There are here special circumstances which should inhibit a court of equity from granting the injunction claimed."

Yet, interesting as those judgments may be, there may be more to the issues raised by *Miller* v *Jackson* than are directly apparent from them. Thus, for instance, were one to suppose that the cricket ground in question were to be closer in reality[225] to the field portrayed in the Norman Nicholas poem excerpted earlier[226] than to the idyllic norm which Lord Denning sought to evoke[227] in *Miller* v *Jackson*, one can only speculate as to whether he himself would have been quite so anxious to protect the cricket club's activities. In addition, Lord Denning, who based his judgment very largely on policy grounds[228] considered that he developers ought not to have been permitted to build houses where they did.[229] This raises, albeit indirectly, the issue of how much the tort of private nuisance impinges on concepts which should relate to land use planning. There is also the difference in approach to the facts of the case by Lord Denning and Geoffrey Lane LJ: Lord Denning emphasised[230] that the case should be determined by reference to modern conditions and avoided reference to earlier case law. When taken together with the rhetoric to be found at the beginning of his judgment, Lord Denning's response to the case at large seems to have been effectively pre-ordained. Put another way, the initial *rhetoric* gave rise to the policy which gave rise to the opinion/judgment. In the light of that, one cannot be blind to the importance of *rhetoric* – including *rhetoric* of a kind which seems more adapted to poetry – in the judicial process. On the other hand, Geoffrey Lane LJ, despite saying that he might have found for the defendants were the case to be regarded as *res integra* (as being independent of earlier authority),[231] found that he was bound by earlier case law in the shape of *Sturges* v *Bridgman*.[232] It should also be mentioned that *Miller* v *Jackson* is discussed by Scott[233] who comments[234] that, "Needless to relate, the Millers were unhappy that the Court of Appeal decided to discharge the injunction. Mrs Miller was reported as saying that she felt 'numbed by the decision' and that she and her husband might consider moving but felt that, because of the publicity, they might lose money if they tried to sell their house." These possible consequences seem to have been overlooked in the Court of Appeal and Lord Denning seemed quite dismissive of them.[235]

Finally, the case is factually, as well as rhetorically, English in its orientation. In that context, Sedley LJ, writing extra-judicially,[236] has stated that, "American judges find it difficult to believe that [English judges] can deliver [judgments] off the cuff. More lay down the law for other cases, judgments are reserved and put in writing, and agreement is sought on them. But the prose form often, at least on appeals remains that of oral judgment, and the oral judgment at base still represents the process of thinking aloud." Throughout the remainder of the book instances of types of judgment/opinion in relation to particular subject matter will be discussed and analysed as well as being related to *rhetoric* both generally and as it relates to poetry.

---

[1] See above Chapter I text at n 248
[2] J. Boyd White, *The Legal Imagination* (Abr. Ed, 1985) at 208 *ff*
[3] Ibid at 208
[4] Indeed, that is a major thrust of Boyd White's book at large.
[5] K Olivecrona, *Preface* to A. Hägerström's, *Inquiries into the Nature of Law and Morals* (1953, Trs Broad) at XVII
[6] Ibid at XIX
[7] K Olivecrona, *Law as Fact* (1971) et 17. For comment, see G MacCormack, "HägerstrÖm's, magical Interpretation of Roman Law" (1969) 4 *Irish Jurist* 153 and, more generally, "Scandinavian Realism" 1970 *Juridical Review* 33
[8] Above n 2 at 209
[9] Boyd White, ibid, also talks of imaginary stories of the past in the sense that the law student reading a case must, "...read with a literary or archeological imagination, reconstructing the facts, the trial, the arguments, ask how a prior case might have been better used, what issues seem to have been omitted or miscast, exactly why things were put this way or that, and how it all might have been better done."
[10] Below text at 87
[11] Above n 2 at 210
[12] Ibid at 211
[13] Sir Philip Sidney, *The Defense of Poesie* (1595).
[14] For example, the late Tony Judt. See T. Garton Ash, "Tony Judt (1948-2010)" (2010) LVII (14) *New York Review of Books* 6
[15] Above n 2 at 212
[16] R. W. Emerson, "The Poet" in *Essays* (2nd Series, 1844)
[17] S. T. Coleridge, *Biographia Literaria* (1817) Ch 14
[18] Above n 2 at 212
[19] B. Schwarz, *A Book of Legal Lists: The Best and Worst in American Law* (1997) at 30
[20] 4 US 37 (1800) This decision upheld the view that France was an *enemy* nation during the undeclared naval war of 1798 and 1799. Moore's view endorsed a 1799 law which allowed the receptor of an American merchant ship, seized by the French, one half of the value of the ship and it s goods as salvaged provided that it took place 96 hours after the original capture.
[21] 5 US 137 (1803) For comment on this decision, see H. A. Johnson, "Marbury v Madison" in *The Oxford Guide to the Supreme Court of the United States (2005 Ed. Hall)* 605.
[22] 5 US 299 (1803) A case decided only six days after *Marbury* v *Madison*, above in 21
[23] Quoted in M. Schmidt, *The Great Modern Poets: An Anthology of the Best Poets and Poetry Since 1900* (2006) at 97
[24] Above n 2 at 212
[25] See above Ch 1 text at n 363 *ff*.
[26] See above Ch 1 text at n 171 *ff*
[27] Above n 2 at 237
[28] See F. Bates, "Which Comforts While it Mocks". Some Paradoxes in Modern Family Law" (2000) 4(2) *Newcastle LR* 17. See also Ch VI at n 12 *ff*.
[29] Ibid at 17 *ff*. Described as, "...the basal paradox."
[30] Ibid at 18. See, for example, A Watson, *The Nature of Law* (1977) at 96
[31] See J. Dewer, "*The Concepts, Coherence and Contact of Family Law*" In *Examining the Law Syllabus: The Core* (1992) 81.
[32] T. C Grey, *The Wallace Stevens Case: Law and the Practice of Poetry* (1991) at 10. Even the title appears to have something of a transposition: thus, one would generally speak of the *Practice of Law* rather than of *Poetry*.

[33] Ibid at 11
[34] Ibid at 13
[35] Two contemporaneous writers whom, according to Grey, ibid, seemed so uncomfortable were John Berryman and Mary McCarthy
[36] The last phrase is owed, according to Grey, ibid at 118, to a conversation between Stevens and Robert Frost, when the former said "The trouble with you is you write about things." Frost replied, "The trouble with you is that you write about bric-a-brac." Stevens, apparently, told this story against himself. See P Brazeau, *Parts of a World: Wallace Stevens Remembered* (1983) at 160.
[37] The last monographic study of the topic is A. H. Robertson, *Characterization in the Conflict of Laws* (1940).
[38] In particular, door-to-door insurance salesmen have been an object of ridicule in Anglophone countries for many years.
[39] John Berryman, "So long? Stevens" in *The Dream Songs* (1969).
[40] See M. Galanter, *Lowering the Bar: Lawyer Joke and Legal Centre* (2005)
[41] Above n 32 at 14
[42] F. Kermode, *Wallace Stevens* (1960) at 1
[43] M. Bates, *Wallace Stevens : A Mythology of Self* (1986) at 85, 158, 201.
[44] Above text at n 9 *ff*
[45] Ibid at 18.
[46] Ibid at 20.
[47] "Sailing After Lunch " in *Ideas of Order* (1936)
[48] Above n 32 at 15.
[49] Above text at n 32
[50] M. Schmidt in above n 23 at 39
[51] Above n 32 at 94
[52] Ibid at 95.
[53] Above text at n 32
[54] Above text at n 52
[55] M. E. Brown, *Wallace Stevens: The Poem as Art* (1970)
[56] Ibid at 65.
[57] Above n 32 at 94
[58] Above n 55 at 66
[59] R. Fernandez, *Messages: Literary Essays* (1927)
[60] M. Benamon, *Wallace Stevens and the Symbolist Imagination* (1972) at 123
[61] H. Steven (ed.) *Letters of Wallace Stevens* (1966) at 823.
[62] Above n 55 at 68
[63] W. W. Bevis, *Mind of Winter: Wallace Stevens, Meditation, and Literature* (1988) at 148
[64] Above text at n 52
[65] Above n 63 at 148
[66] Above n 60 at 14
[67] Above text at n 51
[68] Above n 32 at 65
[69] Ibid at 66
[70] Ibid at 67
[71] See, notably, H. Vendler, *Words Chosen Out of Desire* (1986) at 23 who suggests that the *steel* is an executioner's blade against flesh. She also regards the *sharp flash* as surgical
[72] Above n 32, Chapter IV, "Steel Against Intimation."
[73] Ibid at 66
[74] [1977] QB 966
[75] Below text at n 82
[76] [1977] QB 966 at 976
[77] Author's emphasis
[78] Below Ch VI text at n 63 *ff*

[79] Below text at n 210
[80] In the North of England, where both case and poem are situated, including a league which included the club which was involved in *Miller* v *Jackson*.
[81] F. Muir (Ed) *The Oxford Book of Humorous Prose* (1992) at 721
[82] For other comments on Sir John Squire, see F. Bates and R. McGinty, " 'Arrest Him, he's Indecent, he's Obscene What's More!' The Poems and Paintings of D. H. Lawrence as Part of Cultural History and Moral Outrage" (2006-2008) 10 *Newcastle LR* 91
[83] Above text at n76.
[84] See *R* v *Whitehead* [1929] 1 KB 99 at 102 par Lord Hewart CJ. A significant number of Australian jurisdictions have abolished and replace the corroboration requirement. See *Evidence Act* 1995 (Cth, NSW) s 164.
[85] F. Bates, "Law as Culture: Global Thoughts From a Small Island" (1987) *The Law Teacher* 263 at 268.
[86] For comment on the Scots situation see O.F Robinson, TD Fergus 21, W.M Gordon, *European Legal History* (2nd Ed, 1994) at 224 *ff*; for Scots lack of enthusiasm for English encroachment see T.B Smith, *British Justice: The Scottish Contribution* (1961) at 35*ff*; for comment on the situation in classical times, see J.A Crook, *Law and Life of Rome* (1967) at 7*ff*.
[87] R.A. Posner, *Law and Literature* (1998, Revised and Enlarged Edition) at 255 *ff*
[88] Ibid at 255
[89] Ibid at 256
[90] Posner relies, ibid, on his own book *Overcoming Law* (1995) Ch 24 ("Rhetoric, Legal Advocacy and Legal Reasoning")
[91] R.C.A. Higgins, " 'The Empty Eloquence of Fools' Rhetoric in Classical Greece" in *Rediscovering Rhetoric: Law Language and the Practice of Persuasion* (2008, Ed. Gleeson and Higgins) 3 at 17
[92] Ibid at 20 *ff*.
[93] Ibid at 21.
[94] Just as a doctor, she less convincingly I think, suggests, may lose a patient, while enacting all the medical arts.
[95] Above n 87 at 256
[96] See, for example, P. R. Teachout, "Lapse of Judgment" (1989)77 *California LR* 120; R,. A. Prentice, "Supreme Court Rhetoric" (1983) 25 *Arizona LR* 85
[97] See above n 87 at 305 *ff*. See also Above ChI at n 241.
[98] Above n 91 at 13*ff*
[99] Ibid at 14
[100] Ibid at 15
[101] Above text at n 87
[102] Above n 87 at 255
[103] Ibid at 256
[104] Above text at n 76 *ff*
[105] Below text at n 217 *ff*
[106] P. Goodrich, *Reading the Law: A Critical Introduction to Legal Method and Techniques* (1986) at 173
[107] Ibid at 175
[108] Authors emphasis
[109] Above n 106 at 177
[110] Ibid at 179
[111] Ibid at 179
[112] Above text at n 103
[113] Above n 87 at 257
[114] Posner's view is derived from R. A. Hillman, " ' Instinct with an Obligation' and 'Normative Ambiguity of Rhetorical Power' " (1995) 56 *Ohio State LJ*. 775
[115] Above n 106 at 181
[116] Ibid at 182

[117] Above text at n 111
[118] Above n 106 at 183
[119] Above text at n 115
[120] J. A. Crook. *Law and Life of Rome* (1967) at 33.
[121] Ibid
[122] Pliny. *Ep* VI, 33, 3-4
[123] The period covered by Crook, above n 120 at 8, runs from the legislation of 90-89BC, under which all free people in Italy South of the River Po became entitled to Roman citizenship, to AD 212, which was traditionally the date of the legislation of the Emperor Caracalla under which nearly all free people in the Roman Empire were entitled to Roman citizenship.
[124] Ibid at 33
[125] Ibid at 34
[126] See Horace, *Epistles I*, xvi, 40
[127] Above n 120 at 87
[128] For comment on the role of the *praetor*, see ibid at 74 *ff*
[129] Ibid a 88
[130] Ibid at 89
[131] Ibid at 90
[132] Above at n 123
[133] Above text at n 155
[134] Above text at n 106
[135] Above text at n 118
[136] C. Perelman, *Justice, Law and Argument: Essays on Moral and Legal Reasoning* (1980) at 120
[137] Ibid at 121
[138] Ibid at 122
[139] J. H. Merryman, *The Civil Law Tradition* (1996) at 63
[140] Ibid at 64
[141] 367 F. Supp 373 (1973).
[142] Everything except the list of counsel appearing in the case and a quotation from the relevant statute.
[143] R.E. Megarry, *A New Miscellany – At Law: Yet Another Diversion for Lawyers and Others* (2005 Ed. Garner) 178.
[144] 367 F. Supp 373 (1973) at 374.
[145] Ibid at 376.
[146] 130 SE 2d 251 (1963)
[147] Ibid at 252.
[148] Above text at n 143.
[149] 333 NW 2d 67 (1983)
[150] Bronson PJ, Brennan and Gillies JJ. The Headnote, in verse, reads as follows:

> A way ward Chevy struck a tree
> Whose owner sued defendant three.
> He sued car's owner, driver too,
> And insurer for what was due
> For his oak tree that now may bear
> A lasting need for tender care.
> The Oakland County Circuit
> Court,
> John N. O'Brien, J., set fourth
> The judgment that defendants sought
> And quickly an appeal was brought.
>
> Courts of Appeals, J.H. Gillis, J.,
> Gave thought and then had this to say:

> 1) There is no liability
> Since No-Fault grants immunity;
> 2) No jurisdiction can be found
> Where process service is unsound;
> And thus the judgment, as it's termed,
> And thus the judgment, as it's termed
> Is due to be, and is,
> Affirmed.

[151] Much the same remark could be made regarding the writer of the headnote, above n 150.
[152] Though that poem did include the story of *Peter Grimes*, which was turned into a tragic opera by the great English composer Benjamin Britten.
[153] 667 F. Supp 414 (1982)
[154] Ibid at 414
[155] 579 F 2d 1200 (1978) at 1203.
[156] Above n 143 at 179n
[157] The first, to be found at the end of the second line refers to the shortest *oral* opinion to have been delivered in the United States. At the sentencing of a man convicted of murder. He pleaded, "As god is my judge, I didn't do it, I'm not guilty." the judge is alleged to have replied, "He isn't, I am . You did. You are." That is, of course, well known.
Less well known is the dictum in *Robinson* v *Pioche, Bayerque & Co* 5 Cal. 460 (1855) in the second footnote, which occurs at the end of the judgment. In the *Robinson* case, the plaintiff was injured when he fell into an unguarded hole in the sidewalk at the front of the defendant's store. The defense was that the plaintiff was drunk. The entire opinion was as follows: "The Court below erred in giving the third, fourth, and fifth instructions. If the defendants were at fault in leaving an unguarded hole in the sidewalk of a public street, the intoxication of the plaintiff cannot excuse such gross negligence. A drunken man is as much entitled to a safe street as a sober one, and much more in need of it. "The judgment is reversed and the cause remanded."
[158] Above text as n 141 *ff.*
[159] 216 SE 2d 356 (1975)
[160] Ibid at 357.
[161] In the words of the headnote: Defendant, contending that the State had unfairly won, appealed from judgment of conviction of the Superior Court, Chatham County, Dunbar Harrison, J. The Court of Appeals, Evans, J., being of the view that an opinion in rhyme was just fine, waxed poetic and did proclaim that defendant's prayer for one day's delay so that the jury, twelve good people honest and true, could his missing witness hear should not on deaf judicial ear have fallen and that the appeals judges, in earning their pay, would to be learned trial judge say, "reversed."
[162] 216 SE 2d 356 (1975) at 356.
[163] Above text at n 146
[164] 216 SE 2d 356 (1975) at 357.
[165] 542 P 2d 676 (1975)
[166] The term advisement refers to the consultation of a court after the argument of a cause by counsel and before delivering their opinion. see *Re Holhorst* 150 US 653 (1893) at 662.
[167] 542 P 2d 676 (1975) at 684.
[168] Ibid at 685.
[169] G.R. Smith, "A Primer of Opinion Writing For Four New Judges" (1967) 21 *Arkansas LR* 197 at 210.
[170] 542 P 2d 676 (1975) at 686
[171] Ibid at 685.
[172] Ibid

[173] In the Court's own words, "Respondent who has served as city attorney, as deputy county attorney and county attorney in his home county, and is a respected member of the Kansas bar..."
[174] For comment on this standard, as compared with others, see F. Bates, "Strength or Intensity? Some Reflections on the Modern Standard of Proof in Civil Cases" (1980) 27 *Chitty's L.J.* 335.
[175] 542 P 2d 676 (1975) at 684.
[176] Ibid at 685.
[177] As well as being ordered to pay the costs of the instant hearing.
[178] Above text n 170.
[179] 623 P 2d 1307 (1981).
[180] Ibid at 1312.
[181] 602 F 2d 747 (1979).
[182] Brown CJ, Clark and Vance JJ.
[183] 782 F 2d 1307 (1986).
[184] Goldberg, Jolly and Higginbottom. JJ.
[185] 782 F 2d 1307 (1986) at 1309.
[186] Ibid at 1314.
[187] 604 F 2d 322 (1979).
[188] Goldberg, Ainsworth and Kravitch JJ.
[189] 604 F 2d 322 (1979) at 323.
[190] 437 US 214 (1978).
[191] 589 F 2d 894 (1979).
[192] 604 F 2d 324 (1979).
[193] Above text at n 183.
[194] 465 NE 2d 1391 (1984).
[195] Ibid at 1391.
[196] Given CJ and DeBruler JJ concurred and Prentice J concurred in the result.
[197] The *previous cases* to which Hunter J referred were *Holtscher* v *State* 465 NE 2d 715 (1984); *Avery* v *State* 463 NE 2d 1088 (1984); *Johnson* v *State* 453 NE 2d 975 (1983).
[198] Above n 143 at 179n.
[199] 239 F 3d 1067 (2001). For comment on this case at large, see F. Bates, *International Disorder and the Child Abduction Convention.* (2009) at 31 *ff.*
[200] Kozinski, Thomas and Illston JJ.
[201] See F. Bates above n 199 at 31 *ff.*
[202] 239 F 3d 1067 (2001) at 1072.
[203] (1872), Fit the Second.
[204] 239 F 3d 1067 (2001) at 1073.
[205] See, for example, M. Davies, A.S. Bell, P.L.G. Bereton *Nygh's Conflict of Laws in Australia* (8th Ed, 2010) at 287 *ff.*
[206] Above text at 76.
[207] [1977] QB 966.
[208] Above text at n 77 *ff.*
[209] This description of the facts is largely derived from the judgment of Geoffrey Lane LJ. [1977] QB 966 at 982 *ff.*
[210] [1977] QB 966 at 980.
[211] [1940] AC 880 at 903.
[212] [1977] QB 966 at 981.
[213] [1940] AC 880 at 903.
[214] [1977] QB 966 at 981.
[215] Ibid at 981.
[216] Ibid at 982.
[217] Ibid at 986
[218] (1897) 11 Ch. D. 852.
[219] It was also held that the defence or prescription by means of twenty years use did not apply

as the time would only run from the date that the nuisance occurred, which was when the consulting room was built.
[220] [1977] QB 966 at 987.
[221] Above text at n 216.
[222] [1977] QB 966 at 982
[223] Ibid at 987.
[224] Ibid at 989.
[225] Which, in fact, it was, see above text at n 80.
[226] Above text at n 70.
[227] Above text at n 76.
[228] Above text at n 212.
[229] Above text at n 77.
[230] Above text at n 215.
[231] Above text at n 217.
[232] Above text at n 218.
[233] J. Scott, *Caught in Court: A Selection of Cases with Cricketing Connections* (1989) at 234 *ff.*
[234] Ibid at 237.
[235] Above text at n 214.
[236] S. Sedley, "In the Court of Appeal" (2007) 20(17) *London Review of Books* 26.

Chapter III
Aspects of Rhetoric

1. The Rhetoric of War

a) The Anticipation of War

By international law, as Shearer has noted,[1] State practice as to the commencement of war has varied: until the Sixteenth Century, it was customary to notify an intended war either by herald or by letters of interest. In the following century, it was generally considered that a declaration of war was necessary. The earlier practice had fallen into disuse and several wars were commenced without any formal declaration. However, Shearer comments that, by the Nineteenth Century, it was taken for granted that some kind of preliminary declaration or ultimatum was necessary. Thereafter, there were instances of State practice which were inconsistent with those conventions.

Thus, in 1904, Japan began hostilities against Russia with an unexpected attack on part of the Russian fleet at Port Arthur. Yet, at the same time, Japan had sought to justify her actions on the grounds that negotiations had been broken off with Russia and had, accordingly, notified Russia that she reserved the right to take independent action to protect her own interests. That particular incident led to the rule which was laid down in the *Hague Convention III* in 1907. That Convention stated that hostilities should not be commenced without a prior explicit warning in the form of either a declaration of war, stating the grounds on which it was based, or an ultimatum which contained a conditional declaration of war.

The Convention also provided that the existence of the state of war should be notified to neutral States without delay. Nonetheless in the period between 1935 and 1945, it seems as though little respect was paid to the terms of the Convention, Shearer suggests,[2] with hostilities being begun without any prior declaration. That situation still appears to pertain with disputes such as that between Britain and Argentina over the Malvinas/Falkland Islands being commenced without such a declaration. The result seems to be that parties to such conflicts do not regard themselves as being bound by the rules to be found in the 1907 Convention. The most Shearer seems to be able to offer[3] is that the fact that the rules seem very largely to be ignored, "...does not mean, however, that the procedure of a declaration of war, preceding the commencement of hostilities, is altogether obsolete."

Issues of international law apart, the anticipation of war, both in law and in poetry, presents itself in largely personal terms. Because of this, reactions are bound to be rather mixed, as the material discussed in the following pages will amply demonstrate.

At one end of the scale apparently is Thomas Hardy's poem "Men Who March Away", written in September 1914. The repetitious nature of the rhetorical devices, as illustrated by the first stanza, emphasises a traditional approach to upcoming hostility:

> What of the faith and fire within us
> Men who march away
> Ere the barn-cocks say
> Night is growing gray,
> Leaving all that here can win us;
> What of the faith and fire within us
> Men who march away?

The *faith and fire* is assumed, as is the rhythmic nature of the poem which seeks to evoke marching feet of the soldiers who march away. At the same time Hardy, one of the most influential poets of the Twentieth Century, raises the spectre of scepticism towards the enterprise which is undertaken, after all, by the soldiers themselves whose *faith and fire* it is. In the second stanza, another figure is invoked, who seeks to cast doubt on the activities of narrators:

> Is it a purblind prank, O think you,
> Friend with the musing eye,
> Who watch us stepping by
> With doubt and dolorous sigh?
> Can much pondering so hoodwink you!
> Is it purblind prank, O think you,
> Friend with the musing eye?

However, the person with the *musing eye* is not taken seriously by the soldiers and it is, surely, not without significance that they consider his questioning stance to be that product of excessive *pondering*. Thought is not a part of the soldiers' response, arising from the *faith and fire*. Thus, they respond:

> In our heart of hearts believing
> Victory crowns the just,
> And that braggarts must
> Surely bite the dust,
> Press we to the field ungrieving,
> In our heart of hearts believing
> Victory crowns the just.
> Hence the faith and fire within us...

It may very well be, of course, that the *friend with the musing eye* in the second stanza is the poet himself and the emphasis on emotional responses is not really the subject of approbation and, worse still, may, lead to the continuance of war. The soldiers mistrust of *musing* and *pondering* may lead to their belief in myths such as *Victory crowns the just*. There is certainly room enough in an examination of "Men Who March Away" to be able to extrapolate from it to some of the other attitudes towards the 1914-18 War and towards the horrors which are described in other poems later discussed.[4] Irony is a rhetorical device not unknown in Hardy's work at large and it is a useful weapon to deal with the unthinking, sentimental rationalism which is so damaging, and is not wholly, unfortunately, dead.

Thus, to move almost one hundred years, from the time of the 1914-18 war to the time of Iraq and Afghanistan, we find Kate Brighton's poem "Anthem".[5] The similarities - except, perhaps, for the immediate rejection of the thoughtful observer in "Men Who March Away" are apparent:

> No island is an island
> but when the bright brass band Jerusalem
> of Blake and Parry puts its hand
> on its heart I find I cannot fight
>
> that bead, I feel my face on fire,

my awkward angled arms unfold,
and in my feet of feet desire
to march in step through streets of gold.

From council flat or cotton mill,
as long as we stand singing here
I am as English as the hills,
half only human, half divine,

and shake as overhead, unseen,
the organ's rising voice of god
rings out across the village green
of England's once upon a time.

The references to the words of William Blake's hymn "Jerusalem" are clear, especially in the second stanza. Thus, in Blake's original, *Bring me my chariot of fire* is transmogrified in to *I feel my face on fire* and, in the second line of that stanza *O clouds unfold* is changed into *my awkward angled arms unfold*, *Bring my arrows of desire* into *and in my feet of feet desire*. There is no mention of the *mental fight* which Blake regarded as necessary for the building of Jerusalem, whilst the author is unable to *fight* the beat of the music. The writer describes himself at least whilst in the grip of the anthem, as *English as the hills*, which Blake had earlier described as being clouded. However, at the end, a note, which does not seem deliberately to be decontextualising Blake is struck by means of the last two lines of the last stanza in contradistinction to the first line of the third stanza – *From council flat or cotton mill* – the last two lines refer to the *village green*[6] and, then and most tellingly, *England once upon a time*. Thus, the state of mind induced by Blake's words and Parry's music does not now exist, nor ever really did. Just as, perhaps, the causes for which the men who marched away never really existed, at least not in the way the marchers themselves described them.

As regards "Men Who March Away", it is suggested that the second stanza, with its references to thought process and to observations, regardless of the soldiers' response, is crucial to an understanding of the poem. Why should, in other words, the soldiers marching to fight on the battlefields of the 1914-18 war be regarded as a *purblind prank*? Who, again, is purblind and on whom is the prank being played if, indeed, it is such? After *musing* and *pondering*, the observer concludes that it is the soldiers who are *purblind* and it is on them that the *prank* is being played. It is true that they march away with faith and fire and that *victory crowns the just* and that they vehemently rejected, in the poem's third stanza, the cerebrations of the observer:

> Nay. We well see what we are doing,
> Though some may not see –
> Dalliers as they be –
> England's need are we;
> Her distress would leave us rueing:
> Nay. We well see what we are doing,
> Though some may not see!

The fact the fifth and final stanza repeats the first may well be a dramatic device aimed at emphasising the self delusionary process of the soldiers. However, to find one of the reasons why such a *prank* should have been played on men who, as will be seen,[7] had no genuine idea where their heroic – and no mistake should be made that they were anything else – ideals would take them, another poem must be examined.

That poem is "The Parable of the Old Man and the Young" by Wilfred Owen and written in the same year as "Men Who March Away". It is a retelling, and with a disastrously different ending of the story of Abraham and Isaac from the Old Testament. Its essence refers to some, at least, of the political processes leading up to the 1914-18 War:

> So Abram rose, and clave the wood, and went,
> And took the fire with him, and a knife.
> And as they sojourned both of them together
> Isaac the first-born spake and said, My Father
> Behold the preparations, fire and iron,
> But where the lamb, for this burnt-offering?
> Then Abram bound the youth with belts and straps,
> And builded parapets and trenches there,
> And stretched forth the knife to slay his son.
> When lo! An Angel called him out of heaven,

> Saying, Lay not thy hand upon the lad,
> Neither do anything to him, thy son.
> Behold! Caught in a thicket by its horns,
> A Ram. Offer the Ram of Pride instead.
>
> But the old man would not so, but slew his son,
> and half the seed of Europe, one by one.

The title of Owen's poem is of itself highly significant: first, it is a parable, a story from which a moral can be drawn – a moral fable. Second, it is not entitled the "Parable of Abraham and Isaac", but the *Old* man and the *Young*; of itself, that suggests a much broader base for the parable than simply seeking to draw a moral from a well-known Old Testament story, which concludes with divine intervention and a restoration of the normal familial situation. It is in this restatement, the father, representing an older empowered generation, who kills the son, representing the younger unempowered generation. To draw upon the metaphor in " Men Who March Away", the *purblind prank* has been played, for what reason – though Owen strongly suggests that at the end of "The Parable of the Old Man and the Young". The imagery is powerful from the outset; thus, the phrase *burnt offering* is used in line six strongly suggesting the equation of the end of Isaac with the carnage which was to eventuate in France in the 1914-18 conflict. Then, in lines seven and eight, Isaac, and his generation, is still further disempowered with many of the accoutrements of that war: *with belts and straps* and *parapets and trenches*. Then, in Owen's retelling, the *old man* rejected the divine offer – *The Ram of Pride* – and killed his son and, in the fearful final line, *half the seed of Europe, one by one*.

The target, then, is starkly clear: the overly empowered, overly proud older generation who, for the sole reason that they are possessed of that power and, indeed, are proud of it are prepared to slaughter half a generation which is disempowered. It should be said that "The Parable of the Old Man and the Young" was not uniformly well received. For instance, Welland, in dealing with the poem, comments[8] that Owen's work becomes rhetorical when he is quarrelling with others. The very retelling of a Biblical story which seeks to demonstrate the effectiveness of divine intervention in potentially disastrous situations is an obvious rhetorical device, as are the deliberately anachronistic touches in lines seven and eight. I have already sought to point out the agencies with which Owen found himself quarrelling. It is, *pace* Welland, at least arguable that those rhetorical devices do not but make the poem more effective in seeking to persuade the reader of the intergenerational nature of war with which he quarrels. In addition to Welland, an anonymous review in *The Times/Literary Supplement* in 1921 was apparently disturbed both by the Parable and by "Dulce et Decorum Est", of which more later,[9] and wrote that, "the suggestion is that a nation is divided into two parts, one part which talks of war and sustains it, while the other acts and suffers. We can understand how such a thought might arise, but not how it can persist and find sustenance." It seems clear that the commentator's experience was rather limited. Even solely in the context of the 1914-18 War, as the carnage increased, it is surely apparent that the elements which Owen sought to expose were continuing. Indeed it is a recurrent theme in the poetry of war. Thus, in a poem, "On Hearing a New Escalation", written about the Vietnam War, the American poet Richard Hugo wrote, *inter alia*:

> Killing's still in though glory is out of style.
> And what does it come to, this blood cold
> in the streets and a history book printed
> and bound with such cost saving American
> methods, the names and dates are soon bones?
> Beware certain words: Enemy. Liberty. Freedom.
> Believe those sounds and you're aiming a bomb.

Out of the very same conflict - and the Vietnam War is especially important in the instant context because as Goldensohn has written,[10] "And the civilians who protested the war were usually of one generation, and the soldiers of another; then, too, a bitterness still smacking of class war continues to smoulder in the relation between those of draft age, who had managed to avoid the war, and those who served and felt the consequences of their service – comes W. D. Erhart who, in a poem entitled "Finding My Old Battalion Command Post":

> What we came here to find
> was never ours. After the miles

we've travelled, after the years
we've dreamed if only we could touch
the wound again, we could be whole,
no small wonder to discover
only a lethal past between us,
what we thought a brotherhood
only a mutual recollection of fear.

Of significance is the fact that Hugo was born in 1923 (and died in 1982), whilst Erhart was born in 1948. Thus the intergenerational rupture at time of war does continue, contrary to the view of the *Times Literary Supplement's* critic to be made manifest. It should also be said that intergenerational attitudes towards law and its administration differ. As will become apparent, this is a theme which recurs throughout the book.

The appalling carnage of the 1914-18 War is, now, too well known to need documentation; the English poet Philip Larkin, in 1964, sought to explain the enthusiasm which British people appeared to have to enlist in a War in which, as it went on, they must have known was likely to see them killed or seriously wounded. In his poem "MCMXIV", Larkin seeks initially to establish the context in which the young men sought to enlist at the outbreak of the 1914-18 war. Once again, the intergenerational element is apparent. The poem begins with a striking metaphor:

Those long uneven lines
Standing as patiently
As if they were stretched outside
The Oval or Vila Park,
The crowns of hats, the sun
On moustached archaic faces
Grinning as if it were all
An August Bank Holiday lark;

The parallel drawn by Larkin between the queues of young men seeking to enlist in armed forces in the 1914-18 War and crowds waiting to attend a sporting event or taking part in a holiday activity, suggests something different from reality. The next two stanzas seek to illustrate the difference from the year in which the poem was actually written by drawing attention to change in coinage, the different names by which children were called, the different nature of advertising and the less restricted licensing hours for pubs in 1914 then in 1964 (though it was the 1914-18 War which brought about those restrictions). The third stanza draws attention to changes in rural landscapes and, "The differently dressed servants with tiny rooms in huge mansions."

Having drawn attention to social phenomena at the time of which he was speaking, Larkin then concludes the poem, in the fourth stanza, by an explication, which seems uncannily congruent with the spirit of the marching soldiers in "Men Who March Away":

Never such innocence,
Never before or since,
As changed itself to past
Without a word – the men
Leaving the gardens tidy,
The thousands of marriages
Lasting a little while longer:
Never such innocence again.

Given the nature of "MCMXIV" there has been a not inconsiderable critical reaction: thus, for instance Martin sees[11] the poem in something of an apocalyptic light. He describes the poem as, "...comparing the first waves of enlistees, as shown in photographs...he then surveys some emblems of a way of life which unknown to its participants, would disappear forever... Indeed so struck is he by the consequence of their passing that he purposely chose roman numerals, as on a tombstone, over the Arabic, which he found almost too awful to contemplate and beyond the modest dimensions of his poems. However modest though, this quiet poem captures the essential feel of England in the last years of her innocence and world supremacy in the twentieth century. Because such innocence permeated English life, Larkin has drawn on the great and obscure, in people and objects, to mourn its absence from his contemporary England". Superficially attractive though Martins' thesis might be, it is not factually correct. Although 1918 might have marked something of a milestone in the decline of Britain's military might, it did not bring it wholly to an end, as Britain's role in the 1939-45 War alone attests.

Nor did England's commercial (and legal) international dominance suddenly come to an end. An example is provided by the decision of the Judicial Committee of the Privy Council in *Vita Food Products Inc* v *Unus Shipping Co*[12]. In that case, a cargo of herrings was shipped from Newfoundland to New York in a ship registered in Nova Scotia and the parties to the contract were companies incorporated in Nova Scotia and New York. The ship ran aground in Nova Scotia owing to the captain's negligence. As a result, the cargo was required to be "reconditioned" before it could be sold. The bill of lading stated that the proper law was English law. Therefore, it was perhaps not wholly surprising that the Judicial Committee held that the contract was governed by English law. Yet when one examines the advice prepared by Lord Wright, the situation becomes rather more opaque. "But where the English *rule that intention is the test applies*," Lord Wright stated,[13] "and where there is an express statement by the parties of their intention to select the law of the contract, it is difficult to see what qualifications are possible, provided the intention expressed is bona fide and legal and provided that there is no reason for avoiding the choice on the grounds of public policy." There is, it is suggested a good and clear reason for avoiding the choice – if not on the grounds of public policy *per se* – and that is that there was scant connection between the contract and English law. Lord Wright, though, sought to dispose of that fundamental objection. Most tellingly, I would suggest, Lord Wright emphasised that, in relation to the proper law term in the bill of lading, "...those familiar with international business are aware how frequent such a provision is even where the parties are not English and the transactions are carried out completely outside England." In addition, he continued[14] by commenting that, "...the underwriters are likely to be English. In any case parties may reasonably desire that the familiar principles of English commercial law should apply." It may very well be that, from the point of view of ordinary legal reasoning that view is not especially convincing. However, it is suggested that it is altogether more explicable in historical terms. Thus, in 1891, when England's commercial and maritime power was at a greater height than when *Vita Foods* was decided, the English Court of Appeal was required to decide *Chatenay* v *Brazilian Submarine Telegraph Co.*[15] There, the plaintiff, who was a Brazilian subject, had executed in Brazil, in the Portuguese language, a power of attorney to a broker, who was resident in London, to buy shares.

Accordingly, the broker sold certain of the plaintiff's shares in the defendant company and they were registered in the names of the purchasers. The plaintiff then claimed a rectification of the register on the grounds that the sale was not authorised by the power of attorney. The Court held that the plaintiff's intention was to be ascertained by evidence of competent experts and translators including, if necessary, Brazilian lawyers. If, from that evidence, the intention appeared to be that the authority be acted upon in England, the extent of that authority should be determined by English law. However, although that was the straightforward effect of the decision, there was more to the case than its simple adjudication. Hence, Lindley LJ stated[16] that the trial judge had not been correct in his view that when one is dealing with what takes place in England – being a transfer, or a sale, or some other dealing with shares – recourse must be had to English law. Lord Esher MR was of a similar view when he said[17] that the extent of the authority in any country in which the authority was to be acted on was to be taken to be the law of the country where it is acted upon. Hence, the transactions were subject to English law and, in all likelihood, the jurisdiction of the English courts. On the other hand, it is not hard to see the strength of the arguments to be found in the appeal brought by the defendants: first, the document had been executed in Brazil and, hence, it should be governed by the laws of that country. Second, even assuming, as Lord Esher MR seemed to do, that the document was to be acted on in different countries, it should still only have one interpretation and ought not to be differently construed in each of the countries where it is acted upon - the effect of which would be that the plaintiff might be bound in one country, but not in another, in transactions which were of the same character. The defendants argued that that would not be the situation were the law of Brazil to be held applicable. The point about this discussion is that it demonstrates that attitudes in the area of commercial law had not undergone significant change in the time between the two cases which have been discussed which suggests that Martin's view[18] that 1914 represented the end of England's global dominance is largely misconceived.

There are, inevitably, other ways in which to approach "MCMXIV": Booth writes [19] that Larkin is, "...giving expression to one of those irresistible myths of innocence and beauty through which, in all ages, we seek to come to terms with the suffering and transience of the world". At the same time, given the thrust of the argument which I have sought to advance, from the discussion of "Men Who March Away" onwards, the *innocence* which Larkin seeks to depict may not be a genuine innocence but a quality of *ignorance* and *unknowing* which is instilled in actual ("Men Who March Away") and potential ("MCMXIV") soldiers by an empowered class and generation who became yet further disempowered by the necessary trappings of war itself ("The Parable of the Old Man and the Young"). In view of that, it is not wholly surprising that Booth goes on[20] to state that Larkin's poetic imagination finds no security in patriotism, nor in celebrating his national or class identity. There, of course, is no reason, because Larkin was writing in 1964 about events in 1914 and had the benefits of hindsight and knew what was to follow in consequence of the perceived innocence, why he should.

The issue of that hindsight has, in fact, been raised by Petch who comments,[21] that, "Our shared knowledge of subsequent events between poet and reader which both casts an elegiac aura over the whole poem and makes it very hard to disagree with his valuation of the lost world. Because the poem's attitudes are visualised rather than stated, the very gentleness of this poem's manner coerces us into accepting [Larkin's] attitudes along with the vantage point we are given." The question which, inexorably follows is *why* might we not accept Larkin's view of his own *lost world*. I have already tried to suggest[22] that the *innocence* which Larkin seeks to emphasise, through, *inter alia*, repetition, may be an artificial construct. Further, Larkin's depictions of life in 1914 may not be especially attractive to us almost 100 years later. Thus, the characteristics of the street depicted in the second stanza may not be as appealing as the innately conservative Larkin might have wished them to appear:

> And the shut shops, the bleached
> Established names on the sunblinds,
> The farthings and sovereigns,
> And dark-clothed children at play
> Called after kings and queens,
> The tin advertisements
> For cocoa and twist, and the pubs
> Wide open all day;

In the modern days of unrestricted retail trading hours and decimalised currency, couples with archaically - named children and simplistic advertising may not have been immediately attractive to younger people in 1964 when the poem was written; they seem substantially more at odds with the lifestyle of 2011, when this chapter is being written. More particularly, they are at odds with the experiences of people who were not alive at the time of which Larkin was writing. Hence, it is probably correct to answer Day's rhetorical question[23] that, "Does nostalgia best describe the feeling in the poem?" in the negative because *nostalgia* implies a looking back to something which one has experienced, which most readers of the poem will not. Day, though, asks another question: "What attitude to history does [the poem] imply?" That question is not as easy to answer because more than one attitude is apparent. One such attitude is, essentially and inevitably, *visual* because it is clear, that Larkin is basing his vision on photographs which, in turn, are *one dimensional,* in the sense that they have no depth and, as I have earlier suggested,[24] there may be more to the innocence depicted in the poem than some of the other poems suggest. Day goes on[25] to suggest that the poem verges on the sentimental. This is always an easy charge to make and one which, given the poem's general context, is not easy to refute. In the case of "MCMXIV" it is especially easy to make simply because of the poem's subject matter and readers' knowledge of the consequences of the events which Larkin describes. At the same time, the *innocence* which Larkin describes as having been lost is perceived as somehow valuable in itself. It may be that such a view is simplistic, but on the other hand it may equally be that the innocence is innately of value. Larkin's entire vision is altogether more complex when viewed as a totality.

> I sit in one of the dives
> On Fifty-second Street
> Uncertain and afraid
> As the clever hopes expire
> Of a low dishonest decade:
> Waves of anger and fear
> Circulate over the bright
> And darkened lands of the earth,
> Obsessing our private lives;

> The unmentionable odour of death
> Offends the September night.

The low *dishonest decade*, which Auden describes in his poem '*September 1, 1939*' has, in particular, seen the failure of the policy of appeasement to Hitler and Germany. Whatever other dimensions Auden's dislike of the 1930s may comprise, the instant poem is essentially about the premonition of war and its effects on individuals (*Obsessing our private lives*). In the second stanza, Auden goes on to comment on the history of Germany and the culture which has led up to the events and their consequences:

> Accurate scholarship can
> Unearth the whole offence
> From Luther until now
> That has driven a culture mad,
> Find what occurred at Linz,
> What huge Imago made
> A psychopathic god:
> I and the public know
> What all schoolchildren learn,
> Those to whom evil is done
> Do evil in return.

After psycho-sociological analysis of the entire German and, more particularly, Nazi phenomenon, has failed properly to explain it, Auden suggests, a simpler and more direct explanation is offered in the last four lines of the second stanza. The real answer to the problem, Auden suggests, lies in the *Treaty of Versailles*, which concluded the 1914-18 War and exacted vast reparations from Germany. It has been strongly argued by Taylor[26] that it was these reparations which created the conditions which favoured the rise of Nazism and, hence, the 1939-45 war.

In the fifth stanza, Auden turns his attention to the other drinkers in the bar and their self-deception as to the magnitude (or enormity) of the events which are about to unfold. Auden perceives a plethora of pretence and a total lack of awareness as to the real nature of the plight faced by humanity:

> Faces along the bar
> Cling to their average day:
> The lights must never go out,
> The music must always play,
> All the conventions conspire
> To make this fort assume
> The furniture of home;
> Lest we should see where we are,
> Lost in a haunted wood,
> Children afraid of the night
> Who have never been happy or good.

The truly telling lines in the fifth stanza are the sixth and seventh (*To make this fort assume/The furniture of home*) as they demonstrate, in both military and domestic terms, the lengths that the other denizens of the bar will go to can pretend their present situation to be other than irremedial. That theme is taken up, with more particularity in the sixth and seventh stanzas and, at last, in the eighth, Auden finds himself able to contradict the personalised self-delusion of the ordinary people with whom he has been, in albeit very limited contact. More especially he finds himself able to denounce the public untruths that undermine human beings' collective and personal reliance on one another, which is backed up by official sanction to conceal the fact that human beings face the same present dilemma:

> All I have is a voice
> To undo the folded lie,
> The romantic lie in the brain
> Or the sensual man-in-the-street
> And the lie of Authority
> Whose buildings grope the sky:
> There is no such thing as the State
> And no one exists alone;
> Hunger allows no choice
> To the citizen of the police;
> We must love one another or die.

The last line in that stanza is, clearly, the key which is able to open the box which constricts and yet creates human behaviour. It constricts individuals' capacity for accurate perception and, at the same time, creates a capacity for self delusion. In the final stanza, Auden refuses, despite the apparent hopelessness of the situation which he has depicted, to abandon humanity and find points of light in the general miasma and, ultimately expresses the hope that he will represent such a point and affirm a faith in the future of humanity:

> Defenceless under the night
> Our world in stupor lies;
> Yet, dotted everywhere,
> Ironic points of light
> Flash out wherever the Just
> Exchange their messages:
> May I, composed like them
> Of Eros and of dust,
> Beleaguered by the same
> Negation and despair,
> Show an affirming flame.

As regards the thrust of this poem, which is, at the same time, both deeply pessimistic and wildly optimistic, Hecht has written [27] that, "Something curious or unexpected has happened to Auden in this bar, or, in any case, in this poem. He began by feeling the mixed recognition of fellowship with others and the apprehension of having his privacy and individuality invaded by the overpowering forces of history. Throughout the poem there is a dramatic though unreconciled oscillation between the corporate, or social, and the individual, or private life. The confrontation of these attitudes is finally and unequivocally stated in the paradoxically self contradictory lines. "There is no such thing as the State; and no one exists alone." The poem, therefore, like others before it, employs the ambiguous situation of humans as being at once individuals and part of a social fabric, with advantages or disadvantages in either or both roles. But in the last stanza a new social entity is introduced: in addition to being either private persons or members of a society, we may be, if fortunately endowed, members of an insulated elite, who view the historical calamity not quite with immunity but with the dispassion that makes them 'the Just'. It is with this select group that Auden identifies.

This is an intriguing passage: first there is nothing genuinely paradoxical about being both an individual and, as such, being a part of a social fabric. They are roles which most people are required to play at various parts of their lives. This may, indeed, be especially the case in time of war when an individual may be forced to put off individuality and almost totally assume their role as a distinctive part of the social fabric. It should also be said that I am a little troubled by Hecht's view of an *insulated elite* with which he suggests that Auden identifies in the latter part of the poem. Such select groups would not normally form a part of Auden's *persona*, and although Auden was writing of an abnormal time, the idea articulated by Hecht does seem especially out of character, particularly given the situation which Auden describes.

In addition, Auden, at large, cannot be described as an apolitical poet, and there are necessarily, political references in the poem, both specific and more general. The specific references are to be found in the second stanza with its references to German historical development. Fuller has entered[28] into the political debate, more particularly than had Hecht, at least in some respects. "Actually," he writes, "the mention of Luther was intended to indict far more than Nazism, for Auden at this time blamed the anxieties of modern life largely on those thinkers of the Renaissance and the Enlightenment who were responsible for the economic man." Thus, although the *psychopathic god* referred to in the second stanza may refer to Hitler, it may also refer to the relentless pressures and forces of 1930s capitalism which, in turn, contributed to Auden's description of the 1930s in the first stanza.

Another view of "September 1, 1939" has been expressed by Spears,[29] who suggests that, when reflecting on the political, historical and psychological meaning of what is happening, Auden concludes that the basic fault is that of law. With respect to that commentator, it is suggested that it is not an easy conclusion to maintain. It is not clear what kind of law Spears referred to – if it were International Law, then there could be little doubt that the invading German army would have ignored it, so to that degree, law *qua* law cannot be regarded as having failed.

At the same time, in stanza four, Auden states:

> But who can live for long
> In an euphoric dream;
> Out of the mirror they stare,
> Imperialism's face
> And the international wrong.

In other words, International Law has failed to deal with the wrongs caused by the processes of imperialism. However, the reference as a whole seems to suggest that International Law's effect is, to a significant degree illusory. As regards municipal law, stanza eight suggests that the agents of law may be forced to reinforce, or uphold, the *lie of authority*, which, in terms of wealth and influence, is all pervasive (*Whose buildings grope the sky*). Despite those references, it is, *pace* Spears, a relatively minor thrust of the poem as a whole.

Finally, as regards "December 1, 1939," it appears that Auden, himself, was not especially satisfied with the poem. Callan suggests[30] that Auden believed that his poems should be authentic. By that he meant that the tone of voice, "...must be unmistakeably his own. He defined an authentic poem as one that convinces the reader that the poet has seen its vision of truth with his own eyes, and not through someone else's spectacles." The response to the poem, bearing that comment in mind, must inevitably, be a personal one, unguided by any critical observation, and, hence, the process of authenticising the authentic is quintessentially subjective. One can only suggest that, in "December 1, 1939", Auden has sought to articulate the concerns that not only he but most others would have, were they able to articulate them with the same clarity and grasp of metaphor and of authentic detail.

However, poetry is, essentially, a thoughtful or emotional observation and concern with the approach of war may affect different people in different ways – as the poems hitherto discussed in this chapter suggest. On the other hand, similar concerns might result in more direct and more practical approaches than the writing of poetry. Such direct and practical approaches require a response, or responses, from the law and its agencies. And immediate instance is provided by the decision of the House of Lords in *Chandler* v *DPP*.[31] In that case, the appellants were members of an organisation called the Committee of 100 who sought to further the cause of the Campaign for Nuclear Disarmament by non-violent demonstrations and civil disobedience. In December 1961, they took part in a demonstration at Wethersfield Airfield, which was a *prohibited place* within the meaning of s 3 of the *Official Secrets Act* 1911,[32] and which was then occupied by United States Air Force squadrons assigned by the Supreme Commanders, Allied Forces, Europe. The plan was that, on the day in question, some demonstrators would take up positions outside the entrances to the airfield and remain sitting there for five hours, whilst others would enter the airfield and, by sitting in front of the aircraft, would prevent them from taking off. Many demonstrators, on that day, did travel to the airfield, but were prevented from entering it. The admitted purposes were to ground all aircraft and immobilise the airfield and to reclaim the base for civilian purposes. The appellants were charged, with *inter alia*, conspiring with each other, and others, to commit a breach of s 1 of the *Official Secrets Act* 1911.[33] At trial, a prosecution witness gave evidence to the effect that interference with the ability of aircraft to take off was prejudicial to the safety or interests of the State.[34] However, the judge refused to allow counsel for the appellants to cross examine or call evidence as to the appellants' beliefs that their actions would benefit the State or to show that the appellants' purpose was not, in fact, prejudicial to the State. The appellants were convicted and sentenced to terms of imprisonment. They appealed unsuccessfully to both the Court of Criminal Appeal and to the House of Lords.

In the House of Lords, it was held, first, that the real purpose of the provision was not, as it might *prima facie* appear,[35] limited to acts of espionage[36] but also included acts of sabotage. As Viscount Radcliffe put[37] the matter, "...a prohibited place is not merely something information about which is to be protected from an enemy, but something also which may need to be guarded from destruction, obstruction or interference that would in the result be useful to an enemy. The saboteur just as much as the spy in the ordinary sense is contemplated as an offender under the Act. But, if so, the appellants were saboteurs in this case, for, subject to the question of probative evidence..., it was their avowed purpose to interfere with and obstruct the operation of this airfield, itself a prohibited place within the meaning of the Act." Viscount Radcliffe then went on to consider[38] the *purpose* of the appellants' activities and he did not regard a distinction between *long-term* and *immediate* purposes as being helpful and, hence, that *direct* and *indirect* purposes was more appropriate as being less likely to confuse the issue in the minds of jury. In consequence, Viscount Radcliffe was of the view that, "...if a person's direct purpose in approaching or entering is to cause obstruction or interference, and such obstruction or interference is to be of prejudice to the defence dispositions of the State, an offence is thereby committed, and his indirect purposes or his motives in bringing about the obstruction or interference do not alter the nature or content of his offence." He continued by emphasising that, in the case at hand, the appellants had intended to bring about an obstruction of the airfield for the sake of having an obstruction as nothing else would have served their purpose of using the obstruction as an instrument for furthering their campaign in favour of nuclear disarmament. Likewise, Lord Pearce rejected[39] an argument that the phrase, "...the interests of the State..." to be found in s 1 of the *Official Secrets Act* 1911[40] meant, in the context of *Chandler*, "...the interests of the amorphous populate, without regard to the guiding policies of those in authority, and that proof of possible ultimate benefit to the populace may for the purposes of the Act justify an act of spying or sabotage." Lord Pearce went on to say that, in the context of the Act at large, the interests of the State must mean the interests of the State according to the polices laid down for it by recognised organs of government and authority, in other words, the policies of the State as they are, not, as they ought, in the opinion of a jury, to be.

Viscount Radcliffe was of the opinion[41] that the defence of the State from external enemies was a matter of real concern in time of peace as in war. Further, the, "...disposition, armament and direction of the defence forces of the State are matters decided upon by the Crown and are within its jurisdiction as the executive power of the State. So are treaties and alliances with other States for mutual defence. An airfield maintained for the service of the Royal Air Force or of the air force of one of Her Majesty's allies is an instrument of defence, as are the airplanes operating from the airfield and their armament." The Court, especially Lord Hodson,[42] were fortified in that view by the comment of Lord Parker in *The Zomora*[43] where it was said that, "Those who are responsible for the national security must be the sole judges of what the national security requires. It would be obviously undesirable that such matters should be the subject of evidence in a court of law or otherwise discussed in public". Given the power seemingly vested in the State, Lord Reid discussed what was meant by the phrase, "...the safety or interests of the State..." as used in s 1.[44] Like Lord Pearce,[45] Lord Reid considered[46] that it did not mean, as had been argued on behalf of the appellants, "...the individuals who inhabit these islands. The statute cannot be referring to the interests of all those individuals because those interests may differ and the interests of the majority are not necessarily the same as the interests of the State." At the same time, though, Lord Reid did note that it had all too clearly been seen, in some other jurisdictions, what could happen if the State was personified and deified. In the event, Lord Reid concluded that part of his judgment by saying that, "Perhaps the country or the realm are as good synonyms as one could find and I would be prepared to accept the organised community as coming as near to a definition as one can get."

Having made that valuable point, Lord Reid then stated that he did not subscribe to the view that the Government or a Minister should always have the last word in deciding what is, or is not, in the public interest. However, in the present context, Lord Reid was of the view[47] that, "...the disposition and armament of the armed forces are and for centuries have been within the exclusive discretions of the Crown and that no one can seek a legal remedy on the ground that such discretion has been exercised wrongly... Anyone is entitled, in or out of Parliament, to urge that policy regarding the armed forces should be changed; but until it is changed on a change of government or otherwise, no one is entitled to challenge it in court."

Lord Devlin adopted[48] a slightly different view of the various notions than had Lord Reid. As regards the meaning of *State*, as used in a legal context, Lord Devlin was quite satisfied that it should be used so as to denote the organs of government of any national community. In the context of *Chandler* and the armed forces' situation, the relevant organ was the Crown. "So long as the Crown," Lord Devlin stated, "maintains armed forces for the defence of the realm, it cannot be in its interests that any part of them should be immobilised. It is, of course, arguable that the Crown should not be maintaining the armed forces at all, and that the nation would be safer it the Crown disbanded them. If the Crown was given different advice by the same or different ministers, the result might be that its interests might become different from what they are now. But the statute is not concerned with what the interests of the State might be, or ought to be, but with what they actually are at the time of the alleged offence."

Having said that, Lord Devlin adverted his mind[49] to the issue of the question which the jury was required to answer. First, he answered by saying that they were not inquiring into whether powers of requisition, management or control had been validly exercised. They were inquiring into whether a fact which, by statute, had been constituted as an ingredient of a criminal offence had been proved and that fact which was to be proved[50] was the existence of a purpose prejudicial to the State. However, that purpose was not a purpose which appeared to the State[51] to be prejudicial. "There is no rule of common law," he stated, "that whenever questions of national security are being considered by any court for any purposes, it is what the Crown thinks to be necessary or expedient in fact." The result of all of that, Lord Devlin thought, was that the Crown's opinion as to what was *prejudicial* was as inadmissible as that of the appellants. Though the Crown's evidence about what its interests were an entirely different matter: the interests could be proved by an officer of the Crown whenever it was necessary to do so. Although, in a case such as *Chandler*, it could be presumed that it was prejudicial to the interests of the Crown to have an airfield immobilised, any such presumption was not irrefutable. "Men," Lord Devlin said, "can exaggerate their interests and so can the Crown. The servants of the Crown, like other men animated by the highest motives, are capable of formulating a policy ad hoc so as to prevent the citizen from doing something that the Crown does not want him to do. It is the duty of the courts to be as alert now as they have always been to prevent abuse of the prerogative." However, he considered that, in the case at hand, there was nothing whatsoever to suggest that the Crown's interest in the proper operation of its airfields was not what it might naturally presumed to be, or that it was exaggerating the perils of interference with their effectiveness.

Finally, Lord Devlin emphasised[52] that all questions which concerned the liability of the subject need great care when they are being considered. For Lord Devlin, it was a particular inducement for the courts to take care that the appellants in *Chandler* had not, in his own words, "...traded their liability for gain but for what they sincerely, and however, mistakenly, believe to be the safety of the world. Furthermore (their own expressed determination to break the law notwithstanding), it is the duty of this House to see that men and women who have a creed they want to preach in no case pay any penalty for their faith unless they have taken themselves out of the protection of the law by doing that which the law forbids." Having made that general point, Lord Devlin considered that the House of Lords had discharged that duty, with the result that he concluded that the appellants had committed the crimes with which they had been charged. Lord Pearce, in similar vein, had noted[53] that it had been argued that his view of the *interests of the State*, earlier discussed,[54] constituted an unreasonable infringement of civil liberties. Lord Pearce was not impressed by that argument when he stated that, "...subjects who enter prohibited places for prejudicial reasons know the danger of their liabilities and accept the risk." Lord Pearce also regarded[55] the fact that the Crown is entitled to decide the disposition and order of the armed forces, and that the propriety of any such decision could not be questioned in a court of law was also fatal to any contrary.

So despite their aim of saving the world from nuclear destruction and the courageous methods which they adopted, the appellants were sentenced to terms of imprisonment.[56] The arguments advanced by the House of Lords are quite predictable, based around the power and control of the Crown in respect of the armed services which even the courts cannot redirect. In addition, the ultimate motive of the appellants as described by Lord Reid,[57] in referring to the evidence of the founders of the Committee of 100, was, "... to prevent a nuclear war and their more immediate purpose was to get the facts about nuclear warfare known to the public by any means they could and by pursuing a campaign of non-violent civil disobedience. I should say at once that no one has questioned the sincerity of the accused in their belief in those objectives." Or, as Viscount Radcliffe put the matter[58] in respect of the trial judge's views, "The trial judge did not think that their wishes or hope or beliefs made any difference in this regard. In detail he directed the jury that they should not be influenced by what, he said, was the undisputed fact that the views as to the wrongness and, indeed, unwisdom of nuclear weapons held by the appellants were deeply and passionately held and that they were honest and sincere views."

Motive is generally regarded as being irrelevant, as such, in the criminal law,[59] except to the extent that evidence of motive may be admissible, at common law, from which necessary intent may be inferred.[60] However, colloquially, it may be absolutely crucial in the way in which the arguments of the appellants in *Chandler*, as well as the appellants themselves, were treated. In addition, it seems likely that the appellants were young, whereas the senior judges who made many of the avowedly Statist comments regarding the relationship between the Crown and the armed forces were not. Thus, one may be able to perceive elements of the intergenerational conflict within the same country to which Owen sought to draw attention in the "Parable of the Old Man and the Young", which was discussed[61] earlier in this chapter. Similarly, concern for the survival of humanity, in both the abstract and the actual, which is partly manifested in "December 1, 1939",[62] was clearly a motivating factor for the behaviour of the appellants in *Chandler*. Their attitudes, too, were clearly affected both by the existing political climate – the date on which the offence was committed was at the height of the, so called, Cold War between the United States and its allies, of whom Great Britain was one, and the Soviet Union and its allies. At the same time, the weapons available to both sides were capable of vastly greater destruction than were available in 1914-18 or 1939-45 and, from the comments, especially, of Lord Reid[63] that this was an area of especial concern to the appellants. Given this rather confused context, probably the ultimate decision in *Chandler* was inevitable, but it may also be that, given that same context, the motives of the appellants were given insufficient weight in the course of both the trial and the appellant processes.

b)   The Conduct of War

One of the reasons why there should be such anticipation and, indeed, apprehension of war, is its very conduct which has to be, in an albeit limited sense, controlled by accepted law. Thus, Shearer tells us,[64] "The 'laws of war' consist of the limits set by international law within which the force required to overpower the enemy may be used, and the principles thereunder governing the treatment of individuals in the course of war and armed conflict. In the absence of such rules, the barbarism and brutality of war would have known no bounds." The history of these rules began in the Middle Ages, when, according to Shearer, the influences of Christianity and chivalry combined to restrict aggressive and cruel activities by combatants. As they developed, customary rules relating to such matters as the killing of civilians and ill-treatment of prisoners of war arose. However, from the Nineteenth Century onwards, most rules ceased being of customary origin and became contained in Conventions and

Treaties. In particular, the four Geneva Red Cross Conventions in 1949 brought about a comprehensive codification of these rules. There were numerous other more particular Conventions and Treaties which dealt with discrete topics, such as prohibition of the development and production of biological weapons. It is clear, Shearer suggests further,[65] that, "The essential purpose of these rules is not to provide a code governing the 'game' of war, but for humanitarian reasons to reduce or limit the suffering of individuals, and to circumscribe the area within which the savagery of armed conflict is permissible... Indeed, the currently recognised title for these rules is 'international humanitarian law'..." It is, of course, sadly true that these rules are frequently and seriously ignored and broken and today, as Shearer once again points out, the nature of warfare conducted through directed missiles, "drones" and nuclear weapons has become increasingly depersonalised and, as such, constitutes a grave threat to the useful continuance of international humanitarian law, which different States include as part of their military manuals, which contain instructions to field commanders regarding the major rules and customs of war. It should also be emphasised that these rules are not merely applicable to States but also to individuals – such as Heads of State, Ministers and officials as well as members of the armed forces. The rules are also binding on the United Nations when engaged in armed conflict. That is necessarily the case as the United Nations is a subject of international law and, therefore bound by it, including international humanitarian law.[66] Finally, unless it is otherwise provided in custom or treaty, military necessity cannot justify breaches of international humanitarian law.

From a literary and, more particularly, poetic standpoint, these rules are not likely to avail the individuals, which they are designed to protect, much if they are continually broken. Various specific Treaties or Conventions which might have a bearing on the next poem to be considered – "Dulce Et Decorum Est", written in 1917 by Wilfred Owen – are the *Geneva Convention* of 1864 for the *Amelioration of the Condition of Armies in the Field* and, possibly in consequence of the kind of events described in the poem, the *Geneva Gas and Biological Protocol* 1925.

In "Dulce Et Decorum Est", [as was suggested in relation to "MCMXIV" by Philip Larkin, by Martin[67], the poet was,] "...so struck...by the consequences of [the soldiers] passing that he purposely chose roman numerals, as on a tombstone, over the Arabic which he found almost too awful to contemplate and beyond the modest dimensions of his poems". The title of Owen's poem is to be found in its fuller form, (Dulce Et Decorum Est Pro Patria Mon),[68] on War Memorials in various countries, especially those memorials devoted to those killed in the 1914-18 War. The use of capitalisation (including the word *Et*) can be obviously equated with the Roman numerals in Larkin's poem.

The poems first stanza describes in detail, which is neither sweet not seemly,[69] a retreat by exhausted men from an earlier engagement. The soldiers are exhausted, poorly equipped and demoralised:

> Bent double, like old beggars under sacks,
> Knock-kneed, coughing like hags, we cursed through sludge,
> Till on the haunting flares we turned our backs
> And towards our distant rest began to trudge.
> Men marched asleep. Many had lost their boots
> But limped on, blood-shod. All went lame; all blind;
> Drunk with fatigue; deaf even to the hoots
> Of tired, outstripped Five-Nines that dropped behind.

But worse, if possible, is yet to follow. These men, reduced to entities which are almost less than human by the surrounding conflict, are then subjected to an attack by chlorine gas, which is perceived by the narrator as, "...through the misty panes and thick green light..." One member of the group, though, is unable to fit his gas mask in time. The narrator observes him as if he were drowning, " As under a green sea." The gassed soldier continues (guttering, choking, drowning") to haunt the narrator long after the poem has reached its denunciatory climax and his racked body is thrown on to a cart, which is described in relentlessly repulsive metaphors:

> If in some smothering dreams you too could pace
> Behind the wagon that we flung him in,
> And watch the white eyes writhing in his face,
> His hanging face, like a devil's sick of sin;
> If you could hear, at every jolt, the blood
> Come gargling from the froth-corrupted lungs,
> Obscene as cancer, bitter as the cud

> Of vile, incurable sores on innocent tongues, -

The theme throughout this stanza is manifestly that of *corruption*, there is no sense of any element which is free of it. In every line, apart from the second, a new, and equally coruscating metaphor, allied to corruption appears. There is a clear and rhetorical purpose: that is, to lead in to the final didactic excoriation contained in the poem's last four lines:

> My friend, you would not tell with such high zest
> To children ardent for some desperate glory,
> The old Lie: Dulce et decorum est
> Pro patria mori.

The rhetoric of the stanza previously has done its work effectively: expressions such as *high zest* and *ardent* are in harsh contrast and juxtaposition with metaphors of *corruption* and *cancer* and *incurable sores* to be found therein. In the last four lines, the humanity of the narrator and of his audience is manifest as compared with what might be called the *abhumanity* of the previous stanzas. Further the theme of innocence, which was to be explored in more detail by Larkin in "MCMXIV";[70] thus, the use of the word *children* in the second line of the final stanza implies another manifestation of innocence, which is a theme which recurs in the three poems by English writers discussed in this chapter.

A further manifestation, which bears some resemblance to the language employed by, at least, some of the judges in *Chandler*,[71] is to be found in the much anthologised poem by the United States writer, Rondall Jarrell, "The Death of the Ball Turret Gunner." Perhaps because it is only five lines long, its impact is immediate and stark:

> From my mother's sleep I fell into the State,
> And I hunched in its belly till my wet fur froze.
> Six miles from earth, loosed from its dream of life,
> I woke to black flak and the nightmare fighters.
> When I died they washed me out of the turret with a hose.

Of Randall Jarrell, Goldensohn wrote[72] that he had, "...attempted to canvass the wide, global nature of the conflict being waged, taking in the soldiers who, like himself, trained but never left home, as well as those who were flying bombers or dying on Pacific atolls. Likewise, his poems included the prisoners who came to American shores, as well as the hopeless people dying in concentration camps or under aerial bombardment; for the first time, the children caught in war's meshes apped vividly, recorded with a depth of feeling and observation that goes beyond sentimental portraits of victimization". She also notes[73] that the five lines of "The Death of the Ball Turrett Gunner", "...no doubt comprise the best known American poem about any war."

As regards the poem itself, Jarrell has made an explanatory note to it. "A ball turret," he writes,[74] "was a Plexiglas sphere set into the belly of a B-17 or B-24, and inhabited by two 50 calibre machine-guns and one man, a short, small man. When this gunner tracked with his machine guns a fighter attacking from below, he revolved with the turret; hunched upside-down in his little sphere, he looked like a foetus in the womb. The fighters which attacked him were armed with cannon firing explosive shells. The hose was a steam hose."

Yet there is altogether more to the poem than the rather ghoulish factual background provides, howsoever illuminating that may be . The most striking characteristic of the ball turret gunner is his effective total lack of conscious contact with realities. Thus, from his mother's own unconsciousness, he *fell* into the State, which in turn, carried him along with its own processes, disenabling him from confronting or making decisions on his own destiny. His awareness of his life hitherto is represented as a dream from which he is awakened into momentary reality. Paradoxically, the only real moment of consciousness he has immediately preceeds his violent death. A death so violent that he loses any semblance of human shape, as well as any consciousness. He is even more dehumanised than the soldiers described by Owen in "Dulce Et Decorum Est".[75] However, it is clear, from the arrangement of the poem, that the dehumanisation of the ball turret gunner (as well as his death) has been brought about by the State, into the clutches of which he fell unconscious. We are, after all, told this in the poem's first line. What is disturbing about that, from the point of view of the student of law and literature is that the anonymous and dehumanising agency of the State – namely, the armed forces – seems to have been endorsed by the highest Court of one jurisdiction, at least, as represented in the judgments of the House of Lords in *Chandler*,[76] with the courts not being able to hold the State/Crown to account in respect of the armed forces.

The dehumanisation process described in "Dulce Et Decorum Est" and "The Death of the Ball Turret Gunner" emanates from a combination of war itself and the unbridled, and unreviewable, powers of the State. There are, inevitably, in the theatre of war, other ways in which the process of dehumanisation can occur. An especially graphic instance is provided by the poem "Infantry Assault", written in 1994 by an American poet of the Vietnam War, Doug Anderson. Of the poetry of that tragic, avoidable, carnage, Goldensohn has written[77] that, "The response to the Vietnam War occurred in dominantly free verse, first person narrative. Pervading many of the war poems was the same outpouring of interest in sexual and personal candour, in generational rebellion, and in the overthrow of social conventions that had characterised the sixties and had resulted in the slogan 'the personal is the political'. But the pain and outrage of the soldier poets, their sense of betrayal, brought a moral urgency to their criticism of the debacle of the American involvement in Vietnam, giving their poems a different edge. A verbal saltiness, a canny, ironic politics, and a core of sympathy for the enemy also undercut what might have been the narcissism of a simple insistence on first-person expressivity." Doug Anderson's poem "Infantry Assault" has many of the characteristics to which Goldensohn refers.

Each stanza of "Infantry Assault" begins with the phrase *the way* – most graphically in the second stanza – which speaks of:

> The way they dragged that guy out of the stream,
> cut him to pieces, the stream running red
> with all the bodies in it, and the way the captain
> didn't try to stop them, his silence saying *No prisoners...*

There is no compromise in that stanza: the American soldiers' ("they") barbaric actions compounding earlier barbaric actions and also and, finally, the failure of the armed forces' hierarchy to prevent those actions and, indeed, offering tacit support to the soldiers' actions. Each stanza is connected to the one following by "and", so that the horror in the second stanza is connected to horror found in the first stanza when a depersonalised soldier ("he"):

> ...made that corpse dance
> by emptying one magazine after another into it
> and the way the corpse's face began to peel off...

Ultimately, in the third stanza, the narrator describes *the way* when thirty nine Viet Cong had been killed, and lined up in rows, the American soldiers – heavily ironically referred to as *our boys* – killed all the pigs and chickens in the village until, "...there was no place that was not red and..." then:

> finally, how the thatch was lit, the village burned
> and how afterwards we were quiet riding back
> on the tracks, watching the ancestral serpent rise
> over the village in black coils, and
> how our bones knew what we'd done.

So, in the end, the spectral ancient evil ("the ancestral serpent...in black coils) arises and the soldiers, collectively, aware that they had, through collective dehumanised acts, raised that spectre. Though in "Dulce Et Decorum Est" and "The Death of the Ball Turret Gunner", other forces had dehumanised the soldiers involved, in "Infantry Assault", it was ultimately, the soldiers who had dehumanised themselves and the hierarchy ("the captain") did not prevent them from so doing. In many ways, the vision which "Infantry Assault" gives rise, is the most frightening of all of the visions which have been discussed, so far, in this Chapter.

From those three poems, it is clear that combat, and what happens in its broad context, is the obvious and central feature of the war processes. At the same time, though, other activities, some quite distinct from the scene of combat are not immune, in many facets, from the pervading influence of war. In turn, the legal system and legal concepts may necessarily become involved. Thus, in *Newell* v *Gillingham Corporation*[78], the plaintiff, who was a minor, was bound by a deed of apprenticeship to serve the defendants for a period of five years which ended on March 9th 1941. The deed contained a clause which permitted the defendants to dismiss the plaintiff, "...if he should be wilfully disobedient or, ...slothful or negligent or otherwise grossly misbehave himself." The plaintiff registered as a conscientious objector and, in consequence, the relevant committee of the Corporation passed a motion dispensing with his services. He was dismissed in June 1940 and, subsequently, brought an action to recover damages, claiming loss of wages and postponement of an opportunity to qualify as a surveyor. The major problem which arose was that it was found as a fact that, apart from his registering as a conscientious objector, his behaviour was such as would irritate his workmates and could lead to a loss of his employer's time.

First of all, Atkinson J noted[79] that it was difficult to support an argument that the mere fact alone that the plaintiff was a conscientious objector could justify the corporation in acting as they did. That was the more so because, "The legislature has thought it right to say that if this young man can satisfy the tribunal that he has a conscientious objection to defending his own or the country's liberty or freedom, or from protecting women and children from organised massacre from the air, or protecting our sea-borne supplies of food on which he lives, he shall be exempted from military service, and, if he is a conscientious objector, he has a right to register as such and try to satisfy the tribunal that he has that conscientious objection. He succeeded in satisfying them." It is clear, it seems to this writer, from the rhetoric employed by Atkinson J in the *Newell* case that he was far from impressed with the idea of conscientious objection at large. Indeed, I would go so far as to suggest that the judge was seeking to deny the humanity of conscientious objectors through his references to their, alleged unwillingness to defend women and children or protect food supplies. To a degree, later in his judgment,[80] Atkinson J resiled from that view, but it will be apparent that scorn for the humane attitudes which drive conscientious objectors to take the stance which they do are, for them at least, central to their own humanity. That, attitude the judge appeared to deny.

However, that was not the end of the story by any means: Atkinson J continued[81] by saying that evidence had been presented, which the judge believed, that the plaintiff was not truly a conscientious objector. "He was" as the judge put the matter, "a political conscientious objector." The judge continued by seeking to put himself into the collective mind of the legislature when he said that what Parliament had in mind, in formulating the legislation was a person who, "...on religious grounds thinks it wrong to kill and to resist force by force. He thinks that is the teaching of Christ.

The true conscientious objector remembers other undoubted teachings of Christ – namely, to help the injured, the suffering and the helpless - and remembers that there is such a thing as duty. The true conscientious objector is ready to do ambulance work, rescue work, A.R.P. work and work among the helpless in shelters. There are many conscientious objectors who have proved the genuineness of their belief by that which they have done." Atkinson J then commented[82] that the plaintiff had likened his position to that of Quakers, a stance with which the judge was far from impressed. "Everyone", he stated empathically, "knows the fine work done by Quakers, particularly in the last war. One remembers the work they did on mine-sweepers, probably the most dangerous work there is. They were logical in their views. They recognised their duty to do all they could except to kill if need be. The true conscientious objector is loyal to his country. He is not pro-German. He does not scoff at what other people do, and he is not a defeatist.

The judge then compared the plaintiff's actual conduct with that template and stated[83] that it was plain that the plaintiff was not a true conscientious objector and also expressed the view that the plaintiff's conduct would be most irritating to his fellow–workmen and that his conduct might lead to breaches of the peace and loss of the workman's time. Atkinson J, having noted that none of his fellow workers gave evidence that the plaintiff had ever said that it was wrong or foolish to fight, noted that the plaintiff's attitude was that it was silly to be a member of the A.R.P. or of a rescue squad and that it was, instead of building ships, to produce pots and pans. In addition, the judge stated, he was pro-German. As Atkinson J put the matter, "From what he said, the Germans were always right and we were wrong. He deliberately spread lies, backed up by some correspondence. He was a defeatist. The government were always wrong. The Germans were going to win and we were going to lose. He pooh-poohed everything. His arguments were all based on political considerations and not on religious considerations... He was against the government before the war when they were striving for peace, and he is against them during the war when they are not striving for peace." The plaintiff was asked why he did not do any A.R.P. work and is supposed to have replied that he thought it was a dodge to avoid military service. "An answer of that sort," the judge stated. "...shows the true character of the plaintiff in this case. That sort of conduct is totally alien to that of the conscientious objector."

Atkinson J then went on to comment[84] if his behaviour had been perpetrated by an adult, it might very well be that his employer would be justified in dismissing him. However, the plaintiff was not an adult[85] and was not employed under an ordinary contract of employment, but under a contract of apprenticeship. The judge did not consider that his conduct was such as to entitle the Corporation to put an end to that relationship – unless the plaintiff had been made properly aware by someone in authority of the dangers of his speech and actions. At the same time, the judge stated[86] that although he could, "...well understand the view that employers might take of that sort of conduct...," in the instant case, he felt himself bound to hold that it did not justify the termination of the deed of apprenticeship. Having made that decision, Atkinson J was, then, required to deal with the issue of damages and, on that issue, he stated that the plaintiff had not satisfied him that the damages should be other than nominal, but, because there had been a technical breach of the covenants in the deed, he awarded the plaintiff the sum of £5, though with costs.

Although the plaintiff's conduct does not seem to have been notably attractive, there are still some features of the case which are a little disquieting. Indeed, so unattractive, during wartime, was it that it could not confidently be said that it might not have attracted the attention of authorities beyond his workplace.[87] However, it should be said that the initial rhetoric employed by Atkinson J in respect of conscientious objectors[88] seems intemperate at best and, at worst inaccurate. If Atkinson J is to be taken at face value, it would mean that non-Christians would be unable to claim to be within the relevant statutory provisions to which the judge referred.[89] This, even in 1941, is surely too narrow an interpretation. It is also clear that had the plaintiff been, say, five years older, the judge seemed to consider that, not only would the Corporation have been justified in dismissing the plaintiff, but his workmates might have been justified in taking action, which might properly be called extra-legal, against him.

In an Editorial Note to the case it is stated[90] that, "All that need be said is not based upon the fact that the plaintiff was a conscientious objector, but upon the fact that his conduct and conversation were such as might lead to a waste of time by the other employees." If one were to assume that the plaintiff were of full age[91] and the circumstances had taken place after the conclusion of the war, and the plaintiff's apparent sociopolitical attitudes had generated more than usual political debate during working hours, which disrupted work practices seriously, the question then arises whether the Corporation would have been justified in dismissing him. If the logic of Atkinson J in *Newell* is to be followed, there seems to be little doubt that they would be. Indeed, despite the Editorial Note,[92] it seems, from Atkinson J's judgment,[93] that the only issue which saved the plaintiff's employment was the nature of his employment relationship with the Corporation. Another, by no means unlikely, hypothetical situation would be where the plaintiff were to be employed in a city where there were two major football teams, who were nationally known rivals. Most of the plaintiff's colleagues support one team, whereas the plaintiff aggressively supports the other. In consequence, arguments, usually involving the plaintiff, take place on, especially, Mondays and are disruptive of schedules.

It may, in the end, be that the most appropriate way, given those hypothetical situations, of treating the *Newell* case is to confine it to its germane time and its particular facts. However, one issue which, it is submitted, does arise from the case is that the environment created by wartime does seem to affect the adjudicative and curial processes. The heavily ironic comments initially made by Atkinson J about conscientious objectors have already been noted[94] and the judge's comments on the behaviour of the plaintiff were rather more strongly expressed than one would ordinarily expect in a judgment.[95] Thus, it is suggested, that the fact of war has affected judicial rhetoric in a situation with which the very fact of combat is in a close and apparent relationship. It might also be said that in no other instance considered thus far in the chapter has the rhetoric of the judge and of the poet been so immediately different. The poets have all seen combat as a dehumanising process, whereas, if any group were dehumanised, it was conscientious objectors.

c) The Aftermath of War

Whichever view one takes – and it is hard not to take the view as espoused by the poets, at least in graphic terms, is not the more accurate – about the nature of armed conflict *per se*, it is inevitable that it is going to have consequences – personal, societal and, as a result, legal – in its aftermath. Equally, there can be no doubt that some of those consequences are certain to be of an appalling nature.

As a general principle, the closer to the fact of conflict the aftermath is, the more catastrophic the aftermath appears to be. An immediate instance is provided by Walt Whitman's poem "The Wound-Dresser" written in 1865. The poem, as Ward has pointed out, [96] is set in Washington, where Whitman worked as a government clerk as well as writing articles for New York newspapers. However, it seems as though he considered his real work to be tending the wounded and sick of both sides in the hospitals of that city. The poem begins with the poet explaining how his attitudes towards the War Between the States had come to change in consequence of his experiences:

An old man bending I come among new faces,
Years looking backward resuming in answer to children,
Come tell us old man, as from young men and maidens that love me,
(Arous'd and angry, I'd thought to beat the alarum and urge relentless war,
But soon my fingers fail'd me, my face droop'd and I resign'd myself,
To sit by the wounded and soothe them, or silently watch the dead;)
Years hence of these scenes, of these furious passions, these chances,
Of unsurpass'd heroes, (was one side so brave? the other was equally brave;)
Now be witness again, paint the mightiest armies of earth,
Of those armies so rapid so wondrous what saw you to tell us?
What stays with you latest and deepest? of curious panics,
Of hard-fought engagements or sieges tremendous what deepest remains?

He enters the hospital, which he compares to entry into combat itself and goes on to urge the reader, whom he imagines to be coming with him to, "...follow without noise and be of strong heart." Then, taking courage he goes quickly ("...straight and swift...") to tend to the wounded with whom he rapidly begins to identify. Then, altogether more specifically, he describes the wounds and the condition of the people to whom he tends:

On, on I go, (open doors of time! open hospital doors!)
The crush'd head I dress, (poor crazed hand tear not the bandage away,)

> The neck of the cavalry-man with the bullet through and through I examine,
> Hard the breathing rattles, quite glazed already the eye, yet life struggles hard,
> (Come sweet death! be persuaded O beautiful death!
> In mercy come quickly.)

Each description seems, as the poet moves through the lines of wounded, to build on the previous horror with yet more:

> I dress a wound in the side, deep, deep,
> But a day or two more, for see the frame all wasted and sinking,
> And the yellow-blue countenance see.
> I dress the perforated shoulder, the foot with the bullet-wound,
> Cleanse the one with a gnawing and putrid gangrene, so sickening, so offensive,
> While the attendant stands behind aside me holding the tray and pail.

Nonetheless, the poet does not shrink from his task, but, at the same time, he cannot put his experiences behind him and is forced to relive his experiences in his dreams. However, just as war has dehumanised the soldiers whom he treats, so his determination and care reawaken the humanity of the soldiers:

> Thus in silence in dreams' projections,
> Returning, resuming, I thread my way through the hospitals,
> The hurt and wounded I pacify with soothing hand,
> I sit by the restless all the dark night, some are so young,
> Some suffer so much, I recall the experience sweet and sad,
> (Many soldier's loving arms about this neck have cross'd and rested,
> Many a soldier's kiss dwells on these bearded lips.)

So the poem, with all its ghastly descriptions of wounds, infection and death, ends with a reaffirmation of humanity. The redemption, not only of some of the wounded but, perhaps, of the wound-dresser himself.

In "The Wound-Dresser", it is the effectively immediate aftermath of the combat. It is, indeed, hard to comprehend the scale of the slaughter and carnage which occurred from 1861 to 1865; as Goldensohn points out,[97] the scale of that carnage was appalling in that 618,000 soldiers were killed in that four year period, both sides' armies were comprised of non-professional soldiers and that total was nearly as many as those who were killed in all other American wars taken together.

In the same year as "The Wound-Dresser", Herman Melville wrote "The College Colonel", a poem about the end of the war and a young officer leading his regiment home. The poem examines the changes both the Colonel and his regiment have undergone during the period of the War and how those changes have been more than physical, at least for the officer. The poem begins starkly and cruelly enough:

> He rides at their head;
> A crutch by his saddle just slants into view,
> One slung arm is in splints you see,
> Yet he guides his strong steed – how coldly too...

His return is marked by Melville as demonstrating on the part of the Colonel, a coldness and detachment from the instant event, even though the end of the conflict has brought rejoicing to others:

> There are welcoming shouts, and flags;
> Old men off hat to the Boy,
> Wreaths from gay balconies fall at his feet,
> But to him – there comes alloy.

Even before commenting on that rejoicing, however, Melville has emphasised the effects of what has been experienced already by the young Colonel:

> A still rigidity and pale-
> An Indian aloofness lones his brow;
> He has lived a thousand years
> Compressed in battle's pains and prayers,
> Marches and watches slow.

Of course, the *Indian* aloofness is significant of itself, as Goldensohn, appositely once again has written,[98] by way of example, "The Cherokee nation, seen as an inconvenience lying between Georgian consumers and north-eastern manufacturers, were evacuated by General Winfield Scott in 1838, over what became known as the Trial of Tears. And so it continued on into the gold rush of 1849, where once again Indians sat in possession of what whites wanted for themselves."

However, the real agony which the sensitive, intellectual and young officer has suffered is not the physical, with which the poem opens, and then contradicts:

> It is not that a leg is lost,
> It is not that an arm is maimed,
> It is not that the fever has racked –
> Self he has long disclaimed.

In essence, the stanza continues, the real agony suffered by the Colonel is *spiritual realisation*, which is experienced in all of the various privations which he has undergone, during the course of the war,[99] and, especially, in the heavy fighting in northern Virginia at the end of the war:

> But all through the Seven Days' Fight,
> And deep in the Wilderness grim,
> And in the field-hospital tent,
> And Petersburg crater, and dim
> Lean brooding in Libby, there came –
> Ah heaven! – what *truth* to him.

The spiritual realisation of the *truth* is that all that has happened is fundamentally futile. Although the result of the war might not itself ultimately have been futile. As Julia Ward Howe described the matter in "The Battle Hymn of the Republic", perhaps the greatest battle hymn since the medieval "Vexilla Regis Prodeunt".[100] The final stanza of "The Battle Hymn of the Republic", states the apparent aim of the Union's campaign with the utmost clarity:

> In the beauty of the lilies Christ was born across the sea,

With a glory in his bosom that transfigures you and me:
As he died to make men holy, let us die to make men free,
While God is marching on.

However, the Colonel's concern is not immediately with the ultimate conclusion of the war, at least in the short term, His closest concern is for his own regiment, which like himself, has been shattered by the experience. His concern for the soldiers for whom he has been responsible is apparent from the rhetorical structure of the poem. The second stanza, coming directly after the quatrain describing the Colonel, deals with the condition of the regiment:

He brings his regiment home
Not as they filed two years before,
But a remnant half-tattered, and battered, and worn,
Like castaway sailors, who – stunned
By the surf's loud roar,
Their mates dragged back and seen no more –
Again and again breast the surge,
And at last crawl, spent, to shore.

The Colonel is aware of the relentless carnage [101] to which the soldiers for whom he is responsible have been exposed with calamitous consequences. Although, outwardly, the Colonel is seen as being *cold* and *aloof*, the emphasis on the *College* in the title of the poem inherently suggests intelligence and sensitivity, as well as a naivety. However that naivety has been, in consequence of his wartime experience, shockingly dissipated. The use of the word *heaven* in the last line of the poem is not a description of the truth which the Colonel has discovered. Rather, it is a shocked exclamation or, perhaps, an invocation in the same way as is "Angels and ministers of grace defend us" in Act I Sc 4 of Shakespeare's *Hamlet*. In other words, the reality in the whole context of the poem, is too shocking to be spelled out in secular terms. This is especially true in relation to the, "...remnant half-tattered..." Although the Colonel has himself been grievously wounded, the men for whom he has had responsibility have borne the most severe impact, a matter emphasised by the poem's structure. Thus, a protagonist's actions are certain to have an impact on other people, some of whom may not, or may, be directly involved.

The impact always may be felt by a protagonist's family, notably, and friends. The conditions in the 1914-18 War, as described by Owen, have already been discussed,[102] but the effect of loss on a family has been portrayed (rather than described) by the English writer Rudyard Kipling in a poem, written at the darkest part of 1914-18 War. Thus, as the critic Worthen has written in a study of D. H. Lawrence,[103] "...the war had reached a new pitch of awfulness in 1917, with the long drawn-out horror of Passchendaele; there were nearly 90,000 casualties in the first two months." Kipling in that context was a far from uncontroversial figure – and, indeed, still may be. The United States critic, Bloom, has stated[104] that, "The reaction against Kipling, by postcolonialist zealots and academic imposters was very strong a generation ago, but seems now to have passed. What matters most are *Kim*, many ground short stories and the verse." It is certainly true that Kipling was a paradoxical, even contrary, author and of the poem, "My Boy Jack", Schmidt has written[105] that, "During the First World War he became an elegist. The death of his own son informs 'My Boy Jack', a poem of generalized loss."

The poem, indeed, represents a catastrophe, if not actually a tragedy, in Kipling's own life. *Jack*, in the poem, refers to his son, John, who was killed, as Schmidt noted, in that conflict. It is readily apparent that the war changed many of his attitudes, as well as his style of writing. It transpired that his son, like Kipling himself, was extremely myopic and was, in reality, unfit for military service. Accordingly, Kipling who, frankly, was obsessed with military matters, made a personal arrangement with Lord Roberts of Kandahar, who was himself killed in that war, for John to be accepted into the army. The result haunted Kipling for the remainder of his life.[106]

The poem itself takes the form of a dialogue between an inquiring parent and either the sea itself, or darker forces as represented by the sea.[107] Thus, in the first stanza, the grim, and inevitable, tone is set in the first question and its stern reply:

'Have you news of my boy Jack?'
Not this tide...
'When d'you think that he'll come back?'

Not with this wind blowing, and this tide.

In the second stanza, the process of question and answer continues its inexorable course, though couched, in legal terms in a manner redolent of the evidentiary *presumption of death*. That was clearly enunciated by Sachs J, in *Chard* v *Chard*,[108] "Where as regard A.B. there is no acceptable affirmative evidence that he was alive at some time during a continuous period of seven years or more, then, if it can be proved first, that there are persons who would be likely to have heard of him over that period, secondly that those persons have not heard of him, and thirdly that all due inquiries have been made appropriate to the circumstances, A.B. will be presumed to have died at some time within that period." Although *Chard* was decided significantly later than "My Boy Jack" was written, it represents a distillation of common law experience up to that point.[109] Thus, the poem continues;

'Has anyone else had word of him?'
Not this tide
For what is sunk will hardly swim,
Not with this wind blowing and this tide.

Finally, the inevitable conclusion – from no knowledge, through no hearings, comes no hope – but there is the high probability of pride in filial achievement:

'Oh, dear what comfort can I find?'
None this tide,
Nor any tide,
Except he did not shame his kind –
Nor even with that wind blowing and that tide.
Then hold your head up all the more.
This tide.
And every tide;
Because he was the son you bore,
And gave to that wind blowing and that tide!

Inevitably, parents will be affected by loss in wartime, but so are other relationships affected. In "My Boy Jack", in the last line, Kipling makes reference to the dead soldier's relationship with his natural environment as well as with his mother. Another relationship which is crucial to an appreciation of the rhetoric of war is that between combatants. It is that very relationship which is trenchantly addressed by Thomas Hardy in the poem, "The Man He Killed," written in 1902. The poem begins with the hypothetical situation of the narrator, who has killed another in battle, having encountered the same person in an ordinary social setting:

'Had he and I but met
By some old ancient inn,
We should have sat us down to wet
Right many a nipperkin!

However, the hypothetical nature of that first stanza is emphasised by the second, which starkly addresses the reality of the situation where the two had actually met. The stanza is especially effective because of the typically direct language which Hardy uses:
'But ranged as infantry,
And staring face to face,
I shot at him as he at me,
And killed him in his place.

Hardy then goes on to explain the reason why he killed the other man. The important issue which emerges from the third and fourth stanzas is that the narrator's action is totally impersonal – in other words, it is another instance of the rhetoric of dehumanisation which is a continuing theme in the rhetoric of war – and, further, there is immediate irony in the sense that attention is drawn to the possible similarities between the narrator/poet and his victim. However, as with the first stanza, it is made clear that the similarities which are posited are essentially hypothetical:

'I shot him dead because –
Because he was my foe,
Just so, my foe of course he was;
That's clear enough; although

> 'He thought he'd list, perhaps,
> Off-hand like – just as I –
> Was out of work – had sold his traps –
> No other reason why.

Of course, there might very well have been other reasons why the solder who was killed was taking part in the battle – the most obvious being that he was a fanatical believer in the truth or moral rectitude of his own cause. Hence, the, albeit gentle, irony is not lost.

Finally, though, the reaffirmation of humanity albeit through a hypothetical situation, comes about in the final stanza, which returns to the theme of the first stanza, though with, to heap irony on irony, a seemingly platitudinous comment on the contradictory nature of war itself:

> Yes; quaint and curious war is!
> You shoot a fellow down
> You'd treat if met where any bar is,
> Or help to half-a-crown.'

Before leaving discussion of "The Man He Killed", it should be noted that Wilfred Owen wrote a much anthologised poem, "Strange Meeting", which has a similar theme. However, despite "Strange Meeting" being considerably longer, it seems, to this commentor at least, to lack strangely enough, both the starkness and the complexity of Hardy's poem.

Of course, the issues which have been raised by the various poems hitherto discussed are not mutually exclusive in any respect. Thus, for instance, in Kipling's poem, "Mesopotamia 1917", the intergenerational theme which was considered in relation to Owen's "The Parable of the Old Man and the Young".[110] In "Mesopotamia 1917", Kipling begins with a striking salute to the young men who were killed in that campaign, but each stanza contains a clearly stated comment on the earlier generation whose self-interest and meanness have led to those deaths. Thus, the first stanza reads as follows:

> They shall not return to us, the resolute, the young,
> The eager and whole-hearted whom we gave:

> But the men who left them thriftily to die in their own dung,
> Shall they come with years and honour to the grave?

As the poem continues, the denunciation of the "old men", as categorised by Owen, becomes, if anything, more astringent, so that the fourth stanza is critical of public response to the generational failure:

> Shall we only threaten and be angry for an hour?
> When the storm is ended shall we find
> How softly but how swiftly they have sidled back to power
> By the favour and contrivance of their kind?

Finally, the poem concludes with a ringing denunciation of the previous (Kipling's own, indeed...!) generation and demands moral and electoral reparation:

> Their lives cannot repay us – their death could not undo –
> The shame that they have laid upon our race.
> But the slothfulness that wasted and the arrogance that slew,
> Shall we leave it unabated in its place?

However, one poem that does combine many of the elements which are invoked in the poems which have been discussed, is not derived from that most terrible of waste and carnage, the 1914-18 War, but from the next great conflagration, that of 1939-45. "Vergissmeinnicht" by Keith Douglas, was written nearly at the end of hostilities in the Western theatre and nearly at the end of Douglas's own life. Schmidt has written[111] of him that his, "...love of country and intelligent hunger for experience led him to enlist when the Second World War began, to fight, and to try to make sense of history from within its turbulence. Like the major British poets of the First World War, his art was tried and tempered by the experience, and then curtailed." Bloom takes up the same theme and comments[112] that Douglas was the only British poet of that war who had something of the distinction of Wilfred Owen and Isaac Rosenberg.

In "Vergissmeinnicht", the poet and fellow soldiers have come back to a battleground, three weeks after the combat. The grim landscape is imbued with earlier events and the troops make an equally grim discovery:

> Three weeks gone and the combatants gone
> returning over the nightmare ground
> we found the place again, and found
> the soldier sprawling in the sun.

The body was that of a German soldier who had been in the battle which had taken place earlier and who had, it appeared, played a prominent part by scoring a hit on the poet's own tank, "...with one/like the entry of a demon." Yet the transaction is entirely anonymous, the soldier's personality being, in a paraphrase of Douglas's words, overshadowed by the, "frowning barrel of his gun." Then, suddenly, in death, the dehumanisation of the battle has disappeared:

> Look. Here in the gunpit spoil
> the dishonoured picture of his girl
> who has put: *Steffi Vergissmeinnicht*
> in a copybook gothic script.

The picture was, presumably, not *dishonoured* by its presence on the body of a soldier who, like "My Boy Jack" did not, "...shame his kind...",[113] but by being quite unconsciously involved in the anonymity and dehumanisation of battle and war. The reaction of the poet and his fellow soldiers is deliberately disturbing in that context:

> We see him almost with content,
> abased, and seeming to have paid
> and mocked at by his own equipment
> that's hard and good when he's decayed.

It is the mechanical accoutrements of war which have survived, which are "...hard and good..." and not the, all too, human German soldier. However, despite the almost predictable reaction of the British soldiers, there remains – perhaps the most important – reaction of the author of the inscription of the picture which will, inevitably, be different. But her reaction is to be assessed in the context of the dehumanisation wrought by war:

> But she would weep to see today
> how on his skin the swart flies move;
> the dust upon the paper eye
> and the burst stomach like a cave.

However, albeit in a strange way, it may be possible to synthesise the two truly antithetical elements which arise from the poem. Others, of course, are present (the landscape) or implicit (the intergenerational conflict), but it is the shocking juxtaposition of death and love which gives "Vergissmeinnicht" its impact. But, at the same time, the synthesis which Douglas brings about is just as shocking:

> For here the lover and killer are mingled
> who had one body and one heart.
> And death who had the soldier singled
> Has done the lover mortal hurt.

Schmidt comments,[114] and the final compelling metaphor would seem to bear that out, that Douglas's best poems, "...see death as a force within the object. Perhaps because of this sense of its inherence, unlike the other war poets, Douglas is not an elegist. He accommodates subject matter on its own terms, not blurring it by sentiment or forcing extreme experience into an alien framework or tempering it with a poetic disposition. A violent experience in the foreground is placed in a time context, where it occurs but is limited as experience by its context... He brings individual human situations up close; he exposes us too by evoking his own exposure as calmly as language will allow." The images of corruption wrought by war ("...on his skin the swart flies move"; "...the burst stomach like a cave") bring the reader close to the lover and the killer who, "...had one body and one heart" and, although the images are tied to a place and time, they remain locked there and, so, transcend time.

However, although these poems raise issues which are in effect, timeless, the matters to which the aftermath of war give rise may be altogether more mundane, as well as being more directly legal. One matter which can have very serious consequences, and not merely for former members of the armed services themselves, but for their families, is the matter of service pensions. These benefits can also give rise to legal questions of genuine difficulty.

A valuable illustration is provided by the decision of the Full Court of the Federal Court of Australia (General Division)[115] in *Repatriation Commission v Law*.[116] It was provided in s 101(1)(a) and (b) of the *Repatriation Act* 1920 that the Commonwealth of Australia was liable to pay a pension to a former member of the Australian Military Forces or to his dependants in particular circumstances. Liability arose under s 101(1)(a) if the member's incapacity or death had, "...resulted from any occurrence that happened..." during the period of service and under s 101(1)(b) if it, "...has arisen out of or is attributable to his war service." The legislation also provided a review process which permitted claims for a benefit which had been refused ultimately to be determined by a Repatriation Review Tribunal. This Tribunal was required by s 107VH (2)(a) of the Act to set aside the refusal unless it was, "...satisfied that beyond reasonable doubt that there were insufficient grounds for granting the claim or application."

In *Law*, the respondent was the widow of a former member of the forces, who had died in 1976. His death certificate had recorded the cause of death as a carcinoma of the lung coupled with myocardial infarction. During the 1939-45 War, he had been a prisoner of war of the Japanese and the hardship he had suffered at that time had left him in poor health for the remainder of his life. He also had begun to smoke cigarettes heavily during his period of service and had continued to do so until 1973, when he suffered a heart attack. The respondent claimed a pension on the grounds that her husband's smoking was attributable to war service and that it had caused his fatal carcinoma. That claim was supported by one medical practitioner, whilst two others gave contrary opinions. The respondent unsuccessfully appealed to the Repatriation Review Tribunal from a decision refusing a claim for a pension. She then appealed on questions of law to the Federal Court of Australia,[117] where her appeal was upheld by a single judge. The Repatriation Commission appealed unsuccessfully to the Full Court.

The Full Court held, first,[118] that there was nothing in s 101 of the legislation which could support the argument advanced on behalf of the Commission that a disease which caused death or incapacity must be contracted during war service so as to attract a pension. The legislation[119] could not bear the construction that the disease or infection must be contracted while the member of the forces was on war service.

The Full Court then turned their attention, second, as to whether the widow was entitled to a pension under the legislation. At first instance it had been held that there was no entitlement under the first paragraph as there had been no *occurrence* as was specified in s 101(1) (a). More specifically, it was held that neither the commencement of smoking nor the formation of the habit of smoking amounted to an occurrence within the meaning of the Act. In relation to those findings, the Full Court initially noted[120] that *occurrence* was nowhere defined in the legislation. However, they continued by saying[121] that, in accordance with the view of Stephen J of the High Court of Australia in *Distillers Co Biochemicals (Aust) Pty Ltd v Ajax Insurance Co Ltd*,[122] the word, in the instant context referred, "...to the event, incident or mishap causing incapacity or death... It is an event, incident or mishap which is susceptible of differentiation from the cause of events which constitute the ordinary course of life." It was submitted in that context, on behalf of the respondent that, by reason of s 23 of the Commonwealth *Acts Interpretation Act* 1901, *occurrence* could be understood in its plural sense. Such an interpretation would mean that the repeated act of smoking which occurred during the deceased's war service could be regarded as being *occurrences*. Not especially satisfactorily, it is suggested, the Full Court did not accept that argument. Rather cursorily, the Court stated[123] that the smoking of a cigarette or of an indeterminate number of cigarettes over a period of years, during the deceased's war service could not fairly be described as an *occurrence* or *occurrences*. What, then, one might legitimately ask, was it? If it was not to be so characterised, it might be characterised as a *pattern of behaviour*; in which case, were it connected to war service, then such a description seems to reinforce the widow's case. The Full Court's dismissal of that argument seems unconvincing.

However, and probably thankfully, s 101(1) (a) was not the only ground on which the widow was able to proceed. As regards s 101(1) (b), the court was required to examine the alternative phrases *has arisen out of* and *is attributable to* war service. In respect of the former, the Court noted[124] that it had been considered in a variety of cases,[125] and concluded that, "The precise nature of the relationship denoted by the phrase depends upon the subject matter being dealt with, the context in which the expression is used and the circumstances of the particular case. In the context of the legislation at hand, the phrase, the Court considered, required, "...a consequential relationship of the incapacity or death with the service out of which it was said to arise." The Court further emphasised that it was not useful to attempt to seek to put a gloss on the words to be found in the Act. "The Act" they continued,[126] "does not say death which is 'caused by' or 'results from 'his war service – phrases which connote a proximate causal relationship. The expression 'arisen out of' is satisfied if some less proximate causal relationship is established, that which is fanciful is not sufficient; and a suggested relationship may be so tenuous as to preclude its consideration as answering the description 'arising out of'".

Having made those remarks, without really tying them to the facts of the case as well as to the legislation, the Court then went on to consider the operation of the latter expression used in s 101(1)(b) of the *Repatriation Act* 1920. Once again, they said[127] that the expression, used in different circumstances, had been the subject of judicial analysis in a variety of contexts.[128] In *Law*, the Court sought to synthesise these authorities and concluded[129] that it seemed, "...clear that the expression 'attributable to' in each case involved an element of causation. The cause need not be the sole or dominant cause; it is sufficient to show 'attributability' if the cause is one of a number of causes provided it is a contributing cause. Under s 101(1) (b) it is sufficient to show 'attributability' if a member's was service is a contributing cause to the incapacity or death in respect of which the claim is made."

There can be no doubt that interpretation of the phrase in s 101(1)(b) made the situation very much easier for the widow in *Law*. In addition to that interpretation, the Court then turned their attention to the effect of s 101(1A) on the provision. Section 101(1A) appears, the Court stated,[130] to have be an intended to extend the operation s 101(1) (b). Thus, by way of example, they continued, "...where a person has died from a disease, it renders para (b) applicable if, in the opinion of the Commission, it was due to a disease that was contracted and that would not have been contracted but for his war service or but for changes in his environment consequent on his being on war service. Though causation seems to be required, a 'but for' cause will suffice."[131] Without seeking to become involved in a detailed analysis of the *but for* test as a basis for causation in fact, note should be made of the decision of the High Court of Australia in *March* v

E.M.H Stramere Pty Ltd,[132] where the test was questioned in cases where a superseding cause was alleged to break the chain of causation, where the issue must involve value judgments and infusion of policy issues.

However many value judgments and policy issues were involved in the *Law* decision – and it might be argued that cause in respect of eligibility for pensions is little else – there was one further substantive issue involved in that case. Section 107 VH(2) of the *Repatriation Act* 1920 provides that, where a decision of the Commission which comes before the Tribunal is a decision refusing a claim for a pension, the Tribunal is bound to set aside the decision unless it is satisfied, *beyond reasonable doubt*,[133] that there were insufficient grounds for granting the claim or application.[134] As is notorious, the expression *beyond reasonable doubt* is a formula used to describe to a jury the standard of proof in criminal cases. It is, at the least, unwise to attempt to extrapolate from that formula.[135] The Court were of the view[136] that the expression bore the same meaning in s 107VH(2) as it did in criminal cases. However, they were at pains to point out that, in a criminal trial, the standard was, "...applied to allegations which the Crown bears the onus of proving and these are usually of a positive kind: the Crown seeks to show that conduct has been engaged in, or circumstances or relationships exist. Under s 107VH(2), the standard is applied to a negative proposition..."

The Court then went on to explicate the operation of the provision and noted that, "Where the death of an erstwhile member of the forces might have arisen out of war service or might be attributable to it, a pension cannot be refused unless it is proved beyond reasonable doubt that it was not so related to his war service." The scheme of the Act the Court emphasised, was not to establish an adversarial system of determining claims and applications, but to have the relevant Department make proper investigations and then to require, if there is some evidence that the claimant is eligible to receive a pension, a pension be paid unless the investigations, or course of the proceedings raise[137] information which establishes beyond reasonable doubt that a pension is not payable. As regards that process, the Court stated that it was not for them (or the Tribunal), "...to question whether this provision is excessively generous or to endeavour to read it down so that it does not have an operation beyond that which might be thought reasonable: The legislature has chosen its language and all that remains is to apply it."

In so doing, the Full Court of the Federal Court of Australia was required to deal with the earlier findings in the *Law* case, especially those of the Tribunal. The Court considered[138] that the Repatriation Review Tribunal had misdirected itself in the way it had approached the processes to be found in the Act. "In the present case," the Court said, "the Tribunal seems to have considered its function to be the making of findings on the evidence applying the civil standard of proof and then, having come to a conclusion, to consider, whether its conclusion established beyond reasonable doubt that there were insufficient grounds for granting the claim." The Court did note that the introductory words to s 107VH(2) did provide some support for such an approach. The expression there used – "...after the completion of its consideration in a proceeding on a review..." – suggested that the standard of proof beyond reasonable doubt is not intended to apply during consideration of the facts, but only after that consideration had been completed. The Court rejected that view of the legislation and expressed the view[139] that s 107 VH (2) was, "...obviously intended to operate in favour of claimants and it cannot operate sensibly unless the standard of beyond reasonable doubt is applied at each stage of the inquiry into the facts. Otherwise one cannot attain satisfaction beyond reasonable doubt that there are insufficient grounds for granting the claim."

As regards the Tribunal's inquiry into the facts of *Law* and its findings, the Court were of the opinion that the Tribunal's finding that there was no evidence that the deceased had begun to smoke because of the conditions and demands of his particular war service or because of the conditions in general pertaining to prisoners –of-war was wrong in law. Although, the Court continued, there was no possibility of direct evidence from the deceased (for that very reason), there was evidence of circumstances which raised a very real possibility that he had begun to smoke because of those self-same conditions. "If the question were whether", the Court surmised,[140] "the claimant had proved that that was the correct conclusion, we should not have disagreed with the finding that she had not." However, the Court emphasised, that was not the question which the legislature were posing for the Tribunal, which could not properly be satisfied that the deceased had not begun to smoke for the reasons which had been argued. Further, the Court were doubtful as to whether the findings that the deceased was not psychologically incapable of reducing smoking in the period after the war was of any relevance, but, in any event, the Tribunal could not have been satisfied beyond a reasonable doubt that there were insufficient grounds for granting a claim under s 101(1) (b) of the Act.

But, as the Court properly pointed out, that was not the end of the matter: the next issue was whether, as a matter of law, on the facts *properly found*[141] as well as on the evidence before it, the Tribunal could have been satisfied that there were insufficient grounds for granting the claim under s 101(1) (b). A particular feature of the evidence was a conflict in the medical evidence and it was clear that the Tribunal had preferred the views expressed by two of the medical practitioners involved to that of the others. "In cases involving onus of proof where the civil standard of proof applies," the Court stated, "This may be an acceptable course. Where, however, a Tribunal has to be satisfied that beyond reasonable doubt that a particular finding is not open, notwithstanding that it is supported by medical opinion, it is not sufficient to point to contrary medical opinion which is preferred. It is insufficient unless the contrary medical opinion is such as to destroy the favourable opinion." In *Law*, there was no such contrary opinion and the minority opinion was not shown to be untenable. Hence all that was left was a difference of opinion between reputable medical practitioners.

Finally, the Court encapsulated[142] the evidence, which, they said, showed that the deceased had died from carcinoma of the lung which, in turn, might have been caused by smoking. Further, that his conditions which were peculiar to his war service may well have caused him to commence smoking which was, "...the start of the cumulative process which ultimately produced cancer of the lung which caused his death; that his habit of smoking formed while on war service and continued afterwards ultimately resulted in cancer of the lung and death; and that the debility produced by his war service followed by one debilitating disease after another, interfered with the function of his body referred to as 'immune surveillance' and so damaged the self-protective process of his body against cancer, permitting it to take hold." The Court emphasised that those possibilities were not "fantastic", but *real*.[143]

In the event, the Court concluded[144] that the Tribunal could not possibly be satisfied beyond a reasonable doubt that there were insufficient grounds for granting the claim. Accordingly, the Commission's appeal was dismissed.

Therefore, although in one sense, there was a happy outcome in that the widow ultimately received her benefit, the process by which that was achieved cannot go uncriticised. First, as the Court pointed out,[145] the legislation may be subject to dubious interpretation and, in particular, includes a *standard* of proof [146] which seems hardly appropriate to the subject matter, even if its *onus* is reversed. At best, the legislation's structure might best be described as *unwieldy*. Whilst it might be drawing too long a bow to suggest that the widow in the *Law* case was subjected to the dehumanisation process which war seems to bring about – and which has been so graphically portrayed by the poets whose work has been analysed earlier in the chapter – the processes, on top of her husband's death, which she was forced to undergo are likely to have undermined her personal dignity.

Repatriation Commission v *Law* was considered by the High Court of Australia in *Repatriation Commission* v *O'Brien*,[147] which again demonstrates how convoluted the processes can become. In that case, the respondent had served in the Royal Australian Air Force between 1942 and 1946. During that period, he developed an anxiety neurosis arising out of a number of situations relating to that service. Principal amongst those was his separation from his wife because of his service duties, at a time when she needed his company, and his own desire to serve overseas. The condition persisted after the respondent had been discharged. In 1961, the respondent's anxiety neurosis was accepted as an incapacity due to service. In 1974, he lodged a claim for essential hypertension on the grounds that it was related to his disability of anxiety neurosis, which had been accepted as having arisen from war service. In 1975, that claim was rejected by a Repatriation Board. The appeal from that decision was considered on no less than four separate occasions by the War Pensions Entitlement Appeals Tribunal and five occasions by the Repatriation Commission. The decision not to grant the claim was upheld at all the hearings during that period.

A fifth appeal to the Repatriation Review Tribunal[148] was removed to the Administrative Appeals Tribunal.[149] A challenge was made both to the accepted connection between the anxiety neurosis and military service as well as to the relationship of the essential hypertension to either the anxiety neurosis or to service. The Administrative Appeals Tribunal held that neither disorder was related to military service and, hence rejected the finding of the Repatriation Board in relation to the anxiety neurosis. An appeal to the Full Court of the Federal Court of Australia was successful, the decision of the Administrative Appeals Tribunal being overturned on both issues. The Repatriation Commission then successfully sought leave to appeal to the High Court of Australia. The appeal, however, proved unsuccessful.

The whole Court[150] were of the view that the respondent's anxiety neurosis was, "...attributable to war service..." as was required by the legislation[151] as the causes of his condition, which were separation from his wife and the necessity of serving overseas, were directly attributable to military service. Gibbs CJ, Wilson and Dawson JJ were scathing[152] of the Tribunal's contrary finding. "In our opinion", they stated, "it flies in the face of common sense to say that an anxiety neurosis which is occasioned by reason of the separation of the respondent from his wife because of his war service at a time when she is in desperate need of his company is not attributable to war service". Indeed, those judges went still further when they accepted an argument made on the respondent's behalf that the issue of the connection between the respondent's anxiety neurosis and his war service should not have been the subject of the Tribunal's consideration at all. The reason for that was[153] that the decision granting a pension in respect of the anxiety neurosis had never been challenged and was not one of the matters which had been referred to the Tribunal under the Act.[154] Hence the Tribunal had no jurisdiction, under its own legislation,[155] to review that issue.

Gibbs CJ, Wilson and Dawson JJ then turned their attention[156] to the issue of the respondent's essential hypertension. Once again, they considered [157] that the Tribunal's view could not, "...reasonably be entertained." In reaching that conclusion – which the judges did, "...with a sense of relief that we arrive at a decision which enables this long series of hearings to come to an end." The real issue regarding the hypertension, the judges thought,[158] was, "... the connection, if any, between the accepted disability of anxiety neurosis and the essential hypertension". It was the serious misunderstanding of that question by the Tribunal which undermined the *acceptability* [159] of their decision. "If", the judges continued, "the AAT had accepted, as it was in law obliged to do, that the respondent's anxiety neurosis was attributable to or aggravated by his war service, it would then have been obliged to concentrate its attention on the question of a connection between that neurosis and the hypertension. As it was, having dismissed any relevant relation between the neurosis and the war service, the possibility of a connection between the neurosis and the hypertension became of no importance as a factor supporting the claim for a pension... That being the case it follows that, had the AAT properly instructed itself with respect to the status of the anxiety neurosis as an accepted disability, it could not have been satisfied beyond reasonable doubt that there were insufficient grounds for granting the claim."

There was however, a detailed judgment in dissent by Brennan J, with whom Murphy J agreed. Brennan J's view was conceptually very different from that of the majority: "Where", he stated,[160] "after an investigation has been carried out with reasonable diligence, there is simply no material to raise an hypothesis that the requisite connection exists between a morbid condition and war service, the absence of such a connection can be inferred beyond reasonable doubt. The inference arises from the absence of any material to suggest the contrary." He also noted[161] that there was medical evidence that the respondent's wartime stress was too remote in time to have had any effect in inducing his essential hypertension and that the Administrative Appeals Tribunal was entitled to accept that evidence. The conclusion which the Tribunal had reached, according to Brennan J[162] and, seemingly, accepted by him, was that it was the respondent's natural constitution rather than stress or a stress induced anxiety state which gave rise to the hypertension. A characteristic of Brennan J's dissent was his emphasis on the medical reports regarding the respondent's medical conditions, which the Tribunal had accepted, irrespective of the jurisdictional problems which the majority found so difficult – and properly so - to overcome.

From the point of view of this text, though, it is the rhetoric used by the majority in reaching their decision in favour of the respondent, albeit on narrowly legal grounds. Thus, the emphasis laid by Gibbs CJ, Wilson and Dawson JJ on the separation of the respondent from his wife in difficult circumstances [163] contrasts with the strictly clinical approach to the respondent's situation as demonstrated by Brennan J.

As a general conclusion on the repatriation cases – which, it must be stated, have been selected as wholly exemplary – it seems reasonable to conclude that the processes involved in the legal resolution of the problems are convoluted, time-consuming and are at risk of multiple hearings which are likely to be both time consuming and expensive. Given the circumstances which lead up to these proceedings, and which have been discussed earlier in this chapter,[164] that is a state of affairs which is not satisfactory. It is surely bad enough to subject, sometimes unwillingly or unfit individuals to the dehumanising processes of war, but it is, in totality, worse to subject them to the dehumanising processes of appeals aimed by bureaucracy at preventing their receiving benefits for which their service, and its consequences, should have rendered them eligible. The best which can be said of the two cases which have been discussed is that, in the end, the two claimants did receive the repatriation benefits to which they appeared *prima facie* at least, to be entitled.

Yet the effects of war cannot, nor should be, perceived in entirely legal terms: the medical conditions which were the reasons why the cases were litigated in the first place are real in medical, as well as legal, terms. Other effects have been described and contextualised by the United States writer Howard Nemerov in his poem "Redeployment", which was published in 1987, but its context seems to make it more related to the United State's involvement in the 1939-45 War, than to the chronologically closer Vietnam involvement. "Redeployment" is narrated by a former soldier who begins the narration of his present situation in blood-related terms:

> They say the war is over. But water still
> Comes bloody from the taps, and my pet cat
> In his disorder vomits worms which crawl
> Swiftly away. Maybe they leave the house.
> These worms are white, and flecked with the cat's blood.

Of course, from a medical point of view, if blood is present in parts of the anatomy where it should not be present, it is poisonous. Despite the war's alleged conclusion, the water appears bloody and, hence, poisonous both in retrospect and prospect. Similarly, the narrator's cat to which he closely relates (*pet* in the second line) spews blood flecked worms. The horror continues particularly through the agencies of familiar, or loved, objects. Again, the narrator is concerned that the horror worms will, like the other horrors, continue to pollute his environment.

The second stanza re-emphasises the continuing horror related to the continuance of war and its consequences. It is this stanza which seems to relate the conflict which lurks in the mind of the narrator to World War II, where tales of the collection of dehumanised and dehumanising souvenirs abounded:

> The war may be over. I know a man
> Who keeps a pleasant souvenir, he keeps
> A soldier's dead blue eyeballs that he found
> Somewhere – hard as chalk, and blue as slate.
> He clicks them in his pocket while he talks.

The dehumanisation of both the narrator and the soldier whom he describes is emphasised by the use of *pleasant* in the second line of the stanza. Indeed, the dehumanisation process is completed when, in the fourth line, the narrator equates the dead enemy soldier's, once living, eyeballs to stones. This situation is a present issue for the narrator who has used the present tense effectively throughout the stanza.

As the poem progresses, so does the narrator, into the *now*. But the *now* introduces a fresh horror in the shape of virtually indestructible cockroaches, which seem to enjoy a powerful insecticide:

> And now there are cockroaches in the house,
> They get slightly drunk on DDT,
> Are fast, hard, shifty – can be drowned but not
> Without you hold them under quite some time.
> People say the Mexican kind can fly.

The war *appears* to be over – at least, there is no mention of it – but that has not meant that the horrors have consequentially disappeared. The horrors are, though, not so directly related to the war. Nor will they be when the war is assuredly over and, then, they will prove to be different again, as the fourth stanza illustrates:

> The end of the war. I took it quietly
> Enough. I tried to wash the dirt out of
> My hair and from under my fingernails,
> I dressed in clean white clothes and went to bed.
> I heard the dust falling between the walls.

Thus, even the war's end brings little respite. The narrator fails to celebrate either the war itself ("I took it quietly") or its end, however, he attempts to cleanse himself of the associated filth from his body and dresses – as if, perhaps, he were to be baptised[165] – in white and goes to bed... The symbolism, thereafter, is not a little obvious: the attempt to purge himself or to purge the war from his system *may* have succeeded, but at the cost of his life which he hears falling between the walls. As William Empson had earlier put the matter,[166] "The waste remains, the waste remains and kills." Hence, the condition of the survivor after his part in the hostilities has ceased and after the hostilities have ceased themselves.

But, collectively, the ending of "Redeployment" represents the end for many participants in the whole context of war. Although they may not all be remembered permanently as individuals, they will be collectively remembered, and for many generations. In his poem "Shiloh: A Requiem", written in 1865,[167] Herman Melville, whose poetic work – especially in relation to the Civil War – is characterised by its effective simplicity. In this poem, Melville begins with the swallow, frequently regarded as the symbol of summer, flying over the site of one of the bloodiest battles of that war. The commencing image is, indeed, one of stillness and tranquillity:

> Skimming lightly, wheeling still,
> The swallows fly low
> Over the field in clouded days,
> The forest-field of Shiloh –

Although, immediately, the use of the word *clouded* – even were one not aware of the history involved in the poem – puts the reader on notice that there has been some disturbing happening at the place being described and that the poem is not merely pastoral. The transition is, in fact suddenly made:

> Over the field where April rain
> Solaced the parched ones stretched in pain
> Through the pause of night
> That followed the Sunday fight

Around the church of Shiloh –

Again, stark attention is drawn to the contradictions surrounding the battle, especially the idea of such a battle taking place on a Sunday, the focal point of which was a church. Melville, then, emphasises the relationship between church activities and the aftermath of battle with the cries and moans of the dying being equated to prayer, at least for the purposes of the primitive church building:

> The church so lone, the log-built one,
> That echoed to many a parting groan
> And natural prayer
> Of dying foemen mingled there –

Shortly after, the poet goes on to point out that state of affairs cannot, in the natural order, continue: hence, the relationship of the "dying foemen" in the last line, of necessity, changes, as does their attitude towards the reasons whereby their situation has come about:

> Foemen at morn, but friends at eve –
> Fame or country least their care:
> (What like a bullet can undeceive!)
> But now they lie low,
> While over them the swallows skim,
> And all is hushed at Shiloh.

Very similar sentiments were expressed by a later United States writer, Carl Sandburg, in his poem "Grass", written in 1916, although it seeks to be of more general applicability than the 1914-18 War:

> Pile the bodies high at Austerlitz and Waterloo.
> Shovel them under and let me work –
> I am the grass; I cover all.
> And pile them high at Gettysburg
> And pile them high at Ypres and Verdun.
> Shovel them under and let me work.

However, unlike Melville whose theme, in part, seems to be that, despite the silence over the battlescape, the memory of the dead will remain, in the last three lines of his poem, Sandburg suggests that the sacrifice, the pain and individuality of the dead will be totally forgotten by most people at the very least:

> Two years, ten years, and passengers ask the conductor:
> What place is this?
> Where are we now?

It is not that the passengers to whom Sandburg refers are uninterested in the places which they are passing, there are no signs of what had occurred on the landscapes they were passing. What is also notable in the conclusion to Sanburg's epigrammatic poem is the shortness of the period it has taken the passengers to forget the momentous events in question ("Two years…").

In fine, we have moved from the anticipation of war, including perceptions of the intergenerational nature of the processes of war and its concomitant attitudes.[168] The attitudes of actual and potential participants have been examined through their depiction in various poems written about various wars. In particular, the unreality of many of those attitudes has been explored by those poets.[169] In dealing with wars in which, particularly, Britain was involved, the economic and, related, legal situation as it involved the international scene is considered.[170] The responses of people,[171] both individually and in groups, to the possibility/probability of war, and the law's response to those actions,[172] where it appears as though legal action might be appropriate or necessary.

From the decision in *Chandler* v *DPP*, a consideration of the conduct of war follows almost necessarily. Particular instances[173] of the reality of war – relating to the 1914-18, the 1939-45 and the Vietnam wars – have been discussed in some detail. As well as the realities of combat, the very fact of war has effects on the behaviour, which may also have legal consequences,[174] of non-combatants. The aftermath of war, may also leave lasting impact on non-combatants[175] as well as on the combatants and it is also clear that the effects on the combatants may be lasting and have legal consequences and implications.[176]

Throughout this part of the chapter, the reader will have been made aware of the continuing process of *dehumanisation* which results from effectively every aspect of the rhetoric of war, whether poetic or legal, which has been discussed. The process of *dehumanisation* is continuing because it can be perceived from reaction to the apprehension of war – including, for example, the legal response to protesters against war – through the combat itself and its ghastly aftermath – including demeaning legal process – to the ultimate *dehumanisation* of death and oblivion.

2. Rhetoric in Other Contexts

a) Generally

Strangely enough, much *rhetoric* in contexts than that of *war* arises in the area of *charitable trusts*. In Anglo-American law, the word *charity* has, as Lord Macnaghten pointed out in the leading case of *Commissioners for Special Purposes of Income Tax* v *Pemsel*,[177] a technical meaning. Lord Macnagthen then encapsulated[178] that technical meaning when he stated that, " 'Charity' in its legal sense comprises four principal divisions: trusts for the relief of poverty; trusts for advancement of education; trusts for the advancement of religion; and trusts for the other purposes beneficial to the community, not falling under any of the preceding heads. The trusts last referred to are not the less charitable in the eye of the law, because incidentally they benefit the rich as well as the poor, as indeed, every charity that deserves the name must do either directly or indirectly." However clear that statement, *prima facie*, might seem to be care must be, taken not to apply it excessively rigidly. First, it is clear that some charitable trusts may qualify under more than one head and much may depend on matters such as the surrounding circumstances of the trust.[179] Thus, in *Pemsel's* case itself, by indentures which had been executed in 1813 and 1815, a settler had settled real estate in England on trust to apply the income, "...for the general purposes of maintaining, supporting and advancing the missionary establishments among heathen nations of the Protestant Episcopal Church known by the name of Unitas Fratrum or United Brethren..." commonly known as Moravians. The House of Lords held, with two dissentients,[180] that the words "...charitable purposes..." in the relevant legislation[181] were to be construed in their technical meaning according to English law and, therefore, they were not to be construed as referring only to the relief of poverty. They also held that the purposes of the trusts in question were charitable purposes within the meaning of the legislation and, hence, the rents and profits of the trust property were exempt from tax.

Second, as Dixon and Evatt JJ pointed out in the High Court of Australia's landmark decision in *Attorney General (NSW)* v *Perpetual Trustee Co. Ltd*,[182] "A charitable trust is a trust for a purpose not for a person. The objects of ordinary trusts are individuals, either named or answering a description, whether presently or at some future time. To dispose of property for the fulfilment of ends considered beneficial to the community is an entirely different thing from creating equitable estates and interests and limiting them to beneficiaries. In this fundamental distinction sufficient reason may be found for many of the differences in treatment of charitable and ordinary trusts. As a matter of reason, if not of history, it explains the difference between the interpretation placed on declarations or statements of charitable purposes and the construction and effect given to limitations of estates and interests." The history of the notion of the charitable trust is one, as will be seen,[183] which is of direct relevance in both legal and poetic terms. The judges went on to discuss[184] further the characteristics of the charitable trust when they said that, "The reason why the specific directions given by an instrument creating a charitable trust receive effect is because they tend to a purpose falling within the legal description of charity. The existence of that purpose is, therefore, the foundation of a valid trust. In the next place the very idea of a trust for a purpose beneficial to the community involved a balance between ends and means. If property is devoted to some abstract end or purpose, the details of its application or use must be considered as a means to the end."

Once again, the facts of the case in which these statements of principle were made provides a useful illustration. In *Attorney-General (NSW)* v *Perpetual Trustee Co Ltd*, a testatrix, whose home was a property known as *Milly Milly* made a disposition in her will which stated, "I will and bequeath the whole of the Milly Milly property to be Held by the Perpetual Trustee Co for a training farm for orphan lads being Australians." The property consisted of 3,800 acres of land which was suitable for running sheep and, in part, for the growing of wheat. To use the property as a training farm was impracticable, the homestead being too small and the plant was too old fashioned. Further, the income which the property produced would not be sufficient to support the staff and to meet the expenses which were thought necessary for the project. The High Court of Australia held, by a majority, that the intention that the *Milly Milly* property should be the actual place of training did not form an indispensable or essential condition of the gift, which was dominated by the more general charitable intention of providing training for Australian orphan boys in farming pursuits, which was a guiding purpose to the fulfilment of which the testatrix had bequeathed the property as an appropriate means. However, as the property had proved to be unsuitable as a training farm, it should be applied *cy pres*.[185]

As was noted by Dixon and Evatt JJ in the *Perpetual Trustee Co* case[186] referred to historical issues which, I noted,[187] are relevant in both legal and poetic terms. Although the *Statute of Elizabeth* of 1601[188] was, it appears, aimed at the reform of abuses in the application of property to charitable uses rather than providing a definition of *charity per se*,[189] it has provided a guide to the courts in reaching such a defination. That process continues – no trust can be charitable unless it falls within the spirit and intendment of the preamble to the *Statute of Elizabeth* 1601 as interpreted by the courts and amended by statute – despite the Statute's repeal in 1888.[190]

The list of charitable objects as set out in the Preamble[191] reads, rather quaintly in parts, as follows:

The relief of aged, impotent and poor people; the maintenance of sick and maimed soldiers and mariners, schools of learning, free schools and scholars in universities; the repair of bridges, ports, havens, causeways, churches, sea-banks and highways;
the education and preferment of orphans;
the relief, stock and maintenance of houses of correction;
the marriage of poor maids;
the supportation, aid and help of young tradesmen, handicraftsmen and persons decayed;
the relief or redemption of prisoners or captives;
the aid or ease of any poor inhabitants concerning payment of fifteens, setting out of soldiers and other taxes.

Despite its relative antiquity, the *Statute of Elizabeth* does not represent the beginning of the process. In their book on charities law,

Keeton and Sheridan[192] note that in Langland's poem *The Vision of Piers Plowman*, described, rather unfairly, by Stephen Fry[193] as an allegorical and alliterative poem of great length written in the Fourteenth Century, anxious and wealthy merchants are counselled by Truth so as to obtain remission of their sins and a happy death. They are counselled to use their fortunes for charitable purposes, which are expressed[194] in these terms:

And therewith repair hospitals,
help sick people,
mend bad roads,
build up bridges that had been broken down,
help maidens to marry or to make them nuns,
find food for prisoners and poor people,
put scholars to school or to some other craft,
help religious orders, and
ameliorate rents or taxes.

It will be apparent, as Keeton and Sheridan point out,[195] that *Piers Plowman* strikingly anticipates the language of Preamble to the *Statute of Elizabeth*. They go on to suggest, not that the framers of that Act had consciously borrowed from the poem,[196] but that the essential elements of the Preamble were already well established and were generally known as early as the Fourteenth Century, when *Peirs Plowman* was written. One other matter of interest mentioned by Keeton and Sheridan[197] is that the Preamble's language was derived from an earlier Act of 1597,[198] which that of 1601 replaced. The only significant difference between the list of charitable objectives found in the 1601 Act and earlier formulations, already established in the Middle Ages, is the omission of almost all religious objectives. This is easily accountable through the secularisation of society, at least influential society, during the Tudor dynasty.

However, as the formulation in both the *Statute of Elizabeth* and *Pemsel* might suggest, it is clear that there are very likely to be a number of areas of human activity which gives rise to disputes as to whether bequests or dispositions involving them will be regarded as charitable. Some of these, which involve poetry as well as the law will be discussed next.

b) Animals and their Welfare

The American poet, Edna St Vincent Millay, Schmidt writes,[199] "...accepts and exploits traditional means and is not minded to disrupt or discard them; she writes directly about feelings, even awkward feelings, and the poems are always accessible. She has an old fashioned reverence for poetic beauty and is not ashamed to devote herself to its pursuit." Although Schmidt also comments that she was the outstanding sonnet writer of the Twentieth Century, the poem which will be used to introduce this part of the text is not in that form. "The Fawn", written in 1934 describes the narrator's reaction to coming upon the young deer. The narrator's reaction is initially strangely, almost paradoxically, mixed towards her discovery:

> There it was I saw what I shall never forget
> And never retrieve.
> Monstrous and beautiful to human eyes, hard to believe,
> He lay, yet there he lay,
> Asleep on the moss, his head on his polished cleft small ebony hooves,
> The child of the doe, the dappled child of the deer.

The immediate reaction to that first stanza will be to the poet's description of the fawn as, "Monstrous and beautiful to human eyes, hard to believe." The narrator's reaction is multiple – she sees the fawn in three distinct ways, but then the fawn awakes and "considers" the narrator, whose view of the creative suddenly changes from wonder to yearning:

> I would have given more than I care to say
> To thrifty ears, might I have had him for my friend
> One moment only of that forest day:

The narrator's reaction then changes again, from that initial yearning into a search for being, being a part of the totality of the fawn's environ, which was accepted by the fawn as being a part of nature and of the fawn's consciousness:

> Might I have had the acceptance, not the love

Of those clear eyes;
Might I have been for him in the bough above
Or the root beneath his Forest bed,
A part of the forest, seen without surprise.

Yet, even that wish is effectively momentary and the narrator's dream of assimilation into nature, to which the fawn has introduced her, ends suddenly with the fawn's departure. A departure which is instantly characterised by its clumsiness amongst the innocent landscape:

Was it alarm, or was it the wind of my fear lest he depart
That jerked him to his jointly knees,
And sent him crashing off, leaping and stumbling
On his new legs, between the stems of the white trees?

Again, the poem concludes ambiguously – the narrator is unsure as to whether it is the fawn's or the consciousness of her own fear which has caused his uncertain departure.

The rhetoric used by St Vincent Millay in "The Fawn" is essentially based around *confusion* and *uncertainty*. The fawn itself is confused but whether it is because of his newness in his environment or because, as she fears, of her unfamiliar presence in the relatively familiar environment. The rhetoric of confusion and uncertainty, both in the narrator and her subject seeks to emphasise the utter vulnerability (a theme which St Vincent Millay returns not infrequently in her poetry[200]) of both, but, especially, the fawn. That vulnerability tells us, in turn, how humanity should treat, not merely the fawn itself but all natural objects, anima life in particular.

However, that rhetoric cannot be regarded as being universal and, in that context, the decision of the House of Lords in *National Anti-Vivisection Society* v *Inland Revenue Commissioners*.[201] The issue before the House in that case was whether a society having as its object the total suppression of vivisection (that is, the use of living animals in experimentation) was, "...a body of persons established for charitable purposes only..."[202] so as to be exempt from income tax. The House of Lords held that it was not because, first, a main object of the society was political in nature. Second, and more important for this part of the book, it was held that any assumed public benefit in the advancement of morals would be far outweighed by the detriment to medical science and research and, consequently, to public health. The leading judgment concerned with that issue was delivered by Lord Wright. Lord Wright's starting point[203] was that the position must be judged as a whole: "It is", he said, "arbitrary and unreal to attempt to dissect the problem into what is said to be direct and what is said to be merely consequential. The whole complex of resulting circumstances of whatever kind must be foreseen or imagined in order to estimate whether the change advocated would or would not be beneficial to the community." He then went on to point out that there appeared to be no general consensus of opinion against vivisection, which had originally been permitted by the *Cruelty to Animals Act* 1876. He further expressed the view that people's moral feelings had not been weakened nor their objections to cruelty to animals reduced by the existence of that Act.

At this point in his judgment, Lord Wright became rather more exemplary and specific. If people thought about it all, he continued, "…they think of the immense and incalculable benefits which have resulted from vivisection: if that involves some measure of pain at times to some animals, notwithstanding the Act, they feel that it is due to a regrettable necessity." Lord Wright then sought to relate the issue of the charitable status of the Anti-Vivisection Society to more direct and gastronomically related questions: "Similarly," he said, "a man who has beefsteak for dinner if he thinks at all about the slaughter of the beast reflects that it is inevitable in the present constitution of society." At the same time, he considered that a high degree of regard for animals was a good thing, but also that it must be a regulated regard. On the one hand,[204] cruelty which was purposeless cruelty, "…whether through brutality or through a purpose to satisfy our pleasure or our pride, cannot be forgiven. It is indeed also a penal offence at law." "On the other hand, Lord Wright considered that it was, "…impossible to apply the word cruelty to efforts of the high minded scientists who have devoted themselves to vivisection experiments for the purpose of alleviating human suffering." He went on to note that the physician Harvey would not have been able to publish his major work *De Motu Cordis* in 1628 had he not been given deer from the Royal Park for the purpose of vivisection. "Countless millions," Lord Wright sought to emphasise, "have benefited from that discovery. I do not minimise the suffering of the unfortunate deer. The subject of vivisection is not a consenting party nor does it benefit. But I put against that the benefit to humanity. It has been argued that a court cannot weigh moral and material benefits against each another." Lord Wright, though, did not think that the case at hand was the place to debate abstract notions or to point out that, in ordinary life, people are required to decide between a moral and a material benefit. He did not think that that was a fair statement of the issue and continued by saying that, "The scientist who inflicts pain in the cause of vivisection is fulfilling a moral duty to mankind which is higher in degree than the moralist or sentimentalist who thinks only of the animals. Nor do I agree that animals ought not to be sacrificed to man when necessary. A strictly regulated amount of pain to some hundreds of animals may save and avert incalculable suffering to innumerable millions of mankind, I cannot doubt what the moral choice should be. There is only one single issue."

After having made that point – tendentious though some must surely regard it – Lord Wright went on[205] to be still more graphic and specific. Having noted that he had a great love for animals, as well as, "…some familiarity with certain classes…", Lord Wright expressed regret that, "…rabbits, a weak and innocent but monstrously destructive race, should have to be destroyed in great numbers as they were and are being, to save our people from qualified starvation." Further, he agreed that, "…rats, beetles and other pests if they have to be destroyed should be destroyed with as little cruelty as possible. But destroyed they must be. The lives of animals at best are precarious. Millions have perished in the last frost. That is a regrettable necessity."

Having made that, perhaps rather obvious, point, Lord Wright returned to his essential theme. "But however it is looked at," he stated, "the life and happiness of human beings must be preferred to that of animals. Mankind, of whatever race or breed, is on a higher plane and a different level from even the highest of the animals who are our friends, helpers and companions. No one faced with the decision to choose between saving a man or an animal could hesitate to save the man." Lord Wright then attempted to explain[206] why, despite the fact that he had not, earlier,[207] considered that there was any difficulty in so doing, why he had turned for a while, to issues of fact. That course, he said,[208] "…is inevitable in balancing conflicting values. To my mind the scale of the anti-vivisectionist mounts up and kicks the beam. A statesman is constantly weighing conflicting moral and material utilities." He then adverted his mind to the essential issue in the case, which was whether the *National Anti-Vivisection Society* could, or should be regarded by the Court as being a public charitable object. In view of what he had earlier stated generally, it was not entirely surprising that Lord Wright expressed great doubt as to whether it could so be. Lord Wright could not accept[209] that, "...the object of abolishing vivisection can on any view be regarded as being in law a public charitable object. It is not analogous to any of the objects enumerated in the preamble. Its only claim to be admitted must rest on the fourth head. To get into that class it must be established that it is beneficial to the community." That is, of course, clearly correct;[210] it would be stretching too long a bow to attempt to argue that it would advance religion or education, although, surely, elements of religious and moral education are present in any discussion of the rhetoric used by Lord Wright in the course of his judgment.

As Lord Wright himself noted,[211] in order to be attributed to the fourth class in *Pemsel*, it must necessarily be shown that the purpose is beneficial to the community. Lord Wright was quite unwilling to believe that the organisation in question could so demonstrate. "What it seems to do," he stated,[212] "however is to destroy a source of enormous blessings to mankind. That is a positive and calamitous detriment of appalling magnitude. Nothing is offered by way of counter-weight but a vague and problematical moral elevation. The law may well say that quite apart from any question of balancing values, an assumed prospect, or possibility of gain so vague, intangible and remote cannot justly be treated as benefit to humanity, and that the appellant cannot get into the class of charities at all unless it can establish that benefit. If it fails, it can still continue to carry on such lawful purposes as the members desire and its funds, exiguous as they are, permit." Lord Wright then commented that he could not find any precedent, apart from what he described as the *animal cases*, as support for such an object's being charitable.

The *animal cases,* to which Lord Wright referred, were part of a body of law which operated in addition to the objects set out in the Preamble to the *Statute of Elizabeth*[213] 1601. That body of law, which is no longer regarded as being correct referred to the maintenance of tombs[214] and of animals. The cases to which Lord Wright referred were encapsulated by Swinfen Eady LJ in *Re Wedgewood*,[215] "A gift for the benefit and protection of animals tends to promote and encourage kindness towards them, to discourage cruelty and to ameliorate the condition of the brute creation, and to stimulate humane and generous sentiments in man towards the lower animals, and by these means promote feelings of humanity and morality generally, repress brutality and thus elevate the human race." That *dictum*, which considerably precedes the comments of Lord Wright in *National Anti-Vivisection Society*, seems altogether more specific than Lord Wright seems willing to admit. However, it does appear from other *dicta* in *Re Wedgewood*[216] and, especially, from the subsequent decision of the English Court of Appeal in *Re Grove-Grady*[217] that Swinfen-Eady LJ's generous view is not applicable to all animals. In that case, it was held that a gift for the provision of a, "...refuge or refuges for the preservation of all animals birds or other creatures not human..." was not charitable on the grounds that is lacked public benefit. In the majority,[218] Lord Hanworth MR had said[219] that, "In this proposed refuge all creatures are to find freedom and safety from molestation or destruction by man. Whatever animals, birds or other creatures, ferae naturae, may be living or obtain access thereto, are to find sanctuary. The fox and the rabbit, birds of all sorts with the stoat and the weasel and rats as neighbours, and hawks and crows as spectators, are to live and enjoy themselves after their kind. The struggle for existence is to be given free play – that weapon wherewith nature maintains its balance against over fertility, see Darwin's Origin of Species Ch iii. It is not a sanctuary for any animals of a timid nature whose species is in danger of dying out; nor is it a sanctuary for birds which have almost entirely left our shores and may be attracted once more by a safe seclusion to nest and rear their young. No such purpose is indicated nor indeed possible. The one characteristic of the refuge is that it is free from the molestation of man, while all the fauna in it are to be free to molest and harry one another." The Master of the Rolls concluded[220] that part of his judgment by stating that variety of purpose did not, in his view, afford any advantage to animals that are, in particular, useful to mankind nor did it offer any protection from cruelty to animals generally. Further, it did not denote any elevating lesson for mankind.

In the context of these *dicta*, particularly that of Swinfen Eady LJ, it is interesting to take into account the objects of the *National Anti-Vivisection Society*, which were to, "...awaken the conscious of mankind to the iniquity of torturing animals for any purpose whatever; to draw public attention to the impossibility of any protection from torture being afforded to animals under the present law; and so lead the people of this country to call upon Parliament totally to suppress the practice of vivisection." One must examine these objects with some care as they do, in this writer's view, go some way to undermining the rhetoric of benefit of mankind of vivisection utilised by Lord Wright in the leading case. It is clear from the word *torture* used in the objects, that the *brutality* and *cruelty* adverted to by Lord Wright[221] are the major targets of the Society's campaigns. The word *torture* implies a willingness to inflict pain, effectively, for its own sake. Lord Wright might, one suspects, have been less rhetorical in his stance had he been presented that cruelty was practiced on animals for, say, the purpose of producing cosmetics rather than a process which might save human life.

It is, of course quite clear from the society's object that a major aim is the political one of bringing about legislative change – in other words, having a political objective as a major aim. Lord Simonds had noted[222] that the Charity Commissioners had found that one of the Society's aims was the repeal of the *Cruelty to Animals Act* 1876 and its replacement by a new enactment which entirely abolished vivisection. "This is a finding" Lord Simonds stated, "that the main purpose of the society is the compulsory abolition of vivisection by Act of Parliament. What else can it mean? And how else can it be supposed that vivisection is to be abolished? Abolition and suppression are words that connote some form of compulsion. It can only be by Act of Parliament that that element can be supplied... Coming to the conclusion that it is a main object, if not the main object of the society, to obtain an alteration of the law. I ask whether that can be a charitable object, even if its other purposes were charitable." Lord Simonds went on to conclude[223] that a main object of the society was not established for charitable purposes only.

It should be said that the *political* exception to the *Pemsel* formulation is not especially satisfactory. The reasoning behind denying charitable status to gifts which are regarded as political is the lack of proximity to the spirit of intendment of the Preamble to the *Statute of Elizabeth*. The cases themselves present a confusing picture: thus, obviously, in *Bonar Law Memorial Trust* v *IRC*[224] a trust for a mansion to be used as an educational centre for the British Conservative Party was held not to be charitable and, likewise, in *Re Hopkinson*[225] it was held that a trust for political education in accordance with policies set out in Labour Party Memorandum was not charitable. Those cases are, indeed, obvious but others are less so and objects apparently more in accord with the Preamble have not been held charitable. Thus in *Re Bushnell*,[226] in 1975, it was held that a trust for the teaching of the benefits of socialised medicine was not charitable. More especially, trusts involving international relations have been refused charitable status , though the *fons et origo* of that view may be the older case of *Habershon* v *Vardon*[227] where a trust for the "political restoration of the Jews to Jerusalem and to their own land" was held not to be charitable. Knight-Bruce V-C stated[228] that if the trust was to be understood to mean anything, "...It was to create a revolution in a friendly country. Jews might at present reside in Jerusalem; and if the acquisition of political power by them was intended, the promotion of such an object would not be consistent with our amicable relations with the Sublime Porte." Of course, the use of the word *political* in the trust's objects would not have made the task of those seeking charitable status any easier. It followed that it was held in *Buxton* v *IRC*[229] that a trust for the improvement of international relations was held not to be charitable and neither, in *Anglo-Swedish Society* v *IRC*[230] was a trust seeking to promote a closer and more sympathetic understanding between the English and Swedish peoples.

In many respects, however, even taking into account the Preamble to the *Statute of Elizabeth* which, it will be remembered,[231] includes the, "...relief of prisoners and captives" in the decision of Slade J in *McGovern* v *Attorney General*.[232] The relevant facts in that rather curious case were that the Amnesty International Trust had been set up in 1977 to administer those purposes of Amnesty International which were thought to be charitable. The organisation itself was an unincorporated, non-profit making body formed with the intention of securing, throughout the world, that prisoners of conscious – that is, people who were imprisoned, detained or restricted because of their political, religious or conscientious beliefs or their ethnic origins, sex, colour or language – were treated in accordance with the United Nations *Universal Declaration of Human Rights*. With that end in mind, Amnesty International provided assistance to, and worked to secure the release of, prisoners of conscience by exposing and publicising the situation of such prisoners and by mobilising public opinion and by applying persuasion and pressure on the relevant authorities. Amnesty International operated independently of any government, political faction or religious denomination and, though philanthropic, was admittedly non-charitable.

However, the objects of the trust as were set out in the trust deed were, first, the relief of needy persons within the categories of prisoners of conscience, or who were likely to become prisoners of conscience, or their relatives.[233] Second, attempting to secure the release of prisoners of conscience.[234] Third, procuring the abolition of torture or inhuman or degrading treatment or punishment.[235] Fourth, research into the maintenance and observance of human rights.[236] Fifth, disseminating the results of such research[237] and, finally, doing all such other things as would promote the specific objects. In addition, the deed also provided that the objects of the trust were. "...restricted to those charitable to the law of the United Kingdom, but subject thereto they may be carried out in all parts of the world." The trustees applied to the Charity Commissioners for registration as a charity under relevant legislation.[238] The Commissioners refused and the trustees appealed to the court.[239] Eade J held that, as two of the objects of the trust which Amnesty International had established were non-charitable, the whole trust - the remainder of which was charitable, - was not charitable.

First, the judge took the view[240] that though a trust for the relief of human suffering or distress was capable of being of a charitable nature within the spirit and intendment of the *Statute of Elizabeth*, it did not necessarily follow[241] that, "...a trust established for good compassionate purposes will necessarily qualify as a charity according to English law, any more than it necessarily follows that such a qualification will attach to a trust for the relief of poverty or for the advancement of education or for the advancement of religion." Having noted that there were other requirements which it must satisfy if it were to assume charitable status, Slade J turned his attention to the requirement of public benefit. The judge emphasised[242] that there could be no doubt whatever that a trust of which a principal purpose was to alter the law of *lex fori* could not be regarded as charitable. However, the *McGovern* case was not concerned with changes in that law, but with the law of a foreign country. Slade J, again, was of the view[243] that there were overwhelming reasons why such a trust should not be recognised as charitable. First, it was assumed[244] that, *prima facie* at least, the community which needed to be considered by an English court in deciding whether to regard a trust seeking to change the law of a foreign country was the community of the United Kingdom. As Slade J put the matter: "Assuming that it is the right test, the court in applying it would still be bound to take account of the probable effects of attempts to procure the proposed legislation, or of its actual enactment, on the inhabitants of the country concerned, which would doubtless have a history and social structure quite different from that of the United Kingdom. Whatever might be its view as to the content of the relevant law from the standpoint of an English lawyer, it would, I think, have no satisfactory means of judging such probable effects on the local community." Second, Slade J continued, the court, before deciding the question would be bound to consider the consequences for the United Kingdom as a matter of public policy. "In a number of such a cases", he stated, " there would arise a substantial prima facie risk that such a trust, if enforced, could prejudice the relations of this country with the foreign country concerned. The court would have no satisfactory means of assessing the extent of such a risk, which would not be capable of being readily dealt with by evidence and would be a matter more for political than for legal judgment."[245]

Second, as regards the object of attempting to secure the release of prisoners of conscience, Slade J considered[246] that, "...the persons who are effecting the imprisonment or detention of prisoners of conscience in a foreign country will, ex hypothesis, normally be the government or government authorities concerned exercising a judicial, penal or administrative function, or in some cases acting quite outside the law." Accordingly, the judge did not think that the trust could be construed as being one in which the main purpose was merely to influence public opinion in the country where the imprisonment was taking place as its very terms suggested the direction of moral pressure. Slade J was reinforced in that view by the structure of the relevant object as set out in the trust deed[247] and he commented that, "...the main object of the broadly – defined trust... [must] be regarded as being the procurement of the reversal of the relevant decisions of governments and governmental authorities in those countries where such authorities have decided to detain prisoners of conscience, whether or not in accordance with local law." That could not be regarded as being one method of giving effect to the object, it was, he thought, the principal purpose. Accordingly, following the *National Anti-*

Vivisection Society case, the trust so declared was a trust for political purposes. A particularly disturbing element present in this part of Slade J's judgment relates to his apparent lack of reaction to the admitted fact that governments which restrain prisoners of conscience do so in disregard of their own law!

Third, the judge went on[248] to consider the trust which sought to procure the abolition of torture or inhuman or degrading treatment or punishment. It was argued that the wording of that particular object was similar to Art 3 of the *European Convention for the Protection of Human Rights and Fundamental Freedoms*. In the event, the judge based[249] his view that the trust could not be regarded as charitable on the ground that it included the procurement of changes in the law of the United Kingdom, but also of changes in the laws of foreign countries, as well as the reversal of particular decisions of governmental authorities in those countries.

Fourth, the trusts set out in the remainder of the objects clauses – namely, the promotion of research into the maintenance and observance of human rights and the dissemination of that research – would have, had they stood alone, the judge considered,[250] been charitable. That was because the subject matter of the research was a proper object of study. In Slade J's own words,[251] "...it appears that the study of human rights has become an accepted academic discipline; the subject is taught in many universities, and is part of the curriculum in departments of many schools".

In concluding his judgment, Slade J noted first that counsel for the plaintiffs had made reference to various international conventions to which the United Kingdom was a party and had argued that it was committed to the elimination of unjust laws and actions *whenever those might exist or occur throughout the world*.[252] However, Slade J was not impressed by that argument.[253] "Indisputably", he said, "laws do exist, both in this country and in many foreign countries, which many reasonable people consider unjust. No less indisputably, laws themselves will from time to time be administered by governmental authorities in a manner which many reasonable persons consider unjust, inhuman or degrading. Amnesty International in striving to remedy what its considers to be such injustices, is performing a function which many will regard as being a great value to humanity. Fortunately the laws of this country place very few restrictions on the rights of philanthropic organisations such as this, or individuals, to strive for the remedy of what they regard as instances of injustice, whether occurring here or abroad." Nonetheless on the basis of Lord Parker's statement of policy to be found in *Bowman v Secular Society*[254] where he had stated that, "...a trust for the attainment of political objects has always been held to be invalid, not because it is illegal, for everyone is at liberty to advocate or promote by any lawful means a change in the law, but because the Court has no means of judging whether a proposed change in the law will or will not be for the public benefit and therefore cannot say that a gift to secure the change is a charitable gift." With appropriate respect, it is suggested that this approach represents an evasion of a central issue: Amnesty International, through its objects was seeking to uphold the Rule of Law throughout the world. All that Slade J was doing, in essence, was to handicap it in its work by refusing to permit them charitable status so as to free them from particular taxation impositions. Stevens and Pearce argue[255] that the perception of courts being seen as hostile to particular causes might be overcome if the courts holding were to adopt a policy of adopting purposes as being for the public benefit it they were not illegal, immoral or subversive and were adopted by a significant proportion of the public. It would then be possible, these writers claim, for opposing views both to be considered charitable. It may also be that a distinction ought to be drawn, they suggest, between propagandist trusts and those which seek to influence public and governmental opinion – and perhaps even influence changes in laws though not by means of any pre-ordained view of what is right and wrong,[256] but through reasoned debate. It may be that the position adopted by Pearce and Stevens is Panglossian, but they may be fortified by the fact that, in the subsequent case of *Re Koeppler Will Trusts*,[257] Slade LJ (as he had then become) had sought to distinguish the opinion which he had expressed in *McGovern* on the bases, to a degree, suggested by Pearce and Stevens.

However, there is little doubt in this writer's mind that despite *McGovern* and *Bowman v The Secular Society*, the rhetoric which has dominated the area under consideration is that of Lord Wright in the *National Anti-Vivisection Society* case,[258] both in its mode of expression and in its effect in later cases - it did have considerable effect on Slade J's judgment in *McGovern*. However, his emphasis on the public benefit of vivisection are not the only elements of his judgment which deserve some scrutiny: thus, his comments, on the precarious existence of some animals and their consequent relationship with humanity will not have passed unnoticed.[259] However, early in his judgment,[260] Lord Wright had noted that, "Healthy and manly sports are certainly in fact beneficial to the public, but apart from special concomitants are not general entitled to qualify as charities." That comment, once more, seems to avoid a major issue - namely what kinds of activity should qualify as being a *healthy and manly sport*. Thus, for example, at one time, it was assumed that boxing (which was compulsory at the private school attended by this writer) was assumed to fit into that category. Thus, writing, in general terms, of the attitudes of the Nineteenth Century aristocracy, Holt comments[261] that, "Through sport boys acquire virtues which no books can give them; not merely daring and endurance but better still, temper, self-restraint, fairness, honour, unenvious approbation of another's success and all that 'give and take' of life which stand a man in good stead when he goes forth into the world and without which, indeed, his success is always maimed and partial." Boxing, Gorn suggests[262] was especially highly regarded for those reasons and from the fact that at the major public schools, "...young gentlemen acquired black eyes and split lips along with courage, coolness under pressure and a sense of leadership and command, the moral foundations of the landed classes' rule."

Today, of course, we know different: Anderson has referred[263] to the prohibition in Sweden, in 1969, of professional boxing. The grounds for that prohibition were that the *manly sport* involved severe and life-threatening injuries to the participants, that it had a brutalising effect on the audience and was regulated by dubious financial interests. Although Anderson also notes the criticism that the ban is tokenistic – in the sense that Swedish boxers can always travel to fight in other countries, as can supporters – it is highly symbolic that one of the more advanced European nations has taken the step, and as long ago as they did. All of this is important to the present discussion because, at one time, hunting stag deer with hounds was widely regarded as being a healthy and manly sport as adverted to by Lord Wright. In addition, it was so highly regarded that it generated poetry, such as the *fin de siecle* poet John Davidson's poem, "A Runnable Stag", written in 1906. Indeed, the first stanza emphasises the *healthy* nature of the sport and immediately sets the rhetorical nature of the poem in place:

    WHEN the pods went pop on the broom, green broom,

> And apples began to be golden-skinn'd,
> We harbourd a stag in a Priory coomb,
> And we feather'd his trail up-wind, up-wind,
> We feather'd his trail up-wind –
> A stag of warrant, a stag, a stag
> A runnable stag, a kingly crop,
> Brow, bay and tray and three on top,
> A stag, a runnable stag.

Thus, in the first stanza, the configuration of antlers on the stag's head is referred to as *kingly*. In the second, the stag's *mien* is described as *lordly* and, in the third, the stag is referred to as *wily*. The poem traces the hunt in eleven stanzas with continual reference to the *lordly* configuration of antlers and the skill of the stag in evading the dogs and the huntsmen who are described in the fifth stanza as, "...three hundred gentlemen, able to ride..." A typical instance is to be found in the sixth stanza:

> By perilous paths in coomb and dell,
> The heather, the rocks, and the river-bed,
> The pace grew hot, for the scent lay well,
> And a runnable stag goes right ahead,
> The quarry went right ahead –
> Ahead, ahead, and fast and far;
> His antler'd crest, his cloven hoof,
> Brow, bay and tray and three aloof,
> The stag, the runnable stag.

Inevitably, the stag will be exhausted by a chase of that nature and it is at this point in its repellent course that the poem adds mannered sentimentality to its other manifest deficiencies – such as the fact that its rhythm remains unchanged throughout:

> When he turn'd at bay in the leafy gloom,
> In the emerald gloom where the brook ran deep,
> He heard in the distance the rollers boom,
> And he saw in a vision of peaceful sleep
> In a wonderful vision of sleep,

> A stag of warrant, a stag, a stag,
> A runnable stag in a jewell'd bed,
> Under the sheltering ocean dead,
> A stag, a runnable stag.

The end, in view of that stanza, is just as inevitable: the stag, having avoided his hunters, runs a further thirty miles and, in the final stanza drowns himself in sea which he had heard in the antepenultimate stanza. The final stanza seems, to this commentator at least, even more grotesque than those which preceded it:

> Three hundred gentlemen, able to ride,
> Three hundred horses as gallant and free,
> Beheld him escape on the evening tide,
> Far out till he sank in the Severn Sea,
> Till he sank in the depths of the sea –
> The Stag, the buoyant stag, the stag
> That slept at last in a jewell'd bed
> Under the sheltering ocean spread,
> The stag, the runnable stag.

All in all, "A Runnable Stag" does not present a morally edifying picture: seriously encapsulated, it could be described as *telling the story of three hundred over privileged humans hunting a dignified animal to death*. When one strips the story of the chase, the descriptions of the protagonists and, especially, the stag's romanticised death, the poem becomes both tedious and self justifying. Where it is of interest, perhaps, is that it recreates a sense of *period*, which is of especial importance to contemporary commentators on *hermeneutics* and *rhetoric*.[264] In other words, "A Runnable Stag" can tell us something of the values which pertained at the time when Davidson was writing. Standing alone, and whatever the intention of the poet, the values which are presented are not especially admirable: the stag's only utility lies in chase which he is able to provide for the "...gentlemen, able to ride" and their horses. The poem, likewise demonstrates those people's attitudes towards the work of others when Davidson, in the seventh stanza, writes that:

> For a matter of twenty miles and more
> By the densest hedge and the highest wall,
> Through herds of bullocks he baffled the lore
> Of harbourer, huntsman, hounds and all,
> Of harbourer, hounds and all –

Indeed, all that one seems to have left is a sense of the irresponsibility of the stag hunting classes, whenever they existed...! In view of that kind of behaviour, it is apparent that individuals and groups who were not personally and directly involved with the activity are likely to have a strong response to it, which may involve the law.

Thus, in *R v Somerset County Council, ex parte Fewings*,[265] the respondent local authority, in 1974, appropriated certain common land under s 122(1) of the *Local Government Act* 1972[266] for the purpose specified in s 120(1)(b) of that Act, namely the, "...benefit, improvement or development" of that land. In 1993 the chair of the local authority's environment committee proposed a meeting regarding hunting rights over the land. After reading various reports which had been prepared for the meeting, the committee passed a resolution to recommend that stag hunting be permitted over the land. The reason for that resolution was that the banning of hunting would reduce the deer herd because of indiscriminate shooting and an increase in poaching. However, when the matter came before a full meeting of the local authority, another resolution was passed which meant that deer hunting would be prohibited over the land. That resolution was passed because the majority of the counsellors who voted were deeply opposed to deer hunting and regarded it as morally repulsive. The applicants, who regularly hunted over the land, applied for judicial review of the local authority's decision and queried the legality of the ban on the grounds that it had been made purely on moral grounds and without regard to the legislative provisions.

Laws J was of the view[267] that the language of s 120(1)(b) of the *Local Government Act* 1972 was not sufficiently wide to, "...permit the council to take a decision about activities carried out on this land which is based upon freestanding moral perceptions as opposed to an objective judgment about what will conduce to the better management of the estate." The provision, Laws J went on, was not within the class of such provisions which required a decision maker to have regard to moral considerations *as such*.²⁶⁸ Hence, a prohibition on hunting which manifestly interfered with the lawful freedom of those who take part in the sport could only be justified under the subsection if the council reasonably concluded that the prohibition was objectively necessary as the best means of managing the deer herd, or was otherwise required, on objective grounds, for the preservation or enhancement of land. "The view that hunting is morally repulsive", the judge emphasised, "however pressing its merits, has nothing to do with such questions. Section 120(1)(b) confers no entitlement on a local authority to impose its opinions about the morals of hunting on the neighbourhood. In the present state of the law those opinions, however, sincerely felt, have their proper place only in the private conscience of those who entertain them." The local authority, Laws J reiterated,²⁶⁹ had been given no authority by Parliament to translate such views into public action, there being nothing in the provision to suggest otherwise. Laws J was fortified in his view by the Nineteenth Century decision of *Calder and Hebble Navigation Co v Pilling*²⁷⁰ involving a canal company which made a byelaw which closed a canal on Sundays. The enabling statute authorised the making of byelaws, "...for the good and orderly using the said navigation..." The court held that the byelaw was *ultra vires*, Alderson B stating²⁷¹ that, "The rules which they are empowered to make have nothing to do with the regulation of moral or religious conduct which are left to the general law of the land, and to the laws of God". Though Laws J, in *Fewings*, admitted that *Pilling*'s statutory context was quite different, he would have reached the same conclusion in that later case even without the assistance of *Pilling*. However, *Pilling*, he considered, did provide, "...an instance in practice of...a true proposition, namely that if Parliament intends to confer power on a subordinate body to regulate the morals of other people, it will choose words which make it plain beyond peradventure that that is in truth the ...purpose of the provision."

To take up the point made by Alderson B in *Pilling*, Laws J commented²⁷² that where the activity in question is permitted under the general law, as was deer hunting, it was not to be prohibited only on the grounds of the decision-makers distate or ethical objection where, on its face, the reach of his or her statutory function requires no more than the making of objective judgments for the management of a particular regime. "While", he said, "of course, it is open to Parliament to legislate so as to curtail the activities on individuals on avowedly moral grounds (assuming consistency with the law of the European Union), such restrictions involve a very particular encroachment upon personal liberty; and the court must be alert to see that any action of that kind is strictly justified by law. Where a right so to act is asserted by a subordinate body, whose powers by definition are not at large, the court will presume against it unless the empowering statute positively requires the authority in question to bring its moral views to bear upon the subject in hand, and allows or demands that it treat those views as decisive." If that were not done, Laws J continued, one was required to assume that a discretion remained vested in the authority as to whether or not to impose its morality on the relevant people, even though no practical imperative requires it to do so. The judge could not say, given the present state of the law, that Parliament could not confer such a discretion, but it would require the clearest language. In the present instance, there was no such language.

Such a result, Laws J went on, was wholly unsurprising because, in his *ipsissima verba*, "The morality of hunting is an issue which travels well beyond the boundaries of any local authority area: it is, manifestly, a national issue, upon which well-intentioned people up and down the country entertain strong and diametrically opposed views. While I acknowledge that the issue may not have gained its present profile when the 1972 Act was passed, I consider it highly unlikely that at the time Parliament intended to confer powers on local authorities which would enable them, piecemeal, to impose upon local authorities their individual perceptions of the ethics of the matter. Whether hunting should be banned, or limited, seems to me to be pre-eminently a matter for the national legislature.

Nevertheless, the judge was of the view[273] that the local authority's resolution might still have been lawful had it been passed on the basis of a reasonable perception by that body that the prohibition was necessary for the better management of the herd or for the conservation of the amenities. The judge then emphasised that the decision was not based on any judgment, based on appropriate documentation, that those matters would be enhanced by the prohibition of hunting. In reality, the council determined to prohibit hunting over the land in question because a majority of those voting disapproved of hunting, Laws J considered that they were not entitled to resolve as they did. In consequence, the local authority's decision was unlawful and an order of *certiorari* would be made to quash it. The judge also said that to hear argument as to whether it was appropriate to grant a declaration as to the correct legal position as the importance of the issue was not limited to the facts of the specific decision.

It will be readily apparent that *Fewings* is a case of very considerable interest, even though it is just as clear that not everyone would agree with the ultimate adjudication. What is quite clear, too, is that the majority of the local authority who voted in favour of the prohibition were lacking in tactical skills – even a significant pretence at taking note of documentation might have gained them victory, as Laws J seemed to suggest.[274] Yet, at the same time as he admitted that the issue of a prohibition of stag hunting (or a limitation) transcended the local authority's area of influence, the judge's view of the relevance of morality to the resolution of what is, surely, an essentially moral issue is limited. Put another way, it may very well be that the members of the local authority who reached the decision which they did made that decision after careful thought, even though they were basing their premises on morality, rather than on the simple pragmatics which the sub-committee took into account. In that context, it should also be noted that, in the *National Anti-Vivisection Society* case itself, there was a judgment in dissent by Lord Porter.

Early in his judgment, Lord Porter noted[275] that one of the difficulties present in the case was the determination of what was of benefit to the public and, also, who was to make that determination. A particular question which vexed Lord Porter was the relevance of the earlier decision in *In re Fouveaux*.[276] In that case, Chitty J held that societies for the suppression and abolition of vivisection were charities within the legal definition of the term *charity*.[277] On the issue of morality Chitty J had said,[278] "The mere infliction of pain is not necessarily cruelty; into the question of what is cruelty the moral element largely enters... It may truly be said that the infliction of justifiable pain is not cruelty. The question of what is and what is not justifiable is a question of morals, on which men's minds may reasonably differ and do in fact differ. Cruelty is degrading to man; and a society for the suppression of cruelty to the lower animals whether domestic or not, has for its object, not merely the protection of the animals themselves, but the advancement of morals and education among men. The purpose of these societies, whether they are right or wrong in the opinions they hold, is charitable in the legal sense of the term. The intention is to benefit the community; whether, if they achieved their object, the community would, in fact, be benefited is a question on which I think the Court is not required to express an opinion. The defendant societies may be near the border line, but I think they are charities." In the *National Anti-Vivisection Society* case itself, Lord Porter was of the opinion[279] that the object of the society was the protection of animals from the sufferings believed to be involved in vivisection. That object, he considered, was, in accordance with the earlier cases, charitable, regardless of the finding of the Charity Commissioners that its success would be gravely injurious to the public benefit. Conversely, as might have been expected, Lord Wright, in the *National Anti-Vivisection Society* case, regarded[280] *In re Foveaux* as having been wrongly decided and that it should be reversed. Lord Wright's reasons[281] for so regarding the case were that Chitty J had been inconsistent in holding that the gift was charitable whilst, at the same time, refusing to decide whether it was for the public benefit: unless he so decided in favour of the gift he could not decide that it was charitable. In other words, if he were not satisfied that the propaganda and expenditure for the suppression of vivisection were beneficial to the community, he was not entitled to hold that the society's activities were charitable. Further, Lord Wright considered that Chitty J was wrong in deciding that he could not weigh against each other the detriment inseparable from suppressing vivisection on the one hand and, on the other, the benefit of the community of higher moral standards said to be due to an enhanced regard for the welfare of animals. Lord Wright, once again as might be expected, found no difficulty in weighing what he described as, "...the material benefits of vivisection against the moral benefit which is alleged or assumed as possibly following from the success of the appellant's project." Where Lord Wright's argument is less cogent is because, as will be clear from the discussion as a whole, is that it is far from certain that everyone involved – from the narrators of poems, to protagonists in case law – would necessarily share Lord Wright's rather aggressive certitude! Again, it may very well be, too, that there are those who find the rhetoric of morality, as well as being less harsh than that of Lord Wright, altogether preferable to that of materiality. One issue which is clear from this commentary on animal welfare in poetry and law is that the question of morality cannot be escaped, even though its relevance is accepted only reluctantly by some commentators and, indeed, protagonists.

c) The Rhetoric of Religion

It is quite clear from both Lord McNaghten's formulation in *Pemsel*[282] as well as from the Preamble to the *Statute of Elizabeth*[283] itself, that trusts for the advancement of religion will be regarded by the law as charitable. There are, of course, problems which attach to this apparently straightforward comment: the first is that religious experience is very often a deeply personal matter and may be perceived in different ways by different people (including poets). Second, it is also clear that religious activity may very well have a public aspect which may cause courts some difficulty in deciding how public an activity must be to fulfil the *public benefit* test in respect of a charitable gift and also, possibly, whether a particular activity is, or is not, religious in itself.

However, in some respects at least, the private aspects of religious experience are easier to grasp and provide a more accessible introduction to the topic as it is structured in this part of the text. A simple, direct and accessible introduction is provided by George Herbert's poem "The Elixir". Although Herbert is frequently classified as a *metaphysical* poet, this poem is selected as an illustration of a clearly perceived goal and achievement. The poem begins with the goal, which is set out in the first stanza:

> Teach me, my God and King,
> In all things thee to see,
> And what I do in any thing,
> To do it as for thee:

Herbert then seeks to refine his initial goal by setting out ways of attempting to achieve it. These are not themselves difficult:

> Not rudely as a beast,
> To run into an action;
> But still to make thee prepossest,
> And give it his perfection.
>
> A man that looks on glass,
> Or it may stay his eye;
> Or if he pleaseth, through it pass,
> And then the heav'n espy

The ease of the task is further emphasised by the fourth stanza which seeks to emphasise that the experience sought by the poet is available to everyone who can become transformed for the better by the adoption of Herbert's goal, as enunciated in the first stanza:

> All may of thee partake:
> Nothing can be so mean,
> Which with his tincture (for thy sake)
> Will not grow bright and dean.

The final two stanzas, in effect, reiterate the goal sought to be achieved in the first, though they themselves are written in terms of that very achievement. However, it is clear from the last two verses that the rewards of that achievement can be very considerable indeed and are, themselves, life changing:

> A servant with this clause
> Makes drudgery divine:
> Who sweeps a room, as for thy laws,
> Make that and the action fine.
>
> This is the famous stone
> That turneth all to gold:
> For that which God doth touch and own
> Cannot for less be told.

Thus, the rewards of achieving the goal set, simply, by the poet in the first stanza can make even the most humble (or demeaning) tasks inspiring. Indeed, the initial goal is so valuable and important it is compared with the *philosopher's stone*, at least in personal, spiritual terms. However, as T S Eliot points out,[284] it would be wrong to assume that Herbert's poems are of value only for Christians or, more narrowly still, for members of his own church, although they may provide aids for devotion. Eliot, in fact, goes on to argue that Herbert is a poet that every lover of English poetry, and every student of English poetry, should read irrespective of religious belief or otherwise. Nor, he states, is he concerned primarily with, "...the exquisite craftsmanship, the extraordinary metrical virtuosity or the verbal felicities, but of the content of the poems... These form a record of a spiritual struggle which should touch the feeling, and enlarge the understandings of those readers also who hold no religious belief and find themselves unmoved by religious emotion. Assuming Eliot to be correct in his generalised comment, "The Elixir", which has been discussed as much as for any other reason because this author considers that it has a message which is capable of assimilation by non-Christian readers. Thus, the substitution, say, of "as for a cause" for "as for thy laws" in the penultimate stanza, provides a universal message of which the poem is susceptible in any event. The impression which is, *prima facie*, generated by "The Elixir", though, is that of a continuing religious commitment manifested in a generous ecumenical faith.

Spiritual struggles, however, may be found elsewhere and are demonstrated by the, so called, *terrible sonnets* of Gerard Manley Hopkins. Hence, in "I Wake and Feel the Fell of Dark, Not Day", written in 1885, the poet describes a situation which is familiar to most of us - waking during the night. However, there is an added element, which can vividly be contrasted the poet's stance in "The Elixir", where spiritual involvement can, and does, enoble. Hopkins's experiential torment is certainly not enobling:

> I wake and feel the fell of dark, not day.
> What hours, O what black hours we have spent
> This night! What sights you, heart, saw; ways you went!
> And more must, in yet longer light's delay.
>
> With witness I speak this. But where I say
> Hours I mean years, mean life. And my lament
> Is cries countless, cries like dead letters sent
> To dearest him that lives alas! away.
>
> I am gall, I am heartburn. God's most deep decree
> Bitter would have me taste: my taste was me;
> Bones built in me, flesh filled, blood brimmed the curse.
>
> Self yeast of spirit a dull dough sours. I see

> The lost are like this, and their scourge to be
> As I am mine, their sweating selves; but worse.

Harris, in his study of Hopkins's sonnets, notes[285] that Hopkins, in "I Wake and Feel..." observes his body as a "naturalized counter structure" and, also[286], that, for the poet, Hell was infinite separation from the mercy and goodness of God. The combination of those elements in the poem make for disturbing imagery of isolated self loathing, a theme taken up by McKenzie who writes[287] that Hopkins himself had described the poem as having been "written in blood." McKenzie has also commented[288] himself that the, "...sonnet ends somewhat enigmatically perhaps because [the poet] could not decide whether it was more painful to be an outlaw aware that he was to be justly punished, or be loyal citizen summarily imprisoned on an unknown charge, and left to languish unheard." Although both elements may be present in the poem (and may account for its seemingly bathetic conclusion), there are others which it would be wrong to ignore. Thus, at the end of the initial octet the references to "...cries like dead letters" and to, "...dearest him who lives alas! away" give the impression of a deserted lover rather than the situation to which McKenzie made reference. Of course they are of concern to the main thrusts of this work at large, but so is the thesis which I posit.[289] However one views "I Wake and Feel the Fell..." it clearly represents an agonising personal crisis for the poet.

After George Herbert and Gerard Manley Hopkins, Francis Thompson has generally been regarded as a minor poet, although his major work, "The Hound of Heaven" written in 1893, is still remembered, if only for its striking opening lines:

> I fled Him, down the nights and down the days;
> I fled Him, down the arches of the years;
> I fled Him, down the labyrinthine ways
> Of my own mind; and in the mist of tears
> I hid from Him, and under running laughter.
> Up vistaed hopes I sped;
> And shot, precipitated,
> Adown Titanic glooms of chasmed fears,
> From those strong Feet that followed, followed after.

Evans has commented[290] that "The Hound of Heaven" has, "...a universality which gives it an appeal to many who are not interested in poetry as a whole, nor studious of the niceties of form and vocabulary." Evans then goes on to note that the poem's central theme, which was the pursuit of the soul by God, was already long familiar to mystical writers and, apparently, had been derived by Thompson from the *Confessions* of St Augustine. "Thompson's strength", Evans suggests, lay in his poetry to illustrate that pursuit and, "...seldom has the spiritual experience been wrought with such certainty into the symbols drawn from the images of passable human experience. Here he controlled his decorative virtuosity to a central poetic purpose." At the same time, there are some passages in the poem, which are disturbing, like the Hopkins sonnet, in their intensity:

> Naked I wait Thy love's uplifted stroke!
> My harness piece by piece Thou hast hewn from me,
> And smitten me to my knee;
> I am defenceless utterly.
> I slept, methinks, and woke,
> And slowly gazing, find me stripped in sleep.
> In the rash lustihead of my young powers,
> I shook the pillaring hours
> And pulled my life upon me; grimed with smears,
> I stand amid the dust o' the moulded years –
> My mangles youth lies dead beneath the heap.

The protagonist's defences, including that of his youthful strength, have been ripped from him, leaving only his soul to face God. The poem then concludes, after the relentless pursuit which is emphasised in its inexorability by the *leitmotiv* recurring in slightly different form throughout the poem:

> Still with unhurrying chase,
> And unperturbed pace,
> Deliberate speed, majestic instancy,
> Came on the following Feet,
> And a Voice above their heart –
> 'Naught shelters thee, who wilt nor shelter Me.'

The poem concludes, as it must, with a peaceful awareness of the result of the pursuit as God reaches, despite its endeavour, the soul:

> Halts by me that footfall:
> Is my gloom, after all,
> Shade of His hand, outstretched caressingly?
> 'Ah, fondest, blindest, weakest,
> I am He Whom thou seekest!
> Thou dravest love from thee, who dravest Me.'

The course of the pursuit has been noted by Gurney, who writes[291] that, "The various stratagems whereby the individual soul endeavours to evade the acknowledgement of this holy mystery, fleeing from that presence which exposes the pretence and hollowness of our habitual preoccupations and avoiding that act of contrition which our indifference has rendered a necessity..." That, it is suggested, is an accurate and effective description of a long, and, if presently neglected, remarkable poem of its own period.

After Hopkins's sonnet and, perhaps more particularly, "The Hound of Heaven", it may be surprising to learn that there may be some people who do not seek to evade their spiritual callings. A late poem of Gerard Manley Hopkins, 1918, is "Heaven-Haven", subtitled, "A Nun Takes the Veil". Its point is straightforward and is simply and delicately expressed:

> I have desired to go
> Where springs not fail,
> To fields where flies no sharp and sided hail
> And a few lilies blow.
>
> And I have asked to be
> Where no storms come,
> Where the green swell is in the havens dumb,
> And out of the swing of the sea.

However, whatever the attractions or advantages of the lifestyle (presumably, of a nun in a contemplative order) depicted by Hopkins, it may be that the law takes a view which is not entirely similar. In *Gilmour v Coats*,[292] a gift of £500 had been made to a priory of Carmelite nuns in London. That community comprised an association of strictly cloistered and purely contemplative nuns who devoted their lives entirely to worship, prayers and meditations within the precincts of their convent. They performed no works and engaged in no activities at all for the benefit of anyone outside their association. However, they were regarded, in the belief and teaching of the Roman Catholic Church as causing, by means of their private worship, prayers and meditations, the intervention of God to bring about the spiritual improvement of members of the public (whether Catholic or not) outside their convent and also providing an example of self-denial and concentration on the life of the spirit tending to the spiritual edification of those members of the public. The House of Lords held that the gift was not charitable as there was not the necessary element of benefit to the public as neither intercessory prayer nor edification were within the category of public benefit. Likewise, Lord Simonds regarded[293] any claimed public edification as being too "vague and intangible" to satisfy the appropriate test. In addition, he also rejected[294] the alleged benefit of intercessionary prayer as being, "...manifestly not susceptible of proof." Lord Simonds was also of the view[295] that the courts would not accept as fact whatsoever a particular religion elected to believe.

Although Lord Simonds's view would seem to be emphatic, when it is placed in context, the situation at large becomes less clear. Thus, in *Neville Estates Ltd v Madden*,[296] a trust in favour of a particular Synagogue, which was not open to the public, was held by Cross J to be charitable. The distinction between *Madden* and *Gilmour v Coats* was that, in Cross J's words,[297] the members of the Synagogue, "...spend their lives in the world, whereas the members of the Carmelite Priory live secluded from the world. In addition, it appears as though different considerations apply to gifts for the saying of masses: hence, in *Re Caus*,[298] a Roman Catholic Testator bequeathed £1000 and four houses for the purpose of, "...one foundation Mass to be said for his soul and the souls of my parents and relatives during the space of twenty-five years." Evidence was given that by a *foundation Mass* was meant a mass which was to be paid for from the interest of an invested fund, so that, unless the gift was charitable, it would be void for perpetuity. Luxmore J held that a gift for the saying of masses was charitable as being for the advancement of religion because, first, it enables a ritual act to be performed which is a central part of the religion of a significant proportion of Christian people. Second, because it assisted in the endowment of priests whose duty it is to perform the act.

The water has further been muddied by some more recent decisions. However, as early as 1862, Romilly MR stated [299] that trusts for the advancement of religion which, were, "...not subversive of all morality..." would be regarded as charitable. Indeed, in *Dawkins* v *Gown Suppliers*[300] it was held that a gift in favour of Rastafarianism was charitable. However, this takes us to the next question of what will constitute a *religion*, which will be shortly considered.[301]

At the same time as private religious observances (though, as was seen from *Gilmour* v *Coats*, they must not be too private), there are, in many religions, aspects which involve public participation. These may involve *proselytisation* or *affirmation*. Proselytisation may, of course present its own usually indirect, problems. Thus, for example, in the Australian case of *In the Marriage of Paisio*,[302] in a dispute over custody and visitation, the mother had become involved with the *Jehovah's Witnesses* sect, which is widely known for its active proselytisation. The Full Court of the Family Court of Australia[303] noted[304] that, in the past, it had been held that, "...the doctrines of a particular religion, or at least those doctrines as interpreted by some of its adherents, have been so detrimental to children as to necessitate that the children should not be in the custody of the parent holding such doctrines. In these cases, while the court is necessarily showing disapproval of the practice of a particular religion it is not doing so on any basis that religious teaching is harmful or suggesting that only one form of religion is permissible. The court is doing no more than saying that certain practices, albeit given a veneer of religious justification, are in fact so positively harmful to the welfare of the child that they must be removed from the influence of those who advocate such practices." The Court continued [305] by saying that, in making such a decision, adjudicative bodies must take, "...the utmost care to avoid merely subjective attitudes and steer a careful course between the rights of any citizen to bring children up in certain religious or non-religious beliefs and the point at which the practise of that right will positively end from a proven objective viewpoint obstruct the welfare of children. Liberty is not licence and if, for instance, children were being inculcated in a system of beliefs that condoned violence and murder (and such systems are not unknown)...the Court would not be deterred in acting to protect children merely because such beliefs were claimed to have a 'religious' basis".

Affirmation is an altogether different and healthy matter. There are many groups, not all (one only needs to attend an English football match to be aware of this) which use song as affirmation. However, in religious observance, music and song in particular play an especially significant role. An especially illustrative instance is provided by another work of George Herbert: the hymn, "Antiphon", written in 1633. This triumphal public affirmation, coupled with an awareness of the private aspect of religious belief and its observance brings together many of the aspects which have been considered in this part of the text:

> **Cho**. Let all the world in ev'ry corner sing,
> *My God and King.*
> **Vers**. The heav'ns ate not too high,
> His praise may thither fly:
> The earth is not too low,
> His praises there may grow.
> **Cho**. Let all the world in ev'ry corner sing,
> *My God and King*
> **Vers**. The church with psalms must shout,
> No door can keep them out:
> But above all, the heart
> Must bear the longest part.
> **Cho**. Let all the world in every corner sing,
> *My God and King.*

Though there has been considerable discussion surrounding the classification of trusts for the advancement of religion as charitable, it is also less than certain what *indicia* are required before an organisation is able to claim to be a *religion*. This is the case even after the decision of the High Court of Australia in *Church of the New Faith* v *Commissioner for Pay-Roll Tax (Victoria)*.[306] In that case, the Church of the New Faith Incorporated (hereinafter referred to as the taxpayer) had been incorporated in the State of South Australia in 1969 and was, accordingly, registered as a foreign company in the State of Victoria. Its objects were the presentation, practice and propagation of Scientology,[307] which was a body of teachings devised originally by one L Ron Hubbard. As it was originally presented, the organisation did not seek to place any reliance, in its teachings, on religion in the generally accepted sense of a deity to whom prayers were addressed and the holding of meetings for the purpose of worship. Following decisions of various courts around the world to the effect that the body was not a Church, its approach was varied and its practices then more closely followed those of more conventional churches. It sought exemption from pay-roll tax on the grounds that it was a religious institution entitled to the exemption given to such bodies.

Evidence was given that, under provisions which were identical to that presently being considered, exemption had been granted in the Australian States of New South Wales and South Australia. It had also been held that the taxpayer's income was exempt from income tax and the Commonwealth of Australia's *Tax Assessment Act*. Further, in 1973, the Commonwealth Attorney-General had declared that the organisation was a "recognised denomination" for the purposes of celebrating marriages. Evidence was also given regarding the body's change in attitude and the clarifications which had been made to Hubbard's teachings so as to accord with a new approach that the organisation was a religious body.

At first instance, Crockett J of the Supreme Court of Victoria held that the tax payer's religious pretentions were a sham and that it had merely taken on the appearance of a religious body in order to obtain the legal financial advantages which had been accorded to such bodies. The taxpayer then appealed to the Full Court of the Supreme Court of Victoria which upheld the decision at first instance and decided that the organisation did not possess any *indicia* of a religion. The taxpayer sought special leave to appeal to the High Court of Australia.[308] The High Court held that special leave to appeal should be granted and the appeal allowed.

First, Mason ACJ and Brennan J took the view[309] that special leave should be granted because of the legal importance of religion and the relative paucity of Australian authority on the topic. It was therefore appropriate to grant special leave in order to expound, so far as the facts of the instant case permitted, a concept of religion appropriate to discriminate in law between what is a religion and what is not. Second, these judges expressed the opinion[310] that, "...for the purposes of the law, the criteria of religion are twofold: first, belief in a supernatural Being, Thing or Principle and, second, the acceptance of canons of conduct in order to give effect to that belief, though canons of conduct which offend against the ordinary laws are outside the area of any immunity, privilege or right conferred on the grounds of religion. Those criteria may vary in their comparative importance, and there may be a different intensity of belief or of acceptance of canons of conduct or among the adherents to a religion. The tenets of a religion may give primacy to one particular belief or one particular canon of conduct. Variations in emphasis may distinguish one religion from other religions, but they are irrelevant to the determination of an individual's or a group's freedom to profess and exercise the religion of his, or their, choice". Third, Mason ACJ and Brennan J found[311] that the evidence which had been given in the case supported the finding that the adherents' beliefs satisfied the first of their broad criteria and, also, that a wish to give effect to those supernatural beliefs was a major motive for their acceptance of the dogma contained in Scientological writings.

Wilson and Dean JJ adopted a similar, though rather more fragmented, approach to that of Mason ACJ and Brennan J. They, first of all, noted[312] that the word *religion* was not susceptible of, "...the type of definition which will enable the question of whether a particular system of beliefs and practices is a religion to be determined by use of the syllogism of formal logic...[I]t is appropriate to consider whether it is possible to isolate any essential characteristics without which one cannot have a religion." They went on to say[313] that, in the context of a Western community, there was plainly force in the view that man's recognition of, and his relationship with, a personalised god constituted the essence and essential concern of religion. However, Wilson and Dean JJ stated[314] that the most that courts could do was to formulate the most important of the *indicia* which would go to make up the idea of a religion.

"One of the more important indicia of 'a religion,'" they suggested,[315] "is that the particular collection of ideas and/or practices involves belief in the supernatural, that is to say, belief that reality extends beyond that which is capable of perception by the senses. If that be absent, it is unlikely that one has 'a religion'. Another is that the ideas relate to man's nature and place in the universe and his relation to things supernatural. A third is that the ideas are accepted by adherents as requiring or encouraging them to observe particular standards or codes of conduct or to participate in specific practices having supernatural significance. A fourth is that, however loosely knit and varying in beliefs and practices as adherents may be, they constitute an identifiable group or groups. A fifth, and perhaps more controversial, indicium is that adherents themselves see the collection of ideas and/or practices as constituting a religion." At the same time, the judges emphasised[316] that no one of those *indicia* was necessarily determinative of the question of whether a particular collection of ideas and/or practices should be characterised as a religion – they were no more than aids in determining that question and the assistance which they offered would be determined by the context of the particular case. However, most would be satisfied by leading religions. Conversely, they considered, "It is unlikely that a collection of ideas and/or practices would properly be characterised as a religion if it lacked all or most of them…Ultimately, however, that question will fall to be resolved as a matter of judgment on what the evidence establishes about the claimed religion."

In the end Wilson and Deane JJ, relying on the evidence,[317] concluded that the instant case was not borderline. "Regardless of whether the members of the applicant are gullible or misled," they stated "or whether the practices of Scientology are harmful or objectionable, the evidence, in our view, establishes that Scientology must, for relevant purposes, be accepted as a religion…"

Murphy J adopted a rather different approach although his initial approach was not dissimilar from that of Wilson and Deane JJ. "Because", he said,[318] "so many different beliefs or practices have been generally accepted as religions, any attempt to define religion exhaustively runs into difficulty. There is no single acceptable criterion, no essence of religion." He then went on to state[319] that the better approach was to state what was sufficient, even if not necessary, to bring a body which claims to be religious within the category." Murphy J then noted that some claims to be religious were not serious, but merely a hoax, although to reach that conclusion required an extreme case. At that point, Murphy J reached the central point of his argument when he urged that, "On this approach, any body which claims to be religious, whose beliefs or practices are a revival of, or resemble, earlier cults, is religious. Any body which claims to be religious and to believe in a supernatural Being or Beings, whether physical and visable, such as the sun and the stars, or a physical and invisible God or spirit, or an abstract God or entity, is religious. For example, if a few followers of astrology were to found an institution based on the belief that their destinies were influenced or controlled by the stars and that astrologers can, by reading the stars, divine these destinies, and if it claimed to be religious, it would be a religious institution. Any body which claims to be religious and offers a way to find meaning and purpose in life, is religious. The Aboriginal religion of Australia must be included. The list is not exhaustive; the categories of religion are not closed."

Many may find the rhetoric in Murphy J's judgment a little disquieting, as it seems to suggest that, except in very extreme cases, a claim to the status of religion must necessarily be successful. The comment at the end of the extract from his judgment is redolent of the view expressed in the leading case of *Donoghue* v *Stevenson* [320] that the categories of negligence were never closed. One might do well to take into account Widgery J's *dictum* in *Weller* v *Foot and Mouth Disease Research Institute*[321] that, "The categories of negligence never close, but when the court is asked to recognise a new category it must proceed with some caution." Given his initial view, Murphy J was enthusiastic [322] about finding the Church to be religious: The appellant, he said, had *easily discharged* the onus of showing itself to be religious and the conclusion that the appellant body was a religious organisation was *irresistible*.

It was apparent from all of the judgments that the High Court of Australia considered that the Victorian courts had drawn their vision of the notion of religion too narrowly. Yet it is clear that a crucial element which was central to the decision in *Gilmour* v *Coats*[323] – that of the public benefit – was very largely absent in *The Church of the New Faith*. The Court seemed very much to assume, as it had been in *Thornton* v *Howe*[324] that religion had such benefit unless definitively proved to the contrary. Indeed, at the conclusion of his judgment in the Scientology case, Murphy J stated[325] that, "The Commissioner should not be criticized for attempting to minimize the number of tax exempt bodies. The crushing burden of taxation is heavier because of exemptions in favour of religious institutions many of which have enormous and increasing wealth."

The subjects of gifts which seek to gain charitable status are, as both the Preamble to the *Statute of Elizabeth* and *Pemsel* suggest, both varied and uncertain. So is the rhetoric to be found in the various cases. In the case law and the poems there seems to be a general awareness of the dehumanising process which war involves, even though the manifestations of legal response may leave something to be desired.[326] There is no such discernable pattern in the material on charities, - thus, the distinction in approach between "The Fawn"[327] and "A Runnable Stag"[328] will have been especially apparent. Rhetoric necessarily is represented in various forms, by which form a reader is persuaded is determined by other factors such as the relationship of writer and reader and, in the present text, the relationship of both to the law. Aspects of that tripartite relationship will be considered in the following chapter.

---

[1] I.A. Shearer, *Starke's International Law* (11th Ed 1994) at 483.
[2] Ibid at 484.
[3] Ibid at 484.
[4] Below text at n 7 *ff*.
[5] *The Spectator* 27th November 2010 at 29.
[6] For comment on the *village green* in another context, see above Ch II, text at n 76 *ff*.
[7] Below text at n 67 *ff*.
[8] D Welland, *Wilfred Owen: A Critical Study* (1978) at 61.
[9] Below text at n 66 *ff*.
[10] L Goldensohn, *American War Poetry: An Anthology* (2006) at 286.
[11] B K Martin, *Philip Larkin* (1978) at 38.
[12] [1939] AC 277. For comment on this case, see F. Bates, *The Reality of Conflicts Reasoning: Choice of Law in Torts* (2010) at 265.
[13] Ibid at 290.
[14] Ibid at 291.
[15] [1891] 1 QB 79. For comment on contextual aspects of that case, see F Bates, "Choice of Law in Australian Torts: Or the Truth About Conflicts" (2003) 14 *Caribbean LR* 1 at 20.
[16] Ibid at 85.
[17] Ibid at 84.
[18] Above text at n 11.
[19] J Booth, *Philip Larkin: Writer* (1992) at 73.
[20] Ibid at 74.
[21] S Petch, *The Art of Philip Larkin* (1981) at 80.
[22] Above text at n 19.
[23] R Day, *Larkin* (1987) at 62.
[24] Above text at n 19.
[25] Above n 23 at 63.
[26] A J P Taylor, *The Origins of the Second World War* (1961)
[27] A. Hecht, *The Hidden Law: The Poetry of W. H. Auden* (1993) at 169.
[28] J Fuller, *W. H Auden: A Commentary* (1998) at 291.
[29] M K Spears, *The Poetry of W. H. Auden: The Disenchanted Island* (1963) at 135.
[30] J Callan, *Auden: A Carnival of Intellect* (1983) at 156.
[31] [1964] AC 763. For critical comment, see D Thompson, "The Committee of 100 and the Official Secrets Act 1911" [1963] *Public Law* 201.
[32] Section 1 of the *Official Secrets Act* 1911 provides that, "(1) If any person for any purpose prejudicial to the safety or interests of the State – (a) approaches or is in the neighbourhood of, or enters any prohibited place within the meaning of this Act...he shall be guilty of a felony..."
[33] Above n 32.
[34] Above n 32.
[35] Above n 32.
[36] See particularly, the comments of Lord Hodson, [1964] AC 763 at 799.
[37] [1964] AC 763 at 794.
[38] Ibid at 795.

[39] Ibid at 813.
[40] Above n 32.
[41] [1964] AC 763 at 796.
[42] Ibid at 800.
[43] [1916] 2 AC 77 at 107.
[44] Above n 32.
[45] Above text at n 40.
[46] [1964] 2 AC 763 at 700.
[47] Ibid at 701.
[48] Ibid at 807.
[49] Ibid at 810.
[50] Ibid at 811.
[51] Author's emphasis.
[52] [1964] AC 763 at 812.
[53] Ibid at 813.
[54] Above text at n 40.
[55] [1964] AC 763 at 814.
[56] There were six appellants, five of whom received terms of eighteen months imprisonment, and the other twelve months.
[57] [1964] AC 763 at 787.
[58] Ibid at 794.
[59] See, for example, *Hyam v DPP* [1975] AC 55 at 73 *per* Lord Hailsham.
[60] See, for example, *Plomp v R* (1963) 110 CLR 234 at 242 *per* Dixon C J. For comment on the issue generally, see D Ross, *Ross on Crime* (5th Ed. 2011) at 956 *ff*.
[61] Above text at n 7 *ff*.
[62] Above text at n 26 *ff*.
[63] Above text at n 57.
[64] Above n 1 at 499.
[65] Ibid at 500.
[66] There is also the difficulty which might arise if United Nations forces were no so bound and became involved in military operations against a State, the forces of that State would be bound by international humanitarian law, but not the United Nations force.
[67] Above text at n 11.
[68] It is sweet and seemly to die for one's native country.
[69] Above n 68.
[70] Above text at n 11.
[71] Above text at n 31 *ff*.
[72] Above n 10 at 192.
[73] Ibid at 383.
[74] Quoted ibid at 209.
[75] Above text at 69 *ff*.
[76] Above text a n 31 *ff*.
[77] Above n 10 at 287.
[78] [1941] 1 All ER 552. The author is grateful to Professor Tony Bradney of the University of Keele for drawing this decision to his attention.
[79] Ibid at 553.
[80] Below text at n 82.
[81] [1941] 1 All ER 552 at 553.
[82] Ibid at 554.
[83] Ibid at 554.
[84] Ibid at 554.
[85] He was, at the relevant time, aged twenty. Had the case been decided in 2011, the plaintiff would have been of full age.
[86] [1941] 1 All ER 552 at 555.

[87] A former colleague of the author's told of a person whose behaviour was not dissimilar from that of the plaintiff in *Newell*, although he did express his views publicly, but who was reported to authorities and subsequently convicted.
[88] Above text at n 80.
[89] Above text at n 79.
[90] [1941] 1 All ER 552 at 552.
[91] Above n 87.
[92] Above text at n 90.
[93] Above text a n 86.
[94] Above text a n 80.
[95] Above text a n 83.
[96] C Ward (Ed), *Walt Whitman: Civil War Poetry and Prose* (1995) at iii.
[97] Above n 10 at 56.
[98] Ibid at 109.
[99] The *Libby* to which reference is made in the poem's final stanza was a notorious Confederate prison in Richmond, Virginia, which, after the war, was used by the Union in a similar capacity.
[100] "The banners of the King go on".
[101] Above text at n 97.
[102] Above text a n 67 *ff*.
[103] J Worthen, *D H Lawrence: The Life of An Outsider* (2005) at 191.
[104] H Bloom (Ed), *Till I End My Song: A Gathering of Lost Poems* (2010) at 199.
[105] M Schmidt, *The Great Modern Poets* (2006) at 15.
[106] For further comment, see at n 107 *ff*.
[107] For further comment on "dark forces as represented by the sea", see below Ch VI, text at n 255 *ff*.
[108] [1956] P 259 at 272.
[109] See, for example, G D Nokes, *An Introduction to Evidence* (4th Ed, 1967) at 72.
[110] Above text a n 7.
[111] Above n 105 at 141.
[112] Above n 104 at 347.
[113] Above at text 109.
[114] Above n 111
[115] Bowen C J , Brennan and Lockhart JJ.
[116] (1980) 31 ALR 140.
[117] *Repatriation Act* 1920 s 107 VZZH.
[118] (1980) 31 ALR 140 at 149.
[119] Particularly, *Repatriation Act* 1920 s 101 (A).
[120] (1980) 31 ALR 140 at 149.
[121] After making brief reference to the *Oxford English Dictionary* which defines *occurrence* as, "...something that occurs, happens, or takes place; an event, incident."
[122] (1970) 130 CLR 1 at 19.
[123] (1980) 31 ALR 140 at 150.
[124] Ibid at 150.
[125] See, for example, *Kavanagh v Commonwealth* (1960) 103 CLR 547; *Favelle Mart Ltd v Murray* (1976) 133 CLR 547; *Thom v Sinclair* [1917] AC 127; *Upton v Great Central Railway Co* [1924] AC 302; *Dover Navigation Co v Craig* [1940] AC 190; *Government Insurance Office (NSW) v R J Green and Lloyd Pty Ltd* (1966) 114 CLR 437; *Commercial and General Insurance Co. Ltd v Government Insurance Office (NSW)* (1973) 129 CLR 374
[126] (1980) 31 ALR 140 at 150.
[127] Ibid at 151.
[128] See, *Sneddon v Glasgow Coal Co* (1905) 42 SLR 365; *Richards v Faulls Pty Ltd* [1971] WAR 129; *Marshall v Minister of Pensions* [1947] 2 ALL ER 706; *Walsh v Rother District Council* [1978] 1 All ER 510.
[129] (1980) 31 ALR 140 at 151

[130] Ibid at 151.
[131] In making those comments, ibid, the Court suggested that, as had been observed in *Law* at first instance, the provision seemed to have obviated the distinction drawn by Denning J, as he then was, in *Minister of Pensions* v *Chennell* [1947] KB 250 and *Marshall* v *Minister of Pensions* [1947] 2 All ER 706, between a *cause* and something which should be rather regarded as being a part of the circumstances in which the cause operates.
[132] (1991) 171 CLR 506.
[133] Author's emphasis.
[134] By reason of s 47(2) of the *Repatriation Act* 1920, the Commission itself, or a Board, are bound by the same standard of proof.
[135] See, for example, *Green* v *The Queen* (1971) 126 CLR 28; *La Fontaine* v *The Queen* (1976) 136 CLR 62. For comment, see F. Bates, "Describing the Indescribable – Evaluating the Standard of Proof in Criminal Cases" (1989) 13 *Crim L J* 330.
[136] (1980) 31 ALR 140 at 152.
[137] Or, in the Court's phrase, ibid, "throw up".
[138] (1980) 31 ALR 140 at 152.
[139] Ibid at 153.
[140] Ibid at 153.
[141] Author's emphasis.
[142] (1980) 31 ALR 140 at 154.
[143] Author's emphasis.
[144] (1980) 31 ALR 140 at 154.
[145] Above text at n 137.
[146] Above text a n 135.
[147] (1984) 58 ALR 119.
[148] Which had replaced the War Pensions Entitlement Tribunal in 1979.
[149] See *Repatriation Act* 1920 s 107 VZZB.
[150] Gibbs CJ, Murphy, Wilson, Brennan and Dawson JJ.
[151] *Repatriation Act* 1920 s 101(1)(b)
[152] (1984) 58 ALR 119 at 123.
[153] Ibid at 124.
[154] Above n 149. The only matters which had been referred to the Tribunal for review were the five decisions of the Repatriation Commission where the claim in respect of essential hypertension had been rejected.
[155] *Administrative Appeals Tribunal Act* 1975 s 25.
[156] (1984) 58 ALR 119 at 124.
[157] Ibid at 125.
[158] Ibid at 124.
[159] Author's emphasis.
[160] (1984) 58 ALR 119 at 131.
[161] Ibid at 136.
[162] Ibid at 135.
[163] Above text at n 152.
[164] Especially at n 77 *ff*.
[165] Or *ritually purified*.
[166] W Empson, "Missing Dates" (1935).
[167] The same year as "The Wound Dresser", above text at n 96, and "The College Colonel", above text at n 97.
[168] Above text at n 7 *ff*.
[169] Above text at n 10 *ff*.
[170] Above text at n 12 *ff*.
[171] Above text at n 26 *ff*.
[172] Above text at 31 *ff*.
[173] Above text at 69 *ff*.

[174] Above text at 78 *ff*.
[175] Above text at n 96 *ff*.
[176] Above text at n 116 *ff*.
[177] [1891] AC 531 at 582.
[178] Ibid at 583. This statement is similar to that put in argument by Sir Samuel Romilly in *Morice* v *Bishop of Durham* (1805) 10 Ves 522 at 532.
[179] Such, for example, as the character of the trustees, see *Verge* v *Somerville* [1924] AC 496.
[180] Lord Halsbury LC and Lord Bromwell.
[181] *Income Tax Act* 1842 s 61, Sched A, No VI.
[182] (1940) 63 CLR 209 at 222.
[183] Below text at n 201 *ff*.
[184] (1940) 63 CLR 209 at 223.
[185] That is, that the court will apply the property to some other purpose which is *near enough* (as near as possible) to the original purpose see LA Sheridan and VTH Delany, *The Cy-Pres Doctrine* (1959).
[186] Above text at n 182.
[187] Above n 183.
[188] 43 Eliz 1, c 4, 1601.
[189] See *Royal College of Surgeons of England* v *National Provincial Bank Ltd* [1952] AC 631.
[190] *Mortmain and Charitable Uses Act* 1888 s 13(2). That Act was itself repealed by the *Charities Act* 1960 s 48(2), 7th Sched. This means that the Preamble has wholly disappeared, but is, nonetheless used as a guide by the courts.
[191] The list, as it, generally, appears today is in contemporary orthography.
[192] G W Keeton and L A Sheridan, *The Modern Law of Charities* (2nd Ed. 1971) at 4.
[193] S Fry, *The Fry Chronicles* (2010) at 89.
[194] Again, above n 191, in modern orthography.
[195] Above n 192.
[196] The resemblance had also been noted by J Willard, "Illusions of the Origin of *Cy Pres*" (1894) 8 *Harvard LR* 69 at 70.
[197] Above n 192.
[198] 39 Eliz I, c 6 1597.
[199] Above n 105 at 77. See also below Ch VI text a n 253.
[200] A particular example, selected by Schmidt, above n 105 at 78, is the sonnet "Time does not bring relief; you all have lied".
[201] [1948] AC 31.
[202] *Income Tax Act* 1918 s 37(1)(b).
[203] [1948] AC 31 at 47.
[204] Ibid at 48.
[205] Ibid at 48.
[206] Ibid at 49.
[207] Ibid at 47.
[208] Ibid at 49.
[209] Ibid at 49.
[210] Above text at n 177.
[211] Above text at n 209.
[212] [1948] AC 31 at 49.
[213] Above text at n 188
[214] There was considerable doubt regarding the juristic basis for the inclusion of the maintenance of tombs. See, *Re Tyler* [1891] 3 Ch 252; *Re Dalziel* [1943] Ch 227; *Re Chardon* [1928] Ch 464. These cases cannot now be regarded, at least in Australia, as good law; see *Pedulla* v *Nasti* (1990) 20 NSWLR 720.
[215] [1915] 1 Ch 113 at 122.
[216] Ibid at 121 *per* Kennedy LJ.
[217] [1929]1 Ch 557.

[218] Laurence LJ dissented on the basis of *Re Wedgewood*.
[219] [1929]1 Ch 557 at 573.
[220] Ibid at 574.
[221] Above text at n 204.
[222] [1948] AC 31 at 61.
[223] Ibid at 63
[224] (1933) 47 TLR 295.
[225] [1949] 1 All ER 346.
[226] [1975] 1 WLR 1596.
[227] (1851) 4 De G & Sm 467.
[228] Ibid at 468.
[229] (1962) 41 TC 235.
[230] (1931) 47 TLR 295.
[231] Above text at n 191.
[232] [1981] 3 All ER 493.
[233] Cl 2A.
[234] Cl 2B.
[235] CL 2C.
[236] Cl 2D.
[237] Cl 2E.
[238] *Charities Act* 1960 s 4.
[239] Ibids 5(3). They did so by way of an originating summons seeking a declaration that the trust ought to be registered as a charity.
[240] [1981] 3 All ER 493 at 503.
[241] Ibid at 504.
[242] Ibid at 505. Relying particularly on *dicta* by Lord Parker in *Bowman* v *Secular Society Ltd* [1917] AC 406 at 407 and Lord Simonds in *the National Anti-Vivisection Society* case [1948] AC 31 at 62.
[243] Ibid at 507.
[244] See *Camille and Henry Drefus Foundation Inc* v *IRC* [1954] Ch 672 at 684 *per* Lord Evershed.
[245] See above text at n 227.
[246] [1981] All ER 493 at 514.
[247] Cl 2B. He also took account of the *Amnesty International Handbook* (1977) at 29 which stated that, "Pressure to free prisoners of conscience can mean all of the following: thousands of post cards and letters to the foreign government; distributing leaflets at trade fairs; special appeals signed by prominent individuals; trade union embargoes against goods from the foreign government; continuous international news reports on the human rights violations by the government concerned."
[248] [1981] 3 All ER 493 at 515.
[249] Ibid at 516.
[250] Ibid at 518.
[251] Ibid at 519.
[252] Author's emphasis.
[253] [1981] 3 All ER 493 at 519.
[254] c at 442.
[255] R. Pearce and J Stevens, *The Law of Trusts and Equitable Obligations* (4th Ed, 2006) at 524.
[256] A position which, they note, is taken in all *political* activities.
[257] [1986] Ch 423.
[258] Above text at n 203 *ff*.
[259] Above text at n 205.
[260] [1948] AC 31 at 41.
[261] R. Holt, *Sport and the British: A modern History* (1989) at 93.
[262] E Gorn, *The Manly Art: Bare Knuckle Prize Fighting in America* (1989) at 27.

[263] J Anderson, *The Legality of Boxing : A Punch-Drunk Love?* (2007) at 163.
[264] See above Ch II.
[265] [1995] 1 All ER 513.
[266] This provides that "Subject to the following provisions of this section, a principal council may appropriate for any purpose for which the council are authorised by this or any other enactment to acquire land by agreement any land which belongs to the council and is no longer required for the purpose for which it is held immediately before the appropriation; but the appropriation of land by a council by virtue of this subsection shall be subject to the rights of other persons in, over or in respect of the land concerned."
[267] [1995] 1 All ER 513 at 529.
[268] Laws J's emphasis.
[269] [1995] 1 All ER 513 at 530.
[270] (1845) 14 M & W 76.
[271] Ibid at 88.
[272] [1995] 1 All ER 513 at 530.
[273] Ibid at 531.
[274] Above text at n 273.
[275] [1948] AC 31 at 53.
[276] [1895] 2 Ch 501.
[277] Above text at n 177 *ff*.
[278] [1895] 2 Ch 501 at 507.
[279] [1948] AC 31 at 60.
[280] Ibid at 46.
[281] Ibid at 47.
[282] Above text at n 177.
[283] Above text at n 191.
[284] T S Eliot, *George Herbert: Writers and Their Work* (1962) at 15.
[285] D A Harris, *Inspirations Unbidden: The "Terrible Sonnets" of Gerard Manley Hopkins* (1982) at 59.
[286] Ibid at 110.
[287] N H McKenzie, *A Reader's Guide to Gerard Manley Hopkins* (1981) at 184.
[288] Ibid at 183.
[289] See below Ch IV.
[290] I Evans, *English Poetry in the Late Nineteenth Century* (2nd Ed 1966) at 176.
[291] S Gurney, *British Poetry of the Nineteenth Century* (1993) at 295.
[292] [1949] AC 426.
[293] Ibid at 446.
[294] Ibid at 446.
[295] Ibid at 446.
[296] [1962] Ch 832.
[297] Ibid at 852.
[298] [1934] 1 Ch 162.
[299] *Thornton v Howe* (1862) 31 Beav. 14 at 16.
[300] *The Times*, February 4th 1993.
[301] Below text at n 306 *ff*.
[302] (1979) FLC 90-659. For critical comment, see E Goodman, "The Relevance of Religion in Custody Adjudication" (1981) 7 *Monash ULR* 217.
[303] Evatt CJ, Asche and Marshall JJ.
[304] (1979) FLC 90-659 at 78, 514.
[305] Ibid at 78,515.
[306] (1983) 154 CLR 120.
[307] According to I Crofton, *History Without the Boring Bits* (2007) at 2, the doctrines of Scientology, assert that, "...the galactic tyrant Xenn kidnapped hundreds of billions of individuals from other parts of the galaxy and sent them to Planet Earth to be exterminated.

They arrived by craft that looked like Douglas DC08's but which were in fact powered by rockets. The exiles were then exposed to thermonuclear explosions, prior to being brainwashed by a 36-day-long movie into believing that they were at the same time Jesus, God and the Devil. The victims subsequently parasitized human bodies and can only be removed by advanced Scientological techniques."

In addition, Crofton, ibid at 316, suggests that Hubbard asserted that in 1967, Harold Wilson, the leader of the British Labour Party, was a Soviet agent after he had banned foreign Scientologists from visiting Britain. In fairness to Hubbard though, it should be said that the same allegation had been made, in 1963, by the CIA.

[308] It should be noted that, in the High Court, the Commissioner did not place any relevance on a proposition which had been advanced by Brooking J in the Full Court that the taxpayer's claim to a religious organisation were based on purposes and practices which, by reason of the Victorian *Psychological Practices Act* 1965, were illegal and, hence, that the taxpayer was not entitled to claim the exemption which he sought.

[309] (1983) 154 CLR 120 at 130.
[310] Ibid at 136.
[311] Ibid at 148.
[312] Ibid at 171.
[313] Ibid at 172.
[314] Ibid at 173.
[315] Ibid at 174.
[316] Ibid at 174.
[317] Ibid at 176.
[318] Ibid at 150.
[319] Ibid at 151.
[320] [1932] AC 562.
[321] [1966] 1 QB 569 at 577.
[322] (1983) 154 CLR 120 at 162.
[323] Above text at n 292.
[324] Above n 299.
[325] (1983) 154 CLR 120 at 162.
[326] Above text at n 116 *ff*.
[327] Above text at n 199.
[328] Above text at n 263.

Chapter IV
The Writer in the Law and the Law in the Writer

1. Introductory

The Law and Literature find themselves in one another's company in some peculiar situations: In Chapter III, the rhetoric used by Lord Wright in the *National Anti-Vivisection Society* case.[1] That rhetoric was contextualised within the areas of other case law and poetry. In one situation, the issue of the relationship of law and literature has been brought substantially together in another extraordinary case concerned with the law of charitable trusts. Again, it will be remembered from the discussion of the Preamble to the *Statue of Elizabeth*[2] and in *Pemsel*[3] that trusts for the advancement of *education* would be regarded as being valid charitable trusts. Traditionally the word *education* has been broadly interpreted by the courts in the common law world. Thus, in *IRC* v *McMullen*,[4] Lord Hailsham referred to as being, "...a balanced and systematic process of instruction, training and practice containing...both spiritual, moral, mental and physical elements." Although, the expression clearly subsumes teaching, in its widest sense,[5] and vocational training.[6] However, as Pearce and Stevens seek to point out,[7] Lord Hailsham's *dictum* in *McMullen*[8] did not include *research*. But they qualify that comment by stating that, "Despite a general unwillingness to make value judgments which may be subjective, the courts have sought to distinguish research which is of truly educational value and worthy of charitable status, from that which is not. Research which is of no educational value or of purely esoteric value to the researcher will not be charitable." That, it is suggested, is a valiant attempt to crystallise the various *dicta* and authorities on the area.

On the one hand, is the statement of Harman J in *Re Shaw*[9] that, "...if the object [of the research] be the increase of knowledge, that is not in itself a charitable object unless it be combined with teaching or education." In *Shaw,* the judge had held that a gift by the playwright, George Bernard Shaw had left, in his will a gift, for research into a forty letter alphabet and the translation of one of his plays into it was not charitable. That decision may not stand, in fact, very well beside the judge's own comment. The problems which attach – especially for those people who are not native English speakers – to English pronunciation and spelling are notorious. Hence, research into their simplification through a modification of the alphabet can surely be properly subsumed under *education*. Similarly the translation of one of the testator's plays into the proposed new idiom, by way of illustration of its operation can surely be regarded as combined with *teaching*.

Yet a more complex situation, which confuses Pearce and Steven's view still further, has arisen. In *Re Hopkins*,[10] the testatrix had left a third of her residual estate to the Francis Bacon Society Inc, "...to be earmarked and applied towards finding the Bacon – Shakespeare manuscripts and in the event of the same having been discovered by the date of my death then for the general purposes of the work and propaganda of the society." The trustees of the will took out a summons for the purpose of deciding, *inter alia*, whether the bequest created a valid charitable trust. Wilberforce J was faced with a number of difficulties, the first, as he noted,[11] being the construction of the bequest itself. In other words, what was meant by, "...finding the Bacon-Shakespeare manuscripts..."?

After a consideration of the evidence which was available to him, Wilberforce J took the view[12] that the, "...trusts on which this gift is to be held are to use the money to search for the manuscripts of the plays commonly ascribed to Shakespeare, believed by the testatrix and the society to have been written by Bacon, and that it is these trusts which, if they are to be valid, must be shown to be charitable in the legal sense." Having reached that conclusion, the judge was then forced to deal with an argument advanced by the next of kin that the bequest was made for a purpose which was manifestly futile that it did not even qualify for consideration as a possible charitable gift. Once again, after a broad consideration of the arguments and various opinions on the issue, Wilberforce J concluded[13] that, although the evidence showed that the discovery of any manuscripts of the plays was unlikely, the degree of such improbability would justify the court in placing an initial interdict on the testatrix's benefaction.

That finding then led the judge to consider whether the gift was of a charitable character. In reaching the conclusion[14] that it was of such a character, Wilberforce J stated that, "...the court must decide each case as best it can, on the evidence available to it, as to benefit, and within the moving spirit of decided cases, it would seem to me that a bequest for the purpose of search, or research, for the original manuscripts of England's greatest dramatist (whoever he was) would be well within the law's conception of charitable purposes. The discovery of such manuscripts, or of one such manuscript, would be of the highest value to history and to literature... Without any undue exercise of the imagination, it would surely be a reasonable expectation that the revelation of a manuscript would contribute, possibly decisively, to a solution of the authorship problem and this alone is benefit enough. It might also lead to improvements in the text. It might lead to more accurate dating."

There was, of course, one problem which faced Wilberforce J in *Re Hopkins*, and that, inevitably, was the decision, and *dictum*, of Harman J in *Re Shaw*.[15] In *Hopkins*, the judge interpreted[16] Harman J's *dictum* as meaning that *education*, "...must be used in a wide sense, certainly extending beyond teaching, and that the requirement is that, in order to be charitable, research must either be of educational value to the researcher or must be so directed as to lead to something which will pass into the store of knowledge in an area which education may cover – education in this last context extending to the formation of literary taste and appreciation." Few would question the last extract from Wilberforce J's judgment, though many might query the utility of seeking to find that someone other than the attributed author was the creator of Shakespeare's works.

In *Hopkins*, Wilberforce J noted[17] that two of the experts[18] who gave evidence considered it *certain* that Bacon could not have written the plays and poems in question. They based that view, the judge said,[19] "...on a consideration of the literary style, temperament, cast of mind and attitude to life of Francis Bacon". It is quite safe to say that Bacon, to say the least was a paradoxical character: first, he would, doubtless, have inclined to Harman J's view of the law, rather than to that of Wilberforce J – after all, he took the view[20] relating to judges that, "...their office is *jus dicere*, and not *jus dare*". In other words the judicial duty is to state, rather than change, the law. At the same time, Bacon was instrumental in bringing about the downfall of Lord Chief Justice Coke - in many respects, a far worthier man. As Baker describes[21] the situation: "[Coke] began to release, by habeas corpus, prisoners committed by Ellesmere for contempt of injunctions and he encouraged such prisoners to prosecute their opponents for the crime of impeaching the judgments of the king's courts. Unfortunately for Coke, his hints were taken up by the unworthiest of litigants, and after a misguided attempt by a crank to indict various officials including Ellesmere, the dispute was referred to James I in 1616. Coke was then in political disfavour for other reasons, and Ellesmere combined with Francis Bacon and the Duke of Buckingham to engineer his downfall. Coke was dismissed from office in the same year." The paradoxical nature of Bacon's character has been emphasised by Holdsworth who has written[22] that Bacon was a man of great ideas. In his various roles as a, "...philosopher considering the welfare of mankind, as a statesman considering the solution of the political problems of the day, as a lawyer considering problems of law reform, he never lost sight of those ideals." At the same time, Holdsworth notes that Bacon was no mere academic speculator, "His legal studies had enabled him to earn his living at the bar; and he hoped that his political speculations would give him the high place in the state which he was conscious that he could fill. But in Elizabeth's and James I's courts, such a place could only be won by flattery and intrigue. Bacon stooped to employ these arts, not seeing the fatal effect which their employment was having upon his character. This effect was the more fatal because Bacon had a very unemotional nature, with the result that, having no very keen sense of personal honour, he was too ready to take his tone from the society in which he was placed. But the moral tone of Elizabeth's court was low, and that of James I's court was lower. Being unprotected by a sense of honour, and absorbed in his pursuit of his ideals, he was led to do acts which men of less lofty ideals, but with a keener sense of personal honour, would have instinctively avoided." From that account, it might be relatively easy to suggest that Bacon could very well have written the works traditionally ascribed to Shakespeare! However, it cannot, as Wilberforce J noted in *Hopkins*, be regarded as the whole story. Of course, it is not always the apparently newsworthy poets who give rise to legal issues – thus, for instance, the poet Dylan Thomas, whose life, at any rate according to one biographer,[23] might legitimately be described as *rumbustious*, only gave rise to one reported decision and posthumous at that. *Thomas* v *Times Book Co*[24] involved an action brought by the adminstratrix of Dylan Thomas's estate to recover the original manuscripts of *Under Milk Wood*. The defendant asserted that he had purchased the manuscript from another person who claimed to have received it from the author. The alleged donee, who was a BBC producer, had worked closely with Dylan Thomas during the time when he was working on the play. A few days before the poet was due to leave for the United States where he was to read from his work, the play was completed and the original manuscript was reproduced by the alleged donee. The manuscript was returned to the author who left it in a London public house. Dylan Thomas then called the alleged donee and asked for stencilled copies of the manuscript. When those were delivered, Dylan Thomas then told the alleged donee that, if he was able to find the original manuscript, he could keep it. He also mentioned a number of places where the manuscript could have been left.[25] Whilst the author was in the United States, the alleged donee found the manuscript. However, before returning to England, Dylan Thomas died. The plaintiff alleged that there was no intention to make a gift or, in the alternative, the gift should fail for want of delivery, the only issue being the ownership of the manuscript which was, admittedly, valuable.

Plowman J dismissed the claim, thus deciding that the defendant had established that Dylan Thomas had, in fact, made a gift of the manuscript to the donee. The administratrix, who was also Dylan Thomas's widow, had argued that the story advanced by the defendants was so improbable as to be incredible. Thus, it had been argued, in the words of the judge,[26] that the, "...late Dylan Thomas was always hard up, and on the evidence it appears quite clearly that he was. It is said that he was setting off on this trip to the United States in order to raise some money, and that, no doubt, is equally true. It is said that this is a valuable work of a great poet; that he must have known that the manuscript was of considerable value; that he had previous experience of using his manuscripts as a form, as it were, of currency; that he had sold manuscripts of poems previously for an odd pound or two; that the manuscript was a thing over which he had lavished great care and devotion for a number of years, and that in those circumstances it is really inconceivable that he should have made this present of it..." In the context of all of the other evidence, Plowman J was unwilling to accept those arguments.

Thomas v Times Book Co may be of interest as a matter of strict law in that it refers to issues such as the relative credibility of witnesses, or the burden of proof in regard to claims against a deceased estate or constructive delivery for the purposes of a gift. (Indeed, were it not, it would scarcely have found its way into the law reports). However, what was not argued was the *justice* of the widow/administratrix's claim. This may appear, *prima facie* at least something of a *lacuna* for she was, after all, likely to have been, at the very least, in part dependent on her late husband's rather erratic financial provision. From a literary point of view, the issue of justice is of some interest because of the rather disturbingly rudimentary idea of justice which is apparent from some of his later poems such as "Over Sir John's Hill" and "Lament".[27]

2. The Writer in the Law: The Case of D H Lawrence

a) Lawrence and the Literary/Censorship Laws

Immediately the name of D H Lawrence and law regarding restrictions on literary expression and censorship are mentioned, the cases involving *Lady Chatterley's Lover* and, to a lesser degree, *The Rainbow* and *Women in Love* spring to mind. However, the thrust of this book is not the novel, but poetry, rhetoric and the law. Not altogether surprisingly, however, Lawrence's work as a poet attracted the attention of the legal system. Lawrence's attitude towards censorship, particularly towards depictions (verbal or visual) of the human form can be found in a poem. "Neptune's Little Affair with Freedom", which appeared in a collection entitled *Nettles*, published in 1930.[28]

The poem begins with a somewhat unlikely Father Neptune conjecturing as to where he would live were he not to live in the sea:

Father Neptune one day to freedom did say:
If ever I lived upon dry-y land,
The spot I should hit on would be little Britain –

Said Freedom: Why that's my own I – sland! –

Neptune then emphasises the qualities of his new-found island in naively glowing terms:
"Oh what a bright little I - sland!
A right little, tight little I – sland!
Seek all the world round there's none can be found
So happy as our little I – sland"

But as he walked up the shore, forgetting that, in the sea, he had always lived naked:
So Father Neptune walked up the shore
bright and naked aft and fore
as he's always been, since the Flood and before.

The results become only too apparent:

And instantly rose a great uproar
of Freedom shrieking till her throat was sore:
Arrest him, he's indecent, he's obscene what's more! –

That last stanza inevitably takes us to the distinction between *indecency* and *obscenity*, but, then the law's response becomes immediately apparent:

Policemen and the British nation
threw themselves on him in indignation
with handcuffs, and took him to the police-station.

The sea-god said, in consternation:
But I came at Freedom's invitation! –
So then they charged him with defamation.

The poem clearly contains indirect reference to prosecutions in relation to some of D H Lawrence's art works, where he had offended, some, public sensibility by painting pubic hair on some nude studies.[29] The poem, though, ends with some rather heavy irony, with the denizens on

Neptune's more usual aquatic domain revelling in the time that they thought their King was having in his, in the poem's concluding line, "...right little, tight little I - sland":

> And all the sea-nymphs out at sea
> rocked on the waves and sang lustily
> thinking old Neptune was off on a spree
> with giddy Freedom in the land of the Free

"Neptune's Little Affair with Freedom" cannot truly be regarded as one of Lawrence's major poems, though for the purposes of this book, it does contain features of interest. Implicit, first, in Lawrence's rhetoric is that there is, albeit uncertainly, a gradation between *indecency* and *obscenity*. It is unlikely that many people would disagree that such is the case, but ascertaining how the distinction is to be drawn initially and, therefore, be accurately and appropriately maintained is very much another matter. However, a useful starting point is the decision of the Scottish High Court of Justiciary in *McGowan* v *Langmuir*.[30] Although that case was decided after the incidents involving some of Lawrence's works had occurred, it seems unlikely that the judges who decided it would not have heard of the incidents. The cases involved an initial conviction in respect of the appellant's keeping certain indecent or obscene prints for sale or gain. By a majority, the High Court declined to disturb the conviction, though Lord Justice-General Clyde expressed[31] some doubt as to whether the conviction was, in fact, correct.

For the purpose of the instant discussion, the most important of the judgments was that of Lord Sands, who began[32] by saying that he did not believe that the words *indecent* and *obscene* were synonymous, although the two expressions shaded into one another. There was a difference in meaning, he thought, which was easier to illustrate than to define. "For a male bather," he said "to enter into the water nude in the presence of ladies would be indecent, but it would not be obscene." Lord Sands went on to say that the matter might be expressed in an ascending scale: "Positive – Immodest – Comparative – Indecent; Superlative – Obscene." However, he continued, those were not rigid categories and the same conduct, which in some circumstances, may merit only the milder description may, in other circumstances deserve a harder one. *Indecent*, he said, was a milder term than *obscene*, but it would satisfy the purpose of the case at hand if the prints in question could be regarded as *indecent*. Lord Sand's view, then, seems to accord with that expressed, sardonically, in Lawrence's poem. Lord Sands then emphasised that he was referring to decency and indecency in relation to sex and to nudity and to physiological function.[33] He also necessarily, pointed out that *indecency* referred to that which was contrary to *decency* in relation to "...exposure, conduct, or gesture..." in accordance with the standards which prevailed in the relevant jurisdiction at the time in question. He was also of the view that there was nothing indecent in the human frame *per se*, because, "...that would be a libel on nature." However, that view was subject to obvious exception.

By way of example, the judge then had regard to the conventions which attached to works of art – though, as he himself pointed out, there had been differences of opinion as to how far the conventions ought to extend. "The concession," he stated "if such it is to be regarded, is hedged in certain ways. The nude must be impersonal." Thus, Lord Sands continued, a "...picture of the nude which a man might display in his drawing room as a work of art would, however perfect in that regard, be regarded as grossly indecent if the person depicted were his wife or daughter." That, in the judge's view immediately illustrated the relativity of the notion of indecency and the difficulty of pronouncing upon it apart from surrounding circumstances.[34]

Lord Sands then turned his attention [35] to the very more straightforward (*prima facie* at least) clearer notion of obscenity.[36] The other judges – Lord Justice-General Clyde and Lord Blackburn – were altogether more concerned with the operation of the relevant statutory provision.[37] It must be said, though, the former was doubtful[38] of the relativity argument which had been advanced by Lord Sands and considered that where the indiscriminate exposure of pictures was calculated to prejudice good morals and to suggest impure thoughts to the observer, he had difficulty in, "...seeing why it should not apply to the equally indiscriminate exhibition to the public view of representations of the human form in picture galleries and indeed in many public places still more generally accessible." One supposes that the same considerations might be applicable to say, the broadcasting of lewd poems. *McGowan* v *Langmuir* is an interesting case, and Lord Sands's judgment especially, because it represents a genuine attempt, even though it may not be wholly successful, to distinguish the notions of *indecency* and *obscenity* in a relevant and relative manner. That is, in turn, of importance because there has not been an equivalent attempt so to do in any other common law jurisdiction. The decision has been regarded as being of sufficient importance to have been noted in another major decision [39] which is relevant to the situation in which Lawrence was to find himself. [40] *McGowan* v *Langmuir* has also been anthologised.[41] In Scots Law, it should further be stated that there is a wide *imprimatur* for denunciation and punishment for the dissemination and display of *indecent* matter to be found in Macdonald's[42] statement that, "All shamelessly indecent conduct is criminal." Even though it may actually be open to question, Macdonald's bold statement has been adopted by the High Court of Justiciary in one case.[43] Perhaps, though, more important, there is an analogue in English law: in *R* v *Mayling*,[44] Ashworth J in the Court of Appeal stated that, "It is convenient first to consider the offence alleged to have been committed by the defendant. It is described in the indictment as 'committing an act outraging public decency' and not out of any statute. In the judgment of this court it is now well established that an offence so described is punishable at common law and, indeed, it was not contended on behalf of the defendant that no such offence existed." At the same time, it is certainly true that *Mayling* has little factual connection with the topic under discussion, but the more general tenor of the offence, which appears to date from the 17th Century,[45] has some analogue with Lord Sands's comments, as earlier discussed.[46]

Having, thus, noted the law's uncertainty about what the lesser, as it seems broadly to have been accepted, allegation of *indecency* entails, it does not seem as though the law has fared any better in its view of the greater, as it might seem, allegation of *obscenity*. I am not seeking to provide a detailed disquisition on the law relating to *obscenity* in Lawrence's home jurisdiction as that is beyond the avowed scope of the book and it has been attempted by other writers elsewhere.[47] What I do seek to attempt is to draw attention to the more than slightly confused entity which was used by Freedom in Lawrence's poem.

Originally that test, as is well known, had been enunciated by Lord Cockburn CJ in *R* v *Hicklin*,[48] who had said that, "I think the test of obscenity is this, whether the tendency of the matter charged as obscenity is to deprave and corrupt those whose minds are open to such moral influences and into whose hands a publication of this sort may fall." *Hicklin* is important for the purposes of this discussion, not necessarily because of its subject matter,[49] but because of its procedural history. It involved an appeal from the decision of a Recorder, quashing the order of justices for the destruction of pamphlets [50] under the then applicable legislation.[51] Justices were to figure prominently in one of the incidents involving the works of D H Lawrence.[52] Ultimately, Lord Cockburn CJ's attempted definition became subsumed into statute.[53] But the real question which must now be asked is whether Lord Cockburn CJ's definition in *Hicklin*[54] and its statutory derivatives are what Freedom in the Lawrence poem had in mind? There is certainly evidence from the case law which suggests that, in all probability, it was not. Thus, in *DPP* v *Whyte*,[55] Lord Wilberforce had suggested that was the case when he had said that Lord Cockburn CJ's words in *Hicklin* had largely been ignored in earlier cases – courts simply considered whether the relevant publication could be regarded as being colloquially[56] obscene with any tendency to deprave and corrupt being presumed. That was a position which had, actually, been adopted by Windeyer J of the High Court of Australia in *Crowe* v *Graham*[57] when he stated that, "Writings are obscene by reason of what they describe, express or bring to mind, and the words by which they do it. It is assumed incontrovertibly by the common law that obscene writings do deprave and corrupt morals, by causing dirty mindedness, by creating or pandering to a taste for the obscene." In the *Whyte* case, in contradiistinction, Lord Wilberforce stated that the statutory provision did not deal with articles *which merely shock*, [58] however many people. However, in *Crowe* v *Graham*,[59] Windeyer J emphatically took the view that, "...whatever secondary or additional meanings have been laid upon the word obscene, it has not lost the meaning of filthy, bawdy, lewd and disgusting." In that context, it may not come as much of a surprise that Windeyer J declined, given the context of Lord Sands's judgment in *McGowan* v *Langmuir*,[60] to discuss the meaning of *indecent*, which also appeared in the relevant New South Wales legislation,[61] with which the case was concerned.

Those are not the sole – nor, perhaps, even the most immediate authorities, as Australian law may, at best, be peripheral to the main thrust of the instant discussion. In the central case of *R* v *Anderson*,[62] the Court of Criminal Appeal in England quashed a conviction where the trial judge had, *inter alia*, directed a jury that *obscene* meant "'repulsive', 'filthy', 'loathsome' or 'lewd'". That case involved the, by now notorious *Oz, School Kids Issue* and the views expressed by the trial judge would, certainly, have been endorsed by one commentator in a legal journal,[63] who described the defendants in *Anderson* as "revolting creatures" and "admittedly perverted and evil young editors." At the same time, those same, and predictable, feelings of revulsion gave rise to another issue. In *Anderson*, it was argued by distinguished counsel[64] that, "... many of the illustrations in the magazine were so lewd and unpleasant that they would shock in the first instance and then tend to repel. In other words, it was said that they had an adversive effect and that far from tempting those who had not experienced the acts to take part in them, they would put off those who might be so tempted to conduct themselves." Indeed, the same distinguished counsel had successfully argued that very proposition in an earlier case.[65] All of that can without drawing too long a bow, lead to the strangely paradoxical conclusion that an article might be *obscene* in the sense as used by Freedom in Lawrence's poem, but not into legal sense. Indeed, its very colloquial obscenity might actually preclude its legal obscenity!

The issues and the cases which have been hitherto discussed have largely related to sexual conduct, though that is not the whole extent of the controversy: thus, in one case,[66] it had clearly been held that a particular book could be regarded obscene if it were suggested that the effects of drug taking were such that the practice might be regarded as pleasant or healthful. It seems to follow that one might substitute *any* practices which might be enjoyed by some individuals for the drug abuse which gave rise to that decision. Again, in turn, that gives rise to the position of the decision maker: it is quite clear from some of the decisions which have been mentioned[67] that the question of *obscenity* is solely a matter for the trier of fact.[68] That means there is no room for expert opinion (in the present context, it must be remembered that it is the nature of the concept with which we are presently concerned rather than any statutory defences, such as "public good"[69]). This is probably inevitable, as the decision of the House of Lords in *DPP* v *Jordan*[70] held that expert evidence was inadmissible where, in effect, as Lord Kilbrandon put the matter,[71] the evidence was to be to the effect that it might be for the public good for the public to be depraved or corrupted, quite regardless of any literary or artistic merit which the article in question may or may not possess.

Jordan, and its peculiar submissions, notwithstanding, the position of the trier of fact may not, in any way, be less problematic. That point was effectively made by Stable J in *R v Martin Secker and Warburg*,[72] who stated that the, "...charge is that the tendency of the book is to corrupt and deprave. Then you say: 'Well, corrupt and deprove whom?' to which the answer is: those whose minds are open to such immoral influences and into whose hands a publication of this kind may fall. What exactly does that mean?" That, it is submitted means (if not actually a great deal more) that questions for the trier of fact may be of an especially speculative character. For instance, it should readily be apparent that the same article may or may not be obscene depending on the context of its publication. Thus, many publications would be regarded as tending to deprave or corrupt, say, fourteen year old schoolgirls from a relatively sheltered background and, hence, a distributor who sells such an article in places frequented by such girls would clearly be guilty of an offence. However, were that distributor to retail the same article in a gentlemen's club (of which he might be a member), the answer might be less clear cut. The market might also be relevant to the seller's intent – howsoever relevant that itself may be.[73]

Even assuming some awareness of that convoluted legal background, authors or distributors are not going to find, in the same way as the trier of fact, that an especially easy process, whatever they seek to do. That, in fact, was precisely what happened to D.H. Lawrence. In late 1928 and early 1929, the writer's situation, as described by Worthen,[74] was far from unhappy so, in his own words about life in France, "its sunny here all the time, and quiet and very pleasant: the people are all very nice: why should one hurry away to something worse!"[75] Yet, though matters were seemingly almost idyllic in French Bandol, the effects of Lawrence's notoriety in England were waiting to be felt. In early January 1929, a registered envelope which contained his two typed copies of the almost completed collection of poems to be known as *Pansies* was opened by the English postal authorities. The official reason, as described by Worthen,[76] was a random search of the mail for the purpose of checking "...whether letters or other matters not conveyed at that rate..." were in the package. The reality, Lawrence's biographer comments, was somewhat different: ever since most of the copies of *Lady Chatterley's Lover* had entered

England before the authorities were alerted, any package from Lawrence was, *ipso facto*, suspect.

There was, though, to be an immediate reward for the authorities in the shape of Lawrence's introduction to the poems, which, given the preceding discussion, deserves comment. On a general note, in the forward to *Pansies*, Lawrence wrote that the poems were, "...called *Pansies* because they are rather *Pensées* than anything else. Pascal and Le Bruyére wrote their *Pensées* in prose, but it has always seemed to me that a real thought, a single thought, not an argument can only exist easily in verse, or in some poetic form." Yet the initial interest was almost certainly generated by a passage in *Introduction to Pansies*, where Lawrence discusses. "...the poor simple scapegoat words representing parts of man himself; words that the cowardly and unclean mind has driven out into the limbo of the unconsciousness, whence they return upon us looming and magnified out of all proportion, frightening us beyond all reason."

To illustrate a proposition which many of us today might regard as self evident, Lawrence refers to the well-known poem of Dean Swift's, "Celia", in which every stanza ends with, in Lawrence's own words, the, "...mad, maddened refrain", "But- Celia, Celia, Celia shits!" Swift's coprophobia is by now too well known as to require documentation. Nevertheless, the typescripts were seized and sent to the Home-Office and the Home Secretary, Sir William Joynson-Hicks, who had been advised that there was no, "...possible doubt that these [packages] contained indecent matter and, as such are liable to seizure."[77] Yet on the strength of the Swift quotation, is it possible, even with the benefit of hindsight (howsoever dubious that might be) to justify the Home Office's comment to the Minister? In *McGowan* v *Langmuir*, earlier discussed,[78] Lord Sands seemed to regard *indecency* and *obscenity* as part of a continuum, although he did make an *obiter* reference to physiological function. At the same time, it ought to be clear from Stable J's comment in *Martin Secker and Warburg*[79] that the book in question did, "...deal with candour or, if you prefer it, crudity with the realities of human love and of human intercourse. There is no getting away from that, and the Crown say: 'Well, that is sheer filth' is it? Is the act of sexual passion sheer filth? It may be an error of taste to write about it. It may be a matter in which, perhaps, old fashioned people would mourn the reticence that was observed in these matters yesterday, but is it sheer filth?"

There is sure a clear conceptual difference between the activity described by Stable J and that which aroused the interest of the Home Office. Lawrence, in his *Introduction to Pansies* had the following, surely apposite, comments to make about Swift's attitude to Celia: "His arrogant mind," states Lawrence, "could not see now how much worse it would be if Celia didn't shit. His physical sympathies were too weak, his guts were too cold to sympathise with Celia in her natural functions. His insolent and sickly squeamish mind just turned her into a thing of horror, because she was merely natural and went to the W.C." Put another way, is transference of revulsion, at whatever level, from one bodily function to another in any wise to be justified? Has, then, the law seen anything similar? Of course, both regrettably and contextually, it has. Although it may be thought that the present discussion presents one, rather idiosyncratic author going, as it were, on "...a frolic of his own",[80] the legal obverse is an interesting illustration of the kind of process which seems to have been undertaken in the Home Office with regard to *Pansies*. It is also, in its own way, as perverse.

The issue before the Full Court of the Family Court of Australia in *Re P and P*[81] was the vexed matter of the sterilisation of a young woman with a serious intellectual disability. In that context, the issue of sterilisation as a method of menstrual management arose. The Court[82] did not disagree[83] with the view which had been expressed at first instance that, were that the only factor favouring sterilisation in the instant case, then the operation could not be justified on that ground alone. The Court then went on to note a comment in a Report by the Australian Family Law Council[84] regarding an apparent inconsistency of approach to menstruation compared with other physiological functions such as urinary and faecal control. The Court took the view that that was, "...an invalid comparison as the latter are necessary to maintain life and it could not be seriously suggested that colostomies are an appropriate alternative. Menstruation on the other hand has particular relevance to reproductive functions, but not to the maintenance of life." Unfortunately, the Court was seriously mistaken with respect to the medical history.[85] In Comfort's remarkable book *The Anxiety Makers: Some Curious Sexual Preoccupations of the Medical Profession*[86], published in 1967, the author describes the remarkable career of Sir William Arbuthnot Lane. In cases of chronic intestinal stasis, generally better known as constipation, Lane, not merely urged colostomy, but actually carried it out. In Comfort's *ipsissima verba*: "To treat the disorder he resorted with typical boldness to excision of the colon – a heroic measure which he carried out with superb skill. Cases of all kinds where the cause of the disease was obscure, from rheumatic fever in children to thyroid disease in adults, trusted Lane to remove their colons. Most of them survived the operation; some found their health improved by the ordeal."

From the point of view of this discussion, it is clear that the content of the poems in *Pansies*, as opposed to the introduction, is pornographically and scatologically limited. Worthen, relying on Pollnitz, notes[87] that the words indicative of indecent material were scant enough. There were "turds" and "turd" in "The Jeune Fille" and in "Be A Demon" and "arse" and "member" in "Demon Justice". Of course, there were some rather more obliquely sexual references in other poems – such as the allusions to "Lady Jane", the significance of which will not have been lost on commentators on Lawrence[88] - though those allusions could well have been thoroughly lost on those Home Office functionaries who reported the arrival of the package from Lawrence to Joynson-Hicks.

Inevitably, that was not the end of the story. On 28th of February 1929, there was a Parliamentary Debate on the seizure of *Pansies*,[89] with most of the relevant questions on the order paper standing in the politically sensitive name of Ellen Wilkinson.[90] The recipient was the Home Secretary, Sir William Joynson-Hicks (who has already been mentioned[91] and who later became Lord Brentford) who was described by Lawrence in a contemporaneous letter,[92] as an "imbecile". In the context of that debate, in response to a question from Mr Fredrick Pethic Lawrence,[93] the Home Secretary had stated that, "At present there is no censorship. It is not until a book or any other obscene document is brought to my notice that I exercise my position. A censorship would imply that every book should be read by the body of censors, which would be impossible." As regards *Pansies*, he stated that he had been advised that there was no doubt that the relevant typescripts contained indecent matter and, as such were, "...liable to seizure. I have, however given instructions that they shall be detained for two months to enable the author to establish the contrary if he desires to do so." That response, though, should be read together with an evasive and negative response to the question as to whether, before books were seized, officials had had any literary advice as to their nature.

The same questioner then asked whether, from Sir William's answers to those questions and others, some person or persons had come to a preliminary decision that the book was of an indecent character. Pethick – Lawrence, on behalf of Miss Wilkinson, went on to inquire as to who were those persons who were entitled to give this provisional opinion and what qualifications they did have to make such a literary discrimination. Once again, the Home Secretary's response was less than helpful: "In the first place", he said, "in this case, the Postmaster - General makes the first determination that this is a prima facie and a case of indecency. He then sends it to me and if I agree, I send it on to the Director of Public Prosecutions. It is not a question of literary merit at all and if the hon. Member has any doubt, I will show him this book in question. It contains grossly indecent matter." If the then Home Secretary is to be regarded as correct, then community standards have changed more radically than might usually have been accepted. The previous discussion seems to suggest a pre-adolescent scatological prurience coupled with an obliquity which was unlikely to be immediately recognisable.[94]

The emphasis of the questioning to which the Home Secretary was subjected then changed[95] to the possibility of the privacy of sealed postal packets being violated. The issue of the use of the mails tends to show, it is submitted, that legislature and judiciary have learned little from the rather strange exchanges resulting from the *Pansies* episode. If one were to seek to be charitable, one can only say that the Home Secretary had found himself in a situation where he was defending indefensible practice in a scarcely defensible socio-legal historical context. Not altogether surprisingly, this particular strange continuum did not end with the questions asked in Parliament.

The effectively circular nature of the debate surrounding *Pansies* is well illustrated by the later decision of the English Court of Criminal Appeal in *R* v *Stanley*,[96] which dealt with the transmission of articles through the post, a major issue arising out of the parliamentary questions.[97] *Stanley* dealt with the operation of the United Kingdom *Post Office Act* 1953 which made it an offence to "...send or attempt to send or procure to be sent a postal packet which...encloses any indecent or obscene print, painting, photograph, lithograph, cinematograph film, book, card or written communication, or any indecent or obscene article whether similar to the above or not" .The way in which that legislation was framed suggests that its drafters had taken the conceptual issues raised by the *Pansies* controversies into scant, if any, account. This appears to be more so when the judgment of Lord Parker CJ is taken further into consideration.

In *Stanley*, the jury had reached the conclusion that the articles in question were not obscene, but that they were indecent. It was, hence, argued before the appellate court that the words meant the same and that an alternative verdict was not possible. The legal basis of that view was another Scots case, *Galletly v Laird*.[98] There, Lord Cooper, probably the most prominent Scots judge of his generation,[99] had said[100] that he was willing to accept, in common parlance, that *obscene* was a stronger epithet that *indecent*, and, indeed, to accept the analysis of Lord Sands in *McGowan v Langmuir*,[101] but, at the same time, he did not consider that those matters played any part in the drafting of the legislation in question. In Lord Cooper's opinion, the section had been intentionally drafted in a tautological manner, "…to convey a single idea and a perfectly clear idea at that, and it would be palpably absurd to ask courts to wade through such a collection as has been produced in these cases for the purpose of uselessly classifying the condemned material into different grades of indecency." In *Stanley*, Lord Parker CJ did not regard[102] Lord Cooper as saying anything which could not be gleaned from his *ipsissima verba* – that is, that the two words were expressing the same ideal but in varying degrees. Further to confuse the issue, the Lord Chief Justice then expressed[103] entire agreement with the views of Lord Sands in *McGowan v Langmuir* and did not imagine that Lord Cooper was saying anything other than that, as the words conveyed a simple idea, it was permissible for the charge to be made in the alternative. He went on to say[104] that, "…an indecent article is not necessarily obscene, whereas an obscene article almost certainly must be indecent." However, that statement has clearly failed to take into account conceptual differences, to which Lord Sands had drawn attention, which , though they might have escaped the attention of Freedom in the "Neptune" poem, ought not to have escaped the attention of lawyers or those responsible for the law's administration.

It should be noted that Lawrence's problems with censorship did not end with his poems (or novels). Once again in 1929, Lawrence exhibited a variety of his paintings which attracted not inconsiderable public attention.[105] Trotter described[106] the exhibition in the following terms: "throughout the congestion three schools were clearly distinguishable:

those who condemned the pictures as obscene, but split wide on the question of repressive action; those who defended the pictures as not obscene, and/or asked what, in any case, was meant by obscene and what is its legal definition. The third group, welcome only for its non-use of the hideous word *obscene*, had come in search of dirty pictures and, in varying degrees of forcefulness, expressed disgust at finding none… The daily litter of cast-away catalogues on the stair and landings was interpreted as a manifestation of outraged modesty; but disappointed prurience was at least an equal contributor." Ultimately, the exhibition was interrupted by police on 5th July 1929 and thirteen paintings were impounded until the following month, together with four copies of a book of reproductions of the paintings.

All of that, in turn, led to a hearing before magistrate Mr Frederick Mead. The conduct of the hearing roused the ire of Lawrence in his poem "Innocent England", which appeared in the collection *Nettles* in 1930. At its title might suggest, *Nettles* is altogether more caustic than *Pansies*. "Innocent England" begins with Lawrence setting out, rhetorically, the reason for the hearing's taking place:

> Oh what a pity, Oh! don't you agree
> that figs aren't found in the land of the free!
>
> Fig-trees don't grow in my native land;
> there's never a fig-leaf near at hand
>
> when you want one; so I did without'
> and that is what the row's about

Lawrence then seeks to ridicule the police intervention which, according to Trotter,[107] was clumsy and obvious:

> Virginal, pure policeman came
> and hid their faces for very shame,
>
> while they carried the shameless things away
> to gaol, to be hid from the light of day.

Lawrence then turns his attention to the conduct of the hearing itself. There might, indeed, have been some concern[108] regarding a possible nexus between the magistrate, described less than flatteringly by Lawrence in the following extract, and the prosecuting solicitor, who had appeared for the police in the suppression of Lawrence's novel, *The Rainbow* in 1915. Apart from any other considerations, Mr Mead was aged eighty-two and, according to Trotter, his "preferred victims" were elderly and often distinguished perpetrators of nocturnal incidents in London parks:[109]

> And Mr Mead, that old, old lily
> said: "Gross! coarse! hideous!" – and I, like a silly,
> thought he meant the faces of the police-court officials,
> and how right he was, and I signed my initials
> to confirm what he said; but alas, he meant
> my pictures, and on the proceedings went.

In the event, an undertaking was drafted by the prosecuting solicitor which was agreed by the magistrate and the defence: The case was to be adjourned *sine die* and the pictures were to be restored to their owners, though the books of reproductions were to be destroyed. Lawrence, in "Innocent England", recognised that the apparent affront to the public, was the inclusion of pubic hair on the human objects of his work. All could have been put to rights, he suggested, by dubious concealment:

> The upshot was, my picture must burn
> that English artists might finally learn
> when they painted a nude, to put a cache *sexe* on,
> a cache sexe, a cache sexe, or else begone!
> A fig-leaf; or, if you cannot find it
> a wreath of mist, with nothing behind it.
> A wreath of mist is the usual thing
> in the north, to hide where the turtles sing.

Worthen suggests [110] that the ridiculed magistrate's only real contribution to the faintly farcical proceedings was his suggestion that the paintings' obscenity and their value as works of art were quite independent of one another. This was in spite of the fact that counsel for the defence had, with the aim of showing that the paintings were serious works of art, to call evidence from Sir William Orpen, Glyn Philpot and Augustus John, as well as a number of art professors.[111] The collection of poems entitled *Nettles* was, as might have been guessed from "Innocent England" a response from Lawrence to the events surrounding the exhibition, although, inevitably and deliberately, he extrapolates from them. However, as fate would have it, Lawrence was denied the opportunity to assess the effect of his vitriol: the poems were not published[112] until 13th March 1930, which was eleven days after his death.

b. Lawrence in the Public Law Area

It would be quite wrong, despite the foregoing, to regard, D H Lawrence's involvement with the legal system to concentrate exclusively on his effect on literary and censorship laws. Many other issues arose from his life in England during the 1914-18 War, especially the way his life was to be made all the more difficult as he was unfit for military service. In particular, the events which, indirectly, surround Lawrence's expulsion from Cornwall are of importance both to a study of Lawrence's socio-literary attitudes and to the development of some approaches of areas of public law in England.

From March 1916 until mid-October 1917, at the height of the 1914-18 War, D H Lawrence and his German born wife, Frieda, lived at Higher Tregerthen, a small cluster of buildings, including three cottages, near Zennor in Cornwall. In recent years, a restless disaffection for his fellow English and increasingly pessimistic premonitions of the social, intellectual and moral future of England had seen the gradual development in Lawrence of an almost obsessive compulsion to abandon his homeland and settle in Florida, preferably as part of a colony of like-minded artists and thinkers in an idealised society which they referred to as *Rananim*.[113] However, Lawrence's refusal to attest to his willingness to serve in the British armed forces if so required precluded any chance of his being able to obtain a passport, which left the impoverished Lawrences stranded in Britain[114] and, for a time, Higher Tregerthen did provide a relative haven – it was cheap to rent and there was accommodation for guests and it might have provided a symbolic *Rananim*. On the other hand, it was wartime when patriotic emotions were heightened and suspicion surmounted mundane social activity and interaction. In addition, Government, in this instance supported by an, albeit reluctantly, united Parliament, removed impediments to legislation of a kind which would not normally have been tolerated in the cause of national security.

From the outset, the Lawrences had attracted a hostile reception in Zennor: thus, Stanley Hocking, whose family farm lay just below Higher Tregerthen, has described how even their appearance was regarded as suspicious. "They were different," he was quoted as saying,[115] "There was nobody in the locality who dressed the way he did...[Lawrence's] corduroy suit and slouch hat and Victorian collar and tie were unusual." In addition, it was wartime and this observer stated that, "Then there were the submarines sinking our ships right in view of Lawrence's cottage. People knew he was English enough, but of course since he was married to a German they didn't know ihis loyalties had remained English. And then the remark was being passed "You never know what people are up to. They could have a secret code for signalling to the German submarines and giving the position of our ships.' " Local distrust of the Lawrences intensified with the increase in the successful German U-boat activity as described by Hocking – dozens of British ships being sunk by the week. So serious, at that time, was the British situation that Delaney speculates[116] if those attacks had continued, "...at the same rate Britain would have had to capitulate within a year for lack of food and supplies." The facts of Frieda Lawrence's birth and connections served to heap further suspicion on the couple, which was not ameliorated by the fact that, as Worthen points out,[117] Frieda made no attempt to conceal her pride in the exploits of her distant cousin Manfred von Richthofen – the notorious *Red Baron*. In addition, Delany notes[118] that her mail from Germany, by way of Switzerland, included such newspapers as the *Berliner Tageblatt*. All of this, apparently, tended to make Lawrence himself act defensively and, ultimately, local suspicion escalated into outright spying.

However, it was Lawrence's friends who attracted the first official attention. Robert Mountsier, an Armenian journalist, was questioned by local police during a Christmas stopover with the Lawrences in 1916. On his return to London, Mountsier was arrested, strip-searched, interrogated and detained overnight, as described by Kinkead-Weekes.[119] As incidents of this kind continued, local suspicion of the Lawrences began to develop more officially, led, according to Hocking,[120] by the local vicar. Hence, by late summer 1917, Lawrence began to suspect that his mail was being intercepted and examined. Next when Lawrence and Frieda were returning home from Zennor, they were accosted by two uniformed men who turned out their shopping bag, apparently searching for a camera.[121] Ultimately, as Dehoney reports,[122] the official axe fell on 11th October when, while Lawrence was in Penzance and Frieda at Rosignon, their cottage was ransacked by uniformed men and left in a shambles. The following morning an army major, two detectives and a police sergeant arrived to continue the search. The sergeant of police read a formal expulsion order which had been signed by Major-General Western, from the Southern Command, which directed the Lawrences to, "...leave Cornwall within three days; to report to the police within twenty –four hours after finding a new residence; and to stay out of Class 2 prohibited areas – about one third of England, comprising all coastal regions and major ports." The order was served without explanation and, since it was made under r 14B of the *Defence of the Realm Regulations* there was no means of appeal on the merits.

The legislation, the *Defence of the Realm Acts* 1914-1915, were, initially at least, enabling Acts. The long title of the *Defence of the Realm Act* 1914 is: "An Act to confer on his Majesty in Council power to make regulations during the present war for the *Defence of the Realm*". At the outset, s 1 of the Act makes provision for, "...securing the public safety and the defence of the realm." At the same time, other provisions in the same section authorised the trial by court martial, and provided for the punishment of persons who contravened any regulations designed to, "...prevent persons communicating with the enemy or obtaining information for that purpose or any purpose calculated to jeopardise the success of the operation of any of His Majesty's forces or to assist the enemy"[123] or to "...secure the safety of any means of communication or of railways, docks or harbours".[124] Such trial and punishment was to be administered as though such persons were subject to military law and had, on active service committed analogous offences under military law. Although those powers seem analogous to those enabled under martial law it may be that the analogy can be taken too far. First, the right of the military to exercise abnormal powers in a time of emergency has been recognised by the common law.[125] Second, it seems as though there is no precise test for determining any state of emergency in which martial law does, in fact, exist. However, if such a test does exist, it is submitted that it should be the factual one as to whether civil courts continue to operate during the particular state of emergency. During the period in question, there can be little, if any, doubt that they did continue to do so - a matter which is the more emphasised by the *Defence of the Realm Act* 1915 s 1(i) which provided that any offence against regulations made under the 1914 Act might, instead of being tried by court martial, might, "...be tried by a civil court with a jury, and when so tried the offence shall be deemed to be a felony punishable with the like punishment as might have been inflicted if the offence had been tried by court martial." Thus, although martial law may not strictly have existed during the relevant period, the military powers, nonetheless, remained, rigorous and apparent.[126]

In the situation in which Lawrence found himself, he and Frieda had been served with a *military* exclusion order. However, the orders were enforced by the civilian police rather than by the military *per se*. Indeed, on their return to London, following the order's being carried out, Worthern points out[127] that Lawrence found the police pleasant and, even, sympathetic. All in all, 1917 was an unfortunate time for the Lawrences to have come into contact with the *Defence of the Realm* regulations. Thus, Worthen notes[128] that the war had, "...reached a new pitch of awfulness in 1917, with the long-drawn-out horror of Passchendaele; there were nearly 90,000 causalities in the first two months". That year also saw the House of Lords' decision in the leading case of *R (at the prosecution of Zadig)* v *Halliday*.[129]

In that case, Zadig had been born in Germany of German parents in 1871, but had become a naturalised British subject in 1905. He carried on business in Britain for some years with his brother, who remained a German subject and was hence, an enemy alien. The brother was interned in June 1915, and the appellant was interned in October of the same year. The appellant's internment was at the order of the Home Secretary, which was made under r 14B of the *Defence of the Realm (Consolidation) Regulations 1914*. That regulation empowered the Home Secretary to order the internment of any person where, on the recommendation of a competent naval or military authority or of an advisory committee, it appeared to him in order to secure the public safety or the defence of the realm, expedient in view of the hostile origin or association of that person. If such a person was not a subject of a State which was at war his Majesty, any appeal was to be considered by an advisory committee to be presided over by a person who had held high judicial office. The appellant had unsuccessfully attended before the advisory committee, and, then, obtained from the Divisional Court of King's Bench a rule *nisi* calling upon the respondent (who was the commandant of the place where he was interned) to show cause why a writ of *habeas corpus* should not be issued on the grounds that r 14B was ultra vires the legislation. It should be said that there was no direct suspension of *habeas corpus* during the 1914-18 (or for that matter, the 1939-45) war.

The Divisional Court [130] were of the unanimous view that the regulation was *intra vires* the Act and, so, dismissed the rule. That view was, again unanimously, shared by the Court of Appeal,[131] who dismissed the case, without even calling upon counsel for the respondent, on the grounds that the regulation was in terms authorised by the express language of the Act, which was precise, clear and free from ambiguity. The matter then came before the House of Lords who, again, dismissed the appeal, although with one notable dissentient.[132] From the point of view of Lawrence's situation, r 14B provided that, on appropriate recommendation, "...it appears to the Secretary of State that, for securing the public safety or defence of the realm, it is expedient in view of the hostile origin or of association of any person that they shall be subjected to such obligations and restrictions as are hereinafter mentioned, the Secretary of State may by order require that person forth with to proceed and reside in such places as may be specified in the order and to comply with such directions as reporting to the police, restriction of movement and otherwise as may be specified in the order." It had been argued on behalf of Zadig that some limitation needed to be placed on r 14B as an unrestricted interpretation of its language might involve extreme consequences, including, it was suggested, the infliction of the death penalty without trial. Lord Finlay L. C. was, frankly, dismissive of those submissions. "It appears to me," he stated,[133] "to be no sufficient answer to this argument that it may be necessary at a time of sufficient danger to entrust great powers to His Majesty in Council and that Parliament may do so, feeling certain that such powers will be reasonably exercised... One of the most obvious precautions against dangers such as are enumerated is obviously to impose some restriction on the freedom of movement of persons whom there may be reason to suspect of being disposed to help the enemy. It is to this that regulation 14B is directed. The measure is not punitive but precautionary."

The Lord Chancellor then continued by noting [134] that the enabling legislation was passed at a time of extreme national danger which, contemporaneously, still existed. "The restraint imposed," he went on, "may be a necessary measure of precaution, and in the interests of the whole nation it may be regarded as expedient that an order should be made in appropriate cases. That appears to me to be the meaning of the statute." Further, he commented that every reasonable precaution to alleviate hardship, consistent with the regulation, consistent with the object of the regulation appeared to have been taken.

It would be both simplistic and wrong to ignore the rhetoric of Lord Shaw's judgment in dissent, which seems, albeit with the dubious benefit of long term hindsight, to have been of some significant influence. Lord Shaw inquired [135] whether it might be thought possible to construe the Regulation as meaning not only the grant of a power of prevention from doing certain things, which having been done were punishable, but the reserve of some other and supereminent power of prevention which is distinguishable from punishment? Lord Shaw found no such reserve or distinction in the document, which strongly suggested that none was intended. If the principle of *generality* embraces a power over liberty, might it not, Lord Shaw asked, extend yet further. Put another way: "If the Government judges that particular course to be for public safety or defence, why, on the same principle and in exercise of the same power, may [the person] not be shot out of hand".[136] Still more rhetorically, Lord Shaw sought to emphasise [137] that, under the legislation, the Government had become a Committee of Public Safety (a body which existed at the period of the French Revolution of 1789 generally referred to as *The Terror*), but with wider powers. "It preserved," he continued, "a form of trial, of evidence of interrogations; and the very homage which it paid to law discovered the odium of its procedure to the world"[138] His Lordship further emphasised that, if the power to issue regulations meant warranting a passage from proof to suspicion and from the sphere of action to the sphere of motive on the mind, that involved more than Parliament had surely contemplated and, hence, the words of the Act (and Regulations) could not be so stretched as to involve anything so repugnant to liberty and the law. After an analysis of relevant historical instances Lord Shaw expressed the view [139] that the construction of the legislation implied a repeal of ancient rights and liberties which was of such a comprehensive and radical nature that he believed that Parliament would never have attempted it. Accordingly, he was unwilling to believe that there was any such repeal, "...either in word, in implication or in intention."

Of course *Zadig* was lost and Lawrence never sought to litigate his own case (regardless of any aspect of the *Zadig* decision). Although *Zadig* seemed not to have attracted, as has already been noted, [140] much contemporary interest it clearly did have longer term effects. First, it is possible to contrast the emergency provisions which existed in the 1914-1918 war with those which existed in the 1939-1945 war. The emergency powers which were granted in the later conflagration were both more elaborate and, in consequence, more specific.[141] Those emergency powers, in both wars paved the way for delegated legislation on a scale hitherto uncontemplated and, at least at an early stage resented by, at least, one senior legal figure.[142] Nevertheless, as Allen has properly commented,[143] the result, perhaps because of the *Zadig* case, was that the doctrine of *ultra vires*, at any rate in the present context, had been, "...greatly attenuated and indeed, with regard to a large number of executive powers, it may be said to be completely paralysed."

Although the *Zadig* decision did involve issues which were fundamental, it did not, thankfully, mean that regulations made under the *Defence of the Realm* legislation were not open to successful challenge, albeit after the cessation of hostilities.[144] Thus, in the important case of *Attorney – General* v *Wilts United Dairies*,[145] an attempt by the Food Controller to impose a charge was held to be invalid on the grounds that the regulation contained no power expressly to impose charges on subjects. At the same time, it was doubted whether any regulation which did purport to confer such a power would have fallen within the more general power to make regulations for the public safety or for the defence of the realm. Likewise, in *Chester* v *Bateson*,[146] a regulation which deprived an individual of access to the courts was held to be invalid. The regulation empowered the Minister of Munitions to declare an area where munitions were manufactured, stored or transported to be a *special area*. The effect of that declaration was to prevent any person, without the Minister's consent, from taking proceedings for the recovery of possession of, or for ejectment of a tenant of any dwelling house in the area, if a munition worker was living in it and duly paying rent. It was decided that Parliament had not deliberately denied a citizen resort to the courts and, accordingly, that a regulation framed so as to forbid the owner of property access to legal tribunals was invalid, unless it could be shown that it was a necessary, or even reasonable, way of securing public safety or the defence of the realm. Similarly, in *Newcastle Breweries* v *R*,[147] a regulation was held to be invalid because it purported to authorise the requisitioning of property without fair compensation at market value and without any right to dispute that value in a court of law.

By then, the appropriate approach appeared to have been well encapsulated by Atkin LJ in the *Wilts United Dairies*[148] case when he asserted that, "The circumstances would be rare indeed which would induce the Court to believe that the legislature had sacrificed the well known checks and precautions and, not in express words, but merely by implication, had entrusted a Minister of the Crown with undefined and unlimited powers of imposing charges upon the subject for purposes connected with this department." That view may, of course, be instantly compared with that of Lord Finlay LC in the *Zadig* case.[149] The distinction may, one supposes, be accounted for by the subject matter of the relative proceedings and by the fact that the war was over and not, as it had been at the time of the *Zadig* case, at its height and, also, by the nationalistic impulses which it generated having, to a large degree, dissipated.[150] On the other hand the issues involved in the later cases were less immediate and graphic than those with which *Zadig* was concerned. However, despite the wide powers which the *Defence of the Realm* legislation had indubitably conferred, it is equally clear that numerous irregularities and illegalities were committed under its penumbra. That much is clear from the very fact of legislation which was enacted coterminously with the *Wilts United Dairies, Chester* and *Newcastle Breweries* cases. Thus, s 1(1) of the *Indemnity Act* 1920 provided that, "No action or other legal proceeding whatever, whether civil or criminal shall be instituted in any court of law for or on account of or in respect of any act, matter or thing done, whether within or without his Majesty's dominions, during the war before the passing of his Act, if done in good faith, and done as purported to be done in the execution of his duty or for the defence of the realm or the public safety, or for the enforcement of discipline, or otherwise in the public interest by a person holding office in the service of the Crown in any capacity, whether naval or military, air force or civil, or by any other person acting under the authority of a person so holding office or so employed; and if any such proceeding has been instituted before or after the passing of this Act, it shall be discharged and made void."[151]

That subsequent, comprehensive and retrospective legislation ensured that any complaints which the Lawrences might have been able to make in respect of the conduct which particular individuals manifested towards them[152] was thoroughly obviated; thus, removing any possibility of redress, even assuming that Lawrence had considered the possibility at all! That said, however, he was much distressed by the exclusion order. He wrote[153] to his friend, Lady Cynthic Asquith in the following terms: "The bolt from the blue has fallen this morning, why I know not, any more than you do. I cannot even conceive how I have incurred suspicion – have not the faintest notion. We are as innocent even of pacifist activities, let alone spying in any sort, as the rabbits of the field outside." The tone of that letter was in contradistinction to the attitude which he had earlier assumed, which appeared to observers to be rather more truculent.[154] There can be, over all, little doubt that his time in Cornwall had a strong influence on Lawrence's writing and philosophy, in particular as represented in his novel *Kangaroo*, which was written during a month visit to Australian in 1922. Quite apart from any other factors, the village where he lived during that time was similar in size and remoteness to Zennor.

However, despite the cases which followed the 1914-1918 war's conclusion,[155] the attitudes to be found in Lord Finlay LC's judgment in *Zadig*[156] were not wholly redundant. In 1941, the House of Lords was required to determine the case of *Liversidge* v *Anderson*[157] which raised many of the same issues which had arisen in *Zadig*.[158] The appellant, who had been detained pursuant to an order made by the respondent, who was then the Home Secretary, under r 18B of the *Defence (General) Regulations* 1939, which was couched in terms very similar to those which were in issue in *Zadig*,[159] claimed a declaration that his detention was unlawful. He applied for particulars, first, of the grounds on which the respondent had reasonable cause to believe the appellant to be a person of hostile associations and, second, of the grounds on which the respondent had reasonable cause to believe that by reason of those hostile associations it was necessary to exercise control, by way of detention, over the appellant. A Master of the Supreme Court refused to make any orders and that decision was upheld by a judge in chambers who, however, gave leave to the appellant to appeal to the Court of Appeal. The Court of Appeal held that the appellant, at the present stage, was not entitled to any of the particulars which he was claiming and dismissed his appeal. But, having regard to the great importance of the questions arising out of orders under the particular regulation, the appellant was given further leave to appeal to the House of Lords. The House of Lords[160] dismissed the appeal, with an important dissenting judgment by Lord Atkin, and, in so doing held that where the Secretary of State, acting in good faith under the regulation, makes an order where he states that he has reasonable cause to believe that a person has hostile associations and for that reason it is necessary to exercise control over him and, thus, directs that the person be detained, a court of law may not inquire whether, in fact, the Secretary of State had reasonable grounds for his belief. The matter, in other words, was one for the executive discretion of the Secretary of State. This view was strongly expressed by Viscount Maughan when he said[161] that, "To my mind this is so clearly a matter for executive discretion and nothing else that I cannot myself believe that those responsible for the Order in Council could have contemplated for a moment the possibility of the action of the Secretary of State being subject to the discussion, criticism and control of a judge in a court of law." Further, Viscount Maughan noted[162] that it had been admitted on behalf of the appellant that the Home Secretary could act on hearsay evidence, was not required to obtain any legal evidence in such a case and, most particularly, was not required to summon the person whom he proposes to detain and to hear his objections to the proposed order. It followed that, as the Secretary was not acting judicially in such a case, it would be strange if his decision could be questioned in a court of law.

However, the most important issue, Viscount Maughan considered,[163] was that it was, "obvious that in many cases [the Secretary] will be acting on information of the most confidential character, which could not be communicated to the person detained or disclosed in court without the greatest risk of prejudicing the future efforts of the Secretary of State in this and like matters for the defence of the realm... It is sufficient to say that there must be a large number of cases in which the information on which the Secretary of State is likely to act will be of a very confidential nature. That must have been plain to those responsible in advising His Majesty in regard to the Order in Council, and it constitutes, in my opinion, a very cogent reason for thinking that the words under discussion cannot be read as meaning that the existence of 'reasonable cause' is one which may be discussed in a court which has not the power of eliciting the facts which in the opinion of the Secretary of State amount to 'reasonable cause'." Finally, Viscount Maughan regarded[164] it as important to bear in mind that the Secretary of State was a member of the government and, hence, was answerable to Parliament in respect of a proper discharge of his duties (unlike, say, a police officer). In addition, Viscount Maughan rejected[165] an argument made on behalf of the appellant that an onus was cast on the Secretary to give evidence to show that he had reasonable cause to believe the appellant to be a person of hostile associations and that, by reason of those associations, it was necessary to exercise control over him. In Viscount Maughan's opinion, the maxim *omnia esse rite acta*[166] was applicable to the situation. This meant that, assuming the order to be proved or admitted, it must, *prima facie*, until the contrary is proved, to have been properly made and that the belief of the Secretary of State was complied with.

Although, given the view of Lord Finlay LC in *Zadig*,[167] the approach adopted by Viscount Maughan in *Liversidge v Anderson* was, in all probability, to have been expected, there was, redolent of the strenuous dissent by Lord Shaw in the earlier case,[168] a strongly worded judgment in dissent by Lord Atkin, which Wade, in an early edition of his work on administrative law described[169] as, "...one of the *tours de force* of legal literature." First of all, he emphasised[170] that the phrase "has reasonable cause" had a settled meaning which imparted, "...the existence of a fact or state of facts and not the mere belief by the person challenged that the fact or state of facts existed..." He continued by saying[171] that the words in question were not ambiguous, "...that they have only one plain and natural meaning, that with that meaning, they have been used at common law and in numerous statutes, and that whenever they are used the courts have given them the meaning I suggest, have considered that they give rise to a justiciable issue, and that as to the 'subjective' meaning now contended for by the Secretary of State it has never at any time occurred to the minds of counsel or judges that the words are even capable of meaning anything so fantastic."

Lord Atkin after having further emphasised that the phrase was objective and capable of judicial cognisance, then stated[172] that he viewed with apprehension the attitude of judges who, on most questions of construction, "...when face to face claims involving the liberty of the subject show themselves more executive minded than the executive." Their duty, possibly less in wartime than in time of peace was to give words their natural meaning, leaning, perhaps, towards liberty, but at all times to bed the words of Pollock CB in *Bowditch* v *Balchin*[173] who had said that, in a case in which the liberty of the subject is concerned "we cannot go beyond the natural construction of the statute." In *Liversidge* v *Anderson*, Lord Atkin became still more emphatically denunciatory of those who had sought to elevate the pressures and claims of wartime above the rule of law. It is these *rhetorical* terms of which Wade is especially approbatory:[174] "In this country," Lord Atkin stated, "amid the clash of arms, the laws are not silent. They may be changed, but they speak the same language in war as in peace. It has always been one of the pillars of freedom, one of the principles of liberty for which on recent authority we are now fighting, that the judges are no respecters of persons and stand between the subject and any attempted encroachments on his liberty by the executive, alert to see that any coercive action is justified in law. In this case I have listened to arguments which might have been addressed acceptably to the Court of King's Bench in the time of Charles I." Lord Atkin then went on to encapsulate much of what he had already said, though the rhetorical manner which he adopted in doing so is worthy of quotation: "I protest," he emphasised, "even if I do it alone, against a strained construction put on words with the effect of giving an uncontrolled power of imprisonment to the minister. To recapitulate: The words have only one meaning. They are used with that meaning in statements of common law and in statutes. They have never been used in the sense now imputed to them. They are used in the Defence Regulations in the natural meaning and, when it is intended to express the meaning now imputed to them, different and apt words are used in the regulations generally and in this regulation in particular. Even if it were relevant, which it is not, there is no absurdity or no such degree of public mischief as would lead to a non-natural construction... After all this long discussion the question is whether the words 'If a man has' can mean 'If a man thinks he has'. I am of opinion that they cannot, and that the case should be decided accordingly."

Although the views of Lord Atkin in *Liversidge* v *Anderson* ought to have commended themselves to lawyers, it must be born in mind that the appellant's case failed. Certain of the issues which Lord Atkin had raised in his dissent were contrarily discussed in the judgment of Lord Macmillan:

thus, the judge noted[175] that "If the regulation had been framed so as to read, as the appellant would read it, 'If the Secretary of State has such cause of belief as a court of law would hold to be reasonable.' I doubt it would have commended itself as an emergency measure. Courts may differ as to what is reasonable. A judge of first instance might hold the Secretary of State to be justified in his belief, the Court of Appeal might take another view and this House might take its own view. In a matter at once so vital and so urgent in the interests of national safety, I am unable to accept a reading of the regulation which would prescribe that the Secretary of State may not act in accordance with what commands itself to him as a reasonable cause of belief without incurring the risk that a court of law would disagree with him, and also without the further liability, should the court do so or if he cannot consistently with his duty disclose to the court the grounds of his belief, he will be mulcted in damages for false imprisonment as having acted outwith his powers." Lord Macmillan then went on[176] to examine the more general issue of an individual's freedom under the law which Lord Atkin had raised in his dissentient judgment.[177] "The liberty we so justly extol is," Lord Macmillan stated, "the gift of the law and as Magna Carta recognises may by the law be fortified or abridged. At a time when it is the undoubted law of the land that a citizen may by conscription or requisition be compelled to give up his life and all that he posses for his country's cause it may well be no matter for surprise that there should be confided to the Secretary of State a discretionary power of forcing the relatively mild precaution of detention."

Not altogether surprisingly in view of these differences of opinion, *Liversidge* v *Anderson* has attracted not inconsiderable attention.[178] However, it should be said that it does seem to represent something of an isolated instance which is probably attributable to the extraordinary surrounding circumstances. Indeed, in *Liversidge,* Lord Wright, after having mentioned *Zadig,*[179] noted[180] that, "German methods for effecting the poisonous infiltration among British or allied subjects of their purposes and schemes have been immensely more subtle and rigorous than in the last war. Even a judge may be allowed to take notice of the impact of words like Fifth Columnists and Quislings and the like. It is the duty of the Secretary to check these underground and insidious activities of the enemy and their consequences, whether they result in sabotage or in anti-British propaganda or in weakening the national efforts and endurance." But with

Liversidge v *Anderson* may be compared the decision of the Judicial Committee of the Privy Council in *Nakkuda Ali* v *Jayaratne*[181] which involved the authority of a controller of textiles who had power to cancel a dealer's licence. "...where the Controller has reasonable grounds to believe that any dealer is unfit to be allowed to continue to be a dealer." The Judicial Committee decided that those words imposed a condition that reasonable grounds must be shown to exist to the satisfaction of the court. In that case Lord Radcliffe stated[182] that, "...it would be a very unfortunate thing if the decision of Liversidge's case came to be regarded as laying down any general rule as to the construction of such phrases when they appear in statutory enactments. It is an authority for the proposition that the words 'if AB has reasonable cause to believe' are capable of meaning 'if AB honestly thinks he has reasonable cause to believe'... However read they must be intended to serve in some sense as a condition limiting the exercise of an otherwise arbitrary power. But if the question whether the condition has been satisfied is to be conclusively determined by the man who wields the power, the value of the intended restraint is in effect nothing." In addition, in the later House of Lords decision in *Ridge* v *Baldwin,*[183] a most distinguished member of that Court, Lord Reid, described *Liversidge* v *Anderson* as a "very peculiar decision" and went on to say that he did not think that any decision that the rules of natural justice were excluded from war-time legislation should be regarded as being of any great weight in more modern cases.

3. The Law in the Writer: The Strange Case of A C Swinburne

There is always something almost impenetrably disturbing about the poems of Algernon Charles Swinburne. The reason is not far to seek – even his best work is shot through with masochistic reference. Thus the first stanza in the first great "Chorus" in *Atalanta in Calydon*, written in 1865, begins with a sensuous and vernal metaphor, but ends surprisingly:

> When the hounds of spring are on winter's traces,
> The mother of months in meadow or plain
> Fills the shadows and windy places
> With lisp of leaves and ripple of rain;
> And the brown bright nightingale amorous
> Is half assuaged for Itylus,

> For the Thracian ships and the foreign faces,
> The tongueless vigil, and all the pain.

The final stanza is a likewise varied combination of nature, both real and imagined, but just as in the first stanza, an altogether more sinister figure or metaphor appears deliberately disrupting the idyll of the first lines of each stanza:

> The ivy falls with the Bacchanal's hair
> Over her eyebrows hiding her eyes;
> The wild vine slipping down leaves bare
> Her bright breast shortening into sighs;
> The wild vine slips with the weight of its leaves,
> But the berried ivy catches and cleaves
> To the limbs that glitter, the feet that scare
> The wolf that follows, the fawn that flies.

In addition to those instances of disturbing juxtaposition, there are some other intriguing instances throughout the poem. Thus, at the beginning of the fourth stanza (there are seven in all), in describing winter's end, Swinburne writes that, "For winter's rains and ruins are over/And all the season of snows and sins". One can properly wonder why winter should attract sin more than only other season and, later in the same stanza, Swinburne tells us, that, "Time remembered is grief forgotten", which, even in the context of the poem at large is, effectively, meaningless.

Many similar characteristics are perceptible in the poem "Rococo", written a year later than *Atalanta in Corydon*. The same pattern is apparent at the beginning of the later poem:

> Take hands and part with laughter;
> Touch lips and part with tears;
> Once more and no more after,
> Whatever comes with years.
> We twain shall not remeasure
> The ways that left us twain;
> Nor crush the lees of pleasure
> From sanguine grapes of pain.

The same pattern is apparent throughout the poem – though not consistently. Thus, in the fifth stanza the matter becomes more strongly expressed; the relative metaphors of pleasure and pain – and not emotional, but directly physical, are brutally apparent:

> We have heard from hidden laces
> What love scarce lives and hears:
> We have seen on fervent faces
> The pallor of strange tears:
> We have trod the wine-vat's treasure,
> Whence, ripe to steam and stain,
> Foams round the feet of pleasure
> The blood-read mist of pain.

The same pattern of versification is repeated in the seventh stanza, with the notions of pleasure subsumed into pain - again, bearing in mind that the pain is not primarily emotional, but physical – being both inevitable and inextricable. In addition, in that stanza, the idea of attractive evil being inherent in that involvement:

> The snake that hides and hisses
> In heaven we twain have known;
> The grief of cruel kisses,
> The joy whose mouth makes moan;
> The pulse's pause and measure,
> Where in one furtive vein
> Throbs through the heart of pleasure
> The purple blood of pain.

Another matter which makes "Rococo" more complex than the "Chorus" from *Atalanta in Corydon* is manifest in the seventh stanza of the later poem. Thus, the snake – as representative of the *evil* necessarily in the interaction of pleasure and, as dominated by, pain – is juxtaposed with the *heaven*, as noted in the second line. Further, unlike the "Chorus", "Rococo" does not end with an especially sinister or frightening image. Although the penultimate stanza does end with a pleasure/pain image, it is not presented in the same light as the earlier stanzas which have been considered. This is the penultimate stanza:

> Life treads down love in flying,
> Time withers him at root;
> Bring all dead things and dying,
> Reaped sheaf and ruined fruit,
> Where, crushed by three days' pressure,
> Our three days' love lies slain;
> And earlier leaf of pleasure,
> And latter flower of pain.

In the final stanza, there is, compared with much of the remainder of the poem, an optimistic, if not wholly expectantly so, note:

> Breathe close upon the ashes,
> It may be flame will leap;
> Unclose the soft close lashes,
> Lift up the lids, and weep.
> Light love's extinguished ember,
> Let one tear leave it wet
> For one that you remember
> And then that you forget.

Quite apart from much else – together with a graphic prosody and strikingly infectious rhythm – it must necessarily be said that these poems are possessed of a quite distinctive, and not always an instantly attractive, quality. Sinister image follows upon sinister image and more healthy image is quickly qualified by another sinister, or pain-stressed, image. In order to seek to explain these apparently disturbing matters, it is necessary to place those poems in biographical context.

1866 was the year in which the first volume of Swinburne's *Poems and Ballads* appeared and Colin Wilson draws attention[184] to a review of it in the *Saturday Review* of the 4th of August, which, apparently, drove Swinburne into a fearsome public rage. That, perhaps, is not altogether surprising as the review, as quoted by Wilson, by John Marley included the diatribe: "[The author," wrote Morley, "deserves credit for the audacious courage with which he has revealed to the world a mind all aflame with the feverish carnality of the schoolboy over the dirtiest passages in Lampriére['s] Classical Dictionary]. It is not every one who would ask us all to go and hear him tuning his lyre in a stye." The review concluded with an appeal to the apparently universal moral standards of the time, when it was written that, "We should be sorry to be guilty of anything so offensive to Mr Swinburne as we are quite sure an appeal to the morality of all the wisest and best men would be...but it may be presumed that common sense is not too insulting a standard by which to measure the worth and place of this new volume." It was quite clear, as Wilson points out,[185] that what disturbed Marley especially was the plethora of sado-masochistic reference in *Poems and Ballads*: in particular, a stanza from "Our Lady of Pain":

> By the ravenous teeth that have smitten
> Through the kisses that blossom and bud,
> By lips intertwisted and bitten
> Till the foam has a savour of blood...

That extract may have been regarded in a poor light by the reviewer of *Poems and Ballads*, but his view of an extract from "Faustine" was in a similar vein:

> Stray breaths of Sapphire song that blew
> Through Mitylene
> Shook the fierce quivering blood in you
> By night, Faustine.
>
> The shameless nameless love that makes
> Hell's iron gin
> Shut on you like a trap that breaks
> The soul, Faustine...
>
> Red lips long since half-kissed away
> Still sweet and keen
> You'd give him – poison shall we say?
> Or what, Faustine?

Wilson comments[186] that one does not have to know that Mitylene was the birthplace of Sappho, the lesbian poet, to be aware that, "...something wickedly indecent was being hinted at." Wilson then goes on to comment that even the most innocent-looking poems could be, in his own expression booby-trapped; even the apparently and initially beautiful poem "Itylus", which begins innocently[187] enough:

> Swallow, my sister, O sister swallow,
> How can thine heart be full of spring?

Wilson then states,[188] quite unequivocally, that, "...Swinburne *was* a sexual pervert, although of a fairly harmless variety. Ever since he was a child, he had an obsession with flogging – or rather, being flogged. Most of his biographies assume that this began at Eton, which was notorious for its 'swishings' – one headmaster was said to be more familiar with his pupils' behinds than their faces – but it was almost certainly an inborn tendency."[189] However, despite Wilson's suggestion, as I have elsewhere written,[190] it is very difficult to avoid the influence of Swinburne's school experiences on his personality and on his writing. This view is shared by Swinburne's biographer Henderson[191] who writes that his time there, from 1849-1853, made it seem, "...fairly obvious that Swinburne's lifelong obsession with flagellation had its origin in beatings he witnessed and received at the notorious Eton flogging block...[and] Eton evidently had a good deal to answer for in the development of Swinburne's character." Given such a context, it should be said that the floggings at Nineteenth Century Eton were quite horrible affairs by any remotely acceptable standard: They were inflicted on the child's bare buttocks with a birch rod which was almost five feet long, having three feet of handle and two of bush.[192] At the same time, it must also be emphasised that the extent of Swinburne's flagellomania was quite extraordinary; as George MacBeth puts it[193] when referring to Swinburne's creative output, "...the energy was whipped out (quite literally) in the 1860s." In fact, in the early part of the decade Swinburne had begun work on, in Henderson's words,[194] "...his epic of flagellation, *The Flogging Block,* in which his imagination played delightedly around the whipping of small boys at Eton, and which was to engage him at intervals for the rest of his life. A short quotation is sufficient to give the flavour of this work which, quite apart from its pornographic nature; is characterised by an appalling standard of verse:

> How those great big ridges must smart as they swell!
> How the Master does like to flog Algernon well!
> How each cut makes the blood come in thin little streaks
> From that broad blushing round pain of naked red cheeks.[195]

Swinburne also contributed to *The Pearl*, the notorious Victorian pornographic magazine,[196] as well as to the anonymous collection, *The Whippingham Papers*. In addition, his novel *Lesbia Brandon* (a character almost certainly modelled on his cousin, Mary Gordon[197]) contains copious flagellant references. *In toto*, Swinburne's private life does not present an especially edifying prospect and it is all the more disturbing when I believe that its origins can be readily traced to his school experiences. Wilson, who disputes that, does admit[198] that, at least, some of his school experiences influenced him. Wilson writes that, "In 1849, at the age of twelve, Swinburne was sent to Eton, where he lived with his tutor, James Joynes, and his young wife. Joynes – who was twenty five – had also been a pupil at Eton, so it is just conceivable that he realised how much pleasure he was giving Swinburne with his frequent birchings. He would prepare the flogging room with burnt scent, or make Swinburne put eau-de-cologne on his face before being beaten.

Nor should it be thought that Swinburne's perversion, however harmless it might be, is not reflected in the law. The leading case is the decision of the House of Lords in *R v Brown*[199] where the appellants belonged to a group of sado-masochistic homosexuals, who, over a ten year period from 1978 willingly participated in the commission of acts of violence against one another, including genital torture, for the sexual pleasure which it engendered in the giving and receiving of pain. The passive partner, or victim, in each case consented to the acts being committed and received no permanent injury. The activities took place in private at various locations, including rooms equipped as torture chambers at the home of three of the appellants. Video cameras were used to record the activities and the resulting tapes were then copied and distributed amongst members of the group. The appellants were tried on charges of assault occasioning actual bodily harm, contrary to s 47 of the *Offences*

Against the Person Act 1861, and unlawful wounding contrary to s 20 of the same Act. The case for the prosecution was based largely on the contents of the video tapes. Following a ruling by the trial judge that the consent of the victim afforded no defence to the charges, the appellants appealed against their initial convictions arguing that a person could not be guilty of assault occasioning actual bodily harm or unlawful wounding in respect of acts carried out in private with the consent of the victims. The Court of Appeal dismissed their appeals and the appellants then appealed to the House of Lords who upheld the convictions.

In the majority, Lord Templeman, after having outlined the background to the legislation, noted[200] that, "The assertion was made on behalf of the appellants that the sexual appetites of sadists and masochists can only be satisfied by infliction of bodily harm and that the law should not punish the consensual achievement of sexual satisfaction." To the contention, his Lordship replied that there was no evidence that such activities were essential to the appellants' happiness; indeed, that argument would only be acceptable if sado-masochism were only concerned with sex – as, indeed, the appellants contended. Sado-masochism, Lord Templeman continued,[201] was also concerned with violence: the evidence disclosed that the practices of the appellants were unpredictably dangerous and were degrading both to body and mind and, further, had been developed with increasing barbarity and had been taught to people whose consents were treated as dubious or worthless. That was still further emphasised, Lord Templeman went on[202] to comment the evidence also disclosed that drink and drugs were employed for the purposes of obtaining consent. "The victim", he noted, "was usually manacled so that the sadist could enjoy the thrill of power and the victim could enjoy the thrill of helplessness. The victim had no control over the harm which he sadist, also stimulated by drink and drugs might inflict... I am not prepared to invent a defence of consent for sado-masochistic encounters which breed and glorify cruelty." Having rejected a defence which, "somewhat faintly" relied on Arts 1and 8 of the *European Convention on Human Rights*, Lord Templeman resoundingly concluded[203] his judgment by saying that, "Society is entitled and bound to protect itself against a cult of violence. Pleasure derived from pain is an evil thing. Cruelty is uncivilised."[204]

There was, in particular,[205] a strong dissenting judgment from Lord Slynn, who refused to accept[206] that it was correct to take common assaults as the sole category of assaults to which consent could be a defence and to deny that defence in respect of all other injuries. "In the first place," he continued, "the range of injuries which can fall within 'actual bodily harm' is wide – the description of two beatings in the present case show that one is much more substantial than the other. Further, the same is true of wounding where the test is whether the skin is broken and where it can be more or less serious." Accordingly Lord Slynn could see no significant reason for refusing consent as a defence for the lesser of these cases of actual bodily harm and wounding. Nonetheless, Lord Slynn considered that were a line to be drawn - as it must – it could not be permitted to fluctuate within particular charges and, moreover, in the interests of legal certainty, it had to be accepted that consent could be given to acts which are said to constitute actual bodily harm and wounding. Lord Slynn accepted that grievous bodily harm was different and, so, in cases involving that (or, indeed, death) consent was not a defence. At the same time, his Lordship emphasised,[207] that reasoning did not mean that the acts done were approved of or encouraged – it simply meant that the acts did not constitute an assault within the meaning of the legislative provisions.

The issue then became whether there had been actual consent on the facts of *Brown*; Lord Slynn was of the view[208] that there was consent and, in fact, more than mere consent. "Astonishingly though it may seem," he said, "the persons involved positively wanted, asked for, the acts to be done to them, acts which it seems from the evidence some of them also did to themselves. All the accused were old enough to know what they were doing. The acts were done in private. Neither the applicants nor anyone else complained as to what was done. The matter came to the attention of the police 'coincidentally'; the police were previously unaware that the accused were involved in these practices though some of them had been involved for many years. The acts did not result in any permanent or serious injury or disability or any infection and no medical assistance was required even though there may have been some risk of infection, even injury."

Lord Slynn then turned his attention[209] to an argument to the effect that, if an act was otherwise unlawful, then consent could not be a defence, but it could be a defence if the act was otherwise lawful and in respect of injury which was less than really serious. That, he suggested, would produce the result, in the present case that, if the acts had been done by two men, they would be lawful by reason of s 1 of the *Sexual Offences Act 1967*,[210] even though the acts presently in question were far away from the kinds of homosexual acts which the Wolfenden Committee had had in mind when compiling their report.[211] "If", his Lordship continued,[212] "on the other hand three men took part, the activity would be unlawful under the 1967 Act so that there could be no consent to the acts done. But it would also appear to mean that if these acts were done mutatis mutandis by a man and a woman, or between two men and a woman, or a man and two women, where the activity was entirely heterosexual, consent would prevent there being an offence." Lord Slynn did not find such a distinction as producing an acceptable result.

Lord Slynn concluded by saying that, as the law presently stood, adults could consent to acts done in private which do not result in serious bodily harm and did not amount to criminal assaults for the purposes of the relevant legislation. His Lordship emphasised[213] that his conclusion was in no wise based on any alternative argument that, "for the criminal law to encompass consensual acts done in private would be itself an unlawful invasion of privacy." He further pointed out that, had the acts in question constituted offences under the relevant legislation, there would necessarily be an invasion of privacy. However, whether that invasion would be justified or, particularly, whether it would be within the derogations to be found in the *European Convention on Human Rights*[214] was not a question which it was necessary to answer. He again emphasised[215] that his view was based on the law as it recently stood that he did not consider that was necessary for the House of Lords, "...to give what is called a 'new ruling' based on freedom of expression, public opinion and the consequences of a negative ruling on those whom it is said can only get satisfaction from through these acts". Indeed, Lord Slynn regarded the last criterion as being, at best of little relevance to the decision and nor did he think it to be the responsibility of the Court to make new law so as to bring England into line with other jurisdictions. Such a task was a matter for the legislature.[216]

However, there was another matter which could not be avoided: that was the issue of *policy*, which had been raised by the Director of Public Prosecutions in a written submission.[217] Lord Slynn agreed that the issue was, indeed, a matter of policy in an area where social and moral factors were extremely important and where attitudes could change. "If", he said, "Society takes the view that this kind of behaviour, even though sought after and done in private is either so new or so extensive or so undesirable that it should be brought now for the first time within the criminal law, then it is for the legislature to decide." Nevertheless, Lord Slynn reached the conclusion[218] that, where charges of the present nature had been brought in respect of acts done between adults in private, it must be proved by the prosecution that the person to whom the act was done did not consent to it and, hence, that the convictions should be set aside.

Having discussed the more important aspects of the *Brown* decision, it should be borne in mind that the judgments of both Lord Templeman and Lord Slynn were both essentially conservative in their general approaches to the issue. Thus, Lord Templeman seemed to predicate his approach on the view[219] that the appellants' conduct was not essentially sexual in nature but, rather, the product of an urge to inflict cruelty, or in fact, to receive it. This does not take into, probably proper, account of the complexity of human sexuality. Lord Slynn, on the other hand, strictly applied the law as he considered that it then stood[220] and did not consider that it was the function of the courts, even the jurisdiction's highest appellate court, to change the law in the area without legislative intervention.[221] It may, it seems, apparent, be reducible to issues of *perception* or, perhaps, to words. Thus, Bix points out[222] that, "…the same activity can often be described in different ways. For example, someone speaking at Hyde Park Corner could be described as a 'Nazi sympathiser preaching racial hatred' or as 'a participant in a political debate'. Both descriptions would be accurate, but our inclination to protect the right of the person to speak might depend on the characterization." Hence, he asks, is *Brown* about sexual practices between consenting adults, or is it about a particular, deviant, legally unprotected sexual practice? Much, as will later be seen, will depend, it is suggested, on the context in which the relevant acts take place.[223] "In a similar way", Bix continues,[224] "professional boxing could be characterized as either a sport of skill and strategy which involves violence, or as an activity where the purpose is to cause extreme injury, which is also treated by some, perversely, as a sport." Boxing has already been considered, in the context of its sporting qualities.[225] However, in the present context, what troubles Bix is that there appears to be no reasoned basis for preferring one characterisation rather than another. Therefore, he argues that it is likely that some people may choose one category over another because it supports a conclusion which they wish to reach. It might be thought, in view of the earlier discussion, that there might be a genuinely objective basis for preferring one characterisation to another, but it does seem difficult. Anderson has commented [226] that, "Boxing's veil of credibility and legitimacy has since frayed in the face of its poor, at times egregious, regulatory and medical record. It remains unlikely, however, that boxing's current and precarious legal status will see an individual boxer or the sport become subject to a prosecution. The criminal law alone is too blunt an instrument by which to proscribe the sport. Nevertheless, boxing should not draw too much comfort from that reticence. Fox hunting, despite having a tradition that is established as any other sport and a socio-economic base far more advanced than of boxing, has been banned in England and Wales. The hurt suffered by foxes is not televised, nor do they die in front of a baying crowd. Sometimes boxers do and the next time a high-profile injury or death occurs, will boxing be able to withstand the focus groups, the abolitionists and the medical associations? In that instance, boxing's long history, its popularity, its traditional immunities and assumptions, even the eloquence of the many writers who are drawn to it, may not be sufficient to deter the calls for proscription." Anderson concludes his excellent study by stating simply that, if professional boxing is unable to make particular radical reforms, its status is insufficient to protect it from legislative proscription.[227]

According to Hedley,[228] another commentator on the case, a further difficulty which attaches to *Brown* is that of retrospectivity. "Suppose", he writes, "the police acquire a video of a typical boxing match. They charge all persons present with complicity in the allegedly unlawful violence. What could be said on appeal there that could not have been said here too? Arguments based on pain, cruelty, corruption, and health apply with equal or greater force. Condemnation in the case of public fights goes back centuries. If the consent given here calls for investigation, then so does the consent given by boxers, who run huge risks for what are usually rather paltry financial rewards." What, Hedley asks, do psychiatrists say on that?

Yet there are other – perhaps more mundane – issues which arise out of *Brown* and various comments which have been made on it. In his dissenting judgment,[229] Lord Mustill made reference[230] to particular issues which he regarded as touching on the issue of consent – these were, first prize-fighting, sparring and boxing; second, contact sports (such, in his own words,[231] as the various codes of football) and, third, so-called lawful correction. Fourth, dangerous pastimes, [232] fifth, surgery and, sixth, prostitution and, finally, rough horseplay. Already *boxing* and *lawful correction* have already been touched on.

As regards the former, Lord Murstill adopted a rather different standpoint from, say, Anderson [233] when he stated: [234] "That the court in such cases making a value judgment, not dependant upon any general theory of consent is exposed by the failure of any attempt to deduce why professional boxing appears to be immune from prosecution. For money, not recreation or personal improvement, each boxer tries to hurt the opponent more than he is hurt himself, and aims to end the contest prematurely by inflicting a brain injury serious enough to make the opponent unconscious, or temporarily by impairing his central nervous system through a blow to the midriff, or cutting the skin to a degree which would normally be well within the scope of [the Act]. The boxers display skill, strength and courage, but nobody pretends that they do good to themselves or others. The onlookers derive entertainment, but none of the physical and moral benefits which have been seen as the fruits of engagement in manly sports... It is in my judgment best to regard this as another special situation which for the time being stands outside the ordinary law of violence because society chooses to tolerate it."[235] Lord Mustill's approach to *lawful correction* is very similar: he notes [236] that the infliction of pain must not go too far [237] and for the purpose of correction and not for the purpose of *gratification of passion or rage*.[238] It has, he continues, nothing to do with consent and is, "...only useful as a demonstration that specially exempt situations can exist and that they can involve an upper limit of tolerable harm." The Swinburne story, given that it seems reasonably clear that his personality was shaped to no small extent by his Eton experience, suggests that tolerable harm, as used by Lord Mustill, is something of an amorphous concept.

It may be possible to cloud the issues still further by combining boxing and school discipline. At the (private) school attended by the author, fighting between pupils was frowned upon. If pupils were caught fighting, they were required to take part in a boxing match in the school gymnasium under supervision. In many instances, this procedure was thoroughly unfair and unreasonable in that a bullied child who had lashed out at his tormentor was likely to be assaulted twice, the second time with official approval. The matter was complicated by the fact that contact sports, as referred to by Lord Mustill, were compulsory – including boxing.

Suppose that in one of these supervised fights, a notable bully seriously injures a very much smaller pupil who he has been bullying. The school's liabilities might be (and, in this writer's view, ought to be) serious. Certainly, it is hard to find any legal or ethical, arguments for justifying the school's actions in seeking to resolve one potentially violent situation by means of another.

As Lord Mustill seemed to suggest in his discussion of professional boxing,[239] it is apparent that there are likely to be limits on the operation of the majority view in *Brown*. That such is the case is illustrated by the decision of the English Court of Appeal (Criminal Division) in *R v Wilson*.[240] In that case, the appellant, at his wife's instigation, branded his initials on her buttocks with a hot knife. He was charged with assault occasioning actual bodily harm contrary to the legislation[241] involved in the *Brown* case. At the close of the prosecution case, on a submission of no case to answer the trial judge ruled that, despite the wife's consent, he was bound by authority, including *Brown*, to direct the jury to convict. In light of the ruling, the appellant was not called to give evidence and defence counsel did not make any submissions to the jury. The appellant was convicted and appealed to the Court of Appeal who quashed the initial conviction. In so doing, Russell L J emphasised[242] that, in the Court of Appeal's view, *Brown* was not authority for the proposition that consent is no defence to a charge under the legislation[243] in all circumstances where actual bodily harm had been inflicted deliberately. It was of particular significance that the three judges, including Lord Templeman,[244] had referred to tattooing as being an activity which, if carried out with the consent of an adult did not constitute an offence under the provision, despite the fact that actual bodily harm had been deliberately inflicted. Russell LJ then went on to say[245] that the Court of Appeal, "...could not detect any logical difference between what the appellant did and what he might have done in the way of tattooing. The latter activity apparently requires no state authorisation and the appellant was as entitled to engage in it as anyone else. We do not think that we are entitled to assume that the method adopted by the appellant and his wife was any more dangerous or painful than tattooing. There was simply no evidence to assist the court on this aspect of the matter."

The next question was whether public policy or public interest required that the actions of the appellant should be the subject of criminal proceedings. Having noted that the majority in *Brown* had clearly taken the view that those considerations were relevant, Russell L J then went on to state that the Court of Appeal were, "...firmly of the opinion it is not in the public interest that activities such as the appellant's in this appeal should amount to criminal behaviour. Consensual behaviour between husband and wife, in the privacy of their matrimonial home, is not, in our judgment, a proper matter for criminal investigation, let alone criminal prosecution." In consequence of that view, they regarded the trial judge as having misdirected himself that *Brown, inter alia*, constrained him to rule that consent was no defence as well as to the facts of the case itself. "In this field," Russell L J considered, "...the law should develop a case by case basis rather than upon general propositions to which, in the changing times in which we live, exceptions may arise from time to time not expressly covered by authority."[246]

It is clear that *Wilson* was appropriately decided and for the correct reasons in general. The appellant's actions in *Wilson* were very different in kind from those which were involved in *Brown*. The only concern which is felt by this commentator is that the analogy with tattooing is flawed. Today, when young people in particular, especially in this writer's home Australian State, are enthusiastically tattooed, professional tattoo artists would, doubtless, argue that the conditions under which their operations are carried out are clinically hygienic. It is equally clear from *Wilson*[247] that the operation there cannot be so described. In addition to *Brown*, the court in Wilson distinguished an earlier case, R v *Donovan*,[248] which is altogether more closely connected with the proclivities of the poet Swinburne. In *Donovan*, the appellant had been charged with caning a seventeen years old girl for the purpose of sexual gratification and pleaded in defence that the prosecutrix had consented. In summing up, the Chairman of Quarter-Sessions had directed the jury that, "consent or no consent" was the vital issue in the case. The Court of Criminal Appeal held that there had been a misdirection. The question which should have been put first, to the jury was, the Court considered,[249] whether the blows which were struck were intended to do bodily harm. It was only if this question were answered in the negative that the jury would be required to consider the issue of whether the prosecution had proved absence of consent. In

Wilson, Russell L J noted[250] that the act in *Donovan* had, even though it was carried out in private, an aggressive element. There was no question, in *Donovan*, but that act was done for the purpose of sexual gratification. That, of course, instantly raises the issue of the school floggings witnessed and described by Swinburne: if they were engaged in for the purpose of sexual gratification in respect of the teacher carrying them out, the pupil receiving the flogging or the audience of other pupils (and they seem to have affected Swinburne significantly for the worse) then it does not seem to fit with the notion of *lawful correction*, as raised by Lord Mustill in *Brown*.[251]

4. Some Concluding Thoughts

From the foregoing it is relatively easy to see that both of the writers who have been examined in this chapter have been affected, in one respect or another, by their contacts – sometimes direct and sometimes indirect – with the law.

Insofar as D H Lawrence is concerned, there can be little doubt that his experiences with censorship laws and their enforcement coloured his attitude towards the legal system and its operatives, in England, at least. His poem regarding the Bow Street hearing arising out of the exhibition of his paintings[252] is quite sufficient evidence of that. It is readily apparent that Lawrence regarded the proceedings as themselves as petty and juvenile which they very well might have been. However, it was not, it is suggested, these proceedings which affected Lawrence's work most directly and graphically, but his experiences with the *Defence of the Realm Regulations* during his time in Cornwall. This was as earlier noted,[253] most apparent in his novel *Kangaroo*,[254] where the Lawrence figure, called Somers in the book, is sought after by Cooley, the "Kangaroo" of the title. Cooley is the charismatic Supreme Commander of the Diggers which was a Right Wing organisation of 1914-18 War veterans whose prevailing ideal is a political system based on the organised chain of command which they had known in armed forces in wartime. Cooley's enthusiasm and rhetoric is infectious – "Where there's fire there's change. And where the fire is love, there's creation"[255] – and Somers is all but infected. "[H]e found himself *wanting*," Lawrence writes,[256] "to be convinced, wanted to be carried away." At the same time, behind the benevolent love professed by Cooley, and in the creative "fire" which he urged, Somers could perceive the nascent fascism which had lead to the devastation of Europe and the destruction of British youth in the 1914-18 war. Hence, the memory of his persecution by the "stay-at-home bullies" [257] in England led to a recrudescence of Somers's revulsion of what he perceived as mob rule on a national scale. To survive it, Somers believed, a man, "...must identify himself with the criminal mob, sink his sense of truth, of justice, and of human honour, and bay like some horrible unclean hound, bay...from slavering unclean jaws."[258] Lawrence's disgust at the spectacle of, "...the lowest creatures of mankind spying on the finer creatures to drag them down"[259] and his prophecy regarding the outcome of such a situation may be found in his short poem "Police Spies" which appeared in *Pansies*, ultimately published a year before his death, in 1929:

> Start a system of official spying
> and you've introduced anarchy into your country.

Yet, although that poem might have been a predictable response to Lawrence's Cornish experiences, he wrote two other brief poems in the same collection, which bear directly on his experience and, in the first, Lawrence points to Cooley in *Kangaroo*. [260] It is entitled "New Brooms":

> New brooms sweep clean
> but they often raise such a dust in the sweeping
> that they choke the sweeper.

Finally, the most complete societal response by Lawrence, in *Pansies*, to the manifestations of his treatment in Cornwall and after and, also, a response to the censorship issues involved with both his poems and paintings can be found in "Liberty's Old Old Story."

> Men fight for liberty, and win it with hard knocks.
> Their children, brought up easy, let slip away again,
> poor fools.
> And their grandchildren are once more slaves.

Collecting thoughts about Swinburne's life, literary work and the law is rather more complicated than the process was in the case of D H

Lawrence. The reasons are not far to seek: first, his life and reputation were diffuse and, second, his contact with the law was, effectively, non-existent. An immediate instance of the diffuse nature and effect of his life and work can be illustrated by the effects of Morley's review of *Poems and Ballads* in 1866, to which reference has already been made.[261] As Wilson points out,[262] that review had the instant effect of destroying both the book's short-term sales and Swinburne's reputation. The publication of *Poems and Ballads* was thought by Swinburne's friend, Edmund Gosse, to represent the worst literary scandal since Lord Byron had been forced to leave England fifty years earlier.[263] At the same time, that was not to last: he was read by younger people and within a relatively short time, he was worshipped, according to Wilson, as though he were some kind of deity, with students at Oxford and Cambridge chanting his rhymes and rhythms:

> I will go back to the great sweet mother,
> Mother and lover of men, the sea.
> I will go down to her, I and none other,
> Close with her, kiss her and mix her with me;
> Cling to her, strive with her, hold her fast;
> O fair white mother in days long past
> Born without sister, born without brother,
> Set free my soul as thy soul is free.

Thus, Wilson suggests[264] that, in the medium term, Morley's scabrous review, which had moved Swinburne to rage and depression, proved the best publicity which Swinburne could have had.

Nor did Swinburne escape attention from other notable Victorian figures. In W S Gilbert's operetta *Patience*, one of the central characters is a "fleshly poet" named Reginald Bunthorne, who has long been, and wrongly in my view, assumed to be based upon Oscar Wilde. I have been convinced that, in fact, Swinburne was the model for that character. A key passage occurs towards the end of Act I when the principal characters sing "And the pain that's all but a pleasure will change/ For the pleasure that's all but pain"[265] The sentiments are quite clearly redolent of those to be found in Swinburne's poem "Rocco", quoted earlier.[266] There is also support for the view which I seek to advance, here and elsewhere,[267] in the writings of Jenkins.[268]

Swinburne's lack of direct contact with the law and its machinery was probably largely coincidental: his work (however shocking it may have been to some...!) was never subjected, unlike that of D H Lawrence, to official censorship. It is also clear that he used the services provided by flagellant brothels,[269] though how interested the authorities would have been is, at least, open to question. Wilson, certainly, does not seem to have taken it very seriously, when he wrote[270] that, "Generally speaking, it seems to have been rather tame although the sight of the diminutive naked poet, bounding around the room with mingled cries of agony and delight, pursued by a buxom wench wielding a cat-o-nine-tails, must have been hilarious." It appeared that Swinburne broke his connection with one particular establishment in 1868, when the financial demands of the proprietress became too great; as Wilson[271] puts the matter, "The child in him wanted to indulge the fantasies of 'correction'; the adult objected to being taken for a fool."

Yet Swinburne's obsession, howsoever harmless, lives on not merely in his poetic works, but in the law. The very existence of cases such as, in chronological order, *Donovan*, *Brown* and *Wilson* which have all been discussed in this chapter bear tribute to Swinburne's life in the law. Furthermore, his obsession was shared with other well known cultural figures: thus Bird has described[272] the Australian composer, Percy Grainger, having a similar problem. However, as Wilson points out,[273] it might very well be that some of Grainger's obsession might very well have attracted the quite justifiable, attentions of the law. Wilson quotes him as saying to his pupil, Karen Holten, who he involved in flagellant practices, "I wish to procreate independent children... I propose this: Never to whip them until they are old enough to grasp the meaning of lots of things, then say to them: Look here! I want to ask a favour from you kids. I want to whip you, because it gives me extraordinary pleasure...& when my girls begin to awaken sexually I would gradually like to have carnal knowledge with them... I have always dreamed of having children & whipping them & to have a sensual life with my own daughters." The issues relating to consent which were raised in *Donovan*, *Brown* and *Wilson* are not germane to an incestuously sadistic outburst of this nature. Likewise in his monumental study of the phenomenon,[274] Gibson has drawn attention to another work,[275] which has more of the characteristics of Swinburne, than the altogether more dangerous and distasteful obsessions of Grainger, including school behaviour.

Thus, *in fine*, both the situations of the writer in the law – D H Lawrence – and the law in the writer – A C Swinburne – involved very unhappy people although in very different ways. In the case of Lawrence, the law and is machineries and enforcements are, in essence if not necessarily in actuality, products of the intellect and that, of itself, may have produced antithetical feelings in Lawrence. Wilson argues[276] that Lawrence had, "...an extremely negative attitude to the intellect. And this hatred of the intellect was also bound up with the feeling that modern civilisation condemns people to boredom and futility." If this is correct, and there is much internal evidence in Lawrence's writing at large to suggest that it may well be, then there can be few more alienating than the law, especially when it seems to be involved in seeking to deter or abstract creativity in whatever form. The situation of Swinburne is different and altogether more bizarre. Swinburne is surrounded by the law in both space and, particularly, time. It is impossible to disentangle Swinburne's psychological obsessions from the law's responses, albeit in cases involving other people, and in the future. In truth, it may be that if the poet is not specifically involved with the manifestations of the law, then the poet may be manifested in the law, if not by strict subject matter, but by *rhetoric*.

---

[1] Above Ch III, text at n 203.
[2] Ibid at n 190.
[3] Ibid at n 177.
[4] [1981] AC 1 at 18.
[5] See, for example, *A-G* v *Margaret and Regius Professors in Cambridge* (1682) 1 Vern 55 – the establishment of a professional position.
[6] See, *Construction Industry and Training Board* v *A-G*. [1973] Ch 173 which decided that an organisation with the aim of encouraging craftsmanship and maintaining the standards of both ancient and modern crafts.
[7] R Pearce and J Stevens, *The Law of Trusts and Equitable Obligations* (4th Ed, 2006) at 493.
[8] Above text at n 4.
[9] [1957] 1 WLR 729 at 737.
[10] [1965] Ch 669.
[11] Ibid at 673.
[12] Ibid at 675.
[13] Ibid at 678
[14] Ibid at 679. In making these comments he relied on the judgment of Lord Simonds in *National Anti-Vivisection Society* v *Ireland Revenue Commissioners* [1948] AC 31. See above Ch III text at n 201.
[15] Above text at n 9*ff*.
[16] [1965] Ch 669 at 680.
[17] Ibid at 676.

[18] Professor Muir and Mr Crow.
[19] [1965] Ch 669 at 677.
[20] F Bacon, *The Essays* (1625) at 316.
[21] J H Baker, *An Introduction to English Legal History* (4th Ed. 2002) at 109.
[22] W. Holdsworth, Some Makers of English Law (1938) at 103.
[23] See P Ferris, *Dylan Thomas* (1977) which relates, *passim*, instances which might justify such a description.
[24] [1966] 2 All ER 241.
[25] In the words of the alleged donee, as noted by the judge, ibid at 243, "The only words I can remember him actually saying were that I had saved his life. I said that it had seemed an awful pity that the original had been lost and that it meant an awful lot to me. I had been working on it very closely over six or seven years, and it was the culmination of one of the most interesting things I had produced. He said if I could find it I could keep it. He told me the names of half a dozen pubs, and said if he had not left it there he might have left it in a taxi".
[26] [1966] 2 All ER 241 at 244.
[27] For comment, see F Bates, "Dylan Thomas and the Idea of Justice" in *In Memoriam Senator J William Fulbright 1905-1995* (2010, Eds Magiru, Magiru and Johnson) 15.
[28] The poem appears in a section entitled, "Songs I Learned at School."
[29] For comment, see F Bates and R McGinty, "Arrest him, he's Indecent, he's obscene, what's more." The Poems and Paintings of D H Lawrence as Part of Cultural Heritage and Moral Outrage" (2006) 10 *Newcastle LR* 91 at 108 *ff*.
[30] 1931 SLT 94.
[31] Ibid at 99.
[32] Ibid at 96.
[33] See below text at n 81*ff*. Lord Sands pointed out, in addition, that the words *decent* and *indecent* were frequently used in relation to matters other than those to which he had made specific allusion.
[34] In the judge's own words, 1931 SLT 94 at 96, "[The] picture of Mrs Brown, to which only the very strait-laced might take exception if displayed as a work of art in a remote city, might be grossly indecent if displayed in Brown's drawing room in Edinburgh.
[35] Ibid at 97.
[36] Below text at n 48.
[37] Glasgow *Corporation Order Confirmation Act* 1914 s 21.
[38] 1931 SLT 94 at 99.
[39] *R v Stanley* [1965] 1 QB 327 at 333 per Lord Parker C J. See below text at n 96.
[40] See below text at n 101.
[41] L Blom-Cooper and G Drewny (Eds) *Law and Morality* (1976) at 213 *ff*.
[42] JHA Macdonald, *Practical Treatise on the Criminal Law of Scotland* (1867) at 206. It does not seem as though Macdonald could not be accorded the status of an institutional writer. See D M Walker, *Oxford Companion To Law* (1980) at 791.
[43] *McLoughlan v Boyd* 1934 JC 19.
[44] [1963] 2 QB 717 at 724.
[45] See *R v Sidney* (1663) 1 Sid 168.
[46] Above n 32. Factually, Mayling was concerned factually with observed indecent behaviour in a public lavatory.
[47] See, for example, N St John Stevas, "Obscenity and the Law" [1954] *Criminal L R* 817; DGT Williams, "The Control of Obscenity" [1965] *Criminal LR* 471, 522; G Zellick, "Films and the Law of Obscenity" [1971] Criminal L R 126.
[48] (1868) LR 3 QB 360 at 371.
[49] *Hicklin* was concerned with copies of a pamphlet, entitled "*The Confessional Unmasked;* showing the depravity of the Romish priesthood, the iniquity of the confessional, and the questions put to females in the confession. It appeared that the appellant had not kept these works for profit or gain, but for the purpose of exposing what he believed to be the errors of the Roman Catholic Church.

[50] Above n 49.
[51] *Obscene Publications Act* 1857.
[52] Above n 29 at 112 *ff*.
[53] So that, for instance, s 1(1) of the *Obscene Publications Act* 1959 provided that, "For the purposes of this Act an article shall be deemed to be obscene if its effect (or where the article comprises two or more distinct items) the effect of any one of its items is, if taken as a whole, such as to deprave and corrupt persons who are likely, having regard to all the circumstances, to read, see, or hear the matter contained in it."
[54] Above text at n 48.
[55] [1972] 3 All ER 12 at 18.
[56] Authors emphasis.
[57] (1968) 41 ALJR 402 at 409.
[58] Author's emphasis.
[59] (1968) 41 ALJR 402 at 409.
[60] Above text at n 32.
[61] *Obscene and Indecent Publications Act* 1901-1955 s 16.
[62] [1972] 1 QB 304.
[63] Theo Ruoff, "Links With London" (1971) 45 *Aust LJ* 640 at 641 *ff*.
[64] John Mortimer QC. The statement of his argument is taken from the judgment of Lord Widgery CJ in *Anderson* [1972] QB 304 at 315.
[65] *R v Calder & Boyers Ltd* [1969] 1 QB 151.
[66] *Calder (John) Publications Ltd v Powell* [1965] 1 QB 509.
[67] Above at n 62, 65.
[68] In a serious case, that is the jury, but, in a less serious case, for the judge or magistrate sitting alone.
[69] See, for example, *Obscene Publications Act* 1959 s 4; *R v Penguin Books Ltd* [1961] Criminal LR 176.
[70] [1976] 3 All ER 775. For comment, see F Bates, "Pornography and the Expert Witness" (1978) 20 *Crim LQ* 250.
[71] Ibid at 785.
[72] [1954] 2 All ER 683 at 686.
[73] Ibid at 688, where Stable J told the jury that you will have to, "...consider whether the author was pursuing an honest purpose and an honest thread of thought or whether that was all just a bit of camouflage..." That direction was regarded as being too favourable to the defence.
[74] J Worthen, *D H Lawrence: The Life of an Outsider* (2005) at 388 *ff*.
[75] The only real reason, in Worthern's view, ibid at 388, was that Frieda, Lawrence's wife, wished for a place of her own.
[76] Ibid at 388.
[77] Ibid at 389.
[78] Above text at n 30 *ff*.
[79] [1954] 2 All ER 683 at 687.
[80] *Joel v Morison* (1834) 6 C & P 501 at 503 per Parke B.
[81] (1995) FLC 92-615.
[82] Nicholson CJ, Finn and Fogarty JJ.
[83] (1995) FLC 92-615 at 82, 149.
[84] Family Law Council, *Sterilisation and Other Medical Procedures* (1994) at 48. For other comment on the menstruation taboo, see P Fryer, *Mrs Grundy: Studies in English Prudery* (1963) at 71 *ff*.
[85] *Re P and P* marked a serious disagreement, not merely over that rather peripheral matter, between the Court and the Family Law Council. Such disagreements are rare: for comment on the achievements of the Family Law Council, see B Hughes, *The Family Law Council 1976-1996: A Record of Achievement* (1996).
[86] A Comfort, *The Anxiety Makers: Some Curious Sexual Preoccupations of the Medical Profession* (1967) at 134 *ff*.

[87] Above n 74 at 489.
[88] See also references in *Pansies* to "John Thomas" in "The Little Wowser" and "To Clarinda". It will be remembered that *John Thomas and Lady Jane* was one of the early working titles of *Lady Chatterley's Lover*.
[89] Quoted in E Nehls (Ed) *D H Lawrence: A Composite Biography* Vol 3, 1925-1930 (1959) at 308 *ff*.
[90] (1891-1947) Labour MP for Middlesbrough East, 1924-1931.
[91] Above text at n 77.
[92] 2nd March 1929 to Mobel Dodge Lahan.
[93] Labour MP for Leicester West, who later became Baron Peaslake. Miss Wilkinson was unable to attend the debate owing to a family bereavement.
[94] See above text at n 77.
[95] Under the directed questioning of Mr Charles Ammon, later Baron Camberwell, Labour member for Camberwell North.
[96] [1965] 2 QB 327.
[97] Above text at n 93.
[98] 1953 SC (J) 16.
[99] See T B Smith, "The Contribution of Lord Cooper of Culross to the Law of Scotland" 1955 67 *Jur. Rev* 249.
[100] 1953 SC (J) 16 at 29.
[101] Above text as n 32.
[102] [1965] 2 QB 327 at 332.
[103] Ibid at 333.
[104] Ibid at 334.
[105] For more detailed comment, see above n 29 at 108 *ff*.
[106] P Trotter quoted in above n 89 at 340.
[107] Above n 89 at 342 *ff*.
[108] Ibid at 354.
[109] Ibid at 719.
[110] Above n 74 at 400.
[111] Above n 89 at 386.
[112] By Faber & Faber, as a pamphlet.
[113] From the Hebrew, associated with "Let us Rejoice".
[114] For comment on this time in the Lawrence's lives, see M Kinkead-Weekes, *D H Lawrence: Triumph to Exile 1912-22* (1996) at 293 *ff*.
[115] Quoted in C J Stevens, *Lawrence at Tregerthen* (1988) at 99.
[116] P Delany, *D H Lawrence's Nightmare: The writer and His Circle on the Years of the Great War* (1988) at 99.
[117] Above n 74 at 180.
[118] Above n 116 at 316.
[119] Above n 114 at 347.
[120] Above n 115 at 108.
[121] Above n 114 at 346 *ff*.
[122] Above n 116 at 319 *ff*.
[123] *Defence of the Realm Act* 1914 s 1(a).
[124] Ibid s 1(b)
[125] See, for example, *Marais* v *General Officer Commanding* [1902] AC 109.
[126] In Ireland, the left-wing activist (fated to be executed after the Easter Rising in 1916) expressed, in the Dublin newspaper *Irish Work* (19 December 1914), the opinion that the process established, in an underhand manner, "...martial law as the law of the land." The British Government, he asserted, was "clandestinely and treacherously" seeking to destroy, "...civil liberties while professing a desire to safeguard and protect them."
[127] Above n 74 at 195.
[128] Ibid at 191.

[129] [1917] AC 260. Zadig attracted little in the way of contempory attention, though for a relatively recent commentary, see D Foxford, "*R* v *Holliday ex parte Zadig* in Retrospect" (2003) 119 LQR 455.
[130] Lord Reading CJ, Lawrence, Rowlatt, Atkin and Law JJ.
[131] Swinfen-Eady, Pickford and Bankes LJJ.
[132] Lord Finlay L C. Lords Dunedin, Atkinson, Shaw, and Westbury. Lord Shaw dissenting.
[133] [1917] AC 260 at 268.
[134] Ibid at 270.
[135] Ibid at 290.
[136] Lord Shaw said, ibid at 291, that he had made the same point to the Attorney-General, who had suggested that the latter action seemed to him to be "perfectly logical".
[137] Ibid at 291.
[138] He, then, stated that although, "...the so called principle – the principle of prevention, the comprehensive principle – avoids the odium of that brutality of the Terror. The analogy is with a practice more silent, more sinister – with the *lettres de cachet* of Louis Quatorze. No trial, no proscription. The victim may be 'regulated' – not in his cause of conduct or of action not as to what he should do or is doing. He may be regulated to prison or the scaffold."
[139] [1917] AC 260 at 304.
[140] Above n 129. There was one Note (1917) 33 *LQR* 205, which did not seek to address any of the substantive issues.
[141] For comment, see C P Cotter, "Emergency Detention in Wartime: The British Experience" (1954) 6 *Stanford LR* 238; C Carr, "A Regulated Liberty" (1942) 42 *Columbia LR* 339.
[142] G Hewart, *The New Despotism* (1928). For general comment, see I Jennings, *The Law and the Constitution* (5th Ed, 1959) at 252 *ff*.
[143] C K Allen, *Law in the Making* (7th Ed, 1964) at 565.
[144] It should be said that, apart from the contemporaneous troubles in Ireland and some offshore German activity and a few Zeppolin raids on urban areas, the realm was never genuinely under direct threat.
[145] (1921) 37 TLR 884.
[146] [1920] 1 KB 829.
[147] [1920] 1 KB 854.
[148] (1921) 37 TLR 884 at 886.
[149] Above text at n 133.
[150] See the discussion of Philip Larkin's poem "MCMXIV" in Ch III text at n 10 *ff*.
[151] In addition, a further, separate Act, the *War Charges Act* 1925 was also enacted.
[152] Above text at n 121 *ff*.
[153] D H Lawrence, Letters, iii, at 168.
[154] Above text at n 115.
[155] Above text at n 144 *ff*.
[156] Above text at no 133 *ff*.
[157] [1942] AC 206.
[158] Above text at n 129 *ff*.
[159] Above text at n 129.
[160] Viscount Maughan, Lords Atkin, Macmillan, Wright and Romer.
[161] [1942] AC 206 at 220.
[162] Ibid at 221.
[163] Ibid at 221.
[164] Ibid at 222.
[165] Ibid at 224.
[166] All (official) acts are deemed to have been done correctly.
[167] Above text at n 133 *ff*.
[168] Above text at n 135
[169] H W R Wade, *Administrative Law* (2nd Ed, 1967) at 79.
[170] [1942] AC 206 at 228.

[171] Ibid at 232.
[172] Ibid at 224.
[173] (1850) 5 Ex 378. Cited with approval by Lord Wright in *Bernard v Gorman* [1941] AC 378 at 393.
[174] Above n 168.
[175] [1942] AC 206 at 256.
[176] Ibid at 257.
[177] See particularly above text at n 173.
[178] See especially, A W B Simpson, *In The Highest Degree Odious* (1992); G W Keeton, "*Liversidge v Anderson*" (1942) 5 MLR 162; R F V Heuston, "*Liversidge v Anderson* in Retrospect" (1970) 86 *LQR* 33.
[179] Above text at n 158.
[180] [1942] AC 206 at 265.
[181] [1951] AC 66.
[182] Ibid at 76.
[183] [1964] AC 40 at 73.
[184] C Wilson, *The Misfits: A Study of Sexual Outsiders* (1988) at 142.
[185] Ibid at 142.
[186] Ibid at 143.
[187] Wilson, ibid at 143, points out that, really, the poem tells the story of a mythical king who raped his wife's sister and then cut out her tongue so that she could not tell anyone. His queen avenged herself by killing Itylus, their son, and serving his flesh to his father for dinner.
[188] Ibid at 144.
[189] Wilson, ibid at 144, seeks to back up this view that, long before Swinburne's arrival at Eton, he and his cousin, Mary Gordon (who was three years his junior) used to play flogging games in which they pretended they were pupils at school with savage disciplinary standards.
[190] F Bates, "Corporal Punishment Legal, Historical and Social Context" (1983) 12 *Manitoba L J* 337.
[191] P Henderson, *Swinburne: Portrait of Poet* (1974).
[192] See I Gibson, *The English Vice: Beating Sex and Shame in Victorian England and* After (1978) at 120 *ff.*
[193] G MacBeth (Ed), *The Penguin Book of Victorian Poetry* (1969) at 281.
[194] Above n 190 at 18.
[195] This quotation is taken from "Algernon's Flogging." For comment, see above n 191.
[196] For comment on the position of *The Pearl* in Victorian Society, see, generally, S Marcus, *The Other Victorians: A Study of Sexuality and Pornography in Nineteenth Century England* (1966).
[197] Above n 188.
[198] Above n 183 at 144.
[199] [1994] 1 AC 212.
[200] Ibid at 235.
[201] Ibid at 235.
[202] Ibid at 236.
[203] Ibid at 237.
[204] Lords Jauncey and Lowry delivered judgments agreeing with Lord Templeman.
[205] Lord Mustill also delivered a judgment in dissent.
[206] [1994] 1 AC 212 at 280.
[207] Ibid at 280.
[208] Ibid at 281.
[209] Ibid at 281.
[210] Which decriminalised homosexual acts, which were consensual and in private between two adult males.
[211] *Report of the Committee on Homosexual Offences and Prostitution* (Cmnd 247, 1957) at para 105.

[212] [1994] 1 AC 212 at 281.
[213] Ibid at 282.
[214] See Art 8(2) *European Convention for the Protection of Human Rights and Freedoms* (Rome, 1950).
[215] [1914] 1 AC 212 at 282.
[216] For comment on the issues generally, see L H Leigh, "Sado-masochism, Consent and the Reform of the Criminal Law" (1976) 39 MLR 130.
[217] In the Director's *ipsissima verba*, [1994] 1 AC 212 at 282, "In the end it is a matter of policy. Is/are the state/courts right to adopt a paternalistic attitude as to what is bad or good for subjects, in particular as to deliberate injury".
[218] [1994] 1 AC 212 at 283.
[219] Above text at n 200 *ff*.
[220] Above text at n 206 *ff*.
[221] Above text at n 213 *ff*.
[222] B Bix, "Assault, Sado-masochism and Consent" (1993) 109 LQR 540 at 541.
[223] See the discussion of *R* v *Wilson* [1996] 2 Cr App Rep. 214, below text at n 239 *ff*.
[224] Above at n 221 at 542
[225] Above Ch III at n 261 *ff*.
[226] J Anderson, *The Legality of Boxing: A Punch Drunk Lover?* (2007) at 186.
[227] Ibid at 187. It should also be noted that Anderson, in the preface to his book, status (ibid at xiii) that, "...I am a fan of the sport of boxing. I like its character, its courage and it minimalism. Nonetheless, my love of the sport is often uncomfortable and frequently unfaithful".
[228] S Hedley, "Sado-masochism, Human Rights and the House of Lords" (1993) 52 *CLJ* 194 at 196.
[229] Above n 204
[230] [1994] 1 AC 212 at 262 *ff*.
[231] Ibid at 265.
[232] In which he included (ibid at 266) *bravado*, where a man challenges another to hurt him with a blow and *religious mortification*.
[233] Above text at n 225.
[234] [1994] 1 AC 212 at 265.
[235] Compare the approach of McInerney J of the Supreme Court of Victoria in *Pallante* v *Stadiums Pty Ltd (No. 1)* [1976] VR 231.
[236] [1994] 1 AC 212 at 267.
[237] See *R* v *Hopley* (1860) 2 F & F 202.
[238] Authors' emphasis.
[239] Above text at n 233.
[240] [1997] QB 47.
[241] *Offences Against the Person Act* 1861 s 47.
[242] [1997] QB 47 at 50.
[243] Above n 240.
[244] [1994] 1 AC 212 at 231. The others were Lord Jauncey, ibid at 245 and Lord Slynn, ibid at 277.
[245] [1997] QB 47 at 50.
[246] Russell L J, ibid at 51, concluded his judgment by saying that he shared the trial judge's disquiet that the prosecuting authority had seen fit to bring the proceedings. In his view, they served, "...no useful purpose at considerable public expense."
[247] [1997] QB 47 at 48 *ff*.
[248] [1934] 2 KB 498.
[249] Ibid at 509
[250] [1997] QB 47 at 49.
[251] Above text at n 235.
[252] Above text at n 108.
[253] Above text at n 153.

[254] The edition to which reference is made is that published by Cambridge University Press in 1994 and edited by Bruce Steele.
[255] *Kangaroo* at 132.
[256] Ibid at 132.
[257] Ibid at 212.
[258] Ibid at 212.
[259] Ibid at 249.
[260] Above text at n 253.
[261] Above text at n 183 *ff*.
[262] Above n 183 at 143.
[263] For Wilson's comments on that scandal and other aspects of Lord Byron's life, see ibid at 92 *ff*.
[264] Ibid at 144.
[265] See W S Gilbert, *Original Plays* (3rd Series, 1928) Act I at 112.
[266] Above text at n 182.
[267] Above n 189.
[268] W D Jenkins, "Swinburne, Robert Buchanan and W S Gilbert: "The Pain that is all but a Pleasure" (1972) 69 *Studies in Philology* 369.
[269] Above nn 183, 189, 191. Including one with the name of *The Grove of the Evangelist*.
[270] Above n 183 at 149.
[271] Ibid
[272] J Bird, *Percy Grainger* (1976) generally.
[273] Above n 183 at 205.
[274] Above n 191 at 95 *ff*.
[275] "Y" *The Autobiography of An Englishman* (1975).
[276] Above n 183 at 193.

Chapter V
Crime and Retribution

1. **Introductory : Divine Retribution...?**

Although the terms *crime* and *criminal law* are frequently utilised, both in legal and literary (as well as everyday) parlance, it seems to be a rather more difficult task to devise an encompassing decision. A valuable instance is provided by an attempt by a leading English scholar in the area, Glanville Williams, who considered[1] various definitions. He rejected all of them for various and particular reasons and, ultimately, produced one of his own. It was that, "...a crime is an act capable of being followed by criminal proceedings having a criminal outcome, and a proceeding or is outcome is criminal if it has certain characteristics which mark it as criminal... The features actually taken by the courts as indicative of crime, and the problems that arise in classifying proceedings, must be left for discussion on another occasion." In commenting on that definition, one must seek to be cautious. Williams himself denied that its earlier part was circular in nature and I am sure that the second comment was not intentionally evasive. Despite the fact that even as signal authority as Williams was hard pressed to project a comprehensive definition, the notion of *crime* must surely present some identifiable features. However, as Duff concedes,[2] even that is not without its difficulties and he urges scholars to resist the, "...desire to find some simple concept or value that will capture the essence of crime or *the* essential characteristic in virtue of which crimes are properly punished...in favour of a pluralism that recognises a diversity of reasons for criminalisation, matching the diversity of kinds of wrong which can legitimately be the criminal law's business. Ormerod, though, notes[3] that despite the lack of a generally approved definition, "...it is possible to point to certain characteristics, which are *generally* found in conduct which is criminal, in particular, it usually involves a public wrong and a moral wrong."[4] As regards the *public* nature of crime, Ormerod comments[5] that it is evidenced by the contrast between the rules of criminal and civil procedure: as a general rule, any citizen, in the absence of any specific contrary provision, may bring a criminal prosecution regardless of whether she or he has suffered any special harm over and above any other member of the public. In the case of civil wrongs - such as torts or breaches of conduct - the only person who may sue is the person who has been injured. Of course, in actuality, the vast majority of prosecutions are undertaken by official agencies such as the Director of Public Prosecutions or Crown Prosecution Service, depending on the jurisdiction or subject matter.

In addition to Omerod's explanation, however, there is a related aspect of the *formal* nature of crime. Thus, as the United States commentators Michael and Adler put[6] the matter, "The criminal law is the formal cause of crime... Without a criminal code there would be no crime...the question involved in the formulation or amendment of a criminal code can be stated as what crimes do we wish to cause." Some jurisdictions do not have criminal codes: in Australia, for example, the States of Queensland, Tasmania and Western Australia have criminal codes whereas other jurisdictions do not, though there is a greater or lesser degree of legislative intervention. As Cohen has described[7] the situation, "Acts are criminal not because they *are* harmful, but because they are *deemed* harmful by those who make or interpret the law". This view was also expressed by the distinguished English judge, Lord Atkin, who put the matter another way in the case of *Proprietary Articles Trade Association v Attorney-General for Canada,*[8] "The criminal quality of an act cannot be discussed by intuition; nor can it be discovered by reference to any standard but one: Is that act prohibited with penal consequences. Morality and criminality are far from coextensive; nor is the sphere of criminality necessarily part of a more extensive area covered by morality - unless the moral code necessarily disapproved all acts prohibited by the State, in which case the argument moves in a circle." Or, more brutally, Lord Devlin, speaking[9] extra-judicially, "The criminal law is not a statement of how people ought to behave; it is a statement of what will happen to them if they do not behave." This may appear a strange utterance from a commentator whose essential thesis[10] was that there existed a public morality which helped bind society together and that the State was under an obligation to use the criminal law to preserve that fundamental morality. That view has been replicated in the well known decision of the House of Lords in *Shaw v DPP,*[11] which is deserving of comment. In *Shaw*, the appellant had published a book which was entitled, euphemistically the *Ladies Directory*. That publication contained the names and addresses of various prostitutes together, in some cases, with photographs and particular practices in which they might involve themselves. He was convicted, *inter alia*,[12] of conspiring to corrupt public morals and his subsequent appeals to the Court of Criminal Appeal and the House of Lords were dismissed. As was noted by Lord Simonds,[13] it had been vigorously argued on the appellant's behalf that no such offence was known to the common law. Although Lord Simonds said[14] of himself that he was no advocate of the right of judges to create new criminal offences he went on to say that he entertained no doubt that, "...there remains in the courts of law a residual power to enforce the supreme and fundamental purpose of the law, to conserve not only the safety and order but also the moral welfare of the State, and that it is their duty to guard it against attacks which may be the more insidious because they are novel and unprepared for." Lord Tucker, who delivered what is regarded[15] as the leading majority judgment, emphasised[16] that the decision, both in *Shaw* and similar cases, ought not to depend on the label which was to be attached to a particular conspiracy. "Is it to be said," he rhetorically asked, "that a conspiracy to sell decorated domestic pottery in the home market by means of devices contrived to evade the object of Board of Trade orders is a criminal conspiracy but an agreement to do acts calculated to corrupt public morals is not?" After an analysis of prior authority, Lord Tucker based his argument on the premise that, as there was a crime of conspiring to commit a public mischief, a conspiracy to corrupt public morals must necessarily be a public mischief but, at the same time, he did not reject the view which had been expressed in the court of Criminal Appeal that a conspiracy to corrupt public morals was a substantive crime.[17] Lord Morris, likewise in the majority, stated uncompromisingly[18] that, "There are certain manifestations of conduct which are an affront to and an attack upon recognised public standards of morals and decency, and which all well-disposed persons would stigmatise and condemn as deserving of punishment."[19]

There was, though, a strongly dissentient judgment by Lord Reid who regarded himself[20] as being in fundamental disagreement with the views which have been expressed by Lord Tucker. In Lord Reid's view, "...there is no such general offence known to the law as conspiracy to corrupt public morals. Undoubtedly there is an offence of criminal conspiracy and undoubtedly it is of fairly wide scope." Lord Reid first acknowledged that it was generally thought to have been a creature of the Court of Star Chamber[21] and, after a discussion of earlier case law, he reached the conclusion[22] that, "Even if there is still a vestigial power of this kind it ought not…to be used unless there appears to be general agreement that the offence to which it is to be applied ought to be criminal if committed by an individual. Notoriously, there are wide differences of opinion today as to how far the law ought to punish immoral acts which are not done in the face of the public. Some think that the law already goes too far, others that it does not go far enough. Parliament is the proper place, and I am firmly of opinion the only proper place to settle that. When there is sufficient support from public opinion, Parliament does not hesitate to intervene. Where Parliament fears to tread is not for the courts to rush in". As regards Lord Tucker's suggestion that conspiracy to corrupt public morals was a species of public mischief,[23] Lord Reid took the view[24] that the House of Lords was in no way bound, and ought not to sanction, to accept the extension of *public mischief* to any new field, and certainly not if such an extension would be in any way controversial. "Public mischief" he stated[25] "is the criminal counterpart of public policy, and the criminal law ought to be even more hesitant than the civil law in founding on it in some new respect." Finally, Lord Reid turned his attention[26] to the consequences of deciding that such a very general offence existed. His Lordship considered that it had always been regarded as being of primary importance that the law, especially the criminal law, should be certain. In other words, that a person should be able to know what conduct is, or is not, criminal, especially when heavy penalties were involved. Lord Reid also noted that it had been suggested that it did not matter were the offence to be widely drawn on the grounds that it would rarely be prosecuted, and no jury would convict, were the breach merely venial. However, Lord Reid was of the view that if the jury was to be able to interpret relevant words as they liked, "…the court has transferred to the jury the whole of its functions as censor morum, the law will be whatever any jury may happen to think it ought to be, and this branch of the law will have lost all the certainty which we rightly prize on other branches of the law."

There are two matters which arise from this discussion of *Shaw*: first, it is clear from the comments made by Lord Simonds, Lord Tucker and Lord Morris that it is quite impossible in many circumstances to separate morality (and its enforcement) from the law, as has been suggested by some of the commentators noted earlier.[27] Second, the scope of the enforcement of morality is far from certain, particularly, as Lord Reid trenchantly pointed out,[28] where the offence which purports so to do is as widely drawn as that of which *Shaw* was convicted. The uncertainty which necessarily surrounded *Shaw* was further emphasised by the House of Lord's subsequent decision in *DPP* v *Withers*.[29] In that case, the defendants, in the course of business as an investigation agency, obtained access to confidential information from public officials, banks and other such bodies by falsely pretending that they were entitled to access the information. They were charged with conspiracy to effect a public mischief and the jury were directed that agreement to do deceitful acts which would be injurious to the community at large amounted to the offence. The defendants were convicted, and having appealed unsuccessfully to the Court of Appeal, appealed, this time successfully, to the House of Lords.

Of especial importance, from the point of the present discussion, is the approach of Lord Simon to the *Shaw* decision. As regards Lord Tucker's judgment,[30] Lord Simon stated[31] that, "There were three avenues by any one of which he could have reached his conclusion: (a) that the law recognised an offence when committed by an individual of corrupting public morals, so that an agreement to corrupt public morals is a criminal conspiracy as an agreement to commit a crime, (b) that an examination of the authorities shows that the law has consistently recognised an offence of conspiracy to corrupt public morals; (c) that a conspiracy to corrupt public morals is a sub-genus of the genus conspiracy to commit a public mischief, which the law recognises." Lord Simon commented that Lord Tucker expressly had not rejected the first and undoubtedly relied on the third. However, Lord Simon did go on to say[32] that if the third of Lord Tucker's avenues were to be applied in connection with an earlier case,[33] it would lead to the conclusion that the law recognised a generic offence of conspiracy to effect a public mischief, that term being descriptive of an agreement to perpetrate conduct which is extremely injurious to the public. On the other hand, he continued, were the House of Lords to do so in *Withers*, they would be, "...accepting a judicial situation the practical effect of which is to permit the forensic creation of new criminal offences or the forensic extension of the ambit of old ones... Although, no doubt, the line between, on the one hand, applying to new circumstances a rule which defines and existing offence and, on the other, the extension of an existing offence is one which is different to draw. I have no doubt that the recognition of a generic offence of conspiracy to effect a public mischief would give an uncontrollable dynamism to this branch of the law. This very case illustrates how the generic offence could penetrate into a sphere (privacy) of great delicacy and controversy and where Parliament has assumed cognisance and as yet taken no action. So although I think that the learned trial judge was, on the authorities, bound to direct the jury as he did, and the court of Appeal to uphold the conviction, your Lordships are, in my judgment, free to declare that no such offence as conspiracy to effect a public mischief is known to the law, and should do so."

That, indeed, is what the House, in *Withers*, did: thus, Viscount Delhorne stated[34] that the preferment of charges alleging public mischief appeared to have increased over the recent past. Although he could not be certain as to the cause, if it was, "…due to a feeling that the conduct of the accused has been so heinous that it ought to be dealt with as criminal and that the best way of bringing it within the criminal sphere is to allege public mischief and trust that the courts will fill the gap, if gap there be, in the law. But if the gap there be, it must be left to Parliament to fill." Viscount Dilhorne concluded his judgment by saying that he hoped that, in future, such a vague term as *public mischief* would not be included in criminal charges. It introduced, he said, "…a wide measure of uncertainty and should not be a vehicle for the enlargement of the criminal law or a device to secure its extension to cover acts not previously thought to be criminal." Lord Simon[35] and Lord Kilbrandon[36] both deprecated any tendency to criminalise acts, which would not otherwise have been crimes by attaching the characterisation of conspiracy to them. Lord Diplock was still more emphatic when he said[37] that it would be disingenuous of him to try to conceal his personal conviction that, "…this branch of the criminal law of England is irrational in treating as a criminal offence an agreement to do that which, if done, is not a crime, and that its irrationality becomes injustice if it takes days of legal argument and historical research to appeal to your Lordships' House to discover whether any crime has been committed even though the facts are undisputed." Hence, it was decided, in *Withers*, that there was no crime of conspiracy to effect a public mischief.[38]

Yet conspiracies to effect a public mischief and to corrupt public morals arise in different situations and are different crimes – assuming that they are crimes – and, in *Withers*, the House of Lords were not discussing the latter. However they had done so in a case subsequent to *Shaw*, *DPP* v

Knuller.³⁹ In *Knuller*, the appellants were directors of a company which produced a fortnightly magazine. On an inside page, under a column heading *Males*, advertisements were placed inviting readers to meet the advertisers for the purpose indulging in homosexual practices. The appellants were convicted, *inter alia*,⁴⁰ of conspiracy to corrupt public morals. They appealed on the grounds that an agreement by two or more people to insert advertisements in a magazine for the purpose of homosexual acts taking place between two consenting adult males in private did not constitute the offence of conspiracy to corrupt public morals. Further that the trial judge had misdirected the jury as to the effect of the *Sexual Offences Act* 1967 on that charge. The Court of Appeal applied *Shaw*⁴¹ and dismissed the appeal. The appellants appealed to the House of Lords on the grounds, *inter alia*, that *Shaw* had been wrongly decided. The House of Lords, applying *Shaw*, dismissed the appeal.

Given Lord Reid's stance in *Shaw*,⁴² his approach in *Knuller* is of not inconsiderable interest. He first, pointed to⁴³ his dissent in *Shaw* and stated that he continued to believe that the decision was wrong and did not wish to alter anything which he had there said. However, it did not, he thought, follow that he should now support a motion to reconsider the decision. "In the general interest of certainty in the law," Lord Reid continued, "we must be sure that there is some very good reason before we so act. We were informed that there had been at least 30 and probably many more convictions of this new crime in the ten years which have elapsed since Shaw's case was decided and it does not appear that there has been manifest injustice or that any attempt has been made to widen the scope of the new crime. I do not regard our refusal to reconsider Shaw's case as in any way justifying any attempt to widen the scope of the decision and I would oppose any attempt to do so. But I think that however wrong or anomalous the decision may be it must stand and apply to cases reasonably analogous unless or until it is altered by Parliament." Again, though, Lord Reid was not especially impressed⁴⁴ by the argument that Parliament must have approved of the *Shaw* decision because there had been, several opportunities for legislation intervention disapproving of the decision. Much recent legislative,⁴⁵ his Lordship considered, had all the indications of compromise and, hence, the courts should accept it and interpret it as such. Having said all of that, however, Lord Reid stated⁴⁶ that some matters were in need of clarification: first, he regarded the offence of conspiracy to corrupt public morals as something of a misnomer – it really meant, his Lordship thought, the corruption of the morals of such members of the public as might be influenced by the matter published by the accused. Second, Lord Reid was of the view that the meaning of the word *corrupt* required some clarification and, indeed, one of his objections to the *Shaw* decision was that it left too much to the jury; juries, unlike judges, were not expected to be experts in the use of the English language and ought to have been given some assistance in the *Shaw* case. "I think", Lord Reid stated,[47] "that the jury should be told that although in the end the question of whether the matter is corrupting is for them, they should keep in mind the current standards of ordinary decent people."

His Lordship then turned his attention to the second submission made on behalf of the appellants: namely that, since homosexual acts committed between adult males in private were no longer criminal, it is unreasonable and cannot be the law that people commit an offence if they merely put in touch with one another two males who wish to take part in such acts. Lord Reid emphasised that there was a material difference between merely exempting particular conduct from criminal penalties and making it *lawful*[48] in the full sense. Further, the judge, found, "...nothing in the Act to indicate that Parliament thought or intended to lay down that indulgence in these practices is not corrupting... [T]he Act is saying that, even though it may be corrupting, if people choose to corrupt themselves in this way that is their affair and the law will not interfere. But no licence is given to others to encourage the practice." Accordingly, Lord Reid dismissed the appeal.

In the majority, Lord Simon emphatically stated[49] that *Shaw* laid down *with certainty*[50] that the offence of conspiracy to corrupt public morals was part of the criminal law. He also urged that parliament had recognised[51] that it had been so established and he also noted that a number of people had been prosecuted and convicted on that basis without its being argued that the rule had led to any injustice. In addition, Lord Simon contended that, in addition, there were three features involved in the case at hand which made it undesirable to depart from the decision in *Shaw:* first, that, in *Knuller*, the House of Lords was concerned with highly controversial issues on which there was every sign that neither public no Parliamentary opinion was settled. In that context, Lord Simon referred to *the Sexual Offences Act* 1967 which illustrated, he thought, society's attitude to "homosexualism" [*sic*]. Further, the decision in *Shaw* itself had lacked neither critics nor champions. "Of course", Lord Simon went on, "courts of law do not shrink from decisions which are liable to be controversial when judicial duty demands such decisions. But your Lordships are here in a field where the decisions – at any rate, policy decisions - are best left to Parliament. Certainly, it is the sort of matter in which it is most undesirable that there should be, in effect, an appeal from one Appellate Committee of your Lordships' House to another." The second additional reason advanced by Lord Simon was that there had been several occasions when Parliament had had the opportunity, had it wished so to do, to abrogate the decision in *Shaw*. It had not taken the opportunity.[52] Third, Lord Simon noted[53] that effectively all of the objections which had been advanced against the offence of conspiracy to corrupt public morals were equally as applicable to that of conspiracy to effect a public mischief. It would hardly be possible, he considered,[54] for the House of Lords to review *Shaw* without reviewing the other offence. Of course, Lord Simon was not to know that that was precisely what the House of Lords was, shortly after to do.[55] It can be seen that, within the majority, there was difference of opinion regarding the role of Parliament,[56] *inter alia*.

Another argument, in the majority, can be found in the judgment of Lord Morris who commented[57] that it had continually been suggested that there was an element of uncertainty which attracted to the offence of conspiracy to corrupt public morals. "It is said", Lord Morris pointed out, "that the rules of law ought to be precise so that a person will know the exact consequences of his actions and so that he can regulate his conduct with complete assurance. This, however, it is not possible under any system of law... In many cases there can be no certainty as to what the decision will be. But none of this is a reflection on the law. Nor do I know of any procedure under which someone could be told with precision just how far he may go before he may incur some civil or some criminal liability. Those who skate on thin ice can hardly expect to find a sign which will denote the precise spot where they may fall in." *Shaw*, hence, Lord Morris considered,[58] was not open to any criticism that it created or tolerated a state of uncertainty, it merely affirmed *with certainty*[59] that an offence was known to the law. Lord Morris then noted that it was argued that the law ought not to be used as an instrument to enforce moral standards. However, he continued, whether or not that view should prevail was not a matter for the courts to resolve. "If ," he said, "there be some who think that in relation to the publication of articles or the performances of plays there should be no restraints at all or at least no restraints which involve or require the machinery of the law for their sanction it is for them to persuade Parliament of their views." However, Parliament, in various items of legislation, had shown that it was prepared to lay down standards which it regarded as appropriate.

As might have been expected there was a judgment in dissent – this time by Lord Diplock, who began his judgment[60] by noting that in *Shaw*, the relevant count was cast in conspiracy, as were the counts in *Knuller*, of which he was critical. "The device of charging a defendant with agreeing to do what he did instead of charging him with doing it has become fashionable in recent years. It may have had a tendency to corrupt judicial reasoning, to which I shall revert later." It is to be noted that the rhetoric used by Lord Diplock is, of itself, of some interest – the language which he has used is more than a little redolent of the language to be found in *R v Hicklin*[61] and the legislation which was derived from it. Lord Diplock then continued by saying that his major criticism of the decision in *Shaw* did not depend on the charge having been framed in terms of conspiracy: the criticised reasoning could, Lord Diplock considered, be reduced to a single syllogism. The syllogism is as follows: "Every agreement to do any act which tends to corrupt public morals is a crime at common law. Shaw's act of publishing advertisements for prostitutes soliciting fornication tended to corrupt public morals. Therefore Shaw's agreement to do that act was a crime at common law". In English law, he continued, it was for the judge alone to determine whether the major premise in that syllogism was true; the truth of the minor premise was a question for the jury, provided there was any material upon which a rational being could hold it to be true. Lord Diplock emphasised that he was not critical of the jury's verdict in *Knuller* upon the minor premise. He denied the conclusion because he was convinced that the major premised was false. It is clear that that view represented a striking disagreement from the approach taken by Lord Simon and Lord Morris in *Knuller* and, more especially, that of Lord Simonds in *Shaw* itself. After having examined many of the older authorities (a reiteration of which is beyond the scope of this book), Lord Diplock stated[62] that those were authorities for holding that, "...agreements to do acts not in themselves criminal if done by one person on his own, may nevertheless amount to criminal conspiracies have I believe always been restricted to the field of trade and employment and, in the case of those which have survived into the 20th century to agreements to defraud and deceive. Save to this limited extend, they do not justify the continued existence in the courts of any new power to create new criminal conspiracies to do acts of a kind which have not been held to have been criminal in themselves." He concluded that part of his judgment by stating that, "The constitutional setting in which judges in earlier centuries claimed the power to create new criminal offences has long since passed away. To have reasserted it in 1962 was, in my view, an unacceptable usurpation of what has now become an exclusively legislative power."

The next issue which arose was that which initially had been raised by Lord Reid in *Knuller:*[63] That is, whether, even though *Shaw* was incorrectly decided, it should in the interests of certainty, continue to be followed. Lord Diplock strongly disagreed[64] with any such view when he stated that, "The vice of Shaw's case was that it opened a wide field of uncertainty as to what other conduct was also criminal. Previously it was possible for a citizen to regulate his conduct in the knowledge that what he was minded to do was not specifically prohibited by a criminal statute and did not fall within any of those equally specific categories of conduct which had already been held to be offences at common law, he could do it without incurring punishment even though most of his fellow citizens might be shocked at it as immoral or indecent. As a result of Shaw's case it would seem that any conduct which conflicts with widely held prejudices as to what is immoral or indecent, at any rate if at least two persons are in any way concerned with it, may now ex post facto be held to have been a crime." *In fine*, Lord Diplock assured[65] the other members of the house that overruling *Shaw* would not subject an unwilling public to forced participation in, "…immoralities or exposure to indecencies which are indulged in by a minority in a permissive age. Most conduct which is offensive to public morals or public decency is prohibited by statute or falls within the ambit of some specific misdemeanor at common law which has been recognised in decided cases." If the defendants in *Knuller* were guilty of such specific offences, they were entitled to be charged with them. They were not so charged and the fact that they might have been undeservedly fortunate were *Shaw* to be overruled ought not, Lord Diplock observed, to deter the House of Lords from correcting a previous error.

Although the present writer is wholly sympathetic to the views expressed by Lord Diplock in *Knuller*, there are more central matters which arise out of *Shaw* and the cases which follow on from it. Ormerod, writing particularly of conspiracy to corrupt public morals,[66] considers that there are very strong objections in principle to an offence based on the vague notions of morality which were displayed in *Shaw* and *Knuller*. Further, he considers that it was questionable whether an offence would withstand a challenge based on Art 7 of *European Convention on Human Rights*. [The debate as to the relevance of morality to criminal law, when taken together with resolve other considerations such as the relevance of harm to others.] The crucial case of *R v Brown*[67] has already been discussed in another context and one issue which is clear from that case is that agreement on the relative weights is hard to achieve. The *Wolfenden Committee on Homosexuality and Prostitution*[68] perceived the function of the criminal law as being, "...to preserve public order and decency, to protect the citizen from what is offensive and injurious, and to provide sufficient safeguards against corruption and exploitation of others particularly those who are especially vulnerable... [It is] not the function of the law to intervene in the private life of citizens, or to seek to enforce any particular form of behaviour, further than is necessary to carry out the purposes we have outlined." Although, as has already been noted, some commentators would not accept such a view,[69] to this writer, it seems to be an extremely valuable point of departure. However, it is equally not to say, with Gordon, in the first edition of his compendious work on the criminal law of Scotland,[70] that the criminal law is amoral in itself, however immoral or moral any of its provisions may be. That much should be readily apparent from many of the judicial pronouncements which have appeared in the various cases discussed so far in this chapter, as well as elsewhere in the book.

However, the title of this chapter is *Crime and Retribution* so that some notion of the place of punishment, and the like, is necessary. However, Gordon has written[71] that, "...there does not seem to be anything contradictory in the idea of a crime for which the offender cannot be imprisoned, or, indeed, punished at all in the ordinary sense of the word. Many offences are in fact not visited by punishment, but by other forms of treatment such as absolute discharge or probation." At the same time, though, Gordon does properly point out[72] that such methods of treatment are only used in cases involving behaviours which are also punishable, in other cases, in more usual ways. Gordon concludes the section on the relationship between crime and retribution by saying that *crime* must be defined independently of the manner in which the offender is dealt with.[73]

This discussion is, inevitably, tied to the question of why punishment is effected and, then, to why *retribution* is justifiable. Walker, initially, notes[74] that, although ancient Greek philosophers were rationalist, the mythology was laden with notions of vengeance. In Walker's *ipsissima verba*, "The major deities of the classical pantheon seem to have been concerned only to avenge personal insults or opposition; but there were older and darker goddesses of whom mortals were more afraid. Nemesis arranged 'natural punishments' for the wicked and the overweening. The Erinyes – the Furies in Roman mythology – used men's minds as the instruments of justice, driving them to avenge homicides, rapes and other crimes.[75] Approaching the issue from another direction, Walker refers to the religions which acknowledge Abraham as a prophet – Judaism, Christianity and Islam – all of which attach a special importance to *sin*, which can only be expiated by sacrifice or suffering. "The early Christians," he writes, "expressed this feeling in a formal system of penances: voluntary self-punishment… Most penances, however, had no secular utility: they simply rendered the sinner once more eligible for salvation." Since there was a clear overlap between what the church regarded as *sin* and what the law regarded as *crime*, it was inevitable that the law could be seen as a means of enforcing atonement and, in turn, some judges saw their sentences, not only in utilitarian deterrent terms but as retribution in the sense of what the criminals desert. Walker suggests that that form of desert has, like penance, no secular utility.

The retributive ideal does have some immediate intellectual attractions – unlike utilitarianism, it holds out the promise of certainty. In addition, as Walker points out,[76] "In Christian, Judaic and Islamic cultures there are many people to whom the retributive justification needs no further examination. It has scriptural authority. It is reinforced by dislike of those who flout accepted rules, and by sympathy for the victims of their conduct. To question it seems like questioning the obligations to keep a promise, the very definition of this includes the obligation." Some people may argue that the duty to punish is something which is perceived rather than inferred from reason.[77] Others perceive *retribution* in terms of paying debts to society. Yet, in reality this metaphor is, Walker suggests,[78] confused, in that it fails to distinguish society from the victim. In particular, Walker regards that analogy as breaking down completely when it is remembered that unsuccessful attempts and plans to commit offences are treated as deserving of punishment.

Other justifications which Walker analyses include the metaphorical notion that punishment somehow annuls the crime.[79] In other words, when the punishment has been imposed, it is as if the crime itself was never committed. Of course, the objection to that view is that it is not factually the case: the consequences of, say, a serious assault or rape are likely to last long after the culprit has been caught and the punishment inflicted. In that context, Walker refers to Bosanquet, who had written[80] that, "Some overt act is also necessary…to make sure that the dullest capacity including that of the guilty person… shall not fail to apprehend the intensity of the annulling act." Walker suggests[81] that Bosanquet seems to be suggesting that the function of punishment is conveying a message. These days, at least, most punishment is carried out in private, whereas messages are conveyed, more or less, publicly. Walker argues that it is less nonsensical to argue that public punishment – or, more usually today, the public promise of punishment – is a ritual which helps people to feel that the crime has not taken place. However, he is still not much impressed by the argument. He then refers to the feeling that some people appear to have that the State's execution of a murderer somehow restores the victim to life. Of course it does not in either actual or metaphysical terms! "Sentencing," he suggests, "may have a ritual function, but whatever the ritual celebrates, it is not annulment."

Walker then examines a rather more sophisticated version of the annulment thesis. Under this view, which at various times has been espoused by writers such as Morris[82] and von Hirsch,[83] a law breaker has taken an unfair advantage which can be taken away from him by a penalty. In Walker's own words,[84] "He has usurped property, pleasure or power in a way that is not open to the law-abiding man, who either has to go without or work harder for the same desiratum. Penalties put matters right either by removing what the offender has gained or by imposing a disadvantage, as do penalties in games." As Walker points out, this argument – in part because it is based around analogy, rather than metaphor – is more difficult to refute than the *annulment* argument itself. The fact that it is the product of analogy should not, for that reason discredit it. "As in games," Walker writes, "we feel that the penalty should in some way reflect the seriousness of the offence. If the foul prevented a goal, a goal should be awarded. If a player endangers others, he should be sent off. If a drug- dealer makes a lot of money, he should forfeit it. And many people believe that he who takes a life should forfeit his own, or at least be excluded from the community." In addition, it is not a valid objection to the thesis that there are many ways of *taking advantage* which are not generally felt ought to be the subject of punishment. Thus, for example, a person might succeed in business as a result of having superior sources of capital or a network of similar acquaintances. In the area of games, some athletes have natural physical advantages which are not possessed by others. Where the thesis is deficient, Walker argues, is that what is generally penalised is the *deliberate taking advantage* prohibited by the rules. However, it is unrealistic to regard all law breaking as moves in a competitive game: a person who assaults another is not competing with him in any real sense. The reality, Walker importantly tells us, is that not all crime is instrumental, by any means (that is, with the intention of obtaining some benefit), it may be expressive (in the sense of giving vent to some form of emotion). Again, if a man forces sexual attentions on someone, it is wrong to perceive him as obtaining an unfair advantage over a third person who seeks to use more acceptable means.[85]

It may well be that the fact that Walker has effectively refuted those – and, indeed other [86] – arguments in favour of retribution, does not discourage judges from airing their own views on the issue. Two cases have particularly been noted by Walker,[87] the first being less graphic than the second. In *R v Llewellyn-Jones*,[88] the appellant, who was a County Court Registrar, had been convicted, and sentenced to four years' imprisonment, of misbehaviour in a public office on counts which alleged, in the particulars of offence, that the appellant, being and acting as registrar of the Cardiff County Court with the intention of gaining improper personal advantage and without proper regard to the interests of [the beneficiary], (a) wrote a letter to solicitors acting for the father of the beneficiary 'in terms which he would not otherwise have written' and (b) 'made an order which he would not otherwise have made that £5,000 be paid to [a named person] out of funds in court'." The Court of Appeal (Criminal Division) dismissed his appeal against both conviction and sentence. As regards the factual situation, Lord Parker CJ stated[89] that it was "...indeed a lamentable tale." As regards the sentence, it had been argued that any present sentence would be a drastic punishment for the appellant and also sought to argue that its only purpose could have been to make an example of him. It was further claimed, that there would be little, if any need for a deterrent sentence in regard to people in a similar position. The Lord Chief Justice was far from impressed: "The court is quite satisfied," he stated,[90] "that this is not a deterrent sentence; it is a sentence which is fully merited, in the opinion of this court, as punishment for very grave offences and as expressing the revulsion of the public to the whole circumstances of the case." Given the quite cynically dishonest nature of the crimes, it may be that the public denunciation of the appellant by the Lord Chief Justice might have gone some way towards consoling his victims and of satisfying those members of the public who might have read about them in the media. It may be that, despite Walker's scholarly arguments, a greater urge for retribution, at least as represented by ever longer periods of incarceration, is becoming manifest. In Australia, presently, it seems almost impossible to open a newspaper without reading such demands.

The second case was *R v Sargeant*[91] where the accused had pleaded guilty to affray and had been sentenced to two years imprisonment. The appellant was a night club bouncer who had been involved, largely through his own unnecessary aggression, in a very unpleasant and violent scuffle which had resulted in a customer being seriously injured.[92] The only issue in the appeal was the sentence passed on the particular appellant. Lawton LJ considered the various principles which should affect sentencing in such cases and began[93] with *retribution*. "The Old Testament concept of an eye for an eye and a tooth for a tooth," he commented, "no longer plays any part in our criminal law. There is, however, another aspect of retribution which is frequently overlooked: it is that society, through the courts, must show its abhorrence of particular types of crime, and the only way in which the courts can show this is by the sentences they pass. The courts do not have to reflect public opinion. On the other hand courts must not disregard it. Perhaps the main duty of the court is to lead public opinion." At the same time, Lawton LJ went on to comment on the nature of the crime in question and public opinion, when he said that, "Anyone who surveys the criminal scene at the present time must be alive to the appalling problem of violence. The weapons which the courts have at their disposal for doing so are few. We are satisfied that in most cases fines are not sufficient for senseless violence. The time has come, in the opinion of this Court, when those who indulge in the kind of violence with which we are concerned in this case must expect custodial sentences." Yet he went on to qualify those comments by stating that, although society expects the courts to impose punishment for violence which really hurts, it does not expect the courts to go on hurting for a long time, which, he thought, the sentence which had been imposed at first instance in *Sargeant* was likely to do. In the event, Lawton LJ expressed[94] the view that the sentence was "...for too long". Accordingly, taking into account the time which the appellant had already served, the Court made an order which had the effect of enabling the appellant to be released on the day of the appellate hearing. The factors which affected the decision were clear[95] from Lawton LJ's judgment: first, the appellant, who was twenty six years of age, had no prior convictions; second, he had held a responsible position which he would lose (which, of itself, Lawton LJ considered was a punishment) and that he might find it difficult to obtain another.[96] Third, the appellant had also admitted that he had overreacted to the situation. Nonetheless, it is clear that, despite the reduction on the sentence that the retributive element was especially strong. First, Lawton LJ noted[97] that the judge at first instance had probably passed the sentence as a deterrent; however, Lawton LJ was of the view that it was, "...the experience of the courts that deterrent sentences are of little value in respect of offences which are committed on the spur of the moment. Deterrent sentences may well be of considerable value where crime is premeditated. Burglars, robbers and users of firearms and weapons may very well be put off by deterrent sentences. We think it unlikely that deterrence would be of any value in this case." Second, likewise, Lawton LJ, without detailed explanation considered[98] that a preventative sentence was not called for in the case at hand. Third, similarly, as regards rehabilatory sentence, Lawton LJ took the view that, "This young man does not want prison training. It is not going to do him any good. It is his memory of the clanging of prison gates which is likely to keep him from crime in the future." Hence, it seems as though it is the element of retribution which will provide both the deterrent and rehabilatory functions of the sentence.

However, there are both indefinite and infinite forms of retribution, both in terms of strict law and in more moral terms. The last is especially true of actions which might be more accurately described as *sins*. A commentator on that aspect of the human condition was the 14th Century poet Geoffrey Chaucer. A particular instance is one of the shorter tales from Chaucer's *The Canterbury Tales*, which describes retribution in an especially poetic and, indeed, mystical way. Because of its brevity, "The Pardoner's Tale" has a starkly dramatic impact. The very fact that this tale of riotous living, greed, death and retribution is told by a Pardoner is not without significance or, for that matter, irony: pardoners sold indulgences, or remissions of religious punishment. That of itself brings the subject matter of the tale into stark relief. Initially, the indulgence had been the substitution of one kind of punishment for another – frequently, it involved the substitution of a money payment instead of a physical penalty – the physical penalty involving a period on bread and water or climbing the stairs of the religious building on one's knees. By Chaucer's time, though, the indulgence had become a recognised method of buying time off one's period in purgatory. The Pope alone had authority to issue these indulgences (or pardons) and, hence, all pardoners would claim that their authority to sell indulgences came from Rome. Many pardoners in England, in the Fourteenth Century, were unlicensed and were little more than meretricious frauds. Inevitably, they were far from popular and, in the general Prologue[99] to *The Canterbury Tales*, Chaucer describes him in less than flattering terms: First Chaucer comments on his unprepossessing physical appearance[100] which is then deliberately confused with his trade:

>His wallet bforn hym in his lappe,
>Bret ful of pardon comen from Rome al Hoot.
>A voys he hadde as small as hath a goot;
>No berd hadde he, ne nevere sholde have,
>As smothe it was as it werelate yshave.
>I trowe he were a gelding or a mare.
>But of his craft, fro Berwyk in to Ware [101]

The pardoner's true dishonesty is then exposed by Chaucer when he describes the contents of the Pardoner's bag which is full of fake relics, as his wallet was of fake indulgences, which accounts for his success in his travels through the whole of England.

> For in his male he haddee a pilwe beer
> Which that he seyde was Oure Lady veyl.
> He seyde he hadde a gobet of the seyl
> That Seint Peter hadde whan that he wente
> Upon the see till Jhesu Christ hum hente
> He hadde a croys of latoun full of stones,
> And in a glas he hadde pigges bones.[102]

However, there could equally be no doubt that these false relics proved very successful in the Pardoner's carrying out of what was, clearly, a thoroughly dishonest operation:

> But with thise relikes whan that he fond
> A poure person dwellynge up on lond,
> Upon a day he gat hym moore moneye
> Than that the person gat inmonthes tweye.
> And thus with feyned flaterye and japes
> He made the person and the peple his apes.[103]

Yet that is not the end of the Pardoner's duplicity – he is not above using the rituals and ceremonies of the Church itself to bring about his ends. Despite his unprepossing appearance and his dishonesty, he is possessed of abilities which are useful, and not only to himself:

> But trewely to tellen at laste,
> He was in chirche a noble ecclesiatste;
> Wel koude he rede a lesson or a storie,
> But alderbest he song an offertorie,
> For wel he wiste whan that song was songe,
> He moste preche and wel affile his tonge
> To Wynne silver, as he ful wel koude;
> Therefore he song the murierly and loude.[104]

Now it is the turn of this thoroughly disreputable, dishonest and unattractive character to tell a story to his fellow pilgrims. It begins with a description of the people who were to become the protagonists of the story, and like the tale's teller they are not an instantly likable collection, although, at the same time, the demonstrated hypocrisy of the Pardoner is apparent through the description:

> In Flaundrers whilom was a compaignye
> Of yonge folk that haunteden folye,
> As riot, hazard, stywes and taverns,
> Where as with harpes, lutes and gyternes,
> The daunce and pleyen at dees bothe day
> And nyght,
> And eten also, and drynken over hir might,
> Thurgh which tey doon the devel sacrifise
> Withinne that develes temple is cursed wise
> By superfluytee abhomynable.
> Hir othes been so grete and so dampnable
> That it is grisly for to here hem swere.
> Our blessed lordes body they totere.[105]

The narrator then goes on to link the drunken behaviour of the people to lechery and perverse sexualised behaviour. Including Lot, so drunk that he did not know what he was doing that he slept with his two daughters and Herod who, so full of food and drink that the ordered the execution of the guiltless John the Baptist. Indeed, apart from the description of the group of self indulgent young people, to whom we will return later,[106] almost the first two hundred lines of "The Pardoner's Tale" are taken up with Biblical stories and diatribes against the evils of, especially, drunkenness, gluttony, gambling and swearing. The dramatic purpose of this is twofold: first, it seeks further to emphasised the hypocrisy of the Pardoner himself, who, despite displaying fake relics and deceiving clergy and the people for whom they are responsible, rails loudly at those who take the Lord's name, "…in ydel or amys."[107] Second, this raging pejorative would have the effect of making the other pilgrims, the Pardoner's audience, wait eagerly to hear what was actually going to happen in the tale itself.

Finally, that does happen, and the Pardoner returns to the rioters and their doings, though, now he concentrates on three of them,[108] when they receive something of a shock:

> The riotours thre of whiche I telle,
> Longe erst er prime rong of any belle
> Were set hem in a taverne to drynke
> And as they sat, they herde a belle clynke
> Biforn a cors was carried to his grave.
> That oon of hem gan callen to his knave,
> "Go bet", quod he "and axe" redily
> What cors is this that passeth heer forby,
> And looke that thou reporte his name weel.

The servant knew immediately whose the corpse was: it was a companion of the three who, very drunk, had died in his sleep during the night. Or, in Chaucer's own words:

> And sodeynly he was yslayn tonight,
> Fordronke as he sat on his bench upright.
> Ther cam a privee theef men clepeth
> Deeth,[109]

The servant tells them that Death kills all the people in the country, just as he had killed their friend,. This information, which is confirmed by the Taverner, brings forth a response from one of the rioters:

> "Ye, Goddes armes!" quod this riotour,
> "Is it swich peril with hym for to meete?
> I shal hym seke by wey and eek by street,
> I make avow to Goddes digne bones!
> Herkeneth, felawes; we thre been al ones.
> Lat ech of us holde up his hand til oother,
> And ech of us bicomen otheres brother,
> And we wol sleen this false traytour, deeth.
> He shal be slayn which that so manye Sleeth,

By Goddes dignitee, er it be nyght!"[110]

They then swore further oaths and set off in the direction of a village which had earlier been suggested to them by their servant and the taverner. They had not gone far, and had stepped over a stile when they met poor old man, who greeted them humbly:

> And seyde thus: "Now, lordes, God yow
> See"
> The proudeste of thise riotours three
> Answerede again, "What, carl, with sory
> Grace!
> Why artow al forwrapped save thy face?
> Why lyvestow so longe in so greet age?"
> This olde man gan looke in his visage
> And seyde thus: "For I ne kan nat fynde
> A man, though that I walked into Ynde,
> Neither in cite nor in no village,
> That wolde change his youthe for myn age;
> And therefore moot I han myn age stille,
> As long tyme as it is Goddes wille.
> Ne deeth, llas, ne wol nat han my lyf!
> Thus walke I Lyk a restelees kaityf,
> And on the ground, which is my moodres
> Gate,
> I knokke with my staf bothe erly and late,
> And seye, 'Leeve modder, leet me in!
> Lo, how I vanysshe, flesh and blood and skyn!
> Allas, whan shul my bones been at reste!
> Mooder, with yow wolde I caunge my cheste...[111]

The reason why I have spent such space on this extract is that there has been considerable scholarly debate as to the identity, or nature, of the old man, who is ultimately to guide the three young revellers to Death. Thus, in general terms, Coghill and Tolkien, well known students of the literature of the period and, significantly earlier, write[112] that, "Many critics have argued and conjectured where Chaucer got the idea for him and what he symbolizes. Some have thought that...he was an allegory of old age, some that he was the Wandering Jew, some that he was the Old Adam within us all, some that he was Death himself." There may be internal evidence for all of these and the theme, for instance, of the Wandering Jew has been taken up by Bushnell.[113] Certainly, his earthly wanderings whilst searching for youth or death would he congruent with the myth. At the same time his relationship with the earth might also suggest, contentextually, that he represents something akin to an Earth-elemental who seeks to unify, not merely himself, but all other people with the earth.

How does he bring this about in the present situation? The revellers prevent him from going on and one, outright, accuses him of being an ally of Death and demands that he tell them where Death might be found. The corpse-like figure, whomsoever he might be, gives them directions:

> "Now sires," quod he, "if that ye be so
> Leef
> To fynde deeth, turne up this croked wey
> For in that grove I lafte hym, by my fey,
> Under a tree, and there he wole abyde.
> Noght for youre boost he wole hym no
> Thing hyde.
> Se ye that ook? Right therer ye shal hym
> Fynde.
> God save yow that boghte again mankymde,
> And yow amende." Thus seyde this olde man.
> And everich of thise riotours ran
> Til he cam to that tree, and there they
> Founde
> Of florins fine of gold ycoyned rounde
> Wel ny an eighte bushels, as hem
> Thoughte.
> No lenger thane after death they soughte
> But ech of hem so glad was of that sightte,
> For that the florins been so faire and
> Brighte,
> That doun they sette hem by this precious
> Hoord.[114]

The finding of the treasure is, of course, the fulcrum of the tale and has been pointed in an essentially sinister way by the old man who says that, to find Death, they must go, "...up this croked wey." He also swears by his faith which, axiomatically, he does not truly have, that Death will be waiting for them unconcealed. He leaves them with an open ended and not especially pleasant sounding benediction. They, jointly and severally rush off to find Death and find the treasure. Which is an immediately strange *retribution* for their drunken, obscene and blasphemous behaviour...!

However, difficulties begin almost immediately: after the discovery of the treasure, the first words were spoken by, in Chaucer's own description, "...the worste of hem."[115] This man suggests that it would be unsafe to carry the treasure home by day and so urges that they draw lots to see who should run to the city and buy bread and wine whilst the others would guard the treasure. That was agreed upon and the lot fell on the youngest of the three, who immediately runs into town and the other two devise a plan for when the third returns:

> And two of us shul strenger be than oon.
> Looke whan that he is set, that right anooon
> Arys as though thou woldest with hym
> Pleye,
> And I shall ryve hym thurgh the sides tweye
> Whil that thou stogelest with hym as in game.
> And with the daggere looke thou do the
> Same,
> And thane shal al this gold departed be,
> My deere freend, bitwixen me and thee.
> Thanne may we bothe oure lustes all
> Fulfille,
> And pleye at dees right at oure owene
> Wille."
> And thus accorded been thise shrews tweye
> To sleen the thridde as ye han herd me seye.[116]

However, the youngest of the three had developed his own strategy for obtaining the treasure – "And ate last the feend oure enemy / Putte in

331

his thought the he should poyson beye..."[117] The Pardoner/ Chaucer emphasises that this decision was entirely purposeful and with no possibility of repentance. Thereupon, the third reveller:

>And forth he gooth, no lenger wolde he Tarie.
>Into the toun unto apothecarie
>And preyed hym that he hym wolde selle
>Som poison that he myghte his rates quelle,
>And eek ther was a polcat in his hawe
>That, as he seyed, his capons hadde yslawe,
>And fayn he wolde wreke hym, if he Myghte,
>On vermin that destroyed hym by nyghte[118]

The symbolism of *vermin* and *happy revenge* is not, of course, lost. Having been assured by the apothecary of the lethal qualities of the poison, he goes to the next street and borrows three large bottles. He then pours poison into two, which he tops up with wine, but kept a third, for himself, clear of the poison. His plan, therefore, is every bit as tainted with *mens rea* as is that of the other two. He then returns to the other two and the two plans are duly, and with the assistance of good fortune, put into operation:

>For right as they hadde cast his deeth bilfoore,
>Right so they han hym slayn, and that anon.
>And whan that this was doon, thus spak that Oon:
>"Now lat us sitte and drynke and make us Merie,
>And afterward we wol his body berie."
>And with that word it happed hym par cas
>To take the botel ther the pyson was,
>And drank, and yaf his felawe drynke also,
>For which anon they storven bothe two.
>But certes, I suppose that Avycen
>Wroot nevere in no canon, ne in no fen
>Mo wonder signes of empoisoning

> Than hadde thise wrecches two er hir
> Ending.
> Thus ended been thise homicides two,
> And eek the false empoysonere also.[119]

The Pardoner then denounces the sin of homicide which he groups together with gluttony, lechery and gambling – all of which play some part, direct or indirect, in the tale. He then reverts to plying his trade amongst the pilgrims and proceeds to sell indulgences[120] whilst, simultaneously, and hypocritically denouncing sins. It then becomes quite apparent what the purpose of the whole exercise is:

> Now goode men, God foryeve yow youre
> Trepass,
> And ware yow fro the synne of avarice.
> Myn hooly pardon may how alle warice
> So that ye offer nobels or sterlynges,
> Or elles silver broches, spoones, rynges.
> Boweth youre heed under this hooly bulle.
> Com up, ye wyves, offreth of youre wolle.
> Youre names I entre heer in my rolle anon;
> Into the blisse of hevene shul ye gon.
> I yow assoille by myn heigh power,
> Yow that wol offer as clene and eek as
> Cleer
> As ye were born.[121]

After having told the pilgrims that it is an honour for them to have a Pardoner amongst them, so that – provided they make an appropriate offering – they may be absolved as they ride towards Canterbury. That was especially important as there was a possibility that one of them might fall from a horse and break their neck.[122] The Pardoner then selects a particular pilgrim with, for him, unhappy results:

> I rede that oure Hooste here shal bigynne,
> For he is moost envoluped in synne.
> Com forth, Sire Hoost, and offer first anon,

> And thou shalt kisse my relikes everychon,
> Ye, for a grote! Unbokele anon thy purs![123]

The Host is far from impressed by this suggestion and responds in scabrous and scathological terms, both about the Pardoner and his relics. The Pardoner did not reply because he was so enraged, to which the Host responded by saying that he would not ride with the Pardoner nor any other angry man. However, the difficulty is resolved by the reaction of the pilgrims at large and by the intervention of the Knight:

> But right anon the worthy Knyght bigan,
> Whan that he saugh that al the peple
> Lough:
> "Namoore of this, for it is right ynough.
> Sire pardonerm be glad and myrie of cheere.
> And ye, Sire Hoost, that been to me so deere,
> I preye yow that ye kisse the Pardoner.
> And Pardoner, I preye thee, drawe thee
> Neer,
> And as we diden, lat us laughe and pleye."
> Anon they kiste and ryden forth hir weye.[124]

So the Tale ends happily, through the medium of forgiveness, a commodity - and, in view of the Pardoner's trade, I use the words advisedly – which is not much apparent elsewhere in "The Pardoner's Tale." Although it is readily apparent that the major theme of the story is retribution, there are a number of questions which remain to be answered: first, what is the relationship between the old, all but dead, man at the stile[125] and the treasure, which ultimately brings the three revellers down. If, as I suggested,[126] the corpse-like figure represents some variety of Earth-elemental, it may be that the treasure is another manifestation. Although the text does state that the gold is *coined*, which suggests human manufacture rather any form of manifestation. However, it may be that the use of that word is entirely figurative and that both the man and the treasure are means of enticing humans to become, howsoever, a part of the earth which the elemental manifestations emanate.

The second unanswered question relates to the nature of *retribution* which is a central theme of the tale itself. Indeed, it may be that the Host's violently obscene[127] rejoinder to the manipulation of the pilgrims by the Pardoner may indicate, despite the fact that they kiss and make up, that retribution may be in store for the Pardoner, if not at that juncture, but at some future time. However, we are more immediately concerned with the retribution levied on the three revellers. But, in respect of what? It should be that it was brought about by their riotous living involving drinking, lechery, gambling and blasphemy.[128] It may, alternatively, be that, more directly, the retribution has been visited upon them in respect of the murders of one another. Or it might be a combination of both. One matter, however, is certain and that is that the retribution was not levied in any formal way by an agency or agencies of the State, but, nonetheless, whether in penal or spiritual terms, it was exacted in talionic manner.

2. Aspects of Formal Retribution

The issue of blasphemy has been taken up particularly by the critic Spearing who writes[129] that, "*The Pardoner's Tale* is about blasphemy; it also enacts blasphemy." Although it is obviously true that the context of the Tale, rather than the tale itself, enacts blasphemy: the very conduct of the Pardoner himself, both generally and in respect of the pilgrims, is a graphic instance of the practice of blasphemy. It is rather harder to maintain that blasphemy is the central theme of the tale. The tale itself, as opposed to its context (which is probably more hastily, and funnily, blasphemous than anything else), has many characteristics. Thus, for example, Coghill and Tolkien state[130] that, "…perhaps the supreme thing about the story is, that ministers mostly to its irony, the eeriness. This is partly brought about by the exactitude with which their retribution falls on each of the rioters, the uncanny neatness of the divine arithmetic in their all-unlooked-for punishment. But it is chiefly affected…by Chaucer's invention of the weird old man." In turn, the atmosphere of eeriness is heightened, as those writers have noted,[131] by necessary speculation as to his identity or nature. Much too depends on the way in which the story develops, which has been emphasised by Bishop, who writes[132] that, "The success of the best of Chaucer's shorter tales depends upon the way in which, during the final scene, events move towards their end with an astonishing rapidity and seeming inevitability. But the unimpeded flow of the action at the conclusion of these tales is often made possible only because the author has contrived to introduce into the early part of his narrative much of the information and most of the stage 'properties' that are required for the enactment of the denouement". These of course, are *rhetorical* devices which are designed to involve the reader in the story's development and increasing momentum and inevitable ending. The tension, too, is increased, as Bishop also points out, [133] by the fact that much of the dialogue, of which the tale largely consists, is spoken by the revellers when they are drunk. In addition, that device also seeks to emphasise that the three are not, really at any stage, in command of their own destinies.

The point made by Spearing[134] takes us to an important decision of the House of Lords on the subject of blasphemy which, in turn, raises the issues of crime *qua* crime and of formal retribution. In *R v Lemon and Gay News*,[135] the appellants were the editor and publisher of a magazine entitled *Gay News* the readership of which consisted, almost entirely, of male homosexuals, although it was on sale to the public at some bookstalls. An issue, published in June 1976, contained a poem entitled, "The Love that Dares to Speak its Name" which was accompanied by a drawing illustrating its subject matter. It purported to describe in specific detail acts of sodomy and fellatio committed on the body of Christ immediately after his death. In addition, it ascribed to him during his lifetime, promiscuous homosexual practices with the apostles and other men. A private prosecution was brought against the appellants charging them with blasphemous libel concerning the Christian religion, namely, an obscene poem and illustration vilifying Christ in his life and in his crucifixion. At first instance, the judge directed the jury that, for the appellants to be convicted, it was sufficient if they took the view that the publication complained of vilified Christ in his life and crucifixion and that it was not necessary for the Crown to establish any further intention on the part of the appellants beyond an intention to publish that which, in the jury's view, was a blasphemous libel. The jury convicted the appellants, who appealed unsuccessfully to the Court of Appeal. They, then appealed to the House of Lords who, by a majority,[136] dismissed their appeal.

In the majority, Viscount Dilhorne found himself[137] unable, "...to reach the conclusion that the ingredients of the offence of publishing a blasphemous libel have changed since 1792. Indeed it would, I think, be surprising if they had. If it be accepted, as I think it must, that that which it is sought to prevent is the publication of blasphemous libels, the harm is done by their intentional publication, whether or not the publisher, intended to blaspheme. To hold that it must be proved that he had that intent appears to me to be going some way to making the accused judge in his own cause. If Mr Lemon had testified that he did not regard the poem and drawing as blasphemous, that he had no intention to blaspheme, and, it might be, that it was his intention was to promote the love and affection of some homosexuals for Our Lord, the jury properly directed would surely have been told that unless satisfied beyond reasonable doubt that he intended to blaspheme they should acquit, no matter how blasphemous they thought the publication. Whether or not they would have done so such evidence is a matter of speculation on which views may differ." However, Viscount Dilhorne emphasised[138] that the issue was an issue of law and that he should not be taken as being, in any way, critical of juries. Lord Russell took up some of the points which had been made by Viscount Dilhorne: first of all, he expressed the view,[139] as had Viscount Dilhorne, that it was not the function of the House of Lords to hold that the publication of a blasphemous libel was no longer a criminal offence. Although that very well might be correct, it cannot be without significance that *Lemon* was the first prosecution for fifty years, although it was not to be the last.[140] He noted,[141] though, that, speaking as an ordinary Christian, he found the publication, "…quite appallingly shocking and outrageous." As regards the matter of intent, Lord Russell asked himself, "Why then should this House, faced with a deliberate publication of that which a jury with every justification has held to be a blasphemous libel, consider that it should be for the prosecution to prove, presumably beyond reasonable doubt, that the accused recognised and intended it to be such or regarded it as immaterial whether it was? I see no grounds for that. It does not to my mind make sense; and I consider that sense should retain a function in our criminal law. The reason why the law considers that the publication of a blasphemous libel is an offence is that such publication should not take place, and if it takes place, and the publication is deliberate, I see no justification for holding that there is no offence when the publisher is incapable for some reason peculiar to himself of agreeing with a jury on the true nature of the publication." On the question of evidence, the only evidence, Lord Russell though, which might conceivably have been wrongly excluded was that of the editor's state of mind, of which only he could speak. Expert evidence would have been irrelevant on any footing. His Lordship had no doubt that the editor had a *motive*[142] in producing the publication which justified it for him at least. Supposedly, Lord Russell went on "(though I am guessing) that those of [the editor's] usual readers who were active or passive homosexuals should not feel that they were for that reason excluded from the fellowship of Christianity. But whether intention is or is not an ingredient of the offence, motive is certainly not a defence."

The remaining judge in the majority, Lord Scarman, took an altogether more aggressive approach[143] to the offence. Initially, he stated that he did not subscribe to the view that, "...the common law offence of blasphemous libel serves no useful purpose in the modern law. On the contrary, I think there is a case for legislation extending it to protect the religious beliefs and feelings of non-Christians. The offence belongs to a group of criminal offences designed to safeguard the internal tranquility of the kingdom. In an increasingly plural society such as that of modern Britain it is necessary not only to respect the differing religious beliefs, feelings and practices of all but also protect them from scurrility, vilification, ridicule and contempt." Lord Scarman felt himself fortified in his approach by the words of Kenny, who wrote[144] that, "The common law does not interfere with the bona fide opinion. But it prohibits, and renders punishable, the use of coarse and scurrilous ridicule on subjects which are sacred to most people in this country." Lord Scarman then continued by saying that he had permitted himself those observations because they determined his approach to the appeal – most particularly, he stated that he would not lend his voice to a view of the law relating to blasphemous libel which, "...render it a dead letter, or diminish its efficacy to protect religious feeling from outrage and insult. My criticism of the common law offence of blasphemy is not that it exists but that it is not sufficiently comprehensive. It is shackled by the chains of history." At the same time, he was not prepared to extend the law beyond the limits recognised by the House of Lords in the earlier case of *Bowman* v *Secular Society Ltd*.[145] However, the present appeal did give the House of Lords the opportunity to state the existing law in a form conducive to contemporary social conditions, rather than those which existed in the 17th, 18th or 19th Centuries.

In *Bowman* v *Secular Society Ltd*, Lord Sumner had said,[146] in a speech described by Lord Scarman in *Lemon*[147] as *historic*, that, "The words, as well as the acts which tend to endanger society differ from time to time in proportion as society is stable or insecure in fact, or is believed by its reasonable members to be open to assault. In the present day meetings or processions are held lawful which 150 years ago would have been deemed seditious, and this is not because the law is weaker or has been changed, but because the times having changed, society is stronger than before. In the present day reasonable men do not apprehend the dissolution or the downfall of society because religion is publicly assailed by methods not scandalous. Whether it is possible that in the future religious attacks, designed to undermine fundamental institutions of our society, may come to be criminal in themselves, as constituting a public danger, is a matter that does not arise. The fact that opinion grounded in experience has moved one way does not prelude the possibility of its morning on fresh experience in the other; nor does it bind succeeding generations, when conditions have again changed. After all, the question whether a given opinion is a danger to society is a question of the times and a question of fact. I desire to say nothing that would limit the right to protect itself by process of law from the dangers of the moment, whatever that might be, but only to say that, experience having proved dangers once thought to be real to be now negligible, and dangers once very possibly imminent to have now passed away, there is nothing in the general rules as to blasphemy and religion, as known to the law, which prevents us from varying their application to the particular circumstances of our time in accordance with that experience."

Having quoted Lord Sumner at length, Lord Scarman then went on to say[148] that, for various – and, largely, procedural – reasons, the history of the law provided little guidance. Indeed, Lords Sumner's judgment in *Bowman* suggested very good reasons why it would not: it would be both a learned and courageous court who would be able to place each *dictum*, through the years in its own particular socio-historical context and any attempt genuinely to do so would be to invite criticism unnecessarily. At the same time, although acknowledging that another view could be found – as represented in the instant case by the views of Lords Edmund-Davies and Diplock – he considered[149] that *historically*[150] the law required no more than an intention to publish words found by the jury to be blasphemous.

That being the case, Lord Scarman considered that the issue was one of legal policy in contemporary society. He noted that there was some force in the legally conceptual force that the *mens rea* in all four varieties of criminal libel – seditious, blasphemous, obscene and defamatory – should be the same. "At worst," he said in that context, "the common law may be said to have become fragmented in this area of public order offences: at best it may be said (as I believe to be true) to be moving towards a position in which people who know what they are doing will be criminally liable if the words they choose to publish such as to cause grave offence to the religious feelings of some of their fellow citizens or are such as to tend to deprave and corrupt persons who are likely to read them." Lord Scarman was fortified[151] in his view by recent statutes[152] all of which emphasised the effect of the words in question rather than the intent of the publisher. He concluded that part of his judgment by saying[153] that, "It would be intolerable if by allowing an author or publisher to plead the excellence of his motives and the right of freedom of speech he could evade the penalties of the law even though his words were blasphemous in the sense of constituting an outrage upon the religious feelings of his fellow citizens. This is no way forward for a successful plural society. Accordingly, the test for obscenity by concentrating on the words complained of is, in my judgment, equally valuable as a test of blasphemy. The character of the words in the published matter; but not the motive of the author or publisher." Thus, Lord Scarman finally expressed the view that the modern law of blasphemy had appropriately been formulated in Sir James Fitzjames Stephen's *Digest of the Criminal Law*,[154] written initially in 1877, where it was said that, "every publication is said to be blasphemous which contains any contemptuous, reviling, scurrilous or ludicrous matter relating to God, Jesus Christ or the Bible, or the formularities of the Church of England as by law established. It is not blasphemous to speak or publish opinions hostile to the Christian religion or to deny the existence of God, if the publication is couched in decent or temperate language. The test to be applied is the manner in which the doctrines are advocated and not in the substance of the doctrines themselves."

Lord Scarman's judgment in *Lemon* has attracted the ire of Spencer who writes[155] that it is, "...a remarkable judgment. It consists of a series of *non sequiturs*..." It further involves, Spencer suggests,[156] "...deliberate judicial extension of the criminal law; inflating broad, vague common law offences derived from a society that no longer exists; penalizing in generous terms what the judges on the spur of the moment happen to dislike; resulting in criminal law which Parliament would eject if offered it disinfected on the end of a bargepole." It is certainly true that the judgment contains some confusion –especially insofar as the relevance of historical material is concerned,[157] but the factual situation with which *Lemon* was concerned was not so straightforward as Spencer's bellicose approach would seem to suggest. It seems to the present writer that there might be many Parliamentarians, both at the time when *Lemon* was decided, as well as at the time of the publication of this book, who, as well as being of little religious commitment, might find the subject matter of the prosecution, which was brought at the instance of a member of the public, distressing.[158]

The very complexity of the situation, as well as its societal and political context (which Spencer appears to have overlooked) are illustrated by the bare fact that *Lemon* was decided by a simple majority in the House of Lords.[159] In the minority, Lord Diplock noted, at an early stage in his judgment,[160] that the offence of publishing a blasphemous libel had had a long, and *sometimes inglorious*, history in the common law. He was also, in that context, of the view that it was the responsibility of the House of Lords, in the instant case, to give the operation of the rule of law a degree of certainty which it had previously lacked and, also to do so in a form which would not be inconsistent with the way in which the general law regarding the mental element in criminal matters had developed since *Bowman* v *Secular Society Ltd*[161] in 1917.

After having discussed some of the earlier developments in the law relating to blasphemous libel, Lord Diplock considered[162] that the first major change which had influenced the law was procedural rather than substantive. The *Criminal Evidence Act* 1898 enabled the accused to give evidence on his own behalf – prior to that enactment, it was only possible for the actual intention of he accused person to be ascertained as a matter of inference from what he had been proved to have done and juries were directed that the *presumption* that a man intends the natural and probable consequences of his acts was to be applied. "In the case of blasphemous libel," Lord Diplock explained, "if the jury found that the words published by the accused, looked at objectively had the tendency to produce the effect that it was the policy of the law to prevent, for example, to shock and arouse resentment among believing Christians, then the application of the presumption was sufficient to convert this objective tendency into the actual intention of the accused."

Having made that central point, Lord Diplock then turned his attention[163] to the provisions of s 8 of the *Criminal Justice Act* 1967,[164] by which the House was bound. Lord Diplock commented that the provision threw no light on the question whether an intention to produce a particular effect upon those to whom the blasphemous matter is published is an essential element in the offence of blasphemous libel but, even if it were, the section made the subjective intent of the accused applicable. More particularly, it made the evidence of the actual publisher as to what he intended or foresaw as the result of the publication relevant and admissible to rebut other evidence of the accused's intention. If that were not the case, then, his Lordship stated, the offence of blasphemous libel would revert to the exceptional category of crimes of strict liability. To bring that about Lord Diplock asserted,[165] would be a retrograde step which could not be justified by any considerations of public policy. On that question, his Lordship noted that the usual justification for creating, by statute, a criminal offence of strict liability is, "...the threat that the actus reus of the offence poses to public health, public safety, public morals or public order." He then pointed out that the fact that there had been no prosecutions for blasphemous libel for more than fifty years was, in his view, sufficient to dispose of any suggestion that, "...in modern times a judicial decision to include this common law offence in this exceptional class of offences of strict liability could be justified upon grounds of public morals or public order."

Lord Diplock continued by saying that any fear that by retaining, as a necessary element in the *mens rea* of the offence, the intention of the publisher to shock and arouse resentment among believing Christians, those who are morally blameworthy will be unjustly acquitted appeared to him to manifest a judicial distrust of a jury's capacity to appreciate the meaning which, in English criminal law is ascribed to *intention*. Lord Diplock concluded[166] his judgment by pointing out that his own, "...feeling of outrage at the blasphemous material with which the instant appeal is concerned makes it seem to me improbable that, if Mr Lemon had been permitted to give evidence of his intentions, the jury would have been left in any doubt that, whatever his motives in publishing them may have been, he knew full well that the poem and accompanying drawing were likely to shock and arouse resentment among believing Christians and indeed many unbelievers. Nevertheless, Mr Lemon was entitled to his opportunity of sowing the seed of doubt in the jury's mind. By the judge's ruling he was denied this opportunity. For this reason, if the decision had lain with me, I would have allowed the appeal." It is not hard, it is suggested, to agree with Lord Diplock's line of reasoning regarding his common law offence and it may well also be true that had the accused given evidence as to his actual intention – whatsoever it might have been, and Lord Russell had suggested one[167] - it would have been unlikely to have made a deal of difference to the jury's verdict, which, in any event, was by a majority.

Although, as Lord Diplock had pointed out,[168] *Lemon* had been the first prosecution for blasphemous libel for over fifty years, it was not to be the last. For example, in *R v Chief Metropolitan Magistrate; Ex parte Choudhury*,[169] there had been a private prosecution[170] of the author Salman Rushdie, in respect of his book *The Satanic Verses*, which allegedly blasphemed Allah and other leading Islamic religious figures. It was held that the common law offence was confined to protecting the Christian religion alone and that the Court would not extend the law to cover other religions. The view was taken, in *Choudhury,* that to do so would make it effectively impossible, by means of judicial decision, to set sufficiently clear limits to the offence were it so extended. It will be remembered that such a view was entirely contrary to that which had been expressed by Lord Scarman in *Lemon.*[171] Yet development is, comparatively, far from uniform: thus, in Australia, Harper J of the Supreme Court of Victoria, in *Pell v Trustees of National Gallery*[172] refused an injunction to prevent the exhibition of an artwork – for want of a better expression – entitled "Piss Christ". In so doing, the judge stated[173] that countenance of the action could result in a, "...rebirth as a law protecting much more than the Christian faith."

There was another minority judgment by Lord Edmund-Davies, whose approach was quintessentially historical and, after having analysed the development of the offence,[174] he commented[175] that the "subjective intention to blaspheme or recklessness as to the blasphemous effect of the words published must be brought home in turn to each person charged." By that his Lordship meant that, if the relevant person was the author, then, "...the all important question is what was his state of mind in supplying the material for publication; if he is the editor or publisher of the words of another, it is as to their state of mind in playing their respective roles in the act of publishing. And it would be *nihil ad rem* that one or all of them were motivated by, for example, the desire to make money or to make known the blasphemous words of another."

Lord Edmund-Davies continued[176] by commenting that an analysis of the case law hitherto decided showed that they were so divided in their effect that it was impossible to state with certitude even that the necessity of a subjective intention to blaspheme has hitherto been decisively established over the relevant period. That meant, he went on, that the House of Lords, because it was free in such circumstances to declare what the law is, should now hold that such is, indeed, the law. In addition, he specifically agreed with Lord Diplock regarding the central importance of s 8 of the *Criminal Justice Act* 1967[177] and emphasised that the provision was of significance, "...in relation to the present proceedings in its manifestation of conformity with the increasing tendency in our law to move away from strict liability in relation to statutory offences and to common law crimes." Lord Edmund-Davies accepted that there were others who deprecated the tendency, "But", he responded, "to treat as irrelevant the state of mind of a person charged with blasphemy would be to take a backward step in the evolution of a humane code." That, he considered was what had happened in the instant case. "Accordingly" Lord Edmund-Davies concluded, "despite my strong feelings of revulsion over this deplorable publication, I find myself most reluctantly compelled to answer...in the negative and to hold that these appeals against conviction should be allowed."[178]

Quite apart from its subject matter, *Lemon* is an interesting decision: first, it represents a clear conflict of judicial opinion at a high appellate level on a controversial topic. Second, its whole context suggests that the offence of publishing a blasphemous libel is unlikely to be allowed quietly to die. Third, in view of the last part of this chapter,[179] the sentences passed in the case are not without interest: Lemon was sentenced to nine months imprisonment, which was suspended for eighteen months, and fined £55; the magazine was fined one thousand pounds. It is also readily apparent that the three cases – *Lemon, Chaudhury* and *Pell* – mentioned in this part of the chapter, are all *strong* cases, in the sense that they all involve the arts of self-expression (though only *Lemon* is directly concerned with poetry) and involve sensational instances of blasphemy. There may, of course be other instances where the blasphemous attitudes are not so graphically expressed as in, say, *Lemon* or *Pell*.

An interesting example is provided by Wallace Steven's poem, *"Cy Est Pourtraicte, Madame Ste Ursule, et Les Unze Milles"*[180]

It is a short, albeit heavily nuanced, poem and must be reproduced in its entirety in order to capture properly all of those nuances. It is also deliberately stylised, as its title suggests, being in Norman French. Stevens himself was a lawyer and Norman French, like Latin, is a language associated with the law – it was the official language of English law from 1066 until 1362. However, its usage continued well after that date as English did not become the official law language until 1731. During its period of ascendancy it developed differently from the French spoken in France. *Ste Ursule* requires careful study:

> Ursula, in a garden, found
> A bed of radishes.
> She kneeled upon the ground
> And gathered them,
> With flowers around,
> Blue, gold, pink and green.
>
> She dressed in red and gold brocade
> And in the grass an offering made
> Of radishes and flowers.
>
> She said, "My dear,
> Upon your altars,
> I have placed
> The marguerite and coquelicot,
> And roses
> Frail as April snow;
> But here," she said
> "Where none can see,
> I make an offering, in the grass,
> Of radishes and flowers."

And then she wept
For fear the Lord would not accept.

The good Lord in His garden sought
New leaf and shadowy tinct,
And they were all His thought.
He heard her low accord,
Half prayer and half ditty,
And He felt a subtle quiver,
That was not heavenly love,
Or pity.

This is not writ
In any book.

At first glance, *Ste Ursule* is a gentle, innocent poem involving a gentle, innocent and unworldly act by a rather naive Saint. However, this is not the way in which some commentators have perceived the poem. Thus, Jenkins writes[181] that the title recalls the pornographic novel by Apollinaire, written in 1907, entitled *Les Onze Mille Vierges* and comments that it represents one of Stevens's deliberate and sexual jests at the expense of the pieties. Cook comments[182] on the *secret erotic desire* for Saint Ursula in the poem itself and also refers[183] to similar concealment throughout many of the poems in *Harmonium*, the collection in which "Ste Ursule" appears. She also remarks[184] that Stevens, "...closes the poem mischievously and delicately suggesting that the Lord himself must sublimate sexual feelings from time to time as much as his saints." In fact, it is the conclusion found in the poem's last two lines which more than suggest that Cook's idea of *sublimation* is not always correct and the Deity's sexual feelings are sometimes active, rather than suppressed or reorientated! Much, one supposes, depends upon the priorities of the reader: thus, it must surely be appropriate to inquire as to whether a (very) broadly hinted suggestion that the Deity could have sexual feelings for (at least) one of his Saints is as blasphemous/less blasphemous/more blasphemous than the depiction which was the object of the *Lemon* decision.

Another poem or song which, in my own experience,[185] has been regarded as being blasphemous is "Friday Morning" from the cycle *Songs of Faith and Doubt* by the writer Sydney Carter, which appeared in 1964. The accusation of blasphemy is the more peculiar in this instance when one takes into account that Carter was a Quaker and generally regarded as a deeply spiritual writer and the cycle contains songs such as the well known "Lord of the Dance", derived from a Shaker hymn and "Every Star Shall Sing a Carol" which posits the idea of multiple Christian redemptions taking place throughout the Universe.

"Friday Morning", which Carter himself described as a "one-sided dialogue", retells the story of the crucifixion from the point of the good thief who was said to have been crucified at the same time as Jesus. The narrative begins with the narrator contextualising the situation in which he finds himself:

> It was on a Friday morning
> That they took me from the cell,
> And I saw they had a carpenter
> To crucify as well.

The narrator, more controversially perhaps, then begins to seek to attribute blame for both his, and more particularly, the carpenter's position. In the first stanza, he begins to attribute blame to God. Barabbas, he argues, was a murderer, but was, nonetheless, freed, whilst the innocent carpenter was crucified, with no assistance from his own god:

> And your God is in his heaven
> And he doesn't do a thing
> With a million angels watching,
> And they never move a wing.

Thus, the narrator does not, and cannot, know that the innocent carpenter with whom he hangs is, at the very least, a manifestation of the god whom he blames for their predicament. It is, though, in the final stanza that the massive paradox created by Carter in the earlier part of the poem truly unfolds:

> To hell with Jehova
> To the carpenter I said,
> I wish that a carpenter
> Had made the world instead.
> Goodbye and good luck to you
> And if our ways divide
> Remember me tomorrow
> The man you hung beside.

The key to the whole mystery is the idea of the Holy Trinity – God the Father, God the Son and God the Holy Spirit – the one in three and the three in one. If that is accepted, then of course, the narrator was not only addressing the controller, as it were, of the angels who appeared impotent, but also the creator of the world, who he wishes had done so. "Friday Morning" is based around a paradox, but that, surely, cannot of itself, even though it involved a representation of a manifestation of the Deity in, perhaps, unfamiliar terms, render it blasphemous. To me, when taken together with Carter's other writing, "Friday Morning" represents an instance of spiritual and reverential awareness of the miracle he, and others, have sought to describe.

3. Crime and Consequence

Though blasphemy and related offences are, *Lemon, Choudhury* and *Pell* notwithstanding, uncommon crimes, murder, unfortunately never has been (Chaucer tells us that in the "Pardoner's Tale") so. However, it may be committed in a wide variety of circumstances, which have to be taken into account. The circumstances involved may both be factual and legal, which is well illustrated by the decision of the High Court of Australia in *Boughey* v *The Queen*.[186]

In *Boughey*, the applicant sought special leave to appeal to the High Court of Australia from a decision of the Tasmanian Court of Criminal Appeal who had dismissed his appeal from a conviction for murder. There was little dispute as to the factual situation: it was common ground, said Mason, Wilson and Deane JJ[187], that the appellant killed the victim, "...by applying force or pressure to the region of the carotid arteries on both sides of her neck. The applicant's case at the trial was that he had applied this force or pressure not for the purpose of causing injury to the deceased but for the purpose of causing light-headedness and increased sexual excitement on her part in and for the purposes of sexual activities in which they were engaging at the time." Other connected facts were that the applicant was a qualified medical practitioner and the deceased was a Fijian woman with whom he had corresponded and who had eventually left Fiji to live with the applicant in the Australian State of Tasmania. The applicant also claimed that he had introduced the deceased to certain unconventional sexual practices for which he derived masochistic pleasure and the particular practice [188] of applying pressure to the carotid arteries. The applicant had further claimed that he and the deceased had used this practice on one another on a number of occasions and that he had only applied it to the deceased with her consent.[189]

At the trial, the judge had provided the jury with a written memorandum which related to four sets of circumstances which corresponded to s 157(1) of the Tasmanian *Criminal Code*. This provision is important for all purposes in relation to the factual situation in *Boughey* and reads as follows:

"(1)...Culpable homicide is murder if it is committed

(a) with an intention to cause the death of any person, whether of the person
killed or not;

(b) with an intention to cause to any person, whether the person killed or not, bodily harm which the offender knew to be likely to cause death in the circumstances, although he had no wish to cause death;

(c) by means of any unlawful act or omission which the offender knew, or ought to have known, to be likely to cause death in the circumstances, although he had no wish to cause death or bodily harm to any person."

The third and fourth sets of circumstances which the trial judge had left to the jury as the possible basis of a conviction for murder were based on s 157(1)(c). The third was that that the application of pressure by the accused to the deceased's neck was an unlawful act which the accused knew was likely to cause death of the deceased in the circumstances. The fourth was that such an application of pressure was an unlawful act which the accused *ought to have known* was likely to cause the deceased's death in the circumstances. Mason, Wilson and Dean JJ noted[190] that the parts of the memorandum based on s 157 (1) (b) and (c) contained an element that the accused either *knew* or *ought to have known* that the application of pressure on the deceased's neck in the manner and with the force and for the length of time which he did was likely to cause death in the circumstances. The trial judge and also directed the jury that the phrase *likely to cause death* meant nothing more than that there was *a good chance* that death would follow. It was submitted on behalf of the applicant that the word likely, in the context of s 157, meant *more likely than not*.[191]

In response to that submission, Mason, Wilson and Deane JJ emphasised[192] that the Tasmanian *Criminal Code* contained no definition of the word *likely*. These judges took the view that it was, "...unnecessary for the purposes of the present application to consider whether the knowledge of 'probable' or 'likely' consequences which suffices as an element in common law murder should ever be explained, in directions to a jury, as requiring knowledge of some degree of probability or likelihood such as 'more probable or likely than not' or a minimum percentage figure or maximum gambling odds. It suffices to say that it is plain enough that, in many and perhaps most cases, any such explanation would be undesirable. In the ordinary case where an accused well knows it is probable or likely that his acts will cause death or grievous bodily harm, he will not have the occasion to consider, let alone attempt to calculate, the degree of mathematical probability that death or grievous bodily harm will in fact result. In such a case, it would be liable to mislead or to border on the unreal to direct the jury in terms which required them to convert the knowledge of the accused into some degree of mathematical probability." This is probably, contextually at least, correct: attempts by judges to explain the standard of proof in criminal proceedings have not ended happily.[193]

However, the *Boughey* case was not decided under the rules pertaining to common law murder, but, as the judge at first instance had properly emphasised,[194] under the provisions of s 157(1) of the Tasmanian *Criminal Code*. In that regard, the judges considered[195] that the word *likely* as used in the Code should be given its ordinary meaning – that is, to convey the notion of a *substantial* chance, regardless of whether it was more than 50 per cent. In addition, Mason, Wilson and Deane JJ stated that there was a further reason why one should not superimpose on the Code refinements of meaning which a word did not convey as a matter of ordinary language. "A basic objective," they said, "of any general codification of the criminal law should be, where practicable, the expression of the elements of an offence in terms which can be comprehended by the citizen who is obliged to observe the law and (where appropriate) by a jury of citizens empanelled to participate in its enforcement. History would indicate that the codifier will never achieve the clarity and completeness which would obviate any need for subsequent interpretation or commentary..."[196] It followed, the judges though, that the courts should be wary of the danger of frustrating that fundamental aim of codification by unnecessarily submerging the ordinary meaning of a commonly used word in, "...a circumfluence of synonym, gloss and explanation which is more likely to cause than to resolve ambiguity and difficulty." On the issue arising in the present case, the trial judge, Mason, Wilson and Deane JJ were of the view,[197] had effectively encapsulated the notion when he had sought to convey the meaning that there was a *substantial* or *real* chance as distinct from what was a *mere possibility*. Accordingly, Mason, Wilson and Deane JJ found that there was no substance in that ground for appeal. With respect to three distinguished judges, it may well be that they have overemphasised one aspect of the process of codification. That it should be, in the area of criminal law at any rate, accessible to those who are exposed to it is, of course very desirable, but, at the same time, it should be sufficiently precise and specific to permit the legal advisers of those exposed to it to advise their clients in precise and specific terms. To leave the application of the word *likely* floating in a causative vacuum may very well not have had a desirable effect. To put the matter another way: the degree of likelihood may be unlikely to occur to an accused when the act in question is carried out, but it is another matter entirely for an accused's legal representative not to be able to explain to the accused what the provision means in specific terms.

The judges then turned their attention[198] to the second ground of appeal, which related to the meaning of *unlawful act* within the meaning of s 157(1) of the Tasmanian *Criminal Code*. In *Boughey*, the trial judge had directed the jury to the effect that the application of physical force or pressure to the neck of the deceased would, in the circumstances of the case, have been an unlawful act for the purposes of a 157(1) if it were done without the deceased's consent. On behalf of the applicant, it was submitted that the jury should have been directed that the applicant's act would only have been unlawful if it was done, not only without the deceased's consent, but with positive *hostility* or *hostile intent* on the part of the applicant towards her. Their Honours seemed doubtful as to whether any error on the part of the trial judge would have amounted to being of any great significance in that context, but they regarded it as convenient to consider whether such a direction would have been correct.

The judges then noted the definition of *assault* which was to be found in s 182(1) of the Tasmanian *Code*, which refers to, "...the act of intentionally applying force to the person of another, directly or indirectly, or attempting or threatening by any gesture to the person of another if the person making the attempt or threat has, or causes the other to believe on reasonable grounds that he has, present ability to effect the purpose; or the act of depriving another of his liberty." As regards *Boughey* itself, Mason, Wilson and Deane JJ commented[199] that, "It was not and could not properly be suggested that the fatal and intentional application of force to the deceased's neck in the present case constituted an ordinary incident of sexual intercourse... Indeed, the mere formulation of the proposition that the intentional and fatal application of physical force to the carotid arteries of an unwilling victim cannot constitute common law battery unless accompanied by positive hostility or hostile intent towards the victim suffices to demonstrate its unacceptability". At conclusion of that part of their judgment, where they dismissed that ground of appeal, Mason Wilson and Deane JJ stated[200] that, "...in the present case, however, the applicant's action was neither in a rescue or assistance context nor reasonably necessary for the common intercourse of life. It was an intentional, dangerous and, in the event, fatal application of force. On the assumption it was without the consent of the victim, it satisfied the requirements of a battery at common law and an unlawful assault under the Code regardless of whether it was motivated by positive hostility or hostile intent towards the unwilling victim." The real question, of course, is whether the victim was unwilling or, indeed, how unwilling. In other words, are there some activities to which consent cannot as a matter of law be given – such as the sado-masochist activities in *R* v *Brown*, which was earlier discussed[201] and the kind of activity the applicant and the deceased, much less graphic, except in consequence, appeared to have involved themselves.

Finally, Mason, Wilson and Deane JJ adverted their minds[202] to the meaning of the phrase *ought to have known* is s 157(1) c). It had been argued that the requirement that the accused *ought to have known* that his actions were *likely to cause death in the circumstances* referred only to what the offender actually knew but failed to appreciate because of panic, passion, indifference, willful blindness or the like. It followed that the trial judge was in error in directing the jury to have regard to what the applicant would have found out if he had made inquiries rather than what he actually knew.

In dealing with that submission, Mason, Wilson and Deane JJ stated that the phrase was included in s 157(1)(c) as an alternative to *knew*. "Reliance on them," they argued, "is necessary only in a case where it is not positively established that an accused actually knew that his act was likely to cause death. That does not however mean that the content of the knowledge laid at the door of an accused is to be assessed by reference to the notional knowledge and capacity of some hypothetical person... The relevant question is not whether some hypothetical reasonable person in the position of the accused would have appreciated the likely consequences of teh applicant's act. It is what the particular accused, with his or her actual knowledge and capacity, ought to have known in the circumstances in which he or she was placed". Inevitably, the judges went on,[203] "the word ought required the making of a subjective judgment by a jury, who must be persuaded that the established circumstances were such that the particular accused, with the knowledge and the capacity which he or she actually possessed, ought to have thought about the likely consequences of his or her action. The jury must be persuaded that, if the particular accused had stopped to think to the extent that he ought to have, the result, as a matter of fact, would have been that he or she would have known or appreciated that the relevant act or acts were likely to cause death. In consequence, Mason, Wilson and Deane JJ were of the view that the trial judge's direction adequately conveyed the essence of that present requirement. In particular, the judges noted that, "The repeated reference to the applicant, the emphasis which his Honour placed on factors peculiar to the applicant and the reference to whether the applicant should, in the circumstances, have been alerted to the dangers of his action combined to make it clear that what was relevant was what the applicant himself with his actual knowledge and capacity, ought to have known in the circumstances in which he was placed." That ground of appeal, likewise, failed. Accordingly, special leave to appeal was refused.

Gibbs CJ agreed with Mason, Wilson and Deane JJ. In particular, he agreed[204] that a trial judge, in directing a jury should not seek to put a gloss on the ordinary words of a statutory provision, a difficulty which I have already sought to address.[205] However, the Chief Justice did go on to say that it would be helpful to a jury for them to be instructed that a *possibility*, as opposed to a *probability*, is not enough. "On the other hand" he continued, "it would by potentially misleading to suggest that an act was likely to cause death if there was a chance that it would cause death, since the word 'chance' in its ordinary meaning includes 'possibility' as well as 'probability'." In Gibbs CJ's opinion, "a judge directing a jury... should avoid the use of the word 'chance', even if [it were] qualified by words such as *'good'*, *'substantial'* or *'real'*. However, in all the circumstances of *Boughey*, he did not consider that the trial judge's direction could be taken as meaning that a possibility that the applicant's act would have caused death was sufficient.

There was, though, a judgment in dissent by Brennan J. In so doing, he referred[206] to s 53(b) of Tasmanian *Criminal Code*, which precluded a person from giving consent to the infliction upon himself, "...of an injury likely to cause death." That provision, Brennan J said, "...would have a very wide operation if it precluded the giving of consent to the infliction of an injury which might possibly cause death. In some sports and theatrical performances where consent is given to the infliction of injury there is a possibility that death might result from an injury inflicted, and it would be a curious operation of s 53(b) if it made ineffective a consent to injury in those cases." "On the other hand," he suggested,[207] it would be a sensible interpretation of s 53(b) to make ineffective a consent given to the infliction of an injury which would probably[208] cause death.[209]

Brennan J then went on to note that s 157(1)(c) introduced an "objective, and, hence, novel, mental state as an element of murder. As regards the operation of the phrase *ought to have known,* Brennan J stated that, "The character of the act, the fact that it was likely to cause death (as the accused would have known had he thought about it) and the surrounding circumstances are material to a finding - as to whether the accused 'ought to have known. The criterion to he applied to these facts is whether any sober and reasonable man, having the accused's knowledge, experience and acumen, would have adverted to the possibility that this action might death and, adverting to that possibility, would have known that his action was likely to cause death. If the hypothetical sober and reasonable man would have known that his action was likely to cause death." However, the judge continued, the words *'ought to have known'* do not create a duty to inquire about facts before acting, they relate to *inadvertence* not *ignorance*.

Next Brennan J noted that objection[210] had been taken to the trial judge's direction on the ground that the jury had been invited to find the applicant guilty if he had failed to read his medical texts" – and Mason, Wilson and Deane JJ had taken note of that objection as well[211] - to discover the nature of the danger of applying pressure to the carotid arteries or carotid sinuses before applying such pressure. However, he did not think that the direction had, actually, gone so far. But, Brennan J did consider that there had been a misdirection as to the mental element in s 157(1)(c) of the Code and, hence, would have allowed the appeal and have ordered a retrial.

Boughey is an interesting case on a variety of levels: first, people without much legal (or indeed perhaps, medical) knowledge would, in all probability have regarded the deceased's death as an accident, at least in colloquial terms – the notion of *accident* will be considered, in relation to both poetry and law in more detail later in this book.[212] However, the word as described by Lord Shand in the House of Lords decision in *Fenton* v *J Thorley & Co Ltd*,[213] was, "...to be taken in its popular and ordinary sense. [I]t denotes or includes any unexpected personal injury resulting ...from an unlooked - for mishap or occurrence." In *Boughey*, there seemed to be little doubt as to why the practices were indulged in,[214] and they were not for the purpose of endangering life and the disastrous consequences which did, in fact, eventuate could easily, outwith the context of a 157(1)(c) of the Tasmanian *Criminal Code*, be regarded as an, "...unlooked-for mishap or occurrence." However, the very fact that the applicant was a qualified medical practitioner might very well have affected the jury in the light of, especially, the comment made by the trial judge regarding the need for him to have consulted his medical texts!

As regards the appellate courts, it should be noted that much of the critical comment which has surrounded the *Boughey* decision has related to the issue of *probability* (as opposed to *possibility*) which occurred throughout the judgment in the High Court of Australia. Thus, outwith the factual context of *Boughey*, Waller and Williams have written[215] that, "in some cases foresight of a less than even chance of death or grievous bodily harm may be regarded as sufficient to render the accused guilty of murder if death results. If D places two bullets in a six-chamber revolver and twirls the cylinder, points the gun at V and pulls the trigger once, the chances of V being shot are one in three. It would, however, seem that D could be acting with knowledge that death or grievous bodily harm was a probable outcome of his conduct." Although that may very well be correct as regards the instance which they specify, Waller and Williams do not tell us a great deal about the processes by which the decision in *Boughey* was reached. It seems quite clear that, in that case, not only was there no wish on the part of the applicant to kill the deceased; indeed, his intention, on one level at least, seemed to have been beneficent, yet nowhere was that apparent in the *rhetoric* of the High Court of Australia.

However, the ultimate result of the appellate process was that the applicant's conviction for murder was upheld. The penalty for murder, until relatively recently in most relevant jurisdictions, was death, which still remains pertinent in some jurisdictions/countries even today. Engel, in his compendious study[216] examines the various methods which have been used to effect that end in various jurisdictions. In his preface to that book, Greenspan states[217] that, "Different countries developed different styles of execution. The English excelled at 'drop' hanging, while the Americans invented the 'jerk em up' method. The Americans were also the architects of the Death House which featured the electric chair, the gas chamber and the lethal injection. For sheer depravity, however, it is difficult to match the medieval European method of disposing of condemned women: stitch them into a sack with an ape, a poisonous, snake, a dog, and fling them into a pond to drown." At the same time, Greenspan properly notes[218] his opposition to the death penalty *per se*, when he writes that, "...it is a cruel, barbaric, brutal, useless act that fails to deter crime. It is state-sanctioned vengeance and even the worst murder does not release the state from its obligation to respect the dignity of life, for the state does not honor the victim by emulating the killer. Capital punishment is, at its essence, different from all other forms of punishment by being ultimate, completely irrevocable, irreparable, and final. It is beyond correction."

Of all of the forms of execution to which Greenspan refers, the one which has attracted, particularly, the attention of poets is that of hanging, especially in England. A part of the reason for that was that, prior to 1868, executions were carried out in public in England. One supposes that that was done to act as a deterrent, but such was not the case. In 1783, the principal place of execution in London was moved from Tyburn to Newgate. Engel describes[219] the effect of the change: "In fact, the hour the hangings were scheduled would allow most people to pass in front of Newgate on the way to work. But nothing else was changed. Just as many pockets and purses were picked. The same 'last dying speeches' were hawked. The same refreshments were peddled in the street: oranges, apples, hot meat pies! The great moral lesson still eluded the multitude. People still got maimed when grandstands fell down. Householders nearby rented out windows profitably to the wealthy and socially prominent, who wished to take in the spectacle through their opera glasses." In many respects, the atmosphere at these vile events has been best captured by the Nineteenth Century poet, Coventry Patmore, in his poem "A London Fete", which emphasises, in graphic form, the points made by Engel. First, the poem begins with a description of Newgate prior to the actual hanging and, in particular, Patmore describes the behaviour of the crowd, its being clear to take up Engel's point, that the great moral lesson was lost on the multitude:

> All night fell hammers, shock on shock;
> With echoes Newgate's granite clang'd:
> The scaffold built, at eight o'clock
> They brought the man out to be hang'd
> Then came from all the people there
> A single cry, that shook the air;
> Mothers held up their babes to see,
> Who spread their hands, and crow'd for glee;
> Here a girl form her vesture tore
> A rag to wave with, and join'd the roar;
> There a man, with yelling tired,
> Stopp'd, and the culprit's crime inquired;
> A sot, below the doom'd man dumb,
> Bawl'd his health in the world to come;

> These blasphemed and fought for places;
> Those, half-crush'd, cast frantic faces,
> To windows, where, in freedom sweet,
> Others enjoy'd the wicked treat.

Having, thus, created the atmosphere, Patmore goes on to describe the hanging itself and its consequent and deleterious effect on the crowd. Indeed, it is the effect of the spectacle on the crowd which is the major theme of the poem. The corrupting effect on the crowd, which, doubtless, will be passed on to future generations, is a particular focus of this most effectively stark and graphic poem:

> At last, the show's black crisis pended;
> Struggles for better standings ended;
> The rabble's lips no longer curst,
> But stood agape with horrid thirst;
> Thousands of breasts beat horrid hope;
> Thousands of eyeballs, lit with hell,
> Burnt one way all, to see the rope
> Unslacken as the platform fell.
> The rope flew tight; and then the roar
> Burst forth afresh; less loud, but more
> Confused and affrighting than before.
> A few harsh tongues forever led
> The common din, the chaos of noises,
> But ear could not catch what they said.
> As when the realm of the damn'd rejoices
> At winning a soul to its will,
> That clatter and clangour of hateful voices
> Sicken'd and stunn'd the air, until
> The dangling corpse hung straight and still.

Thus, the hellish noise, which represents the crowd's dehumanisation is momentarily quelled, though, again the dehumanisation is apparent in other ways ("Thousands of eyeballs, lit with hell"). The poem concludes as the crowd disperses and Patmore emphasises the corrupting effect, not only of the execution itself, of the crowd's behaviour and reemphasises that the crowd's vicious and abhuman behaviour is unlikely to disappear with the generation of adults which are represented in it. Similarly, he notes, at both the beginning and end of the following extract, that the execution itself has no moral or educative function:

> The show complete, the pleasure past,
> The solid masses loosen'd fast:
> A thief slunk off, with ample spoil,
> To ply elsewhere his daily toil;
> A baby strung its doll to a stick;
> A mother praised the pretty trick;
> Two children caught and hang'd a cat;
> Two friends walk'd on, in lively chat;
> And two, who had disputed places,
> Went forth to fight, with murderous faces.

Engel, in fact, likewise comments[220] that, "...the unruliness of the spectators went a long way to convincing responsible people that public executions belonged to a bygone and barbaric age... The ending of public executions relieved public opinion. One might parody Lord Macaulay and say that some abolitionists at least had public hanging, not because it gave pain to the condemned, but because it gave pleasure to the spectators."

After 1868, hangings were conducted inside prisons, but that did not mean that there was no effect on people other than the condemned prisoner. This point together with comments on other forms of retribution which will be later considered,[221] was powerfully made by Oscar Wilde in his last poem (written in France after his won release from prison). Bloom considers[222] that, "Wilde's poetry [except for the "Ballad of Reading Gaol"] is weak and forgettable. His *Ballad* owes rather too much to Coleridge's *The Rime of the Ancient Mariner* but is rescued by its somber intensity." The poem describes, as Engel points out[223] the execution of Charles Wooldridge, a former trooper in the Royal Horse Guards. The poem begins with, a rather romanticised, description of Wooldbridge at exercise in the prison yard:

> He did not wear his scarlet coat
> For blood and wine are red,

> And blood and wine were on his hands
> Then they found him with the dead,
> The poor dead woman whom he loved,
> And murdered in her bed.
>
> He walked amongst the Trial Men
> In a suit of shabby grey;
> A cricket cap was on his head,
> And his step seemed light and gay;
> But I never saw a man who looked
> So wistfully at the day.

There follows the discovery that the man is shortly to be executed for the murder mentioned in the first stanza, but, in Wilde's interpretation, for doing that which is, in one form or another, common to all:

> Some love too little, some love too long,
> Some sell, and others buy;
> Some do the deed with many tears,
> And some without a sigh:
> For each man kills the thing he loves
> Yet each man does not die.

There then follows a deliberately harrowing depiction of the events leading up to the execution itself:

> He does not wake at dawn to see
> Dread figures throng his room,
> The shivering Chaplain robed in white,
> The Sheriff stern with gloom,
> And the Governor all in shiny black,
> With the yellow face of Doom.
>
> He does not rise in piteous haste
> To put on convict-clothes,
> While some coarse-mouthed Doctor gloats, and notes

Each new and nerve-twitched pose,
Fingering a watch whose little ticks
Are like horrible hammer-blows.
He does not feel that sickening thirst
That sands one's throat, before
The hangman with his gardener's gloves
Comes through the padded door,
And binds one with three leathern thongs,
That the throat may thirst no more.

He does not bend his head to hear
The Burial Office read,
Nor, while the anguish of his soul
Tells him he is not dead,
Cross his own coffin, as he moves
Into the hideous shed.

Although it might – with some justification – be thought that Wilde is too dramatic in the versified description, it is, in fact, not too inaccurate. Thus, Engel quotes[224] James Berry, the public executioner at about the time[225] Wilde himself was writing of the procedure. Berry states that, "I enter the cell punctually at three minutes to eight. When we enter the condemned cell the chaplain is already there, and he has been for some time. The attendants who have watched through the convict's last night on earth are also present. At my appearance the convict takes leave of his attendants to whom he generally gives some small token or keep-sake, and I at once proceed to pinion his arms. As soon as the pinioning is done a procession is formed. On the way from the cell to the scaffold the chaplain reads the service for the burial of the dead, and, as the procession moves, I place the white cap upon the head of the convict. Just as we reach the scaffold I pull the cap over his eyes. Then I place the convict under the beam, pinion his legs just below the knees, adjust the rope, pull the bolt and the trap falls. Death is instantaneous." According to Engel, Berry had some additional personal thoughts on the matter and believed that a special bond existed between the executioner and his victim, which excluded all others.[226]

Sometimes, inevitably, matters did not go as well as Berry had suggested. Thus, Engel describes[227] Berry's hanging of Robert Goodale on November 30th 1885. Goodale, apparently, was a heavy man, who weighed fourteen stones. His death was, indeed, instantaneous though he had not been hanged as such, but decapitated. For Berry, Engel says, "...all hell broke loose and a long shadow was cast on his career and livelihood." In consequence, a committee was set up in the House of Lords to inquire into all aspects of judicial hanging. This committee took evidence, "...from leading authorities both practical and medical about the best way of insuring instant death without a hitch, if possible. The medical people contradicted one another which confused everybody." Ultimately, after another accident similar to the Goodale experience,[228] Berry resigned. In 1913, he committed suicide, being described on the death certificate as *Evangelist*.

4. Other Consequences

One particular issue which Oscar Wilde raised in the latter part of "The Ballad of Reading Gaol" was the morbid effect of the execution on other prisoners, who, of course, knew full well what was taking place:

> We had no other thing to do,
> Save to wait for the sign to come:
> So, like things of stone in a valley lone,
> Quiet we sat and dumb:
> But each man's heart beat thick and quick,
> Like a madman on a drum!
>
> With sudden shock the prison-clock
> Smote on the shivering air,
> And from all the gaol rose up a wail
> Of impotent despair,
> Like the sound that frightened marshes hear
> From some leper in his lair.

It is an easy and logical step to move from that stance to a critique of the prison system as such and Wilde does not fail to take advantage of that opportunity and of his own experience:

> This too I know – and wise it were
> If each could know the same –
> That every prison that men build
> Is built with bricks of shame,
> And bound with bars lest Christ should see
> How men their brothers maim.

Wilde then goes on to examine, in strongly rhetorical terms, the corrupting and dehumanising effects of life in a Nineteenth Century prison:

> The vilest deeds like poison weeds,
> Bloom well in prison-air;
> It is only what is good in Man
> That wastes and withers there:
> Pale Anguish keeps the heavy gate,
> And the Warder is Despair.
>
> For they stave the little frightened child
> Till it weeps both night and day:
> And they scourge the weak, and flog the fool,
> And gibe the old and grey,
> And none a word may say.
>
> Each narrow cell in which we dwell
> Is a foul and dark latrine,
> And the fetid breath of living Death
> Chokes up each grated screen,
> And all, but Lust, is turned to dust
> In Humanity's machine.

One tends to assume that conditions – both physical and spiritual – are improved since Wilde wrote this still powerful and rhetorically stark poem. The modern reality may not, in any real sense, justify any such assumption. Thus, Hogg has written[229] that, "Prisons in Australia, with some exceptions, are organised around a cell confinement of inmates. Most, but not all, cells are designed to house a single prisoner. Prisons are carefully designed to hold a designated maximum or optimum number of inmates. Prison use rate is a measure of the relationship between the actual number of prisoners and the designated capacity of the prison system. As such it affords a general guide to levels of prison overcrowding (as well as perhaps the efficient use of public resources)." Such overcrowding, Hogg continues, means that a not inconsiderable number of prisoners are accommodated by putting two, or more in a cell originally designed for one. In addition, that writer notes that such overcrowding means that, "…imprisonment involves much more than separation from the outside world and loss of freedom of movement and association. It also typically involves a severe deprivation of autonomy and privacy within the confines of the prison and forced association with persons not of the individual prisoner's choosing.

That problem may further be exacerbated by continuing increases in the prison population which, according to writers such as Bartlett, appears to be a globally increasing process.[230] Increasing imprisonment rates, Bartlett suggests, are generally based on policy choices which, in turn, are influenced by public attitudes, which, presently, favour severity. "Public fear of crime", Bartlett writes, "real or perceived has been compounded by a lack of confidence in the criminal justice system. These sentiments, fuelled by the mass media have promoted ill-informed legislative response. As criminal policy has become a favourite item in the toolkit of general politics, legislative emphasis has returned to retribution and deterrence as the hopeful goals of punishment." Bartlett continues by saying that, in many jurisdictions, long sentences are continuing to be pursued as the primary deterrent against crime which, in turn, means that societies are sending an increasing number of people into prison systems which are dysfunctional.

The chronic overcrowding in prison systems has led, Bartlett argues,[231] to major societal consequences at large. Particularly, he suggests, the high costs which are associated with the use of imprisonment have given rise to significant difficulties in some countries. Thus, he comments that, although custodial corrections often directly compete with funding for health, education and other vital services, the public is rarely aware of how large correctional budgets actually are. In many developing countries, very substantial sums are diverted away from needy communities so that offenders – many of whom are serving long sentences for minor crimes – may be incarcerated. For many countries, especially industrialised countries, the immediate response, at vast expense, has been to build more prisons which may, in turn lead to further additions to the prison population. Another response has been the use of amnesties and mass pardons to reduce prison populations.[232] At the same time, Bartlett suggests, alternatives to custodial sentences such as bail, conditional release, probation and the like – are either not available or not much utilised.

In view of the foregoing comments, it might readily be thought that the future might better be served through awareness of both presently existing and prior deficiencies in the system of custodial sentencing. Thus, the distinguished commentor, Wilson, has been guardedly pessimistic[233] about the efficiency of the process. Wilson suggests that the modern, and supposed aims of imprisonment – punishment, rehabilitation and deterrence – have been replaced by the goal of *incapacitation* in recent times. That goal can simply be stated by reference to the political catch-cry "Prison works," which simply means that criminals who are put in prison are thereby prevented from further victimising innocent citizens. Wilson believes the argument, at best, to be simplistic and short-sighted if only because almost all offenders, many alienated and brutalised, will ultimately be returned to the community with little hope of avoiding crime. Wilson's essential point is that a prison sentence can never be a neutral experience. It is imperative, he argues, that young people, especially, who are sent to prison experience an environment which is challenging, constructive and needs based. He further suggests that education training and care are essential if those people's decline into a life of crime and destitution is to be prevented. In other words, young people sentenced to prison must be equipped to deal with the problems they face and motivated to avoid their reoffending. Until that happens, Wilson states, any prison sentence will be counterproductive.

The points made by Wilson reiterate, to no little degree, the view of the prison experience which Oscar Wilde demonstrated in the later part of the "The Ballad of Reading Gaol." Perhaps his most graphic description of the alienating and dehumanising effect of the sterile prison experience, effectively denounced by Wilson, is to be found at the end of the poem:

And never human voice comes near

To speak a gentle word
And the eye that watches through the door
Is pitiless and hard:
And by all forgot, we tot and rot,
With soul and body marred.

And thus we rust Life's iron chain
Degraded and alone:
And some men curse, and some men weep,
And some men make no moan:
But God's eternal Laws are kind
And break the heart of stone.

Wilson is particularly concerned about the incarceration of young people and believes that young offenders should be diverted from prison whenever possible. That, though, is one instance of a more central problem: that there are many different groups of prisoners for whom many different objectives must be sought. He suggests that with a wide ranging prison population – which ranges from people awaiting trial, through the addicted and drug dependent, from the inadequate to the violent to the young or elderly – it would seem to be impossible that the product will suit all of those variants or will be able effectively to assist all of those people to lead useful and law abiding lives on their release. However, that cause is not helped by political figures who assert that a large prison population means that government was taking action on crime.

It seems to follow that the process by which people, especially young people, find themselves in a system which cannot itself work well is itself unsatisfactory. Of course, there are different levels of crime, and criminality for that matter, a fact which is initially demonstrated by the decision of the New Zealand Court of Appeal in *Melser* v *Police*.[234] The four appellants in this case were found by the police chained to the pillars at the entrance to Parliament House in Wellington, the capital of New Zealand. These pillars were immediately overlooking the main steps to the main building. The chains were not only round the pillars but round the demonstrators' bodies and padlocked so that it was impossible to release them from the pillars without either the chains being cut or the padlocks unlocked. They explained that they were demonstrating against the visit of the Vice-President of the United States later that day. They also stated that they did not have the keys to the padlocks and intended to stay there until after the Vice-President's arrival. They had chained themselves in such a way that the Vice-President could not have entered by the main steps without passing between them. There had been a small crowd during the morning in the Parliament grounds in front of the steps, but, during the afternoon, it had swelled to between two and three hundred people, many of whom carried banners protesting against American participation in the Vietnam War. The police did not interfere in any way with the demonstrators, except to enable people who were entering Parliament Buildings reasonably to use the main entrance. Had the four appellants been content to join the other demonstrators, the police would have taken no action. However, the police did ask the appellants to join the other demonstrators and they refused, at which point they were arrested. They were convicted under s 3D of the *Police Offences Act* 1927. That section provides that, "Every person commits an offence…who in or within view of any public place as defined in s 40 hereof or within the hearing of any person therein, behaves in a riotous, offensive, threatening, insulting or disorderly manner uses any threatening, abusive or insulting words." They appealed to the New Zealand Court of Appeal, who, unanimously upheld their convictions.

North P disposed of the appeal with some expedition; he noted[235] that he was not persuaded that the conduct of the appellants was not, at least, likely to cause annoyance to other persons who were present at the time. He also agreed with the trial judge who had found that the appellants' conduct was likely to cause a breach of peace. North P considered that it was "quite idle" for the appellants' counsel to argue that their conduct in chaining themselves to the Parliament House pillars on the occasion of the visit of a distinguished guest was not likely to annoy some of the persons who were present. It had also been submitted, on the appellants' behalf, that there was insufficient proof that the appellants' conduct was within the view of a place open to, or used by the public. North P agreed[236] with the trial judge that there was such evidence as brought the appellants within the legislation's purview. Further, were there any deficiency in proof, the President thought, the Court was entitled to take judicial notice of the fact that it was common knowledge that Parliament grounds were a place open to, and used by, the public.

Turner J agreed with North P, but added[237] that it was, "...not easy to define with exactitude in words what is or is not 'disorderly' conduct... [I]t is a matter of degree whether such conduct is in any case sufficiently grave to bring it within the ambit of some particular section of a criminal statute... Disorderly conduct is conduct which is disorderly; it is conduct which, while sufficiently ill-mannered or in bad taste, to meet with the disapproval of well-conducted and reasonable men and women, is also something more – it must in my opinion tend to annoy or insult such persons who are faced with it – and sufficiently deeply or seriously to warrant the interference of the criminal law." At the same time, Turner J continued, it was not enough, especially in the context of legitimate public protests, that the conduct should not be merely ill-mannered or in bad taste nor, indeed, that it should go so far as to be likely to cause a breach of the peace, which would be dealt with elsewhere. In the present context, Turner J explained,[238] it might not have been disorderly conduct on the appellants' part had they made more orderly public protests against an administration of whose policies they disapproved, which did not include chaining themselves at the place and time which they did. Nor might it have been disorderly conduct if they had chained themselves to pillars or posts on different days or times, and in some other place, less calculated to arouse serious annoyance to the public. "But" he said emphatically, "to chain themselves to the pillars of Parliament buildings on the day, at the time, and in the circumstances of this particular protest went further. It is impossible not to say that it went some considerable distance towards provoking a breach of the peace even though it did not do so, and it was certainly calculated to give serious annoyance to the public, whether a breach of the peace was rendered likely or not."

McCarthy J adopted a rather different approach to the issue than had North P and Turner J. He began his judgment[239] by noting that, throughout the submissions of the appellants' counsel, was a theme that, were the convictions to be upheld, the Court of Appeal would be giving judicial approval to a denial of democratic rights of expression of opinion and of protest against political decisions. In order for him to deal with that assertion, which had been seriously made after appropriate consideration, he was required to say something regarding the Court's function in defining the rights of citizens in the context of s 3D of the *Police Offences Act*. Primarily McCarthy J accepted that, "...freedom of opinion including the right to protest against political decisions is now accepted as a fundamental human right in any modern society which deserves to be called democratic. Its general acceptance is one of the most precious of our individual freedoms. It needed no Charter of the United Nations to make it acceptable to us; it has long been part of our way of life. But a democracy is compound of many different freedoms, some of which conflict with others..." Accordingly, the task of law was to define the limitations which society, for its own social health, has placed on such freedoms.

As regards the application of s 3D, the judge noted,[240] and accepted unhesitatingly, the appellants' right to protest. However, he also referred to the members of the House of Representatives who had a reciprocal right to freedom from interference at the doorway of the House and their right freely to entertain their visitors, unembarrassed by unseemly behaviour on the part of intruders. McCarthy J continued by saying that the appellants had chosen to exercise their freedom in a way which interfered with the rights of others. That seemed to the judge to be beyond all question and, "...to be the central feature of the case. It is not the fact that the appellants made a protest, but rather the way in which they made that protest which is objected to. The prosecution claim that that way was unecessarily objectionable." However, McCarthy J further noted that offences against good manners, taste or morality, although contrary to public opinion were insufficient to constitute an offence under s 3D. "There must," he said, "be conduct which can not only be fairly characterised as disorderly, but is also likely to cause a disturbance or to annoy others considerably." McCarthy J agreed with Turner J that, in the ultimate, the question was one of degree. Thus, in the event, McCarthy J took the view that the appellants' conduct was, "...unnecessarily disorderly and objectionable. It was likely to engender annoyance..."

Melser is an interesting case for various reasons: first, the Court of Appeal seemed to be concerned, McCarthy J most particularly,[241] with matters other than a direct application of the statutory provision. This is interesting as the approach of the Court does not seem to accord with the words used in s 3D itself. Second, the heralded breach of the peace, as was pointed out, never eventuated, but that was mostly because the other protesters were, at least, sympathetic to the appellants.

The third point, of most interest in the *Melser* case is its aftermath, in all senses with which this is concerned: legal, poetic, rhetorical and social.

From a legal point of view, the operation of s 3D of the *Police Offences Act 1927* and *Melser* were considered by Woodhouse J of the Supreme Court of New Zealand in an appeal from a Magistrate in *Kinney* v *Police*.[242] The appellant had been convicted of an offence under s 3D after a daylight festival of amplified pop music in a city's Botanical Gardens, which had been attended by some three thousand people. As regards the conduct of the festival, the judge referred.[243] to a press cutting concerning the event which, he said, provided, "...a pleasing description of the way many young people commendably set to work to tidy up at the end of the function by collecting and removing numerous drumloads of litter. The police were obliged to put an occasional brake on some developing exuberance, and three or four arrests were made; but overall this large holiday gathering was well behaved and good humoured." After the music had finished, and there were a few bystanders present, the appellant waded up to his knees in an ornamental lake and, after a minute or two, and at the instruction of a police officer, returned to the bank where he was arrested. The appellant appealed against his conviction to the Supreme Court, where it was upheld.

As regards the effect of the appellant's conduct, Woodhouse J noted[244] that, "The ducks seemed unperturbed – they remained on the surface of the water with scarcely an increase in their rate of stroke. The attitude of the goldfish is unknown. As for bystanders, there were few people about at the time, although there is evidence that some persons were looking across towards the Gardens from their homes on the far side of the road. The judge then noted *Melser* and commented that *disorderly behaviour* was necessarily a somewhat nebulous term, but it was, "...clear that the conduct under review must be something more than unmannerly, or disturbing, or annoying before it can be the basis for a conviction in terms of the section." Woodhouse J was also of the opinion that the provision, "...should not be allowed to scoop up all sorts of minor troubles and it certainly is not designed to enable the police to discipline every irregular or inconvenient or exhibitionist activity or to put a criminal sanction on over-exuberant behaviour, even when it might be possible to discern a few conventional hands raised in protest or surprise."[245]

From the description of the events by the judge in *Kinney*, it is clear that the charge was not taken particularly seriously. The explicit rhetoric lies in the judge's description of the responses of the ducks and goldfish.[246] By concentrating on the periphery of the case, Woodhouse J was seeking to trivialise the prosecution. Perhaps he should have attempted to deliver his judgment in verse.[247] *Melser*, though, was to be severely modified by the, then, recently created Supreme Court of New Zealand in *Brooker v Police*.[248] That case decided that the legislation[249] when taken together with the *New Zealand Bill of Rights Act* 1990, was intended to protect public order. Hence, for behaviour to be regarded as disorderly, it had to be disruptive of public order in the particular circumstances of time and place.

In *Brooker*, the appellant believed that the police, especially one officer, had acted unfairly towards him. In response, one morning after 9am, he went to that officer's house, knowing, as was found by the District Court, that she had been on duty overnight. He rang and knocked until she opened the door and told him to go away. At that juncture, he went to the grass verge of the road where he sang songs in a normal singing voice and played his guitar while displaying a placard which made reference to police behaviour. The officer called for assistance and an inspector and other police arrived. After talking to the complainant officer, the police told the appellant that he would be arrested for intimidation if he did not desist. He did not desist and was arrested. Perhaps significantly, there was no evidence of complaint from other residents of the neighbourhood. The District Court judge amended the charge to one of the disorderly conduct as there was no evidence of an intent to intimidate. The appellant appealed on the grounds that his behaviour could not be described as *disorderly* within the meaning of the legislation when read together with s 14 of the 1990 Act, which protects freedom of expression. The Supreme Court held[250] that, in addition to the matters already noted,[251] the fact that the behaviour took place in a residential area might be relevant to applying the standard to the facts, but it could not be determinative and the fact that the conduct concerned involved a genuine exercise of freedom of expression was also relevant. In addition, Blanchard, Tipping and McGrath JJ were of the view[252] that private annoyance was not sufficient – disturbance or anxiety beyond what reasonable citzens should be required to bear was required. Hence, insofar as it had dealt with those matters, *Melser* was overruled.

However, it must be remembered that the appellants in *Melser* were convicted, as was *Kinney* at first instance, in that context, it should be borne in mind that young offenders and less serious offenders are/may/should be placed in institutions which are separate and different from those in which offenders who fall into the other groups mentioned by Wilson are placed.[253] Of both kinds of institutions, Liebling has stated[254] that research suggests that human beings, including prisoners, need to be in environments which treat them with dignity and permit their development. Such well-being, it is argued, depends, at least in part, on fair and respectful treatment. However, Bob Dylan paints a different picture, in his lyric "Walls of Red Wing", written in 1963. He begins by mentioning the ages of those confined and shortly describes their treatment in the first stanza of the lyric:

> Oh, the age of inmates
> I remember quite freely:
> No younger than twelve
> No older 'n seventeen
> Thrown in like bandits
> And cast off like criminals
> Inside the walls
> The walls of Red Wing

In the third stanza, Dylan writes of the philosophy adopted by the inmates to avoid difficulties in the institution. Effectively all of these are negative in the their intention and effect:

> Oh, the gates are cast iron
> And the walls are barbed wire
> Stay far from the fence
> With the 'lectricity sting
> And it's keep down your head
> And stay in your number
> Inside the walls
> The walls of Red Wing.

In the fifth stanza, Dylan points sharply to the attitude of the prison officers. Once again, as with the third stanza, the atmosphere which has been created in the institution seems to be the antithesis of the kind of environment which Liebling regarded as being both necessary and desirable:

> Its many a guard
> That stands around smilin'
> Holdin' his club
> Like he was a king
> Hopin' to get you
> Behind a wood pilin'
> Inside the walls
> The walls of Red Wing

As might be expected, finally, attention is drawn to the results of the experience within the institution. Perhaps the only really surprising suggestion which is made by the writer in the final stanza is that some of the inmates might ultimately prove to be successful. Although the phrase, "...lawyers and things..." suggests that that profession may not be much more respectable than the criminals who were produced by Red Wing:

> Oh, some of us'll end up
> In St. Cloud Prison
> And some of us'll wind up
> To be lawyers and things
> And some of us'll stand up
> To meet you on your crossroads
> From inside the walls
> The walls of Red Wing

In respect of younger offenders, the approach adopted in the sentencing process is of especial importance. That was considered by Crawford CJ of the Supreme Court of Tasmania in *Cashman* v *Jordan*[255] where the applicant had been sentenced to eight months imprisonment, with four months being suspended on the condition that for a period of two years following his release from prison he commit no further offences under specified legislation [256] or drive while disqualified or without a licence. In addition, he was disqualified from driving for a period of eighteen months commencing on his release from prison. The sentence, Crawford CJ pointed out[257] was a global one and was imposed in respect of ten offences committed between November 2008 and March 2009. Those offences included driving while disqualified, a penalty which had been imposed at the beginning of the relevant period. The Chief Justice then referred[258] to other relevant matters: at the time of the offences, he was twenty years of age and did not have a significant record, although he had earlier been disqualified from driving for three months for having an excessive number of demerit points. That was significant, Crawford CJ considered, because, "…the first two offences of driving while disqualified were committed not only in breach of a court order of disqualification but also in breach of that disqualification notice. It emphasise the contempt he demonstrated for the law and authority." He applied for the sentence to be reviewed on the grounds, first, that it was manifestly excessive and, second, that the Magistrate had given insufficient weight to the applicant's prospects of rehabilitation.

It was argued on the applicant's behalf that he was employed, was a youthful offender and had excellent prospects for rehabilitation. It was also said that he had sold his vehicle so as to ensure that he was not tempted to drive in the future. His employer had offered to assist him getting to and from work. In the course of that argument, the applicant's counsel had referred to the earlier decision of the same Court in *Lahey* v *Sanderson*,[259] where Burbury CJ had emphasised that the public interest was best served if an offender is induced to turn from a criminal course. This meant, Burbury CJ had continued, that, "…a court rarely sends a youth to gaol except in the case of a crime of considerable gravity (such as a crime of violence) or in the case of a persistent offender who has shown himself not amenable to disciplinary methods short of gaol." The Chief Justice, in *Lahey*, also referred to the dangers of exposing a young person to corrupting influences and confirming him in criminal ways, were he sent to prison. Burbury CJ had also emphasised that, in the case of a youthful offender, reformation was always an important consideration and, "…in the ordinary run of crime the dominant consideration." In *Cashman*, Crawford CJ noted[260] that Burbury CJ's formulation had been previously applied in cases involving driving while disqualified.[261] It was also argued on the applicant's behalf that he should have been given an opportunity to reform before sending him to prison for the first time and that a sentence less severe than actual imprisonment should have been imposed. The Chief Justice interpreted[262] that submission as suggesting that any youthful offender should not be sent to prison until he or she has been subjected to less severe punishments in an ascending order of severity: first, community service; second, suspended imprisonment and finally, actual imprisonment. "However", he said, "there is no principle that binds a sentencing court to conform with that regime. If that was the case, youthful offenders would soon learn that they can commit offences without concern of severe punishment."

Having said that, Crawford CJ commented[263] that his first response to the sentence was that it was, as had been claimed, manifestly excessive, even though the applicant's "...contemptuous attitude particularly displayed by failure to comply with court orders, deserved a punishment that will teach him a lesson, but nevertheless that could have been achieved with a young offender with a far less severe sentence than the one imposed, and one that did not require immediate incarceration. The length of the imprisonment was commensurate with sentences imposed in other cases for far worse offending or in the light of a far worse record for similar offences." However, he continued[264] by saying that those comments were not to be taken as meaning that driving while disqualified was not a serious offence – they merely meant that the punishment which had been imposed was more severe than was warranted. Accordingly, Crawford CJ set aside the whole of the sentence[265] and stated that in its place, he was considering a suspended sentence of imprisonment, together with a community service order and disqualification.[266]

The *Cashman* case demonstrates the dilemma faced by a sentencing court in a case in which there were clearly contradictory issues involved. The case can validly be contrasted with the decision of the New South Wales Court of Criminal Appeal in *R v Bond*,[267] which dealt with altogether more serious offences. In *Bond*, the applicant had pleaded guilty to charges of manslaughter, inflicting grievous bodily harm with intent to have sexual intercourse and robbery with striking. He sought leave to appeal against sentences aggregating to twenty years penal servitude with a non-parole period of fifteen years.[268] The offences had occurred when the applicant had agreed to walk the victim home from a club late at night. In a park near where the victim lived, the applicant became enraged when a proposition to the victim was rejected and he admitted such to the police. In reality, though, he inflicted such severe injuries on the victim that she died in hospital some sixteen days later without regaining consciousness. The applicant did have a record of prior assaults on women, although he could not properly be described as a hardened criminal. His personality was badly affected by alcohol and he was of low average intelligence. The trial judge had given credit for the applicant's plea of guilty, but did not refer to the fact that, when the applicant was initially approached by police, he had fully co-operated with them. The Court of Criminal Appeal granted leave to appeal, but dismissed the appeal.

Badgery-Parker J, with whom Wood J agreed noted,[269] first, that having regard to the extent of the beating inflicted must place the offence very high in the scale of manslaughter offences. The judge accepted that it did not, "…fall in the category of the worst possible case, for which indeed a life sentence is sometimes appropriate. Nevertheless if it came to be considered on its own, there being no associated charges, it would be relevant to note, as an aggravating circumstance, that the offence was committed in the course of an attempt to have sexual intercourse." As regards the remainder of the offences excluding the theft, which was committed on the spur of the moment, Badgery-Parker J considered that they were of the utmost gravity. "The gravity of the particular offence," he said,[270] "…must, in large measure be determined by the extent of harm inflicted – and in this case, the beating was so severe that ultimately, over a fortnight later, the victim died. I find it difficult to imagine a case more deserving of the maximum sentence. Perhaps it is a question for philosophers rather than lawyers whether the malicious infliction of harm causing death is or not worse than the malicious infliction of harm leaving the victim so disabled that life itself becomes a cruel burden. For my part, although imagination may conceive worse cases, I am satisfied that this was indeed, objectively considered, one of the worst category of cases… and one to which, subject of course to the existence of any relevant mitigating circumstances and subjective matters, the maximum penalty was appropriate." Badgery-Parker J then went on[271] to consider the effects of the attitude of the applicant and he noted that, whilst there were circumstances where co-operation with police would entitle an offender to very substantial sentencing discounts, it was not the case that, whenever an offender confesses his guilt and facilitates the establishment of the details of his offence by the police, that a discount would be given over and above that attracted by a plea of guilty and expressions of remorse.[272] It was on that issue that Kirby P dissented and he regarded[273] the present state of criminal law as specifying it as appropriate to provide a due allowance in sentencing for co-operation with authorities and pleas of guilty as a factor distinct from, and additional to, evidence of personal contrition or the fact that co-operation leads to the solution of other crimes.[274]

The rhetoric employed by sentencing judges may not seem attractive to many – especially, of course, the person being sentenced. Thus, the categorisation of the applicant's conduct in *Bond* by Badgery-Parker J may not have endeared him to relatives, say, of the applicant and, similarly, Kirby P's slightly differently orientated rhetoric might have not been appreciated by family and friends of the deceased. On both sides, there could well have been a lack of comprehension of the legal process at large. It may also, therefore, present a selective and particularised image of judges. It is all of that which brings us to Ted Hughes's narrative poem *Cave Birds,* published in 1978.

The essential narrative structure of *Cave Birds* is that the protagonist is accused of an obscure crime, is tried, convicted, executed, goes to the underworld and is reborn. All of the protagonists – judge, accused, summoner, interrogator, and so on - are played by birds. The poem was published originally together with drawings by Leonard Baskin, an American artist. That edition has not been republished and, apparently, some of the individual poems are rather obscure without the drawings. The judge is not flatteringly portrayed:

> The pondering body of the law teeters across
> A web-glistening geometry.
>
> Lolling, he receives and transmits
> Cosmic equipoise.
>
> The offal-sack of everything that is not
> The Absolute on to whose throne he lowers his buttocks.
>
> Clowning, half-imbecile,
> A Nero of the unalterable.
>
> Hi gluttony
> Is a strange one – his leavings are guilt and sentence.

> Hung with precedents as with obsolete armour
> His banqueting court is as airy as any idea.
>
> At all hours he comes wobbling out
> To fatten on the appeal of those who have fouled
>
> His tarred and starry web.
>
> Or squats listening
> To his digestion and the solar silence.

Robinson comments,[275] particularly, on two facets of the description of the judge: his gluttony and his urge to keep things as they are. The former refers to the poet's way of describing the excesses of the intellect which drain life of its energies. Second, the concern with stasis makes, according to Robinson, "…the judge a 'Nero of the unalterable,' refusing to acknowledge change, fiddling while the city burns, pretending, against all the evidence, that all will continue as before." Scigay regards[276] those aspects in a different light. He suggests that the figure of the judge represents an abstract intellect in human consciousness or a paradoxical faculty which devours all phenomena which it perceives yet it is not itself a physiological organ (the garbage sack of everything is not). Hughes responds to the apparent oafishness of the original drawing by Baskin, Scigay suggests, by, "…figuring forth the abstracting intellect as a faculty that has physiological roots, but whose only leavings are 'guilt and sentence.'" However, another view is taken by Sager, who describes[277] the defendant's being brought face to face with the judge and states that, "…the representative of natural law is a gross spider squatting obscenely at the centre of his cosmic web… and therefore of everything that lives to disturb 'cosmic equipoise' and break the 'solar silence'". When he has removed the substance of those who have fouled his 'tarred and starry web,' all that remains is the, "…unalterable – guilt and sentence."[278]

Gifford and Roberts appear to emphasise[279] the paradoxical nature of Hughes's vision of the judge – at least in an abstract or cosmic setting. These commentators suggest that the portrait of the judge must present something of a shock to the reader, because of its difference from the other legal figures in *Cave Birds*. "This figure," they write, "is an abstraction...who is at the same time a physical denial of abstraction... This figure results from an attempt to reconcile two conceptions of nature. First, there is the idea that a figure presiding over the universe is preserving equilibrium... Against this conception is the voracious view of nature represented by the judge's gluttony. The judge seems to think that his fat buttocks will sit with dignity on the throne of the absolute. The capital betrays the grand illusion at the centre of the parody." Ultimately, Gifford and Roberts note that these two concepts of nature cannot be reconciled and also that there can be no genuine judgment because the physical processes are unalterable.[280]

Whichever approach one adopts towards the various critical stances which have been adopted towards Hughes's portrait of the judge, there are, indeed, various characteristics which are clearly apparent: the first is that he figure either is, or perceives himself as, a central figure in the infinite cosmic scape. Second he is resistant to change in that the precedents on which he must rely so as to protect himself (the *obsolete armour*) are firmly based in the past. Third, the process in which he is involved is circular in that he feeds on the remains of the litigation which he must adjudicate. Hughes's view of the law, at least as represented by that figure, is one of self-indulgence, self-propagating and, literally self-centred.

In reality, though, the judges must be judged, and may judge themselves, in a far more mundane light. Thus, Lee, writing effectively of the English scene,[281] quotes Lord Reid, who stated that, "Those with a taste for fairy tales seem to have thought that in some Aladdin's cave there is hidden the Common Law in all splendour and that on a judge's appointment there descends on him knowledge of the magic words Open Sesame. Bad decisions are given when the judge has muddled the password and the wrong door opens. But we do not believe any fairy tales anymore." In view, especially, of Robinson's approach[282] to Ted Hughes's depiction of the cosmic judge, one might think that fairy tales have been too quickly abandoned...!

In view of some of the comments about the shortcomings of the penal system, it is, as Wilson noted,[283] quite possible to find oneself in prison without the commission of any offence having been proved. In *Bond*, for example, Badgery-Parker J required[284] that the time which the applicant had already spent in prison should be taken into account in the calculation of the period of his sentence which should actually be served.

From the point of view of both rhetoric and poetry, the English writer and folk singer Bill Bragg, in his lyric "Rotting on Remand", which appeared in 1990, has dealt with the issues of the use of remand and the conditions of remand yards, which he suggests might actually be worse than those in prison itself. The matters are described especially graphically by Bragg because of the extremely direct style of rhetoric which he adopts. The poem opens with the narrator being remanded in custody by a judge, who when the narrator asks for justice, tells him that his court is a court of law, rather than a court of justice. Still more tellingly, Bragg, in the second stanza, tells of his treatment within the system and its effect on his chances of ultimately escaping conviction:

> They first sent me to Windsor
> And then to Stoke on Trent
> In a holding cell in Liverpool
> Three days and nights I spent
> My solicitor can't find me
> And my family don't know
> I keep telling them that I'm innocent
> They just say, "Come on son, in you go."

Bragg then goes, in the fourth and fifth stanzas to describe the conditions in remand, which are reminiscent of conditions fifty years prior to when the song was written:

> I ended up in this jail
> Built in 1882
> When one man to one prison cell
> Was a Victorian value
> Now three of us are squeezed in here
> And you can't escape the smell
> Of that bucket in the corner
> And we eat in here as well
>
> They let me out of this cage
> To slop that bucket out
> To get my food and bring it back

And if I'm lucky, get a shower
Apart from one hour's exercise
I'm locked in here all day
You don't turn criminals into citizens
By treating them this way.

The last two lines of the fifth stanza are especially significant and lead to the inevitable conclusion of "Rotting on Remand":

Is the price of law and order the stench of Wormwood Scrubs?
With judges quick to sentence more down from above
It's a cruel unusual punishment that society demands
Innocent till proven guilty, rotting on remand.

Although the rhetoric espoused by Bragg in this stark and vividly descriptive poem may seem a little outrageous to some, its description of conditions on remand is essentially borne out by the relevant social science literature. An especially apposite finding is made by Ashworth,[285] who writes that, "Remand prisoners have always tended to be placed in the most overcrowded conditions in the system, since they are sent to local prisons. In the 1980s the number of remand prisoners increased at a far higher rate than the number of convicted prisoners… This was certainly inconsistent with the proper treatment of people who have not yet been convicted, even if it was not formally in breach of the presumption of innocence." The way in which that factual statement relates to Billy Bragg's experiential account is uncanny.

Although both Bragg and Ashworth were writing of English conditions, their comments cannot be restricted to that jurisdiction. Thus, Bartlett has commented [286] that, "Most developing countries and particularly parts of South America and Asia have extremely high percentages of unconvicted prisoners." Yet, as that commentator notes, approximately twenty percent of Australia's prison population are on remand and proportions of between 15 and 25 percent are found in Israel, the United Kingdom and the United States, Canada , Russia and Poland. Most of these cannot be characterised as *developing* countries. The problems seems global. Bartlett goes on to say that, "High remand populations are also supported by hard-line criminal justice policies. In certain countries 'preventative' imprisonment has become the rule rather than the exception. Often, unsentenced prisoners can spend months or years awaiting trial. The status, proportions and imprisonment conditions of remand inmates have become a global human rights issue and high on the United Nations agenda for criminal justice reform. Gross breaches of international treatment standards tend to be commonplace whenever high proportions of remandees exist."

There may be other serious consequences: thus, Ashworth asks,[287] in view of the matters raised by the poet and by criminologists, why it is necessary to remand so many people in custody, and for so long, even as a means of public protection. On one level, it might be argued, that the public will be protected if the commission of crime is precluded by a custodial remand. Hence, for instance, remands in custody of people with a record of shop thefts might be seen as desirable – as it appears that people charged with that particular offence have a forty per cent chance of reoffending whilst on bail. On the other hand the words of Vinson CJ, of the United States Supreme Court in *Stack* v *Boyle*[288] ought not to be forgotten. There, the Chief Justice had said that, "...the traditional right to freedom before conviction permits the unhampered preparation of a defence and serves to prevent an infliction of punishment prior to conviction. Unless this right to bail before trial is preserved, the presumption of innocence, secured only after centuries of struggle, would lose its meaning."

In response, perhaps, to that dictum, Ashworth concludes[289] that where, for whatever reason, a custodial remand, is necessary – its duration should be kept to a minimum. In particular, the matter of delay in bringing cases to court must be given urgent and high profile attention. This, he suggests, is not only because people who, after all, might not actually be guilty have lost time out of their lives, but because of the cost that this wasteful incarceration is costing the state too much. For those who are so remanded, Ashworth urges that the conditions in which remandees are kept be drastically improved. Finally, he urges, "...the creation of a new middle path between custodial remand and conditional bail. This might take the form of release upon undertaking with properly funded supervision from the Probation Service. If successful, it should avoid loss of liberty and show proper respect for the rights of defendants and victims."

All in all, it seems as though the poem by Billy Bragg, when taken together with the various commentaries which have been considered, is a case of life imitating art, or, at the very least, art and life proceeding down parallel paths.

The story so told has, this far at any rate, been one of unrelieved iniquity, ineptitude and, more than any other single matter, of failure. Failure of individuals, failure of institutions and, perhaps above all, failure of redemptive communication. Indeed, the failure of the last suggests that much of the process of crime and retribution as depicted in this chapter is irremediable. One writer who does not appear to think so is the seminal United States poet, Walt Whitman, whose work has already been discussed in another context.[290] In "The Singer in the Prison", Whitman seeks to describe the visit of the soprano Parepa Rosa to Sing Sing Prison. The poem begins, by way of introduction, by describing the general effect on the narrator and the prison guards in terms which, legitimately, can only be described as highly dramaticised:

> *O sight of pity, shame and dole!*
> *O fearful though a convict soul.*
> Rang the refrain along the hall, the prison,
> Rose to the roof, the vaults of heaven above,
> Pouring in floods of melody in tones so pensive sweet and
> strong the like whereof was never heard,
> Reaching the far-off sentry and the armed guards, who
> ceas'd their pacing,
> Making the hearer's pulses stop for ecstasy and awe.

The second part of the poem is more specific and detailed and begins with the arrival of the singer, together with her two children, at Sunday church at the prison. Whitman compares her with the waiting inmates of the prison:

> The sun was low in the west one winter day,
> When down a narrow aisle amid the thieves and outlaws of the
> land,
> (There by the hundreds seated, sear-faced murderers, wily
> counterfeiters,

> Gather'd to Sunday church in prison walls, the keepers round,
> Plenteous, well-armed, watching with vigilant eyes,)
> Calmly a lady walk'd holding a little innocent child by either hand,
> Whom seating on their stools beside her on the platform,
> She, first preluding with the instrument a low and musical prelude,
> In voice surpassing all, sang forth a quaint old hymn.

Whitman sets out the text of the entire hymn, which concludes, in scarcely optimistic vein, with a view towards the ultimate release of the prisoners whom Whitman had earlier described:

> Dear prison'd soul bear up a space,
> For soon or late the certain grace;
> To set thee free and bear thee home,
> The heavenly pardoner, death shall come,
> *Convict no more, nor shame, nor dole!*
> *Depart – a God-enfranchis'd soul!*

At this rather platitudinous conclusion, and not one which might, one would have thought, brought a deal of consolation to the prisoners, the singer concludes. The effect, though on the prison population is quite magical:

> While, upon all, convicts and armed keepers ere they stirr'd,
> (Convict forgetting prison, keeper his loaded pistol,)
> A hush and pause fell down a wonderous minute,
> With deep half-stifled sobs and sound of bad men bow'd
> and moved to weeping,
> And youth's convulsive breathings, memories of home,
> The mother's voice in lullaby, the sister's care, the happy childhood,
> The long pent spirit rous'd to reminiscence,
> A wonderous minute then – but after in the solitary night to
> many, many there,
> Years after, even in the hour of death, the sad refrain, the
> tune, the voice, the words,

> Resumed, the large calm lady walks the narrow aisle,
> The wailing melody again, the singer in the prison sings,
> *O sight of pity, shame and dole, shame and dole!*
> *O fearful thought – a convict soul.*

Perhaps, not altogether surprisingly, the critical reception of "The Singer in the Prison" was not a little mixed: thus, Fausset is not much impressed[291] with the poem and comments that Whitman's, "...capacity too, to communicate simple sentiment without lapsing into sentimentality was less sure, as in "The Singer in the Prison" [moves with] all the unction of a revivalist tract." It is difficult to grasp, in some respects, that 'The Wound Dresser", to which reference was made in Chapter III, and "The Singer in the Prison" were written by the same author. That might be accounted for by Allen who wrote[292] that, subsequent to the Civil War, Whitman felt the necessity of giving poems a *topical connotation*. Allen's reason for making that suggestion was that the war had, "...enabled him to enter more fully into the life of the nation and think less about himself." The difficulty to which Allen points in Whitman's work can be illustrated by one of the stanzas from the hymn sung in "The Singer in the Prison":

> It was not I that sinn'd the sin,
> The ruthless body dragg'd me in;
> Though long I strove courageously,
> The body was too much for me.

Although that was purportedly sung about a woman prisoner, it could well have been written by Whitman about himself...!

5. A Concluding Reflection

This chapter has considered a variety of crimes and the retribution which has been exacted by the formal processes of the law. It has, likewise, noted the entirely dehumanising process which seems to be a necessary part of the retributive process - whatever its weaknesses as a poem, it has been necessary to include "The Singer in the Prison" by Walt Whitman in that discussion because it does suggest that sometimes, and from extraneous sources, that process of dehumanisation can be diverted, if not entirely halted.

However, a particularly humanised approach to retribution[293] may be found in Dylan Thomas's late poem "Lament". That poem is characterised, according to Tindall, [294] by, "…humour, irony, gusto and bouncing rhythm." Tindall also suggests strongly that the poem contains an autobiographical element, a point which, if fairly made, would make the personalised element more poignant. Moynihan, additionally, notes[295] that its very ironic humour represents an indirect attack on religion. Indeed, the references in the second lines of each of the first four stanzas and their ecclestical context – "…the black spit of the chapel fold"; "And the black beast of the beetles' pews"; "And the black cross of the holy house"; "And serve me right as the preachers warn" – would seem to bear that out, both in blasphemous[296] and self-personalised senses. The description of his own activities in the second stanza corroborates, in turn, some of those quasi-moral judgments:

> Whenever I dove in a breast high shoal,
> Whenever I ramped in the clover quilts
> Whatsoever I did in the coal –
> Black night, I left my quivering prints'

Inevitably, of course, retribution arrives in the fifth and final stanza, First, there is, in Moynihan's words,[297] "…the unhappy dotage and death [which] are scarcely to be envied":

> Now I am a man no more no more
> And a black reward for a roaring life
> (Sighed the old ramrod, dying of strangers)
> Tidy and cursed in my dove cooed room
> I lie down thin and hear the good bells jaw

Second, though, there is the truly personal and paradoxical but, in view of the past, just retribution is visited on the narrator, with which the poem culminates and which, in turn, seems far worse than inevitable natural decay:

> For, oh, my soul found a Sunday wife
> In the coal black sky and she bore angels!

Harpies around me out of her womb!
Chastity prays for me, piety sings,
Innocence sweetens my last black breath,
Modesty hides my thighs in her wings,
And all the deadly virtues plague my death.

Clearly, "Lament" does not directly concern itself with the law, its processes, institutions and machinery, though that is not to say that some of the narrator's activities might not have attracted the attention of the law or, for that matter, the attention of husbands and fathers. However, it is discussed because it suggests that retribution can be considered, as it was in the "Pardoner's Tale",[298] in terms other than legalistic. Indeed, in terms which are personal to the protagonist or the narrator; put another way, the ultimate retribution meted out to the narrator in "Lament" is scarcely the retribution which might be feared by other protagonists in the cases and poems with which this book is concerned. At least this chapter, after dealing with dehumanising processes to a significant extent, concludes with an individual and human perspective.

---

[1] G L Williams, "The Definition of Crime" (1955) 8 *Current Legal Problems* 107 at 126.
[2] R A Duff, *Answering for Crime* (2004) at 139.
[3] D Ormerod, Smith and Hogan: *Criminal Law* (12th Ed, 2008) at 10.
[4] He notes, ibid, that the last 25 years or so have seen substantial writing on the theory of criminal law. See, particularly, R A Duff, "Theorising About Criminal law" (2005) 25 *OJLS* 353.
[5] Ibid at 11.
[6] J Michael and M Adler, *Crime, Law and Social Science* (1933) at 5.
[7] M R Cohen, *Reason and Law* (1950) at 25.
[8] [1931] AC 310 at 324.
[9] P Devlin, "The Enforcement of Morals" (1959) 45 *Proc. British Academy* 129 at 146.
[10] P Devlin, *The Enforcement of Morals* (1965) at 1.
[11] [1962] AC 220.
[12] He was also convicted of living off the earnings of prostitution, contrary to s 30 of the, now repealed, *Sexual Offences Act* 1956 and of publishing an obscene article, contrary to s 21 of the *Obscene Publications Act* 1959.
[13] [1962] AC 220 at 266.
[14] Ibid at 267.
[15] Above n 3 at 429.
[16] [1962] AC 220 at 285.
[17] Ibid at 289.
[18] Ibid at 292.
[19] Lord Hodson delivered a concurring judgment.
[20] [1962] AC 220 at 272.
[21] For comment on the Court of Star Chamber, see M Stuckey, "A Consideration of the Emergence and Exercise of Judicial Authority in the Star Chamber" (1993) 19 *Monash ULR* 117.

[22] [1962] AC 220 at 274.
[23] Above text at n 16.
[24] [1962] AC 220 at 275.
[25] Ibid at 276..
[26] Ibid at 281.
[27] Avoce text at n 7 *ff*.
[28] Above text at n 22 *ff*.
[29] [1975] AC 824.
[30] Above text at n 15 *ff*.
[31] [1975] AC 842 at 871.
[32] Ibid at 872.
[33] *Mirehouse* v *Rennell* (1833) 1 Cl & F 527.
[34] [1975] AC 842 at 861.
[35] Ibid at 871.
[36] Ibid at 875.
[37] Ibid at 862.
[38] Lord Reid concurred in Viscount Dilhorne's judgment.
[39] [1973] AC 435.
[40] They were also convicted of conspiring to outrage public decency. See *R* v *Mayling* [1963] 2 QB 717
[41] Above text as n 11 *ff*.
[42] Above text at n 20 *ff*.
[43] [1973] AC 435 at 454.
[44] Ibid at 455.
[45] See for example, *Obscene Publications Act* 1959 s 2(4).
[46] [1973] AC 435 at 456.
[47] Ibid at 457.
[48] Author's emphasis.
[49] [1973] AC 435 at 489.
[50] Author's emphasis.
[51] *Theatres Act* 1968.
[52] Lord Simon then cited Lord Reid's comment in *Shaw*, quoted above text at n 22.
[53] [1973] AC 435 at 489.
[54] Ibid at 490.
[55] Above text at n 29 *ff*.
[56] Above text at n 44.
[57] [1973] AC 435 at 463.
[58] Ibid at 464.
[59] Author's emphasis.
[60] [1973] AC 435 at 470.
[61] (1868) LR 3 QB 360. For comment, see above Ch IV text at n 48.
[62] [1973] AC 435 at 479.
[63] Above text at n 43.
[64] [1973] AC 435 at 480.
[65] Ibid at 481.
[66] Above n 3 at 430.
[67] [1994] AC 212. For comment, see above Ch IV text at n 198 *ff*.
[68] (1957) Cmnd 247 para 13.
[69] Above text at n 9 *ff*.
[70] G H Gordon, *The Criminal Law of Scotland* (1967) at 13.
[71] Ibid at 11.
[72] Ibid at 12.
[73] Though he does state, ibid, that any such definition must take into account the procedure by which the offender is dealt with.

[74] N Walker, *Why Punish?* (1991) at 7.
[75] Walker, ibid, especially notes that Clytemnestra felt obliged to avenge Iphigenia on Agamemnon, her son felt obliged to avenge his father on her, and so on down the dynasty.
[76] Ibid at 72.
[77] These people are referred to by Walker, ibid, as *intuitionists* who, he considers, are not yet extinct, but are not common.
[78] Ibid at 73.
[79] Ibid at 74.
[80] B Bosanquet, *Some Suggestions in Ethics* (1918).
[81] Above n 74 at 74.
[82] H Morris "Persons and Punishment" (1968) 52 *Monist* 475. Walker notes, ibid at 151, that Morris changed his view towards it "A Paternalistic Theory of Punishment" (1981) 18 (4) *Am. Phil* Q 263.
[83] A von Hirsch, *Doing Justice: The Choice of Punishments. Report for the Study of Incarceration* (1976). Walker, ibid 151, notes that von Hirsch has also changed his view to that of a symbolic justification in A von Hirsch, *Past or Future Crimes* (1985).
[84] Ibid at 75.
[85] Ibid at 76
[86] The other theories to which Walker turns his critical attention are, first, the Kantian theory of the *categorical imperative*; second, the spiritual improvement to the offender; third, retribution as communication, and finally, Nozick's theory of connection and communication. See, ibid at 76 *ff*.
[87] Ibid at 22.
[88] (1967) 51 Cr. App Rep 204.
[89] Ibid at 208.
[90] Ibid at 212.
[91] (1974) 60 Cr. App. Rep 74.
[92] Another bouncer had been sentenced to three years imprisonment, three others were acquitted and yet another had only recently been arrested.
[93] (1974) 60 Cr. App. Rep. 74 at 77.
[94] Ibid at 78.
[95] Ibid at 76.
[96] One can only speculate as to what the court's approach would have been had the appellant and victim's roles been reversed – that is, had the assaults been committed on the bouncer who, after all, is employed as a protector of property!
[97] (1974) 60 Cr App. Rep. 74 at 77.
[98] Ibid at 78.
[99] Line 675 *ff*.
[100] Lines 675 – 684.
[101] Lines 684 – 693. "The travelling bag he carried in his lap was brimful of pardons come all hot from Rome. He had a voice as quiet as a goat's and had no beard, nor ever should have had for his face was as smooth as it had just been shaved. I think he was a eunuch or a woman, though he plied his trade from Berwick (North) to Ware (South)."
[102] Lines 694 – 700. "For in his bag there was a pillow case which he said was the Virgin Mary's veil. He said that he had a piece of the sail of St Peter's boat when he went on the sea and Jesus caught hold of him [and saved him]. He had a copper cross covered with [fake precious] stones and in a glass he had a pig's bones.
[103] Lines 701 – 706. "But with those relics, when he found a poor clergyman living in the country, in a day he got him more money than the clergyman would have had in two months. So with feigned flattery and tricks he made both the clergyman and the people his dupes".
[104] Lines 707-714. "But, in conclusion, to the tell truly, in church he was a noble churchman. He could read a lesson or a story well. But, best of all, he sang offertory, for he knew well that, when that song was sung, he must preach and talk smoothly, to gain money – as he could do well; therefore he sang more merrily and louder."

[105] "The Pardoners Tale", lines 1-12. "There was once in Flanders a group of young people who hunted folly through gambling, and going to brothels and taverns, where they, with harps, lutes and other such instruments, dance and play at dice both day and night. Also they eat and drink more than they can hold, through which behaviour they make sacrifices to the devil in the devil's temple [that is, the tavern] in a cursed manner through an abominable superfluity. Their oaths are so great and damnable, that it is horrible to hear them swear, and, by so doing, they tear our blessed Lord's body [that is, they swear by different parts of Christ's body]."

[106] Below text at n 108.

[107] Line 180. "in vain ar amiss."

[108] Lines 199 – 207. " These hoons, three of whom I now speak, long before the prime ring of any bell [that is, before 9am] were sitting in a tavern, drinking. As they sat there, they heard a bell clink in front of a corpse being carried to its grave and one called out to his servant 'Go quickly' he said, 'and ask wisely whose body is that which passes by here and be sure that you report his name correctly."

[109] Lines 211 – 213. "And suddenly he was slain tonight, well drunk, a he was sitting upright on his bench, there came a stealthy thief whom men call Death".

[110] Lines 229 – 239. "By Gods, arms" shouts this hoon, is it such a danger to meet him. I will seek him by road and also by street, I make this vow by God's worthy bones! Listen fellows, we three are really one, let each of us hold up his hand to the other each become one another's brothers, and we will kill this false traitor death and he will be slain who has slain so many others by God's dignity before night falls!"

[111] Lines 253-272. "And then he said, 'Now, lords may God preserve you!' But the most aggressive of the three hoons answered him back, 'What, fellow, not you! Why are you so covered up and why have you lived so long at such great age?' The old man looked him straight in the eye and said, 'For I cannot find a man, even if I walked to India, neither in city or in village who would change his youth for my age; and, therefore, I must carry my age for such time as God wills. No death has anything worse than my life! So I walk around like a restless wretch. And on the ground which is my mother's gate, I knock with my staff both late and early and say 'Dear Mother, let me in – look how I vanish, flesh and blood and skin! Alas, when shall my bones be laid to rest? Mother, with you would I change my clothes chest'".

[112] N Coghill and C Tolkein, *The Pardoner's Tale (Introduction)* (1958) at 37.

[113] N S Bushnell, "The Wandering Jew and *The Pardoner's Tale*" (1931) 28 *Studies in Philology* 450.

[114] Lines 298 – 313. " 'Now gentlemen,' he said 'if that is your wish to find Death, turn up this crooked lane for in that grove I left him, by my faith, under a tree and there he will remain, nor for your boast, he will hide nothing, Do you see that oak? You shall find him right there. God save you that bought against mankind and amend you'. Thus said the old man and each of the hoons ran till he came to the tree and there they found coins of coined gold weighing very nearly eight bushels, they guessed. Now, they no longer looked for Death, but now each one was so glad of the sight of the coins which were so bright and beautiful, but sat down by the precious hoard."

[115] Line 314. He says of himself (Line 316) as, "My wit is greet, though that I bourde and playe." [My brain is great, although I joke and play].

[116] Lines 363 – 373. "...and two of us should be stronger than one. 'Look, when he is sat, right away arise as if you would play with him and I shall stab him in both sides as you struggle with him as in a game and, with a dagger, you look to do too. Then the gold shall be divided, my dear friend between you and me. Then we can fulfil all our desires and play at dice as we like'. So agreed those two rats to kill the third as you have heard me say".

[117] Lines 382 – 384. "And at last the fiend, our enemy, put in his mind that he should poison both".

[118] Lines 389 – 396. And forth he went, no longer would he stay [but went] into the town to an apothecary and asked him whether he could sell him some poison that would kill his rats and also there was a weasel in his hedge which, he said, had killed his chickens and happily he would take revenge on such vermin which had destroyed him by night."

[119] Lines 418-432. "For just as they had planned his death before, so have they killed him. And when that was done, the first conspirator said, 'Now let us sit and drink and make merry and afterwards we will bury his corpse.' And with that very word it happened, by chance, the hoon took a poisoned bottle and gave his friend drink also. For which, ultimately, they both died. And certainly, I think that Avicenna had never written in either a text or section about such wonderful signs of poisoning then had these two wretches at their deaths. This is how the murderers and the false poisoner met their ends."

[120] Above text at n 99.

[121] Lines 438 – 452. "Now good men, God forgive your sins and beware of the sin of avarice. My holy pardon may well heal you all, provided that you offer gold or silver coins or else silver brooches, spoons or rings. Bow your heads under this holy [papal] bull. Come up you wives and offer up your wool. Your names I will enter in my roll in time and you will go into the bliss of heaven. I absolve you by my own high power, you that will offer, as clean and clear as you were born."

[122] Lines 469 475.

[123] Lines 479 – 483. "I tell you that our host will begin since he is most embroiled in sin. Come here, sir host, and offer, first, now and you can kiss my relics everyone. Yes, only for a groat! Unbuckle your purse!

[124] Lines 498 - 502. "But immediately the worthy Knight began, when he saw that all the people were laughing, 'No more of this, for it is right enough. Sir Pardoner, be glad and of merry cheer. And you, Sir Host, who has been so dear to me, I ask you to kiss the Pardoner. And, Pardoner, I ask you to come near; and as we once did, let us laugh and play'. And so they kissed, and rode along their way."

[125] Above text at n 112.

[126] Ibid.

[127] Above text at n 123.

[128] Above text at no 105.

[129] A C Spearing, "The Canterbury Tales IV: Exemplum and Fable" in *The Cambridge Chaucer Companion* (1986) at 167.

[130] Above n 112 at 36.

[131] Above n 112.

[132] I Bishop, "The Narrative Art of the Pardoner's Tale" in *The Canterbury Tales: A Casebook* (1974 Ed. Anderson) at 215.

[133] Ibid at 217.

[134] Above text at n 129.

[135] [1979] AC 617.

[136] Lords Diplock and Edmund – Davies dissenting.

[137] [1979] AC 617 at 645.

[138] Ibid at 646.

[139] Ibid at 656.

[140] See below text at n 168 *ff*.

[141] [1979] AC 617 at 657.

[142] Lord Russell's emphasis.

[143] [1979] AC 617 at 658.

[144] C S Kenny, "The Evolution of the Law of Blasphemy" (1922) 1 *CLJ* 127 at 127.

[145] [1917] AC 406.

[146] Ibid at 466 *ff*.

[147] [1979] AC 617 at 659.

[148] Ibid at 663.

[149] Ibid at 664.

[150] Author's emphasis.

[151] [1979] AC 617 at 665.

[152] *Obscene Publications Act* 1959, *Public Order Act* 1938 s 5A; *Race Relations Act* 1976 s 70 (2).

[153] [1979] AC 617 at 665.
[154] (9th Ed, 1950) at Art 214.
[155] J R Spencer, "Blasphemous Libel Resurrected – Gay News and Grim Tidings" [1979] *CLJ* 245 at 249.
[156] Ibid at 249.
[157] Above text as n 146 *ff.*
[158] Mrs Mary Whitehouse, was a notoriously courageous and aggressive campaigner on issues of public morality or, as others might have it, a campaigner who regarded the law as representing an extension of her own prejudices.
[159] Above at 136.
[160] [1979] AC 617 at 633.
[161] Above n 146.
[162] [1979] AC 617 at 636.
[163] Ibid at 637.
[164] This provision states that, "…a court or jury, in determining whether a person has committed an offence, - (a) shall not be bound in law to infer that he intended or foresaw a result of his actions by reason only of its being a natural and probable consequence of those actions; but (b) shall decide whether he did intend or foresee that result by reference to all the evidence, drawing such inferences from the evidence as appears proper in the circumstances."
[165] [1979] AC 617 at 638.
[166] Ibid at 639.
[167] Above text at n 142.
[168] Above text at n 165.
[169] [1991] 1 QB 429.
[170] Above n 158.
[171] Above text at n 143 *ff.*
[172] [1998] 2 VR 391.
[173] Ibid at 394.
[174] [1979] AC 617 at 646 *ff.*
[175] Ibid at 655.
[176] Ibid at 656.
[177] Above text at n 164.
[178] Lord Edmund-Davies concluded, [1979] AC 617 at 656, by expressing in the view that a submission made on behalf of the accused that, in order to justify a conviction for blasphemous libel, the publication must tend to lead to a breach of the peace should be rejected.
[179] Below text at n 255 *ff.*
[180] In *Harmonium* (1923).
[181] L M Jenkins, *Wallace Stevens: Rage for Order* (2000) at 24.
[182] E Cook, *Poetry, Word-Play and Word-War in Wallace Stevens* (1988) at 65.
[183] Ibid at 67.
[184] Ibid at 102.
[185] In the 1960s the present writer, a person of no great religious belief, but who (at the time) had some pretension as a singer, offered to sing "Friday Morning" at some Easter festivities. The offer was refused on the grounds that the song was blasphemous.
[186] (1986) 161 CLR 10.
[187] Ibid at 15.
[188] The applicant had, apparently, ibid at 16, referred to it as a *technique*.
[189] In addition, though, ibid at 16, the applicant had initially told the police that, at the relevant time, the deceased had gone to bed early and that he had fallen asleep elsewhere. When he awoke, he went into the bedroom and found that the deceased was not breathing and unsuccessfully tried to revive her.
[190] Ibid at 18.
[191] Or *odds on* or *more than a 50 per cent chance.*
[192] (1986) 161 CLR 10 at 19.

[193] See F Bates, "Describing the Indescribable – Evaluating the Standard of Proof in Criminal Cases" (1989) 13 *Crim LJ* 330.
[194] Above text at n 189.
[195] (1986) 161 CLR 10 at 21.
[196] See H F Jolowicz, *Historical Introduction to the Study of Roman Law* (1939) at 491 *ff*, J C Gray, *The Nature and Sources of the Law* (1909) at 176 *ff*.
[197] (1986) 161 CLR 10 at 22.
[198] Ibid at 23.
[199] Ibid at 25.
[200] Ibid at 27.
[201] Above Ch IV text at n 198 *ff*.
[202] (1986) 161 CLR 10 at 28.
[203] Ibid at 29.
[204] Ibid at 15.
[205] Above text at n 197 *ff*.
[206] (1986) 161 CLR 10 at 44.
[207] Ibid at 45.
[208] Author's emphasis.
[209] In all the provisions of the Code, Brennan J stated, (1986) 161 CLR 10 at 45, that *likely* meant *probable*; whilst in none did it mean *possible*.
[210] (1986) 161 CLR 10 at 46.
[211] Ibid at 29.
[212] Below Ch VII
[213] [1903] AC 443 at 451.
[214] Above text at n 187.
[215] PL Waller and C R Williams, *Criminal Law: Text and Cases* (10th Ed. 2005) at 167.
[216] H Engel, *Lord High Executioners: An Unashamed Look at Hangmen, Headsmen and Their Kind* (1998).
[217] E L Greenspan, ibid at 7.
[218] Ibid at 8.
[219] Ibid at 44.
[220] Ibid at 55.
[221] Below text at n 293 *ff*.
[222] H Bloom, *Till I End My Song: A Gathering of Last Poems* (2010) at 193.
[223] Above n 216 at 85.
[224] Ibid at 75.
[225] Berry was executioner from 1884 until 1891. "The Ballad of Reading Gaol" was published in 1897. The executioner who hanged Wooldridge in 1896 was James Billington.
[226] Above n 216 at 75.
[227] Ibid at 79.
[228] Ibid at 80.
[229] R Hogg, "Prisoners and the Penal Estate in Australia" in *Prisoners as Citizens: Human Rights in Australian Prisons* (Ed Brown and Wilkie, 2002) 3 at 5.
[230] M Bartlett, "World Correctional Population Trends and Issues" in *Corrections Criminology* (Ed. O'Toole and Eyland, 2005) 8 at 11.
[231] Ibid at 12.
[232] Bartlett, ibid, notes that, in 2003, Los Angeles County gave early release to 50,000 inmates in response to budget cuts of $US166m over the previous two years. Some of the released offenders had served only ten per cent of their sentences.
[233] P Wilson, "What Future for the Prison?" in *Corrections Criminology* (Ed. O'Toole and Eyland 2005) 230.
[234] [1967] NZLR 437. The statement of facts is adopted from that of Tomkins J at first instance.
[235] Ibid at 443.
[236] Ibid at 444.

[237] Ibid at 444.
[238] Ibid at 445.
[239] Ibid at 445.
[240] Ibid at 446.
[241] McCarthy J, Ibid at 445, stated that his discussion was to deal with issues which, "...are as much sociological as legal."
[242] [1971] NZLR 924.
[243] Ibid at 925.
[244] Ibid at 925.
[245] Woodhouse J did go so far as to suggest, ibid at 926, that if conduct of the kind involved in *Kinney* was to be discouraged, it remained, in Woodhouse J's *ipsissima verba*, "...open to the local authority to issue an edict in the form of a bylaw regulating the paddling by persons in the City ponds, should so solemn an injunction seem necessary."
[246] Woodhouse J, ibid at 925, did note that the arresting officer had suggested that the several people observing the scene from their homes might have been offended by the appellant's behaviour because of the presence of the gold fish in the pond.
[247] See above Ch II Text at n 141 *ff*.
[248] [2007] 3 NZLR 91.
[249] Now contained in s 4(1) of the *Summary Offences Act* 1981.
[250] Elias CJ, Blanchard, Tipping and McGrath JJ Thomas J dissenting.
[251] Above text at n 248.
[252] [2007] 3 NZLR 91 at 114 *per* Blanchard J; ibid at 124 *per* Tipping J; ibid at 135 *per* McGrath J.
[253] Above text at n 233.
[254] A Liebling, "Measuring Prisons and Their Moral Performance" in *Correction Criminology* (Ed. O'Toole and Eyland, 2005) 199 at 204.
[255] [2009] TASSC112.
[256] *Road Safety (Alcohol & Drugs) Act* 1970.
[257] [2009] TASSC 112 at [2].
[258] Ibid at [4].
[259] [1959] Tas SR 17 at 21.
[260] [2009] TASSC 112 at [9].
[261] See the unreported decisions of *Rigby* v *Dillon* 56/1984; *Van Zelm* v *Guinan* 41/1978.
[262] [2009] TASSC 112 at [10].
[263] Ibid at [15].
[264] Ibid at [16].
[265] Ibid at [17].
[266] The Chief Justice, ibid, also said that he would obtain a report as to the applicant's suitability for community service.
[267] (1990) 48 A Crim R 1.
[268] By reason of intervening legislation, the New South Wales *Sentencing Act* 1989 Sch 2, the sentence had been redetermined to a minimum term of nine years, five months and fourteen days with an additional term of three years, one month and four days.
[269] (1990) 48 A Crim R 1 at 13.
[270] Ibid at 13.
[271] Ibid at 14.
[272] See generally, *R* v *Ellis* (1986) 6 NSWLR 603; *R* v *Perez Varges* (1986) 8 NSWLR 559; R v *Cartwright* (1989) 17 NSWLR 243.
[273] (1990) 48 A Crim R 1 at 6.
[274] See generally, *R* v *Shannon* (1979) 21 SASR 442; *R* v *Slater* (1984) 36 SASR 524; *Jago* v *District Court of New South Wales* (1989) 168 CLR 23.
[275] C Robinson, *Ted Hughes as a Shepherd of Being* (1989) at 115.
[276] L M Scigay, *The Poetry of Ted Hughes: Form and Imagination* (1986) at 211.
[277] K Sager, *The Art of Ted Hughes* (2nd Ed. 1978) at 175.

[278] Sager, ibid at 243, notes that Baskin had shown Hughes a series of nine drawings of which that chosen by Hughes to represent the judge had been entitled, "An Oven-Ready Piranha Bird".
[279] T Gifford and N Roberts, *Ted Hughes: A Critical Study* (1981) at 209.
[280] These writers, additionally, suggest that, possibly, the law figures may be perceived as representatives of the hero/defendant's physical nature, rather than as independent controlling forces.
[281] S Lee, Judging Judges (1989) at 3.
[282] Above text at n 275.
[283] Above text at n 233.
[284] (1990) 48 A Crim R 1 at 15.
[285] A Ashworth, *The Criminal Process: An Evaluative Study* (2nd Ed, 1998) at 218.
[286] Above n 230 at 10.
[287] Above n 285 at 226.
[288] 342 US 1 (1951) at 4.
[289] Above n 285 at 240.
[290] Above Ch 3 text at n 96 *ff*.
[291] H I Fousset, *Walt Whitman: Poet of Democracy* (1966) at 236.
[292] G W Allen, *The New Walt Whitman Hanbook* (1975) at 34.
[293] This *humanised*, or, perhaps more accurately *personalised* view of retribution can be compared with that to be found in another late poem, "Over Sir John's Hill" See F Bates "Dylan Thomas and the Idea of Justice" in *In Memoriam Senator J William Fulbright 1905- 1995* (Ed. Magiru, Magiru and Johnson 2010) 15.
[294] W Y Tindall, *Reader's Guide to Dylan Thomas* (1962) at 301.
[295] W T Moynihan, *The Craft and Art of Dylan Thomas* (1966) at 173.
[296] Above text at n 135 *ff*.
[297] Above n 295 at 174.
[298] Above text at n 104 *ff*.

Chapter VI
Love, Pain, Marriage and the Whole...

1. An Overview

From the point of view of the commentator on Law, Poetry and Rhetoric, a major difficulty in any consideration of law and its consequences can be found in Carol Ann Duffy's poem "Words, Wide Night"[1] a poem which brings out much of the uncertainty of love's taxonomy. The narrator, at a distance, is thinking of the loved one:

> This is pleasurable. Or shall I cross that out and say
> it is sad? In one of the tenses I am singing
> An impossible song of desire that you cannot hear.
>
> La lala la. See? I close my eyes and imagine
> the dark hills I would have to cross
> to reach you. For I am in love with you and this
>
> is what it is like or what it is like in words.

Much of this extract is taken up with a verbal camouflage: first, the narrator is uncertain as to whether the nature of her instant experience is pleasurable or sad. Second, the narrator *imagines* hazards ("the dark hills") which separate them. Finally, at the end of the poem, the narrator is uncompromising about how she feels and how the feeling is experienced. At the same time, though, both the feeling and the experience are qualified by the final comment that the feeling and the experience are limited by the way in which they can be expressed. As will be observed throughout this chapter, there are difficulties in communication which Duffy has so delicately and deftly exposed in the appositely entitled "Words, Wide Night".

In addition to the issues raised in that poem, the Seventeenth Century poet Samuel Daniel in his poem "Love", written in 1623, has, just as graphically, pointed to another paradox – that of lack of reciprocity:

> Love is a sickness full of woes,

All remedies refusing;
A plant that with most cutting grows,
Most barren with best using.
Why so?

More we enjoy it, more it dies;
If not enjoyed, it sighing cries,
Heigh ho!

Love is a torment of the mind,
A tempest everlasting;
And Jove hath made it of a kind
Not well, nor full, nor fasting.
Why so?
More we enjoy it, more it dies;
If not enjoyed, it sighing cries,
Heigh ho!

It should be said, as the present writer has sought elsewhere to point out,[2] that the area generally designated as *Family Law* is not immune, like Daniel's poem, from the paradox, which operates at an especially basal level. Before going on to discuss the application of the paradox to particular factual situations, and, it must be said that it will suffuse, directly or indirectly, the remainder of the chapter, it should be stated what, essentially, the term *paradox* involves. Thus, the *Shorter Oxford English Dictionary* defines[3] *paradox* as *inter alia*, "A phenomenon that exhibits some contradiction or conflict with preconceived notions of what is reasonable or probable." The same source also purportedly defines[4] the phenomenon as being "...a seemingly absurd or self-contradictory statement or proposition which when investigated or explained may well prove to be well founded or true."

In all likelihood, the most basal paradox is to be found in the very label which is attached to the topic under scrutiny. In other words, is *Family Law* as Law? One ought to be able to assume, without more, that, as the label includes the word *Law*, the question need not be asked in the first instance. However, asked it most assuredly is. Thus, for example, in a history of one of Australia's older Law Schools, it was noted[5] that the Chief

Justice of the relevant jurisdiction regarded the areas of Evidence, Conveyancing and Family Law as being unsuitable for academic study in 1966. It may, indeed, be that one of the reasons for such a stance is that the subject itself was of relatively recent origin. Thus, in 1955, Stone had noted[6] that six English law teachers had met, "...to consider this strange if not exactly esoteric subject." Five years later, that same distinguished commentator was still seeking to justify the subject's being taught[7] and concluding[8] that, "...university law faculties can make contributions of analysis, rationalisation and integration which this branch of the law so urgently needs." Today, however, as family law is now an established part of the law curriculum throughout the common law world, and beyond, any novelty which it might have had fifty or so years ago has long since dissipated. Logically, it would, hence, seem as though the fact that the discussion continues must be the product of other factors or combinations of such factors. At the same time, it should be said that family law is not alone in being the object of discussions along the same lines, the most obvious of such areas being public international law. However, it is well known that the view that public international law is not, in the strict sense, *Law* is derived from the writings of Austin and Hegel. The former regarded[9] public international law not as positive law, but as positive morality and that the, "...so-called law of nations consists of opinions and statements current amongst nations generally. It is therefore not law properly so called." Similarly, there was no equivalent to Austin's sovereign or sanction. Hegel adopted[10] a similar approach, taking the view that sovereign states were not answerable to any external authority and, hence even the principle of *pacta sunt servanda* which, according to Kelsen,[11] is the supreme rule of public international law is not positive, merely normative.

All of that notwithstanding, arguments opposing family law's characterisation as positive law seem to have different bases. In 1986, O'Donovan wrote[12] that that view appeared to be gaining credence. However, that situation had not come about through recourse to Austinian or Hegelian models but rather asserts that the law is unable to deal with family disputes and family behaviour and that legal structures and methodologies in respect of conflict resolution and behaviour guidance are not applicable to family and personal life. She suggests that that particular attempt to demonstrate family law's deficiencies are tripartite in its attack.

First, she argues, that it posits *inability* - put another way, the law is not in a position to tell people how to behave in their own homes because they will not obey such instructions and, hence, rules become unenforceable because crucial information is not available. Therefore, it is better not to attempt to legislate. Indeed, there have been some respectable advocates of such a view. Watson[13] and Stein and Shand[14] have expressed the view that, generally, family relationships are an area from where the law both does, and should, seek to distance itself However, in the contemporary climate, it is a view which is continually harder to justify either in factual or in policy terms. Community knowledge and awareness of the internal dynamics of family life – especially the unhappy ones – is being increased and, in turn, is manifested in crucial decisions.

There are numerous examples, though one, at the present juncture, will suffice: in *Blanch v Blanch and Crawford,*[15] the husband, who was aged thirty and the wife, who was aged 27, began cohabitating in 1987 and were married in February 1990. There were three children of the marriage who were aged respectively eight, six and three. In October 1990, the wife was raped by an unknown assailant and claimed that, after that, the husband became violent towards her. The parties separated in January 1997, when the husband left the former matrimonial home with the children. The wife immediately applied for a residence order, as it was then known, though she withdrew the application while the parties attempted a reconciliation. Apart from a period of about one month, when the youngest child lived with the wife in 1997, the children all lived with the husband at his mother's home since the separation. In January 1997, the wife began a relationship with one T who, in addition to having assaulted the husband on at least one occasion, had convictions for assault which dated back to the 1980's. In June 1997, the husband consented to an Apprehended Violence Order sought by the wife and cross-applied to her fresh application for residence. In November of that year, consent orders were made providing that the husband had interim residence and that the wife had contact every weekend.

At the time of the initial hearing, the wife had separated from T and the future of their relationship was in considerable doubt. The wife was living with her mother whilst T, and his son from a prior relationship, were living in the former matrimonial home. In April 1998, orders were made that the children reside with the husband, save for two consecutive weekends every three, as well as half of all school holidays, when they were to reside with the wife. In making those orders, the trial judge found that, since the separation, the husband had been the children's primary carer and, also, that the mother had played a significant role in their lives. The judge who was assisted by the evidence of a court counsellor. who regarded each party as being an adequate parent, found that the children had an excellent relationship with each parent. The judge, though, doubted whether the counsellor's finding that the children's primary attachment was to the mother since that view had been based entirely on their responses during one procedure and on the observed interaction between the children and their parents. In addition, although the trial judge was not satisfied that the husband was an inherently violent man, and finding that his aggressive attitude towards the wife to be attributable to circumstances arising during the marriage, he did express concern regarding certain aspects of the wife's relationship with T. In reaching the conclusion that the best interests of the children required that they remain with the husband, the judge had emphasised that he had not regarded himself as being bound by the recommendations of the children's representative, who had supported the mother's case; he did, though, note that he was conscious that he had departed from them. The wife's appeal to the Full Court of the Family Law Court of Australia was largely concerned with two matters: first, the trial judge's treatment of the evidence regarding primary attachment and, second, his treatment of the issue of domestic violence.

As regards the first ground, Lindenmayer J, who delivered what might be described as the major judgment, stated[16] that, had it been the only issue in the appeal, he would have been disposed to uphold it. In the event, the Full Court did allow the appeal and remitted the matter for rehearing. As regards the issue of domestic violence, which he regarded as being "more substantial", Lindenmeyer J, first of all, commented[17] that it was, "...not always necessary, or even desirable, for a trial judge to make specific findings in relation to every issue presented by the parties, even ones they clearly regard as important... [I]n cases such as this, where a case of sustained and severe domestic violence by one party is advanced by the other, the court is obliged to give a clear indication whether it accepts or rejects that case and, in either event, to explain why it reached that conclusion. Lindenmeyer J then went on to state that the legislation, as it then stood,[18] had made the importance of domestic violence as a factor in the making of parenting orders *very clear*.[19] At the same time, though, Lindenmeyer J referred to an earlier version of the Act. Of particular importance, it is suggested, are the comments of Chisholm J in *JG and BG*[20] who had said that, "...[v]iolence associated with a pattern of dominance, for example, may be particularly serious. For children to grow up in a climate of potentially violent and dominating relationships between their parents seems to be an unacceptable model of family relationships, and would be very likely to create a situation of stress and fear that may be damaging over a period. It is quite wrong...to assume that violence can be relevant only if it is directed to children or takes place in their presence."[21]

In the broad context of the trial judge's treatment of violence, Lindenmeyer J in *Blanch* found[22] that his Honour's finding that the husband's treatment of the wife was the product of the marital relationship rather than the husband's personality was, "...less than entirely satisfactory..." Lindenmeyer J went on to explicate that view, when in relation to the issue of violence, he said[23] that, apart from the failure to address, "...the issue of the potential damage to children of exposure to a violent role model in their home environment... [it] includes a finding which was not open to his Honour on the evidence before him, namely that such violence as the husband demonstrated towards the wife during the marriage was somehow the product of the relationship between the parties rather than of the husband's personality." Lindenmeyer J continued by extrapolating from that statement, when he stated that, "As a general proposition, that sort of finding indicates an attribution of responsibility for the domestic violence perpetrated by the husband to the wife (who was even on his Honour's modest findings, the victim) or at least to an interaction between the parties." Yet more emphatically, Lindenmeyer J was of the expressed view that, "As a general proposition such an attribution of responsibility away from the perpetrator towards the victim is simply not acceptable, at least in the absence of any evidence of an expert nature to the effect that the sort of behaviour attributed to the victim by other evidence in the case was of such a nature as to be likely to provoke a violent response from *any* reasonable person, and the actual response of the perpetrator to that provocation was not disproportionate to the provocation offered."[24]

So far as it seems to go, both Lindenmeyer J's argument and *rhetoric* is consonant with other, non-judicial, writing on the topic. However, the real question is whether they go sufficiently far – especially in awakening interdisciplinary awareness of the subject matter at large. Thus, for instance, Alexander draws attention[25] to various *myths* or *misconceptions* regarding domestic violence which must be exposed so that members of the relevant professions who are entrusted with helping victims do not themselves make hasty judgments, perhaps subconsciously, regarding the victim. More important, from the standpoint of the discussion of the *Blanch* decision, Alexander writes[26] that, "...[m]ost of these myths have the effect of sharing fault or transferring responsibility for the violence to the victim. They may even be believed by the victim who blames herself for the violence and feels ashamed for failing in her role as wife and mother." More particularly, she refers to the myth whereby it is perceived that the victim has somehow provoked the violence. Of that suggestion, she trenchantly comments, and it is a view which I would strenuously endorse, that, "Even if the victim has done this, it is no excuse for physical violence. But in many cases the 'provocation' is imagined or concocted by the violent party. For example, it is not uncommon for a male to be obsessively jealous and to 'see' signs of unfaithfulness in his partner where none exist."

In the context of those comments, the views of Mullane and Kay JJ become the more apposite as they, unlike Lindenmeyer J's judgment, contained no reference to abstractions such as female provocation. Thus, Mullane J stated[27] that, "The proposition that if the father used abusive behaviour it was not because of his personality but because of the parties' relationship and surrounding circumstances seems to shift responsibility from the father for his behaviour and run contrary to the fact that some people do use violence in their dealings with other people, but most people don't". Mullane J noted that there was neither[28] adequate explanation nor any evidence to support any such conclusion. Kay J emphasised that, in his view, any suggestion that there was any symmetry in the spouses' conduct was inappropriate, even though it had found its way into the reasons given by the trial judge. In Kay J's view, "...any such suggestion does not do justice to the victim in all the circumstances."

Earlier, Mullane J had made especial reference to the position of the children: first, he pointed out[29] that the trial judge had overlooked the wider and more serious dangers that an abusive parent presents to children than that of physical harm. "In addition to that harm," he said "children can suffer, insecurity, fear, unhappiness, and hyper vigilance from witnessing abusive behaviour by a parent. Such effects present a threat to their emotional development." Second, though, the judge went on to say that probably the worst danger was the role model which a violent parent could provide which might lead children themselves coming to suffer the serious social disability of using violence in their dealings with other people, including those they love. "Such as disability," Mullane J went on, "can destroy the most intimate relationship and bring the person into conflict with other people, the police and the law. Abusive behaviour by way of putting down a child can also lead to serious long term emotional problems such as poor self esteem and lack of self confidence."

For the purposes of the present discussion, it will be apparent that courts will now and, if necessary in some detail, examine both the internal and external dynamics of the family. Given factual situations of the kind which pertained in *Blanch* it is, surely, quite proper that they should do so. Further, from the point of view of one of this book's major thrusts, it is important, as *Blanch* must assuredly tell us, that in presenting their findings and expressing their conclusions, judges must speak with appropriate rhetorical emphasis so as to attempt to dispel the mythology which has grown up around family function and, indeed dysfunction. *Rhetoric* is important when courts are dealing with areas of human behaviour about which people hold strong ideas to which they are equally strongly attached – howsoever inaccurate and misinformed they might be. Mullane J, had sought especially and effectively to clarify some of the central issues which arose out of the case. That same judge was to make similar comments at first instance in *M* v *M*[30] : "the father's abusive behaviour," he said, "presents a multi-faceted danger to the children. There is a risk of violence to them personally and injury. There is a risk that violence poses when it involves living with fear, insecurity and vigilance. There is the danger of ongoing fear that the father will emotionally or physically abuse the mother they love... There is a danger that both children will come to believe from their father's abuse of the mother, that women are lesser beings." More particularly, Mullane J continued by saying that the greatest danger was that the elder child, especially, would, "...learn from his father's behaviour that physical and emotional abuse are acceptable ways of dealing with other persons and thus come to share his father's disability."[31]

Once again, the views of Mullane J seem to be congruent with extra-legal writing: in particular, Kempe and Kempe, in their seminal study,[32] wrote as early as 1978 that, "Emotional abuse, in the absence of physical damage, is difficult to document, but its effects can be crippling: they tend to be diagnosed by psychiatrists and psychologists only years after the event, as the symptoms of emotional disturbance become more obvious. *A priori*, we assume that physical abuse and neglect imply the presence of at least some emotional abuse, but the opposite may not always be true. Sometimes the abuse is primarily verbal, and the child is continually told that he is hated, ugly, unlovable, stupid or an unwanted burden. He may not even be spoken to by name, but called 'you' or 'freak' or 'Hey, Stupid'. Such a child may find himself made into the family scapegoat, and it even may be that his brothers and sisters are actively encouraged and perhaps even rewarded for abusing and ignoring him."

All of this analysis and commentary reinforces the view that there can be little, if any, validity in the suggestions, noted earlier,[33] that the law should stay clear of intra-familial responsibilities. Further, it is also desirable that judicial rhetoric and the rhetoric utilised by social science commentators were directed to the same ends and couched in similar terms. It would be too much to expect them to be couched in the same terms because, although similar goals sought to be achieved, they are achieved through different skills and methodologies.

The second group of arguments noted by O'Donovan[34] is based around the thesis that the law is an unsuitable mechanism for dealing with personal behaviour or feelings and emotions. The law is perceived as cold, antagonistic, adversarial, and alienating, whereas families are concerned with love and trust. "What", she writes, "is being expressed here is a statement about the limits of law in the resolution of disputes." That is a point which has been directly taken up by McClean who states[35] that, "Whenever law is dealing with family relationships, it is at best a clumsy instrument. Law cannot make people be wise or responsible or happy or good." There are various issues which arise out of that seemingly innocent statement: first, and almost self-evident, is that were that the only goal of legal intervention, a great deal of it would be declassified. A major function of legal intervention and activity is to help prevent people from being unwise, irresponsible, unhappy or, more especially, bad. That is surely the case when the law is dealing with family relationships as it is, say, with crime. Indeed, in the areas of domestic violence and child abuse, the analogy with crime is notably apposite. In that context, a valuable instance is provided by the decision of Moore J of the Family Court of Australia in *T and N*,[36] where the issue was the future arrangements for two children (TN and JT, who were aged four and two years respectively at the time of the hearing). The parties had begun a relationship in May 1998, which had ended in April 2001, when Ms N had left with the children when Mr T was at work. She conceled her whereabouts, thereafter, from T, the reason being that their relationship had been turbulent. The relationship had included allegedly violent conduct and abusive conduct by T towards N and JT. On one occasion, T had been charged with assault, and an apprehended violence order[37] had been made in N's favour. On several other occasions, she had applied for such orders but had not proceeded with the applications. N also alleged that after the birth of JT, the violence towards her increased and that T had bitten JT on the fingers, face and ears when he cried. It was alleged further that T regularly smoked marijuana, which caused them financial problems, and that, in such situations, he became violent.

In addition, the parties had requested that the court make consent orders which provided for supervised contact, leading to unsupervised contact. These were coupled with various undertakings to be given by the father, which included his undertaking not consuming marijuana or alcohol for 24 hours prior to any contact, not using physical discipline on the children and attending an anger management course.

In the event, Moore J made orders only for supervised contact[38] but at the same time, noted[39] that, notwithstanding the terms of any order, the parties would be free to agree informally regarding unsupervised contact arrangements. Hence, she referred the matter to the relevant State Departments to alert them that there might be such informal arrangements. In doing so, the judge emphasised[40] that no findings could be made without the evidence having been tested and that, "...long experience teaches that findings must abide the close of the evidence when everything is shown in quite a different light." However, she expressed the view that the evidence in *N and T* did, *prima facie*, establish a risk to the children if orders for unsupervised contact were made and that the magnitude of that risk was unacceptable.[41] "That," she stated "flowed from the unchallenged evidence of Ms N and Mr T's conduct and included, in some instances, his own concessions." The judge also noted[42] that, were the allegations against T established, they strongly indicated him to be a violent and abusive person who represented a high degree of harm to the children. It followed, Moore J continued, that the undertakings which T had given were wholly inadequate to address the risk of harm to the children and required a more profound and therapeutic approach, especially in view of his conduct towards the baby, than merely an anger management course.

The judge then went on to discuss the potential effects on the children. There was, she stated, "...an abundance of research from social scientists about the highly detrimental effects upon young children of exposure to violence and the serious consequences such experiences have for their personality formation. They are terrified and simultaneously come to accept it as acceptable behaviour and an integral part of intimate relationships; or that violence or fear may be used to exert control over family members; they may suffer significant emotional trauma from fear, anxiety, confusion, anger, helplessness and disruption in their lives; they may have higher levels of aggression than children who did not have that level of exposure; and they may suffer from higher anxiety, more behavioural problems and lower self esteem than children not exposed to violence." Moore J then went on to say that clinical profiles for such children included, "...post-traumatic play, diminished ability to regulate effect in the form of hyper-arousal, numbness, emotional constriction, a low frustration threshold, nightmares, and other sleep disturbances, aggressive behaviour, intense and multiple fears, regression in developmental achievements and disturbances in peer relationships." The final substantive point made by Moore J referred to the use of marijuana by the male party. She was strongly of the view[43] that, if he could not be alert and free from substance abuse, he would not properly be able to care for young children who were dependant on him to have their needs met. In the end, it was the responsibility of the Court to make orders which were in the best interests of the children, regardless of agreements which might be reached by the parties.

Quite apart from the discussion of the consequences to children of exposure to violence and abuse, the facts of *T and N* themselves strongly suggest that the law is the only societal entity which is capable of dealing with situations such as those. The acts in *T and N* involve various assaults, grossly criminal abuse of a child and proscribed substances. Given those facts, an analogue with the criminal law is surely apposite. Hence, the second approach noted by O'Donovan seems, in reality, to be little more than a variant of the first, and is just as easily refuted.

The third approach to which O'Donovan refers seeks to point to the bad effects of using law on the family, in that law operates only as a negative force which destroys what it is intending to help. Once again, this argument is merely another manifestation of the thesis that the law's operation, in the context of familial relations, is necessarily limited. However, it is suggested that the truth of the matter is that it is familial circumstances which led up to the legal intervention, rather than the intervention itself, which has caused any damage. To take one instant example, in the Australian case of *In the Marriage of Schwarzkopff*,[44] the parties had married in 1981, there being three children of the marriage. They separated in March 1991, when the wife and children left the matrimonial home and went to a refuge. The following week, consent orders were made at a Magistrates' Court regarding custody, guardianship and access. More particularly, orders were made under s 114 of the *Family Law Act 1975* which sought to restrain the husband from assaulting, harassing, threatening or interfering with the wife and from attending at or near any premises where she might be working, living or visiting. Between 29th of March and 3rd of April, 1991, the husband committed various breaches of these orders and, on March 9th, the wife applied under s 112AD of the Act, which set out the sanctions which were available to the courts in dealing with contraventions of orders made under the Act, for the husband to be dealt with for those breaches. The following month, the Family Court made orders which were similar in terms to those which had earlier been made. The wife's application under s 112AD was heard in the same month and the Family Court found that the husband had breached the orders made in March. He was ordered to enter into a recognisance that he be of good behaviour and comply with the Family Court orders. However, he continued to breach the orders, so that, by July 20th, there were twenty further breaches, including two serious ones. On July 3rd, the wife applied to the Family Court in respect of those breaches and, consequently, the husband was arrested and remanded in custody for two days after which he was released on his own recognizance on various conditions. Nonetheless, his breaches of the orders continued, including two more serious ones later in the month. As a result, the wife made a further application under s

112AD which, again led to the husband's being arrested and remanded in custody until his trial which began on August 22nd. The trial judge found the husband guilty of 29 of the 32 alleged breaches of the orders and sentenced him to two years imprisonment. The husband appealed to the Full Court of the Family Court of Australia on the grounds that the sentence was manifestly excessive.

In dismissing the appeal, the Full Court[45] commented generally[46] that, "One of the fundamental purposes of a legal system in a civilized society is the protection of members of the community from acts of violence. Until recent times the criminal law, which makes acts of this kind an offence, was not properly enforced in cases where violence occurred within the family. Such violence was considered private in nature and beyond the reach of the law except in the most serious cases. However, in the last 20 years increasing attention has been focussed on the prevalence of crimes of violence within the family and attitudes which tolerate family violence are now condemned by law." After noting the various legislation which had come into force in Australia between 1982 and 1989, the Court further emphasised the law's public role when it was said that, "Personal relationships, especially within the family, are rightly protected by privacy, but that privacy must not be allowed to hide violence. Family violence is not a private matter and must be treated seriously by the Courts, not only when prosecuted as a criminal offence in the ordinary way, but also where violence is an element of a breach of an order of the Family Court." As regards the facts of the case at hand, the Court regarded the sentence as being far from excessive and that it was appropriate as meeting the case's situation. "The Court" it was said, "has an obligation to the wife who seeks its protection. Society is entitled to expect that the Court will meet conduct of this type in an appropriate way and the Court has an obligation to itself to ensure that orders which it has made are complied with and that persistent, deliberate and serious breaches are dealt with in a firm and clear way." Although, in the event, it seems very clear that the sentence which was passed on the husband was very likely to bring the marriage to a formal end, it surely cannot be reasonably argued that it was the law's intervention which destroyed the marriage. The genuine cause of the breakdown of the relationship, which led to the necessary intervention of the law, was the husband's behaviour which was of a kind that, as the Full Court pointed out, the law could not ignore either as a matter of both fact and policy.[47]

There is, however, a further issue, raised by O'Donovan[48] – this matter, for some purposes at least, is more serious and may be more difficult to refute, initially at least. This matter, O'Donovan writes, arises from, "...the conferral on the judiciary and on administrators by the Parliament of discretion in deciding matters of custody, childcare, divorce, maintenance, matrimonial properly and inheritance. Discretion permits the individualisation of justice according to the particular facts of each case. Criticism of this laments the loss of law's hortatory function in laying down rules for the future, lack of predictability; universality or generality of the law, the undermining of the moral authority of the judiciary, and the expansion of litigation as each case seeks its individual adjudication." That argument has been expressed rather more strongly by Dewar, who writes[49] that academic colleagues regard family law as inherently inferior because it represents, "...a falling away from the rigorous discipline of common law reasoning, or a mutation into a discretionary gloop that is beneath serious intellectual endeavour."

Elsewhere, I have sought to refute this attitude[50] by suggesting that post 1975 developments in family law, at least in Australia, have seen a steady diminution in the utilisation of discretions, especially in relation to post separation care of children. Thus, in 1976, when the *Family Law Act 1975* came into force, all that the courts were required to take into account were that the welfare of the child should be the paramount consideration[51] and that courts should not make an order contrary to the wishes of children who had attained the age of fourteen years, unless, by reason of special circumstances, it was necessary to do so.[52] Subject to those provisions, courts might make such orders as they thought proper.[53] Those provisions stand in stark contrast to those introduced by the *Family Law Amendment (Shared Responsibility) Act* 2006,[54] which considerably restricts court's discretionary powers. Further, as was noted by Dewar himself,[55] aspects of public law are beginning to encroach on traditionally perceived private areas. He specifically refers to the *Children Act* 1989 in the United Kingdom which sought to provide a code in relation to both private and public matters as they related to children.[56] There are other instances in Australia, such as child support[57] and family based social security provisions.[58] This process inevitably engages the attention of the lawyers of whom Dewar spoke[59] and, hence, the validity of their argument is, at the very least, questionable.

However, at this stage in the discussion, it may be that the concluding word should be left with Dewar who is aware of, some anyway, of the unavoidable issues and who posits something of a solution which is the mainstream of this book's direction. "That family law should be in a chaotic state," he writes,[60] "is perhaps scarcely surprising, given the social facts with which it routinely deals. Family law engages the passions as no other part of our legal system does; and it is the hallmark of passion that it must exceed rationality." He further points out[61] that it is diffuse and de-differentiated and must accommodate a certain level of contradiction. Dewar continues[62] by urging a higher status for family law on the basis that it is not solely directed at judges and litigants and that it offers a range of rhetorical structures for resolving issues which cannot be resolved by other means. How accurate his comments may be it is hoped that the remainder of this chapter will go some way towards answering. Perhaps it may also go some way towards answering how far passion does exceed rationality…

2. An Intriguing and Illustrative Case

In the light of the previous discussion and, especially in the light of the poem by Samuel Daniel quoted at the beginning of the present chapter, the High Court of Australia in *Louth* v *Diprose*[63] presents a pointed and striking instance of some matters alluded to by Dewar[64] and the present writer. [65] The facts of the case were, of themselves somewhat extraordinary: a man of relatively modest means[66] gave some $58,000 to a woman with whom he was infatuated, but who was largely indifferent to him, for the purchase of a house for occupation by herself and the children of a previous marriage. The woman was registered as proprietor. Later, the parties fell out and, in the male party's action to recover the land, the trial judge found that the male party had become emotionally dependent on the woman who, as a result, had had great influence on his actions and decisions. He found further that the woman tolerated the man's attentions because of the material advantages which had resulted and that she had manufactured an atmosphere of crisis about her ability to continue living in the rental accommodation and did so in order to influence him to provide money for the purchase of the house. In addition, that she had played upon his love for her by making threats of suicide in relation to her accommodation, and that she was aware of his infatuation, which she manipulated, and of his consequent inability to judge what was in his best interests and, also, that her manufacture of an atmosphere of crisis was dishonest. Accordingly, the woman was ordered to transfer the property to the man. On appeal to the Supreme Court of South Australia, the findings of fact by the judge at first instance were upheld and her appeal was dismissed. She then appealed to the High Court of Australia, which, by a majority of six[67] to one,[68] held that the facts found by the trial judge were supported by evidence and led to the conclusion that the woman had been guilty of unconscionable conduct in procuring and retaining the gift.

After having discussed the process of the case through the courts below, Deane J commented[69] that it had "...long been established that the jurisdiction of the courts of equity to relieve against unconscionable dealing extends generally to circumstances in which (i) a party to a transaction was under a special disability in dealing with the other party to the transaction with the consequence that there was an obsence of any reasonable degree of equality between them and (ii) that special disability was sufficiently evident to the other party to make it *prima facie* unfair or 'unconscionable' that the other party procure, accept or retain the benefit of, the disadvantaged party's assent to the impugned transaction in the circumstances in which he or she procured or accepted it. Where such circumstances are shown to have existed, an onus is cast on the stronger party to show that the transaction was fair, just and reasonable..." Deane J then referred[70] to the High Court's decision in *Blomley* v *Ryan*,[71] where Fullagar J had listed some instances of *special disability* – although, Deane J in *Louth* v *Diprose* had noted that they might take a wide variety of forms and were not susceptible of being comprehensively catalogued. Nonetheless, Fullagar J referred to, "...poverty or need of any kind, sickness, age, sex, infirmity of body or mind, drunkenness, illiteracy or lack of education, lack of assistance or explanation where assistance or explanation is necessary." Fullegar J had gone on, in *Blomley* v *Ryan*, to say that the common characteristic of those circumstances, "...seems to be that they have the effect of placing one party at a serious disadvantage vis-à-vis the other."

The very facts in *Blomley* v *Ryan* illustrate the operation of Fullagar J's remarks, albeit in a rather less controversial context than those in *Louth* v *Diprose*. In *Blomley* v *Ryan,* the respondent was an elderly farmer who had sold his property, at significantly lower value than it was worth, to the appellant, a neighbouring grazier. The negotiations were conducted through the appellant and his agent who was the manager of the area's stock and station store. The court found that the respondent had a notorious propensity for drink and both the appellant and the agent knew of the respondent's indulgence in heavy drinking bouts and, in fact, the respondent bought rum at the agent's store. Further, at the time the respondent was required to negotiate with the others, he had been drinking heavily for some days. Many witnesses had said that he looked both old and ill at the relevant time, although the appellant and his agent said that they had seen nothing untoward in his appearance. The Court was incredulous of that story and found that the appellant and the agent did have actual knowledge of his disability. The High Court attached particular importance to the fact that the appellant and the agent had produced a bottle of rum at the negotiations and, so, suggested that they knew of the respondent's weakness and had helped him to maintain his state of intoxication when he entered into a transaction which was not in his best interests. In the event, the High Court of Australia refused to grant the appellant a decree of specific performance on the grounds that the contract was unconscionable. It should, though, be said that it was not the respondent's inebriation *per se* which was regarded as a disability rendering him unable to enter into a valid contract, but rather as a characteristic which caused weakness, which was known and exploited by the appellant. That exploitation was readily apparent from the highly favourable terms received by the appellant and the consequent improvidence of the transaction for the respondent.

In *Louth* v *Diprose*, Deane J commented[72] that, on the findings of the trial judge, "...the relationship between the respondent and the appellant at the time of the impugned gift was plainly such that the respondent was under a special disability in dealing with the appellant. That special disability arose not merely from the respondent's infatuation. It extended to the extraordinary vulnerability of the respondent in the false 'atmosphere of crisis' in which he believed that the woman with whom he was 'completely in love' and upon whom he was emotionally dependent was facing eviction from her home and suicide unless he provided the money for the purchase of the house. The appellant was aware of that special disability. Indeed, to a significant extent, she had deliberately created it.

She manipulated it to her advantage to influence the respondent to make the gift of the money to purchase the house. When asked for restitution she refused. From the respondent's point of view, the whole transaction was plainly a most improvident one." In the context of the trial judge's findings of fact, the case, Deane J considered, was not simply one in which the respondent, under the influence of his love for the appellant, made an imprudent gift in her favour: "The case," he stated, "was one in which the appellant deliberately used that love or infatuation and her own deceit to create a situation in which she could unconscientiously manipulate the respondent to part with a large proportion of his own property. The intervention of equity is not merely to relieve the plaintiff from the consequences of his own foolishness. It is to prevent his victimization."

Of course, the judgment of Fullagar J in *Blomley* v *Ryan*[73] is not the only attempt by the High Court of Australia to set out what one might call the *indicia* of *special disability*. Thus, in *Commercial Bank of Australia* v *Amadio*,[74] two judges, who took part in the final appeal in *Louth* v *Diprose*, had made apposite remarks in that regard. First, Mason J had said[75] that if, "…A having knowledge that B occupies a situation of special disadvantage in relation to an intended transaction, so that B cannot make a judgment as to what is in his own interests, takes unfair advantage of his (A's) superior bargaining power or position by entering into the transaction , his conduct in doing so is unconscionable. And, if, instead of having actual knowledge of that situation, A is aware that the situation may exist or is aware of facts that would have raised that possibility in the mind of any reasonable person, the result will be the same." Similarly, Deane J considered[76] the issue to be whether the disability was sufficiently, "…evident to the stronger party to make it prima facie unfair or 'unconscientious' that he procure, or accept the weaker party's assent to the impugned transactions in the circumstances in which he procured or accepted it." Both *Amadio* and *Blomley* v *Ryan* were alluded to by Brennan J in his judgment. However, that facts of *Amadio* are sufficiently notable, in the instant context to be worthy of mention. The central feature of that case related to the situation of the respondents, who had, unwisely, guaranteed an increased overdraft relating to their son's collapsing building business. Their circumstances were noted[77] by Dean J, "They were advanced in years. Their grasp of written English was limited. They relied on [their son] for the management of their business affairs and believed that he and Amadio Builders were prosperous and successful. They were approached in their kitchen by the bank…at a time when Mr Amadio was reading the newspaper after lunch and Mrs Amadio was washing dishes. They were presented with a complicated and lengthy document for their immediate signature. They had received no independent advice in relation to the transaction which that document embodied and about which they learned only hours earlier from [their son] who…had misled them as regards the extent and duration of their potential liability under it. Apart from indicating that the guarantee/mortgage was unlimited in point of time, [the bank] made no personal attempt to explain it to them." The majority of the High Court[78] based their decision on principles of unconscionability and, not surprisingly, found the respondents to have been in a position of special disadvantage. Mason J regarded[79] the *special disadvantage* as requiring that, "…the disabling condition is one which seriously affects the ability of the innocent party to make a judgment as to his own best interest."

In *Louth* v *Diprose*, Brennan J pointed out[80] that, "… a gift may be impeached where the evidence shows that in fact it was procured by unconscionable conduct. Where a gift is impeached on the ground that it was obtained by unconscionable conduct consisting in an unconscionable exploitation of an antecedent relationship, the relationship is one in which one party stands in a position of special disadvantage vis-à-vis the other." By that Brennan J meant that, in matters where the parties' interests did not coincide, the donor's capacity to make a decision as to his or her own best interest is particularly susceptible to control or influence by the donee. That was a point which had been strongly made by Mason J in *Amadio*.[81] As regards the findings of fact in the lower courts, Brennan J stated[82] that, given those findings, the relationship between the respondent and the appellant was so different in degree as to be different in kind from the ordinary relationship of a man courting a women. It had been found that the personal relationship between them was such that the plaintiff was extremely susceptible to influence by the appellant as she knew. More controversially, Brennan J suggested[83] that that made the relationship analogous to that existing between an engaged couple, as was suggested by Lord Langdale MR in *Page* v *Horne*.[84] In that case, a gift by a woman to her fiancé was set aside, the Master of the Rolls commenting that, "…no one can say what might be the extent of the influence of a man over a woman, whose consent to marriage he has obtained." The analogy, on one plane at least, may be suspect: in his dissenting judgment, Toohey J, in stating the facts in some detail, noted[85] at the time of the parties' initial meeting, the respondent was still married to his second wife (although the final separation was about to occur) and during the seven years of their peculiar relationship sexual relations had only taken place on two occasions, at an early part of the story.

In *Louth* v *Diprose*, Brennan J pointed out[86] that the appellant had argued that, whatever view might be taken of her conduct, the only proper conclusion which could be reached on the evidence was that the respondent had made the gift to her because he wished to do so – how ever imprudent the gift might have been. If that was the right conclusion, Brennan J said, so that the gift was not the result of unconscionable conduct on the appellant's part, then the plaintiff could not recover the gift. Brennan J then referred to the decision of Salmond J in *Brusewitz* v *Brown*[87] where it was said that, "The law in general terms leaves every man at liberty to make such bargains as he pleases, and to dispose of his own property as he chooses. However improvident, unreasonable or unjust such bargains or dispositions may be, they are binding on every party to them unless he can prove affirmatively the existence of one of the recognised invalidating circumstances, such as fraud or undue influence." Salmond J, however, then went on to distinguish the legal situation in cases involving undue influence, when he stated that, "This general principle, however, is subject to an important exception. Where there is not merely an absence or inadequacy of consideration for the transfer of property, but also exists between the grantor and the grantee some special relation of confidence, control, domination, influence, or other form of superiority, such as to render reasonable a presumption that the transaction was procured by the grantee through some unconscientious use of his power over the grantor, the law will make the presumption, and will place on the grantee the burden of supporting the transaction by which he so benefits, and of rebutting the presumption of its invalidity. In such cases, it is necessary for the grantee to prove that the suspected transaction has not its source in any improper influence over the mind or will of the grantor, or in any fraud, misrepresentation, mistake or concealment of material facts which ought to have been disclosed by the grantee to the grantor in view of the relation between them. Unless the grantee can prove this the transaction will be set aside at the suit of the grantor." In *Louth* v *Diprose*, Brennan J took the view[88] that the same approach leads to the same conclusion where the evidence shows unconscionable conduct on the part of the donee. "Once," he said, "it is proved that substantial property has been given by a donor to a donee after the donee has exploited the donor's known position of special disadvantage, an inference may be drawn that the gift is the product of exploitation. Such an inference must arise, however, from the facts of the case; it is not a presumption which arises by operation of law. The inference may be drawn unless the donee can rely on countervailing evidence to show that the donee's exploitive conduct was not a cause of the gift. At the end of the day, however, it is to the party impeaching the gift to show that it is the product of the donee's exploitive conduct. This is the final and necessary link in the chain of proof of unconscionable conduct leading to a decree setting aside the gift." Brennan J was of the opinion that the respondent, based on the findings of fact in the courts below had discharged the necessary onus. The other judges in the majority, Dawson, Gaudron and McHugh JJ, in a joint judgment, and Mason CJ, were concerned largely with the factual conclusions to be drawn from the evidence and were of the view that there had been no appealable error.

There was, however, as has already been noted,[89] a dissenting judgment by Toohey J, which Radsan and Stewart have described[90] as *vigorous*. After having set out the facts in some detail and referred to *Blomley*[91] and *Amadio*,[92] Toohey J remarked[93] that there could be no doubt regarding the strength of the respondent's feelings for the appellant and the lengths, including the financial lengths, to which he was prepared to go to express those feelings. "But," Toohey J continued, "equally, while the appellant was content to accept the many benefits she received from the respondent, there can be no doubt that she made her position in the relationship quite clear. It was the respondent who continued to seek her out. She did not mislead him in regard to her position; she did not hold out any false hopes to him. They were both adults; each had been married before (the respondent twice); and the respondent was a practising solicitor who must have appreciated fully the consequences that the law would ordinarily attach to the gifts he made to the appellant, including the money involved in the purchase of the [relevant] house. It was the respondent's idea to buy the house not the appellant's. In those circumstances, there is much force in the appellant's criticism of certain expressions used by the trial judge... [which] tend to give an unbalanced picture of the relationship between the parties by placing undue emphasis on one of them." Yet, despite its limitations and apparent disadvantages, Toohey J noted that the respondent was prepared to accept the relationship; its sexual element was extremely limited and it might have been the case, the judge thought, that the respondent might have sublimated through what he called *The Mary Poems*, which he had written and had sent to her. Toohey J stated that whether or not that was actually the case could, "…only be a matter of speculation though there are precedents in history and literature for the kind of relationship that existed here."[94]

At this point of his judgment, Toohey J then began to question the findings of the South Australian courts. Particularly, be considered[95] that one aspect of the facts which required particular attention related to the purchase of the relevant house itself. In the Full Court of the Supreme Court of South Australia, King CJ had found that the appellant had manufactured an atmosphere of crisis so as to influence the respondent to provide the money for the purchase of the house and her threats of suicide in that regard. In particular, the Chief Justice had said that that behaviour had involved the manufacture of a crisis where existed, "…was dishonest and smacked of fraud…" which, in turn, led to his conclusion of unconscionability. Toohey J did not regard that finding as being supported by the evidence, even though he considered that it was necessary to put aside the evidence of the appellant herself as King CJ had found her evidence relating to the circumstances leading up to the purchase to be "…quite unimpressive." However, there was evidence from another witness[96] which, seemed to Toohey J to put the matter in a different light.

That witness had given evidence to the effect that the respondent had told him that he accepted the fact that the appellant would never marry him, but, nonetheless, he wanted her to be happy and secure, which is why he bought the house for her. However, Toohey J did admit[97] that there was some ambiguity in the record of the witness's evidence – it was not clear beyond argument that, at that point, he was continuing his account of the conversation with the respondent or simply giving evidence of his own state of mind. However, in the light of the evidence, Toohey J regarded,[98] as had the Chief Justice of South Australia, the starting point as being the fact that there was a gift of the house to the appellant. "It was," said Toohey J "of course a very generous gift in the circumstances; it was a gift that the respondent's children might justifiably have resented; and it was a gift that the respondent himself might have regretted and later did regret." However, Toohey J did regard[99] the law as being clear and as represented in the *dictum* of Salmond J in *Brusewitz* v *Brown*.[100] However, Toohey J did note that Salmond J's reference to *invalidating circumstances* must be read in the light of the High Court of Australia's decisions in *Blomley* and *Amadio* – as well, one might add, of the remainder of Salmond J's own discussion in *Brusewitz*, earlier noted.[101]

Toohey J then sought to draw together his view of the situation by way of conclusion. First, he noted[102] that, although the concept of unconscionability had been expressed in fairly wide terms, the courts were exercising an equitable jurisdiction according to equitable principles and they were, "…not armed with a general power to set aside bargains simply because, in the eyes of the judges, they appear to be unfair, harsh or unconscionable."[103] As regards the notion of *special disability*, Toohey J referred to *Amadio*,[104] and the respondents' unfamiliarity with written English therein, and *Wilton* v *Farnworth*,[105] which involved deafness. He then emphasised that the conditions in those cases could have been readily apparent, which was not so in *Louth* v *Diprose*.

Second, although Toohey J found the appellant's attack on the trial judge's findings generally persuasive it was not necessary to make contrary findings in order to reach a contrary conclusion because those findings were of a general nature which bore on the parties' relationship. However, he did find[106] that the appellant's complaint that those findings focussed unduly on the position of the respondent and failed to have due regard to the totality of the parties' relationship was well founded. In so doing, he reiterated his view that the assessment that the appellant had manufactured an atmosphere of crisis where none existed[107] was, "…not so much a finding as an inference. In either case, it does not find great support in the evidence."

Third, the judge continued by seeking to emphasise that, "…the important thing is that the respondent failed to make good the proposition that his relationship with the appellant placed him in some special situation of disadvantage so that he should be recognised as the beneficial owner of the [relevant] house. The relationship was one which might be thought to have little to offer him but it was one in which he was content to persist and which the appellant in no way misrepresented or disguised." In other words, the respondent was fully aware of all the circumstances, his actions and their consequences. That applied especially, the judge thought, to the purchase of the house. "That knowledge," Toohey J emphatically concluded, "and his clear appreciation of the consequences of what he was doing ran directly counter to a conclusion that he was suffering from some special disability or was placed in some special situation of disadvantage. It is clear that the respondent was emotionally involved with the appellant. But it does not follow that he was emotionally dependent on her in any legal sense."

It will be clear from the foregoing discussion that *Louth* v *Diprose* is not an easy case to evaluate. That is clear from the various reactions of Australian text writers to the case. Thus, Duggan describes[108] *Louth* v *Diprose* in these terms: "[T]he plaintiff was a male solicitor with, presumably, some experience of worldly affairs, while the defendant was a woman experiencing financial hardship and personal difficulties. Nevertheless, the trial judge had found that the relationship was an unusual one, and that the defendant manipulated the plaintiff's feelings for her so as to induce the gift. In particular, the judge held that the defendant had deliberately manipulated an atmosphere of crisis in relation to her living arrangements (she had at one point threated suicide) and that this was dishonest and smacked of fraud. Although some reservations were expressed in the High Court about these findings, the majority was not prepared to overturn them. Taking the findings as given, the case was a clear one". With respect to that writer, the case, as will later be seen,[109] was anything but clear, especially when Toohey J's dissent is contextualised and it is apparent from the three judgments which I have considered in detail that the view which is likely to be taken of the case is likely to be dependent on the emphasis which an observer is going to place on particular issues. Hence, Meagher, Heydon and Leeming have emphasised[110] the importance of the appellant's threats of suicide.

The majority of judges at all three levels of the case's hearings seem to regard the nature of the parties' relationship, and the respondent's consequent disability, as being the central issue. Thus, Evans suggests[111] that *Louth* v *Diprose* should not be seen as. "…opening up a new field of equitable assistance for the love-struck. The peculiar twist to the case that attracted equitable intervention was the position of special advantage given to Ms Louth by Mr Diprose's infatuation and the manipulative and calculated manner in which she sought to take advantage of it to secure for herself the benefit of a sizeable and improvident transaction, without ever having the intention of accepting any comparable burden. Dal Pont and Cockburn state[112] that the majority of the High Court of Australia found, "...the respondent to be in a position of special disadvantage arising out of his emotional dependence on the woman even though he was a solicitor, and had ample time in which to consider the wisdom or otherwise of the proposed transaction." Hepburn is rather more cautious and, at the same time, more overarching when she comments[113] that the decision of the majority in the High Court, "...has been criticised because of the subjective evaluation intrinsic in an assessment of emotional dependency. It is very difficult to establish whether or not one person is emotionally 'infatuated' with another, and to further allege that such dependency constitutes a special disability to ground an action in unconscientious dealing. The mere purchase of large gifts does not necessarily connote dependency; it may simply be evidence of persuasion or hope as to how a relationship may develop. Nevertheless, the decision in *Louth* v *Diprose* illustrates the reluctance of appellate courts to overturn the findings of trial judges in cases concerning unconscionable dealings." Finally, Radan and Stewart comment[114] that, "Throughout the case, reference is repeatedly made to the 'emotional dependence' and 'infatuation' of Diprose, but it is clear from many judgments...that it was the 'manipulation' by Louth that gave Diprose's unrequited love its status as a 'special disadvantage'. While the other party's behaviour is obviously relevant to the later elements of the unconscionability doctrine, reference to it at the initial stage of determining the 'special disadvantage' of an applicant would seem to be at odds with the previous case law. However where the special disadvantage derived from a relationship, such considerations would seem necessary and valid."

In the context of such different approaches, or emphases, one particular dispute – and one which is within the rhetorical thrust of this text – is that between Sarmas and Heerey regarding *Louth* v *Diprose*. The dispute had its origins in a paper by Sarmas,[115] where she concluded[116] by describing her paper as, "...a critique of *Louth* v *Diprose* using the methods and insights of legal storytelling. The story I have told has been a bleak one. It has been about the persistence of gender stereotypes and a judicial inability to acknowledge class and gender power. But it has also been about possibilities, the possibilities which emerge when we realise that there is nothing essential, objective or neutral about the current legal order.

This realisation brings with it a responsibility to engage in scholarship which challenges that order. Legal storytelling does just that." The first issue which arises from that necessarily grim conclusion is: what characteristics does *legal storytelling* possess? Sarmas notes [117] that, although there is considerable diversity amongst those engaged in the activity,[118] a number of themes were immediately identifiable. First, she suggests that its adherents are largely drawn from those scholars who are involved in critical race theory and from feminists who emphasise the control role of *narrative* in legal analysis; that is "...the stories told and untold in law, rather than its abstract rules and principles. Stylistically, they often use stories, parables and dialogues as a means of persuasion in their work." Second, Sarmas writes that emphasis on narrative, rather than on abstract rules and facts deposits legal storytelling in a rather wider intellectual context of what is generally referred to as *postmodernism.*[119] That emphasis, Sarmas goes on, assumes the constructed and partial nature of facts and rules and problematises the distinction between them. To put the matter another way, the process of adjudication is perceived as the adoption of a particular story in order to resolve a case, rather than as the application of objective rules to objective facts. Third, it is also claimed, Sarmas argues, that the stories adopted by decision makers, notably judges, are not arbitrary. They are stories which are part of, and reinforce, the dominant discourse. It follows that legal narratives are likely to be structured in such ways to exclude, as well as silence or oppress, people who are not members of the dominant culture – such as people of colour, women and the poor – a characteristic which, inevitably, politicises the processes of legal storytelling. Fourth, Sarmas refers to[120] the issue of *voice*, which refers to the identity of the storyteller which, in turn makes a difference to the variety of story which is told. Hence, the telling of stories by those who are not a part of the dominant legal culture, or the telling of *counter stories*,[121] represent a means of challenging dominant legal stories and, hence, changing the legal system so that it is more inclusive and responsive to the needs of other groups. Inevitably, there is likely, as Sarmas points out,[122] to be debate about the success of the process, especially in the light of the need for sympathy from adjudicators which, in Sarmas's *ipsisimma verba*, has led to, "...some proponents of legal storytelling to advocate the need to tell the stories of outsider clients in the courtroom, in ways which create empathy on the part of decision makers with the outsider group. Others have become increasingly pessimistic about the ability or the willingness of those with power (judges and other decision makers) to participate in and contribute to progressive change."

Sarmas seeks in her article to utilise the notion of legal storytelling to explore the official court stories *in Louth* v *Diprose*; by which she means the particular narratives utilised by the judges who decided the case. Her avowed aim in so doing is to demonstrate that those stories were *stock stories* [123] about women, men and social class and, also, that they determined the specific outcome of the actual case and, what is more, determined the development of the doctrine of unconscionable dealing, upon which the decision was ostensibly based. She seeks to do this by means of a fictitious classroom dialogue which she states [124] tells three stories about *Louth* v *Diprose*, each quite different, though all derived from the same facts presented at the trial. "Not only," Sarmas urges, "does the interpretation of that evidence differ from story to story, but the 'facts', the same 'facts', are indeed different in each story. Some 'facts' are included, some excluded in the process of developing each particular narrative."

The three stories (which she entitles "STOCK STORIES: DAMNED WHORES; ROMANTIC FOOLS, DAMSELS IN DISTRESS AND KINDLY GENTLEMEN"). The first is told by the trial judge and repeated by the majority judges on appeal "Diprose", she writes, "is depicted as the classical romantic fool who is powerless in the face of love. He is so utterly in her power that he pursues her and showers her with gifts *even though he gets no sex in return for it*. He is also a very nice man. Not only is he generous, but he is helpful and supportive, he wants marriage; he is a loving father whose concern extends beyond his own children to her children. His generosity is more significant for the fact that his assets are limited. In contradistinction, the appellant is depicted as, in Sarmas's words,[125] "...she is slovenly, conniving and materialistic. Her morals are suspect. Her sexuality is dangerous. She uses it to get what she wants, but she persists in denying that which she has been well paid for. She is not a nice woman. She is a tease. *She* has power over *him*." The immediate point of that stereotypical set of images is that, once it is grasped, it is readily assumed that the appellant must lose!

A second story is that told by the minority judges (only, after all, two from eleven: Matheson J in the Full Court of the Supreme Court of South Australia and Toohey J in the High Court of Australia). In this story, the appellant is rather less suspect; in fact she deserves to be pitied. However, as Sarmas puts the matter, the stereotype is reversed rather than eliminated – she turns, "...from undeserving whore into pitiful victim, a status which makes it acceptable for the minority to find that she should keep the house in the circumstances (those circumstances being that it was given to her as an outright gift and that it would be stretching the doctrine of unconscionable dealing beyond its previous parameters to set it aside on that basis)." At the same time though, the image of the respondent as a benign and romantic suitor persists in that second story as well as in the first.

The central point made by Sarmas about those two stories is that they are *stock stories*[126] – she goes on to say that, "Whether it's whore or victim, kindly gentlemen or romantic fool, these images not only fail to capture the complex nature of human subjectivity, but they also reinforce dominant stereotypes about women, particularly poor woman, and about men." Sarmas then suggests that the construction of the appellant (woman) as the more powerful party by the majority *and*[127] the construction, by the minority, of the power relationship between them as being relatively equal ignores the structural inequities in that relationship based on the respondent's position as a moneyed man. That issue had, in fact, been noted by Dawson, Gaudron and McHugh JJ in their joint judgment in *Louth v Diprose*, when they said[128] that, "The trial judge's conclusions are not conclusions which would readily be reached in relation to persons of the same background as the parties. The respondent is a male solicitor with, presumably some experience of worldly affairs and the appellant is a woman to whom he was emotionally attached and who, at the time, was experiencing financial hardship and emotional difficulties. Given the ordinary expectations with respect to men of professional standing and the assumptions generally made with respect to the relationships between men and women, it may be taken that the respondent's case was one involving a substantial evidentiary burden." Nevertheless, Dawson, Gaudron and McHugh JJ nonetheless upheld the trial judge's finding on the facts! Both narratives, though, Sarmas argues, render gender and social class irrelevant whilst, at the same time, reproaching stereotypes based on those very categories. In particular, she notes[129] that one of the protagonists in her hypothetical classroom discussion[130] has alerted readers to the extent of the inconsistency involved in the trial judge's characterisation of both parties and, in that protagonist's narrative, is the juxtaposition of the respondent's economic and social power as a professional man with the appellant's position at the bottom of the class hierarchy. Whilst one may, and I believe should, deplore the reduction of the people involved in the narrative to gender or socio-economic stereotypes, one is left with the feeling that Sarmas is guilty of the same offence which she has claimed the judges in *Louth* v *Diprose* have committed. Thus, the respondent is a professional man (and, therefore, moneyed and socially empowered) and has, for that reason (if for no other), exploited the appellant who (because she is female) is liable to exploitation, the more so because, *ex hypothesi*, she is at the lower (lowest...?) band of the socio-economic spectrum.

Sarmas then goes on [131] to seek to examine how the narrative employed by the majority ensured a victory for the respondent. In that regard, the first point she makes is that, if the respondent were to succeed, it was necessary for the majority to construct powerful images of both parties because his legal case was not, of itself strong. In the earlier cases of *Blomley* v *Ryan*,[132] *Wilton* v *Farnworth*[133] and *Commercial Bank of Australia* v *Amadio*[134] there was an obvious power disparity, an absence, in Deane J's words in the last case, "...any reasonable degree of equality." However, in *Louth* v *Diprose*, if the respondent were to succeed, the courts would have to fit a rather different factual situation into the template created in the earlier cases. Sarmas claims [135] that, although the facts themselves were readily apparent. "...it was necessary for the majority to do some very fancy foot work to construct him as the 'weaker party' and [the appellant] as the 'stronger party'. This was achieved, in part, by the juxtaposition of the powerful images of [the respondent] as pathetic, utterly infatuated and emotionally dependent romantic fool, and [the appellant] as dangerous, undeserving and calculating." Yet that was by no means the end of the story because, to allow the matter to have rested there, might have permitted speculative claims in unconscionable dealings where a party entered into a transaction with someone upon whom they were emotionally dependent. Thus, were proof of emotional dependence, together with knowledge of it by the stronger party to create a *prima facie* case of unconscionable dealings, women might properly use the doctrine to escape transactions entered into for the benefit of their spouses.[136] Accordingly, suggests Sarmas[137] the additional , and constricting, factor was discovered in the, "...finding that [the appellant] manufactured a false atmosphere of crisis, that is she manipulated [the respondent] into purchasing the house." Sarmas emphasises that the trial judges and the majority judges on appeal regarded the presence of that factor as *essential*[138] to their conclusion that the respondent should recover the house on the basis of unconscionable dealing.[139]

Sarmas then goes on to examine what might have been done to make a difference to *Louth* v *Diprose*, both in terms of the actual result and, in the broader sense, of combating the stock stories on which that decision was based. The first issue she discusses[140] is the case presented for the appellant in terms of a romantic suitor making a gift. In that context, Sarmas suggests that the appellant's case as it was actually presented to the court did, in reality, facilitate the construction of the narratives utilised by the Courts in reaching a decision which was unfavourable to her. Initially, it contributed to the construction of the respondent as, in Sarmas's own words, "...a benign romantic fool." *The Mary Poems*,[141] of which there were 91, were introduced as evidence in her defence and the respondent was, Sarmas states, allowed, "...enormous scope and leeway to discuss his poetry before the Court. At no stage during the presentation of her case was it suggested as a possibility that she might have felt threatened or harassed on receipt of the poems. [The respondent's] advances towards [the appellant] and her annoyance at them were brought up only in the context of demonstrating that [he] wanted an intimate relationship with her rather than to suggest that he might have been harassing her." Further, the legal strategy which was presented on her behalf did not involve making an issue out of the structural inequity between the parties and, thus, did not provide a *counter narrative*[142] to the prevailing view that the power relationship between them was either equal or in the respondent's favour. Sarmas considers that that strategy was comprehensible if it was assumed that the result of the case turned on whether the gift was outright or whether it was subject to a retransfer (the initial action does, of itself, suggest that the respondent, the original plaintiff, decided, at some stage that he wanted it to be returned). What Sarmas argues is that, if it could be shown that the respondent was a romantic person who was actually in love with the appellant, then the suggestion of an outright gift would be plausible. Sarmas then suggests that that device worked insofar as the gift argument was concerned, but did not do so[143] when the trial judge did indeed use that image of the respondent to support an argument that he was suffering from a *special disability*. All of that meant, Sarmas claims,[144] was that the appellant's own case, "...ended up supporting the narratives which ultimately led to a finding against her. Moreover, it served to reinforce rather than challenge the stock stories which rendered her experience and her reality invisible."

Sarmas then goes on to suggest that the telling of outsiders' stories may very well challenge dominant legal stories and, hence, contribute to progressive legal change. In that context, she quotes[145] Fajer who contends[146] that, in the context of gay rights litigation advocates must tell stories of the lives of lesbian and gay men in order to seek to create empathy amongst judges and to attempt to destroy the myths about gay life which they might believe. A similar view has also been advanced by a critical race theorist, Delgado.[147] However, quite appositely, Sarmas inquires as to whether the stereotypes, if challenged in *Louth* v *Diprose*, would ultimately have been rejected by the courts. A major difficulty, it is suggested, is that if the stereotype of the appellant, which Sarmas suggests was accepted by the courts, were replaced with another stereotype – that is, of a societal and personal victim – that does not mean necessarily that it would change the ultimate decision. Sarmas admits as much when she writes[148] that, "...because dominant narratives are seen as the 'natural' state of affairs, because they have the power of 'truth', then it is most unlikely that counter-narratives will persuade people to think otherwise. They are more likely to generate resistance rather than conversion, particularly amongst those who have a stake in the status quo." Nevertheless, Sarmas does not give up on that particular strategy: lawyers, she says,[149] who have a commitment to the outsider cause, need to develop such strategies aimed at taking advantage of the gaps which exist in the dominant discourse. She admits that the, "...telling of outsiders' stories in an out of court might not achieve change overnight, but it may assist in the gradual process of fracturing dominant narratives and creating larger spaces in the gaps which appear. It can also help create a viable opposition through community building and consciousness raising within outsider groups."[150]

Sarmas continues by investigating the relationship between storytelling and *voice*.[151] Sarmas is concerned that the protagonist in the hypothetical classroom discussion may, in fact, be seeking to impose a *feminist* and *class-conscious* voice on the appellant which she might not, in fact have had. To use Sarmas's own words,[152] the appellant, "...may not have perceived or named [the respondent's] behaviour as sexual harassment or otherwise threatening; she may even have considered it to be romantic; she may not have been conscious of issues of structural power; and it is possible that she saw herself as a victim, or as undeserving." Now that, as Sarmas herself points out, identifies the problems which are inherent in a strategy which seeks to value the voices of outsiders but, at the same time, requires, or hopes, that those voices do, in fact, question or refute the dominant discourse rather than speaking directly as a part of it. Further, and this, it is suggested, is an especially salient point: Sarmas points to the risk which proponents of this strategy run if they use their own positions of relative power to silence the genuine voices of others and replace them with the strategists' own, and more privileged, voice. Sarmas notes, too, that this central issue has been debated elsewhere,[153] but nonetheless she raises it because it is a factor which must be borne in mind when considering strategies which might be employed towards achieving progressive change. The issues which have just been raised must, she urges, remind relevant strategists of the need to be vigilant about the effect that their strategies can have on those whose situations are being so utilised. It must continually be asked, she reminds us, what will be the consequences of employing particular strategies for particular groups or individuals. In turn, for the purpose of the present, and limited, discussion that raises the question of how should the appellant's case, in *Louth* v *Diprose*, have been formed *from her point of view*. Or, in other words, how, in retrospect, should her story have been told?

In seeking to answer that question, Sarmas, rightly, emphasises[154] that it is, from the appellant's point of view, not to lose sight of the fact that a major (if not the sole) concern for her was whether she should win her case and, so, keep the house. This raises the instant dilemma of whether to use a dominant narrative which would win the case, rather than strategies which might challenge those dominant narratives. Sarmas suggests, supported by Freeman,[155] that, although the former course might give rise to a successful outcome, it may also very well reinforce any negative self-image or injure the participant's self-esteem or reinforce those narratives which ultimately work against them. Applying those considerations[156] to the appellant's case in *Louth* v *Diprose*, Sarmas suggests that, if her defence was structured in such a way as to support the narrative embraced by the minority judges, it might have increased her chances of a successful outcome. On the other hand, their construction of the appellant as a victim might also have reinforced any feelings of helplessness which she might have had and the failure to denounce the respondent's behaviour as being sexual harassment or otherwise threatening might have left her with the feeling that her experience had been, in part at least, invalidated. In addition, Sarmas refers to the work of Bottomley,[157] and suggests that the achievement of a favourable result in *Louth* v *Diprose* by means of that construction and using the appellant as a victim might create a situation where women who are unable to fit such a stereotype are likely to be denied success in later cases. Finally, she argues that the very use of dominant narratives in argument will reinforce their legitimacy and contribute in their persistence to the detriment of outsiders in general.

What is clear is that, as Sarmas herself readily admits,[158] there can be no *Grand Theory* or *Grand Strategy* which will produce the right result in all cases. There is no one formula which is able to do that. It is necessary, she urges, to evaluate strategies from the point of view of what they can achieve in a particular case, at a particular point in time. In other words, she suggests, one should think in terms of *contingent*[159] strategies and, by way of illustration she ends with a quotation from Hutchinson who writes[160] that, "the core idea is to act in a guerrilla – like way – within a broad set of progressive objectives to seize the possibilities of any contingent moment in order to achieve judicial decisions that heighten the status quo's contradictions and open up space for lasting political action." Sarmas's paper is, I would venture to suggest, a bold and interesting way of examining a rather intriguing and illustrative decision. There are, of course, other ways of deconstructing *Louth* v *Diprose*: instead of regarding it as a manifestation of *class* (meaning *power*) and *gender* (meaning *power*) it could be regarded in an entirely socio-personal light – in terms of relative personal inadequacy.[161] Of course, it is clear that different results are likely to be achieved if different facts or, indeed different emphases are found and applied. A good example of that occurs in a case already discussed in an earlier chapter:[162] in *Miller* v *Jackson*,[163] had Lord Denning, in particular, not had such a clear affection for village cricket nor such a beneficent view of its qualities and considered that the housing needs of the local community of more importance, then, it is very likely that the results of the case would have been different. It is, after all, not too hard to find sympathy for the plaintiffs in that case. It is also to be anticipated that

Sarmas's view is open to disagreement from those, especially, who are more accustomed to the traditional approach to the common law and its processes.

So, indeed, it was to prove: Heerey J, of the Federal Court of Australia, writing extrajudicially, has discussed[164] Sarmas's approach to *Louth v Diprose*, in altogether more traditional terms and, inevitably has come up with rather different conclusions. Heerey, at the outset, noted[165] that *Louth v Diprose* is, "...unusual as a story of how a man and a woman treated each other, and in the sense that there are not many similar stories which have reached the courts. It is perhaps paradoxical that much of the academic discussion which the case has generated concerns whether the issue was dealt with by the courts in terms of stereotypes, that is to say whether the case was treated as a familiar type of story." Heerey goes on to say that, in his view, much of the academic commentary[166] has ignored the forensic constraints which necessarily restricted the way in which the case was presented to the various courts and, therefore, decided by them. Further, Heerey writes[167] that he will seek to establish that much of that commentary involves replacing one stereotype with another and, "...using litigation as a weapon for the correction of perceived injustice to classes within a society rather than justice according to law between the parties to a particular case." Thus, Heerey's ground rules, or battle lines have been clearly drawn, at the very outset of his argument.

Heerey then goes on to detail the facts and, then, to analyse[168] the arguments presented by Sarmas, though probably, not in the same detail which has here been attempted.[169] In the law, Heerey, states,[170] "...[w]ithout storytelling there could be no litigation. But without facts – true, half-true or false – there could be no stories." In litigation, *inter parties* at any rate, both parties have a story to tell *but* the legal system as Heerey tell us, "...imposes constraints on the way their stories are told. Most of these constraints would strike even ardent reformers as reasonable, and are in any event applicable equally to all litigation, not just cases which raise sensitive class and gender issues." The constraints, subject to some limited exceptions,[171] are that the story has to be told in a formal setting – a courtroom – on oath or affirmation and in a witness box so that the storyteller is isolated from supporters and friends. Further, the story must be told in response to questions from lawyers, both on behalf of, or opposed to the storyteller, or from less frequently, the judge. In addition, as Heerey points out[172] there is the storytelling of lawyer to judge: that being what the lawyer tells the judge about what has happened in the courtroom. That story is itself constrained by the fact that the judge has been in the courtroom and listened to the stories told by the parties. Further, Heerey states, the storytelling in court resonates with an earlier storytelling -that of the party/client to her or his lawyer during and before the trial. Ultimately, Heerey suggests, the judge tells a story in her or his reasons for judgment and that story is a story about the other stories - what the witnesses have said and what the lawyers have argued. As there would not be a case if the parties had not disagreed, inevitably, the judge will be required to accept some parts of the stories and to reject others. As regards stories *per se*, Heerey comments[173] that stories are normally told for a purpose, even though that purpose may be no more than amusement; however, stories in court are always told for a serious purpose, which is to win the case, which is necessarily important for the storyteller. Consequently, the storyteller's interest will be affected, for good or ill, by the judge's belief, or lack thereof, in the story. In other words, Heerey suggests, a, "...litigation story presents as truth and not fiction. Literally truth, the whole truth and nothing but the truth. The teller of litigation stories usually does not believe that there is such as thing as objective fact – if he or she does, it is a mental reservation unlikely to be disclosed to the judge." In addition to those matters raised by Heerey, there is another which is of direct relevance to the thesis advanced in this book at large: the stories told in litigation, if they are to be accepted by the court, must be told in accordance with the *rules of evidence*, which serve, not only to constrain, but to expand the range of the story as it is told. Thus, in *Craig* v *R*,[174] Evatt and McTiernan JJ, in the High Court of Australia, pointed to that very problem, when they said that, "An honest witness who says that 'The prisoner is the man who drove the car' while appearing to affirm a simple, clear and impressive proposition is really asserting: (1) that he observed the driver, (2) that the observation became impressed on his mind, (3) that he still retains the original impression, (4) that such impression has not been affected, altered, or replaced by published portraits of the prisoner, and (5) the resemblance between the original impression and the prisoner is sufficient to base a judgment, not of resemblance, but of identity." That comment notwithstanding, most evidentiary rules are exclusionary in nature, - that is, concerned with what items may not be received. In one sense, they correspond in poetic terms with verse forms such, for instance, as the *sonnet*. However, the constrictions which the sonnet forms might impose may, indeed prove liberating. As Wordsworth wrote in his sonnet, about that form:

> Nuns fret not at their convent's narrow room;
> And hermits are contented with their cells;
> And students with their pensive citadels;
> Maids at the wheel, the weaver at his loom,
> Sit blithe and happy; bees that soar for bloom,
> High as the highest Peak of Furness-fells,
> Will murmur by the hour in foxglove bells;
> In truth the prison, unto which we doom
> Ourselves, no prison is: and hence for me,
> In sundry moods, 'twas pastime to be bound
> Within the Sonnet's scanty plot of ground;
> Pleased if some Souls (for such there needs must be)
> Who have felt the weight of too much liberty,
> Should find brief solace there, as I have found.

As regard the rules of evidence themselves, Glanville Williams has written[175] that, "The common law of evidence is distinctive chiefly in the determined way in which it excludes certain evidence which, although logically relevant, is regarded as unfair or as dangerously misleading." Although, he was writing of criminal proceedings, Glanville Williams's comments are just as apposite to civil proceedings, such as *Louth* v *Diprose*. The rules, in effect, tell each story teller how to tell, and within what parameters, his story should be, or should not be told.

As regards the process of adjudication, Heerey, whilst admitting that litigation does involve storytelling, points out that, "...the competing stories are dealt with by the judge in a way that is dictated by the law and the judging craft. It is not as though the judge goes to a theatre, watches the plaintiff's and the defendant's plays, and votes for the more appealing one. A more accurate metaphor is the mosaic made up of many different pieces... [T]he judge's mosaic take pieces from both and adds some of his or her own." The operation of that process meant, in the context of *Louth* v

Diprose, that the respondent might be disbelieved in respect of one aspect of his story, but could still win his case.

Heerey then changes[176] his approach slightly by referring to the *judicial function*, which he regards as the decision of the particular case and he emphasises that, "It is fundamentally at odds with that function that witnesses and in particular the parties themselves, should be believed or disbelieved depending upon their membership of a particular class or gender." However, he notes that law had not always adhered to that principle as steadfastly as it ought, especially in relation to the evidence of complaints in rape or other sexual offences,[177] though that is no longer the case in Australia at the present day.[178] At the same time, there did remain some rules which related to classes or categories of witness as which were, nevertheless, justifiable – not on the basis of the personal characteristics of the individual concerned - but rather on the witness's particular involvement in the events with which the case is concerned.[179] Heerey continues by pointing out that a judge's task is made the more difficult by the fact that people can either lie or be honestly mistaken or can tell a story which is partly true or partly false. The judge must, therefore, try to find the true facts, or, perhaps more accurately, the facts more likely than not to be true.[180]

He then[181] turned his attention to applying those principles to the facts of *Louth* v *Diprose*, and in particular, to the questionable veracity of the respondent. First, there appeared to have been some doubt in relation to a proposed retransfer of the house and, indeed, Matheson J in the Full Court of the Supreme Court of South Australia was of the view[182] that the respondent "...plainly gave false evidence." Second, as Heerey points out,[183] the respondent had organised an application for a government grant for first home buyers which had seriously misstated the true position. The application had claimed that the appellant had received the money for the purchase of the house by way of loan from the respondent's employer. The appellant, who signed the application and received the grant, may have been more aware of this untruth than was indicated by her evidence, although the initiative appeared to have emanated from the respondent. However, Heerey, at this point, is at pains to emphasise that the trial judge had seen and heard the parties' stories at first hand – which was more than the appellate judges had been able to do, as well as the commentators on the case, including himself. Third, Heerey suggests [184] that *reconstruction*[185] may have taken place when the respondent was giving evidence at the first instance hearing. By that is meant that the respondent was seeking to understate the extent of his infatuation for the appellant and had sought, instead, to present the rather less unflattering image of a kindly uncle.

On the other hand, quite apart from the incident regarding the government grant,[186] there was the issue of the appellant's real attitude towards the respondent. Was it, asks Heerey,[187] "Sympathetic friendship,? Mild affection? Insipid neutrality? Vapid nonchalence?" There was some evidence to the effect that it was none of these, but rather *intense dislike*[188] at the same time that he was regularly visiting her and was paying her children's private school fees! Further, as regards the appellant's apparent veracity, Heerey notes the finding that, despite her denials, she had made threats of suicide at the time of discussions about the house. The falsity of the denials, Heerey suggests,[189] rather suggests that the threat was made with an ulterior motive, and, in consequence, King CJ's findings in the Full Court of the Supreme Court of South Australia[190] that the appellant had engaged in manipulative and calculated conduct of a material kind were well founded. Heerey also argues that the Chief Justice's conclusion was not based on any acceptance of a *stock story*,[191] but on his findings as to specific events, some of which were disputed (though many were not). Heerey reinforces his view by commenting that, if that conclusion looks like a familiar story found in literature and human experience, it does not follow that the latter gave birth to the former. Still less can his Honour's conclusion be treated as one based on the presumption that women, or some women are inherently likely to act [in that manner]. That interpretation, of course, flies directly in the face of Sarmas's view.[192]

Having made that point, Heerey remarks[193] that, "Courtrooms are busy places. In any given case there will be issues raised by the parties for the judge's decision. It is about these issues that litigation stories are told. Harsh as it may seem, judges are not interested in material which does not bear on those issues." Heerey then discusses various incidents relating to Sarmas's suggestion that the respondent had engaged in violence and harassment represented, in part, by the *Mary Poems*. Heerey, from a strictly lawyerly standpoint, inquires[194] as how the depiction of the respondent as being involved in sexual harassment or violence could have helped the appellant's case. "Remember," he states, "she is resisting a claim that she hand over a house, the title to which is in her name, because she had allegedly (i) agreed to transfer it to [the respondent] or, alternatively (ii) unconscionably exploited his disadvantage flowing from his emotional dependence. As to physical violence, such as it was, the only incident suggested came three years after the critical events and partly, if not mainly involved acts of [the appellant] herself. [The respondent] may have had his faults but does not seem to have been a basher of women."[195] As regards sexual harassment, Heerey suggests that it is hard to perceive any strategic advantage to the appellant in portraying the respondent as a sexual harasser rather than as romantic and infatuated and, thus, less likely to have wanted a retransfer of the property.

Heerey then turns his attention[196] to the central pillar of Sarmas's thesis: namely, that the courts' treatment of the appellant was predicated on class and gender discrimination. As regards the first, Heerey finds it to be unconvincing, "[The] stories of Mary and Louis," he writes, "do not present as a meeting across class boundaries, like Professor Higgins and Eliza Doolittle or Constance Chatterley and Mellors the gamekeeper to cite a few stories." Heerey, tellingly, in this commentator's view, notes that the respondent was a lawyer, although not an especially distinguished one (by his mid-forties he was working as an employed solicitor, having terminated an unsuccessful partnership in the small Australian State of Tasmania). Again, Heerey points out that, in Australia, it would not be totally unremarkable for a doctor or lawyer to marry a secretary or nurse. It also seemed as though the social circles of the parties were not mutually exclusive. Heerey claims[197] that there did not appear (though he has admitted that he had not directly observed the parties[198]) that no class differentiation could be detected in their speech. Nor, Heerey argues[199] that there was any significant difference in their ages[200] and, material possessions aside, there was nothing to suggest that the appellant had abandoned her prior social status, nor her family and friends. Heerey, in that context, notes that the retention of social class despite financial decline is a recognisable phenomenon, perhaps even a stock story.

In sum, Heerey strongly argues that any, "…story in which any emotional and sexual power [the appellant] might have had over [the respondent] is negated or mitigated by [the respondent's] membership of a superior social class would be reconstruction of the most synthetic kind. That is to say that it would be untrue on the facts – and not obviously helpful to [the appellant's case]. If [the appellant] were of a distinctly lower social class than [the respondent], it might be thought the less likely that he would have made an outright gift of the house to her – amongst other things to the disadvantage of his own children, who belonged of course to his own class." Heerey is equally sceptical[201] of Sarmas's suggestion[202] that the respondent's having more money than the appellant gave him power over her. Heerey claims that power involves the ability to have others act as the holders of the power desires and, if need be, as those others would prefer not to act. "Power as between two individuals," Heerey goes on, "can be formal and low – backed like the lecturer's power to pass or fail a student or the judge's power to uphold or dismiss a plaintiff's claim. What however is in issue here is power that is suggested as flowing in an informal and social setting from the personal attributes and advantages or lack thereof – money, class, gender, sexual and emotional attraction, strength of personality, harassment or violence." The question, though, is, in reality what motivates the person holding the power to exercise it in a particular way. There may, as *Louth* v *Diprose* itself illustrates, be disputes may actually be about who does, in fact, hold the power. Heerey concludes[203] that part of his argument by suggesting that the respondent was unable to persuade the appellant to do, or refrain from doing, anything because he had more money had than she. There were other reasons for that's being the case: she positively disliked him,[204] so that she had the choice of tolerating the annoyance which he caused her or of ridding her life of him, but, if she were to adopt that course, she would lose the material benefits which the respondent provided for her children and herself.

In Sarmas's paper, she inquires[205] as to the kind of story which would have best presented the appellant's case. Heerey seeks to answer that question[206] by suggesting that closer attention should be paid, initially by storytelling, by client to lawyer. The client tells the lawyer what happened, but that is storytelling for a particular purpose, because the client wants to win the case and the telling of the story to the lawyer is the first step on the way to that goal. The client, accordingly, will tell the lawyer the story and, in so doing, will emphasise the facts which seem to be important to her or to him. However, it is likely that there will be other facts, which might very well have legal significance, but are not so instantly apparent to the client. The lawyer must, therefore, inquire after such facts: it is, at the very least possible that a client may never have heard, say, of *unconscionability*. The process of civil procedure, then, involves the respective lawyers learning what the other party's story is and the lawyer will ask her or his clients what their responses are to particular allegations. "The process," Heerey emphasises, "assumes that there is such a thing as historical fact, that as to some critical facts there may be dispute, and that the lawyer will attempt to persuade the judge that his or her client's version of these facts is the true one."

However, although lawyers will have the same ultimate objective as their clients, there may be constraints which are imposed upon the lawyer when retelling a client's story to the judge and these constraints apply to the lawyer's assisting witnesses in telling it. The first, as I have already noted[207] is the rules of evidence (though Heerey specifically only refers to rules concerning *admissibility* and *relevance*.) Second, the lawyer does not personally vouch for the truth of his client's story.[208] Third, a lawyer may not manufacture facts or suggest to the client that a particular fact would help the client's case, Heerey wisely comments[209] that such breaches might happen, "…with little risk of detection and with great personal benefit to lawyers. Because it is so fundamental the rule is not explicitly discussed. But breaches would be very destructive of any system of justice and certainly of any legitimate role for the legal profession." Fourth, lawyers must bear in mind that it is the client's case, as the result of a case – such as *Louth* v *Diprose* – may be of very considerable importance to the lives of the clients. "The client," asserts Heerey, "is entitled to be treated as an individual whose story deserves attention and skilful presentation. The client's supposed ignorance of wider political and sociological issues should not result in him or her being patronised or used as guerrilla-fodder." This last comment, is presumably aimed at the adherents of the school of scholars with whom Sarmas claims adherence and whom she is palpably addressing.[210] Sarmas makes little secret of that, so that, perhaps, Heerey's comment was more than a little unnecessary.

However, that was not to be the end of the dialogue: Sarmas sought to reply to Heerey's comments on her initial paper.[211] Indeed, not unlike Heerey,[212] she strongly urged[213] that, "…it was important for advocates to ensure that the client's voice is heard and listened to in the course of the litigation." She then goes on[214] to attempt to refute Heerey's criticisms of the approach in her original article. First, she notes that Heerey implicitly criticises regarding her question the findings of fact in *Louth v Diprose*. She responds[215] by stating that his analysis in that regard[216] is deficient in that it ignores, "...the fact that 'law' and 'the judging craft' do not exist in a vacuum. They exist in the social world and are constituted by it. The dominant discourses or stock stories in the world will invariably impact on the 'law' and the 'judging craft'." Thus, she argues,[217] even simple narratives take place in a context[218] and that context is there before, after and during the trial as well as being in the judge's conscious. It is therefore, integral to the whole process. Second, she notes that Heerey had criticised her earlier analysis for ignoring the formal restraints which restrict the way in which the case is presented to, and decided by, the judge. In particular, Sarmas takes up[219] the matter of *evidentiary relevance* as raised by Heerey.[220] She expresses the view that, by restricting the information that may be presented in court to a narrow range of *legally relevant* material, rules of evidence may well have a profound impact on the court's construction of both "what happened" in the cases, and the characters of the parties who are involved. In particular, Sarmas is critical of Heerey's suggestion[221] that it would not have done much good for the appellant's case for the respondent to have been depicted as being culpable in respect of sexual harassment and violence. Thus, she writes[222] that, "...had the [trial] judge obtained a broader picture of who [the appellant] was and what she did (i.e. that she had trained as a nurse and had resumed work in that area), then it may have been more difficult for him to have depicted her in the one-dimensional and demonised way in which he did. And the trial judge's construction of [her] character *did* have a lot to do with the eventual outcome of the case, because the trial judge found her an unreliable witness and preferred [the respondent's] evidence over her account of what happened." Still further, Sarmas argues that evidence of any sexual harassment and violence might well have helped the appellant's case because it tended to demonstrate the nature of the generated power relationship between her and the male plaintiff. When examined in context, Sarmas argues,[223] these issues are relevant to the more strictly legal issues in the case – the issue of unconscionable dealing – because that doctrine envisages some kind of power relationship through the requirement that one party be at a *special disadvantage* as regards the other. It followed that, if the male party possessed gendered power over the female, then it is difficult to see how the courts could have reached a conclusion that *he* was at a disadvantage as regards *her*.[224] Fourth, Sarmas takes issue with Heerey regarding the class disparity between the parties. In so doing, she contends[225] that a *fair*[226] assessment of the socio-economic circumstances of the parties indicated that the respondent had more economic power than the appellant. In addition to the facts as Sarmas found them, she notes a large body of research[227] which demonstrates that families in which women are solely responsible for the care of their children are likely to be living in poverty. This was the position in which the appellant had found herself. The appellant's experience was, Sarmas argues,[228] a part of that widespread phenomenon rather than being the product of short term misfortune and, after all, "…poverty is based on gender, as well as class. Gender and class intersect in ways that exacerbate the disadvantage." In that context, Sarmas is especially critical of Heerey's view that the fact that the respondent had more money than the appellant did not necessarily give him power over her.[229] To Heerey's comments, Sarmas asks, "But isn't the ability to provide or withdraw material benefits to another, especially if that other is living in poverty, one of the most obvious and explicit ways of wielding power over that person?" She, further, is critical of Heerey's emphasis on *choice* on the grounds that the concept is itself problematic. Next, Sarmas refers to Heerey's suggestion[230] that she had, in her initial paper, replaced one alleged stereotype with another. She argues[231] that, if Heerey's suggestion is that by attributing gender and class identities to the parties she was engaged in stereotyping, Sarmas, once again, emphasises that it is essential that the social context in which people live is appropriately recognised. The real risk, I suspect, is that, probably subconsciously, Sarmas has substituted one process of demonisation (if not caricature) for another. Instead of the dotingly obsessive suitor trapped into an unconscionable bargain by an unscrupulous woman, Sarmas would present us with a plot scenario beloved of the creators of Nineteenth Century novelists and playwrights, usually not of the first order. In other words, though with considerable subtlety, she has created a situation where an impoverished younger woman is importuned by a wealthy, and older, man who seeks to take advantage of her gendered disadvantage! That view may seem to be a little harsh but it was one which came quickly to mind when I first read Sarmas's initial paper. Sarmas concludes her remarks on that issue by stating that acknowledging the context must also mean acknowledging the fact that, "…people come before the courts as already marked by gender, class, race and other such identities. To acknowledge that such characteristics are social and that they have social consequences does not necessarily involve stereotyping. To ignore those factors in the name of a hollow liberal individualism merely serves to reinforce existing structural inequalities." Whilst it is hard to disagree with that comment, its strength is surely modified by one of the processes undertaken by Sarmas herself. At the same time, I am not to be taken as saying that stereotypes are not part either of the literary or the legal process or that we should not try to rid ourselves of them in both areas of intellectual endeavour. If we are genuinely to do so, then all parties must be aware of the phenomena and the issues raised by both Sarmas and Heerey in their debate on *Louth* v *Diprose*.

Finally, Sarmas is critical[232] of Heerey's conclusions, especially and with justification, of his comment regarding litigants being treated as *guerrilla-fodder*.[233] Her instant response is that Heerey has misrepresented her position which was taken in her original article and that they, "...miss the central theoretical point which [she made] about narrative and storytelling." The point which Sarmas states that she was seeking to make in her initial article was that, "...the telling of facts is *always* going to be an interpretive and reconstructive process. It has to be because we can never objectively represent the past. This means that there are a number of ways of *legitimately* presenting 'the facts' of a case. This is exactly what lawyers mean when they talk of 'trial strategy'." Her most fundamental criticism of Heerey's response was that his accusation that she supposed the appellant to be ignorant of wider social and political issues and advocated that outsider clients be treated as "guerrilla-fodder" meant that he had missed the point of what she was trying to say. More particularly, Sarmas was concerned[234] that Heerey's criticisms represented a real message that critical academic debate about the facts of specific legal cases was somewhat illegitimate. Although that implication may well be open, I read Heerey's comment as expressing a concern that manipulation of the facts of such cases, as he suggested that Sarmas and those on whom she drew had been doing, could well lead to litigants from outsider groups being used as tools of propagandists. Nonetheless, it is still a disturbing allegation to have made. The dispute between Sarmas and Heerey has proved interesting and will, for various reasons, continue so to be and it is important that the various points of view be expressed. With that in mind, I should give Sarmas the last word, as she concludes by saying, "The legitimacy, indeed the *necessity* for such debate is made clearly by the fact that it has got us talking. To be sure, the stakes are high". The importance of the issues is illustrated by her quotation from the feminist legal scholar, Thornton, who has written[235] that, "Neutrality is a central value of law, legality and adjudication. Partiality, bias and vested interests detract from the authority of law or delegitimate it altogether. Feminist legal scholarship has unequivocally demonstrated that claims to neutrality, objectivity and universality are spurious."

The discussion of the reactions of Sarmas and Heerey to *Louth* v *Diprose* will, as I have just written, continue to be of interest and value for various reasons. The first of these is that *Louth* v *Diprose* has spawned a mutant offspring in the shape of the decision of the High Court of Australia in *Bridgewater* v *Leahy*.[236] In that case, an owner of grazing land entered into a contract to sell it to his nephew and his nephew's wife for $696,811 and, at the same time, executed transfers of the land and a deed of forgiveness for $546,811 of the price. The nephew had himself suggested a price of $150,000 and he paid the balance some months later and the transfers were completed. The owner of the land had four daughters, but the nephew had worked on the land for some years. The uncle, the original owner, had wanted the land not to be broken up after his death and was dependent on the nephew for management of the land as he was aged 84. Immediately before executing the transfers and the release, the owner was examined by a medical practitioner and found to be of sound mind and capable of making decisions about his personal affairs, he died, though, the following year. By a will which was dated some three years before the contract of the sale of the land, he had given his nephew an option to purchase specified property, which included the land in question, for $200,000. The residuary estate was left to his four daughters. The nephew exercised the option, paying $200,000 for the property described in the will, excluding the property which had already been transferred. The original owner's wife and daughters made applications for family provision, which were dismissed for want of prosecution. They also brought proceedings for a declaration that the transfers and deed of forgiveness were of no effect because they had been obtained by undue influence or unconscionable conduct or a combination of both. The High Court held, by a majority of three to two, that the deeds were of no effect.

The majority, Gaudron, Gummow and Kirby JJ, were of the view that the uncle's strong emotional dependence on, or attachment to, his nephew placed him in a position of disadvantage so that it was unconscionable for the nephew and his wife to retain the benefit of the deed of forgiveness.[237]

There are clear differences between *Bridgewater* v *Leahy* and *Louth* v *Diprose*, though their effect is uncertain, and it is that very uncertainty which has troubled critics such as Finlay.[238] In *Bridgewater*, the nephew had, at least, worked and managed the land for a significant period of time; there were other people to whom the owner, in *Bridgewater* owed a paternal and spousal responsibility of provision. These matters were not really present, or only peripherally so, in *Louth* v *Diprose*. The minority, Gleeson CJ and Callinan J, took a wholly different and factual view of the situation in *Bridgewater* and considered that there were concurrent findings of fact to the effect that the uncle was not under any special disability which ought not to be disturbed. Yet, in the event, the majority, in setting the transaction aside called *Louth* v *Diprose, inter alia*, into aid[239] at the very outset of their judgment.

The second reason why, at least for the purposes of this book, the discussion of *Louth* v *Diprose* will continue to be of importance is because of its inherent relationship with *rhetoric*, which it will be remembered from Chapter III is one of the major thrusts of this text. In relation to the commentators in *Louth* v *Diprose*, I have already noted,[240] these commentators are likely to be addressing specific audiences: Sarmas has outlined the likely adherents of *legal storytelling*,[241] whilst Heerey will be attempting to address those of a more traditionally lawyerly bent.[242] Such attention to audience is an important part of the *rhetorical* tradition, at least according to Goodrich.[243] To describe matters another way, it may be easier to convert the already half-converted. In Chapter II, I suggested[244] that *rhetoric*, in the light of the views of various commentators and of examples, might be described as, "…any combination of rhetorical devices, designed according to context and audience, to persuade, or describe, a view or an attitude to that audience." The contributions of Sarmas and Heerey are examples, surely of the appropriateness of that approach.

It may be argued, of course, that *Louth* v *Diprose* and its associated commentary have no real bearing on poetry, at least as such, though it will be remembered that Heerey did mention that the story of that case was of a kind that not many had reached the courts.[245] That he also, deprecatingly, referred [246] to *Pygmalion*, by George Bernard Shaw and to *Lady Chatterley's Lover* by D H Lawrence and he also noted[247] that the parties' story looked as though it might have been drawn from literature (as well as human experience). However, and both Heerey and Sarmas would agree on that, the parties' story involved a narrative and, additionally, a narrative which has legal implications. There is, of course, nothing new about narrative poems with legal themes as their core: thus, "Michael": A Pastoral Poem" by William Wordsworth is concerned with the legal notion of *primogeniture*[248] and "Enoch Arden" by Alfred, Lord Tennyson, which is concerned with the *presumption of death.*[249] These are both well-known poems by famous poets, but one suspects that the story of the parties – whatever view one may take of the facts in issue – is a better narrative than either, both of which are predictable in their outcomes. *Louth* v *Diprose* has generated an intriguing critical debate, one wonders whether it could engender a creative response.

One issue which has already arisen in relation to *Louth* v *Diprose*, is the matter of *verse form*, which I sought to compare, in effect, with the rules of evidence as they affect the processes of legal storytelling. To that end, the sonnet by Wordsworth was quoted.[250] The sonnet is itself an especially effective verse form for the communication of strong emotion. As Stephen Fry has described the sonnet form,[251] "It is the Goldilocks form: when others seem too long, too short, too intricate, too shapeless, too heavy, too light, too simple or too demanding the sonnet is always just right. It has the compactness to contain a single thought and feeling, but space enough for narrative, development and change." As well, it should be said, as being able to do both. Schmidt suggests[252] that the outstanding sonnet writer of the Twentieth Century was the American Edna St Vincent Millay. Schmidt's reasons for so saying are clearly connected with Fry's comments about the sonnet as verse form. Schmidt states[253] that Millay writes, "...directly about feelings, even awkward feelings, and the poems are always accessible. She has an old-fashioned reverence for poetic beauty and is not ashamed to devote herself to its pursuit. Her sense of life's ironies is acute, especially those treacherous ironies of love and a relationship developing and dying in time. She is not embarrassed by the exclamation mark – the vocative, the unabashed declaration... [L]ater this developed into resigned and eloquent philosophical and nature poetry."[254] Nowhere are all of these more apparent than in her sonnet "Time Does Not

Bring Relief...", which also adds a cosmic quality to the natural quality of the irony of a dead relationship which will not allow itself to be shed:

> Time does not bring relief; you all have lied
> Who told me time would ease me of my pain!
> I miss him in the weeping of the rain;
> I want him at the shrinking of the tide;
> The old snows melt from every mountain-side,
> And last year's leaves are smoke in every lane;
> But last year's bitter loving must remain
> Heaped on my heart, and my old thoughts abide
>
> There are a hundred places where I fear
> To go, - so with his memory they brim
> And entering with relief some quiet place
> Where never fell his foot or shone his face
> I say, "There is no memory of him here!"
> And so stand stricken, so remembering him!

In this poem, the narrator's experience is melded with natural phenomena – "the weeping of the rain," "the shrinking of the tide" – gives the experience an elemental or cosmic quality. From the point of view of the relationship of poetry and law, as represented in *Louth* v *Diprose*, if one assumes that the respondent's feelings for the appellant were, in any real sense, genuine, Millay's poem should provide a valid point of reference. Because of the elemental nature of the experience which the poem describes, the causes of that cosmic condition have become all embracing and conscious absorbing. Even when in places where she knows her love object has never been, her experience is such that that knowledge is as devastating as in places where they have been, together in the past. The word *devastating* which I use in commenting on this poem is, internally, entirely justified by the line, "And last year's leaves are smoke in every lane", that is especially so when contrasted with the previous line which suggests the possibility of regeneration. There is an echo in the last line in the use of the word *stricken*. There is no regeneration of the parties in *Louth* v *Diprose*, of any kind.

3. Love's Aftermath

One is almost accustomed to assume that what will happen when matters actually do work out between the parties and there is no shortage of poetic examples – though few from the law – to tell us of the genuine benefits bestowed by domestic partnership. Yet there is always the disastrous marriage and it is poems with such a theme which can be more readily related to legal considerations, which have already been adverted to earlier in the chapter.[255] In that context, one remarkable poem presents itself for discussion that is "Eros Turannos" by another American, Edwin Arlington Robinson, who has been described by Bloom[256] as, "One of the major American poets, now rather neglected." In view of that comment, coupled with the fact that I regard "Eros Turannos" as being one of the genuinely great poems in the language, it is necessary, it is suggested, to place Robinson in his contemporary cultural context as it can go some way towards providing an explanation for his prosody. At the outset, the commentator Van Doren observed[257] that Robinson saw, "...life in that profound perspective which permits of its being observed from two angles at once. He sees it realistically at the same moment that he sees it ideally." That perception, or those perceptions, may not tell the reader a great deal, though Van Doren seems more accurately descriptive of Robinson's characteristics as a poet when he writes that the lines represented by realism and idealism[258] meet, "...in the lives of people; the struggle between sun and shadow is studied by him in the characters of men. For he is above all else dramatic in his imagination, and one can conceive him as being quite helpless in the face of such difficulties... had he not had specific human cases to consider."[259]

That last point was taken up by Barnard who, having noted Robinson's (like his friend Robert Frost's) initial critical rejection, comments[260] that both poets, "...were trying...to bring poetry back into touch with life; to take it out of the drawing room, out of the realm of hearts and flowers, and onto drab small town streets and dusty country roads; to tell the stories of humdrum and even sordid lives and show that these were after all the lives of human beings; and to tell the stories in 'the real language of men'". Robinson had put his faith to the test, Barnard continues,[261] "...in the abrasive snarl of Aaron Stark," the inarticulate grief of 'Reuben Bright,' and the shop worn courtesy of 'The Clerks'".

Barnard, interestingly, traces[262] the pattern of Robinson's reputation which, he suggests, replicates that of no other United States poet; "...nearly total neglect for the first twenty years of a late starting career; a dozen years of acknowledged national supremacy; and thirty years of slow return to obscurity." Much of the earlier period, at any rate, can be accounted for by historical factors: thus, at the time Robinson was writing, poetry, as Barnard has graphically put it,[263] was one thing and reality another – "Poetry was for ladies and lady-like professors; the mode for men was action." As regards Robinson personally, Barnard noted[264] that, "A belated strain of Puritanism and grimness of his personal experience were stronger in effect than his formulation of faith. And the society around him had little interest in either." The last phase, Bernard suggests[265] was the result of fashions in criticism: a particular source of alienation from the New Criticism was, "...that Robinson was primarily interested in *people* – simply for their own sake, as unique individuals. The anthologists' liking for 'Richard Corey' and 'Miniver Cheevey' has been based at least on a sound perception of where Robinson's own concern chiefly lies."[266]

That of course, is never the whole story: Yvor Winters writes[267] that, "Much praise has fallen to Mr Robinson because he deals with people, 'humanity' and this is a fallacy of inaccurate brains. Humanity is simply Mr Robinson's physical milieu; the thing, the compound of the things, he sees. It is not the material that makes a poem great, but the perception and organisation of that material. Mr Robinson's greatness lie not in the people of whom he has written but in the perfect balance, the infallible precision, with which he has stated their cases."

Nonetheless, it is surely impossible to dissociate Robinson's subject matter from its articulation and, more specifically, from its organisation. Zabel has noted[268] that, "Robinson's art at its best, derives from his sense of the plainest use of speech. Even his lyrics are written in taciturn English that lies between the purely logical and the obviously colloquial style. His lyric perceptions, like his human values, are rooted in the known and the possible – the capacities of man which survive even in the sorriest condition of stultification and confusion." Zabel goes on to say that it is those very firm roots, not only in experience, but in language, which bind Robinson to his moment in (modern) history. However, I regard that view as unnecessarily limiting. Zabel seems to suggest that the moral conflict, the economics and social conditions, the political crises and, especially the human claims are somehow unique and render Robinson's vision, as well as his diction, unique as well. This is surely, as will later be seen,[269] not true, as Zabel himself seems, albeit cautiously, later to admit. "[The] attenuated rumination, impassioned hair-splitting, and bleak aphorism," of which Zabel writes,[270] are appropriate to all of the subject matter on which Robinson's work touches or which he explores.[271] Indeed, Zabel takes a further step back from any impressionistic base when he writes that, "The grey monotone of [Robinson's] collected works is deceptive for within it may be discovered both the sweep and anger of righteous denunciation and the sudden and lavish beauty of such lines as the endings of "Eros Turannos" and *The Sheaves*".[272]

As might have been expected, Barnard's vision of Robinson's place in literature is altogether broader based and, perhaps, less apologetic than that of Zabel. "The medium", he writes,[273] "is not the message. The message is never new though the medium may change. The message is always man... And in Robinson's poetry also, there is a vision of life that assuredly the world will not let die; a vision rendered, not rarely, through the medium of inevitable words and flawless form; a vision whose intensity is sometimes scarcely bearable, though presented with irony as well as sympathy and with humour as well as pathos; a vision that reveals without the luxury of rage or the patronage of pity or the vanity of piety, the human character in all its grime and glory, its abasement or exhaltation, its endurance of fate and its dream of freedom, and all the other attributes that poets incarnate – and that critics anatomize."

These general comments on Robinson's artistic achievement ultimately conclude that this vision is timeless, in general terms at least. My own view is that even those of his poems which are centred in particular time and place can, by a process of simple extrapolation, readily be interpreted in that light. There are , of course, some poems which, by their very nature, transcend notions of time and place and can readily be placed in any appropriate context – such a poem is "Eros Turannos", which is much anthologised and has already been mentioned both by Zabel[274] and myself.[275] It initially appeared in his collection, *The Man Against the Sky*, which appeared in 1916. Since the poem itself and its contextualisation, in both poetic and legal terms, represent a central thrust of this chapter and, perhaps, of the book at large, it is necessary to set it out, at this stage of the argument, *in toto*:

She fears him, and will always ask
What fated her to choose him;
She meets in his engaging mask
All reason to refuse him.
But what she meets and what she fears
Are less than are the downward years,
Drawn slowly to the foamless weirs
Of age, were she to lose him.

Between a blurred sagacity
That once had power to sound him,
And Love, that will not let him be
The Judas that she found him,
Her pride assuages her almost
As if it were alone the cost –
He sees that he will not be lost,
And waits, and looks around him.

A sense of ocean and old trees
Envelops and allures him;
Tradition, touching all he sees,
Beguiles and reassures him.
And all her <u>doubts</u> of what he says
Are dimmed by what she knows of days,
Till even Prejudice delays
And fades, and she secures him.

The falling leaf inaugurates
The reign of her confusion;
The pounding wave reverberates
The dirge of her illusion.
And Home, where passion lived and died,
Becomes a place where she can hide,
While all the town and harbour side
Vibrate with her seclusion.

We tell you, tapping on our brows,
The story as it should be,
As if the story of a house
Were told, or ever could be.
We'll have no kindly veil between
Her visions and those we have seen—
As if we guessed what hers have been,
Or what they are or would be.

Meanwhile we do no harm, for they
That with a god have striven,
Not hearing much of what we say,
Or like a changed familiar tree,
Or like a stairway to the sea,
Where down the blind are driven.

Having called upon critical aid in order to place Robinson in the American literary scene, it seems appropriate to do the same in respect of a particular poem – especially one which is so generally a well known part of the Robinson canon, even if, as Bloom suggested,[276] the canon at large may not be as well known as it might (or ought) to be. Accordingly, Squires has described[277] "Eros Turannos" as, "...his finest poem." Stivek is rather more particular and comments[278] that, "...it is probably the finest example of Robinson's mature style for short poems." His reason for that statement is something of a specification of Zabel's comments, earlier quoted.[279] "Eros Turannos", he states,[280] "...combines its distinctive techniques of blending character portrayal, implicit narrative, and abstract, generalized statement, his sparing but careful employment of allusion... his considered use of regular and restrictive verse form, and a meticulous adjustment of all aspects of a poem in complete equipoise" Barnard describes[281] the poem as, "...possibly Robinson's most admired poem." Winters (himself a not inconsiderable poet) refers to it[282] as one of Robinson's greatest poems and a universal tragedy in a Maine setting.[283] Coxe perceives[284] "Eros Turannos" as the Robinsonian archetype in which he reaches, "...an ultimate kind of equipoise of statement and suggestion, generalization and concretion." Thus, there can be no question of the foremost place of "Eros Turannos" in the Robinsonian canon.

As regards critical interpretation of the poem: first, Winters notes[285] that, in the first three stanzas of the poem, there is an exact description of the personal motives of the actions and the implication of their social motives; in the fourth stanza, the tragic outcomes; and, in the last two stanzas, the generalised comments. Winters, then states that, "In such a poem we can see to an extraordinary degree the generalising power of poetic method: for this piece has the substance of a short novel or of a tragic drama, yet its brevity has resulted in no poverty – its brevity has resulted, rather, in a concentration of meaning and power."

Coxe tells us[286] that the poem contains two complementary parts: the abstract, generalised statement and the symbolic counterpart of that statement, each constituting a kind of gloss upon the other; each moves through the poem parallel with the other, until, at the end, they become fused in the concrete images. As regards the poem's subject matter, Coxe says[287] that, "We grasp readily enough the pathos of the [central figure's] situation: a woman with a worthless husband, proud and sensitive to what the world is whispering yet ready to submit to any indignity, to close her eyes and ears rather than live alone". He had earlier commented[288] that, "Important though obtrusive imagery not only reinforces and enriches the exposition by the calculated ambiguity, as well as sets a tone of suspense and fatality. The man wears a mask: he conceals something that at once repels and attracts her..." In the end,[289] the wife's security will only exist by, in effect, blinding herself and seeing her husband as she would wish to see him. "Eros Turannos", Coxe then comments,[290] is, "...about the marriage of untrue minds, but specifically it is not just about untrueness and minds; it is about untrue man A suffering self-deluding woman B, as well as about those worldly wise men who conjecture and have all the dope."

Having now placed the poem in its critical landscape, what next can justify finding it a place in modern family relationships, particularly as represented in law? A first, though not perhaps totally convincing, reason is that the present writer has used the poem in his own work in the area, on two occasions, without having attracted undue criticism. The first instance directly involved discussion of a family law issue[291] – albeit a somewhat speculative one. The second was what might be best described as a contemplative discourse[292] with autobiographical overtones, but which might be considered, by some, to have family law implications. Second, the universal application of Robinson's work has already been noted[293] and aspects of both the story and the prosody of "Eros Turrannos" have been with us always, surely, as part of the human condition.[294] The function of the law with regard to family relationships is largely reactive and only, to a lesser extent, proactive. Although one must, at the very least, bear in mind the view of Watson and Stein and Shand, who have earlier been discussed,[295] that, as has already been emphasised, cannot be the end of the story.[296] The law, for example, must now at least, adjust to new forms of family organisation.[297]

Another way of approaching the issue is to suggest that Family Law can often, at least to a protagonist, represent a *transition*, as represented in turn by poetic metaphor. Hence, an appropriate result may appear, to some litigants, in Davenant's words, "A short dark passage to eternal light".[298] Some individuals, for whatever reasons – and some examples have been given in the form of case law earlier in the chapter[299] – may not have had such a happy experience with either the law itself or with the situations leading up to the litigation. Thus, the United States poet, Richard Wilbur has written,[300] in a rather different vein, that:

"...the stuff of her young life is a great cargo and some of it heavy:
I wish her a lucky passage".

At the same time, the existence of the processes of Family Law does not mean that advantage needs to be, or in fact is, taken of them. Hence, T S Eliot's more generally, and aphoristically, based comment[301] perhaps remains the most apposite:

'Footfalls echo in the memory
Down the passage which we did not take
Towards the door we never opened
Into the rose-garden

Clearly, all of this abstract discussion can, though, be related to the content and prosody of "Eros Turannos." As Coxe points out,[302] the first three words of the poem ("She fears him...") set the tone and provide the key to that which the remainder of the poem will later develop. *Fear*, of whatsoever kind, seems over a long period of time to have become endemic in so many family relationships, leading to legal involvement so that a legal (and poetic) response is needed – even though the fear may have been long term and the responses may not now be adequate. Coxe further refers[303] to the epigrammatic tone of the poem's first stanza when he writes that, "[W]e are aware that there is a kind of expository writing that is capable in its generality of evoking a good deal more than the words state. Important though unobtrusive imagery not only reinforces and enriches the exposition but by calculated ambiguity as well sets a tone of suspense and finality." Yet both the poem and Coxe's comment are, more than coincidently perhaps, reflected in actual situations and the legal response to them.

In addition, we are reminded from time to time, throughout "Eros Turannos", that the developments of the plot, as Coxe called them, and, in consequence, the various transitions that are perceived through some entities who refer to themselves as *we*. These entities seem unsure of their roles: in the fifth stanza, they tell the story, "...as it should be," though in the same stanza they refuse to obscure the characters with, "...a kindly veil." Finally, in the last, great metaphysical stanza, they claim that *they*, "...do no harm" and that, "...they/That with a good have striven/ not hearing much of what to say/Take what the god has given." Who *they/we* are is unclear. Coxe has referred to them in a passage earlier quoted.[304] Yet their eumenidean quality is undermined, at least, when the last stanza of Robinson's other coterminous and reflective poem, "The Unforgiven" is taken into consideration. That poem concludes, after having described another disastrous marriage, by commenting, "Although to the serene outsider/There still would seem to be a way." As regards the relationship between the poems, Stevik states[305] that both have, "...two characters, husband and wife, caught in a domestic tragedy of unsuccessful marriage. The discord arises from deception experienced by the characters as a result of Love's clouding their judgment. One is superior, the other inferior: the callous husband of "Eros Turannos" is matched in the other poem by the vindictive wife." Stevick's view[306] of the commentators in both poems is cautious when he suggests that each situation, "...is rationalized by an outsider whose understanding (or misunderstanding) we are able to take into account in providing part of the tension of the poem." At the same time, the certitude in the final stanza of "The Unforgiven" is greater than anything provided by Coxe's *worldly wisemen* – all the dope, or not – in "Eros Turannos."

Yet perception through other agencies is a part of the process of observing the law – even in some of its crudest instances and, as will be seen, it may be hard to break through those alien perceptions. Thus, in the case of *Fitzgibbon* v *Baker, Gardner and Leader Associated Newspapers: Re Schwazkopff*,[307] a case which has been noted earlier,[308] the respondents were allegedly the proprietor, publisher and editor of a suburban newspaper. They were charged with contempt of the Family Court of Australia in that they had published an account of a demonstration protesting at the imprisonment of one "Linsee Schwarzkopff" who, the demonstrators claimed had been "...jailed for two years only because he wanted to see his children." The reality, as we know,[309] was more than a little different: the true reason, as has been observed, why the subject of that demonstration had been imprisoned was repeated breaches of non-molestation orders aimed at the protection of the wife.[310] In addition to those comments, the Court, in the earlier hearing had emphasised[311] that violence of the kind which the husband was culpable could no longer be regarded as a private matter. Specifically, the Court in *Schwarzkopff* was referring to developments in the last twenty or so years,[312] but it must not be thought that material conduct of a vicious kind was much new. Thus, closer to Edwin Arlington Robinson's own time (he was born at Head Tide, Maine in 1869), the early feminist writer, Frances Cobbe, in 1878, had written[313] of public indifference towards and, indeed, trivialisation of, family violence.

Of course there is nothing directly in "Eros Turannos" which relates to violence *qua* violence, though, at the same time, there is the "engaging mask" – in Coxe's words:[314] "The man wears a mask: he conceals something that at once attracts and repels her. Though this is less than the foamless weirs of age". Again, according to Coxe,[315] the man finds a solace and security in the love of his wife and in her solid place in the community. Yet, the first stanza tells us, the wife is unsure of what fated her to choose him (the use of the word *fated* implies some kind of *inevitability*, perhaps, indeed tragic inevitability) but her daily meetings and fears are less than her long term fear of being alone, which is the product of the inevitable aging process. But that, itself, is innately paradoxical, and, as such, it is redolent of the situation in which Scarman LJ was to find himself in *Bradley* v *Bradley*.[316] In that case, a wife had obtained two non-cohabitation orders on the grounds of persistent cruelty, but a local authority had refused to rehouse her until she had obtained a divorce. Lord Scarman commented,[317] albeit in graphic terms, that, "There are many, many reasons why a woman will go on living with a beast of a husband. Sometimes she may live with him because she fears the consequences of leaving. Sometimes it may be physical duress, but very often a woman will willingly make the best of living with a beast of a husband because she believes it to be in the true interest of the children. Is such a woman to be denied the opportunity (which, of course, is what has happened here) of calling evidence to show that, although she is living with him, yet the family situation is such that she cannot reasonably be excepted to do so?"[318]

At the same time as all of that, the protagonist was unsure, "...what fated her to choose him." The law has never been especially helpful to those, whether fated or otherwise, make, of themselves, a wrong choice. The grounds for nullity, which could provide an appropriate remedy, do not generally do so. Thus, as early as 1818, Sir William Scott, Lord Stowell, in *Sullivan v Sullivan*,[319] stated emphatically that, "the strongest case you could establish of the most deliberate plot, leading to a marriage, the most unseemly in all disproportions of rank, of fortune, of habits of life, and even age itself would not enable this court to free [the petitioner] from chains which, though forged by others, he had riveted on himself." That was the law when Robinson wrote and remains, generally, the same today. Thus, an aggrieved party must await such remedies, as well as time constraints, as exist in the law relating to dissolution of marriage, Hence, for a multiplicity of reasons, we are told in the second stanza that the husband, in calculated manner, "...sees that he will not be lost/And waits and looks around him."

Exploration of the institution, and condition, of marriage, for whatever reason, is far from unknown and the response of the law, once again, has been far from either uniform or truly satisfactory. Thus, in instances of fraud, one might have thought that the immediate remedy of nullity might provide a solution – as in one Australian case it was found to do. In *In the Marriage of Deniz*[320] the female applicant was of Lebanese family. The respondent was Turkish and, at the relevant time, was seeking permanent residence in Australia. In order further to establish a basis for his application, he sought to marry an Australian citizen. He obtained the permission of the applicant's parents and she left High School in Fourth

Form convinced that he loved her and went through a ceremony of marriage with him. The marriage was never consummated and the applicant, on being told the respondent's reasons for so behaving, attempted suicide. The respondent's application for residence was refused and he was returned whence he came. There was also evidence that divorce would be an especially serious matter for a person of the applicant's background and, indeed, she told the Court that she would rather die than be divorced. Frederico J granted the application for nullity on the grounds of fraud, although he noted[321] that the fraud must go to the very basis of the marriage relationship and that care ought to be taken as there, "...would be general consternation if an application was granted on the basis of fraud by reason of one party deceiving the other as to being possessed of natural teeth. The case of the person who marries to gain money, rank or title would also cause concern." However, on the facts of *Deniz*, Frederico J stated that, "The respondent has not had the slightest intention of fulfilling in any respect the obligations of marriage. He has used the unfortunate applicant as a tool of his own convenience. His conduct amounts to a total rejection of the institution of marriage and what it stands for. He clearly deceived the applicant into marriage for his own personal motives and with the intention summarily of rejecting her immediately after the ceremony." Although, first, it should be said that *Deniz* has not, for good or ill, generally found favour in Australia[322] and elsewhere, [323] it should be emphasised, second, that the substantial reservations expressed by Frederico J[324] would have ensured that this most exclusionary of all tests for fraud in nullity of marriage would be inapplicable to the situation of the wife in "Eros Turrannos." Thus, the remedy, assuming one to be available at all, must lie in divorce – with necessarily attendant delays and potential social difficulties.

Nonetheless, the third and fourth stanzas show how, and at what cost,[325] the wife's position has been, at least in her own mind, secured. But that is illusory, as such perceptions frequently are – and the legal instances utilised in this chapter bear that out. The fourth stanza emphasises her seclusion both within the, "...home where passion lived and died" as well as outside, where the wife's situation is emphasised still further by the dreadful final lines of that stanza, "While all the town and harbour side/Vibrate with her seclusion." Hence, there can be no escape from her self-delusive situation. However, a legal escape might be a possibility, but whether that will inevitably lead to the "eternal light", as presaged by Davenant,[326] is another matter. In the case of *In the Marriage of Tye*,[327] the husband had left Australia after informing his wife that, after he had settled abroad, he would send for her to join him. Instead, some two months later, she received a letter telling her that he would not resume cohabitation. Until she received that latter, she firmly believed that there was no actual, or impending, breach of the matrimonial relationship and that the *consortium vitae* was still intact. At the hearing, the husband gave evidence that he had made up his mind to end the matrimonial relationship within a week or so after leaving Australia. In holding the ground for dissolution of marriage,[328] Emery J commented[329] that, "The conduct of the husband towards the wife in my opinion reflects complete lack of any moral obligation to his wife and a degree of cruelty which makes it very difficult to believe that he never had any regard at all for her." So that, as in "Eros Turannos" in addition to the private anguish which must have been suffered by the wife, the public judicial denunciation of her husband further isolates her. Indeed, on appeal on another matter,[330] the Full Court of the Family Court of Australia noted[331] that, "...a doctor certified that she was suffering from a severe anxiety state and was close to a nervous breakdown. [Emery J]'s observation of the wife in the witness box bore out this opinion." So that in the legal action, as in the poem, as Coxe points out,[332] that *dictum* seems to form the climax of the plot.

The themes of illusion and reality, apparent from the decision in *Tye* are also apparent in the fifth stanza. There again, as Coxe has pointed,[333] the *story*[334] which has unfolded is replete with concealment and deceit, but, perhaps even more clearly, with uncertainty ("As if the story of a house/Were told or ever could be") even though it is already known that the house was, "...where passion lived and died"). Yet, even on a more straightforward plane, telling the story of a house might not be capable of easy narrative.

Hence, in *Phillips and Phillips*,[335] the Full Court of the Family Court of Australia was required to deal with an appeal by the wife against property settlement orders. She had sought to retain, and remain living in, the former matrimonial home. However, the judge at first instance was unable to resolve differences between two property valuers. Accordingly, he had proposed orders for the division of the property which assumed that the former home was valued as the husband's valuer had suggested. At the same time, though, as the trial judge could not fashion orders which satisfied the wife (that is, by transferring most of the assets other than the home to the husband), the home should be sold. The Full Court[336] allowed the appeal and, on the issue of the mechanics of valuation stated[337] that a trial judge ought not to approach the question on the basis that there is an obligation to prefer one approach over the other. "However", they continued, "the ability of a trial judge to reach a separate opinion as to value depends on the evidence and other considerations such as the type of property being valued and the appropriate method of valuation." As regards the matrimonial home itself, the Court took the view[338] that, in all the circumstances, to order the sale of the family home, where the wife and children had lived since the separation and intended to continue to do so, was inappropriate. That intangible consideration was an issue which the trial judge should have taken into consideration. Hence, in attempting a valuation, a process itself shot through with value judgment,[339] intangible factors may be of crucial import. So that the story of a house may not properly be told or, indeed, valued. This is the more so when the story, the protagonist's aims and visions are obscured by a veil – however erroneously kindly that veil might seem to be.

Finally, in "Eros Turannos" comes the great metaphysical conclusion. The Chorus admit, initially, their total powerlessness. They admit the best that they can do is remain harmless, the more so as the victims (*the tortured* wife and the *secured* husband), in Squires's words[340], do not, or will not, hear much of any attempted intervention. Squires though, it should be said, perceives the Chorus as more active than the last stanza seems to suggest when he writes that, "[They] cannot absorb all of the pain that is pressed into the one image of 'the foamless weirs/of age', but the chorus can take in as much of it as can modulate the water image. In this way, the chorus mediates in the classical manner between tragedy and society." At the same time, the central figures, having striven with their god, take what that entity has given Stevick assumes[341] that the god is representative of *love*, howsoever the two individuals stand in relation to it. Given the context (and, indeed, the title) that is the god's distributive function – but it need not, in the Robinson canon at large be wholly exclusive. Thus, for instance in the well known sonnet "Reuben Bright,"[342] the unspoken god is *death* and its gift a radical change of lifestyle.

However, the god's gifts in "Eros Turannos" are alternative and, in Coxe's words,[343] "...thematic, narrative and symbolic materials merge in the three images that accumulate power as they move from the simple to the complex, from the active to the passive from the less to the more terrible." The movement in the poem is significant: Robinson, Coxe suggests, has packed the final stanza with words that suggest descent, depth and removal from sight, so that the terrible acceptance of the idea that "What the god has given" must be accepted. At the same time, too, the sea to which the blind are driven is represented as having a doomstruck quality. Thus, in the words of the Scots poet Iain Crichton Smith, who writes that, "The sea is darker than anyone dares to know".[344] At the same time, as I have elsewhere sought to suggest,[345] the divine gift may not, howsoever unfamiliar, necessarily be quite so frightening as the metaphor might initially suggest, even though its consequential effects are not to be known. In addition to Coxe's perception of the final stanza as being centred on descent, much of its awesome quality is its descent through declining levels of familiarity and predictability. Thus, "breaking waves" are both familiar and uniformly predictable, though the "changed familiar tree" is not so familiar, but in its distortion of familiarity it may nevertheless, be if itself, disturbing. The final metaphor dealing with an unfamiliar, unpredictable and potentially frightening idea adds the likelihood of grim finality both in the poem itself and to all of the processes described, or hinted at, in it.

Yvor Winter wrote[346] that "Eros Turannos" is, "...in forty-eight lines, as complete as a Lawrence novel." I have sought to place that quite remarkable poem within the context, not only of personal relationships themselves, but of the law which seeks to regulate some aspects of those relationships. It is an attempt of which Coxe, the literary critic, would not, I fear, have approved. At the conclusion of his essay, to which considerable reference has been made, Coxe wrote[347] that, "Time and fashion will have their effects, true enough, but unless we can rise above the predilections of the movement in our reading, there is little possibility of our understanding what we read." The moral dilemmas and fears raised in "Eros Turannos" have not, and probably cannot be, solved by law, even by laws which are more advanced than those which existed when Robinson originally wrote this remarkable and perceptive poem.

Of course, not all marriages are as disastrous as that which was explored in "Eros Turannos" – but, as Tolstoy wrote at the beginning of

Anna Karenina, all happy families have qualities in common, but each unhappy family is unhappy in its own way." One poem which describes another kind of marriage or family to that dissected in "Eros Turannos" is "Because", written by the Australian poet James McAuley in 1969. The Australian commentator Clive James, in a relatively recent article,[348] has said of the poem that, "One of Australia's artistic treasures, James McAuley's poem 'Because' is only a slight thing physically. Ten spare quatrains, swinging lithely along on a lattice of conversational iambic pentameter, it is over as soon as begun." The poem, which, as James tells us[349] was a late work begins by being about his dead parents and it begins starkly and suddenly:

> My father and my mother never quarreled.
> They were united in a kind of love
> As daily as the *Sydney Morning Herald,*
> Rather than like the eagle or the dove.

Since, James goes on, we already know that there was something wrong with the way the poet's parents were united, the first three lines of the second stanza come, really, as no surprise:

> I never saw them casually touch,
> Or show a moment's joy in on another.
> Why should this matter to me now so much?

James then comments [350] that, "Any trainee poet amongst his readership would have been impressed by the boldness of this *démarche*, where the story suddenly turns into a rhetorical question." The reason, of course, why it does matter is that the poem shortly states that, just as the poet's father could not demonstrate affection to his wife and the poet's mother he could not so demonstrate to his son. His father, McAuley notes in the third stanza's last line, "Had stiffened into stone and creaking wood." In the fifth and sixth stanzas of the poem, McAuley describes an attempt to draw some affection from his father, which, inevitably, was sharply rebuffed:

> Small things can pit the memory like a cyst:

> Having seen other fathers greet their sons,
> I put my childish face up to be kissed
> After an absence. The rebuff still stuns
> My blood. The poor man's curt embarrassment
> At such a delicate proffer of affection
> Cut like a saw. But home the lesson went:
> My tenderness thenceforth escaped detection.

James then suggests[351] that, in this seemingly slight poem, there are really two dramas being played out, even relatively early in the poem. The first is the apparent lack of love between his parents and, on attendant lack, between father and son which may have serious consequences for the poet/son at the poem's ultimate conslusion. Although James does not draw that conclusion, as he might, have. The poem ends with an indirect reference to earlier events, after all :

> It's my own judgment day that I draw near,
> Descending in the past, without a clue,
> Down to that central deadness: the despair
> Older than any hope I ever knew.

That final stanza refers particularly to the seventh stanza, which contains, in context, the poem's title and relates it to the situation in which the three protagonists are caught:

> My mother sang *Because*, and *Annie Laurie,*
> *White Wings*, and other songs; her voice was sweet.
> I never gave enough, and I am sorry;
> But we were all closed in the same defeat.

Yet being caught *in the same defeat* does not necessarily imply criticism by the narrator of the other people so trapped and this is admitted, not grudgingly, by the poet in the seventh stanza:

> People do what they can; they were good people,
> They cared for us and loved us. Once they stood
> Tall in my childhood as the school, the steeple.

How can I judge without ingratitude?

According to James,[352] it is the question contained in the last line of that stanza which begins the "wind-up" (in James's words) to the poem. "The narrative is put aside," he writes, "...there was nothing more to be wrung out of it – and the tone suddenly becomes declarative. Young writers who were still learning about the freedoms that verse could allow them could learn from the poem's penultimate stanza that if you got the build-up well enough detailed you could form a climax out of generalities and sound sonorous instead of ponderous." The stanza to which James refers is as follows:

> Judgment is simply trying to reject
> A part of what we are because it hurts.
> The living cannot call the dead collect:
> They won't accept the charge, and it reverts.

James then goes on to agree that whatever McAuley's childhood deprivation may have been, it helped generate a lyricism which was all the more musical for being free of any limit of standardised beautification. "In that regard," James states,[353] "the poem is prosaic: its poetics are without poeticism. But a simpler way of putting it would be to say this is a poem made up out of the fullest possible intensity of prose. Good prose is an arrangement, and a great poem makes the arrangement a part of the subject."

It must be said that James's view of the poem is not shared by every other commentator and James is attempting to make a point about Australian writing at large. Thus, McCredden has taken the view[354] that "Because" is unnecessarily complex and she writes that, "...the reader's confusion must surely be caused by the neatly framed iambic pentameters, as well as the moral platitudes... Taking this drama of rejection and identification at its linguistic level, the pained measuredness of the autobiographical thematics collapses into the measureless failure to answer, failure to signify and failure of self to emerge." She continues by saying that the poem's initial attempts at summarising the parental relationship draw attention to the linguistic platitudes as much as summarising the truth.

Of the two views of the poem, the present writer would incline to that of James, rather than that of McCredden. However, it should be borne in mind that, from the analysis of one poem, James was seeking to make a general point about the importance of Australian prosody.[355] "When McAuley wrote 'Because'," James extrapolates, "he wrote a poem fit to conquer the world, and since then it has; or at any rate the tone of voice exemplified by it has become universally recognisable." But he also states that, on the whole, McAuley's poetry was a "joy-free" zone, but James is of the view that it is individual poems which make an initial impact, rather a body of work. For him, "Because" has had such an impact. The general point which James makes,[356] and it is clearly derived from that last, is that, "A treasure more important than nationalism, a fully developed poetic language is the only patriotism that matters… What it can't do without, what it embodies, is a way of speaking about justice and freedom at once. Not just by luck but by thought and endeavour, Australia is well placed to do that… That important place was as much built as found and McAuley's little poem was one of the things that built it." It may be, in part answer to McCredden's strictures,[357] that the form which McAuley chose for his poem (and I do not find it unduly complex) is to emphasise the ordinariness of the poet's parents' situation.

There are other manifestations of marital dysfunction which are altogether more graphic than that described in "Because" – or even, perhaps, "Eros Turrannos". Probably the most obvious is infidelity, which used to be represented in family law by the matrimonial offence of adultery. However, legislative approaches have radically changed: thus, in Australia, for example, adultery no longer plays any part in the process of dissolution of marriage *per se*.[358] In other jurisdictions, in England for instance, it continues so to remain.[359] However, it is not simply sufficient to prove that the respondent committed adultery, it must additionally be shown that the petitioner finds it intolerable to live with the respondent. There are difficulties in relation to the last requirement: namely, whether the adultery and the intolerability must be connected. In *Roper* v *Roper*,[360] it was held that they need not be. Hence, in the words of Harris-Short and Miles,[361] a wife could take the occurrence of her husband's adultery to get the divorce she always wanted because of the irritating way in which the husband blew his nose. On the other hand, in *Cleary* v *Cleary*,[362] Denning LJ took a contrary view. In his own words, "Take this very case. The husband proves that the wife committed adultery and that he forgave her and took her back. That is one fact. He then proves that after she comes back, she behaves in a way that makes it quite intolerable to live with her. She corresponds with the other man and goes out at night and finally leaves her husband, taking the children with her. That is another fact. It is in consequence of that second fact that he finds it intolerable – not in consequence of the previous adultery." Even before the addition of the second requirement, which was the subject of *Roper* and *Cleary*, problems existed regarding the nature of adultery: in *Dennis* v *Dennis*,[363] Singleton LJ stated that, "I do not think it can be said that adultery is proved unless there is some penetration. It is not necessary that the complete act of sexual intercourse should take place."[364] Note, though should be taken of the comment of Orde J of the Ontario Supreme Court in *Orford* v *Orford*[365] that, "Sexual intercourse is adulterous because in the case of the woman it involves the possibility of introducing into the family of the husband a false strain of blood."

Although, that last statement, made ninety years ago would, in all reasonable probability, not be taken seriously today, it does raise one serious issue which has been taken up by two poets in relatively recent times. That is, that adultery may well have consequences which the people involved have never anticipated or wanted. This theme is especially taken up by the United States poet Donald Hall in his poem, "When the Young Husband", which appeared in 1993. The poem begins with the protagonist collecting his friend's wife for lunch, which, inevitably, is intended as a prelude to an afternoon's adultery. Suddenly, unexpectedly, his car on the way to the assignation is stuck in a traffic jam:

> midtown traffic gridlocked and was abruptly still.
> for one moment before klaxons started honking,
> a prophetic voice spoke in his mind's ear despite
> his pulse's erotic thudding:

The *prophetic voice* describes, in the fourth, fifth and sixth stanzas of this nine stanza poem, the lunch and the immediate aftermath. But the voice is warning from the very outset in the fourth stanza with the grim warning contained in its first two lines:

The misery you undertake this afternoon
will accompany you to the ends of your lives...

Indeed the prophetic narrative has already begun (unlike the traffic) to accelerate: immediately after "...the taxi back, and the furtive kiss of goodbye." The emphasis changes from the description of the squalid encounter to something great verydifferent. By the latter two lines of the sixth stanza where an altogether darker future is presaged:

Then, by turn, treachery, anger, betrayal;
marriages and houses destroyed;

Thereafter, the momentum becomes inexorable: the poem then, from the seventh stanza, disaster is piled upon disaster involving the abandonment of inconsolable children, destruction of property, possessions and wealth, dependence on drugs, alcohol and promiscuity. At this point, the poem's structure is tight, leading the parties to what can only properly be described as a vortex of catastrophe until the final, sudden line:

small children abandoned and inconsolable
their foursquare estates disestablished forever;
the unreadable advocates; the wretchedness
of passion outworn; anguished nights
sleepless in a bare room; whiskey, meth, cocaine; new
love essayed in loneliness with miserable
strangers, that comforts nothing but skin; hours with sons
and daughters studious always
to maintain distrust; the daily desire to die
and the daily agony of the requirement
to survive, until only the quarrel endures.
Prophecy stopped; traffic started.

The prophetic voice ends in desolation with the promise of broken relationships and lives emptied of all useful meaning. What is more, the final line holds out no hope for the protagonist – the traffic has restarted, the prophecy must take its wretched course.

The same theme is taken up by the English poet Carol Anne Duffy in her poem "Adultery",[366] which tells a similar kind of tale. The warning, though, in Duffy's poem is not as sudden, but is more picturesque in it intensity in the first stanza:

> Wear dark glasses in the rain.
> Regard what was unhurt
> as though through a bruise.
> Guilt. A sick, green tint.

The decline she depicts is not so cataclysmic as that depicted by Hall, though, like Hall she describes the taxi back from the assignation to her own married life which, "…crumbles like a wedding cake". The return home is, inevitably, disastrous:

> Then, selfish autobiographical sleep
> in a marital bed, the tarnished spoon of your body
> stirring betrayal, your heart overripe at the core.
> You're an expert, darling; your flowers
> dumb and explicit on nobody's birthday.
>
> So write the script – illness and debt,
> a ring thrown away in a garden
> no moon can heal, your own words
> commuting to bile in your mouth, terror –
>
> and all for the same thing twice. And all
> for the same thing twice. You did it.

Where Duffy's approach differs from Hall's is that the reproach is directed firmly at herself, whereas there cannot really be any reproach, only potential, or more likely, actual disaster as in Hall's *scéne de la vie future*.

The difference between the poet and the lawyer in relation to phenomena of this kind is that it is the function of the poet to analyse it in personal terms, whereas it is the function of the lawyer and her or his apparatus to attempt to do something in personal terms which will prove beneficial to the parties, and others involved and will do so in a manner which gives a broader impression of fairness in a broader context. A useful instance is a case which has already been noted[367] – the decision of Wood SJ of the Family Court of Australia in *In the Marriage of Gillie*.[368] In that case, the wife had applied for an injunction under s 114 of the *Family Law Act* 1975, which gives the Court wide powers to make injunctions in respect to the parties' matrimonial relationship. She sought an order that the husband deliver up possession of the matrimonial home to her so that she could live in it with the children of the marriage. She also sought orders restraining him from entering the premises except for the purpose of access, a further order relieving her from any obligation to perform marital services or render conjugal rights to her husband as well as interim custody of the children and maintenance in respect of them. The wife argued that the husband's conduct towards her had forced her to leave the home and that throughout the marriage she had been frequently assaulted and treated with violence, Conversely, the husband claimed that there was a substantial degree of sexual incompatibility between the parties and that minimal help had been sought to alleviate the situation. He also complained of the wife's admitted adultery shortly before she left the home. The wife earned a good salary as a radiographer, though the husband, who was a self-employed contractor, relied on orders through the telephone at home and his business depended to a large degree on his mental state. The parties had tried to resolve their differences but the wife then had had a brief affair with a work-mate as solace for her unhappiness.

Wood SJ granted the wife the injunction for the order which she had sought. In so doing, he took into account the view which had earlier been expressed by the Full Court of the Family Court of Australia i*n the Marriage of Davis*[369] to the effect that, "…one of the criteria which would justify the exercise of the Court's power under s 114(1) to exclude one spouse from the matrimonial home would include the conduct of one party (where relevant) which may justify the other party in leaving the home or in asking for the expulsion from the home of the first party." Wood SJ continued by saying[370] that the manner in which that *dictum* had been expressed indicated that the conduct involved must be regarded objectively by the Court and that its gravity must be measured after a consideration of all relevant facts including those which constitute provocation or mitigating factors. He concluded[371] that part of his judgment by stating that the assaults perpetrated by the husband after hearing of his wife's adultery, were not justifiable and would, in any event, have entitled the wife to leave the home. Hence, she was entitled to an order relieving her from any obligation to perform marital services or render conjugal rights.

As regards the occupancy of the matrimonial home, some additional considerations, the judge thought, arose in *Gillie*. In *Davis*,[372] it had been said that s 114(1) gave the Court, "...wide power to deal with the use and occupancy of the matrimonial home and make such order as it thinks proper. This power may be exercised even if the home is solely owned by one spouse and where the other spouse has no legal or equitable interest in the home. Where dissolution proceedings are instituted it is appropriate that the question of occupation be considered together with any other maintenance and property issues." In that context, Wood SJ took the view[373] that the means and needs of the parties in seeking possession of the home were of equal weight. However, both parties needed accommodation and, in that sense, the wife was in a better position than that of the husband. Finally, it was said by the Full Court in *Davis*[374] that matters which should be considered included the needs of the children and hardship to either party or the children. In *Gillie*, Wood SJ considered[375] it to be desirable that the children have the best parenting available to them now that their parents have separated. Although, the judge concluded[376] on that issue, "...both [parents] are very depressed and extremely tense as a result of the shattering events of the past few weeks, the mother is showing more resilience and a more realistic appraisal of the situation. That leads me to conclude that the interests of the children are best served if the more stable of the parents resides in the house with them."

He concluded his judgment with a comment[377] on the behaviour of the wife who, he said, was, "...blameworthy by reason of having committed adultery. But it must be allowed that the conduct of her husband had conduced or at least contributed to this state of affairs and she has, as a result of her infidelity, lost a substantial amount of face in the eyes of her children, and has been subjected to anguish as the result of an affair which I think may have brought her some comfort at the time but little joy in the long run." Thus, it does seem as though, in one aspect of family relations at least, poet and judge are, if not in total agreement, at least on the same plane. Although there is little evidence of marital discord having led to the act in Hall's poem, though, it is at least left open in Duffy's, the consequences, though not quite so devastating as those presaged by Hall, are congruent in poetry as in law.

This chapter has, and there are reasons for it, given, I fear, an impression of unrelieved gloom. The reasons are not far to seek: the law deals, in the areas of personal and family relationships with situations which are necessarily pathological. Hence, relationships and families which are not in a pathological state will not come to the attention of the law and its attendant apparatuses and processes. Similarly, it is situations, such as separations or relationship breakdown, which provide material for the poetic imagination. However, it is time to redress the balance.

This is done through the medium of a poem by the noted Australian poet Margaret Scott (1934 – 2005), "Twilight"[378] which is all but wholly idyllic in its portrait of a loving, steady-state relationship:

> The room is quiet, grey with evening silence.
> The hills stoop down to drink the twilight river.
> You sit, placidly reading, eyes hooded.
> My turning is relentless and unperceived
> as the coming of darkness.
> You have never been faithless, never angry or jealous.
> Civility has stroked the air to silver.
> Habitual kindness lies on our home like dust.
> When you turn the page, your hand glimmers a moment
> with light from a distant, half-imagined star.
> Children's cries from the city drift up muted,
> meaningless as the words we'll speak when I rise
> to cross the room, switch on the reading lamp,
> and stand beside you, ringed about by shadows.

The poem exudes an aura of gentleness which, in the end is productive of regeneration in the form of the children's cries. It might be argued that there is no reference to law in the poem at all; however, that would not be correct. The phrase "habitual kindness" stands in contradistinction to the ground for divorce in Australia of *habitual cruelty*[379] with which both the poet and her subject would have been familiar. In addition, it is clear from other of Margaret Scott's poems, that the subject was a legal scholar.[380] The partnership, in love, law and poetry of two skilled in law and poetry as represented in "Twilight" is as effective an antidote to much of the rest of the chapter as there is possible to be.

---

[1] *The Other Country* (1990).
[2] F Bates, " 'Which Comforts While it Mocks': Some Paradoxes in Modern Family Law" (2000) 4 (2) *Newcastle LR* 17
[3] L Brown (Ed.) *The New Shorter English Dictionary on Historical Principles* (1993) at 2003.
[4] Ibid
[5] R Davis, *100 Years: A Centenary History of the Faculty of Law, University of Tasmania 1893 – 1993* (1993) at 65.
[6] O M Stone, "Family Law" in "Symposium on the Teaching of Various Subjects" (1953) 3 *JSPTL* 107 at 113
[7] O M Stone, "University Teaching of Family Law" (1960) 5 *JSPTL* 130.
[8] Ibid at 139.
[9] J Austin, *The Province of Jurisprudence Determined* (1832) at 184.
[10] GWF Hegel, *Outlines of the Philosophy of Right* (1821) para 331
[11] H Kelsen, *General Theory of Law and State* (1945, Trs Wedberg) at 369.
[12] K O'Donovan, "Family Law and Legal Theory" in *Legal Theory and Common Law* (1986) at 185.
[13] A Watson, The Nature of Law (1977) at 96.
[14] P Stein and J Shand, *Legal Values in Western Society* (1974) at 21.
[15] (1999) FLC 92-837. For comment on this on related cases, see F Bates, "Children and Family Violence in Australia: An Aberation in the Law Reform Process" (2005) 13 *Asia Pacific LR* 63
[16] (1999) FLC 92-837 at 85,743.
[17] Ibid t 85, 745.
[18] *Family Law Act* 1975, as amended in 1995, ss 68F (2) (g), (h) and (i).
[19] Author's emphasis.
[20] (1994) FLC 92-515 at 81,317. See also the comments of Baker J in *Patsalou and Patsalou* (1995) FLC 92-580 at 81,752.
[21] Chilsom J did continue, in *JG and BG* by saying, (1994) FLC 92-515 at 81,317, that, "It is equally wrong to assume that violent behaviour will be repeated, or to assume too readily that it will harm children, or to give it excessive importance..."
[22] (1999) FLC 92-837 at 85,745.
[23] Ibid at 85,746.
[24] Lindenmayer J's emphasis.
[25] R Alexander, *Domestic Violence in Australia* (3rd Ed, 2002) at 8.
[26] Ibid at 9.
[27] (1999) FLC 92-837 at 85,749.
[28] Ibid at 85,749.
[29] Ibid at 85,748.
[30] (2000) FLC 93-006 at 87, 159.
[31] Mullane J concluded, ibid, that part of his judgment in *M* in terms still more redolent of what he had said in *Blanch*, above text at n 29, by saying that, "...such a disability would mar his dealing and relationships with others, including those he loves, bring him into contact with the police, the Courts and the Community, and result in him being penalised and even being imprisoned."
[32] R S Kempe and C H Kempe, *Child Abuse* (1978) at 24.
[33] Above text at n 13.
[34] Above n 12 at 185.
[35] J D McClean, "The Battered Baby and the Limits of the Law" (1978) 5 *Monash ULR* 1 at 15.
[36] (2003) FLC 93-172.
[37] For a discussion of the operation of these orders see above n 25 at 104 *ff*.
[38] (2003) FLC 93-172 at 78,762.
[39] Ibid at 78,757.

[40] Ibid at 78,757.
[41] See *M v M* (1989) 166 CLR 69.
[42] (2003) FLC 93-172 at 78,760.
[43] Ibid at 78,761.
[44] (1992) FLC 92-303. For comment on the aftermath of that decision in the later case of *Fitzgibbon v Barker, Gardner and Leader Associated Newspapers*; *Re Schwarzkopff* (1993) FLC 92-381, see F Bates, "Scandalising the Court: Some Peculiarly Australian Developments" (1994) 13 *Civil Justice* Q 241.
[45] Barblett DCJ, Fogarty and Moore JJ.
[46] (1992) FLC 92-303 at 79,291.
[47] For a Canadian case which provided an analogous factual situation and, additionally, children see *Plesh v Plesh* (1992) 41 RFL (3d) 102. For comment, see F Bates, "Finding the Truth in Child Sexual Abuse Cases: Some Comparative Developments" (1993) 5 *J Child L* 178.
[48] Above n 12 at 186.
[49] J Dewar, "The Concepts, Coherence and Contact of Family Law" in *Examining the Law Syllabus: The Core* (Ed Birks 1992) at 81.
[50] Above n 2 at 22 *ff*.
[51] *Family Law Act* 1975 s 64 (1) (a).
[52] Ibid s 64 (i) (b).
[53] Ibid s 64 (2) (c).
[54] For comment, see F Bates, "Blunting the Sword of Solomon – Australian Family Law in 2006" in *International Survey of Family Law* (Ed Atkin 2008) 21.
[55] Above n 49 at 81.
[56] Such a code is impossible, apart from the State of Western Australia, in Australia for constitutional reasons, See L Young and G Monahan, *Family Law in Australia* (7th Ed 2009) at 96 *ff*.
[57] See ibid at 532 *ff*.
[58] Above n 2 at 25 *ff*.
[59] Above text at n 49
[60] J Dewar, "The Normal Chaos of Family Law" (1998) 61 *MLR* 467 at 484.
[61] Ibid at 485
[62] Ibid at 485.
[63] (1992) 175 CLR 621.
[64] Above text at n 60.
[65] Above n 2.
[66] In the words of Deane J (1992) 175 CLR 621 at 636, "In 1985, the respondent, who is a solicitor, was in his early forties. After two unsuccessful marriages, he was living in rented accommodation in Adelaide with the three children of his first marriage. Putting to one side an old car, a Chipmunk aeroplane (worth less than $30,000) and a share in a house owned with other members of his family in Tasmania, his net assets totalled less than $100,000. The appellant, who had been married and divorced, was living in Adelaide with her two children in a rented house owned by her sister's husband. She had few assets of her own and was living in straitened circumstances."
[67] Mason CJ, Brennan, Deane, Dawson, Gaudron and McHugh JJ.
[68] Toohey J.
[69] (1992) 175 CLR 621 at 637.
[70] Ibid at 638.
[71] (1956) 99 CLR 632 at 405.
[72] (1992) 175 CLR 621 at 638.
[73] Above text at n 71 *ff*.
[74] (1983) 151 CLR 447.
[75] Ibid at 467.
[76] Ibid at 474.
[77] Ibid at 476.

[78] Mason, Wilson and Deane JJ.
[79] (1983) 151 CLR 447 at 462.
[80] (1992) 175 CLR 621 at 628.
[81] (1983) 151 CLR 447 at 462.
[82] (1992) 175 CLR 621 at 629.
[83] Ibid at 630.
[84] (1848) 11 Beav. 227 at 235.
[85] (1992) 175 CLR 621 at 644.
[86] Ibid at 631.
[87] [1923] NZLR 1106 at 1109.
[88] (1992) 175 CLR 621 at 632.
[89] Above text at nn 68, 85.
[90] P Radan and C Stewart, *Principles of Australian Equity and Trusts* (2010) at 237.
[91] Above text at n 71 *ff*.
[92] Above text at n 74 *ff*.
[93] (1992) 175 CLR 621 at 651.
[94] Toohey J also noted, ibid, that the respondent continued, whatever the limitations imposed upon him by the appellant, to involve himself in her domestic life and the two families seemed to have had a close relationship.
[95] Ibid at 652.
[96] A Mr Volkhardt, who was the appellant's brother in law.
[97] (1992) 175 CLR 621 at 652.
[98] Ibid at 653.
[99] Ibid at 654.
[100] Above text at n 87.
[101] Ibid.
[102] (1992) 175 CLR 621 at 654.
[103] That stands in contradistinction to legislation which allows courts to exercise a wide discretion to control contracts which appear to be harsh, oppressive, unjust or unconscionable. For a review of such legislation, see M Cope, *Duress, Undue Influence and Unconscientious Bargains* (1985) at 188.
[104] Above text at n 74.
[105] (1948) 76 CLR 646.
[106] (1992) 175 CLR 621 at 655.
[107] Above text at n 95.
[108] A J Duggan, "Unconscientious Dealing" in *The Principles of Equity* (Ed. Parkinson, 2nd Ed, 2003) 127 at 133.
[109] Below text at n 115 *ff*.
[110] R P Meagher, J D Heydon and M Leeming, *Equity: Doctrines and Remedies* (4th Ed, 2002) at 526.
[111] M Evans, *Equity and Trusts* (3rd Ed, 2003) at 194.
[112] G Dal Pont and T Cockburn, *Equity and Trusts in Principle* (2004) at 124.
[113] S Hepburn, *Principles of Equity and Trusts* (2nd Ed, 2001) at 149.
[114] Above n 90 at 238.
[115] L Sarmas, "Storytelling and the Law: A Case Study of *Louth* v *Diprose*" (1994) 19 *Melbourne ULR* 701.
[116] Ibid at 728.
[117] Ibid at 702.
[118] For some general comment on legal storytelling, see, for example, M Scheppele, "Forward: Telling Stories (1989) *Michigan LR* 2073; R Delgado, "When a Story is Just a Story: Does Voice Really Matter?" (1990) 76 *Virginia LR* 95; J W Singer, "Persuasion" (1989) 87 *Michigan LR* 2442; S Winter, "The Cognitive Dimension of the *Agon* Between Legal Power and Narrative Meaning" (1989) 87 *Michigan LR* 2228; M Matsuda, "Looking to the Bottom: Critical Legal

Studies and Reparations" (1987) 22 *Harvard Civil Rights – Civil Liberties* LR 323. A more detailed list can be found at above n 115 at 201 n 3.

[119] See, for example, A Hunt, "The Big Fear: Law Confronts Postmodernism" (1990) 35 *McGill LJ* 507; A Hutchinson, "Inessentially Speaking (Is there Politics After Postmodernism?)" (1991) 91 *Michigan LR* 1549.

[120] Above n 115 at 703.

[121] See R Delgado, "Storytelling for Opportunists and Others: A Plea for Narrative" (1989) 87 *Michigan LR* 2411.

[122] Above n 115 at 703.

[123] See above text at n 119 *ff*. That is, stories which are part of, and reinforce, the dominant discourse.

[124] Above n 115 at 718.

[125] Ibid at 719.

[126] Ibid at 720.

[127] Sarmas's emphasis.

[128] (1992) 175 CLR 621 at 639.

[129] Above n 115 at 721.

[130] Above text at n 124.

[131] Above n 115 at 721.

[132] (1956) 99 CLR 362. Above text at n 71 *ff*.

[133] (1948) 76 CLR 646. Above text at n 105.

[134] (1983) 151 CLR 447. Above text at n 74 *ff*.

[135] Above n 115 at 722.

[136] Sarmas, ibid n 144, points to the issue of "sexually transmitted debt," where women are left bearing the burden of debts left by their male partners as the result of having signed guarantees on their behalf.

[137] Above n 115 at 723.

[138] Sarmas's emphasis.

[139] See, for example, the comments of Deane J above text at n 72.

[140] Above n 115 at 724.

[141] Above text at n 93.

[142] Above text at n 121.

[143] "Back-fired" in Sarmas's own word.

[144] Above n 115 at 724.

[145] Ibid at 725.

[146] M Fajer, "Can Two Real Men Eat Quiche Together? Storytelling, Gender-Role Stereotypes and Legal Protection for Lesbians and Gay Men" (1992) 46 *U Miami LR* 511.

[147] R Delgado, "Storytelling for Opportunists and Others: A Plea for Narrative" (1989) 87 *Michigan LR* 2411.

[148] Above n 115 at 725. She relies on R Delgado and J Stefencic, "Norms and Narratives: Can Judges Avoid Serious Moral Error?" (1991) 69 *Texas LR* 1929.

[149] Ibid at 726.

[150] Sarmas also notes, ibid n 156, that that process should not be seen in isolation from non-legal areas of activity, such as direct and indirect political action, educational campaigning and the like.

[151] Above text at n 120.

[152] Above n 115 at 727.

[153] See, for example, A Harris, "Race and Existentialism in Feminist Legal Theory" (1990) 42 *Stanford LR* 581; M Matsuda, "Pragmatism Modified and the False Consciousness Problem" (1990) 63 S *California LR* 1763; R Delgado, "When a Story Is Just a Story: Does Voice Really Matter?" (1990) 76 *Virginia LR* 95; R Kennedy, "Racial Critiques of Legal Academia" (1989) 102 *Harvard LR* 1745.

[154] Above n 115 at 727.

[155] J Freeman, "Constitutive Rhetoric: Law as a Literary Activity" (1991) 14 *Harvard Women's LJ* 305.
[156] Above n 115 at 728.
[157] A Bottomley, "Self and Subjectivities; Languages of Claim in Property Law" (1993) 20 *J Law and Society* 56 at 58.
[158] Above n 115 at 728.
[159] Sarmas's emphasis.
[160] A Hutchinson, "Initially Speaking (Is There Politics After Postmodernism?) (1991) 89 *Michigan LR* 1549 at 1568.
[161] See above text at n 126.
[162] See below Ch II at n 76.
[163] [1977] QB 966.
[164] P Heerey, "Truth, Lies and Stereotype: Stories of Mary and Louis" (1996) 1 (3) *Newcastle LR* 1.
[165] Ibid at 1.
[166] In addition to Sarmas, above n 115, see D Otto, "A Barren Future? Equity's Conscience and Women's Inequality" (1991) 18 *Melbourne ULR* 808: S Hepburn, "Equity and Infatuation" (1993) 18 *Alternative LJ* 208.
[167] Ibid at 2.
[168] Ibid at 13 *ff*.
[169] Above text at n 115 *ff*.
[170] Author's emphasis.
[171] Heerey refers, above n 164 at 17 n 59, to Aboriginal land claims, which are frequently conducted *in situ*.
[172] Above n 164 at 17.
[173] Ibid.
[174] (1993) 49 CLR 426 at 446.
[175] G Williams, *The Proof of Guilt: A Study of the English Criminal Trial* (3rd Ed 1963) at 195.
[176] Above n 164 at 19.
[177] See *Kelleher v R* (1974) 131 CLR 534; *R v Henry* (1968) 53 Cr App Rep 150.
[178] See *Longman v R* (1980) 168 CLR 79.
[179] Notably the evidence of accomplices, see *Davis v DPP* [1954] AC 378 at 400 *per* Lord Simonds LC; *Sneddon v Stevenson* [1967] 1 WLR 1051 at 1058 *per* Walker J.
[180] *More probable than not* is the standard of proof in civil cases, more usually referred to as the *balance (or preponderance) of probabilities*. See F Bates, " 'Strength or Intensity?' Some Reflections on the Modern Standard of Proof in Civil Cases" (1978) 27 *Chitty's Law Journal* 335.
[181] Above n 164 at 20.
[182] *Louth v Diprose* (1990) 54 SASR 438 at 480.
[183] Above n 164 at 20.
[184] Ibid at 19
[185] Author's emphasis.
[186] Above text at n 183.
[187] Above n 164 at 20.
[188] Ibid at 21.
[189] Ibid at 21.
[190] *Louth v Diprose* (1990) 54 SASR 438 at 447.
[191] Above text at n 126.
[192] Above text at n 125.
[193] Above n 164 at 22.
[194] Ibid at 24.
[195] For a description of the alleged incident, see ibid at 23.
[196] Above n 164 at 26.
[197] Ibid at 27.

[198] Above text at n 183.
[199] Above n 164 at 28.
[200] At the relevant time, the appellant was aged 41 and the respondent 43.
[201] Above n 164 at 28.
[202] Above n 115 at 720. Above text at n 127.
[203] Above n 164 at 28.
[204] Above text at n 188.
[205] Above text at n 153.
[206] Above n 164 at 29.
[207] Above text at n 174.
[208] Above n 164 at 30.
[209] Ibid at 31.
[210] Above text at n 118.
[211] L Sarmas, "A Response to Justice Peter Heerey" (1998) 3 (1) *Newcastle LR* 82.
[212] Above text at n 209.
[213] Above n 211 at 85.
[214] Ibid at 86 *ff*.
[215] Ibid at 87.
[216] Notably at above text at n 175 *ff*.
[217] Above n 211 at 87.
[218] Samaras's emphasis.
[219] Above n 211 at 89.
[220] Above text at n 207.
[221] Above text at n 195.
[222] Above n 211 at 89.
[223] Ibid at 90.
[224] Sarmas's emphasis.
[225] Above n 211 at 90.
[226] Author's emphasis.
[227] See, for example, R Graycar and J Morgan, *The Hidden Gender of Law* (1990) at 69 *ff*.
[228] Above n 211 at 91.
[229] Above text at n 201 *ff*.
[230] Above text at n 167.
[231] Above n 211 at 91.
[232] Ibid at 92.
[233] Above text at n 209.
[234] Above n 211 at 93.
[235] M Thornton, "Discord in the Legal Academy: The Case of the Feminist Scholar" (1993) 3 *Aust. Feminist LJ* 53.
[236] (1998) 194 CLR 457.
[237] It should be noted that the majority ordered that the amount stipulated in the deed of forgiveness be invalidated, but not the purchase of the land. The matter was, thus, remitted to the Supreme Court of Queensland to determine the amount to be forgiven from the purchase debt after taking account of the adequate provision for the wife and daughters from that property.
[238] A Finlay, "Can We See the Chancellor's Footprint: *Bridgewater* v *Leahy*" (1999) 14 *J Contract L* 265.
[239] (1998) 194 CLR 457 at 474.
[240] Above text at 167 *ff*.
[241] Above text at n 118 *ff*.
[242] Above text at n 194.
[243] Above Ch II text at n 107.
[244] Ibid text at n 135.
[245] Above text at n 165.

[246] Above text at 156
[247] Above text at 191.
[248] This is a rule whereby the whole of an inheritance of land descends entirely to the eldest son to the exclusion of all other relatives. It survived, long after its rationale had ceased, until 1926 in England.
[249] In *Chard* v *Chard* [1956] P 259 at 272, Sachs LJ stated that, "Where as regards AB there is no affirmative evidence that he was alive at some time during a continuous period of seven years or more, then, if it can be proved that there are persons who would be likely to have heard of him over that period, secondly that those persons have not heard of him, and thirdly that all due inquiries have been made appropriate to the circumstances, AB will be presumed to have died at some time during the period." For comment, see G H Treitel, "The Presumption of Death" (1954) 17 *MLR* 530.
[250] Above text at n 174.
[251] S Fry, *The Ode Not Taken: Unlocking the Poet Within* (2007) at 281. Fry goes on to discuss the differences between the *Petrarchean* and the *Shakespearian* sonnet as well as variants such as the *curtal* and *caudate* sonnets.
[252] M Schmidt, *The Great Modern Poets: An Anthology of the Best Poets and Poetry Since 1990* (2006) at 77.
[253] Ibid.
[254] For another instance of Millay's approaches to nature, see the discussion of "The Fawn", below Ch III text at n 199. The comments made by Schmidt are applicable to both poems and so should be immediately applied to both.
[255] Above text at n 12.
[256] H Bloom, *Till I End My Song: A Gathering of Last Poems* (2010) at 211.
[257] M Van Doren, *Edwin Arlington Robinson* (1927) at 30.
[258] Ibid at 33. Robinson has, "...indicated the delicate balance which the universe seems to preserve between good and evil, between day and night, between light and dark, between beauty and deformity, between music and noise."
[259] My colleague and co-author in other enterprises, Dr Ronan McGinty, has described Robinson's artistic quality as an exploration of the deepest parts of human misery through an examination of particular individuals. Van Doren though, ibid at 32, suggests that Robinson is, "...as far as anyone from the cheaper varieties of gloom."
[260] E Barnard, "Robinson's Literary Reputation" in *Edwin Arlington Robinson: Centenary Essays* (Ed Barnard. 1969) 1 at 2.
[261] Ibid at 5.
[262] Ibid at 2.
[263] Ibid at 2.
[264] Ibid at 3.
[265] Ibid at 9.
[266] "In contrast," Barnard writes, "contemporary poetry and contemporary criticism have generally not been concerned with people as such, but have preferred fleshless mythic figures in symbolic garb." In passing that comment, Barnard, ibid at 10, makes a useful statement regarding approaches to "Eros Turannos."
[267] Y Winters, "A Cool Master" in *Edwin Arlington Robinson: A Collection of Critical Essays* (Ed Murphy 1970) 8 at 9.
[268] M D Zabel, "Robinson in America" in, ibid, 29 at 31.
[269] Below text at n 289
[270] Above n 268.
[271] In Zabel's own words, above n 268 at 32, "He writes searching judgments, not only on tragedies of love, jealousy and envy but also on the crimes of imperialism, the folly of the Eighteenth Amendment and the toppling recklessness of industrial inflation."
[272] The ending of "Eros Turannos", will be discussed below, text at n 344 "The Sheaves" ends with the following lines:
So in a land where all days are not fair,

> Fair days went on till on another day
> A thousand golden sheaves were lying there,
> Shining and still, but not for long to stay –
> As if a thousand girls with golden hair
> Might rise from where they slept and go away.

[273] Above n 260 at 14.
[274] Above text at n 273.
[275] Above text at n 255.
[276] Above text at n 256.
[277] R Squires, "Tilbury Town Today" in above n 260, 175 at 183.
[278] R D Stevick, "The Metrical Style of E A Robinson" ibid, 54 at 56.
[279] Above text at n 268.
[280] Above n 279.
[281] Above n 260.
[282] Y Winters, "The Shorter Poems" in above n 267, 40 at 42.
[283] See below text at n 286 *ff*.
[284] L O Coxe, "The Lost Tradition" in above n 267, 60 at 65.
[285] Above n 284.
[286] Above n 285 at 30.
[287] Ibid at 67.
[288] Ibid at 66.
[289] Ibid at 67.
[290] Ibid at 70.
[291] F Bates, " 'We Prize Not to the Worth' – Some Thoughts on the Valuation of Property Under the Family Law Act" (2005) 7 (2) *Newcastle LR* 35, in which reference is made to the fifth stanza.
[292] F Bates, "On the Mat and Up the Wall" (2005) XLIX (10) *Quadrant* 44, in which reference is made to the sixth stanza.
[293] Above text at n 274 *ff*.
[294] Coxe, above n 285 at 70, likens it to *Madame Bovary*.
[295] Above text at n 13 *ff*. To them, one might also add the overtly theocratic Finnis, see J Finnis, *Natural Law and Natural Rights* (1990), who holds views not dissimilar from the other commentators, though he approaches the matter from a rather different standpoint. For comment, see F bates, "Some Theoretical Aspects of Modern Family Law" (1984) 100 *South African LJ* 664.
[296] Above text at n 15 *ff*.
[297] See, for example, F Bates, "Artificial Families – Upside Down? A View from Australia" [2004] *International Fam L.* 82.
[298] William Davenant, (1606 – 1668), "The Christian's Reply to the Philosopher".
[299] Above text at n 15 *ff*.
[300] Richard Wilbur (1921), "The Winter".
[301] T S Eliot (1888-1965) "Burnt Norton" from *Four Quartets* (1936).
[302] Above n 285 at 65.
[303] Ibid at 66.
[304] Above n 291.
[305] Above n 279 at 55.
[306] Ibid at 57.
[307] (1993) FLC 92-381.
[308] Above n 44.
[309] Above text at n 44
[310] The comments made by the Full Court of the Family Court of Australia regarding the husband's behaviour are set out above text at n 45.
[311] Above text at n 46.

[312] This matter had also been earlier referred to by Woods J of the Family Court of Australia in *In the Marriage of Gillie* (1978) FLC 90 – 442 at 77,260, who had said that the husband in that case, "…unfortunately can see little wrong in his conduct towards his wife which this court in this day and age must condemn. Violence of a kind which he has practised towards his wife is totally out of keeping with present norms in society, and the civilised, behaviour which is to be expected between people, and in particular between husband and wife."

[313] F B Cobbe, (1878) 32 *The Contemporary Review* 57. For more detailed commentary on that article, see F Bates, "The Family and Society: Reality and Myth" (1980) 15 (n.s.) *Irish Jurist* 195 at 200 *ff*.

[314] Above n 285 at 66.

[315] Ibid at 66.

[316] [1973] 3 All ER 750.

[317] Ibid at 753.

[318] In the event, the Court of Appeal decided that the fact that the wife was living in the same house as her husband did not prelude her from petitioning for divorce under the legislation as it existed in England.

[319] (1818) 2 Hag Con 238 at 248. For general comment, see A Dickey, *Family Law* (5th Ed, 2007) at 153 *ff*.

[320] (1977) FLC 90-252. For comment, see F Bates, "Consent to Marriage Obtained by Fraud – A New Development" (1978) 128 *New LJ* 403.

[321] Ibid at 76, 355.

[322] In Australia, see, for example, see *In the Marriage of Otway* (1987) FLC 91-807; *In the Marriage of Osman and Mourrali* (1989) 96 FLR 362.

[323] See, for example, in Canada, *Iantsis* v *Papapatheodrou* (1971) 15 DLR (3d) 53.

[324] Above text at n 322 *ff*.

[325] Above text at n 290.

[326] Above text at n 299.

[327] (1976) FLC 90-028.

[328] See *Family Law Act* 1975 ss 48, 49.

[329] (1976) FLC 90-028 at 75,122.

[330] *In the Marriage of Tye (No 2)* (1976) FLC 90-048.

[331] Ibid at 75,202 *per* Evatt CJ, Demack and Watson JJ. That Court upheld the trial judge's findings on maintenance.

[332] Above n 285 at 67.

[333] Ibid at 68.

[334] See above text at n 117 *ff*.

[335] (2002) FLC 93-104. For a differently focussed commentary, see F. Bates, "Transition and Translation in Literature and Law – *Eros Turanos* Revisited" (2008) 18 *Caribbean LR* 1.

[336] Finn, Kay and O'Ryan JJ. For more detailed commentary see above n 292.

[337] (2002) FLC 93-104 at 88 893.

[338] Ibid at 88,986.

[339] See above n 292

[340] See above n 278 at 183.

[341] Above n 279 at 56.

[342] *In Children of the Night* (1890-1897).

[343] Above n 285 at 68.

[344] This is an especially grim instance and is derived from "The Banquet [15]" in *Poems for SJ* (1971). The poem is as follows:

> You brought me a bouquet, salt with brine.
> Neither was it your fault. The sea is salt.
>
> The sea is darker than anyone dares to know
> The lights more bright for vaster distances.

[345] Above n 293.

[346] Above n 283 at 12.
[347] Above n 285 at 76.
[348] C James, "There You Come Home" (2011) LV (4) *Quadrant* 12 at 12.
[349] Ibid.
[350] Ibid.
[351] Ibid at 13.
[352] Ibid.
[353] Ibid.
[354] L McCredden, *James McAuley* (1992) at 82.
[355] Above n 349 at 14.
[356] Ibid
[357] Above text at n 355.
[358] See *Family Law Act* 1975 ss 48, 49.
[359] *Matrimonial Causes Act* 1973 s 12(a).
[360] [1972] 1 WLR 1314.
[361] S Harris-Short and J Miles, *Family Law: Text Cases and Materials* (2007) at 251.
[362] [1974] 1 WLR 73 at 76.
[363] [1955] P 153 at 160.
[364] See also *Locke* v *Locke* (1956) 95 CLR 165; *McKinnon* v *McKinnon* [1942] SASR 107; *McLellan* v *McLennan* 1958 SC 105.
[365] (1921) 58 DLR 251 at 258.
[366] In *Mean Time* (1993).
[367] Above n 313.
[368] (1978) FLC 90-442.
[369] (1976) FLC 90-062 at 75,309 *per* Evatt CJ, Powley and Ellis JJ.
[370] (1978) FLC 90-4442 at 77,257.
[371] Ibid at 77,259.
[372] (1976) FLC 90-062 at 75,309.
[373] (1978) FLC 90-442 at 77,259.
[374] (1967) FLC 90-062 at 75,309.
[375] (1978) FLC 90-442 at 77,259.
[376] Ibid at 77,260.
[377] Ibid at 77,261.
[378] From *Visited* (1983).
[379] *Matrimonial Causes Act* 1959 s 28 (d). For comment on the operation of that provision see F Bates, "Habitual Cruelty – The Right Approach?" (1973) 47 *Aust LJ* 30.
[380] See, To a Scholar's Ghost" in *Tricks of Memory* (1980), "Elegies M.F.C.S. 1928-1984" in *The Black Swans* (1988). For comment on his academic career, see R Davis, above n 5 at 58, F.Bates, "In Memory of Michael Scott" (1984) 8 U *Tasmania LR* 1.

Chapter VII
Accidents, Neighbours and other Nuisances

1. Accidents

"The word 'accident'", said Lord Lindley in *Fenton* v *Thorley*,[1] "is not a technical legal term with a clearly defined meaning. Speaking generally, but with reference to legal liabilities, an accident means any unintended and unexpected occurrence which produces hurt or loss. But it is often used to denote an unexpected loss or hurt apart from its cause; and if the cause is not known, the loss or hurt itself would certainly be called an accident. The word 'accident' is also often used to denote both the cause and the effect, no attempt being made to discriminate between them. The great majority of what are called accidents are occasioned by carelessness; but for legal purposes it is often important to distinguish careless from other unintended and unexpected events." In *Fenton* v *Thorley*, a workman employed by the respondents in their machinery shop ruptured himself by an act of over-exertion in trying to turn a wheel. The House of Lords held that the workman had suffered an, "…injury by accident as was required by relevant legislation,[2] with Lord Lindley also noting that the word *accident* had been used extremely loosely in that legislation. Lord Lindley also stated[3] that, it was, "…impossible to read the Act without coming to the conclusion that the object of the Legislature was to throw upon certain classes of employers of labour the obligation to compensate their workmen for personal injuries for which such employers were not responsible before, and it becomes necessary to determine what injuries are within the Act and what are not."

Hence, it was the legislation which provided the appellant in *Fenton* v *Thorley* with a remedy – if there had not been legislation, or if it had been differently framed, the result might very well have been different. Another, well-known, decision provides a valuable example. In *Palsgraf* v *Long Island Railroad Co*,[4] the plaintiff was standing on a platform of the defendant's railroad after having bought a ticket. A train bound for another destination stopped at the station. Two men ran to catch it. One of the men reached the platform of the car without mishap, even though the train was already moving. The other man, carrying a package, jumped aboard the car, but seemed unsteady as if about to fall. A guard on the car, who had held the door open, reached forward to help him in, and another guard on the platform pushed him from behind. In this act, the parcel was dislodged and fell upon the rails. It was a package of small size, about fifteen inches long, and was covered in a newspaper. In fact, it contained fireworks, but there was nothing in its appearance to give notice of its contents. The fireworks, when they fell, exploded. The shock of the explosion threw down some scales at the other end of the platform many feet away. The scales struck the plaintiff, who sued the railroad company. The New York Court of Appeals held that the company was not liable as there was no breach of duty to the plaintiff herself. Cardozo CJ, a judge of international standing,[5] stated[6] that, "The conduct of the defendant's guard, if a wrong in relation to the holder of the package, was not a wrong in relation to the plaintiff standing far away. Relative to her it was not negligence at all... What the plaintiff must show is 'a wrong' to herself; i.e. a violation of her own right... The risk reasonably to be perceived defines the duty to be obeyed..." Yet, of course, there may be other issues involved: Cardozo CJ seemed to regard *policy* as central to the necessary decision, when he said[7] that, "A different conclusion will involve us, and swiftly too, in a maze of contradictions. A guard stumbles over a package which has been left upon a platform. It seems to be a bundle of newspapers. It turns out to be a can of dynamite. To the eye of ordinary vigilance, the bundle is abandoned waste which may be kicked or trod on with impurity...[The] orbit of the danger as disclosed to the eye of reasonable vigilance would be the orbit of the duty... The wrongdoer as to them is the man who carries the bomb not the one who explodes it without suspicion of the danger. Life will have to be made over, and human nature transformed, before prevision so extravagant can be accepted as the norm of conduct, the customary standard to which behaviour must conform."

Smith, though, seems to suggest[8] that *Palsgraf* might not be described in the same way today because courts are willing to limit the ambit of liability to the confines of the original risk, which was damage to the package which the guard's negligent conduct caused. Although, he goes on, courts may pay up lip–service to a doctrine which he calls *privily of fault*. But they will then go on to find the damage to persons, who would not fall within that initial risk, to be reasonably foreseeable if they find the damage, for unarticulated reasons, not to be too remote. Even if the damage does fall within the risk, courts will even then conclude that it is *not* reasonably foreseeable if for other unarticulated reasons, they consider the damage to be too remote. With respect to that learned commentator, one suspects that Cardozo CJ had actually dealt with that issue in his judgment, when he stated [9] that, "The law of causation, remote or proximate, is thus foreign to the cause before us. The question of liability is always anterior to the question of the measure of the consequences that go with liability. If there is no tort to be redressed, there is no occasion to consider what damage might be recovered if there were a finding of a tort." In other words, there was no duty to *that* plaintiff in *those* circumstances.

There was, as might have been expected from the *prima facie* risible factual situation in *Palsgraf*, a dissent by Andrews J who took a rather different view of the function of tort law than had Cardozo CJ. "Every one owes to the world at large," Andrews J stated,[10] "the duty of refraining from those acts that may unreasonably threaten the safety of others . Such an act occurs, Not only is he wronged to whom harm might reasonably be expected to result but he also is in fact injured, even if he is outside what would generally be thought to be outside the danger zone. There needs to be duty due to the one complaining, but this is not duty to a particular individual because as to him harm might be expected. Harm to some one being the natural result of the act, not only that one alone, but all those in fact injured may complain." Again, Cardozo CJ appears to have headed off that particular line of reasoning when he suggested[11] that, were it to be accepted, life would have to be made over!

Other complexities – legislation and the plaintiff's relative position notwithstanding – may arise. The English case of *Roberts v Ramsbottom*[12] provides an instance of where the balancing of various criteria must be undertaken by the courts. In that case, the defendant had, unknown to himself, suffered a cerebral haemorrhage, entered and drove his car on an urban road. He was unaware that he was unfit to drive throughout the processes involved, even though his consciousness was impaired or clouded. He did, though, have some awareness of his surroundings and the traffic conditions and made a series of deliberate and voluntary, even though they were inefficient, movements with his hands and legs so as to manipulate the controls of the car. He, suddenly, experienced feelings of disorientation and collided with a stationary van. Still unaware that he was unfit to drive, he drove away and then collided with a vehicle which was parked at the roadside on his rear side. As a result, the parked vehicle was damaged and the driver and a passenger were injured, The plaintiffs, who were the vehicle owner, the driver and the passenger, claimed damages from the defendant for loss and personal injuries caused by his negligent driving. The defendant denied negligence and pleaded that he was acting in a state of automatism and, hence, was not responsible for his actions.

Neill J gave judgment for the plaintiffs. As regards the applicable law, the first point made by the judge[13] was that the standard of care by which a driver's actions were to be judged in an action based on negligence was an objective standard. Neill J based his view on a comment made by Lord Denning MR in *Nettleship* v *Weston*,[14] where it had been said that every driver, including a learner driver, "...must drive in as good a manner as a driver of skill, experience and care, who is sound in wind and limb, who makes no errors of judgment, has good eyesight and hearing and is free from any infirmity..."[15] *Nettleship* v *Weston* is, for the purpose of the instant discussion, an important decision because, in *Roberts* v *Ramsbottom*, Neill J placed considerable reliance on it.

In *Nettleship* v *Weston*, the plaintiff, who was an experienced driver, agreed to give a friend's wife some driving lessons in her husband's car after satisfying himself that the car was insured against risk of injury to a passenger, He took the wife out on the road and found her to be an assiduous learner, However, on the third occasion, when she was holding the steering wheel and controlling the pedals and he was moving the gear lever and the handbrake, she failed to straighten out after turning left, and panicked, Despite the fact that the car was moving at walking pace and the plaintiff's efforts to straighten out, the car mounted the kerb and struck a lamp standard. The plaintiff sustained injuries, including a broken knee-cap. The learner was subsequently convicted of driving without due care and attention. The plaintiff then brought an action for damages in respect of the learner's negligence. The defendant denied negligence, alleged contributory negligence and, alternatively, claimed that the plaintiff had implicitly consented to run the risk of injury. At first instance, the plaintiff's claim was dismissed on the grounds, *inter alia*, that the plaintiff had voluntarily assumed the risk of injury and that, in any event, the learner was not in breach of the only duty to her instructor, which was to do her best. The standard of care was, in the circumstances, reduced by reason of the parties' special relationship. The trial judge also made an alternative finding that, if there were a breach of duty, the plaintiff had been contributorily negligent, and that both parties were equally to blame. The plaintiff successfully appealed to the Court of Appeal.

In delivering a judgment in favour of the appellant, Lord Denning MR, apart from the *dictum* earlier quoted,[16] referred[17] to the statement of Dixon J in the High Court of Australia's decision in *The Insurance Commissioner* v *Joyce*[18] where it was said that "If a man accepts a lift from a car driver whom he knows to have lost a limb or an eye or to be deaf, he cannot complain if he does not exhibit the skill and competence of a driver who suffers from no defect... If he knowingly accepts the voluntary services of a driver affected by drink, he cannot complain of improper driving caused by his condition, because it involved no breach of duty." Lord Denning did not agree with Dixon J's view. "The driver," he said, "owes a duty of care to every passenger in the car, just as he does to every pedestrian on the road: and he must attain the same standard of care in respect of each. If the driver were to be excused according to the knowledge of the passenger, it would result in endless confusion and injustice. One of the passengers may know that the learner driver is a mere novice. Another passenger may believe him to be entirely competent. One of the passengers may believe the driver to have had only two drinks. Another passenger may know that he has had a dozen. Is the one passenger to recover and the other not? Rather than embark on such inquiries, the law holds that the driver must attain the same standard of care for passengers as for pedestrians. The knowledge of the passenger may go to show that he was guilty of contributory negligence in ever accepting the lift – and this reduce his damages – but it does not take away the duty of care, nor does it diminish the standard of care which the law requires of the driver." Lord Denning MR went on[19] to discuss the position of the defendant as regards the plaintiff. He was of the view that that relationship did not prelude the plaintiff from maintaining an action unless he had agreed to waive any claim in respect to injury. However, he might have been guilty of contributory negligence; "He may," in Lord Denning's words, "for instance, have let the learner take control too soon, he may not have been quick enough to correct his errors, or he may have participated in the negligent act." Lord Denning MR was, in addition, of the view that the defence of *volenti non fit injuria* had been so severely restricted that it, presently, had no application to negligence where the duty was based on proximity.[20] Lord Denning ultimately concluded[21] that, where a driver is being taught to drive a car under the tuition of an experienced driver, if the car runs off the road and there is an accident in which one or other is injured, "...it should be regarded as the fault of one or other or both of them. In the absense of any evidence enabling the court to draw a distinction between them, they should be regarded as equally to blame, with the result that the injured one gets damages from the other, but they are reduced one half owing to his own contributory negligence." The Master of the Rolls was of the view that the only alternative was to hold that the accident was the fault of neither, with the result that the injured person received compensation from no-one. In his Lordship's opinion, in the days of compulsory insurance, that was not an acceptable solution.

Megaw LJ agreed with Lord Denning MR, except in that he would have allowed the appeal in full.[22] However, like Lord Denning MR, he was extremely critical of Dixon J's comments in *The Insurance Commissioner v Joyce*[23] which he regarded as not being attractive in principle. He commented[24] that, "...if this doctrine of varying standards is to be accepted as part of the law on these facts, it could not logistically be confined to the duty of care owed by learner drivers. There is no reason in logic why it should not operate in a much wider sphere. The disadvantages of the resulting unpredictability, uncertainty and, indeed, impossibility of arriving at fair and consistent decisions outweigh the advantages. The certainty of a general standard is preferable to the vagaries of a fluctuating standard." After having considered various issues relating to the driver and passenger relationship, Megaw L J emphasised[25] that he did not think that the legal process could satisfactorily or successfully cope with the task of assessing fairly, or applying to the facts of, particular cases such varying standards, dependent on complex and elusive factors which would include an assessment by the court, not merely of a person's actual skill or experience, but of another person's knowledge or assessment of that skill or experience at a particular moment in time. If one were to accept the notion in relation to the driving of motor vehicles, there was no logical reason why it would not apply in other fields: "Suppose." Megaw LJ stated,[26] "that to the knowledge of the patient a young surgeon, whom the patient has chosen to operate on him, has only just qualified. If the operation goes wrong because of the surgeon's inexperience, is there a defence on the basis that the standard of skill and care is lower than that of a competent and experienced surgeon? Does the young, newly qualified solicitor owe a lower standard of skill and care, when the client chooses to instruct him with the knowledge of his inexperience?" Although, in those two hypothetical situations, Megaw LJ admitted that there were elements of contract law which might govern the questions, that was not an issue in the present, or a similar, case. It was preferable, he urged, "...that there should be a reasonably certain and reasonably ascertainable standard of care, even if on occasion that may appear to work hardly against an inexperienced driver, or his insurers. The standard of care required by the law is the standard of the competent and experienced driver: and this is so, as defining the driver's duty towards a passenger who knows of his inexperience, as much as towards a member of the public outside the car, and as much in civil as in criminal proceedings."

Salmon LJ began[27] his judgment by agreeing with what Lord Denning MR had said regarding the responsibility of learner drivers, both to passengers and the public at large. However, he continued by saying that, with minor reservations, and unlike Lord Denning MR. he agreed with the comments of Dixon J in *The Insurance Commissioner* v *Joyce*.[28] In particular, he did not agree that, "...the mere fact that the driver, has to the knowledge of his passenger, lost a limb, an eye or is deaf can affect the duty which he owes the passenger to drive safely. It is well known that many drivers suffering from such disabilities drive with no less skill and competence that the ordinary man." On the other hand, the situation, Salmon LJ considered,[29] was wholly different when, to the passenger's knowledge, the driver is, "...so drunk as to be incapable of driving safely. Quite apart from being negligent, a passenger who accepts a lift in such circumstances clearly cannot expect the driver to drive other than dangerously." The key to Salmon LJ's argument is that he postulates that the duty of care springs from *relationship* and, by accepting a lift in the circumstances described by Salmon LJ, he has created a special relationship whereby he cannot expect the driver to discharge a duty of care or a skill which, *ex hypothesi*, he knows the driver is incapable of discharging. As there were no authorities on the duty owed by a learner driver to his instructor, Salmon LJ posited an analogy between the two situations, even though the analogy was by no means exact. The relationship between the driver and the instructor was such, Salmon LJ considered,[30] that, "...the beginner does not owe the instructor a duty to drive with the skill and competence to be expected of an experienced driver. The instructor knows that the learner does not possess such skill and competence. The alternative way of putting the case is that the instructor voluntarily agrees to run the risk of injury resulting from the learner's lack of skill and experience." That relationship, though, will cease to exist if, for example, the learner refuses to obey instructions or suddenly accelerates or pays no attention to what he is doing and, as a result, the instructor is injured, the learner will be in breach of duty and, hence, liable in damages. However, the duty was still that of using reasonable care and skill in all the relevant circumstances. What is reasonable depends on the special relationship existing between the learner and the instructor. That relationship, in Salmon LJ's view, made the learner's lack of skill and experience a highly relevant circumstance. Salmon LJ, further, did not consider that, "...the learner is usually liable to his instructor if an accident occurs as a result of some mistake which any prudent beginner doing his best can be expected to make. I recognise that on this view, cases in which a driving instructor is injured when a pupil is driving may raise difficult questions of fact and degree." At the same time, the judge properly noted that equally difficult questions of fact and degree are being assessed and decided by the courts every day. "The law," Salmon LJ, again properly, stated, "laid down principles but not rules of thumb for deciding issues arising out of any special relationship between the parties – though, if such a rule of thumb existed, it might remove difficulties, but could hardly produce justice either in practice or in theory." In addition, the fact that the appellant had made inquiries of the respondent's husband regarding whether he was covered by insurance was an integral part of the relationship between the parties. But the fact that the assurance had been given to the appellant before the appellant had agreed to teach the respondent disposed of any possible defence of *volenti non fit injuria*. In the event, Salmon LJ was of the view,[31] which he expressed with some doubt, that the assurance given to the appellant by the respondent and her husband altered the nature of the relationship which have existed between the parties but for the assurance, which resulted in a relationship which would under which the respondent accepted responsibility for any injury which the appellant might have suffered in consequence of any failure on her part to exercise the ordinary driver's standards of reasonable care and skill. As regards the issue of contributory negligence, Salmon LJ agreed with Lord Denning and stated[32] that,

"...neither was guilty of serious negligence, but both were at fault and equally to blame. She panicked as beginners sometimes do, and he did not react as quickly as he should have done." Accordingly, Salmon LJ allowed the appeal and agreed with Lord Denning MR regarding the apportionment of damages.

The next issue which arose in *Roberts* v *Ramsbottom*[33] was how far the strict standard which had generally been applied in *Nettleship* v *Weston* was relevant. Neill J was clearly of the view that the liability of a driver in tort was not strict – in other words, there may be cases where a driver might be able to raise some matter sufficient to avoid the influence of fault. So, in the criminal case of *R* v *Spurge*,[34] Salmon J, as he then was, stated that, "If, however, a motor-car endangers the public solely by reason sudden overwhelming misfortune suffered by the man at the wheel for which he is in no way to blame – if, for example, he suddenly has an epileptic fit or passes into a coma, or is attacked by a swarm of bees or stunned by a blow to the head from a stone, then he is not guilty of driving in a manner dangerous to the public... It would be otherwise if he had felt an illness coming on but still continued to drive, for that would have been a manifestly dangerous thing to do." He later, sought to explain that what he described as the *sudden affliction* case could be expected on the basis that the defendant was not really *driving* at all.

That possibility had earlier been raised by Lord Goddard CJ in *Hill* v *Baxter*.[35] There, the defendant had driven across a road junction at high speed, ignoring an illuminated *Halt* sign, and colliding with a car. The van then continued for a short distance and overturned. In hospital, the defendant said that he was unable to recall what had occurred.[36] At the hearing before justices, the only evidence for the defence was that of the defendant himself, but, there being no objection by the prosecution, the justices allowed two medical reports from the doctor, who had examined the defendant, to be put in. Those reports showed no abnormality and it was impossible to say whether the defendant had lapsed from consciousness or not. The defendant argued that he became unconscious as a result of being overcome by a sudden illness. The justices found that the defendant must have exercised skill in being able to reach the road junction, but were of the opinion that he was not conscious of what he was doing for some little time before reaching the junction and was not capable of forming any intention as to his manner of driving so that, accordingly, the charges were dismissed. The Divisional Court[37] were of the view that, because the legislation contained an absolute prohibition against dangerous driving, the defendant's intention at the relevant time was immaterial. It followed that the justices had come to a wrong conclusion in law.

In coming to that conclusion, Lord Goddard CJ said[38] that, "…there may be cases where the circumstances are such that the accused could not really be said to be driving at all. Suppose he had a stroke or an epileptic fit, both instances of what might properly be called acts of God; he might well be in the driver's seat even with his hands on the wheel, but in such a state of unconsciousness that he could not properly be said to be driving." Pearson J adopted[39] a similar approach; "On the facts," he said, "if he was driving at all he was unquestionably driving dangerously, and therefore the question at issue was whether he was driving the car. In any ordinary case, when once it has been proved that the accused was in the driving seat of a moving car, there is, prima facie, an obvious and irresistible inference that he was driving it. No dispute or doubt will arise on this point unless and until there is evidence tending to show that by some extraordinary mischance he was rendered unconscious or otherwise incapacitated from controlling the car. In *Roberts* v *Ramsbottom*,[40] Neill J, after referring to other authority,[41] noted that, in particular, *Hill* v *Baxter* provided support for the view that, in law, a state of automatism involved a complete lack of consciousness.

However, the cases, including *Hill* v *Baxter,* were criminal cases, but Neill J considered that a similar approach ought to be taken in civil actions and he encapsulated the legal position in the following terms: "The driver will be able to escape liability if his actions at the relevant time were wholly beyond his control. The most obvious case is sudden unconsciousness. But if he retained some control, albeit imperfect control, and his driving, judged objectively was below the required standard, he remains liable. His position is the same as a driver who is old or infirm. In my judgment unless the facts establish what the law recognises as automatism the driver cannot avoid liability on the basis that owing to some malfunction of the brain his consciousness was impaired. [Counsel] put the matter accurately when he said "One cannot accept exculpation from anything less than total loss of consciousness." The judge, at that point, admitted that a doctor had described the defendant's condition as being one of *automatism*; however, Neill J was satisfied that the relevant condition did not amount to automatism as t had been described in the decided cases. Hence, the judge decided that the defendant was liable, in law for his driving when he collided with the second car. In addition, he was also of the opinion that the plaintiffs would be entitled to succeed, should it be necessary, on the grounds that the defendant had continued to drive after he was unfit to do so and when he should have been aware of his unfitness. As Neill J put the matter,[42] "He was aware that the was feeling queer and had to appreciate that he should have stopped. As I have said, and I repeat, the defendant was in no way morally to blame, but that is irrelevant to the question of legal liability in this case. An impairment to judgment does not provide a defence. I consider that the defendant was in law guilty of negligence in continuing to drive because he was aware of his disabling symptoms and of his first collision even though he was not able to appreciate their proper significance."

Not wholly surprisingly, it is suggested, *Roberts* v *Ramsbottom* has not gone uncriticised, Thus, Stanton had described[43] the decision as being even harsher than *Nettleship* v *Weston*,[44] although Stanton himself is not unsympathetic to the eventual decisions in both of those cases on the grounds that a stringent standard of care will ensure that the victim obtains access to insurance funds. At the same time, and I suggest that this is an important point, Stanton points out that, "The objective standard of care ensures that the compensatory purpose of tort is not undermined by an argument founded on moral responsibility and the need to achieve effective deterrence. The result in motoring cases is that what is formally an obligation to take reasonable care acquires the appearance of strict liability." However, there is more to the matter than that of itself: in *Hill* v *Baxter*,[45] it will be remembered that the Divisional Court were of the view that, because the Act contained an absolute prohibition against dangerous driving, the intention of the driver at the relevant time was immaterial.[46] Since considerable reliance appeared to have been placed on *Hill* v *Baxter* in *Roberts* v *Ramsbottom*, at least an element of strict liability seems to have been introduced. At the same time, in the case of *R* v *Gosney*,[47] to which reference was also made in *Roberts*,[48] Megaw LJ had stated that the offence of dangerous driving was, "...not an absolute offence. In order to justify a conviction there must be , not only a situation which, viewed objectively, was dangerous, but there must also have been some fault on the part of the driver, causing that situation. 'Fault' certainly does not necessarily involve deliberate misconduct or recklessness or intention to drive in a manner inconsistent with proper standards of driving. Nor does fault necessarily involve moral blame. There is fault if an inexperienced or naturally poor driver, while straining every nerve to do the right thing, falls below the standard of a competent and careful driver. Fault indicates a failure, a falling below the care or skill of a competent and experienced driver, in relation to the manner of the driving and to the relevant circumstances of the case. A fault in that sense, even though it be slight, even though it be a momentary lapse, even though no danger would normally have resulted." It may be legitimately be thought that, despite Megaw LJ's first statement in that extract from his judgment, he was close to suggesting a standard so severe that it was close to strict liability. That thought is likely further to be reinforced by a later *dictum* of Megaw LJ in *Gosney*[49] that, "Such a fault will often be sufficiently proved as an inference from the very facts of the situation." Though, as has been observed in the prior discussion,[50] there may be some *exceptional*[51] situations where the driver may be able to raise some matter which may be sufficient to enable any such inference to be drawn.

What conclusions can be drawn from the discussion of these various cases? The first is that it is apparent that courts will take an extremely restrictive view of any defendant who claims that a disability affected his ability to drive from which an accident resulted. To take *Roberts* v *Ramsbottom's* factual situation as a starting point: there can be few sudden-onset conditions as serious as a cerebral haemorrhage (as, indeed, the writer knows from his own experience[52]). Although the defendant in *Ramsbottom* might have been aware that he was feeling ill, it is highly unlikely that he was instantly aware of the cause of his apparent illness, The reason for this, when coupled with the rejection of the *Joyce* approach by Lord Denning MR and Megaw LJ in *Nettleship* v *Weston*,[53] is that, by seeking to apply objective standards of care, courts are seeking to bring about quick and cheap resolutions of the issues arising out of *accidents*.[54] In *Ramsbottom*, Neill J clearly expressed the view that the defendant was in no way morally to blame for the incident.[55] Second, there does seem to be some juristic difficulty in dealing with the phenomenon of the accident: it does seem a little incongruous that, albeit in wholly different factual situations, to hold the defendants in *Palsgraf* not to be liable when negligence was clearly found and to hold the defendant in *Roberts* v *Ramsbottom* liable, despite a clearly documented disability.

Liability apart, the plaintiff in *Palsgraf*, and, doubtless, her family, as well as the plaintiffs in *Roberts* v *Ramsbottom*, would have suffered varying degrees of distress and, at least, surprise. There are some accidents which are, in fact, just that and will not give rise to legal issues – we can probably put *Palsgraf* into that category, except that it did give rise to legal proceedings. An example is provided by a poem, written in 1953, by the United States writer, Theodore Roethke, "Elegy for Jane", and subtitled, "My student thrown by a horse." Of the poem, Ross-Bryant writes[56] that Roethke, "...succeeds in creating for us Jane and, as the focal point of the poem, his feelings for her and his sense of loss at her death. This is done very simply and subtly through her association with nature and though the final statement of his live." The poem begins, thus, with a description of Jane and her closeness, rather than mere association, with nature:

> I remember the neckcurls, limp and damp tendrils;
> And her quick look, a sidelong pickerel smile;
> And how, once started into talk, the light syllables leaped for her.
> And she balanced in the delight of her thought,
> A wren, happy, tail into the wind,
> Her song trembling the twigs and small branches.
> The shade sang with her;
> The leaves, their whispers turned to kissing,
> And the mould sang in the bleached valleys under the rose.

Ross-Bryant goes to comment[57] that both Jane's lost presence and the poet's sorrow received expression through the concrete world. The second stanza goes on to emphasise the poet's loss and its relationship with those entities to which Ross-Bryant has referred:

> Oh, when she was sad, she cast herself down into such a pure depth,
> Even a father could not find her:
> Scraping her cheek against straw,
> Stirring the clearest water.
> My sparrow, you are not here,
> Waiting like a fern, making a spiney shadow.

The sides of wet stones cannot console me,
Nor the moss, wound with the last light.

As regards these first two stanzas, the commentator Wolfe goes beyond the apparent simplicities found in the poem and writes[58] that Roethke is, "...intent on celebrating the loveliness of Jane's spirit; he is also writing in the form of a biblical Psalm." That was done, he points out, not by rhyme at the end of the lines, but by the structure at the lines at the beginning, notably the last three lines in the first stanza. In the last line of the second stanza, the use of the word *wound* in the last line is, it is suggested, especially telling – it is of course, the past participle of *wind*, describing how the poet cannot be consoled by even a beautiful natural image. However, the word can also be interpreted as being a synonym for *injury*: in other words, Jane's death has *wounded* the poet, as if the death has become the poet's injury. But, in the end, as Ross-Bryant has herself commented,[59] "...the loss comes to one who loved her."

The nature of the poet's relationship with Jane and his true feelings for her are revealed in the final stanza. Wolfe, in his description of the way in which the poem develops and unfolds, remarks[60] that, as the details relating to Jane accumulate with increasing thoroughness, they symbolise the motions of her spirit and the poet's increasing attachment to her. He, despite her absence, moves towards a greater closeness:

If only I could nudge you from this sleep,
My maimed darling, my skitter pigeon.
Over this damp grave I speak the words of my love:
I, with no rights in this matter.
Neither father nor lover.

But at the same time, he denies – after all, he is a teacher and she a student – any right to love or, indeed probably, even to grieve.

On the other hand, Parini suggests[61] that Jane's death is the occasion for a poem invoking a particular emotional state: the poet's feelings of grief and pity transcend the occasion, Parini also discusses the process of composition and posits that Roethke has used, particularly in the first stanza, many phrases which he has accumulated, in his notebook, over the years. That, he seems to suggest, has had consequences for the thrust of the poem generally. "In the elegy," Parini states, "Roethke associates the girl with elemental aspects of nature: the plant tendrils, the pickerel, the wren; this has the autarchy effect of defusing the pathos of her death. The romantic views death as merely a stage; the lesson of the plants points to some kind of rebirth" Parini concludes[62] that, as the poem stands, Roethke is mourning, not only one particularised student whom, after all, he knew only slightly, but the deaths of us all.

It may very be that all of the elements which have been referred to by these commentators are, indeed, present in the poem. After all , it is widely regarded as the most successful of Roethke's elegies and it brings together natural metaphors which seem to represent unity of a kind envisaged by other poets such as Wordsworth, Hardy and Dylan Thomas. Thus, in the first stanza of "A Refusal to Mourn the Death by Fire, of a Child in London,"[63] there is a more concentrated awareness of the surrounding phenomena and forces of nature:

> Never until the mankind making
> Bird beast and flower
> Fathering and all humbling darkness
> Tells with silence the last light breaking
> And the still hour
> Is come of the sea tumbling in harness

After that striking beginning, the poet moves closer to his subject, although he rejoices, rather than grieves over the child's ultimate union, both physical and metaphysical, with that very nature:

> Deep with the first dead lies London's daughter,
> Robed in the long friends,
> The grains beyond age, the dark veins of her mother,
> Secret by the unmourning water
> Of the riding Thames.
> After the first death, there is no other.

Roethke's response, though, is altogether more humanised than Thomas's overly fatalistic and pantheistic approach, though he does acknowledge his victim's Jewish origins in the second stanza ("And I must enter again the round/Zion of the water bead/And the synagogue of the ear of corn"). Although Thomas's rhetoric may be more immediate, it is surely, Roethke's which is closer to everyday experience and emotion.

Inevitably, not all accidents are so personal in the various senses which may be represented in Theodore Roethke's poem. There may be some accidents which are more material in their consequences than that in "Elegy for Jane". Disasters at work may be of such a kind. "The Trimdon Grange Explosion", written in 1882, describes the consequences of an explosion at a colliery in the north-east of England. Mining in the Nineteenth Century was a fraught occupation and the poem, by Thomas Armstrong (1848-1920), describes the consequences of a particular explosion. The background to the poem is that, on February 16th 1882, the colliery at Trimdon Grange, County Durham, exploded killing seventy four miners. The poem begins, in true Victorian manner, with a warning which is both moral and spiritual and goes on to describe the situations of various families affected by the disaster and concludes with both another warning and hope for resurrection. It, thus, comports with the form used in many folk-poems of its kind and is, in its own dignified way, perfectly formed and balanced:

> Let us not think of to-morrow,
> Lest we disappointed be; Our joys may turn to sorrow,
> As we may daily see.
> Today we're strong and healthy,
> But how soon there comes a change,
> As we may see from the explosion
> That has been at Trimdon Grange
>
> Men and boys left home that morning
> For to earn their daily bread,
> Little thought before the evening
> They'd be numbered with the dead;
> Let us think of Mrs Burnett
> Once had sons and now has none –
> With the Trimdon Grange explosion,
> Joseph, George and James are gone.

February left behind it
What will never forget;
Weeping widows, helpless children
May be found in many a cot.
Little children kind and loving.
From their homes each day would run;
For to meet their father's coming.
As each day's work was done.

Now they ask if father's left them.
And the mother hangs her head,
 With a weeping widow's feelings,
Tells the child its father's dead.
Homes that once were blessed with comfort,
Guided by a father's care
Now are solemn, sad and gloomy,
Since the father is not there.

God protect the lonely widow,
Help to raise each drooping head;
Be a Father to the orphans.
Never let them cry for bread.
Death will pay us all a visit;
They have only gone before.
We may meet the Trimdon victims
Where explosions are no more.

Since that rather remarkable poem is not generally well known outside of its area of origin, it is important to say something of its author.[64] Armstrong was, indeed, described by the great English folksong collector A L Lloyd as, "...the bard of the Durham coalfield and one of the most remarkable of all working-class songmakers." Lloyd went on to describe him as being, "...a small bow legged man with a huge family (fourteen children) and an indomitable thirst. Out of his wages as a miner, little was left over for Tommy's own pleasures and he became accustomed to making songs, getting them cheaply printed and selling the broadsheets round public houses at weekends, a penny a time, to raise beer-money. His son

William, himself a song maker locally called 'Poety Armstrong' told me [Lloyd], "Me dad's muse was a mug of ale.'"

Ultimately, Armstrong's fame developed to such a degree that he was frequently called upon to write poems or songs on important events in the life of the West Stanley/Tanfield community where he spent all his working life.[65] Hence, he wrote on such matters as disasters or strikes. The latter were especially noteworthy,[66] as the later years of the Nineteenth Century were marked by industrial unrest caused, in the mine owners which led to struggles. Of particular note, regarding Armstrong's work, is that the songs and poems which he wrote on such matters tended to be written in a closer approximation to standard English than those which he wrote about less formal matters, which were written in the local dialect. His best known song of the latter type is entitled, "Wor Nannie's a Maisor", which translates, approximately as, "My wife Ann is possessed of surprising characteristics."[67]

Armstrong, particularly, took his commitments and responsibilities as a formal commentator extremely seriously. He is on record, according to A L Lloyd, as having said that, "When you're the pitman's poet and looked up to for it, wey, if a disaster or a strike goes by wi'oot a song fre ye, they say: 'What's wi' Tommy Armstrong? Has someone druv a spigot in him and let oot aal the inspiration?'" "The Trimdon Grange Explosion" which was certainly the product of a remarkable inspiration was written to be sold on streets and in Mechanics' Halls to raise money for the widows and orphans of the disaster. It remains a remarkable example of folk-poetry at its very best – straightforward, simple in its prosody and direct in its description and imagery.

As was clear from "The Trimdon Grange Explosion", major disasters can affect the lives of people who might be less directly involved than the families of the Trimdon victims in Armstrong's poem. An especially striking instance of that, and the legal response to it is to be found in the decision of the House of Lords in *Alcock* v *Chief Constable of South Yorkshire*.[68] There, the defendant was responsible for the policing of a major football match at which, as a result of overcrowding in part of the stadium, ninety five people were killed and many more received serious injuries through crushing. As the magnitude of the disaster became apparent, live pictures of the events were broadcast on television. The plaintiffs were all related to, or were friends of, spectators who had been involved in the disaster. Some saw events from other parts of the ground. One plaintiff, who was outside the ground, saw the events on television and went to search for his missing son. Other plaintiffs were at home and watched the events on live television broadcasts or heard of them from friends or through radio reports, though only later saw recorded television pictures, All of the plaintiffs, alleging that the impact of what they had seen and heard had caused them severe shock resulting in psychiatric illness, claimed damages from the defendant. On the issue of liability, the trial judge held that the category of plaintiffs who were entitled to claim damages for nervous shock including a sibling as well as a parent or spouse of a victim, and that those plaintiffs present or immediately outside the stadium at the time of the disaster or who had watched it live on television were sufficiently close in time or place to be reasonably foreseeable and that what they had seen would cause them to suffer psychiatric illness. Accordingly, nine of the plaintiffs, who were either parents, spouses or siblings of the victims and who were eye-witnesses of the disaster or who saw it live on television, were held to be entitled to claim damages for nervous shock. The remaining six plaintiffs were excluded because they were in a more remote relationship or because they had heard about the disaster by some means other than the live television broadcast. The Court of Appeal allowed the defendant's appeal and dismissed the cross-appeal of the unsuccessful plaintiffs. The plaintiff appealed to the House of Lords, who affirmed the decision of the Court of Appeal.

First, Lord Keith noted[69] that injury by a psychiatric illness was more subtle than direct physical injury[70] as, in the present type of case, it was a, "...secondary source of injury brought about by the infliction of physical injury or the risk of physical injury, upon another person." That , he continued, could affect those closely connected with the injured person in a variety of ways – one way was by subjecting a close relative to the stress of caring for that person over what might be long period of time. However, injury hitherto, resulting from such stress had not been regarded as founding a claim for damages. "So", he said, "I am of the opinion that in addition to reasonable foreseeability, liability in the form of psychiatric illness must depend in addition upon a requisite relationship of proximity between the claimant and the party said to woe the duty." The persons to whom the duty was owed had been described by Lord Atkin in *Donoghue* v *Stevenson*[71] as being. "...persons who are so closely and directly affected by my act that I ought reasonably to have them in contemplation as being so affected when I am directing my mind to the acts or omissions which are called in question." The concept, Lord Keith stated,[72] of a person being closely and directly affected had, for convenience, been labelled proximity and had been applied in a variety of cases, especially those concerned with pure economic loss, so as to limit and control the consequences which would follow were reasonable foresseability the sole criterion. Having said that, Lord Keith considered that as regards the class of people to whom a duty may be owed to take reasonable care to avoid inflicting psychiatric illness through nervous shock sustained by reason of physical injury or risk to another, reasonable foreseebility should the guide. The reason for that apparently contradictory stance was that he was unwilling to limit the class by reference to particular family relationships. However, the closeness of the tie would have to be proved by the plaintiff, though, doubtless, it might be presumed in appropriate cases. By way of example, Lord Keith referred to , "The case of a bystander unconnected with the victim of an accident is difficult. Psychiatric injury to him would not ordinarily...be within the range of reasonable foreseeability, but could not perhaps be entirely excluded from it if the circumstances of a catastrophe occurring very close to him were particularly horrific." Further, in the case of those who came within the sphere of reasonable foreseeability, the proximity factors mentioned by Lord Wilberforce in *McLoughlin* v *O'Brien*[73] must be taken into account in determining whether a duty of care existed. In that case, Lord Wilberforce had said that, "As regards proximity to the accident, it is obvious that this must be close in both time and space. It is after all, the fact and consequence of the defendant's negligence that must be proved to have caused the 'nervous shock'. Experience has shown that it insists on direct and immediate sight or hearing would be impractical and unjust and that under what might be called the 'aftermath' doctrine, one who, form close proximity comes very soon on the scene, should not be excluded... Finally, and by way of reinforcement of 'aftermath' cases, I would accept, by analogy with 'rescue' situations, that a person of whom it could be said that one could expect nothing else than that he or she would come immediately to the scene (normally a parent or spouse) could be regarded as being within the scope of foresight and duty. Where there is no immediate presence, account must be taken of the possibility of alterations in the circumstances, for which the defendant should be responsible...

Subject only to those qualifications, I think that a strict test of proximity by sight or hearing should be applied by the courts." In *McLoughlin* v *O'Brien*, the plaintiff had remained at home whilst her husband was out with three of the children in their car, the eldest child driving. At about 5.00pm, a friend arrived with the news that, about an hour previously, the car had been involved in a very serious accident some two miles away. The friend drove her to the hospital where she found her husband and sons hurt, screaming and disorientated. She also learnt that her eldest daughter had been killed. These events, caused by the defendant's negligence, resulted in her suffering severe shock, organic depression and a change of personality, all the time its being assumed that she was a person of normal fortitude. At first instance, it was held that her claim should fail on the grounds that the possibility of her suffering injury by nervous shock was not reasonably foreseeable. The Court of Appeal upheld the decision at first instance, though on other grounds: first, Stephenson LJ was of the view that the possibility of such an injury to the plaintiff was reasonably foreseeable and that the defendants did owe the plaintiff a duty of care. However, she was precluded from recovery on policy grounds. Griffiths LJ took the approach that injury through nervous shock was reasonably foreseeable but that the defendants owed no duty to the plaintiff, the duty being limited to those who were on the road nearby. Cumming-Bruce LJ appeared to agree with both judgments. However, the House of Lords allowed the original plaintiff's appeal.

To return to *Alcock*, Lord Keith concentrated, in applying Lord Wilberforce's comments in *McLaughlin*, on the appellants who had seen the disaster on television and he noted [74] that none of the television coverage depicted the suffering of recognisable individuals (which was prohibited by the broadcasting code of ethics). In Lord Keith's opinion, the viewing of those televised scenes could not be regarded as being in accord with the view of Lord Wilberforce in *McLoughlin* v *O'Brien*[75] and nor could the scenes be regarded as giving rise to shock, in the sense of a sudden assault on the nervous system. "They were capable," he concluded, "of giving rise to anxiety for the safety of relatives known or believed to be present in the area affected by the crush, and undoubtedly did so but that is very different from seeing the fate of the relative or his condition shortly after the event. The viewing of the television scenes did not create the necessary degree of proximity."

Lord Ackner began his judgment[76] by saying that, were sympathy alone to be determining factor in these claims, they would never have been contested. Further, he also noted[77] that the respondent had admitted that he owed a duty to those who died or were injured in the disaster and that he was in breach of that duty. Lord Ackner then went on[78] to examine the nature of the cause of action, which he reduced to five propositions, after having said that the reasonable foresight test, of itself, was not operative. The first proposition was that, even though the risk of psychiatric illness was reasonably foreseeable, the law would not award damages if the psychiatric injury was not induced by shock. This, in turn, meant that, "Psychiatric illness caused in other ways, such as from the experience of having to cope with the deprivation consequent upon the death of loved ones, attracts no damages." In that context, Lord Ackner referred to examples quoted by Brennan J in the High Court of Australia's decision in *Jaensch* v *Coffey*[79] – these were, the spouse who has been worn down by caring for a tortiously injured husband or wife and who, as a result, suffers psychiatric illness and the parent who is rendered distraught by the wayward conduct of a brain damaged child and who suffers psychiatric illness in consequence will neither be able to obtain compensation by way of damages. Second, Lord Ackner stated[80] that, "Even where the nervous shock and the subsequent psychiatric illness caused it could both have been reasonably foreseen, it has generally been accepted that damages for merely being informed of, or reading or hearing about the accident are not generally recoverable."[81] Third, Lord Ackner emphasised[82] that mere mental suffering, although reasonably foreseeable, if unaccompanied by physical injury was not a basis for a claim in damages.[83] Fourth, Lord Ackner noted that, as yet, there was no authority establishing that there was liability on the part of the injured person[84] for mere psychiatric injury which was sustained by another by reason of shock, as a result of a self-inflicted death, injury or peril of the negligent person, in circumstances where the risk of such psychiatric injury was reasonably foreseeable. Despite Lord Ackner's somewhat convoluted prose, that, in effect, meant that some extraneous limit, other than reasonable foresight, was placed on the duty to third parties. Thus, in *Bourhill* v *Young*, at first instance, the Lord Ordinary (Lord Robertson) was unwilling to accept[85] a suggestion that a negligent window cleaner who loses his grip and fell from a height and impales himself on spiked railings would be liable for shock-induced psychiatric illness occasioned to a pregnant woman looking out of the window of a house on the other side of the street. Fifth, Lord Ackner considered[86] that, in the present context, the notion of *shock* involved, "...the sudden appreciation by sight or sound of a horrifying event, which violently agitated the mind. It has yet to include psychiatric illness caused by the accumulation over a period of time of more gradual assaults on the nervous system."

In the context of all of that, Lord Ackner was not surprised that the reasonable foresight test was restrained. In that view, he was reinforced by the comments of Deane J in *Jaensch* v *Coffey*[87] that, "Reasonable foreseeability on its own indicates no more than that such as duty of care will exist if, and to the extent that, it is not precluded or modified by some applicable overriding requirement or limitation. It is to do little more than to state a truism to say that the essential function of such requirements or limitations is to confine the existence of a duty to take reasonable care to avoid reasonably foreseeable injury to the circumstances or classes of case in which it is the policy of the law to admit it. Such overriding requirements or limitations shape the frontiers of the common law of negligence." In addition, Lord Ackner was of the view[88] that the satisfaction of the reasonable foreseeability test did not satisfy the principle which had been set out by Lord Atkin in *Donoghue* v *Stevenson*, to which reference has earlier been made.[89] Lord Ackner was at pains to point out that Lord Atkin had emphasised that the formulation of a duty of care, couched solely in terms of reasonable foresight, would be too wide unless it was limited to the restriction of the duty to a *neighbour*, by which was meant the notion of proximity. The next question which arose was the specific nature of the limitation. That was important as Lord Wilberforce had emphasised in *McLoughlin* v *O'Brien*,[90] that there was a genuine need for the law to place some limitations upon the extent of admissible claims. Those elements introduced the requirement of proximity as conditioning the duty of care and were: first, the class of persons whose claims should be recognised. Secondly, the proximity of such persons to the accidents in time and space and, third, the means by which the shock has been caused.

As regards the first element, Lord Wilberforce had said in *McLaughlin*[91] that, "The closer the tie (not merely in relationship; but in care) the greater the claim for compensation, The claim, in any case, has to be judged in the light of the other factors such as proximity to the scene in time and place and the nature of the accident, Lord Ackner found himself with the same problem as had Atkin LJ in *Hambrook v Stokes Bros*.[92] That is, how is it possible to explain why a duty is confined, say, to parent and child whilst not extended to other intimate associations and not, ultimately, extended to bystanders? Lord Ackner then referred[93] to an instance, raised in argument, of "…a petrol tanker careering out of control into a school in session and bursting into flames". Lord Ackner said that he would not be prepared to rule out a potential claim by a passer-by so shocked by the scene as to suffer psychiatric illness, assuming that person to be reasonably strong-nerved. Similar considerations were applicable to the close family relationships referred to by Lord Wilberforce in *McLoughlin*, the justification. Lord Ackner considered, for admitting such claims was a, "…presumption, which I would accept as rebuttable, that the love and affection normally associated with persons in those relationships is such that a defendant ought reasonably to contemplate that they may be so closely and directly affected by his conduct as to suffer shock resulting in psychiatric illness. While as a generalisation more remote relatives and, a fortiori, friends, can reasonably be expected not to suffer illness from the shock, there can well be relatives and friends whose relationship is so close and intimate that their love and affection for the victim is comparable to that of the normal parent spouse or child of the victim and should for the purpose of this cause of action be so treated."[94] Lord Ackner encapsulated[95] these principles when he said that, "Whether the degree of love and affection in any given relationship, be it that of relative or friend, is such that the defendant, in the light of the plaintiff's proximity to the scene of the accident in time and space and its nature, should reasonably have foreseen the shock - induced psychiatric illness - has to be decided on a case by case basis." In that view, he was, once more, fortified by a comment made by Deane J of the High Court of Australia in *Jaensch v Coffey*,[96] who had said that, "While it must now be accepted that a realistic assessment of the reasonably foreseeable consequences of an accident involving actual or threatened serious bodily injury must, in appropriate case, include the possibility of injury in the form of nervous shock being sustained by a wide range of persons not physically injured in the accident, the outer limits of reasonable foreseeability of more psychiatric injury cannot be identified in the abstract or in advance. Much may depend upon the nature of the negligent act or omission, on the gravity or apparent gravity of an actual or apprehended injury and on any expert evidence about the nature and explanation of the particular psychiatric injury which the plaintiff has sustained."

Lord Ackner then turned his attention to the remaining two elements. As regards the proximity of the plaintiff to the accident, his Lordship noted that it was generally accepted that proximity to the accident must be close in space and time, even though direct or immediate sight or hearing was not requisite, It was reasonably foreseeable that injury by shock could be caused to a plaintiff, not only through sight or hearing of the accident, but of its immediacy. On the facts of *Alcock*, only two of the plaintiffs were at the stadium at the relevant time. One, though, identified his brother-in-law in a mortuary some eight hours after the accident. Lord Ackner did not consider[97] that that situation could be described as being a part of the *immediate aftermath*, even if it were a part of the aftermath. Unlike the plaintiff in *McLoughlin*,[98] who had arrived at the hospital within an hour, in the post-accident identification cases in *Alcock*, there was not sufficient proximity in time and space to the accident. In regard to the means by which the shock was caused, Lord Ackner noted[99] that whilst the television pictures had certainly given rise to feelings of the deepest anxiety and distress, it could not properly be said that they could be equated with being in sight or hearing of the event or its immediate aftermath. Having said that, Lord Ackner stated that simultaneous broadcasts of a disaster could not always be ruled out as providing such an equivalent. For example, a film of an event of children travelling in a balloon, which showed the balloon bursting into flames might well have an appropriate effect and, in his own words, "Many other such situations could be imagined where the impact of the simultaneous television pictures would be as great, it not greater than the actual sight of the accident." Although Lord Ackner made, and suggested, many inroads into the strict operation of the *McLoughlin* principle, he, nevertheless, agreed[100] that the appeals should be dismissed.

Lord Oliver began his judgment by saying that there was nothing unusual or peculiar in the recognition by the law that compensatible injury could be caused by a direct assault upon the mind or nervous system as much as by direct physical contact with the body. "This", he went on,[101] "is no more than the natural and inevitable result of the growing appreciation by modern medical science of recognisable casual connections between shock to the nervous system and physical or psychiatric illness.

Cases in which damages are claimed for directly inflicted injuries of this nature may present greater difficulties of proof but they are not, in their essential elements, any different from cases where the damages claimed arise from indirect physical injury and they present no very difficult problems of analysis where the plaintiff has himself been directly involved in the accident from which the injury is said to arise." He continued by pointing out that it was customary to classify cases in which damages were claimed for injury occasioned in that way under a single generic heading as cases involving *liability for* nervous shock. Lord Oliver, though, regarded that label as convenient but, in fact, misleading to the extent, at least, that it was assumed to lead to a conclusion that they had more in common than the factual similarity of the medium through which the injury is sustained. In reality, the cases, he said, broadly divide into two categories: first, those cases in which the plaintiff was involved either mediately or immediately as a participant and, second, those in which the plaintiff was the passive and unwilling witness of injury caused to others. Lord Oliver considered that cases on the former situation[102] were not especially helpful.[103] As regards the situation in the *Alcock* case, the situation became rather more complex: "The infliction of injury on an individual," Lord Oliver stated,[104] "whether through carelessness or deliberation, necessarily produces consequences beyond those to the immediate victim. Inevitably the impact of the event and its aftermath, whether immediate or prolonged, is going to be felt in greater or lesser degree by those with whom the victim is connected by ties of affection, of beloved relationship, of duty or simply of business." Lord Oliver went on to comment[105] that the general failure of the law to compensate for injuries sustained by persons unconnected with the event,[106] which had been precipitated by a defendant's negligence, must, he thought, impart the lack of any legal duty owed by the defendant to such people – it could not be attributable to an arbitrary, if undefined, rule of *policy*, nor could it rationally be argued that such injury is outside the scope of foreseeability. It must he said,[107] "...be attributable simply to the fact that such persons are not, in contemplation of law, in a relationship of sufficient proximity to or directness with the tortfeasor as to give rise to a duty of care, though no doubt 'policy', if that is the right word, or perhaps more properly the impracticability or unreasonableness of entertaining claims to the ultimate limits of the consequences of human activity, necessarily plays a part in the court's perception of what is sufficiently proximate." He further noted that an exception had been made in those cases where the event of injury to the primary victim had actually been witnessed by the plaintiff and the injury is established as resulting from that. What was unclear, Lord Oliver considered,[108] was the ambit of the duty in such cases or, alternatively described, what was the essential characteristic of such cases which delineated them from those cases of injury to uninvolved people whom the law denies any remedy for injury of an identical type.

Although it might be convenient to describe the plaintiff in that kind of case as a secondary victim, Lord Oliver urged that that description not be permitted to obscure the necessity of establishing that any duty owed by the defendant rested, not only on *reasonable foreseeability* but on the *proximity* or *directness* of the relationship between the parties. The real problem, Lord Oliver thought, lay in identifying the features which distinguished between people who suffered identical injuries, one being present at the accident and the other not. Thus, for example, the traumatic effect on a mother of the death of her child is as foreseeable if described by an eye witness at an inquest as it would be when she learns of it in a hospital immediately after the event. It also cannot be any factor of suddenness or unexpectedness, as news brought by a policeman hours after an event may be as sudden and unexpected as to an observer. "The answer has, as it seems to me," said Lord Oliver, "to be found in the existence of a combination of circumstances form which the necessary degree of 'proximity' between the plaintiff and the defendant can be deduced". However, having said that, his Lordship then emphasised that it had to be accepted that, "...the concept of 'proximity' is an artificial one which depends more on the court's perception of what is the reasonable are for the imposition of liability than upon any logical process of analogical deduction." In view of some of the criticisms of the *Alcock* decision, that seems a fair point. [109]

That area was then delineated from prior case law by Lord Oliver, who regarded five matters as being crucial for the determination: first, that there was a marital or parental relationship; second, that the injury arose from the sudden and unexpected shock to the plaintiff's nervous system; third, that the plaintiff was either personally present at the scene of the accident or was in the more or less immediate vicinity and witnessed the aftermath shortly afterwards; fourth, that the injury arose from witnessing the death or extreme danger or injury and discomfort suffered by the primary victim; fifth, that there was not only an element of physical proximity to the event but a close temporal connection between the event and the plaintiff's reception of it combined with a close relationship of affection between the plaintiff and the primary victim. In addition, there was the requirement of reasonable foreseeability on the part of the defendant that, in the combination of circumstances, there was a real risk of injury of the type sustained by the plaintiff in consequence of a concern for the primary victim. "There may", Lord Oliver went on,[110] "indeed, be no primary 'victim' in fact. It is, for instance, readily conceivable that a parent may suffer injury, whether physical or psychiatric, as a result of witnessing a negligent which places his or her child in extreme jeopardy but from which, in the event, the child escapes unharmed."[111]   After considering *McLoughlin* v *O'Brien*,[112] Lord Oliver saw,[113] "...no logic and no virtue in seeking to lay down as a matter of 'policy' categories of relationship within which claims may succeed and without which they are doomed to failure in limine. So rigid an approach would, I think, work great injustices and cannot rationally be justified. Obviously a claim for damages for psychiatric injury by a remote relative of the primary victim will require more cautions scrutiny and faces considerable evidentiary difficulties. Equally obviously, the foreseeability of such injury to such a person will be more difficult to establish than similar injury to a spouse or parent of the primary victim. But these are factual difficulties..."

However, Lord Oliver went on to emphasise[114] that, in every case, the "underlying and essential postulate" was the relationship of *proximity* between the defendant and plaintiff and must be regarded as the determining factor in the *Alcock* case. "The necessary element of proximity between plaintiff and defendant, " he said, "is furnished, at least in part by both physical and temporal propinquity and also by the sudden and direct visual impression on the plaintiff's mind of actually witnessing the event or its immediate aftermath." He then went on state that grief, sorrow, deprivation and the necessity of caring for loved ones who have suffered injury and misfortune, he regarded as being a part of the, "...ordinary and inevitable incidents of life, regardless of individual susceptibilities, must be sustained without compensation." Lord Oliver was unwilling to extend the law so as to cover a more gradual realisation of consequences, as to do so was not justified by pressing policy considerations and for which there was no logical stopping point. In other words, his Lordship was of the view that, "...the necessary proximity cannot be said to exist where the elements of immediacy, closeness of time and space, and direct visual or aural perceptions are absent... To extend the notion of proximity in cases of immediately created nervous shock to this more elongated and, to some extent, retrospective process may seem a logical analogical development. But the law in this area is not wholly logical."

Finally, Lord Oliver took up that point[115] in his conclusion: he could not regard the law as being either entirely satisfactory or logically desirable. By way of example, Lord Oliver referred to a situation where a mother suffered shock and psychiatric injury through watching the death of her son who has negligently walked in front of a moving car. It would be difficult to envisage a greater proximity or a greater degree of foreseeability and, hence, if liability was to be denied it could only be because of the law's *policy*, which prohibits the action. Depending on the degree of negligence contributed to the accident by the primary victim, it might be quite unjust to hold the driver of the car liable to the mother. It followed, Lord Oliver thought,[116] that such considerations of policy might better be enshrined in, and limited by, legislation.[117]

Lastly,[118] Lord Jauncey agreed[119] with Lord Wilberforce in *McLoughlin* that cases involving less close relatives should be carefully scrutinised, though he emphasised that they must not *ipso facto* be excluded. In Lord Jauncey's view, the proper approach was, "...to examine each case on its own facts in order to see whether the claimant has established so close a relationship of love and affection to the victim as might reasonably be expected in the case of spouses and children. If the claimant has so established and all other requirements of the claim are satisfied be or she will succeed since shock to him or her will be within the reasonable contemplation of the tortfeasor. If such a relationship is not established the claim will fail."

As regards the issue of proximity, Lord Jauncey, despite Lord Wilberforce's view in *McLoughlin*, did not regard[120] a claimant who watched a normal television programme displaying the events as they happened satisfied the test of proximity. He took that view for two reasons: first, a defendant could normally anticipate, given broadcasting guidelines, that pictures of people dying and suffering would not be transmitted. Second, that, such programs would be edited, Hence, it could not be said that such programmes were equivalent to actual sight or hearing at an accident or its aftermath and a claimant who listened to a radio broadcast or saw a subsequent television recording fell even shorter of Lord Wilberforce's requirement. As regards the issue of the constitution of the aftermath, Lord Jauncey considered that it must necessarily depend upon the surrounding circumstances. By way of illustration his Lordship referred to *McLoughlin* v *O'Brien*, where the plaintiff had taken approximately an hour to reach the hospital, but found her family in much the same condition as they would have been had she seen them at the accident itself. That seemed to Lord Jauncey[121] to be a wholly different situation from that where a relative identifies the victim in a mortuary some time after the event. Accordingly, the appeals were unanimously dismissed.

In view of the various approaches taken to a difficult area – from the juristic approach of Lord Oliver, through the systematic approach of Lord Ackner to the more pragmatic approaches of Lords Keith and Jauncey – it would have been surprising had not *Alcock* been productive of not inconsiderable critical comment. Thus, Handford is highly critical of the decision[122] which, he argues that, "No basis other than policy is advanced to veto this particular variety of mental illness. Apart from encouraging claim distortion and being medically too imprecise to cater for the vast majority of psychiatric abnormalities, it seems obvious that a person may suffer as much of an emotional and psychological disturbance from seeing (or learning of) a loved one's deterioration or slow death as seeing him or her killed suddenly or coming upon the aftermath."

Further, as regards *proximity*, to which much attention had been paid by the House of Lords in *Alcock*, Handford notes[123] that the notion of *aftermath*, similarly employed, was, "...ill-equipped to deal with cases where the consequences of a tortfeasor's wrongdoing take a while to become apparent. Cases...the essence of which is ignorance of events and uncertainty of outcome, seem to penalise the family, friends and others of those who linger, rather than die immediately as a result of the defendant's carelessness, or who are caught up in chaos and confusion of large-scale catastrophes where it is inevitable that a clear picture of true facts will not emerge for some time."

From those comments, Handford's judgment on the case is, itself, quite foreseeable. He urges[124] that what matters is whether psychiatric illness is foreseeable in the circumstances. The existence of a close relationship is probably the most powerful factor in such a finding, but rather the existence of such a relationship, nor presence at the accident or its aftermath, nor any other factor, should be regarded as an essential precondition to liability if the foreseeable criteria are satisfied." Although that view has the not inconsiderable attraction of simplicity, it may lead to uncertainty in the sense that it may not be so simple to predict who might incur some liability. Thus, in the case of media broadcasters, as in *Alcock*, it may be reasonable to foresee that a distressful account may well affect the mental health of watcher, listeners or readers and, when one takes Handford's other strictures into account, particularly if media are not acting ethically or in accord with prescribed codes, there is little logical reason for denying those appropriately affected a remedy.

As regards *proximity* itself, in one jurisdiction at any rate, it has effectively been dismissed as a proper basis for liability. In *Perre* v *Anand Pty Ltd*,[125] the High Court of Australia so decided, at least in cases involving pure economic loss, However, the High Court did not replace it with an alternative criterion. From some of the discussion in the House of Lords, as well as from Handford's critique, it would appear that *policy* might well replace it.

In addition to Handford's aware commentary, there have been other approaches toward the *Alcock* decision: first, Teff comments[126] that such publicised disasters, "...provide ammunition for root and branch reformers of the tort system, impatient with tortured and elaborate consideration of whether to add an hour or two to the aftermath, precisely where to draw the line between sudden and gradual assaults on the nervous system or where live TV can be 'equiporated' with actual sight or hearing." That, indeed is a very fair point and I would venture to agree with that commentator when he concluded[127] that the, "...deficiencies of nervous shock arise not from an appeal to policy considerations as such, but from arbitrary distinctions based on exaggerated concern about limitless liability." One of the more important reasons for this state of affairs, he argues, is a general reluctance of judges either to address, or to internalise, the medical insights into nervous shock, which would have informed their judgment as a result of a progressive understanding of mental illness. That is borne out by the fact that, in all the judgments in the House of Lords in *Alcock*, there was not a single explicit reference to the medical determinations of psychiatric illness.

There are, inevitably other views: thus, Lynch has stated[128] that, "Considerable advantage can be seen in the pragmatic approach adopted. The concession that *proximity* is merely a convenient term for describing the factual requirements for liability as dictated by common sense in particularly welcome." This, I fear, is a rather strange comment – if Lynch is suggesting that the use of the word *proximity* means something other than that term is legally ordinarily understood, then, especially in view of their Lordships' continual reference to the *McLoughlin* case[129] would not appear to bear that out. Second, I have never been enamoured to recourse to common sense as applicable to law: as I suggested, albeit in another context,[130] one person's common sense is another person's idiocy. Lynch is also critical of attempts, as urged in *Alcock*, to legislate.[131] She urges that it is impossible to legislate to cover all possible situations which, in turn, would mean that the most difficult problems would return to the courts, but rather confused by the apparatus of statutory interpretation.

The issues raised in all of these commentaries had been distilled by Nasir, who suggested[132] that three changes might best serve the interests of justice: first, that the requirement of direct perception of the accident or of its immediate aftermath should be abandoned, Second, that should a restriction on liability be deemed necessary, the categories of plaintiff afforded a remedy should be restricted to those involving close familial ties (or the equivalent) to primary victim – to include parents, spouses and, possibly, siblings. Such a limitation would be without prejudice to the requirement of foreseeability. Third, a threshold period for recovery should be introduced. Although, *prima facie*, that might seem fair, it could, conceivably lead to some strange combinations of circumstances being recognised.

However, this book is about law, rhetoric and poetry and, as Lord Keith pointed out,[133] the catastrophe which was the subject of *Alcock* involved the deaths of 95 people and over 400 physically injured. Yet, perhaps as might be expected, the language and rhetoric, even though Lord Ackner did say, at the beginning of his judgment[134] that, were sympathy alone to be determining fact,or the claims in *Alcock* would not have been contested. Put another way: it seems as though the legal concepts of *proximity*, *foreseeability, aftermath* and so on, seem designed as an interposition to protect the reader from the magnitude (and enormity) of the calamity itself. Apart from "The Trimdon Grange Explosion", earlier discussed,[135] poetry, too does not seem to have served the victims of disasters especially well. Perhaps the best known of what we might call *disaster poets* was William Topaz McGonagall[136] who, although best known for that genre,[137] wrote over two hundred poems in his long lifetime. "The Tay Bridge Disaster" is probably the poem for which he is best remembered and begins with a brief introduction, setting out the poem's subject matter:

> Beautiful Railway Bridge of the Silv'ry Tay!
> Alas! I am very sorry to say
> That ninety lives have been taken away
> On the last Sabbath day of 1879,
> Which will be remember'd for a very long time.

The poem continues with a description of the weather and then goes on to describe the moods of passengers, some of whom seemed more apprehensive than others:

> When the train left Edinburgh
> The passengers' hearts were light and felt no sorrow,
> But Boreas blew a terrific gale,
> Which made their hearts for to quail,
> And many of the passengers with fear did say –
> "I hope God will send us safe across the Bridge of Tay."

The poet notes the increasingly bad weather and then, once again, personalises the perceived feelings of the passengers regarding their trip and its intended completion:

> So the train sped on with all its might,
> And Bonnie Dundee soon hove in sight,
> And the passengers' hearts felt light,
> Thinking they would enjoy themselves on the New Year,
> With their friends at home they lov'd most dear,
> And wish them all a happy New Year.

Finally, inexorably, the train reaches the railway bridge and the driver, as if realising the possibility of danger, slows down:

> So the train mov'd slowly along the Bridge of Tay,
> Until it was about midway,
> Then the central girders with a crash gave way,
> And down went the train and passengers into the Tay!
> The Storm Fiend did loudly bray,
> Because ninety lives had been taken away,
> On the last Sabbath day of 1879,
> Which will be remember'd for a very long time.

The poem's concluding stanza is representative, despite its distinctly odd prosody, of the conclusion of much Victorian poetry as it seeks to draw both a practical and a moral conclusion from a particular event:

> It must have been an awful sight,
> To witness in the dusky moonlight,
> While the Storm Fiend did laugh, and angry did bray,
> Along the Railway Bridge of the Silv'ry Tay,
> I must now conclude my lay
> By telling the world fearlessly without the least dismay,
> That your central girders would not have given way,
> At least many sensible men do say,
> Had they been supported on each side with buttresses,
> At least many sensible men confesses,
> For the stronger we our houses do build,
> The less chance we have of being killed.

I am not seeking to claim that "The Tay Bridge Disaster" is an important social document or, indeed, that it is not a truly appallingly bad piece of versification. Thus, Fry has written[138] that, "Almost everything that can go wrong with a poem has gone wrong here. One might argue that McGonagall has brilliantly memorialised a doomed and structurally flawed bridge in congruently doomed and structurally flawed verse. His poem is a disaster for a disaster: it *is* the Tay Bridge, crashing hopelessly to its destruction and dragging every innocent word with it. It is not buttressed by metre, rhyme, sense or reason and even as we read it we feel it collapse under the weight of its own absurdity and ineptitude." But Fry goes on[139] to examine two other disaster poems by established poets - "The Wreck of the Deutschland" by Gerard Manley Hopkins and "The Convergence of the Twain" by Thomas Hardy – and seems genuinely unmoved by either; he then moves[140] to military disasters in the shape of "The Charge of the Light Brigade" by Alfred, Lord Tennyson, which is too well known to require reproduction. He emphasised[141] that the rhyming is perfect:[142] "The rhyming" states Fry, "quite as much as the rhythm helps generate all the pity, pride and excitement for which the poem is renowned." It very well may be, but it is, in all likelihood, the subject matter of the poem which causes the utilisation of both rhythm and rhyme to provide the effect which it creates. In Fry's own words,[143] "We should recognise that Tennyson's is a poem written for the nation while the Hopkins and Hardy are essentially inward looking. Indeed, 'The Wreck of the Deutschland' is much more an autobiographical contemplation of the poet's religious development rather than the commemoration of a shipwreck." At the same time, Fry suggests[144] that, had it not been for Tennyson's poem, the disastrous charge would have vanished into history. Fry's view of "The Charge of the Light Brigade" may have had many subscribers at the time the poem was written and, for a time, after but, today, it is more likely to be perceived as hackneyed doggerel.

Having said that about other disaster poems, is there anything which can be said in favour of "The Tay Bridge Disaster", especially in the light of Fry's devastating critique?[145] Surprisingly enough, especially when compared with other poems discussed by Fry, I believe that there is. In none of the other poems is there any attempt to personalise/humanise the victims. In "The Tay Bridge Disaster", however unfortunately they may actually be portrayed, McGonagall does attempt to empathise his readers with the aspirations, hope and fears of the passengers. He may not be as successful in doing so as Tommy Armstrong in "The Trimdon Grange Explosion", but he has not sought to detach himself from seeking to utilise such techniques in versification as he possesses to *humanise* a disastrous event.[146]

In those poems, the victims' injuries were physical and often leading to death, whereas, in the *Alcock* case, the injuries for which damages were claimed were psychological. In that context, it will be remembered that Teff has been critical[147] of the House of Lords for failing to take into account the medical insights into psychological disability. Whatever may be said of the House of Lords' failure of proper analysis, poets have not shirked such analysis, notably from an internal perspective. A straightforward account of psychological injury or illness and the damage it causes, and the results ,can be found in Rudyard Kipling's poem "The Mothers Son", written in 1932. The poem begins with a simple statement of the poem's subject:

> I have a dream - -a dreadful dream –
> A dream that is never done.
> I watch a man go out of his mind,
> And he is My Mother's Son.

From that introductory verse, which strongly suggests that the narrator is, in fact, writing of himself, the poem, in the second stanza, moves to the result of the sickness:

> They pushed him into a Mental Home,
> And that is like the grave:
> For they do not let you sleep upstairs,
> And you aren't allowed to shave.

Having this disposed of the victim, the narrator seeks to explain how that came, or did not come, to happen. Given the time the poem was written, it is not wholly surprising to see psychiatric illness separated from physical illness in an apparently arbitrary manner. Similarly, given that modern medication had not been devised when Kipling was writing, seemingly invasive, and resented, safety measures were implemented.

The poem then discusses the reasons for the narrator's incarceration which, again, differentiate between psychiatric and physical illness, but, at the same time, crystallising the importance of stress as a causative factor:

> And it was not disease or crime
> Which got him landed there,
> But because They laid on My Mother's Son

More than a man could bear.

What with noise, and fear of death,
Walking, and wounds and cold,
They filled the Cup for My Mother's Son
Fuller than it could hold.

At that point, the focus of Kipling's poem seems to shift and the narrator now seems readier to equate psychiatric with physical illness; his experience in the mental home having both physical and psychological effects:

They broke his body and his mind
And yet They made him live,
And They asked more of My Mother's Son
Than any man could give.

The following stanza continues with that theme and seeks to distinguish psychiatric illness not only from physical illness, but also from death and health itself. The distinguishing factor to which Kipling points is the degrading and isolating nature of the treatment inflicted on the narrator:

For, just because he had not died,
Nor been discharged nor sick,
They dragged it out with My Mother's Son
Longer than he could stick...

Finally, when the uncertainty of the narrator's position is revealed, so is his identity, which had been left unrevealed, though more than hinted at, in the first stanza. Also, in the first line, physical and psychiatric illness is finally equated, though the continuing fate of the poet/narrator is, and, probably cannot be, ultimately decided:

And no one knows when he'll get well - -
So, there he'll have to be:
And, 'spite of the beard in the looking-glass
I know that man is me!

Kipling's poem, it is suggested, is oddly disquieting despite its apparently simple form. The central theme appears to be lack of comprehension – lack of comprehension of the relationship between physical and psychological illness, lack of comprehension of treatment which the poet/narrator is receiving and, more disturbing still, the lack of comprehension of the poet's own identity in the scheme of things at large.

While the treatment of that large theme is not consciously tied to the treatment received by the poet/narrator and, as such, is not treated as a metaphysical phenomenon, its prosody seems to make it all the more compelling. Its deliberate lack of a metaphysical basis can be contrasted with a later treatment, "In a Dark Time" by Theodore Roethke, written in 1964. "In A Dark Time" is an important part of the Roethke canon, as Malkoff has commented that it has received more attention than any other of Roethke's lyrics.[148]

"In A Dark Time" begins symptomatically – that is, the poet, who was himself subject to severe breakdowns, describes, in the first stanza, what is happening to him. He describes it in the terms of a mystical relationship with nature as derived from a heightened perception:

> In a dark time, the eye begins to see,
> I meet my shadow in the deepening shade;
> I hear my echo in the echoing wood - -
> A lord of nature weeping to a tree.
> I live between the heron and the wren,
> Beasts of the hill and serpents of the den.

At that point, the poet seeks to come to terms with the disorder of his mind, which he unhesitatingly describes as *madness*, which once again, this time more threateningly, affects his perception of natural phenomena. The first two lines of the second stanza seem to be of particular significance as Roethke is quoted[149] as having said that, " 'Madness' is a sociological term a good deal of the time. What is madness in the Northwest is normal conduct in Italy, and a hero's privilege in western Ireland." In fact, from the natural descriptions in "In A Dark Time", the landscape seems very much, from the first three stanzas, to be rooted in the physical structures of the Pacific Northwest of the United States. Thus, we must ask how

Roethke contextually regards his state of mind. He does though, know that he is in a situation of uncertainty regarding his future perception and, indeed, development:

> What's madness but nobility of soul
> At odds with circumstance? The day's on fire!
> I know the purity of pure despair,
> My shadow pinned against a sweating wall.
> That place among the rocks - - is it a cave.
> Or a winding path? The edge is what I have.

The third stanza confirms his confusion of perceptions, which, finally in their confusion, make him realise his loss of identity surrounded by juxtapositions, some ("correspondences") normal and natural whilst others are the reverse (see the imagery in the third and sixth lines of the stanza):

> A steady storm of correspondences!
> A night flowing with birds, a ragged moon,
> And in broad day the midnight come again!
> A man goes far to find out what he is - -
> Death of the self in a long, tearless night,
> All natural shapes blazing unnatural light.

The final stanza, which has attracted the most critical attention, reaffirms, through an initial paradox, the poet's crisis of identity. But in the end, he finds himself as part of a metaphysical trinity of himself, his mind, as representative of God, and God, all blown together by natural forces:

> Dark, dark light, and darker my desire.
> My soul, like some heat-maddened summer fly,
> Keeps buzzing at the sill. Which I is I?
> A fallen men, I climb out of my fear.
> The mind enters itself, and God the mind,
> And one is One, free in the tearing wind.

So, in the end, the poet's being is complete and that completeness is, finally, brought about by those very forces which could have (or the poet's perception of them) have ultimately destroyed it. In critical terms, the response to the poem has been mixed: for Malkoff,[150] the poet's condition is to be equated with mystical experience. Thus, he writes that even though the poet has hit the depths, "...he weeps for the agonies of the human condition, which he has not yet transcended. He calls upon the magical powers of the world to save him, to help move beyond himself, he is also calling upon the prehuman within, lurking in the depths of his unconscious." In the final stanza, Malkoff considers[151] that Roethke demonstrates that mystic experience is not an end in itself; mystic union undeniably brings news of God and the universe, but that news does not of itself provide meaning for our lives nor put an end to fears.

In contrast, Parini regards[152] much of the poem, especially in the context of the final stanza, as ironic in nature. This, he considers must be kept in mind so that the surface of the poem not be too highly valued. "The modern Romantic poet," he asserts, "*needs* this saving edge of irony, however there." Thus, in the final stanza, the word *fallen* has to read ironically because, according to Parini, the fall is from flesh *to* spirit, hence, out of fear. The notion of the mind entering itself and God entering the mind, Parini argues, "...suggests the dissolution of all boundaries between self and soul, between soul and God. All contrarieties are resolved, and a new, somewhat terrifying freedom is granted. There is no guarantee that the condition of union will continue. The mystic like anyone else, has to live in the temporal while participating in the eternal one – until his final release in death." The difficulty with Parini's thesis is that there is no internal evidence in the poem to suggest any justification for an ironic interpretation of anything whatever in it: in particular, the poet's damaged perception of natural phenomena and objects would seem strongly to militate against it.

So, we have examined the nature of *accident* as a legal concept, considered accidents as perceived by some poets and discussed the relationship between the two. A particularly catastrophic legal instance has been analysed in some detail and the poetic response to the kind of injury suffered by the plaintiffs in the *Alcock* case has been discussed. If a general conclusion can legitimately be drawn, it has been observed that the law, through both its policies and its language, has generally sought to distance itself from the human consequences of what we describe as *accidents*, the poetic response, though its form and *rhetoric*, to humanise understanding of both relationships leading to accidents and to humanise and personalise their consequences.

2. Disputes Between Neighbours

There is one well known, and major, poem about the relationship between neighbours, and their separation: that poem is "Mending Wall", written by the leading United States poet Robert Frost in 1914. The poem begins with a striking first line which describes the situations in an ordinary spring when the narrator, as usual, find that a winter cold has caused the wall to collapse at intervals:

> Something there is that doesn't love a wall,
> That sends the frozen-ground-swell under it,
> And spills the upper boulders in the sun;
> And makes gaps even two can pass abreast.

However, damage which has been deliberately caused by hunters is more difficult to repair and more extensive and done for no constructive purpose. The narrator hints pointedly that it is damage of the latter kind that the narrator (and his neighbour) must mend:

> The work of hunters is another thing:
> I have come after then and made repair
> Where they have left not one stone on a stone,
> But they would have the rabbit out of hiding,
> To please the yelping dogs. The gaps I mean,
> No one has seen them made or heard them made,
> But at spring mending-time we find them there.

Accordingly, the narrator informs his neighbour, who lives some distance away and they arrange to mend the walls. As they do so, symbolically, they keep the wall between them and deal only with the stones which have fallen on their respective sides. It is harder to replace some rocks than others and, hence, an elemental spirituality is invoked:

> I let my neighbour know beyond the hill;
> And on a day we meet to walk the line
> And set the wall between us once again.
> We keep the wall between us as we go.
> To each the boulders that have fallen to each.
> And some are loaves and some so nearly balls
> We have to use a spell to make them balance:
> "Stay where you are until our backs are turned!"

Rebuilding the wall is hard work, though the narrator compares it to a game – which, in reality, it is. It is apparent that the wall fulfils no real purpose because the two properties are both populated by trees, of different types, rather than by livestock which might necessitate a wall. The neighbour, on being informed of that, comes back with an enigmatic reply:

> We wear our fingers rough with handling them.
> Oh, just another kind of out-door game,
> One on a side. It comes to little more:
> There where it is we do not need the wall:
> He is all pine and I am apple orchard.
> My apple trees will never get across
> And eat the cones under his pines, I tell him.
> He only says, "Good fences make good neighbours."

The enigmatic reply evokes a response from the narrator who feels as though he might point out the absence of livestock and suggest that, before a wall was built, it ought to be decided what was to be walled in, or out, and to whom the wall might cause offence:

> Spring is the mischief in me, and I wonder
> If I could put a notion in his head:
> "Why do they make good neighbours? Isn't it
> Where there are cows? But here there are no cows.
> Before I build a wall I'd ask to know
> What I was walling in or walling out,
> And to whom I was like to give offence.

The narrator is then forced to return to the poem's first line and ask himself *what* might want it down. He feels that he might tell his neighbour that it might be *Elves*, but that would not be the precise answer and he notes the elemental nature of his neighbour's presence and his return to his original enigmatic answer:

> Something there is that doesn't love a wall,
> That wants it down." I could say "Elves" to him,
> But it's not elves exactly, and I'd rather
> He said it for himself. I see him there
> Bringing a stone grasped firmly by the top
> In each hand, like an old-stone savage armed.
> He moves into darkness as it seems to me,
> Not of woods only and the shade of trees.
> He will not go behind his father's saying,
> And he likes having thought of it so well
> He says again, "Good fences make good neighbours."

Inevitably, the symbolism of the poet, and, especially the wall has attracted critical attention. Thus, Gerber [153] comments that the poem involves two neighbours who, "...labor so closely together that their hands can touch and they engage in extended conversation. Yet between them stands a wall of solid rock which holds one apart from the other; the men are engaged in raising this wall even more solidly and securely. But the wall of field-stone is a relatively insubstantial symbol of the real barriers dividing men. That particular wall can come down. In fact it does every fall and winter. Were it not for spring mending time, it would topple altogether." Gerber continues[154] by suggesting that between the neighbours is another wall, built slowly of set ways and habits, mortared firmly of "...tradition, upbringing and environment. One neighbour recites over and over his creed: 'Good fences make good neighbours' To the passing eye, Gerber writes that the that two men give the appearance of working closely, although their co-operation is deceptive because, "In actuality, they stand so far from each other that even the simplest communicative act proves futile. The closed mind slows harder then granite against an unwelcome idea." One might be forgiven for thinking that those two views are more than a little contradictory: in fact, the evidence from the poem itself leads to the second the interpretation as being the correct one. After all, there is no internal evidence that although they could do so if they wished, the neighbours do not indulge in extended conversation. Similarly, although their hand could touch, they do not do so.

On the other hand, Berry regards[155] the relationship between the narrator and his neighbour in a more complex light. Although, like Gerber, she views the wall as representing a symbol which acts as a focus for two conflicting attitudes, there is more, she urges, to the matter than that. "The balance of sympathy," she suggests, seems to lie with the narrator, and an inattentive reader might be led to assume that the poem simply advocates the abolition of walls." The two arguments are justified carefully: the narrator's argument is, "...practical and sensible, his voice easygoing and tolerant. His common sense is based solidly on visible facts..." The neighbours, contrarily, opposes the empirical argument, "...by tradition. It too is based on the practicalities of living. But he has inherited his country wisdom unthinkingly..." Berry then states[156] that, "...all reasonableness is on the narrator's side. Yet it is not ultimately convincing. Despite his good humoured condescension toward the old man he continues with the job. In fact, it was he who instigated the mending..." She concludes by saying that, ultimately, the poem would seem not to be about simple conflicts of attitudes as about the different modes of thinking which inform both attitudes. Berry is of the ultimate view that each of those attitudes – the purely empirical and the purely traditional – are wanting. In her own words, "The conflict is, thus, deliberately unresolved and...the total effect of the poem is ironically, more thoughtful and subtle, more true to human experience..." That equivocation, Berry suggests,[157] is reflective of Frost's own feeling that the consciousness of individuals and the instrumental, intuitive interaction – which he referred to as *passionate preference* – were, for Frost, the only viable premises for human action and creative thought. Hence, in Berry's view, "The function of a wall as a symbol, then lies not in the fact that it shuts people off from each other...or that it may be rationally unnecessary...but that it focuses the constant tension of opposing elements, which Frost saw as the essence of the human condition."

In addition, Lynen raises[158] the issue of the difficulties presented by the poem's symbolism and he comments[159] that (as has already been observed) there has been a great deal of speculation as to what the wall really represents. "Does it," he asks, "signify class division, the barriers of racial prejudice, the misunderstanding between nations, or differences of religion? Similarly the opposed opinions of the speaker and the old farmer seem to invite a comparison with political, philosophical or ethical positions. One might see the poem as a contrast between the liberal and the conservative, the instinctualist and the rationalist, the man of clarity and the man of justice." Lynen then comments[160] that any such interpretation, which lacks supporting evidence anyway, cannot account for the broad range of symbolic meaning which gives the poem its beauty and interest. Thus, in general terms, Lynen writes "That the symbolism of 'Mending Wall' is general does not meant that it is indefinite...Frost has exactly defined the nature of the problem he portrays, so that it represents, not vague classes or experience, by only other problems of the same kind. Though one may see in 'Mending Wall' allusions to specific things outside the poem, even reminiscences of one's past experience, their meaning will always have a certain fundamental similarity."

In the context of Lynen's last point, it may be that the reason why the narrator's neighbour was keen to rebuild the wall was that he wished to build a wall to protect what he perceives as his own vulnerability. The building of such personal walls may be necessary for many reason. The poem "Ears in the Turrets Hear" by Dylan Thomas which Tindall notes,[161] is readily accessible, unlike much of Thomas's other work. Tindall is not much impressed: "All is neat and clear. Assonance, dissonance and internal rhyme provide a little relief. But Thomas is better when rich and strange." The poem's first stanza clearly and neatly, indeed, states the narrator's situation – he is frightened by the importunity of a stranger who seeks to disturb his introverted and isolate condition:

> Ears in the turrets hear
> Hands grumble on the door,
> Eyes in the gables see
> The fingers at the locks.
> Shall I unbolt or stay
> Alone till the day I die
> Unseen by stranger-eyes
> In this house?
> Hands, hold you poison or grapes?

The second stanza reinforces the impression of that first stanza by emphasising the vulnerability of the narrator's protection, of his body, and the peacefulness, in an absolute sense, of his present condition. The third stanza provides him with a choice of either staying as he is and ignoring the overtures of the strangers and the ships which are anchored off the island which he both inhabits and represents. Thus, he asks himself:

> Shall I run to the ships
> With the wind in my hair,
> Or stay till the day I die
> And welcome no sailor?
> Ships, hold you poison or grapes?

As might have been expected, the answer he ultimately reaches is inconclusive and, in that context, it is clearly not without significance that the poem was written about the time Dylan Thomas left known and familiar south Wales for an unknown and unfamiliar London. Thus, the poem ends, perhaps with a beginning:

> Hands grumble on the door,
> Ships anchor off the bay,
> Rain beats the sand and slates.
> Shall I let in the stranger,
> Shall I welcome the sailor,
> Or stay till the day I die?
>
> Hands of the stranger and hold of the ships,
> Hold you poison or grapes?

As regards the specifically autobiographical aspects of the poem, Glyn Lewis writes [162] that, "...the poet is debating the desirability of moving away from the solipsistic attitude, feeling his way to a decision whether to remain isolated in his subjectivism or to open windows and doors upon the objective social world. Either decision carries with it terrifying possibilities." That point has been taken up by Tindall, who is rather more circumspect when he states [163] that, "Turreted house and womblike island insulate him from the mainland which sends menacing

523

intruders. Going out for this egregious man is as frightening as staying home." However, it is suggested that in going out, the poet may have the opportunity to experience a sense of ecstatic freedom ("With the wind in my hair") which is otherwise impossible. The key to real understanding of the nature of the poem may be provided by Ackerman who considers[164] that, at that stage of his artistic development, Dylan Thomas was, "...apt to relate all experience to himself... he does not write outside the orbit of his own personal emotions, but seems also, at times, to hide is naked inner self..." Another view is represented by Moynihan who suggests[165] that any ambiguity in the poem is based on the image of the human being as an island and maybe understood on at least two levels. It may first, be read as a meditation by a woman on whether or not to receive a man, or, second, as a meditation by any human being as to whether or not to trust human beings. In either interpretation the question ("Hands of the stranger...?) is translated as "Is life evil or good, is sexual passion and its result bitter or sweet?"

Assuming Moynihans's second interpretation to be the more likely, which, given Dylan Thomas's experiential and emotional development, seems the more plausible, if the creation of emotional walls in personal and poetic life is not an infrequent occurrence, what is the position in law? In that context, it is suggested that the law may, from time to time, be required to provide walls of its own creation when actual walls have failed to achieve their purpose. A useful example is provided by the decision of McMullin J of the New Zealand Supreme Court in *Matheson* v *Northcote College Board of Governors*.[166] In that case, the plaintiffs, who were the occupiers and owners of a residential property, which was built on a section of land which adjoined the college, sought an injunction to restrain the defendants from permitting their pupils from committing various acts which were alleged to constitute an actionable nuisance. They sought an injunction and sued in nuisance, negligence and under the rule in *Rylands* v *Fletcher*. The acts alleged were that the defendants,[167] "...wrongfully permitted pupils and others from the school to throw firecrackers and other objects and to strike golf balls onto the plaintiff's land and to trespass thereon, stealing fruit therefrom and disturbing and interfering with the plaintiff's use and enjoyment of their land and causing nuisance annoyance and damage thereto." These acts were alleged to have taken place in a period between February 1966 and November 1973 and there were 35 specific instances alleged in the plaintiff's statement of claim. It was also accepted by the judge that the plaintiffs were in a position to be able to prove all of the acts alleged.

Initially, it had been argued that only the actual trespassers were liable to the plaintiffs either in trespass or nuisance because the defendants had not themselves committed the acts and nor were the pupils their agents or servants. To that submission, it was replied, on behalf of the plaintiffs, that the defendants had so badly supervised and controlled the school that pupils were not prevented from committing acts of trespass and that the board had not taken steps in the way of erecting fences to prevent the acts and, hence, that the damage was a consequence of the state of affairs for which the board was responsible and, therefore, accounted to a private nuisance. That submission was accepted by the trial judge and, in so doing, McMullin J referred[168] to various cases where people or organisations who have attracted crowds, members of which who have committed acts of trespass, were liable in both public and private nuisance. "It is not hard to see," said the judge,[169] "why the law has afforded a remedy in nuisance to persons aggrieved by the acts of individual trespassers against the 'controller'. Such individuals may differ from time to time and be difficult to identify. If the aggrieved party were allowed a remedy against them only, the difficulties of proof and enforcement might such as to make the remedy of little value.[170] Although many of the cases to which he made reference were brought in public nuisance, many of the same considerations applied to each instance.[171] Accordingly, the activities alleged in the relevant paragraphs of the plaintiffs' statement of claim might constitute an actionable nuisance.

The second issue which arose in McMullin J's judgment was the defendant's potential liability under the rule in *Rylands* v *Fletcher*. It was argued on behalf of the defendants that the rule only applied to a non-natural user of land and bringing children onto school playing fields did not constitute a non-natural user of land and, further, that the rule only applied to things rather than people. However, the judge made reference[172] to the enunciation of the rule itself by Blackburn J in delivering the judgment of the Exchequer Chamber:[173] "...the person who for his own purposes brings on his lands and keeps and collects there anything likely to do mischief if it escapes, must keep it in at his peril, and, if he does not do so , is prima facie answerable for all the damage which is the natural consequence of its escape. He can excuse himself by showing that the escape was owing to the plaintiff's default, or perhaps that the escape was the consequence of vis major, or the act of God, but as nothing of this sort exists here it is unnecessary to inquire what excuse would be sufficient." Prior to applying those principles to the facts of the case at hand, the judge noted that the *non-natural* user referred to by the defendants' counsel had been refined by the Judicial Committee of the Privy Council it as being some special use bringing with it increased danger to others and must not be the ordinary use of the land or such other use as is proper for the general benefit of the community.[174] Also, he noted that counsel for the plaintiff had admitted that the authorities in *Rylands* v *Fletcher* were not as strong as those in nuisance.

In *Matheson*, McMullin J continued,[175] it might be argued that either the golf balls which were hit on the plaintiffs' land, or the pupils who trespassed on it, were *things* for the purposes of the rule in *Reynolds* v *Fletcher*. As regards the first, the judge was not prepared to apply the rule to the escape of balls used in sport: he noted that Lord Reid, in *Bolton* v *Stone*[176] had refused to cricket balls escaping from a field where the game had been played for many years. "A cricket ball," he said, "is not a thing which is dangerous in itself nor is the playing of cricket in School grounds a non-natural user of land. Nor is a golf ball a thing dangerous in itself not is the playing of golf in school grounds non-natural user of land. The playing of a game of cricket would amount to a social utility to which the rule of *Rylands* v *Fletcher* in this modern day applications would not apply." Hence, the rule in *Rylands* v *Fletcher* had no application to the present case, insofar as the escape of the ball was concerned. With respect to McMullin J, it is hard to agree with some of his earlier statements: a stationary cricket ball is not normally a dangerous thing, although it could, hand-held, amount to an *offensive weapon* if used aggressively. However, when projected with appropriate velocity by a motivated pace bowler or struck with sufficient force it can be a very dangerous thing indeed. It is certainly perceived as such, as the very fact that *Miller* v *Jackson*[177] was litigated at all strongly suggests. The danger is generally not so great in so many different ways as might be presented by a cricket ball in the case of a golf ball, although, once again, the facts of *Castle* v *St Augustine's Golf Links Ltd*[178] are not without interest. In that case, a taxi driver[179] who lost an eye from a sliced ball recovered damages from a golf club where a hole was so near a road as to constitute a public nuisance. In addition, though, golf balls were repeatedly sliced on to the road and there was consequent and substantial interference with the use of the road. In that context, the *rhetoric* employed by McMullin J in *Matheson* seems positively Denningesque!

McMullin J then turned his attention [180] to the pupils as *things escaping from the school's premises*. In that context, the judge reiterated his earlier rhetorical comment [181] when he said that, "Children cannot be said to be dangerous per se nor their playing on a school ground a non-natural user of the land." That, he considered, was, of itself enough to dispose of the application of *Rylands* v *Fletcher* to the acts of trespass by the children. However, there was one contrary authority in the shape of the decision of Bennett J in the English case of *Attorney-General* v *Corke*.[182] There, the owner of a disused brickfield allowed people to bring caravans on to the field and live there at a weekly rent. Some of the occupants of the caravans committed acts on the land adjoining the field which amounted to a nuisance and were a menace to the health of the community, such as depositing human excrement, breaking down fences, trespassing, and permitting their horses to trespass, on the adjoining property and creating disturbances by noise in the neighbourhood of the property. Bennett J held that the owner of the property was bound to prevent the occupants from committing the acts in question and an injunction was granted restraining him from permitting the occupants to commit the acts in question. In making that order, Bennett J stated [183] that, "...the principle in *Rylands* v *Fletcher* affords in my judgment a basis upon which the defendant can be made responsible in law for the nuisance which undoubtedly exists, on the facts, in the vicinity of this camp, and which nuisance is caused by some of the people whom he brings there for his own profit. On that principle I hold that the defendant is responsible and that an injunction must be granted against him". Apart from a seeming confusion between the notions of *Rylands* v *Fletcher* and nuisance, *Corke* has been strongly criticised, especially by Holdsworth, who suggested [184] that, first, if *Rylands* v *Fletcher* did properly apply, then the defendant would have been under a duty to keep the caravan dwellers on his land. Had he done so, he might have rendered himself liable in false imprisonment to the dwellers themselves! Second, a recognised defence to actions in *Rylands* v *Fletcher* is that the escape was caused by someone other than the defendant. In

Corke, the caravan dwellers were neither the defendant's servants nor, even, independent contractors with whom he had business relations. In addition, McMullin J noted[185] that he was not aware of any case where *Corke* had been followed.[186] In particular, in the leading case of *Dorset Yacht Co Ltd* v *Home Office*,[187] the House of Lords had held the Home Office liable for the escape of borstal boys, but not in *Rylands* v *Fletcher*. "Prison authorities, "said McMullin J,[188] are in a greater position to exert control over other human beings than any other groups or individuals and much more so than school board. If *Rylands* v *Fletcher* has not been accepted as applying to prison escapees, it is not likely to find acceptance in the case of school pupils." Accordingly, no action in respect of the pupil trespasses lay in *Rylands* v *Fletcher*. Before leaving that particular topic, it should be noted that, in *Burnie Port Authority* v *General Jones*,[189] the High Court of Australia absorbed the rule in *Rylands* v *Fletcher* into the tort of negligence.[190]

It seems logically to follow that the next major issue arising in *Matheson* was the possibility of the defendants being liable in negligence. It was argued on their behalf that the defendants did not owe a duty of care to prevent people on tis playing fields from committing acts of trespass on the plaintiffs' land. It was, further, argued that a duty of care could only arise in three specific relationships – a duty could arise it either, first, the defendant owed a duty of care to the plaintiff by reason of being the occupier of land, or, second, the defendant owed a duty by reason of being a school authority; or, third, the defendant owed a duty by reason of having control or custody of school pupils.

As regards the first category, it was argued that the law did not impose any duty of care on the occupier of land which arose independently of the duties of an occupier to prevent a nuisance arising from the uses of land and any duty under *Rylands* v *Fletcher*. In respect of the second, counsel for the defendants noted the decision of the High Court of Australia in *Smith* v *Leurs*,[191] where Dixon J had said[192] that, "It is, however, exceptional to find in the law a duty to control another's actions to prevent harm to strangers. The general rule is that one man is under no duty of controlling another man to prevent his doing damage to a third. There are, however, special relations which are the source of a duty of this nature . It appears now to be recognised that it is incumbent upon a parent who maintains control over a young child to take reasonable care so to exercise that control as to avoid conduct on his part exposing the person or property of others to unreasonable danger." *Smith* v *Leurs*, was an action for damages in negligence resulting from damage to the sight of a boy who was hit in the eye by a stone fired from a shanghai of another boy. The action was brought against that boy's parents. There was no evidence of vicious propensities on the part of the boy, but his parents knew that he had a shanghai in his possession. Nonetheless, the High Court of Australia held that the parents were not liable in damages. Dixon J's *dictum* in *Smith* v *Leurs* was adopted by Lord Morris in the *Dorset Yacht Co* case,[193] although he did find that a special relationship did exist so as to render the Home Office liable. As regards the third category, in *Dorset Yacht Co. Ltd* v *Home Office*, Lord Morris had said[194] that, "If A can reasonably foresee that some act or omission of his may have the result that loss or damage may be suffered by B who is someone who would be closely and directly affected by the act or omission, there will be some circumstances in which a legal duty will be owed by A to B and some in which it will not. The question arises as to what is the dividing line and on which side the present case falls. The fact that the immediate damage suffered by B may have been caused by C does not affect the question A owed a duty to B; such fact would only relation to the question of whether the act or omission of A did result in damage to B. Some act on the part of C might be the very kind of thing which would be likely to happen if there was a breach of duty by A." It was, therefore, argued that the defendant as a school authority had no duty of care in relation to the custody of pupils and that no analogy could be drawn between the escapees from prison in *Dorset Yacht Club* and the pupils in the instant case.

Counsel for the plaintiffs disputed the defendants' breakdown at a fundamental level [195] and, accordingly, McMullin J was cautious in deciding on the future of that claim. However, he did say[196] that, whilst he was mindful that, before a new category of negligence was recognised, the courts must be satisfied that there is a need for it and that due weight is given to established principles,[197] one must also guard against too narrow a categorisation of the duties of care. In the light of that statement he was not prepared to decide conclusively - negligence being a matter which depended so much on time, circumstance and proximity that no duty of care could exist on the part of the defendants to the plaintiffs. Accordingly, he permitted the claims based on nuisance and negligence, though not that based on *Rylands* v *Fletcher,* to go forward for trial on the facts.

By way of comment on the proceedings at large, it is necessary to return to Robert Frost's poem "Mending Wall"[198] and, in particular, to the neighbour's enigmatic response to the building of a quite useless wall. If "Good Fences Make Good Neighbours", then it might very well have been that better fences kept neighbours out of court. Thus, to resist the plaintiff's claim in nuisance,[199] the defendants might have done better had they erected fences which would have helped keep projectiles out and sought to act as a deterrent to pupils entering on to the plaintiffs' property. As regards nuisance itself, it appears from the *Matheson* decision that liability may be imposed for the creation of a nuisance committed by someone over whom the defendants have control, regardless of any adoption or continuance by the defendants. Thus, it might very well be that if some of the alleged incidents had been committed by supporters of the teams of other schools playing sporting fixtures against Northcote College, the governing body might well be liable. The point of the previous discussion is that, for whatever reason, the building of fences between properties and between people seems to be a basic human need, whether, objectively, necessary or not. Thus, the narrator's neighbour in "Mending Wall" needed to rebuild the vulnerable wall, even though its existence was futile. In "Ears in the Turrets Hear", assuming it to be broadly autobiographical, the narrator did leave his walled life, with very mixed results, In *Matheson*, insufficient walls led to unnecessary legal action. The walls may be physical, spiritual or legal but it is clear from a concluding passage in "Mending Wall", when the narrator describes his perception of his older neighbour, that the urge and need to build them is truly elemental.[200]

3. Privacy, Rights and Relationships

In this final, substantive section of this rather speculative and eclectic book, it is proposed to examine the three interrelated topics of privacy, protection of human rights and relationships. A way of introducing these apparently diffuse topics is, inevitably, through poetry – in the instant case a lyric by Bob Dylan, the first stanza of which is as follows:

As I went out one morning

> To breathe the air around Tom Paine's
> I spied the fairest damsel
> That ever did walk in chains
> I offer'd her my hand
> She took me by the arm
> I knew that very instant
> She meant to do me harm

Immediately, there is both a legal and contemporary sense in the poem in the reference in the second line. Tom Paine (1737-1809) was a radical English writer[201] who, having spent over ten years in America, wrote *The Rights of Man*, which was published in two parts in 1791 and 1792, initially in response to Edmund Burke's reflections on the *Revolution in France*, published in 1790, which represented a forceful attack on the activities of the revolutionaries. Paine's most famous work prompted the British Government to introduce a law against seditious publication, of which he was convicted in his absence, his having to flee to France, There, he was no more successful, being imprisoned from 1793 to 1795, and narrowly escaping execution, on account of his opposition to the execution of the King, Whilst in prison, he wrote *The Age of Reason* which was a savage critique of traditional religious beliefs and practices. His last years, from 1802, were spent in America but, by then, Walker suggests,[202] his popularity had waned significantly. Assuming, as it is very easy to do with Dylan's lyrics, that "As I Went Out One Morning" is allegorical, it could depict the woman as either representing *The Right of Man* or *The Age of Reason*; in other words the chains worn by the woman could either represent infringements of human rights as perceived by Paine or traditional religion. Given some of Dylan's religious output, it is more convincing, I would suggest, that the *air* about Tom Paine's habitation is Paine's *rights* thesis, rather than the critique of religion represented by *The Age of Reason*.

In the area of human rights, there is one particular issue which has been especially productive of controversy in various aspects of human activity – and that is the right to privacy. A useful and interesting example of the application of this notion is provided by the decision of the High Court of Australia in *Australian Broadcasting Corporation v Lenah Game Meats*.[203] In that case, an injunction had been sought to restrain the publication of a video, by the Corporation, which had been taken of the slaughtering process used by Lenah Game Meats when butchering possum carcasses. The film had been recorded by hidden cameras which had been placed by supporters of Animal Liberation inside the respondent's' building. It had been assumed that those people had trespassed when placing the cameras in the building. The video was then given to the Corporation who broadcast it after an original application for an injunction had been refused. The major issue involved in the dispute was whether the Corporation could be restrained by an injunction given that it had not committed an in actionable wrong in obtaining the video. It was also argued that it would be unconscionable to broadcast the video further as the corporation knew that it had been obtained by way of a trespass and that that unconscionability would, of itself, justify the grant of an injunction.

The High Court of Australia rejected the application, with Callinan J dissenting. In particular, Gleeson CJ, although he supported the view that, under certain circumstances, equity could intervene to prevent the publication of photographic material which had been improperly obtained, it could only do so where the material could be regarded as *private*. That was so because it could only be regarded as being unconscionable in those circumstances. Therefore, the idea of privacy was crucial to the decision. In that context, the Chief Justice stated[204] that, "There is no bright line which can be drawn between what is private and what is not. Use of the term 'public' is often a convenient method of contrast but there is a large area between what is necessarily public and what is necessarily private. An activity is not private because it is not done in public. It does not suffice to make an act private that, because it occurs on private property, it has such a measure of protection from the public gaze as to the characteristics of the property, the nature of the activity, the locality, and the disposition of the property owner combine to afford. Certain kinds of information about a person, such as information relating to health, personal relationships, or finances, may be easy to identify as private; as may certain kinds of activity, which are reasonable person, applying contemporary standards of morals and behaviour, would understand to be meant to be unobserved. The requirement that disclosure or observation of information or conduct would be highly offensive to a reasonable person of ordinary sensibilities is in many circumstances a useful practical test..." In all the circumstances, Gleeson CJ was of the view[205] that the activities portrayed on the film were in private. Thus, he emphasised that, "...an act does not become private simply because the owner of land would prefer that it were unobserved. The reasons for such preference might be personal, or financial. They might be good or bad. An owner of land does not have to justify refusal of entry to a member of the public, or of the press. The right to choose who may enter, and who will be excluded, is an aspect of ownership. It may mean that a person who enters without permission is a trespasser; but that does not mean that every activity observed by the trespasser is private." Accordingly, it followed that, as the video was private, it was not unconscionable for the Corporation to publish it. However, the situation would have been different had the Corporation itself been the trespasser[206] or the video been of a private nature.[207]

Gummow and Hayne JJ, with whom Gaudron J agreed, were of the view[208] that the case of *Victoria Park Racing and Recreation Grounds Co v Taylor*[209] did not stand in the path of the development of a tort protecting rights of privacy. In *Taylor*, the plaintiff company conducted, for profit, race meetings as a racecourse which it owned in a Sydney suburb. Inside the grounds, signals and noticeboards displayed details of each race some twenty minutes before it was run. The three defendants, who were the owner and occupier of adjoining land and one of the employees of a radio station, had entered an observation platform on the land and broadcast the details to the public. The plaintiff sought injunctions to restrain the defendants' activities. They failed both at first instance and in the High Court of Australia when claiming on the grounds of copyright infringement and in actions in nuisance and *Rylands* v *Fletcher*.[210] However, in *Lenah Game Meats*, those judges also stated[211] that the respondents' reliance on an emergent tort of invasion of privacy was misplaced. "Whatever developments may take place in that field will be to the benefit of natural not artificial persons. It may be that development is best achieved by looking across the range of already established legal and equitable wrongs. On the other hand, in some respects these may be seen as representing species of a genus, being a principle protecting the interests of the individual, to some reasonable extent, a secluded and private life, the words of the Restatement, 'free form the prying eyes, ears and publications of others.' Nothing said is these reasons should be understood as foreclosing any such debate or indicating any particular outcome."

Kirby J, even though he did not support the grant of the injunction in the case at hand, was of the view[212] that Australian courts had responded to new circumstances which had involved serious affronts to conscience. "Such circumstances, "he said, "will arise in a case where information which lacks the quality of confidence had nevertheless been obtained illegally, tortiously, surreptitiously or otherwise improperly. In such cases the preservation of the confidentiality or secrecy of the information may be of substantial concern to the applicant for relief. The jurisdiction to restrain the use of confidential information has long been exercised against third parties who have received the information from someone else, By extension such jurisdiction may now be exercised in a case where the information in question has been obtained illegally, tortiously, surreptitiously or improperly, even where the possessor is itself innocent of wrongdoing. The reason for providing the relief is to uphold the obligation of conscience and to prevent publication in circumstances where such publication would be unconscionable." Nevertheless, Kirby J did not agree to the award of an injunction because he regarded[213] the discretion vested in the Court below as having miscarried to the extent that it had, "...failed to give proper weight to the constitutional consideration favouring discussion in the appellant's television programme of animal welfare as a legitimate matter of governmental and political concern." This was a matter of especial concern in the present case because the product involved was wholly exported and the appellant was the national broadcaster established by federal law with national functions. When the constitutional consideration favouring the free discussion of government and political issue of animal welfare in this context is given due weight, a proper exercise of the discretion obliged that the interlocutory injunction be refused. The power to grant an injunction existed. But the exercise of that power miscarried. Such exercise should have upheld free speech.

In dissent, Callinan J made his initial standpoint clear, when he stated[214] that, "If journalists and publishers may not improperly obtain matter for publication, why should they be permitted, it may be asked, to publish material improperly, in this case criminally, obtained by others? I cannot accept that the nature of the source and the reprehensibility, especially criminal, of the conduct by which information and matter have been obtained may not be a highly relevant consideration to a determination whether its publication should b e permitted." On the issue of unconscionability, Callinan J was of the view[215] that where an item of valuable property has been obtained in violation of a person's right to exclusive possession in circumstances in which the defendant knows, or ought to have known, of the violation , it is to be regarded as unconscionably obtained and to be delivered to the person whose rights have been so violated, Callinan J went on to apply that view to the facts of *Lenah Game Meats*, when he commented[216] that his view also represented the, "...reality of the value of images. If they have value, the right to control the making of them plainly has value. If there is no right to control the making of them, that is, for example, if they can be made in, or form a public place or places upon which their maker may go, then on the current state of the law, the maker will not be able to be restricted from using them. But if the position, as here, be otherwise then an occupier should not be denied rights in respect of them because their maker has been able, surreptitiously, to violate the occupier's rights." The judge also argued[217] that his stance was justifiable on policy grounds in that it should serve as a deterrent to others who might be prepared to obtain illegally, or to use illegally obtained material, for their own financial or other benefit to the detriment of people whose rights had been infringed. Further, it paid proper regard to the long established common law principle that people were entitled to secure and protect their property and to deny access to whom they please. It followed that the injunction sought by the respondents should be upheld.[218]

The *rhetoric*, with the exception of Callinan J, was couched generally in terms of privacy and the decision, including the judgment of Callinan J, certainly laid open the way to the recognition, or creation of a tort based around the protection of privacy. However, as has been pointed out by Johnston,[219] other courts in Australia, at least, have not been so immediately enthusiastic. However, the ways in which cognisance of the problems which might arise in relation to some of the issues is considered shortly.[220]

In the second stanza of the Bob Dylan lyric which was earlier noted,[221] the narrator describes a conversation he had with the "...fairest damsel that ever did walk in chains..." He does so, suspiciously as, it will be remembered from the first stanza, the narrator had become aware that the woman had meant to harm him. Against that background, the stanza is as follows:

> "Depart from me this moment"
> I told her with my voice
> Said she, "But I don't wish to"
> Said I, But you have no choice"
> "I beg you, sir," she pleaded
> From the corners of her mouth
> "I will secretly accept you
> And together we'll fly south"

The whole communication exercise is deceptive: although the narrator tells the woman to leave, he only does so *with his voice* which suggests that even though he says the words, he does not mean them and wishes that he could override his initial feelings. However, the woman's response, although apparently directly offering him some kind of idyllic relationship – "...together we'll fly south" implies warm climates and scenic surrounds – but it is truly oblique, being said *from the corners of her mouth*. The private nature of what she offers is further emphasised by the use of the word *secretly* in the penultimate line. Since she is the product of the *airs* which surround Tom Paine's residence, *rights of privacy* are instantly hinted at and the kind of relationship which the woman seemed to be offering the narrator is pervasively personal and such relationships are normally private. How does all that poetic rhetoric relate to the discipline of Law?

First of all, the issue of privacy as it refers to the intimate human relationships is far from unknown in the common law. In the rather notorious case of *Duchess of Argyll* v *Duke of Argyll*,[222] Ungoed Thomas J had stated[223] that, "The confidential nature of the [marriage] relationship is of its very essence and so very obviously and necessarily implicit in it that there is no need for it to be expressed. To express it is superfluous: it is clear to the least intelligent. So it seems to me that confidences between husband and wife during marriage are not excluded from the court's protection..." In that, far from edifying, case an injunction was granted where the defendant had proposed to write a series of articles for a newspaper, some of which contained information relating to the plaintiff's private life, personal affairs and conduct which had been communicated in confidence to the defendant during the subsistence of the marriage. The grant of the injunction was, of itself, of some interest because, first, there was no direct[224] authority which governed the claim and, second, there was an application of the equitable maxim *[S]he who comes to Equity must come with clean hands*. That latter was important because it appeared that the plaintiff had written earlier newspaper articles herself – although they were not as salacious as those projected and of which she was complaining. Also, she had apparently been guilty of the most flagrant immorality. Those matters, Ungoed Thomas J considered,[225] were not sufficient to enliven the maxim's application.[226]

Since 1965, when *Argyll* was decided, the whole context surrounding the kind of activities and relationships involved has dramatically changed. That may clearly be seen from the facts of the decision of Eady J of the Queen's Bench Division of the English Supreme Court in *CC v AB*.[227] There, the claimant had conducted, over some months, an adulterous affair with the defendant's wife. The defendant had made it clear, in a number of hostile communications, that he wished to make the relationship public by way of relevant media publicity. He was motivated partly by a desire for revenge and partly by an urge to make money. Neither the claimant not the claimant's wife wished the fact of the relationship, or any of its details, to be made public. The claimant, in the aftermath of the relationship, was seeking to reconstruct his own family life. Hence, he was concerned for the welfare and interests of his own wife and their young children. In particular, his wife was receiving medical attention for anxiety and stress and her conditions were likely to be exacerbated by media exposure. Indeed, there was also a fear that the wife was self-harming and might attempt suicide.

Accordingly, the claimant brought an action to prevent publication of the story on the basis that such communication would be a breach of confidence or, in the alternative, that it would amount to harassment. Conversely, the defendant took the view that any harm which the claimant's wife might suffer was attributable to the behaviour of the claimant himself and he argued that a party to an adulterous relationship could never obtain injunctive relief against a wronged party so as to prevent the relationship's disclosure.

Ultimately, Eady, J who initially described[228] the matter as, "...involving no direct precedent for this so far as I am aware, and it does not at first glance appear to be a very compelling case...", granted on interlocutory injunction which restrained the defendant from direct or indirect communication with the media, or on the internet, regarding the claimant's former relationship with the defendant's wife. He also granted an interim order under relevant legislation. [229] Despite his initially deprecatory remarks,[230] Eady J's first inquiry was into the nature of the cause of action.[231] The instant point which he made was that, were reliance being placed by the claimants on defamation, there would be no prospect of an injunction. That is a long established view, represented by the decision of the Court of Appeal in *Bonnard v Perryman*.[232] There, Lord Coleridge CJ had commented[233] that, "The right of free speech is one which it is for the public interest that individuals should possess, and, indeed, that they should exercise without impediment so long as no wrongful act is done; and unless an alleged libel is untrue, it is not clear that any right has been infringed and the importance of leaving free speech unfettered is a strong reason in cases of libel for dealing most cautiously and warily with the granting of interlocutory injunctions... In the particular case before us, indeed, the libellous character of the publication is beyond dispute, but the effect of it upon the Defendant can be disposed of only by a jury, and we cannot feel sure that the defence of justification is one which, on the facts which may be before them, the jury might find to be wholly unfounded: nor can we tell what damages may be recoverable."

At the same time, however, there was a judgment in dissent by Kay LJ, who took the view[234] that, congruent with ordinary practice, courts should decide whether to grant an injunction in such circumstances, "...by the consideration of what is commonly termed the balance convenience and inconvenience." Kay LJ then considered the issue which might guide courts. Hence, were the injunction to be continued, it would not prevent the defendant from seeking to protect the public by means of other statements which he might legitimately make against the plaintiffs, but would only preclude him from repeating the particular allegation. On the other hand, if the defendant were permitted to repeat the statement, as apparently the intended to do, then very considerable injury might be caused to the plaintiff. Hence, were the injunction to be denied, such injury might very well consequently result.

Thus, it very well may be that the principle enunciated by Eady J in *CC v AB* regarding injunctions in defamation matters might not be so clear cut as was made out. Eady J then continued[235] by saying that, as English domestic law did not recognise an enforceable right to privacy as such, the issue had been put on the basis that any relevant communication must be treated as being a breach of confidence. In *CC v AB* defamation was not, *per se*, in issue. However, as a most distinguished torts scholar, Fridman, has pointed out [236] in his discussion of *Australian Broadcasting Corporation v Lenah Game Meats*,[237] issues of privacy and defamation may, in fact, be inextricably entangled, so that, once again, assertion of principle may not, so far as Australia is concerned, be wholly or comprehensively accurate.

In *CC v AB*, the first cause of action relied upon entailed, in Eady J's *ipsissima verba*,[238] "...the striking proposition that a spouse whose partner has committed adultery owes a duty to the third party adulterer to keep quiet about it – even without any voluntary assumption of such an obligation." In that context, it was necessary to examine various elements which had been revealed by the evidence in *CC v AB*. First, it appeared that the defendant had, in a number of threatening communications as well as in evidence before the court, said that he wished to reveal the information partly out of revenge and partly to make money by selling his story to the media. That gave rise immediately to the issue of whether the citizen's right of free speech was dependant on motive. Thus, in *Cheng Albert v Tse Wai Chun Paul*,[239] Lord Nicholls seemed to be of the view[240] that the right to free speech was not dependent on the motives which might govern its exercise when he said that, "Commentators of all shades of opinion are entitled to 'have their own agenda.' Politicians, social reformers, busybodies, those with political or other ambitious or none all can grind their axes." In addition, Lord Nicholls was not prepared, and this is important for the purpose of the present discussion, to permit courts to distinguish between *public* or *private* purposes, or between purposes which they might regard as socially or politically desirable or those which they regarded as undesirable. "That would," he said, "be a highly dangerous course. That way lies censorship. That would defeat the purpose for which the law accords the defence of freedom to make comments on matters of general interest." Thus, it would appear not to matter whether the defendant in *CC v AB* had acted from his clearly expressed and bad motives or had, say, sought to expose the moral frailties of a particular and influential group of people.

A contrary view can be found in the view of the majority of the House of Lords in *Campbell* v *MGN Ltd*,[241] who seemed to be of the opinion that the purpose for which defendants sought to exercise their freedom of speech might be relevant. A useful instance was provided by Baroness Hale who commented[242] that, "Not every statement about a person's health will carry the badge of confidentiality or risk dong harm to the person's physical or moral integrity. The privacy interest in the fact that a public figure has a cold or a broken leg is unlikely to be strong enough to justify the press's freedom to report it. What harm could it possibly do? Sometimes there will be other justifications for publishing, especially where the information is relevant to the capacity of a public figure to do the job. But that is not the case and, in this case, as the judge found, a risk that publication would do harm."

Of course, the factual situations in *Cheng* and *Campbell* were different: *Cheng* involved the publicity attaching to the arrest of a tour escort for drug trafficking, which might give rise immediately to the second instance noted by Baroness Hale in *Campbell. Campbell* itself concerned photographs of an internationally known fashion model taken when she was emerging from therapy, provided by a self-help group, for drug addiction. In *Campbell*, her claim was successful, even though the claimant had earlier asserted to the media that she did not take drugs. In *Chen*, the claim, more surprisingly perhaps, was also successful because the defendant's motives had supplanted genuineness of belief in respect of the defence of fair comment. Thus bearing out Fridman's view[243] that privacy laws and the law of defamation are thoroughly – if, perhaps, confusingly – intermingled.

Having made those general points, the judge in CC v *AB* went on to examine[244] the specific features of the case. First, the evidence indicated that neither of the parties to the adulterous relationship wished either the existence or the details relating to its conduct to be made public. There is surely nothing much exceptional about that – indeed, unless either party, or both of them, was given to a peculiarly exhibitionistic urge, one would normally expect that to be the case. Eady J then went on to extrapolate from the parties' proper reticence and stated that, "There is a powerful argument that the conduct of an intimate or sexual relationship is a matter in respect of which there is a 'reasonable or legitimate expectation of privacy.' Accordingly, anyone who obtains such information would be expected to recognise that expectations, either from the nature of the information itself or of the circumstances in which it was imparted. If that is so for journalists or for scandal mongers in general, it is a matter for consideration whether, and to what extent, a 'cuckolded' husband is under a lesser obligation."

That is a comment of some interest, as it brings Baroness Hale's comment in *Campbell*[245] into immediate focus. Suppose, for example, that the adulterous relationship had involved a public figure whose self-appointed mission had been the improvement of moral standards in public life, then *journalists and scandal mongers in general* might very well have a proper interest in the dissemination of such information. Similarly, were that public figure married and female, and advocated the virtues of fidelity in marriage, then the same criteria might well be applicable to that person's deceived husband!

The next matter to which Eady J then adverted was the assertion by the claimant that he was seeking to reconstruct his own family life and that he was seeking to reconstruct his own family life and that he was concerned for the welfare of his wife and young children. It was argued on his behalf that there was no reason why those people should suffer more than was necessary, especially by reason of the effects of intervision by the media. It was further argued that the courts should have regard to the rights of the wife and children, particularly in the context of Art 8 of the *European Convention for the Protection of Human Rights and Fundamental Freedoms* 1950 in determining the dispute, even though the wife and children were not parties.

A further, connected issue arising from the case which Eady J regarded as, "...even more troubling..." was the claimant's wife's medical condition.[246] That concern had in fact, led editors to refrain from publication of the story which, consequently, meant that the defendant had hitherto been frustrated in publishing the narrative for gain. Nonetheless, the defendant had not been deterred by that situation in the least, even though the editors were exhibiting a degree of responsibility which they had failed to do in, for example, the *Campbell* case. The defendant rudely dismissed any suggestion that he was in any way responsible for the wife's condition and, further, sought to portray himself as a victim who should be absolved of any responsibility for the consequences of his actions. "His attitude," said the judge,[247] "is that he is entitled to his revenge on the claimant, and if possible also to some financial gain; if his own wife, or the claimant's wife or his children, suffer incidental fallout, then that is the claimant's fault." Extra-legally, individuals might be forgiven for thinking that the defendant's wife was not wholly unjustified in seeking solace elsewhere!

On the other hand, it was the claimant's case (though contested) that he did not know that the defendant's wife was married, as she did not wear a wedding ring and had made no mention of having a current partner. One cannot help but feel that the claimant, in present times, was not a little disingenuous: it is very far from unknown for married women to continue, for example, to use their single names, to abstain from wearing traditional ornamentation and, less so perhaps, to maintain confidentiality regarding their personal relationships.

Against the background, it was strongly argued, on behalf of the defendant, that there was a general principle to the effect that *a party to an adulterous relationship never, as a matter of law, obtain injunctive relief (interim or permanent) against the wronged party preventing him from disclosing the relationship.*[248] Not altogether surprisingly, Eady J was frankly sceptical[249] of the existence of any such principle, when he said that, if no such principle could be demonstrated from Nineteenth or Twentieth Century case law, it was curious that it had emerged fully formed in the Twenty-first! Furthermore, domestic courts were not directed, by the 1950 Convention, to refrain from purporting to create general principles of law but, rather, to bring an *intense focus* on the circumstances of particular cases, especially where they are required to adjudicate on particular conflicts between Convention rights. Since the claimant had brought the convention into the arena, the methodology in that context was necessarily germane.

Thus, in *A Local Authority v W, L, W, T and R (by the Children's Guardian)*,[250] Potter P had stated that, once it was clear that conflicting Convention rights were involved in a particular case, "The exercise to be performed is one of parallel analysis in which the starting point is presumptive parity in that neither Article has precedence over or 'trumps' the others. The exercise of parallel analysis requires the court to examine the justification of interfering with each right and the issue of proportionality is to be considered in respect of each. It is not a mechanical exercise to decide on the basis of rival generalities. An intense focus upon the comparative importance of the specific rights being claimed in an individual case is necessary before the ultimate balancing act that in terms of proportionality is carried out."

In attempting to apply Potter P's rather tortured formula, Eady J in *CC v AB* considered [251] that the general principle which had been constructed on the defendant's behalf could properly be described as a *generality* which would pre-empt *parallel analysis* or *intense focus* on the case itself. The outcome, accordingly, was likely to be decided , as Potter P suggested, in terms of proportionality. On that issue, in *Douglas v Hello! Ltd,* [252] Sedley LJ had referred to, "...the principles of legality and proportionality which, as always, constitute the mechanism by which the court reaches its conclusion on countervailing or qualified rights. It will be remembered that in the jurisprudence of the Convention proportionality is tested by, among other things, the standard of what is necessary in a democratic society" From there, it had to be determined whether relevant Convention rights were engaged. Eady J had no doubt that the defendant's right of freedom of expression was engaged. That immediately brought Art 10(1) of the Convention into operation: that provision states that, "The freedom to hold opinions and to receive and impart information and ideas without interference by public authority..." shall be enjoyed by everyone. The whole aim of the proceeding was to restrain the defendant from imparting information and, at the same time, it is a freedom under the Convention to which especial importance appears to be attached." Thus, in the European Court of Human Rights decision in *The Observer and the Guardian v United Kingdom*,[253] it was stated that, "...the dangers inherent in prior restraints are such that they call for the most careful scrutiny on the part of the Court. This is especially so far as the press is concerned, for news is a perishable commodity and to delay its publication, even for a shot period, may well deprive it of its value and interest." Again, in *Wingrove v United Kingdom*,[254] the European Commission of Human Rights stated that, "The dangers inherent in prior restraints are such that they call for the most careful scrutiny on the part of the Convention organs." Those two cases had little in common factually with *CC v AB*: the newspapers' case involved a potential breach of national security and *Wingrove* an issue of blasphemy and, arguably, pornography.[255]

In domestic law, international Conventions apart, like sentiments may be found. Thus, in the judgment of Sedley LJ in *Douglas v Hello!*

Ltd, to which reference has already been made,[256] the judgment of Hoffman LJ in *R v Central Independent Television plc*[257] was noted. There, Hoffman LJ had said that, "Newspapers are sometimes irresponsible and their motives in a market economy cannot be expected to be unalloyed by considerations of a commercial advantage. Publication may cause needless distress and damage to individuals or harm to other aspects of the public interest. But a freedom which is restricted to what judges think to be responsible or in the public interest is no freedom. Freedom means the right to publish things which government and judges, however well motivated to say things which 'right-thinking people' regard as dangerous and irresponsible. This freedom is subject only to clearly defined exceptions laid down by common law or statute." If that were not sufficiently emphatic, Hoffman LJ continued by saying that, "It cannot be too strongly emphasised that outside the established exceptions, or any new ones which Parliament may enact in accordance with its obligations under the Convention, there is no question of balancing freedom of speech against other interests. It is a trump card which always wins." In the context of all of that, in *CC v AB*, Eady J said that he accepted the view of Munro, who had written[258] that, "There cannot as yet be said to be a 'bright line' rule against judicial prior restraint in the law under the Convention. However, it is clear that prior restraints are viewed as pernicious and that, to be upheld as justifiable, their use will have to be viewed as appropriate, proportionate and absolutely necessary."

Of course, Art 10 (2) of the Convention does provide for exceptions to the general statement laid down in Art 10 (1) and from which the comments of Hoffman LJ and Munro are necessarily derived Art 10 (2) provides that the exercise of the freedoms to be found in Art 10 (1), "May be subject to such formalities, conditions, restrictions or penalties as are prescribed by law and are necessary in a democratic society... [including]... the protection of the reputation or rights of others." It followed, according to Eady J in *CC v AB*,[259] that the relevant question was, having applied careful scrutiny and intense focus to the disclosed facts of the case, that there was a, "...countervailing requirement of public policy which renders it necessary and proportionate to restrain the defendant from communicating certain information in order to protect the Convention rights of any other person(s)."

As part of the process, the judge went on, it would be necessary to pay close attention to what the defendant would be likely to say and to whom, and them to evaluate the type of speech involved in each scenario. That, immediately, is a process fraught with immediate and obvious difficulty: in every type of family law matter, prediction, as I have pointed out elsewhere,[260] on both a personal and institutional level, is notoriously hazardous, being predicated on information which courts and commentators simply do not have and which may be all but impossible to obtain. In *CC v AB*, Eady J seemed properly to be aware of that difficulty when he said[261] that, "For example, while it may conceivably be right to restrain the sale of celebrity tittle tattle in which there is no real public interest, on the other hand, there would be no necessity or proportionate countervailing advantage in preventing him from conversing with relatives, friends or (say) doctors or counsellors about the subject of his own nervous breakdown and what may have contributed to it." It is not clear from the report what positions in the world the claimant and the defendant occupied, but it does seem safe to say that the defendant, at any rate, seemed to consider that his story would be of media interest. Were he, say, a Law Professor, it would be generally unlikely that his story would be of any real media interest. However, were he for instance, a highly placed clergyman or an entertainment celebrity, then it very well might. After all, *Douglas v Hello! Ltd*[262] involved the wedding of celebrated film actors, and *Campbell v MGN Ltd*[263] involved the extra-mural activities of an internationally known fashion model. These matters, if not of public interest, were clearly matter of interest to the public. Of more direct, or legitimate, public interest and concern would have been had the defendant been a government minister and the claimant a suspected espionage agent of an allegedly hostile power. Unfortunately perhaps, Eady J was silent as to that kind of situation.

The next issue which arose was whether there was any countervailing Convention right against which the rights of the defendant needed to be balanced. Inevitably, it was argued on behalf of the defendant that, in view of cases such as *R v Central Independent Television plc*,[264] the process of balancing could not even be reached in the instant case. However, a contrary provision, as initially raised by the claimant, exists in Art 8(1) of the Convention which specifies that, "… everyone has the right to respect for his private and family life...". In that regard, Eady J noted[265] that, in personal and sexual relationships, the courts had, for some time, recognised a reasonable and legitimate expectation of privacy. Hence, in *Campbell* v *MGN Ltd*,[266] Lord Nicholls had commented, in fairly general terms, that, "information about an individual's private life would not, in ordinary usage, be called 'confidential'. The more natural description today is that such information is private. The essence of the tort is better encapsulated now as misuse of private information. In the case of individuals, this tort, however labelled, affords respect for one aspect of an individual's privacy. That is the value underlying this cause of action." In *Von Hannover* v *Germany*,[267] the European Court of Human Rights had said, first, that they had, "...indicated that, in certain circumstances, a person had a 'legitimate expectation and respect for his or her private life." They had also, more emphatically, stated that, "the Court reiterates the fundamental importance of protecting private life from the point of view of the development of ever human being's personality. That protection...extends beyond the private family circle and also includes a social dimension. The Court considers that anyone, even if they are known to the general public, must be able to enjoy a 'legitimate expectation' of protection of respect for their private lives."

From those *dicta*, it is imperative in determining what is to be encompassed by the notions of *family* and *private* life, especially in the rather strange context of *CC* v *AB*. After noting *Hannover* and *Campbell*, Eady J was initially reminded of the earlier decision in *Stephens* v *Avery*,[268] where Brown-Wilkinson V-C had said that he could, "...see no reason why information relating to the most private sector of everyone's life, namely sexual conduct, cannot be the subject of a legally enforceable duty of confidentiality." The sexual conduct involved in the *Stephens* case related to a female homosexual relationship. Yet it is also apparent from the case law which succeeded *Stephens* v *Avery* that much might depend on the nature of the relationship involved, as well as the person(s) to whom disclosure was made. Thus, in *Theakston* v *MGN Ltd*,[269] Ouseley J had said, first, that the impact of disclosure of an adulterous relationship on others, notably the children of one of the parties, might be especially relevant to the very existence of confidentiality, As regards the nature of relationships generally, Ouseley J said that, "...the protection of confidentiality in relation to any particular set of circumstances is also affected by the nature of the person to whom disclosure is proposed to be made, whether to partner, friend or lawyer or to the press for wider publication." In *CC* v *AB*, there was, of course, no doubt as to whom the defendant intended to disclose the relationship or, indeed, why he intended so to do. More generally, though equally germane, Ouseley J commented that the nature of the disclosure might be equally relevant. "Sexual relations within marriage," he said, at home would be at one end of the range or matrix of circumstances to be protected from most forms of disclosure; a one night stand with a recent acquaintance in a hotel bedroom might very well be protected from press publicity. A transitory engagement in a brothel is yet further away." Although, in general terms, Ouseley J cannot be properly criticised, much is bound to depend on the contextual situations to which judicial allusion has been made must surely be taken into account. Thus, in all of the situations to which Ouseley J referred, protection might be less readily afforded were sado-masochistic practices of the kind referred to in Chapter IV involved.[270]

However, the points which Ouseley J raised in *Theakston* were taken up both by Lord Woolf CJ in *A* v *B plc*[271] and Eady J in *CC* v *AB*.[272] In the former case, the Lord Chief Justice stated that, though he was not to be taken as saying that no confidentiality could exist where one party to a relationship does not want confidentiality, the fact that, in *A* v *B plc*, two parties, C and D, had elected to disclose their relationship to B did affect A's right to protection of the information. For the position to be otherwise, he thought, would fail to acknowledge C and D's own right to freedom of expression. The trial judge in that case had apparently regarded a disclosure to friends as not being objectionable, but publication to the media as being so. Lord Woolf CJ considered that that approach ignored the importance to be attached to free press, In *CC* v *AB*, Eady J took the view that, although it might be necessary to have regard to the nature of the relationship, '...it may yet be the case, for example, that a fleeting one night encounter will attract less protection, if any, than a long-term relationship. This is an uncertain area because it is by no means fully determined how appropriate it is for individual judges to apply moral evaluation to such encounters." However, the judge did not regard that as an issue which he needed presently to address closely. At the same time, he was not prepared to accept a submission made on the defendant's behalf that there could be no legitimate expectation of privacy for a person who conducts a relationship with another person's wife. Or, indeed one supposes, with another person's husband...

As regards Ouseley J's scale of privacy protection, it should not be thought that it is invariable. Thus, for instance, the fact that a campaigner against family violence is given to sadistic practices in his own marital relationship may very well not be deserving of protection, whilst the circumstances surrounding a transitory encounter in a brothel may sometimes deserve, or even necessitate, protection.

In *CC* v *AB*, it was argued on behalf of the claimant that since, in *Stephens* v *Avery*,[273] one of the protagonists was herself married, it was scarcely likely that a modern court would regard an adulterer as, "...beyond the pale when it comes to the protection of intimate relationships." The case relied on was the House of Lords' decision in *Polanski* v *Condé Nast Publications Ltd.*[274] There, it had been held that an internationally renowned film director was entitled to bring proceedings in England so as to protect his civil rights, notwithstanding that he was a fugitive from criminal proceedings in another jurisdiction.[275] Thus, it was argued that, as the commission of a crime might not deprive a person of protection under Art 8 of the Convention, it was difficult to see how adultery could. Eady J's response [276] to that suggestion is unlikely to receive universal approbation: "Judges", he emphatically stated, "need to be wary of giving the impression that they are ventilating, while affording, of refusing legal redress, some personal moral or social views, and especially at a time when society is far less homogenous than in the past." In more particular vein, the judge continued by commenting that, "At one time, when there was, or was perceived to be, a commonly accepted standard in such matters as sexual morality, it may have been acceptable for the courts to give effect to the standard in exercising discretion or in interpreting legal rights or obligations." Yet, more emphatically, he continued by saying that, "Now, however, there is a strong argument for not holding forth about adultery or attaching greater inherent worth to a relationship which has been formalised by marriage than to any other relationship."

In the context of *CC* v *AB*, one might assume therefore, that, had the defendant and his wife elected not to marry, then effectively the same issue would arise, although the terms *adultery* and *adulterer* would have lacked the impetus which they carried in *CC* v *AB*. In other words, if Art 8 could be used to protect homosexual relationships, at least those subsisting over the medium term, then it clearly ought to offer protection to those involved in uniformalised relationships, even though denunciatory elements might be less than in cases such as the present! Eady J continued in similar vein: "A judge like everyone else, is obviously entitled to hold personal moral views about the issues of the day, but it is important not to let them intrude when interpreting an applying the law. Such issues are best avoided – at least without some statutory sanction. No doubt many people, especially those with a strong religious faith, will disapprove of adultery." That, no doubt, ought to go without saying, but Eady J's next comment is likely to cause more global concern. "Many others," he said, "on the other hand, will not give it a second thought while moving easily through a series of medium or short-term relationships as they feel it appropriate." Yet, in the Australian context at least, it would probably not have been so easy for Eady J to be quite so dismissive of notions relating to traditional marriage: thus, s 43 (a) of the *Family Law Act* 1975 provides, as one of the principles which courts exercising jurisdiction under the Act shall have regard to, "...the need to preserve and protect the institution of marriage as the union of a man and a woman to the exclusion of all others voluntarily entered into for life". Thus, it is immediately apparent that Eady J's ready acceptance of adultery as a part of social fabric does not sit well with that legislative statement. It is probably true to say that the provisions, together with the remainder of s 43 has had relatively little in the way of direct effect,[277] though it does seem to say that marriage cannot be entered into for limited periods and its content cannot be so entered into[278] and its content cannot be interpreted as any kind of approval of adultery,[279] either as a social fact or as a desirable cause of action.

The judge then went on[280] to comment that, with such a wide range of differing views in society – perhaps more than for many generations – judges must guard against allowing legal judgments to be coloured by personal attitudes. There was no doubt, of course that, even amongst judges, there was a wide range of personal opinion. In turn, that meant it was, "...all the more important, therefore, that the outcome of a particular case should not be determined by the judge's personal views or, as it used to be said, by 'the length of the Chancellor's foot.' There is a risk that with greater emphasis on applying on 'intense focus' to the particular facts, with the room this leaves for the making of individual judgments, differing outcomes on what may seem to be broadly comparable facts may be interpreted by onlookers as being explicable on the basis of arbitrary personal difference between the judges." Eady J also remarked that that was plainly undesirable, "…because it would undermine faith in the rule of law, but the danger has to be recognised as inherent in the 'new methodology of balancing Convention rights'. That might, indeed, be a most trenchant warning and one which advocates of the adoption of similar Conventions into Australian, or analogous, law or who urge the creation of Charters (or Bills) of Rights (or Freedoms) might do well to bear continually in mind. In other words, we might care to ask ourselves who will most likely gain from the adoption or creation of Charters which may contain clauses which might patently be contradictory.

As regards the instant Convention, Eady J then noted that it was a secular document which applied either to all religions or none. Hence, it was not for judges to, "…give an appearance of sanctimony damning adulterers or seeking [as was urged on behalf of the defendant] to vindicate the state of matrimony." Indeed, the judge stated emphatically that, "…if the defendant is pretending that his desire 'to spill the beans' to a tabloid newspaper has anything to do with 'vindicating' the institution of marriage, that would be remarkable hypocrisy in the light of his own evidence. He wished to expose and humiliate the claimant but also incidentally his own wife and to do so, on his own admission, for revenge and for financial profit."[281] Altogether, one might reasonably think, a motive more relevant to, say "The Pardoner's Tale"[282] by Chaucer rather than a case in the 21st Century regarding the operation of a *Convention for the Protection of Human Rights and Fundamental Freedoms*. It is certainly proper to inquire whose rights and freedoms were being compromised. In an Australian context, earlier noted,[283] s 43 (c) of the *Family Law Act* 1975 refers to, "…the need to protect the rights of children and to promote their welfare." Whatever may or may not have been the merits of the claimant's own behaviour, ostensibly, at least, he was seeking to protect his children from conduct which, although conduced perhaps by his own, on the part of the defendant which could very well have damaged them.

In the event, Eady J concluded[284] that there could be no rule of generality that an adulterer could *never*[285] obtain an injunction to restrain the publication of matters which related to his adulterous relationship. Put another way,[286] "…even an adulterous relationship may attract, at least in certain respects, a legitimate expectation of privacy." Therefore, there was no rule which exempted a husband from restraint, by reason of his status. Although in any given situation, there might be particular aspects in which the right of freedom of speech might be given greater priority. In turn, it followed that the Art 8 rights of the other party to the adulterous relationship (in the present case, the defendant's wife) must be taken into account. It was clear, the judge considered, from *A v B plc*[287] that courts would be less likely to protect the rights of one party to such a relationship if the other wished to reveal what had happened. As was apparent from the facts in *CC v AB*, no such issue was applicable. Eady J further concluded[288] that what was required was *an intense focus on the particular facts so as to achieve an appropriate balance between the competing rights*.[289] At the same time, it should be borne in mind that freedom of speech should only be constrained if it was necessary to protect the rights of the other persons concerned – what is more, any such restraint should be limited to what is proportionate. Thus, Eady J's general emphasis is now made clear, even though I might venture to suggest that, in the context of *CC v AB*, it might not be wholly appropriate.

The judge then turned his attention to the remedy sought by the claimant: which , of course, was an interlocutory injunction, but, additionally, it was sought in the context of s 12 (3) of the *Human Rights Act* 1998. That provision had been discussed by the House of Lords in *Cream Holdings Ltd v Banerjee*.[290] The provision itself states that no such interlocutory relief, which might affect the exercise of the Convention right to freedom of expression is to be granted, "…so as to restrain publication before trial unless the court is satisfied that the applicant is likely to establish that publication should not be allowed." The major concern of the House of Lords in *Banerjee* was the meaning of the word *likely*. That, of itself, as Lord Nicholls pointed out,[291] was innately productive of difficulty as the word had, "…several shades of meaning". Lord Nicholls took the view[292] that the principle purpose for which the provision had been enacted was to support the protection given to freedom of speech at the interlocutory stage by setting a higher threshold for the grant of interlocutory injunctions against the media than had previously been the case.[293] Accordingly, Lord Nicholls stated[294] that s 12 (3) made likelihood of success at trial an essential element in the court's consideration as to whether to make an interlocutory order. Though, to achieve a necessary degree of flexibility, the likelihood of success must depend upon the circumstances.

In *CC* v *AB*, Eady J said[295] that he ought to grant an injunction unless he was satisfied that the claimant was likely to gain an order in similar terms at trial. He could only decide that in the light of the evidence which was before him and should not speculate as to what might eventuate, Eady J recognised immediately that the claimant was unlikely to obtain a blanket restraint on *any*[296] communication regarding the adulterous relationship. In the present situation, the judge considered that what in issue was, "...the defendant's desire, directly or indirectly, to put the relationship into the public domain through the press and to support it with detail." The distinction which the judge regarded himself as having drawn could, he thought be analysed in terms of differing categories of speech. In that context, selling a story to the tabloids – whether for money, revenge or other purpose – would be accorded a lower priority. A distinction had been drawn shortly before in the House of Lord's decision in *Jameel* v *Wall Street Journal Europe SPRL*,[297] where Baroness Hale had commented that there was no right to, "...a free-for-all to publish without being damned." Her Ladyship continued by saying that the public only had a right to be told if two conditions were satisfied. "First," she said, "there must be a real public interest in communicating and receiving he information, This is, as we all know, very different from saying that it is information which interests the public – the most vapid tittle-tattle about the activities of footballer's wives and girlfriends interests large sections of the public but no-one could claim any real public interest in our being told about it. It is also different from the test...of whether the information is 'newsworthy'. That is too subjective a test, based on the target audience, inclinations and interests of the particular publication. There must be some real public interest in having this interest in the public domain. But this is less than a test that the public 'need to know', which would be far too limited." Despite Baroness Hale's comments, the House of Lords in *Jameel* held[298] that disclosure of matters which related to the trading activities of a bank, and companies related to it, as they involved relationships with terrorist organisations were protected under defamation law.

In *CC* v *AB*, Eady J pointed out that the distinction drawn by Baroness Hale in *Jameel* was one which had long been recognised. Thus in *British Steel Corporation* v *Granada Television Ltd*,[299] Lord Wilberforce had said that, "...there is wide difference between what is interesting to the public and what is in the public interest to make known". That was a distinction, Eady J though,[300] which was of equal validity in assessing the relative value of different kinds of *speech*. In other words, "The communication of material to the world at large in which there is a genuine public interest is naturally to be rated more highly than the right to sell what is mere 'tittle-tattle.'" In making those comments, the judge noted, a matter to which reference has already been made,[301] that information about the sexual relationships of people, whether *public figures* or not, who were in the public eye were likely to be interesting to the public but might very well not be of genuine public interest, Sometimes, though, a case will fulfil both criteria – the fact that, in the past, a Minister for War, at the height of the Cold War, had shared a mistress with a Soviet diplomat, who might have been engaged in espionage, clearly fulfilled both such criteria![302]

However, the judge went on, courts would recognise a legitimate expectation of privacy, not on the basis of the means by which the information was imparted, but rather because of the nature of the information itself, "Quite often, for a variety of reasons, people prefer," Eady J stated, "to conduct sexual relationships, at least temporarily, on a secret basis. They would appear to be entitled to do so and, until they choose to 'go public', to enjoy a legitimate expectation of privacy vis-a-vis the world at large. This is to say such information is capable of being regarded as confidential." In *CC* v *AB* it had been argued that the adulterous relationship had been conducted in public, at least in the sense that the claimant and the defendant's wife had been seen in various locations, not merely in England, but in Europe and the United States. They had not been recognised, but the judge noted that it seemed as though they had "taken the chance" of being so. Nonetheless, the judge doubted whether that could be regarded as synonymous with "going public". In that context, Eady J referred to the decision of the European Court of Human Rights in *Von Hannover* v *Germany*,[303] which has already been noted,[304] where it was recognised that the law was capable of extending its protection to public places and also to a *social dimension* in respect of the relationship which people have with one another, Thus, the judge found it difficult to accept[305] that a clear distinction could, presently at least, be drawn between private documents and the bare (as it were) fact of a relationship. All depended on the surrounding circumstances, which were to be carefully scrutinised.

In *CC* v *AB*, the relationship had ceased and the respective parties wished to disperse. On the face of it, the judge said,[306] those involved, "...ought to be able to keep their past indiscretions to themselves rather than suffer public humiliation and embarrassment – not only for themselves but for completely 'innocent' third parties such as the claimant's wife and children," Indeed, further exposure in the press of the state of affairs at large could only frustrate the claimant's ongoing relationship with his wife and damage any rebuilding process as well as the wife's already delicate mental state. Eady J stated that he needed to act compatibly with the Convention and protect the claimant's family life.[307] It followed that were the judge to attempt so to do, it would be necessary to prevent the defendant from going, either directly or indirectly, to the media. His motivation was little better than spite, money-grubbing or "tittle-tattle" and the court might well be obliged to restrain him from so doing. The fact that the defendant saw himself as an *injured party* did not accord[308] him, a special status, which inherently raised the value of the communications which he was seeking to make to the tabloids newspapers, "...on to some higher plane or [render] them more valuable in Art 10 Convention terms."

At the same time, though, there remained the issue of Art 8 of the Convention which had, at most times hitherto throughout Eady J's discussion, to have been subordinate to Art 10, perhaps because of the volume of the defendant's submissions. In that regard, the judge, first, refused to accept an argument by the defendant to the effect that the claimant's own voluntary conduct had placed his marriage and family life in jeopardy. Eady J responded[309] by saying that that factor did not absolve the court from having to take the impact on the claimant's family life into account. Indeed, it appeared to have been acknowledged that the position of the claimant's wife had become relevant were the claimant held to have a reasonable expectation of privacy in respect of the adulterous relationship. At the same time, however, the defendant had argued that it would be wrong for much weight to be attached to the position of the claimant's wife and she was neither a party nor had provided any evidence herself. That argument was, once again, rejected[310] by Eady J, who stated that, even before the Convention and the *Human Rights Act* 1998, "...the courts always had an eye to the rights of any third party affected by the grant of an injunction. Now a judge is certainly required to ensure that court orders and determinations are compatible with the Convention, and thus to have regard to such rights in arriving at decisions." This is, of course, a very fair, sensible and apposite comment in respect of the operation of injunctions, indeed, as early as 1865, it was stated[311] by Kindersley V-C that courts, "...will not ordinarily and without special necessity interfere by injunction, where the injunction will have the effect of very materially injuring the rights of third parties not before the court." The rights to which the Vice-Chancellor alluded need not now[312] be proprietary in nature.[313] More recently in *Miller* v *Jackson*,[314] it will be remembered, the Court of Appeal in England took account of hardship which would result to third party inhabitants of a village were an injunction granted to prevent the playing of cricket on a particular ground, Cumming-Bruce LJ stated[315] that where the plaintiff, "...has prima facie a right to specific relief, a court of equity will, if occasion should arise weigh the disadvantage or hardship which would be caused to third persons or the public generally if relief were granted."

Further, Eady J refused[316] to accept the analogy which had been drawn by Ouseley J in *Theakston* v *MGN Ltd*[317] regarding the visit to the brothel, in respect of which he had refused relief, Again, it is suggested that Eady J's point is fair: there is a clear and readily apparent distinction between a visit to a brothel and a relationship, even though adulterous, lasting even for a relatively brief period, Another argument advanced by the defendant was to the effect that, once the wronged party was entitled to tell some people, the information could not, as such, be protected in any meaningful way. Eady J considered that, as a matter of law, that submission could not be regarded as correct. Exceptions," he said,[318] "are regularly incorporated in the terms of court orders to enable initial communications to take place, the most typical example being to facilitate discussions with lawyers or expert witnesses. If the defendant were restricted from communicating with the press, but chose to do so through a friend or family member, he would be on risk of imprisonment for contempt of court." The judge was likewise dismissive of a submission that it would be wrong to restrain the defendant when the claimant, his wife and the defendant's wife were not so restrained. An injunction, Eady J considered, was granted because there was evidence that, otherwise, the party to be restricted would commit a wrong. There was obviously no point in granting injunctions in respect of other people where no such possibility arose. Both of those propositions are all but self-evident and one might be legitimately surprised that they were advanced at all.

Once, again, as earlier noted,[319] it was argued that, as the claimant had a *public persona* and that the relationship went towards informing that *persona*. Hence, there was a public interest in the disclosure of the relationship. In *A* v *B plc*,[320] Lord Woolf CJ, in addition to the other points which he had made which were relevant to the facts of *CC* v *AB*, had commented[321] that "Where an individual is a public figure, he is entitled to have his privacy respected in appropriate circumstance. A public figure is entitled to his private life." At the same time, though, the Lord Chief Justice pointed out that, "The individual should recognise that because of his public position he must expect and accept that his actions will be more closely scrutinised by the media." Indeed, he further continued by saying that, "In many of these situations it would be overstating the position to say that there is a public interest in the information being published. It would be more accurate to say that the public have an understandable and so a legitimate interest in being told the information, if this is the situation then it can be appropriately taken into account by the court when deciding on which side of a line a case falls. The courts must not ignore the fact that if newspapers do not publish that which the public are interested in there will be fewer newspapers published, which will not be in the public interest. The same is true in relation to other parts of the media."

Yet, in *CC* v *AB*, Eady J was at pains to note[322] specifically that the case at hand was not the same as *Campbell* v *MGN Ltd*,[323] where the plaintiff had misled the public by false denials, and nor had the claimant in *CC* v *AB* moralised publicly on family life or his own continence in sexual matters. Hence, the judge could not accept that there was any genuine interest in the disclosure of this information so far as the public was concerned. In addition, the judge considered that it was also important to have regard to the attitude of the defendant as was demonstrated by an e-mail and a telephone call made by him to the claimant. These were both threatening and obscene in both nature and content.[324] Further, the defendant had sought to utilise what had been described as the *divorce ruse*, in that he had threatened to use divorce proceedings as means of bringing the claimant's name to the attention of media: that, of course, meant, quite unnecessarily, joining the claimant as co-respondent. That, the judge considered,[325] suggested of itself that the defendant was intending to abuse the process of the court of a collateral purpose.

Such abuses have long been regarded as amounting to contempt of court: thus, for instance in *Apted* v *Apted and Bliss*,[326] a petitioner who had deliberately included falsehoods in a divorce petition was held to be in contempt. In so deciding, Lord Merrivale P emphasised [327] the state's interest in the integrity of marriage. Likewise, a barrister, in *Linwood* v *Andrews and Moore*,[328] who was instrumented in procuring the making of an affidavit which he knew to be false, and which he read to the court, was held to be in contempt. Although it may very well be, as Lord Goddard CJ seemed to suggest in *Weisz; ex p Hector McDonald Ltd*[329] that it is not every abuse of court process which will amount to contempt, but any, "...attempt to deceive the court by disguising the true nature of the complaint is a contempt." By reason of that last comment, and by analogy with *Apted* and *Linwood*, the defendant might very well, once again, be in danger of committal for contempt.

All in all,, Eady J regarded the various documents,[330] in that context, as laying a clear foundation for a reasonable apprehension that, unless restrained by a court order, the defendant would publish as many details as he knew of the claimant's relationship – regardless of the consequences for the claimant's wife and children. In addition to those documents, there were some communications by the defendant on the internet. The information was still regarded as confidential, those statements notwithstanding; to put the matter another way, those statements had not removed the issue from the area of confidentiality. Or, again, to use the language of Lord Goff in *A-G v Guardian Newspapers* (No 2),[331] the first limiting principle which regulates confidential information, "...only applies to information to the extent that it is confidential. In particular, once it has entered what is usually called the public domain (which means no more than the information in question is so generally accessible that, in all the circumstances it cannot be regarded as confidential) then, as a general rule, the principle of confidentiality can have no application to it." Eady J did not regard the information, as yet at least, as having reached that stage. Accordingly, as he was satisfied that the claimant was likely to obtain a permanent injunction in terms similar to those which he was to propose, Eady J granted an injunction.

It is apparent that *CC* v *AB* is a case which involves many important and controversial issues – and not only concerned with privacy matters but with the major themes of this book. However, it would be wrong to ignore the more strictly legal aspects of the case, both substantive and remedial. Indeed, the first and most immediate matter raised by the case is the grant of the injunction itself. In *Argyll*,[332] for instance, the injunction was granted, as it was to be in *CC* v *AB*, and the applicant/claimant's own conduct was held to be insufficiently culpable to preclude its grant. In the latter case, it was the conduct of the defendant which was sufficiently gross to permit the grant of the inunction and which seemed to extinguish, or outweigh, the claimant's initially immoral behaviour. The grant of the inunction also took into account the likely effect of the disclosure of the information on third parties – the claimant's wife and children, rather than those of the defendant, although the defendant seemed largely heedless of the effect which the disclosure might have had on his own. Thus, the view that an injunction will lie to protect the interests (non-proprietary, as well as proprietary) of innocent third parties has been further emphasised. In that context, it is worth considering the interests of the claimant's wife and children which would be protected by the injunction. That is, *ex necessitate*, a difficult task – not least because of the uncertainty which has surrounded, in legal terms at least, the notion of *family*, both in *definitional*[333] and *functional*[334] forms. Hitherto, it does not appear to have stood high in any supposed hierarchy of legal concepts. Thus, in *Schaefer v Schuhmann*[335] a majority of the Judicial Committee of the Privy Council seemed to place family rights based legislation below a contractual obligation to a non-family member. In *CC* v *AB*, most obviously there seemed to be evidence that the claimant's wife might be potentially suicidal or self-harming, although the defendant had been quite deprecatory of any such suggestion.[336] Indeed, that response seemed to be included in Eady J's accumulated assessment of the defendant's conduct[337] and its effect on the application. That issue is complicated, as has already been considered,[338] by attitudes towards family life and its relationship with law which are frequently significantly disparate. One such attitude is that, save in the most extreme situations, the law does not, and should not, it is argued, involved itself in the way in which obligations are worked out within the particular family. These are further complicated by various new forms of family organisation with which the law is being required to deal, but which are beyond the scope of the present book.

Yet the connecting thread which runs through the present part of this chapter of the book is the lyric "As I Went Out One Morning" by Bob Dylan. Its final stanza emerges with a sudden and dramatic shift in direction which is pertinent to Paine's own work, *The Rights of Man*[339] and to issues arising out of *CC* v *AB*. In the final stanza, the narrator finds himself rescued both in an unexpected way and by an unexpected person:

> Just then Tom Paine, himself
> Came running from across the field
> Shouting at this lovely girl
> And commanding her to yield
> And she was letting go her grip
> Up Tom Paine did run
> "I'm sorry, sir" he said to me
> "I'm sorry for what she's done"

Thus the poem ends with an apology from Tom Paine for the acts of his creature, who had sought to ensnare the narrator. Although the young woman was attractive and, indeed, seductive, her behaviour had not found favour with the narrator – who may very well be representative of the humanity whose rights and freedoms were initially to be protected by Tom Paine's original vision. Hence, although it possible to perceive *CC* v *AB* in terms of personal and family relationships, it is impossible to avoid the relevance and applicability of the *European Convention for the Protection of Human Rights and Fundamental Freedoms*. From an Australian perspective, this aspect of *CC* v *AB* is of especial and instant importance: in the words of a retired Australian State Supreme Court Chief Justice, [340] "The question of whether Australia should have a *Bill of Rights* has been the subject of a great deal of public discussion and debate. The omission of a *Bill of Rights* from our Constitution is one of the elements which marked it as different to the United States Constitution from which a number of propositions were derived. The omission was not by accident." Although Malcolm refers to, and agrees with, Spiegelman CJ, writing extra – judicially, [341] who has warned that a failure to keep abreast of other common law countries in respect of human rights could result in significant intellectual isolation for Australia, he is not blind to some of the innate difficulties which the area at large might contain. Thus he writes[342] that, "In the absence of a carefully drafted instrument there is a political danger that certain judicially implied rights may conflict with other rights which are also fundamental. An obvious example is the right to freedom of speech as against the right not to be defamed."[343]

However, and this is quite clear from the discussion of *CC v AB*, even in an apparently carefully drafted document, such conflicts may be revealed even went an immediate conflict might not spring to mind. In other words, even in an already established document, such as the *European Convention*, conflicts between the rights to freedom of speech and the protection of family life may suddenly, given the right case, come to light. *CC v AB* was one such case. Further, the factual situation in that case, unedifying and unhappy as it might have been for the protagonists, may, for some observers at any rate, be little more than risible. Thus, one might properly question how *fundamental* the provisions of the Convention were, as such, to the facts of the case. In general terms, there may be an inherent danger that the provisions of any such document might become clogged by factual instances which, although at the instant, they might seemed urgent to the protagonists, objectively they might only serve to trivialise the concept at large, which may have the effect that the document fails to achieve the appropriate protection for which might prove to be genuinely serious infringements.

By way of example, first, in *Collins v Brantford Police Services Board*,[344] the Ontario Court of Appeal was required to deal with the plaintiff, who, it must be admitted, had a history of neighbourhood disputes, had sprayed a neighbour with a hose. The neighbour called the police and the investigating officer decided to arrest the plaintiff without a warrant. The officers had knocked on the plaintiff's front door and had entered his house after the plaintiff had motioned them in. The officers cautioned the plaintiff as to his rights, arrested him and took him to the police station. After the plaintiff had entered into a recognisance requiring him to refrain from contact with his neighbours, he was released two hours after the initial arrest. Subsequently, he was convicted of assaulting the neighbour. Approximately a year after the arrest, the plaintiff brought an action against the Police Services Board for damages in respect of the tort of unlawful arrest and for breach of his right to protection from arbitrary detention under s 9 of the *Canadian Charter of Rights and Freedoms*.[345] The Board argued contrarily on the basis of s 495 (2) of the Canadian *Criminal Code* 1985. That provision specifies that an officer shall not arrest a person without a warrant for an offence in any case where he believes on reasonable grounds that, "...the public interest, having regard to all the circumstances including the need to...protect the continuation or repetition of the offence or the commission of another offence without so arresting the person."[346] The trial judge found that the arrest was not necessary to prevent the continuation or repetition of an offence, or the commission of another offence and awarded damaged.

The Police Board appealed to the Divisional Court, which held that the tort claim was statute barred,[347] but upheld the award of damages under the Charter. The Board then appealed to the Ontario Court of Appeal, which allowed the appeal, In so doing, Rosenberg JA,[348] who delivered the Court's judgment, was of the view that both the trial judge and the Divisional Court had erred in concluding that the issue was determined by the finding that the arrest was not necessary to prevent the continuation or repetition of the offence or the commission of another offence.[349] Further, the onus of proving that the action was unlawful was cast on the plaintiff [350] and he had failed to discharge that onus of proof in relation to s 459 (2). However, even if he had established that the arrest was unlawful, the action ought still to have been dismissed. The reason for that was that it was not every unlawful arrest which fell within the phrase arbitrarily detained in s 9 of the Charter. That condition could only be fulfilled if, in the words of the Ontario Court of Appeal in *R v Coyer*,[351] were it, "...capricious, despotic or unjustifiable." That, Rosenberg JA considered, was not an apt description of the police conduct on the relevant occasion, hence, the finding of liability under the Charter could not stand.

Collins, despite its seemingly trivial aspects, can, together with the unrelated factual situation in *CC v AB*, help to tell us some rather disturbing things about documents aimed at enumerating protected rights and freedoms. Not only, as Malcolm has properly pointed out,[352] must the document be carefully drafted itself so as to avoid conflicts of the kind which occurred in *CC v AB*, as well as complex statutory devices which seek to eliminate them – but care must be taken to avoid conflicts with other statutory provisions which seek, for instance, the protection of the public. That suggestion ought to be self-evident, but, if *Collins* is a useful example, it may be a difficult object to attain. Further indications may also be found in the volume of case law generated by the Canadian Charter.[353] It may very well be that unintended by-products resulting from such Charters and like documents will have to be as closely subject to curial scrutiny as were those rights and freedoms which were initially created by judges themselves.

There is also the omnipresent danger that some particular factual situations will arise which will give rise to some of the problems which have already been outlined, but may also tend to bring the very notion of Charter/Bills of Rights and Freedoms into disrepute. An example may be provided by the decision of the Supreme Court of Canada in *Weatherall v Canada (Attorney General)*.[354] There, a male prison inmate, in the Federal Court, challenged the constitutionality of *frisk searching* and patrolling of cell ranges conducted in male prisons by female guards. The frisk search consisted of a hand search of a clothed inmate from head to foot with touching of the genital area, though not specifically prohibited, generally avoided. The surveillance patrols consisted of regular cell patrols (known as *counts*) and unannounced patrols conducted at random times every hour (known as *winds*). The inmate to the cross-gender touching which occurred during a frisk search and to the female guards possible viewing of inmates while undressed or while using lavatory facilities during the *counts* and *winds*. The trial judge concluded that the cross-gender *frisk searches* did not violate ss 7, 8 and 15 of the *Canadian Charter of Rights and Freedoms*, but that the *winds* conducted by female guards did constitute an invasion of the privacy of male inmates contrary to s 9. The Federal Court of Appeal set the judgment aside, holding that neither the cross-gender *frisk searches* not the cross-gender *winds* were unconstitutional. The claimant appealed to the Supreme Court of Canada, who dismissed the appeal. La Forest J, who delivered the judgment of the Supreme Court,[355] began by noting[356] that, "The possible inappropriate effects of the practices are minimized by the provision of special training to ensure they are professionally executed with due regard for the dignity of the inmate. Few complaints are received from inmates regarding invasions of privacy by virtue of having been searched by a female officer. Regarding the winds. The occasions when an inmate might be seen unclothed or tending to personal functions are rare and fleeting: One or two times a year according to the appellant, for the two or three seconds it takes a guard to view acell.

Modesty barriers, which are placed in front of the cell toilets so that officers can only view the inmates from the waist up while using the facilities, are present in certain cell blocks." At the same time, though, La Forest J pointed out that imprisonment necessarily entailed surveillance, searching and scrutiny and, to that end, a prison cell is exposed and subject to observation. All of the practices to which the inmate took objection were all necessary in a prison for the purposes of protecting the security of the institution, the public and, indeed, the inmates themselves. Most particularly, the judge emphasised that a substantially reduced level of privacy was present in such a setting and, "...a prisoner cannot hold a reasonable expectation of privacy with respect to those practices. This conclusion is unaffected by the fact that the practices at times may be conducted by female guards." Therefore, La Forest J considered that, as there was no reasonable expectation of privacy, the provisions of the Charter which related to privacy could not be invoked.

The judge was also of the view that it could not be argued that the practices were discriminatory in their treatment of male prisoners, as might have been proscribed by s 15(1) of the Charter. Further, he did not accept the appellant's argument that the female inmates were not subjected to frisk searches and other cross-gender forms of surveillance. "The jurisprudence of this Court," said La Forest J,[357] "is clear, equality does not necessarily connote identical treatment and, in fact, different treatment may be called for in certain circumstances to promote equality. Given the historical biological and sociological differences between men and women, equality does not demand that practices which are forbidden where male officers guard female inmates must also be banned where female officers guard male inmates... Biologically, a frisk search or surveillance of a man's chest area conducted by a female guard does not implicate the same concerns as the same practice by a male guard in relation to a female inmate. Moreover, women generally occupy a disadvantaged position in society in relation to men. Viewed in this light, it becomes clear that the effect of cross-gender searching in different and more threatening for women than for men. The different treatment to which the appellant objects may not e discrimination at all."

Finally, La Forest J noted[358] that the assignment of women to the surveillance of male inmates, with all of the consequent duties, was a relatively recent phenomenon. He was of the view that the governmental ends of inmate rehabilitation and institutional security were promoted as the result of the humanising effect of having women in such positions. Further, the parliamentary goal of achieving employment equity is given material application by way of initiative, and hence, the proportionality of the means used to the importance of those ends would justify the breach of s 15 (1) of the *Charter*, if any had, in fact, occurred.

There are two general points to be made in relation to *Collins* and *Weatherall*: the first is that both actions, which were heard by appellate courts, arose out of incidents which many people (not necessarily the author) might regard as being essentially trivial. In turn, that might well lead those same people to the conclusion that the *Charter* is being involved in matters which are personal and in which the law has no business being involved. The effect of that is that the very notion of *Bills/Charters of Rights and Freedoms* may be seriously undermined, The second point is inextricably involved with the first: although the matters involved in the two cases can easily be perceived as trivial, there were three hearings in each case and each ended in a high appellate court, one in the highest court in Canada. Litigation is widely, and generally correctly, perceived as an expensive activity especially at the highest appellate level. It is certainly true that, in the *Weatherall* case, in addition to the parties themselves, the Attorneys General for the Provinces of British Columbia, Ontario and Quebec, the Coalition of Provincial Organisations of the Handicapped, the Women's Legal Education and Action Fund and the Minority Advocacy and Rights Council were all involved as interveners. Although that might have helped to defray some of the costs involved in the appeal to the Supreme Court of Canada, all the interveners were represented by lawyers. The conclusion which, thus, might be drawn is that the only people – and it should be remembered that both the actions considered in this chapter failed – who are likely to benefit from such Charters are members of the legal profession. Whether Bob Dylan, in "As I went Out One Morning" was hinting at issues of this kind must, of course, remain speculative...

However, this book has not been entirely concerned with the substantive law of privacy or the operation of *Charters of Rights*, it is concerned with poetry and rhetoric. In one sense, the cases which have been discussed in this part of the book are about *rhetoric*, especially Eady J's decision in *CC* v *AB*.[359] The nature of *rhetoric* has already been considered[360] and it is apparent from the various writings that are therein considered that the immediate purpose of *rhetoric* is *persuasion*, although that must be understood in terms of its various contexts,[361] which include the audience.[362] In *CC* v *AB*, the rhetoric used by Eady J is of considerable interest: first, he began by utilising the rhetoric of privacy,[363] which he must needs tread cautiously, as the law generally was in a somewhat uncertain state, particularly as regards the relationship between privacy *per se* and defamation which was not directly in issue in the case at hand. His rhetoric then changed[364] to the rhetoric of freedom of speech. Once again, the judge seemed not a little cautious, although there were good reasons for such caution. Not only was there prior conflicting authority, but the facts of the case were such as to be *sui generis* with regard to preceding case law. In addition, reliance on freedom of speech would have resulted in a almost inevitable victory for the defendant when it became clear that there were conflicting Convention rights.[365] The issue was, of course, further complicated by the question raised, *inter alia*, by Lord Wilberforce in *British Steel Corporation* v *Granada Television Ltd*[366] when he said that, "...there is a wide difference between what is interesting to the public and what is in the public interest to make known." At that point the orientation in Eady J's rhetoric began to change and to become more forceful: the focus, by now, as his conclusion began to approach, was not on privacy and freedom of speech but on responsibility for others – in this case, the claimant's family and the protection which was provided for them by the Convention. Eady J admitted the rhetorical nature of his judgment, which ended favourably for the claimant (and his family) when he referred to varying kinds of speech. Finally, the judge tied the rhetoric together when he referred to the Convention and to the notion of privacy with he had begun his judgment. By his reference to different kinds of *speech* and the adjudicative function of the judge, Eady J was acknowledging the place of rhetoric, as discussed in Chapter III, in the litigation process at large. Eady J's judgment itself represents a rhetorical process which is aimed at convincing the *parties* of the appropriateness of his ultimate decision, but also the general reader. He does this by structuring his judgment in the manner which I have described.

    It is probably appropriate to conclude this final substantive chapter with a comment from a poet who, in his own lifetime, was not an uncontroversial figure.[367] It is probably appropriate to do so, because much of this part of the commentary has been held together by the Bob Dylan lyric "As I Went Out one Morning." In 1862, Arthur Hugh Clough published, "The Latest Decalogue" in which he advised the reader:

Do not adultery commit
Advantage rarely comes of it

At least one party in *CC* v *AB* could have well needed that advice!

---

[1] [1903] AC 443 at 453.
[2] *Workmen's Compensation Act* 1897 s 1 (1)
[3] Above n 1 at 454.
[4] 248 N.Y. 339 (1928). The statement of facts is taken from the judgment of Cardozo CJ.
[5] See R Polenburg, *The World of Benjamin Cardozo: Personal Value and the Judicial Process* (1997).
[6] 248 NY 339 (1928) at 341.
[7] Ibid at 342.
[8] J C Smith, *Liability in Negligence* (1984) at 119.
[9] 248 NY 339 (1928) at 346.
[10] Ibid at 350.
[11] Above text at n 7.
[12] [1980] I WLR 823.
[13] Ibid at 829.
[14] [1971] 2 QB 691 at 699.
[15] Neil J noted, ibid, that that was the same standard as applied in the criminal law in relation to the offences of dangerous driving and driving without due care. See; *R v Gosney* [1971] 2 QB 691; *R v Spurge* [1961] 2 QB 205.
[16] Above text at n 14.
[17] [1971] 2 QB 691 at 700.
[18] (1948) 77 CLR 39 at 56.
[19] [1917] 2 QB 691 at 701.
[20] See *Wooldridge* v *Summer* [1963] 2 QB 43 at 69.
[21] [1971] 2 QB 691 at 703.
[22] Ibid at 711.
[23] Above text at n 18.
[24] [1971] 2 QB 691 at 707.
[25] Ibid at 708.
[26] Ibid at 709.
[27] Ibid at 703.
[28] Above text at n 18
[29] [1971] 2 QB 691 at 704.
[30] Ibid at 705.
[31] Ibid at 706.
[32] Ibid at 707.
[33] {1908] 1 WLR 823 at 830.
[34] [1961] 2 QB 205 at 210.
[35] [158] 1 QB 277.
[36] He was charged with dangerous driving and failing to conform to a traffic sign, contrary to ss 11(1) and 49 (b) respectively of the *Road Traffic Act* 1930.
[37] Lord Goddard CJ, Delvin and Pearson JJ.
[38] [1958] 1 QB 227 at 283.
[39] Ibid at 286.

[40] [1980] 1 WLR 823 at 832.
[41] *Waugh v James K Allen Ltd* [1964] 2 Lloyds Rep 1; *Jones v Dennison* [1971] RTR 174; *Watmore v Jenkins* [1962] 2 QB 572; *R v Isitt* [1978] TR 211.
[42] [1980]1 WLR 823 at 833.
[43] K M Stanton, *The Modern Law of Tort* (1994) at 69.
[44] Above text at n 14 *ff*.
[45] Above text a n 35 *ff*.
[46] Above text at n 37.
[47] [1971] 2 QB 674 at 680.
[48] [1980] 1 LWLR 823 at 830.
[49] [1971] 2 QB 674 at 680
[50] Above text at n 34 *ff*.
[51] Author's emphasis.
[52] See F Bates, "On the Mat and Up the Wall" (2005) XLIX (10) *Quadrant* 44.
[53] Above text at n 14 *ff*.
[54] Author's emphasis.
[55] Above text at n 43
[56] L Ross-Bryant, *Theodore Roethke: Poetry of the Earth...Poetry of the Spirit* (1981) at 74.
[57] Ibid
[58] G Wolfe, Theodore Roethke (1981) at 61.
[59] Above n 56 at 75.
[60] Above n 58 at 64.
[61] J Parini, *Theodore Roethke: The American Romantic* (1979) at 138.
[62] Ibid at 130
[63] From *Death and Entrances* (1946)
[64] For what follows I am indebted to a variety of formal and mainly informal sources. For a very recent study, see R Tilly Tommy Armstrong: *The Pitman Poet* (2010). The author is the poet's grandson,
[65] He did spend some time in Whitley Bay, Northumberland, from 1902 and worked as a newsagent.
[66] See particularly, "The South Medomsley Strike" (1885). The last stanza of which reads as follows, demonstrating the bitterness involved:

> Commander Potsick gave the word, they started with their work,
> Though they were done at five O'clock, they dursent stop till dark,
> And when they'd done all they could and finished for the day,
> The bobbies guarded Postick and his dorty dogs away.
>
> Fisick was a tyrant and the owners was the same,
> for the torn oot of the strike, they were the men to blame,
> Neither them not Postick need expect they'll ever thrive,
> For what they did to Dipton Men in eighteen eighty five.

The chorus of the song carries the same message:

> The moners of South Medomsley the're gannin te mek some stew
> The gannin' te boil Postick and his dorty candy crew,
> The maistors should have nowt but soup as long as their alive
> In memory of their dorty tricks in eighteen eighty fice

[67] The first verse of that song and its chorus are as follows:

> Wor Nan and me made up wer minds t gan and catch the train,
> For teg an te the Toon te buy some clathes for wor little Billy and Jane;
> But when we got to Rowlands Gill the mornin' train was gone,
> And there was ne mair te gammin' that way till fifteen minutes to one.
> So as says te wor Nan, "Its lang way te gan," aa saw by her fyece she was vext;
> But aa say, "never mind, we hev plenty of time, so we'll stop and gan in with the next"

> She gave a bit smile, when aa spoke up an said, "There's a public-hoose alang here-
> We'll gan alang there an hev wersels warmed, and a glass of the best bitter beer"
> Nan was se' stout aa knew she couldn't walk, and she didn's seem willing te try;
> When aa think of the trouble aa had wiv her that day, If aa liked aa could borst oot and cry,
>
> Chorus; Aye,, wor Nannie's a maisor, and a maisor she'll remain,
> As long as aa live, aa'll never foget, the day we lost the train.

[68] [1992] 1 AC 310.
[69] Ibid at 396.
[70] See *Bourhill* v *Young* [1943] AC 92 at 103 *per* Lord Macmillan
[71] [1932] AC 562 at 580.
[72] [1992 1 AC 310 at 397.
[73] [1983] 1 AC 410 at 422.
[74] [1992] 1 AC 310 at 398.
[75] Above text at n 73.
[76] [1992] ! AC 310 at 398.
[77] Ibid at 399.
[78] Ibid at 400.
[79] (1984) 155 CLR 549 at 569.
[80] [1992] 1 AC 310 at 400.
[81] See *Bourhill* v *Young* [1943] AC 92 at 103 *per* Lord Macmillan; *Jaensch* v *Coffey* (1984) 155 CLR 549 at 567 *per* Brennan J; *Hambrook* v *Stokes Bros* [1925] 1 KB 141 at 152 *per* Bankes LJ.
[82] [1992] 1 AC 310 at 401.
[83] Lord Ackner, ibid, pointed out that view represented a gap in the law which had, in part, been filled by s 3 of the *Administration of Justice Act* 1983, which inserted a new s 1A in to the *Fatal Accidents Act* 1976 enabling actions for bereavement to be brought.
[84] On her or his estate.
[85] 1941 SC 395 at 339.
[86] [1992] 1 AC 310 at 401.
[87] (1984) 155 CLR 549 at 583.
[88] [1992] 1 AC 310 at 402.
[89] Above text at n 71.
[90] [1983] 1 AC 410 at 422. See above text at n 73.
[91] Ibid
[92] [1925] 1 KB 141 at 158.
[93] [1992] 1 AC 310 at 403.
[94] Lord Ackner noted, ibid, that similar views had been adopted y Stoker and Nolan LJJ in the Court of Appeal, he also made reference , ibid at 404, to s 4(5) of the New South Wales *Law Reform (Miscellaneous Provisions) Act* 1944, which provides that the term, " ' Member of the Family' means the husband, wife, parent, child, brother, sister, half-brother or half-sister of the person in relation to whom the expression is used, 'Parent' includes father, mother grandfather, grandmother, stepfather, stepmother, and any person standing in loco parentis to another. 'Child' includes son, daughter, grandson, granddaughter, stepson, stepdaughter, and any person to whom another stands in loco parentis."
[95] [1992] 1 AC 310 at 404.
[96] (1984) 155 CLR 549 at 610.
[97] [1992] 1 AC 310 at 405.
[98] Above text a n 73 *ff.*
[99] [1993] 1 AC 310 at 405.
[100] Ibid at 406.
[101] Ibid at 407.
[102] See, for example, *Dulieu* v *White & Sons* [1991] 2 KB 669; *Bell* v *Great Northern Railway Co of Ireland* (1980) 26 LR Ir 438; *Schnieder* v *Eisovitch* [1960] 2 QB 430. In *Alcock*, Lord

Oliver, ibid at 408, was of the view that the *rescue cases* fell into the same category: see, *Chadwick v British Transport Commission* [1967] 1 WLR 912 as well as cases such as *Dooley v Cammell Laird & Co Ltd* [1951] 1 Lloyds Rep. 217; *Galt v British Railways Board* (1986) 136 NLJ 446.
[103] Except to the extent that they were the source of some interesting dicta.
[104] [1992] 1 AC 310 at 408.
[105] Ibid at 410.
[106] See, for instance, *Kirkham v Boughey* [1958] 2 QB 338; *Best v Samuel Fox & Co* [1953] AC 716.
[107] [1992] 1 AC 310 at 410.
[108] Ibid at 411.
[109] Below text at n 122 *ff*.
[110] [1992] 1 AC 310 at 412.
[111] See *King v Phillips* [1953] 1 QB 429; *Hambrook v Stokes Bros* [1925] 1 KB 141; *Owens v Liverpool Corporation* [1939] 1 KB 394, though disapproved by the House of Lords in *Bourhill v Young* [1943] AC 92 at 100, 110, 116.
[112] Above text at n 73 *ff*.
[113] [1992] 1 AC 310 at 415.
[114] Ibid at 416.
[115] Ibid at 418.
[116] Ibid at 419.
[117] Above n 94.
[118] Lord Lowry intimated that he, too, would disallow the appeals.
[119] [19912] 1 AC 310 at 422.
[120] Ibid at 423.
[121] Ibid at 424.
[122] P R Handford, *Mullaly and Handford's Tort Liability for Psychiatric Injury* (2nd Ed. 2006) at 310.
[123] Ibid at 239.
[124] Ibid at 284.
[125] (1999) 198 CLR 180. For comment on that case, see JLR Davis, "Liability for Careless Acts Causing Pure Economic Loss" (2000) 8 *Tort LJ,* 123.
[126] H Teff, "Liability for Psychiatric Illness after Hillsborough" (1992) 12 *Oxford J Legal Studies* 440 at 451.
[127] Ibid at 453.
[128] B Lynch, "A Victory for Pragmatism? Nervous Shock Reconsidered" (1992) 108 *LQR* 367 at 370.
[129] Above text at n 73 *ff*.
[130] F Bates, "Psychiatric Evidence of Character" (1976) 5 *Anglo-Am LR* 99 at 103.
[131] Above n 128 at 371.
[132] K J Nasir, "Nervous Shock and *Alcock*: The Judicial Buck Stops" (1992) 55 MLR 705.
[133] [1992] 1 AC 310 at 396.
[134] Above text at n 63 *ff*.
[135] Above text at n 63 *ff*.
[136] McGonagall, who died in 1902, represents, *The Dandy* and *The Beano* apart, the City of Dundee's major contribution to United Kingdom culture.
[137] I counted some 36 poems in the McGonagall *oevre* of which the majority (twenty) were sea disasters.
[138] S Fry, *The Ode Not Taken: Unlocking the Poet* Within (2007) at 154.
[139] Ibid at 155.
[140] Ibid at 158 *ff*.
[141] Ibid at 162/
[142] Author's emphasis.
[143] Above n 139 at 162.

[144] Ibid at 163
[145] Above text at n 139.
[146] For the comment of this issue, see above C III text at n 69 *ff*.
[147] Above text at n 126 *ff*.
[148] K Malkoff, *Theodore Roethke: An Introduction to the Poetry* (1966) at 206.
[149] Ibid
[150] Above n 149 at 207.
[151] Ibid at 209.
[152] Above n 61 at 178.
[153] PL Gerber, *Robert Frost* (Rev, Ed. 1982) at 124.
[154] Ibid at 125.
[155] E Berry, *Robert Frost* (1973) at 110.
[156] Ibid at 112.
[157] Ibid at 111.
[158] J F Lynen, The Pastoral Art of Robert Frost (1960) at 27 *ff*.
[159] Ibid at 29.
[160] Ibid at 30.
[161] W.Y Tindall. *A Reader's Guide to Dylan Thomas:* (1962) at 121.
[162] E Glyn Lewis, "Dylan Thomas" in *Dylan Thomas The Legend and the* Poet (1960) Ed Tedlock) 168 at 181.
[163] Above n 162 at 120.
[164] J Ackerman, *Dylan Thomas: His Life and Work* (1964) at 71.
[165] W T Moynihan, *The Craft and Art of Dylan Thomas* (1966) at 191.
[166] [1975] 2 NZLR 106.
[167] [1975] 2 NZLR 106 at 108.
[168] Ibid at 113. See *R* v *Moore* (1832) 3 B & Ad 184 at 188 per Lord Tenterden CJ; *Lyons, Sons & Co* v *Gulliver* [1914] 1 Ch 631 at 674 per Swinfen Eady J; *Newell* v *Izzard* [1944] 3 DLR 114.
[169] Ibid at 113.
[170] See also *Attorney-General* v *Stone* (1895) 12 TLR 76.
[171] See *Castle* v *St Augustine's Golf Links Ltd* (1922) 38 TLR 615 and *Lester-Travers* v *City of Frankstone* [1970] VR 2.
[172] [1975] n NXLR 106 at 115.
[173] (1866) LR 1 Ex 265 at 279.
[174] *Rickards* v *Lothian* [1913] AC 263 at 280 *per* Lord Moulton.
[175] [1975] 2 NZLR 106 at 117.
[176] [1951] AC 850 at 867.
[177] Above Ch II text at n 76 *ff*.
[178] Above n 172.
[179] Who had been driver to a General throughout the 1914-18 War without injury.
[180] [1975] NZLR 106 at 117.
[181] Above text at n 177.
[182] [1933] Ch 89.
[183] Ibid at 94.
[184] W S Holdsworth, "Note" (1933) 49 LQR 158.
[185] [1975] 2 NZLR 106 at 118.
[186] Although, in *Smith* v *Scott* [1973] Ch 314, it had been distinguished, and Pennycuick V-C had suggested that *Corke* ought to have been decided on the basis of nuisance.
[187] [1970] AC 1004. See also *Greenwell* v *Prison Commissioners* [1951] 101 L J 486.
[188] [1975] 2 NZLR 106 at 118.
[189] (1994) 170 CLR 520.
[190] With the caveat that, in situations falling within the scope of *Rylands* v *Fletcher*, the duty would be non-delegable. See C Sapideen and P Vines (Eds) *Fleming's The Law of Torts* (19th Ed 2011) at 386.

[191] (1945) 70 CLR 256. For comment on this case and others, see F Bates, "Accident, Trespass and Burden of Proof" (1978) 11 *Irish Jurist* (ns) 88.
[192] Ibid at 262.
[193] [1970] AC 1004 at 1038. See also Lord Diplock, ibid at 1063.
[194] Ibid at 1037.
[195] See *Bolton v Stone* [1951] AC 850 at 856 *ff per* Lord Reid.
[196] [1975] 2 NZLR 106 at 121.
[197] In New Zealand, see *Marx v Attorney General* [1914] 1 NZLR 164; in England, *Weller & Co v Foot and Mouth Disease Research Institute* [1966] 1 QB 569.
[198] Above text at 154.
[199] Above text at n 169 *ff*.
[200] There may be something paradoxical; after all the motto of Northcote College is *Ut Prosim Allis* (Let me be of service to others).
[201] For a contemporaneous account, see M D Conway, *The Life of Thomas Paine* (1892).
[202] D M Walker, *The Oxford Companion to Law* (1980) at 912.
[203] (2001) 208 CLR 199. For comment on that case, see GH L Fridman, "A Scandal in Tasmania: The Tort that Never Was" (2003) 22 *U Tasmania LR* 84.
[204] Ibid at 226.
[205] Ibid at 227.
[206] See *Lincoln Hunt Australia Pty Ltd v Willesee* (1986) 4 NSWLR 457.
[207] See *Donnelly v Amalgamated Television Services Pty Ltd* (1998) 45 NSWLR 570.
[208] (2001) 208 CLR 199 at 248.
[209] (1937) 58 CLR 479.
[210] Above text at n 167 *ff*.
[211] (2001) 208 CLR 199 at 257.
[212] Ibid at 272.
[213] Ibid at 288.
[214] Ibid at 305.
[215] Ibid at 315.
[216] Ibid at 318.
[217] Ibid at 319.
[218] Ibid at 341.
[219] M Johnston, "Should Australia Force the Square Peg of Privacy into the Round Hole of Confidence or Look for a New Tort?" (2007) 12 *Media and Arts LR* 44.
[220] Below text at n 227 ff.
[221] Above text at n 202.
[222] [1965] 1 All ER 611. For comment on that case and others see F Bates, "Marital Confidences" (1980) 10 *Fam L* 178.
[223] Ibid at 619.
[224] Ungoed Thomas j sought to extrapolate from *Prince Albert v Strange* (1849) 1 I & T 1 and *Pollard v Photographic Co* [1889] Ch D 345.
[225] [1965] 1 All ER 611 at 625.
[226] In the article, above n 223 at 179, the present writer inquired as to what conduct might so enliven it. See also, *In the Marriage of Simpson* (1978) FLC 40-497; *In the Marriage of Gibb (No 2)* (1979) FLC 90-649. In these subsequent Australian cases, it was decided that the confidences were insufficient to justify such protection.
[227] [2007] 2 FLR 301.
[228] Ibid at 303.
[229] *Protection from Harassment Act* 1997.
[230] Above text at n 229.
[231] [2007] 2 FLR 301 at 303.
[232] [1891] 2 Ch 269.
[233] Ibid at 284. Lord Esher MR, Lindley, Bowen and Lopes LJJ concurred in Lord Coleridge's judgment.

[234] Ibid at 288.
[235] [2007] 2 FLR 301 at 303.
[236] Above n 204.
[237] Above text at n 204 *ff*.
[238] [2007] 2 FLR 301 at 331.
[239] (2000) 10 BHRC 525.
[240] Ibid at 534.
[241] [2004] 2 AC 457. Lord Nicholls and Hoffman dissented.
[242] Ibid at 501.
[243] Above text at n 237.
[244] [2007] 2 FLR 301 at 304.
[245] Above text at n 243.
[246] See above text at n 228.
[247] [2007] 2 FLR 301 at 304.
[248] Authors Emphasis.
[249] [2007] 2 FLR 301 at 304.
[250] [2006] 1 FLR 1 at 19.
[251] [2007] 2 FLR 301 at 305.
[252] [2001] QB 967 at 1005.
[253] (1991) 14 EHHR 153 at 191.
[254] (1996) 24 EHHR 1 at 20.
[255] For a description of the activities depicted in the video which was the subject of the case, see ibid at 6.
[256] Above text at n 253.
[257] [1994] Fam. 192 at 203.
[258] C Munro, "Prior Restraint of the Media and Human Rights Law" 2002 *Jur Rev 1 at 23*.
[259] [2007] 2 FLR 301 at 306.
[260] F Bates, *An Introduction to Family Law* (1987) at 212.
[261] [2007] 2 FLR 301 at 306.
[262] Above text at n 253.
[263] Above text at n 242.
[264] [1994] Fam 192.
[265] [2007] 2 FLR 301 at 306.
[266] [2004] 2 AC 457 at 465.
[267] (2005) 40 EHRR 24 at 27.
[268] [1988] 1 Ch 449 at 455.
[269] [2002] EMLR 398 at 410.
[270] Above Ch IV text at n 198 *ff*.
[271] [2003] QB 195 at 216.
[272] [2007] 2 FLR 301 at 306.
[273] Above text at n 269.
[274] [2005] 1 WLR 637.
[275] In the American State of California, where he had pleaded guilty to a charge of unlawful sexual intercourse with a thirteen year old girl, but had fled before sentence would be passed.
[276] [2007] 2 FLR 301 at 307.
[277] See, for example, F Bates, "Principle and the Family Law Act: The Uses and Abuses of Section 43" (1981) 55 *Aust LJ* 181.
[278] See *Re S* (1980) FLC 90-820 at 75, 177 *per* Watson S J; although "for life" in all probability means "hopefully for life", continuing adultery presumably is not subsumed in it!
[279] See above Ch VI text at n 363 *ff*.
[280] [2007] 2 FLR 301 at 307.
[281] Eady J noted, ibid, that, in the context of adultery, reference had been made by both counsel in the case of *Tammer* v *Estonia* (2001) 29 EHRR CD 257. In that case, a criminal sanction had been imposed over insults directed at an individual.

[282] See above Ch V text at n 99 *ff*.
[283] Above text at n 278.
[284] [2007] 2 FLR 301 at 307.
[285] Eady J's emphasis.
[286] [2007] 2 FLR 301 at 308.
[287] Above n 272.
[288] [2007] 2 FLR 301 at 308.
[289] Author's emphasis.
[290] [2005] 1 AC 253.
[291] Ibid at 259. Lord Wolf CJ, Lords Hoffman and Scott and Baroness Hale agreed with Lord Nicholls.
[292] Ibid at 260.
[293] The previous test that been that of a real prospect of succeeding at trial in a claim for a permanent injunction. See *American Cynamid Co* v *Ethican Ltd* [1975] AC 396.
[294] [2005] 1 AC 253 at 261.
[295] [2007] 2 FLR 301 at 308.
[296] Eady J's emphasis. In his own words, "It would not be proportionate to any reasonable expectation on the claimant's part to prevent the defendant, for example, discussing his wife's adultery with a close friend, or with members of the family, or (if he needed to do so) with a family doctor, counsellor or social worker, or with his lawyers."
[297] [2007] 1 AC 359 at 408.
[298] Lords Bingham,, Hope and Scott, Lord Hoffman and Baroness Hale dissented.
[299] [1981] AC 1096 t 1168.
[300] [2007] 2 FLR 301 at 309.
[301] Above text at n 298.
[302] The *Profumo* scandal. For comment, see P Knightley and C Kennedy, *An Affair of State: The Profumo Case and the Framing of Stephen Ward* (1987).
[303] (2005) 40 EHRR1
[304] Above text at n 255.
[305] [2007] 2 FLR 301 at 310.
[306] Ibid.
[307] Above text a n 265 *ff*.
[308] [2007] 2 FLR 301 at 310.
[309] Ibid.
[310] Ibid.
[311] *The Hartlepool Gas & Water Co* v *West Hartlepool Harbour Co* (1865) 12 LT 336 at 338.
[312] See the High Court of Australia's decision in *Cowell* v *Rosehill Racecourse Co Ltd* (1937) 56 CLR 605.
[313] See, for example, *Ansell Rubber Co Pty Ltd* v *Allied Rubber Industries* [1967] VR 37, where it was decided that a proprietary right was not needed to restrain breaches of confidence.
[314] [1977] QB 966. See above Ch II at 96 *ff*.
[315] Ibid at 988.
[316] [2007] 2 FLR 301 at 310.
[317] Above text at n 270.
[318] [2007] 2 FLR 301 at 311.
[319] Above text at n 242 *ff*.
[320] Above text at n 272.
[321] [2003] QB 195 at 208.
[322] [2007] 2 FLR 301 at 311.
[323] Above text at n 242 *ff*.
[324] For the relevant text, see [2007] 2 FLR 301 at 311.
[325] [2007] 2 FLR 301 at 312.
[326] [1930] P 246.
[327] Ibid at 260.

[328] (1888) 58 LT 612.
[329] [1951] 2 KB 611 at 617.
[330] [2007] 2 FLR 301 at 312. He also took the view that they gave rise to the need for an interim order under the *Protection From Harassment Act* 1997, which was not opposed.
[331] [1990] 1 AC 109 at 282.
[332] Above text at n 223 *ff*.
[333] See, A Dickey, "The Notion of 'Family' in Law" (1982) 14 *UWALR* 417.
[334] See F Bates, "Does the Family Have Legal Functions?" (1987) 1 *Can J Fam L* 455.
[335] [1972] AC 572. For comment, see F Bates, *An Introduction to Family Law* (1987) at 17.
[336] [2007] 2 FLC 301 at 311.
[337] Above text at n 245 *ff*.
[338] Above Ch II text at n 12 *ff*.
[339] Above text at n 202.
[340] D Malcolm, "A Human Rights Act for Australia" (2006) 8 *U Notre Dame Australia LR* 19 at 20.
[341] J Spiegelman, "Access to Justice and Human Rights Treaties" (2000) 22 *Sydney LR* 141 at 150.
[342] Above n 341 at 23.
[343] See *(1994) 124 ALR 1*.
[344] (2001) 158 CCC (3d) 405.
[345] This provides that everyone has the right not to be arbitrarily detained or imprisoned.
[346] Section 459 (2) is qualified by s 459(3) which provides that the previous subsection notwithstanding an officer making an arrest without warrant, "…is deemed to be acting lawfully and in the execution of his duty…" for the purposes of other proceedings, unless in any such proceedings it is alleged and established by the person making the allegation that the officer making the arrest did not comply with the requirements s 459 (2).
[347] See *Public Authorities Protection Act* 1990 s 7.
[348] With Osbourne ACJO and Laskin JA agreeing .
[349] (2001) 158 CCC (3d) 405 at 413.
[350] *Criminal Code* s 459 (3).
[351] (1988) 20 OAC 105 at 115.
[352] An indication may be found in the fact that, in the volume of *Canadian Criminal Cases* in which *Collins* was reported there were nineteen cases concerned with the application of the Charter.
[353] L'Heureux-Dubé, Sopinka, Gonthier, McLachlin, Iacobucci and Major JJ concured.
[354] [1993] 2 SCR 872.
[355] [1993] 2 SCR 872 at para 4.
[356] Ibid at para 5.
[357] Ibid at para 6.
[358] Above text at n 228 *ff*.
[359] Above Ch II text at n 87 *ff*.
[360] Ibid text at n 106.
[361] Ibid text at n 109.
[362] Above text at n 232 *ff*.
[363] Above text at n 239 *ff*.
[364] Above text at n 251.
[365] [1981] AC 1096 at 1168.
[366] Above text at n 270.
[367] See A Kenny, *Arthur Hugh Clough: A Poet's Life* (2006)

Chapter VIII
Concluding Reflections

This book has covered a great deal of ground in relation both to poetry and law. In it, I have sought not to encumber the topic with too much in the way of either legal or literary theory because, all too often, I suspect that such theoretical considerations can obfuscate, rather than illuminate the book's subject matter. Instead, I have continually sought to direct attention to texts, both in terms of poetry and especially case law and to tie them together through the medium of rhetoric. It has, of course been impossible to avoid theoretical considerations entirely: thus, for example, theoretical contributions may, at an introductory stage, assist in drawing together poetry and law through the medium of rhetoric, so that some discussion has been necessitated.[1] There are some generally broad issues involved in both poetry and law in an obvious sense, these will have been apparent throughout the book's explorations.

The first is that both are concerned, at a very basal level, with words and the ways in which those words are used. These are sometimes quite complex and derivative in both poetry and in the law. The relationship between contemporary instances and what has gone before is of especial importance and interest in the relative contexts of poetry and law. Thus, to take some instances from the first chapter of the book. Carol Anne Duffy's remarkable poem "Passing Bells"[2] which concluded that Chapter, could not have been written, at least not in its existing form, had Wilfred Owen not written "Anthem for Doomed Youth"[3] nearly a century earlier, and its reference to *passing-bells* in its first line. In the same way, the decision in *Lewis* v *Avery*[4] would not have been decided in the same way and, more particularly, in the same terms had it not been for the two decisions which preceded it.

Yet, in those instances, it is quite clear that the words in which either the poems or the legal disputes are expressed and the actions, or feelings, of the protagonists or narrators in the poems and the parties to the legal proceedings interrelate and interact. An especially graphic instance of that interaction is Kenneth Koch's poem "Permanently", written in 1962. In the first stanza, the narrator describes, in wholly objective terms, the development of the sentence:

> One day the Nouns were clustered in the street.
> An Adjective walked by, with her dark beauty.
> The Nouns were struck, moved, changed.
> The next day a Verb drove up, and created the Sentence.

In the succeeding stanza, the function of the sentence is described in exemplary manner – that is, by using examples of the kind of matters which a sentence can be made to relate. The matters chosen by Koch are, as might have been expected, drawn from varieties of human activity and experience: first, Koch relates the sentence to that which he has previously described in his outline of the sentence's creation and then moves on to the altogether more mundane uses to which the sentence may be put:

> Each Sentence says one thing for example, "Although it was a dark rainy
> day when the Adjective walked by, I shall remember the pure and sweet
> expression on her face until the day I perish from the green, effective earth."
> Or, "Will you please close the window, Andrew?"
> Or, for example, "Thank you, the pink pot of flowers on the window sill has
> changed color recently to a light yellow, due to the heat from the boiler
> factory which exists nearby."

It will have been noted that the objective has largely been subsumed into the structure of the sentence and, thus, loses the individuality which has initially moved all of the other varieties of word with which she – and Koch has emphasised the adjective's influences on the other kinds of word by feminising her - and had enlivened their various roles. By this point in the poem, the adjective has been wholly subsumed and cannot be disentangled from the structure of the various sentences themselves:

> In the springtime the Sentences and Nouns lay silently on the grass.
> A lonely Conjunction here and there would call, "And! But!"

But the Adjective did not emerge.

However, of itself, the analysis of sentence structures in terms of Nouns, Conjunctions and Adjectives is essentially a sterile exercise. But, at the same time, if it is related to human thought or feelings, it can be a useful comparative exercise. Thus, the mood of the poem altogether changes:

As the adjective is lost in the sentence,
So I am lost in your eyes, ears, nose, and throat –
You have enchanted me with a single kiss
Which can never be undone
Until the destruction of language.

Hence, the power of words, and their organisation into sentences ,can be transferred to an activity, or a state of affairs, which is, innately and necessarily, a part of all human life and experience. From the structure of Koch's poem, it seems clear that he is seeking to link, through language, abstract concepts to direct human experience. From many of the examples of the operation of case law which have been considered throughout this book, the process is repeated in the processes of the law. Thus, abstract notions are required to be refined so that they may be applied to particular factual situations, of which the legal response may only represent a part. It is language – often the language of rhetoric – which brings the law into contact with the reality of its subject matter. The same, as has been observed, is true of poetry – the language whether rhetorical or not – ties the abstraction to the observed manifestation which may, in many cases, give rise to awareness of the abstraction. Of course, the language which is used is not the same in each context, but there may be similarities which are not immediately, or readily, apparent. Although they may both, from time to time, approximate to ordinary speech, the language in which both operate is distinctive. Thus, by way of example, Bloom has said[5] of Kenneth Koch that he was, "An adroit comedian of the spirit [and] refreshes by vivacity, high good humor and surrealistic jests." "Permanently," though making a point which is central to the thrust of this book, does so by means of one of Bloom's *surrealistic jests*!

The fundamental nature of the language used in both law and poetry – that of *rhetoric* was considered in Chapter II, entitled *Poetry, Rhetoric and Law: The Sound and The Fury*. In the early part of that chapter,[6] I sought to draw on the work of such disparate commentators as Karl Olivecrona and James Boyd White who suggest that language, and its form and utilisation, can have a *magical* and *controlling* effect on people other than the narrator for the time being. The latter writer is also especially emphatic[7] regarding the *imaginative* powers and roles of lawyers, which is a characteristic normally more associated with poets. Boyd White's view is not, perhaps strangely, original – owing its genesis, in part at least, to the Sixteenth Century philosopher, soldier and poet, Sidney.[8] Where Boyd White's view is original lies in the manner in which he has juxtaposed the poetic and legal imaginations. Boyd White, and this has been amply illustrated, thus suggests that a concentrated or encapsulated statement of a poetic concept or legal principle may be more effective, by way of impact, than a more detailed explication might be, especially if, thereby, attention is drawn to paradoxes, for instance, which exist in poetry or law, at large.[9]

In order to attempt to exemplify the ideas which have been generally expressed by Boyd White in particular, Chapter II goes on to consider the United States poet Wallace Stevens, who was himself legally trained, and more directly his poem "The Idea of Order at Key West" and its interpretation in the light of Stevens's perceived paradoxical position. With the implications of the poem and its environs considered, I seek to relate its rhetoric[10] to that, particularly, of Lord Denning in the decision of the English Court of Appeal in *Miller* v *Jackson*.[11] There can be little doubt that both of these contributions, in poetry and in the law, are rooted in the interstices of *rhetoric*[12], which were discussed in the first chapter. Indeed, the *rhetoric* to be found in Lord Denning's judgment is far more accessible than that in Stevens's poem, almost certainly because it is concerned with matters which are of more immediate concern to people than the metaphysical issues arising out of a quest for a possibly mythical idea of *order*. Indeed, the *rhetoric* of the poet is not always as obvious as that of the lawyer. That, it is suggested is readily apparent from Norman Nicholson's less romantic vision of village cricket. Experientially, I consider that Nicholson's vision and imaginative interpretations is more accurate thus Lord Denning's in *Miller* v *Jackson*, which, in turn, is redolent of A C McDonnell's humorous account.[13]

Having seized on varieties of rhetoric, which is the thread which links the various types of imagination to their less abstract sources, it becomes necessary to analyse the nature of the concept. The views of various commentators are encapsulated.[14] It is easy to oversimplify the notion of *rhetoric* as such, especially in the present context and to confuse it with issues such as *style* and to neglect ethical considerations. In addition, in order to fulfil its persuasive function, a speech, judgment or, indeed, a poem must be appropriate to its audience. These devices are well known, and have been so for a very long time, in both poetry and law.

But one may be used as a device in respect of the other: thus, Chapter II goes on to examine the way in which *law* and *rhetoric* relate to one another in jurisdictions which are different in concept and structure, as in Roman law based systems. In addition, analysis is attempted of a variety of cases from the United States where judgments were delivered in verse (it would not be apposite to describe it as *poetry*). In many instances, it is apparent that the use of verse of quite graphic ineptitude is intended to trivialise the action or a particular argument. Had a more dignified or sophisticated poetic form been adopted, it might have been possible to draw some other conclusion, but the use of juvenile couplets in, even, relatively trivial situations, can lead to no other.

Chapter II concludes by relating the decision in *Miller v Jackson*, and the rationative processes which led up to it, to the rhetorical position with which Lord Denning began his opinion. It is clear that the two are related in that, by the initial rhetorical introduction, the Master of Rolls was making it generally clear in which camp he stood – and it was not that of the original plaintiffs. Indeed, Lord Denning's original rhetorical standpoint is confirmed[15] by his legal justification which was, inevitably from the initial rhetoric, favourable to the defendants. The other judges in the Court of Appeal[16] did not begin with Lord Denning's rhetorical stance, so that their judgments sound all the more restrained and, thus, perhaps the more immediately acceptable to the legally trained reader, rather than the more populist approach demonstrated in Lord Denning's judgment. The general considerations which have been analysed and developed in the first two chapters were applied in various different contexts. So that judicial rhetoric as represented in those contexts has been examined in relation to notions of rhetoric in general and to those employed in poetry.

The first of these *aspects of rhetoric* which is considered in Chapter III is *the rhetoric of war*. There can be few areas of human activity (for better or worse) which have given rise, directly or indirectly, to both litigation and poetry in such quantities. There are obvious reasons why that should be: both are concerned with the effects of what is, after all, an abnormal situation which gives rise to abnormal or disastrous results which are described, discussed and interpreted by relevant bodies and people. There are particular periods of activity associated with war. First, the anticipation of war, which may very well be based on assumptions which are patently false[17] or, worse, have been, for whatever reason, deliberately falsified by the empowered classes.[18] Above all, perhaps, there are the *generational* factors as represented in the poems which are analysed in that section of Chapter III. These are not solely the exploitive nature of intergenerational relationships as depicted by Wilfred Owen, but in the repetitious attitudes handed down through generations.[19] Furthermore, it is impossible to dissociate the phenomenon of war from socio-political considerations which pertain at the same time. But the anticipation of war has *micro*, as well as *macro*, effects: that is individuals are affected by the premonition of war and may act in a manner other than that in which they ordinarily might. That reaction may manifest itself in a poetic response or in a physical response, which, in turn, may very well (and in the event, does) result in legal response. The legal response may also, and this is contextually important, be representative of the intergenerational conflict apparent in attitudinal responses to the anticipation of war.[20]

After the premonition comes the reality and both poetry and law must necessarily be concerned with the *conduct of war*. On one level, the solider is *corrupted* by having his humanity destroyed by the devices used by the enemy or, more simply, by the acts involved with fighting in dehumanising conditions.[21] At the same time, though, the dehumanising process may be brought about by the behaviour of combatants themselves.[22] But it may very well be that the State's relations with all of the individuals caught up in the dehumanising processes of armed conflict is the necessary key to understanding how war is conducted. In fact, the conduct of the war may affect more than actual combatants, and relationships with State authorities, including the law, may once again be brought into play and the generational divide may once again become apparent.[23]

However, even after actual combat has ceased or particular individuals have ceased to take part in it, the task of the lawyer and the poet is not necessarily finished. The consequences to people who had, both directly and indirectly, been caught up in the processes and machinery of war may well be both horrific and complicated and, hence, requiring both the insights of the poet and lawyer. The most obvious victims of war are those who have been seriously injured. Some of the more seriously wounded may find themselves in the horrors of a military hospital which, in many ways, may properly be equated with combat itself.[24] Even if the wounds are not as serious physically, there may be additionally spiritual damage. Both the physical and spiritual damage to individuals, both directly and vicariously, are dehumanising unless their implications are realised and faced,[25] Included, especially, in the *vicarious* repercussions of the processes of war are combatants' family,[26] though, paradoxically, there may be a cryptorelationship between the combatants themselves.[27]

There are, of course, less abstract issues which arise consequently out of law, but which, at the same time, can add to the entire process of dehumanisation. That is the organisation and administration of service pensions, which may have serious implications for both those who have been involved in active service and their families and dependants.[28] If the proceedings, before various courts and tribunals, are subsumed in unnecessarily complex and arcane legislation, similar procedures may add to the process of dehumanisation which armed conflict itself may very well have begun. Even out with the socio-legal area of benefits, the treatment of veterans of armed conflict may be less than satisfactory and, despite the war's (or the former combatant's part in it) being over, it does not mean that the horrors which were experienced during combat have *ipso facto* disappeared. A further instance of the process of dehumanisation which war has brought about from its apprehension, through its conduct, is its almost equally traumatic aftermath.

The ultimate dehumanisation – although an inevitable part of the condition – is death itself. Various poets have emphasised[29] the finality of death and the transitory nature of life and, in the ultimate, its total nullity. Yet despite the overpowering need for rhetoric to justify, perhaps, the process of war, it is by no means the only area of poetic or legal endeavour where rhetoric has been called into aid – and in some rather unlikely situations at that. In other words, a dreadful phenomenon such as modern warfare would seem quaintly juxtaposed with something as apparently beneficent as a charitable trust.[30] However, as can be perceived from the case law, many decisions seem to be aimed at frustrating such beneficent designs. Chapter III then goes on to consider particular situations: animal protection, which has attracted the attention of both poet and lawyer,[31] and, in that context, the rhetoric to be found in both poem and judgment is various and diffuse and becomes so varied depending on the context in which it arises and in which it is placed by the various narrators. In consequence the traditional view of *charity* cannot be regarded as presenting an especially coherent picture containing, especially, a number of *lacunae*. Furthermore, much of the more conservative rhetoric is, when compared with empirical study, inaccurate, In particular, much of this rhetoric can be transferred from animal protection's justification (or otherwise) to sport,[32] either involving animals or not. At this point, the rhetoric seems from time to time, sadly misplaced. However, it might be that the law,[33] if it does not become too entangled in its own processes, might be able to render other rhetoric less divisive.

From the discussion of animal protection, it is clear that it is impossible to avoid issues relating to general morality and, therefrom, it is not a huge step to a consideration of law, poetry and rhetoric as it applies to religion, which is inherently connected with the notion of the charitable trust[34] itself. The difficulty which has arisen in relation to religion in this context is the question of how far any *public* element is involved - much religious feeling and belief is intensely personal[35] and, although intensely personal, may vary significantly in its nature and, consequently in its *rhetoric*. The law though, too, must deal directly[36] with that problem and, perhaps because of rhetorical considerations, its solutions may not always appear uncontradictory or coherent. At the same time, there may well be a clearly public aspect represented, in rhetorical terms, by proselytisation, which may present its own problems for the law and its agencies, which may have to take account of those rhetorical terms and respond to them in their own.

However, a still more fundamental question may arise – namely, what will constitute a *religion* for legal and, indeed, rhetorical purposes? This is a question which courts have been forced to answer, especially in relation to less than orthodox practices.[37] In general, the policy has been to identify the various interstices which are possessed by less unorthodox religions and, then, to see how far the particular group in question fits into the template. Although there may well be, as some of the rhetoric in the case law would seem to suggest, an assumption that religions belief and practice is necessarily beneficial, it is important that the rhetoric be carefully scrutinised. Indeed, the rhetoric should be carefully scrutinised in all of the instances which were considered in Chapter III.

There is generally good reason for such scrutiny and, indeed, yet further scrutiny of the contexts in which the rhetoric has been used. Rhetoric is essentially persuasive in character and ,whether it is used by poet or by judge, it is important to evaluate the context, as there is necessarily a tripartite relationship between the rhetoric, as used, the reader or listener and the law.

That is graphically borne out by Chapter IV, which sought to first explore that relationship through an examination of the writer's contact with the law and, usually, his rhetorical response to that contact. Second, the chapter examined the law which was to be found in the rhetoric employed by a particular writer and how that link, contextually, came into being. That has been effected by initially introducing the notion of *education* – and especially research – as it has been applied in the area.[38] Again, the judicial views which have been expressed on the matter are, inevitably, various and inconsistent. That is inevitable because many of the writers whose work was the subject of the case law were themselves individualistic and idiosyncratic in both their ideas and lifestyles.

The writer's relationship with legal processes and institutions is illustrated by some of D H Lawrence's experiences, especially in relation to reaction to his poems, paintings and the law's rhetorical reaction to them, as well as to Lawrence's interaction with the law's response to the 1914-18 War.[39] Much of the controversy surrounding some (and not by any means most) of Lawrence's work does take us into semantic territory occupied by lawyers when issues about the relative notions of, say indecency and obscenity are canvassed. Indeed, it is correct to say that some of the particular instances have become landmarks in the application of the law.[40] Tests devised by the law must, of course, be applied to fact specific situations and may be at odds with more conventional attitudes to the issues raised in the initial cases so that their very application might be a fraught process. In addition, the processes of the law themselves may not be conducive to creative endeavours and that situation may very well be exacerbated when political considerations are added to an already potent mix. The core of the problem, which can arise in a variety of situations, is that lawyers, politicians and, indeed, poets may apply generic tests to situations which may have little in common.[41] In turn, that may lead to the legal and administrative process being brought into play, and which were in Lawrence's case, subjected to public scrutiny. That scrutiny may raise crucial issues – such as violation of privacy – in the public arena, even though the rhetoric of the law may circumscribe appropriately wide ranging discussion.

Lawrence's paintings similarly raised issues far beyond their immediate visual impact. Once again, it may be that the processes of the law, both in terms of substance and procedure, are not suited to dealing with issues arising from creative endeavours.[42] As with his poems, though possibly even more directly, Lawrence's paintings were likely, especially at the time they were exhibited, to produce a reaction which would not be favourable to the paintings and which would not be susceptible to rational and professional persuasion.[43] In addition, the rhetoric of the legal discourse, which was ridiculed by Lawrence, may seem strange to modern ears.

It must also be borne in mind that D H Lawrence's encounters with legal process was not solely connected with his creative output. It could well be that his experience with law and governmental agencies during the 1914-18 War might very well have added to his views of them. However, Lawrence's adventures in the public law area are generally interesting and might have been of considerable developmental importance. It is also probably fair to say that – given the moral climate of the time – Lawrence (and his associates) might not have made their own difficulties.[44] Nevertheless, Lawrence was forced, largely through the implementation of *ad hoc* legislation,[45] to change his place of residence. All of that was played out against a backcloth of confused and confusing litigation at high appellate level.

The second writer who is discussed in Chapter IV is effectively the obverse of D H Lawrence – he was never genuinely in difficulty with the law, its agencies, processes or rhetoric. At the same time, implicit in much of his work and, indeed, in his perverse personality was much that might have attracted both the action and rhetoric of the law. Masochistic reference remains a thoroughly unhealthy preoccupation in the poetry of A

C Swinburne. Even in his best, and best known work, this unfortunate tendency is instantly apparent.[46] It is interesting to trace the origins of Swinburne's psychopathology, which is clearly attributable to early, especially educational,[47] experience. This is the more disturbing when one considers that, as in so many other instances, the law may be forced to react to some of the manifestations of Swinburne's disorder which is so clearly revealed in his poetry. There have been a number of major cases, largely from the criminal law,[48] which give rise to issues which are of very considerable importance – not merely in relation to strict law, but in relation to issues such as civil liberties, realities of consent and public policy.

It is clear that both Lawrence and Swinburne were both affected – one very directly and the other rather less so – by their dealings with the law. Lawrence may well have had his whole attitude to authority, in whatever form,[49] coloured by his experiences both in the 1914-18 War and by experience of censorship. Swinburne's lack of direct contact with the law was largely coincidental, but he did not escape the attention of some establishment figures and the law, more metaphysically perhaps, permeates Swinburne's obsessional verse, even though, at the time, he may well not have considered it.

Both of those writers were, as was observed in Chapter IV, involved in the interstices of the criminal law, though rather differently and it, consequently, must be asked what is the relationship between poetry, rhetoric and the criminal law. In colloquial terms, after all, it is the criminal law which is the area of legal activity which comes first to mind. Further, it is the area which gives rise, probably, to the most media-based rhetoric, with calls for changes to the law of evidence, for ever increasingly severe sentences and punishments and so on...! Yet, in reality, there is scant agreement as to what a *crime* should be regarded as and what activities should be designated as crimes.[50] There is continuing argument between the relativities of *formalism* and *moralism*[51] ,and also as regards the extent to which the courts can create new offences. All of that gives rise to the deeper question as to how far it is ever possible to separate legal issues from considerations of morality. There have been various important cases in which that issue has been directly raised, if not, in the end, directly answered. Of course, inevitably connected with these basal matters is the issue of consequences attaching to a finding that a crime has been committed by a particular person. Central to the notion of punishment is the relevance of *retribution* and the various other theoretical justifications which are made for the imposition of punishment, many of which do not stand up well to detailed analytical scrutiny.

It is at this point that poetry becomes relevant, as the rhetoric to be found in some of the case law is couched in the language of *sin* and consequent *retribution*. However, from various sources, it will be apparent that retribution can take many forms emanating from many areas, quite apart from the formalism associated with judicial sentencing. The example which I have chosen to discuss is "The Pardoner's Tale" from Geoffrey Chaucer's cycle *The Canterbury Tales*,[52] which is a relatively short and stark tale of retribution emanating either from a malign external entity or from the cupidity of the major protagonists. In addition to the central theme of retribution, there are elements of poetic mysticism and trenchant social comment. The tale, in part because of its brevity, is one of the most graphic of *The Canterbury Tales* and tells a story through rhymed couplets which serve to heighten the tension, rather than trivialise proceedings as did their use in the cases discussed in Chapter II.[53] The description of the Pardoner and his tale ends, unlike the tale itself, happily through the ministrations of the Knight.[54] At the same time, it should be said that the tale, rather than its context, leaves a number of crucial questions unanswered, including, for present purposes, some relating to the nature of retribution.[55] There is, of course, more than an element of inevitability about the way in which the tale unfolds and ends as it seems that the three protagonists are not in genuine control of their own destinies.

Another view of "The Pardoner's Tale" is that it is centrally concerned with blasphemy,[56] with which both the law and rhetoric; as well as poetry are necessarily concerned.[57] It is, perhaps, unfortunate that much of the case law which,h has arisen has been concerned with very extreme instances (including a poem) with the result that the rhetoric which is used in them is itself extreme and tends to further entrench attitudes which have been already deeply entrenched. Yet, there can be just as clearly no doubt that issues of *policy* ought not to be concealed behind walls of rhetoric. Inevitably, too, much of the rhetoric has attracted quite severe criticism which, likewise, uses extreme rhetorical devices.[58] The situation is still further confused by the fact that there is some confusion as to what offences involving blasphemy actually entail and to whom they are applicable.

This is not to say that blasphemous reference may not be found in poetry,[59] and, in some situations at least, poetry may be a useful medium on occasion to conceal views which might otherwise be regarded as blasphemous. At the same time, in other contexts, a poem which might initially be regarded as blasphemous might not, on closer inspection, prove to be anything of the kind.

Of course, blasphemy related offences (or the prosecution thereof) may be uncommon, although they may give rise to interesting issues in law, rhetoric and policy, but *murder* is less so - although it has been with us for at least as long. It may be committed in a wide variety of situations, which involve both factual and legal matters, many of which must be taken into account in the attribution of guilt and the application of penalty. Much may depend, as so often in the law, on matters of semantics and interpretation. This may be particularly important where the offence is contained in a statute which may differ from the common law. Any complexity of that nature may cause difficulties in the preparation of, particularly, a defence case, as it may not be easy for a legal representative to explain the meaning to a client charged with murder. This is important as very serious consequences may result from a finding of guilt.[60] Further, complex notions of *probability* as opposed, say, to *possibility* may become relevant.

Despite the deficiencies in the trial process, until quite recently, the penalty was irrecoverable and the death penalty, though opposed by a great many lawyers who are generally aware of the difficulties involved, is still competent in some developed jurisdictions. In particular, the mode of execution which attracted poetic attention was hanging, whether conducted publicly or within the confines of a prison. Poets, especially, have noted the corrupting effect of executions on those involved, even indirectly.[61] The poetic vision is corroborated by historical and related studies, which seem to suggest that the poems discussed on the topic in Chapter V are accurate.[62] it is a logical step, which one of the poems makes to a general critique of the prison system at large, and, again, that critique seems to be borne out of sociological research into the prison system as it presently exists, the more so as, in response to political demands, the prison population increases.

In addition, there is little general awareness of the disparity of prison populations – a fact which is inescapable because of the variety of crimes committed, for a wide variety of reasons, especially by young people who should, generally, be kept out of prison. This fact can be readily established by a consideration of the cases which are discussed at the relevant part of Chapter V.[63] More unfortunately, attempts to provide appropriate accommodation for young offenders may very well have the opposite effect from that which was intended.[64] It must, though, be borne in mind that the sentencing process itself is far from easy and judges will frequently go to considerable lengths to protect the interests of young offenders.[65] However there will inevitably be cases where a long custodial sentence should be imposed and can be justified,[66] although such justification may well be open to argument. Further, these justifications may also reinforce already held public perceptions of judicial behaviour and it would struthious to attempt to pretend that poetic imagination has not been affected by them.[67] However, they may be affected in different ways: thus, one perception may be cosmic in its grasp, whereas another, for instance, might focus on the conditions of prisoners on remand,[68] and, once more, that poetic view is reinforced by socio-legal study.

However, I do seek to end Chapter V on a more inspiring and poetic note than much of what has preceded it. There may, often unexpectedly, be creative or artistic incidents which have the effect of lifting people above the depths where they have found themselves as a result of their own conduct. But, as was suggested in relation to the discussion of "The Pardoner's Tale", retribution may not always be inflicted by the formal processes of the law. Similarly, it may well be inflicted in a humanising way in a personal situation,[69] which might not always be criminal.

The personal uncertainty of the conclusions to Chapter V takes us, almost by natural progression, to a consideration of a wider spectrum of personal relationships (which I have called, "Love, Pain, Marriage and the Whole..."). At the outset, it must be said that the kind of personal relationship which is canvassed in this chapter is characterised by uncertainty[70] and, paradoxically, lack of reciprocity. The area of the law which is most deeply concerned with personal relationships is that which is designated as *Family Law* (perhaps for want of any better designation) which is likewise characterised by uncertainty and paradox, even at a basal level.[71] However, arguments that family/personal relationships ought not to be subject to legal scrutiny do not stand up well in the face of hard facts as represented by case law from various jurisdictions, which tend to be consonant with extra-legal commentary.[72] Issues such as family violence must not be permitted to escape the proper attention of the law and its agencies. Nonetheless, arguments in favour of non-intervention and Family Law's not being genuine *law* continue to be made, even though they can easily be refuted and do not stand up to scrutiny. This is especially the case when relatively recent times have seen a reduction in the amount of discretion given to courts by legislation.[73]

The chapter then goes on[74] to consider in depth a case which is illustrative of the uncertainly and the paradoxical nature of certain personal relationships and their relationship both with the law and with issues relating to rhetoric, though rhetoric derived from storytelling rather than poetry, although there was poetry involved in the case's facts. It is worthy of note that the case did not come from the area of Family Law, as such as it concerned an attempt, which was unsuccessful, to establish a relationship rather than the formal termination of a formal relationship, and its consequences, with which Family Law is concerned. The various reactions to the case which seek to examine more than the strict law[75] tend, inevitably perhaps, to be gender based. The case also gave rise to disagreement between those who favour a traditional approach towards the processes of the law. Indeed, it is apparent that there is little in the way of common ground between those entrenched positions. If one perceives the case as being about *gender* and *class*, it is unlikely that one will have much in common with someone who regards it in terms of strict legal process. Nevertheless, the case and its context provides an interesting illustration of the ways in which the law and literary devices can interact – even if not especially constructively, because of the rhetoric used by adherents of each position. It may also be that, as case law develops, the dispute, in literary terms, may well continue.[76] However, the parent case's importance is likely to continue because of its relationship to rhetoric and the audiences sought to be addressed by the various commentators.

Yet the crucial case led to nothing constructive for either of the parties – even though the rhetoric, both internal and external, can easily be tied to poetry. Apparently positive outcomes, such as marriage, may not ultimately prove to be what the parties had aspired to, hoped for and, more certainly, wished for by the parties. There are poets who observe that kind of failure and comment on it, in some cases in explicit and resounding detail[77] – notably in one poem, which I consider to be among the greatest in the language. It deals with motive, with deceit, with misunderstanding and, finally, with metaphysical consequence. The disappointment of expectation as well as the various transitions experienced in the relationship. Yet many of the unhappinesses described in the poetry may be reflected in the law's responses to them. However, the law's responses may be both limited – in the sense that the law does not respond to all manifestations of marital dysfunction – and not especially coherent.[78] It is clear from a study of both the poetry and the law that exploitation of both the social institution and of people are not unusual events, but, however acutely the poet may describe them in rhetorical terms, the law's responses may be inadequate and actually or potentially dehumanising. Problems may also arise in areas which might not be immediately regarded as giving rise to failures of expectation.[79]

Finally, the damage described in the poem may not be physical, emotional or, perhaps, financial, but metaphysical or spiritual. By this is meant, the sense of motivation and direction which people normally possess is destroyed;[80] thus, leaving them lost and at the apparent mercy of metaphysical forces which they cannot know but are forced, through their own blindness, to follow.

Of course, not all marriages are as disastrous as that described in a truly effective and concentrated poem. Others, however, may be unsatisfying and may also have been commented on in significant poems.[81] In such marriages, where there are children especially, the initial lack of love and sympathy between the parties could, and in the poem used as an illustration did, result in a lack of those qualities between parents and children. Although it is not the same dreadful trap as in the earlier poem, it remains a trap nonetheless, as the only way in which the rebuffed child seems able to escape is through his own death. All of that has come about even though the parties to the marriage were far from wicked people and the poem's prosody emphasises their own, as well as their situation's ordinariness. A particularly ordinary manifestation of marital dysfunction is infidelity and there have been both poems and, less regularly, legal response towards it. The legal responses have, necessarily because of statutory proscription, tended towards its legally recognisable characteristics. Conversely, the poems which are discussed on this topic in

Chapter VI have tended to focus on the personal and social consequences of the act. The difference probably exists because the poet is able to perceive in entirely personalised terms, whereas the lawyer is required to look through personalisation to larger societal ends, and may find itself sacrificing and dehumanising participants in so doing – that, at least in part, is apparent from some of the case law.[82]

But, at the same time, despite the traps and the (self-inflicted?) misery that Chapter VI has considered, it should be said that there are, indeed some marriages, or other relationships, which can, and do, fulfil the needs, aspirations and wants of the parties to them. It is probably best to end this part of the conclusions on such a note!

Although the previous chapters fell into cognisable groupings, it is equally apparent that characterising topics, in law, rhetoric and poetry may not always be so simple – hence, the generic title of Chapter VII. The legal notion (rather than concept) of *accident* is discussed and illustrated. The issue of ultimate liability is not easy to predict, by reason of the multiplicity of factual circumstances which may arise and the difficulty of applying what might be regarded as settled law to particular circumstances, rather than any deficiencies in the law itself. At the same time, it may be difficult to formulate statements of law which can readily be made applicable to factual circumstances,[83] as even small distinctions of a factual kind may make a difference to the attribution of liability. It may be that, in attempting to attribute liability, courts have failed to take into account characteristics which seem part of the human condition *per se*.[84] Put another way, it may be unfortunate if legal responsibility and moral responsibility are permitted to drift too far apart.

There are, of course, some accidents which will not give rise to legal liability though these may leave behind consequences as devastating as those which give rise to curial discussion of liability attribution,[85] they are not the concern of the law.

However, those consequences and other contexts are appropriate objects of observation by poets, who are not generally concerned with guilt or liability but with the contextualised and spiritual implications of an accident, and the accidents which are to be found in poems tend to be fatal. They may be individual or, in industrial instances, collective.

Clearly, the larger the disaster, the wider implications it is likely to have for both the student of law and the student of poetry, to say nothing of relatives and friends of those involved in the disaster. This is the subject of inquiry in both law and poetry. The law's immediate question will concern attribution of liability but also on who may be able to recover, apart from those directly involved in the collective accident. A tendency can be observed from the case law not to permit those who are too far away in, effectively, all terms to recover compensation from the person to whom liability is to be attributed.[86] However, it may ultimately be, with the notion of *proximity* having been abandoned in at least one jurisdiction,[87] that that may not finally be the case, although the *policy* behind its adoption may continue and arguments have been advanced coherently on both sides.[88] However, from another point of view, it may be that *legal rhetoric* may be designed to objectify the reader from the reality of an accident's consequences. The rhetoric of poetry, on the other hand, even in bad poetry,[89] does seek to connect readers with the fears hopes and aspirations of victims.

Inevitably, the nature of the damage and the rhetoric which attaches to it is of interest both to the law and the poet. Psychological damage is harder to evaluate than physical in both contexts. Again, both poetry and the law are concerned with psychological injury and its causes as well as the methods of treating those hurts. Yet the two rhetorics seem, just as in the discussion of accidents at large, to be disparate, though in the same contexts: legal rhetoric seems to seek to objectify itself from the realities with which it is forced to deal. Conversely, poetic rhetoric aims to personalise and humanise the people affected directly or indirectly by the phenomena characterised as accidents.

The question of disputes between neighbours, although both legal and poetic rhetoric is relevant, is different in that the context is relative isolation. Indeed, in the poems discussed under this head in Chapter VII the theme of self-protection is emphasised.[90] Thus, for example, walls are perceived as agents to be used to protect protagonists or narrators from their own perceived vulnerability. Walls or turrets may be both symbolic and real and can represent refuges and isolation from one's own kind. However, it remains not a little unclear how successful the protection is or even can be. In one poem the protagonist, rather than the narrator, seems permanently, locked into a pointless network of walls, whereas, in the other, despite the narrator/protagonist's uncertainty, he is likely to break down the barriers and find out for himself whether the risk has been worth it.[91]

In the law, the position is different in that the tasks of the law are the creation of artificial walls and fences, where real obstructions have not achieved their purpose.[92] However, the artificial, conceptual walls so created, are often arbitrary and technically complex in their construction. The interplay of case law demonstrates legal development or, indeed, the lack of it.[93] It may be that, for legal purposes at least, better fences may have restricted chances of litigation. In the end, for whatever reason, actual or futile, the urge to build walls, of whatsoever kind seems.

The final substantive area of Chapter VII is concerned with the interrelationship between privacy, and protection of human rights and relationships as perceived in the rhetoric of law and poetry. In fact, the topics are brought initially together through a poem[94] and the history of such protections. The issue of the protection of privacy though the law and its agencies has been a vexed matter and, in recent times, has become an issue of definition. It may be that the way has been opened so as to permit the creation or recognition of a tort based around the protection of privacy,[95] but whether advantage will be taken of that opportunity remains to be seen. At the same time, the rhetoric of *privacy* seems entrenched in both law and poetry, often in some rather unusual circumstances.[96] Indeed the very basis of any such tort is, at least questionable[97] and *policy* considerations cannot be evaded. In formulating policy, it would be fallacious to ignore the purposes for which freedoms especially of speech, were being exercised. However, views of the purposes' relevance could, in particular instances, be in dispute. There may, indeed, be dispute as to the relationship between such privacy laws as presently exist and other areas of law – notably defamation laws.[98]

In these areas, problems have arisen where jurisdictions have sought to entrench these matters by way of legislation which is often aimed at implementing an international Convention. For various, often historical, reasons, these Conventions may not have been especially carefully drafted and may contain contrary provisions[99] and it is a task which the courts are required to resolve. That, and related, tasks have not proved generally easy. Further, for reasons of policy, unlimited freedom of media speech may not be desirable for numerous reasons especially in relation to personal relationships which might well have unhappy consequences for people involved in them, but also for others.[100] In that context, the provision of an appropriate remedy which balances the interests of all relevant persons is of the essence. In seeking to find an appropriate remedy, the courts could recognise a legitimate expectation of privacy.

The point of this discussion is that well-meaning notions may well come back to have precisely the opposite effect from that which was initially intended. Thus, the *rights* notion may, through complex litigation and unpopular legislation, damage its own image and impact. The poem which represents the theme of the section did conclude[101] with the originator of the *rights* thesis apologising for his creation's misdeed. Instances from another jurisdiction[102] likewise suggest that the complexity, both intrinsically and extrinsically, of provisions may bring the provisions themselves into question. Thus, instances of trivial litigation may very well have such an effect.

Those, then, are some general reflections on the detail of the book at large in its passage. Is it possible to devise some overarching view of the relationship between law, rhetoric and poetry? The most obvious answer, though so obvious that it may sometimes be missed, is that all three involve particular and contextual uses of words.[103] The key is how those words are used and rhetoric, which is persuasive in both intent and purpose, may act as a link between law and poetry. Both lawyer and poet seek to persuade. In so doing, both areas of human activity use different *styles* or *conventions* which at first sight, may appear to have little to nothing in common. However, it is suggested that a major purpose of the rhetoric which is used in both poetry and law is the resolution of *doubt*. In law, the fact that the cases which have been discussed in the preceding pages were heard in court at all immediately suggests that a doubt existed in the minds of the parties to the litigation, or, at least, their legal representatives had some doubt either as to the outcome of the proceedings or as to the law which governed the factual situation. The function of the court is, using legally appropriate devices, to resolve the dispute.

The *doubts* which exist in poetry necessarily cover much wider experiental areas than they do in law, but, on many occasions, their subject material will overlap to a very considerable extent. Thus, as I suggested in Chapter VI,[104] poems have been written about legal notions by established poets and, doubtless, a narrative poem might well have been written on the factual situation in the case which is one of the focal points of that chapter.

An especially moving and graphic instance of a figure in a narrative poem seeking to come to terms with doubt is provided by a passage from "Tristram", which is a longer poem, written in 1927, by Edwin Arlington Robinson, based around the Arthurian legend.[105] The critic Van Doren, an avowed Robinson enthusiast, comments on the passage[106] that, "Not only is it finely representative of his poetry at its most tactful, its most beautiful; it is also as compendious a statement as he would probably care to make concerning the degree of felicity attainable by men in this existence which is a battle between passion and intellect, between chance and purpose, between destiny and wisdom. The only wisdom is that which comes after the event. Wisdom before experience is only words; wisdom after experience is of no avail. The wise man is a sad man who can only claim that this was so. And he will not claim that he might have ordered things better than they went. His respect for the brute strength of determined deeds prohibits such folly; his respect for the mind saves him, however, from weak wailing against fate. Perhaps it was better thus, perhaps it was not. Passion has its victories no less than reason. The tragic picture would be incomplete without either of them."

In the passage in question, Tristram and Isolt have been killed by Andred, a baron responsible to Isolt's husband, King Mark. Mark, who is more usually depicted as an unmitigated villain, is portrayed by Robinson, in Davis's words,[107] "...as a man, self-indulgent, sensual and fallible, but retaining a measure of fairness. More important, he struggles vainly to understand a problem which is, he admits, beyond him." He stands on the parapet where the lovers were killed, looking out to sea – a point regarded by Davis[108] as crucial, as the sea represents, at that time and in that space,[109] "...the movement of life, reflecting, at one moment, despair and acute unhappiness, and, at another, delight and ecstasy, but these impressions are illusory, since the sea, finally, is indifferent to men's fortunes. It comprehends them all and stands for ceaseless change." Thus:

> By the same parapet that overlooked
> The same sea, lying like sound now that was dead,
> Mark sat alone, watching an unknown ship
> That without motion moved from hour to hour,
> Farther way. There was no other thing
> Anywhere that was not as fixed and still

> As two that were now safe within the walls
> Below him, and like two that were asleep.
> "There was no more for them," he said again,
> To himself or to the ship, "and this is peace.
> I should have never praise or thanks of them
> If power were mine and I should waken them;
> And what might once have been if I had known
> Before – I do not know. So men will say
> In darkness, after daylight that was darkness,
> Till the world ends and there are not more kings
> And men to say it. If I were the world's maker,
> I should say fate was mightier than I was,
> Who made these two that are so silent now,
> And for an end like this...
>   There are some ills and evils
> Awaiting us that God could not invent;
> There are mistakes too monstrous for remorse
> To fondle or to dally with, and failures
> That only fate's worst fumbling in the dark
> Could have arranged so well...
>   There is too much in this
> That intimates a more than random issue;
> And this is peace – whatever it is for me.
> Now it is done, it may be well for them,
> And well for me when I have followed them,
> I do not know."

Many of the poems which have been analysed and contextualised in the course of this book express doubt about various experiential matters. The law must, by its nature seek to resolve doubt even though, often, it will not do so to the satisfaction of all those involved in its processes. Similarly, in poetry, the act of writing the poem brings awareness of the doubt to the conscious, even though it may not be able to resolve it. But that is, surely, a part of the condition of humanity. A major characteristic shared, surely, by both poetry and law, which are tied together through rhetorical device, is that they seek to resolve problems relating to our humanity and are, thus, humane studies. As Grayling has written,[110] in reference to the work of Collins,[111] the humanities explore what it means to be human; the words, ideas, narratives and artefacts that help us to make sense of our lives and the world we live in; how we created it and are created by it. The humanities, he goes on, involve judgment not measurement and that must include both law and poetry, bound together with rhetorical technique. They are all part of the seamless web of our cultures[112] and humanity.

At the same time, too, law and poetry – and not only because of their connection through rhetoric, however important that may be – have an especial affinity. Thus, that extraordinary and exemplary United States writer and feminist, Adrienne Rich, who recently died, said,[113] in 2006, of poetry that it, "...is not a healing lotion, an emotional massage, a kind of linguistic aromatherapy. Neither is it a blueprint, nor an instruction manual, nor a billboard." She was still more specific when she related poetry to the major problems of her time and, ultimately to an end of law, when she stated[114] that, "We may feel bitterly how little our poems can do in the face of seemingly out-of-control technological power and seemingly limitless corporate greed, yet it has always been true that poetry can break isolation, show us to ourselves when we are outlawed or made invisible, remind us of beauty where no beauty seems possible, remind us of kinship where all is represented as separation... Maturity in poetry, as in ordinary life, surely means taking our place in history, in accountability, in a web of responsibilities met or failed, of received and changing forms, arguments with community or tradition, a long dialogue between art and justice."

It is apparent that the qualities which Rich searches for and admires in poetry are solidly reflected in many of the poems, whether new or old, which have been discussed, analysed and contextualised throughout this book. Yet many of those same qualities may be apparent in some of the law which is similarly discussed, analysed and criticised in the book. Where the law does not have the qualities which Rich wants poetry to possess, it stands out in such stark contrast – because we, the readers, know its consequences!

---

[1] See above Ch I text at n 225 *ff*.
[2] Ibid text at n 363.
[3] Ibid text at n 362.
[4] Ibid text at n 198.
[5] H Bloom, *Till I End My Song: A Gathering of Last Poems* (2010) at 35.
[6] Above Ch II text at n 5 *ff*.
[7] Ibid text at n 9.

[8] Ibid text at n 13.
[9] Ibid text at n 28.
[10] Ibid text at n 24 *ff*.
[11] [1977] QB 966.
[12] Above Ch II text at n 79.
[13] Ibid text at n 82.
[14] Ibid text at n87 *ff*.
[15] Ibid text at n 210 *ff*.
[16] Ibid text at n 217 *ff*.
[17] Above Ch III text at n 3 *ff*.
[18] Ibid text at n 7.
[19] Ibid text at n 9 *ff*.
[20] Ibid text at n 60 *ff*.
[21] Ibid text at n 69 *ff*.
[22] Ibid text at n 77 *ff*.
[23] Ibid text at n 78*ff*.
[24] Ibid text at n 96 *ff*.
[25] Ibid text at n 97 *ff*.
[26] Ibid text at n 102 *ff*.
[27] Ibid text at n 109 *ff*.
[28] Ibid text at n 116 *ff*.
[29] Ibid text at n 167 *ff*.
[30] Ibid text at n 177 *ff*.
[31] Ibid text at n 199 *ff*.
[32] Ibid text at n 260 *ff*.
[33] Ibid text at n 265 *ff*.
[34] Ibid text at n 177 *ff*.
[35] Ibid text at n 283 *ff*.
[36] Ibid text at n 292 *ff*.
[37] Ibid text at n 306 *ff*.
[38] Chapter IV text at n 1 *ff*.
[39] Ibid text at n 28 *ff*.
[40] See, for example, ibid text at n 62 *ff*.
[41] Ibid text at n 74 *ff*.
[42] Ibid text at n 105 *ff*.
[43] Ibid text at n 111 *ff*.
[44] Ibid text at n 116 *ff*.
[45] Ibid text at n 123 *ff*.
[46] Ibid text at n 184.
[47] Ibid text at n 189 *ff*.
[48] Ibid text at n 198 *ff*.
[49] Ibid text at n 253 *ff*.
[50] See Chapter V text at n 1 *ff*.
[51] Ibid text at n 11 *ff*.
[52] Ibid at n 99 *ff*.
[53] Above chapter II text at n ???? ff.
[54] Chapter V text at n 124.
[55] Ibid text at n 125 *ff*.
[56] Ibid text at n 129.
[57] Ibid text at n 135 *ff*.
[58] Ibid text at n 155 *ff*.
[59] Ibid text at n 180 *ff*.
[60] Ibid text at n 216 *ff*.
[61] Ibid text at n 213 *ff*.

[62] Ibid text at n 225 *ff*.
[63] Ibid text at n 234 *ff*.
[64] Ibid text at n 254 *ff*.
[65] Ibid text at n 255 *ff*.
[66] Ibid text at n 267 *ff*.
[67] Ibid text at n 274 *ff*.
[68] Ibid text at n 285 *ff*.
[69] Ibid text at n 293 *ff*.
[70] Above Ch VI text at n 1 *ff*.
[71] Ibid text at n 5 *ff*.
[72] Ibid text at n 15 *ff*.
[73] Ibid text at n50 *ff*.
[74] Ibid text at n 63 *ff*.
[75] Ibid text at n 115 *ff*.
[76] Ibid text at n 236.
[77] Ibid text at n 276 *ff*.
[78] Ibid text at n 317 *ff*.
[79] Ibid text at n 336 *ff*.
[80] Ibid text at n 341 *ff*.
[81] Ibid text at n 349 *ff*.
[82] Ibid text at n 369 *ff*.
[83] Above Ch VII text at n 23 *ff*.
[84] Ibid text at n 51 *ff*.
[85] Ibid text at n 56 *ff*.
[86] Ibid text at n 68 *ff*.
[87] Ibid text at n 125.
[88] Ibid text at n 122 *ff*.
[89] Ibid text at n 136 *ff*.
[90] Ibid text at n 155 *ff*.
[91] Ibid text at n 163 *ff*.
[92] Ibid text at n 167 *ff*.
[93] Ibid text at n 181 *ff*.
[94] Ibid text at n 202 *ff*.
[95] Ibid text at n 205 *ff*.
[96] Ibid text at n 224 *ff*.
[97] Ibid text at n 236 *ff*.
[98] Ibid text at n 244 *ff*.
[99] Ibid text at n 251 *ff*.
[100] Ibid text at n 270.
[101] Ibid text at n 340.
[102] Ibid text at n 345 *ff*.
[103] Above text at n 1.
[104] Above Ch VI txt at n 248.
[105] The others being "Merlin" (1917) and "Lancelot" (1919).
[106] M Van Doren, *Edwin Arlington Robinson* (1927) at 89.
[107] C T Davis, "Robinson's Road to Camelot" in *Edwin Arlington Robinson: Centenary Essays* (1969 Ed. Barnard) 88 at 99.
[108] Ibid at 101.
[109] For another view see above Ch VI text at n 346 *ff*.
[110] A C Grayling, "The Rise and Fall of the Ivory Tower" (2012) 395 *Literary Review* 50 at 50.
[111] S Collini, *What Are Universities For?* (2011)
[112] For additional comment, see F Bates, "Law as Culture: Global Thoughts from a Small Island" (1998) 21 *The Law Teacher* 263.

[113] Quoted in an obitrary in *The New York Times* by M Fox, reproduced in *The Sydney Morning Herald* of April 6 – 8th 2012.
[114] Quoted in D Lehman (Ed) *The Oxford Book of American Poetry* (2006) at 867.

Bibliography

Ackerman, J. *The Craft and Art of Dylan Thomas* (1966)
Alexander, R. *Domestic Violence in Australia* (3rd ed, 2002)
Allen, C.K. *Law in the Making* (7th Ed, 1964)
Allen, G.W. *The New Walt Whitman Handbook* (1975)
Amnesty International Handbook (1977)
Anderson, J *The Legality of Boxing: A Punch Drunk Love?* (2007)
Ashworth, A. *The Criminal Process: An Evaluative Study* (2nd ed. 1998)
Austin, J. *The Province of Jurisprudence Determined* (1832)
Bacon, .*The Essays* (1625)
Baker, J.H. *An Introduction to English Legal History* (4th ed. 2002)
Barnard, E. "Robinson's Literary Reputation" in *Edwin Arlington Robinson: Centenary Essays* (Ed Barnard, 1969) 1
Bartlett, M. "World Correctional Population Trends and Issues" in *Corrections Criminology* (Ed. O'Toole and Eyland 2005) 8
Bates, F. "A Reflection upon Law and Literature" (1981) 28 *Chitty's LJ* 13
Bates, F. *An Introduction to Family Law* (1987)
Bates, F. "'Like an Unwelcome Guest': the Moral Crisis in Modern Legal Education" (1985) 18 *The Law Teacher* 181
Bates, F. "Artificial Families – Upside Down? A View from Australia" [2004] *International Fam L* 82
Bates, F. "Benefits for Children with Disabilities: A Light at the End of the Tunnel" (1999) 20 *Statute LR* 154
Bates, F. "Benefits for Handicapped Children in Australian Family Law: A Disaster in Statutory Interpretation and Reform" (1991) 11 *Statute LR* 108
Bates, F. "Blunting the Sword of Solomon – Australian Family Law in 2006" (2008) in *The International Survey of Family Law* (2008, Ed, Atkin) 2
Bates, F. "'Completing the Charm' – the Relevance of Children's Wishes in Contested Cases" (2004) 5(2) *Newcastle LR* 97
Bates, F. "Children and Family Violence in Australia: An Aberration in the Law Reform Process"(2005) 13 *Asia Pacific LR* 63
Bates, F. "Children's Best Interests in Australia: Camouflage, Persiflage or What?" (2005) *International Fam. L.* 138
Bates, F. "Choice of Law in Australian Torts: Or the Truth about Conflicts" (2003) 14 *Caribbean LR* 1

Bates, F. "Consent to Marriage Obtained by Fraud – A New Development" (1978) 128 *New LJ* 403

Bates, F. "Corporal Punishment: Legal, Historical and Social Context" (1983) 12 *Manitoba LJ* 337

Bates, F. "Describing the Indescribable – Evaluating the Standard of Proof in Criminal Cases" (1989) 13 *Crim LJ* 330

Bates, F. "Does the Family Have Legal Function" (1987) 1 *Can J Fam L* 455

Bates, F. "Dylan Thomas and the Idea of Justice" in *In Memoriam Senator J William Fulbright 1905-1995* (2010, Eds Magiru, Magiru and Johnson) 15

Bates, F. "Dylan Thomas and the Idea of Law: (2007) VIII (3) *Down Under Milk Wood* 13

Bates, F. "Finding the Truth in Child Sexual Abuse Cases: Some Comparative Developments" (1993) 5 *J Child L* 178

Bates, F. "Improperly Obtained Evidence and Public Policy: An Australian Perspective" (1994) 43 *ICLQ* 379

Bates, F. "In Memory of Michael Scott" (1984) 8 *U Tasmania LR* 1

Bates, F. *International Disorder and the Hague Child Abduction Convention: A Discursive Commentary* (2009)

Bates, F. "Law as Culture: Global Thoughts from a Small Island" (1987) *The Law Teacher* 263

Bates, F. "'Like an Unwelcome Guest': the Moral Crisis in Modern Legal Education" (1985) 18 *The Law Teacher* 181

Bates, F. "Marital Confidences" (1980) 10 *Fam LJ* 178

Bates, F. "On the Mat and Up the Wall" (2005) LIX (10) *Quadrant* 44

Bates, F. "Pornography and the Expert Witness" (1978) 20 *Crim LQ* 250

Bates, F. "Principle and the Family Law Act: the Uses and Abuses of Section 43" (1981) 55 *Aust LJ* 181

Bates, F. "Psychiatric Evidence of Character" (1976) 5 *Anglo-Am LR* 99

Bates, F. "Same Sex Marriages, Conflict of Law and Public Policy – A Modern Commentary" (1999) 21 *Liverpool LR* 49

Bates, F. "Scandalising the Court: Some Peculiarly Australian Developments" (1994) 13 *Civil Justice Q* 241

Bates, F. "Social Security Law and Children with Disabilities: Change and Decay in Australian Statute Law" (1997) *Statute LR* 215

Bates, F "Some Theoretical Aspects of Modern Family Law" (1984) 100

South African LJ 664

Bates, F. "Strength or Intensity? Some Reflections on the Modern Standard of Proof in Civil Cases" (1980) 27 *Chitty's LJ* 33

Bates, F. "The Family and Society: Reality and Myth" (1980) 15 (n.s.) *Irish Jurist* 19

Bates, F. "The Perils of the Small Law School *Or* A Lesson from *Captain Carpenter*" (1984) 5 *Otago LR* 458

Bates, F. *The Reality of Conflicts Reasoning: Choice of Law in Torts* (2010)

Bates, F. "The Responsibility of the Law School" (1982) 15 *The Law Teacher* 172

Bates, F. "Violence, Money and Informal Families in Australia and New Zealand" (1999) 7 *Asia Pacific Law Review* 1

Bates, F. "War and Disorder: the Hague Child Abduction Convention – Australia Law in Context" (2010) 13 *Asia Pacific LR* 133

Bates, F. "'We Prize Not to the Worth' – Some Thoughts on the Valuation of Property Under the Family Law Act" (2005) 7 (2) *Newcastle LR* 35

Bates, F. "'Which Comforts While It Mocks': Some Paradoxes in Modern Family Law" (2000) 4(2) *Newcastle LR* 17

Bates, F., McGinty, R. "'Arrest Him, He's Indecent, He's Obscene What's More!' the Poems and Paintings of D.H. Lawrence as Part of Cultural History and Moral Outrage" (2006-2008) 10 *Newcastle LR* 91

Bates, M. *Wallace Stevens: A Mythology of Self* (1986)

Bell, J. *Policy Arguments in Judicial Decisions* (1983)

Benamon, M. *Wallace Stevens and the Symbolist Imagination* (1972)

Berry, E. *Robert Frost* (1973)

Bevis, W.W. *Mind of Winter: Wallace Stevens, Meditation and Literature* (1988)

Bishop, I. "The Narrative Art of The Pardoner's Tale" in *The Canterbury Tales: A Casebook* (1974 Ed. Anderson) 215

Bix, B. "Assault, Sado-masochism and Consent" (1933) 109 *LQR* 540

Blom-Cooper, L, Drewry, G (Eds) *Law and Morality* (1976)

Bloom, H. (ed.) *Till I End My Song: A Gathering of Last Poems* (2010)

Booth, J. *Philip Larkin: Writer* (1992)

Bosanquet, B. *Some Suggestions in Ethics* (1918)

Bottomley, A. "Self and Subjectivities: Language of Claim in Property Law" (1993) 89 *Michigan LR* 11549

Boyd White, J. *The Legal Imagination (Abr. Ed, 1985)*
Brazeau, P. *Parts of a World: Wallace Stevens Remembered* (1983)
Brown, B.J. *Shibboleths of Law: Reification, Plain-English and Popular Legal Symbolism* (1987)
Brown, L (Ed.) *The New Shorter English Dictionary of Historical Principles* (1993)
Brown, M.E. *Wallace Stevens: The Poem as Art* (1970)
Bushell,N.S. "The Wandering Jew and The Pardoner's Tale" (1931) 28 *Studies in Philology* 450
Carr, C. "Regulated Liberty" 1942) 42 *Columbia LR* 339
Cavers, D.F. "Legal Education in the United States" in *Talks on American Law* (Rev. Ed., 1971. Ed.Berman)
Cobbe, F.B. (1878) 32 *The Contemporary Review* 57
Coghill, N., Tolkein, C. *The Pardoner's Tale* (Introduction) (1958)
Cohen, M.R. *Reason and Law* (1950
Coleridge, S.T. *Biographia Literaria* (1817)
Collier, J.G. *Conflict of Laws* (3rd Ed. 2001)
Collini, S. *What Are Universities For? (2011)*
Comfort, A. *The Anxiety Makers: Some Curious Sexual Preoccupations of the Medical Profession* (1967)
Conway, M.D. *The Life of Thomas Payne (1892)*
Cook, E. *Poetry, Word-Play and Word-War in Wallace Stevens* (1988)
Cook, N. "Shakespeare Comes to the Law School." (1988) 68 *Denver ULR* 387.
Cook, "An Impossible Distinction" (1991) 107 *LQR* 46
Cooke, D. *Rich Law, Poor Law: Different Responses to Tax and Supplemenetary Benefit Fraud* (1989)
Cope, M. *Duress, Undue Influence and Unconscientious Bargains* (1985)
Cotter, C.P. "Emergency Detention in Wartime: The British Experience'(1954) 6 *StanfordLR* 238
Coxe, L.O. "The Lost Tradition" in *Edwin Arlington Robinson: A Collection of Critical Essays* (Ed. Murphy,1970) 60
Craig, P. "Negligence in the Exercise of Statutory Power" (1978) 94 *LQR* 428
Crofton, I. *History Without The Boring Bits* (2007)
Crook, J.A. *Law and Life of Rome* (1967
Culler, J. *On Deconstruction*(1983)

Dal Pont, G., Cockburn, T. *Equity and Trusts in Principles* (2004)
Davenant, William (1606 – 1668). "The Christian's Reply to the Philosopher."
Davis, C.T. "Robinson's Road to Camelot" in *Edwin Arlington Robinson: Centenary Essays* (1969 Ed. Barnard) 88
Davis, J.L.R. "Liability for Careless Acts Causing Pure Economic Loss" (2000) 8 *Tort LJ* 123
Davis, R. *100 Years" A Centenary History of the Faculty of Law, University of Tasmania 1893-1993* (1993)
Day, R. *Larkin* (1987)
Delany, P. *D.H. Lawrence: The Writer and His Circle in the Years of the Great War* (1988)
Delgado, R. "Storytelling for Opportunists and Others: A Plea for Narrative" (1989) 87 *Michigan LR* 2411
Delgado, R. "Whan a Story is Just a Story: Does Voice Really Matter?" (1990) 76 *Virginia LR* 95
Delgado, R., Stefancic, J. "Norms and Narratives: Can Judges Avoid Serious Moral Error?" (1991) 69 *Texas LR* 1929
Devlin, P "The Enforcement of Morals" (1959) 45 *Proc. British Academy* 129
Devlin, P *The Enforcement of Morals* (1965)
Dewar, J "The Concepts, Coherence and Contact of Family Law" in *Examining the Law Syllabus: The Core* (Ed. Binks 1992)
Dewar, J. "The Normal Chaos of Family Law" (1998) 61 *MLR* 467
Dickey, A. "The Notion of 'Family' in Law" (1982) 14 *UWALR* 417
Dickey, A. *Family Law* (5th Ed, 2007)
Duff, R.A. *Answering for Crime* (2004)
Duff, R.A. "Theorising about Criminal Law" (2005) *25 OJL 353*
Duggan, A.J. "Unconscientious Dealing" in *The Principles of Equity* (Ed. Parakinson, 2nd Ed, 2003) 127
Dworkin, R. *Law's Empire* (1986)
Dworkin, R. *Taking Rights Seriously* (1997)
Eekelaar, J.M. "The Emergence of Children's Rights" (1986) 6 *Oxf J Legal Studies* 161
Eliot, T.S. *George Herbert: Writers and Their Work* (1967)
Emerson, R.W. "The Poet" in *Essays* (2nd series, 1844)
Engel, H. *Lord High Executioners: An Unashamed Look at Hangmen,*

Headsmen and Their Kind (1998)

Enonchong, N. "Illegal Transactions: the Future" (2000) 8 *Restitution LR* 82

Enonchong, N. "Illegality : The Fading Flame of Public Policy" (1994) 14 *OJLS* 295

Eskridge, W.N. *The Case for Same-Sex Marriage: From Sexual Liberty to Civilized Commitment* (1996)

Evans, I. *English Poetry of the Late Nineteenth Century* (2nd ed 1966)

Evans, M. *Equity and Trusts* (3rd Ed, 2003)

Fajer, M. "Can Two Real Men Eat Qiche Together? Storytelling, Gender Role Stereotypes and Legal Protection for Lesbians and Gay Men" (1992) 46 *U Miami LR 511*

Family Law Council. *Sterilisation and Other Medical Procedures* (1994)

Fernandez, R. *Messages: Literary Essays* (1927)

Finkelman, P. "Law of Slavery" in *Oxford Guide to American Law* (2002. Ed. Hall)

Finlay, A. "Can We See the Chancellor's Footprint: *Bridgewater v Leahy*" (1999) 14 *J Contract L* 265

Finlay, H.A. *To Have But Not to Hold: A History of Attitudes to Marriage and Divorce in Australia 1858-1975* (2005)

Finnis, J. *Natural Law and Natural Rights* (1990)

Fitzpatrick, P, Hunt, A. "Critical Legal Studies: An Introduction" in *Critical Legal Studies* (1987, eds. Fitzpatrick and Hunt)

Fousset, H.I. *Walt Whitman: Poet of Democracy* (1966)

Foxford, D. "*R v Holliday ex parte Zadig* in Retrospect" (2003) 119 *LQR* 455

Freeman, J. "Constitutive Rhetoric: Law as a Literary Activity" (1991) 14 *Harvard Women's LJ* 305

Fridman, G.H.L. "A Scandal in Tasmania: The Tort that Never Was" (2003) 22 *U Tasmania LR* 84

Fried, C. "Sonnet LXV and the 'Black Ink' of the Framers Intention" (1987) 100 *Harvard LR* 761

Frued, A. "Child Observation and Prediction of Development: A Lecture in Honour of Ernst Kris" (1958) 13 *The Psychoanalytical Study of the Child* 97

Fry, S. *The Fry Chronicles* (2010)

Fry, S. *The Ode Not Taken: Unlocking the Poet Within* (2007)

Fryer, P. *Mrs Grundy: Studies in English Prudery* (1963)
Fuller, J. *W.H. Auden: A Commentary* (1998)
Gadamer, H. *Truth and Method* (1979)
Galanter, M. *Lowering the Bar: Lawyer Jokes and Legal Culture* (2005)
Garton Ash, T. "Tony Judt (1948-2010)" (2010) LVII (14) *New York Review of Books* 6
Gerber, P.L. *Robert Frost* (Rev Ed, 1982)
Getman, J. "Voices" (1988) 66 *Texas LR* 577
Gibson, I. *The English Vice: Beating, Sex and Shame in Victorian England and After* (1978)
Gifford, T., Roberts, N. *Ted Hughes: A Critical Study* (1981)
Glyn Lewis, E. "Dylan Thomas" in *Dylan Thomas" The Legend and the Poet* (Ed. Tedlock,1960 168
Goldensohn, L, ed. *American War Poetry: An Anthology* (2006)
Goodhart, A.L. "Mistake as to Identity in the Law of Contract" (1941) 57 *L.Q.R* 228
Goodman, E. "The Relevance of Religion in Custody Adjudication" (1981) 7 *Monash ULR* 217
Goodrich, P. *Reading the Law: A Critical Introduction to Legal Method and Techniques* (1986)
Gordon, G.H. *The Criminal Law of Scotland* (1967)
Gorn, E. *The Manly Art: Bare Knuckle Prize Fighting in America* (1989)
Gottlieb, S.R. "Cardozo, Benjamin Nathan" in *The Oxford Guide to the Supreme Court* (2nd Ed 2005, Ed. Hall) 148
Gray, J.C. *The Nature and Sources of Law* (1909)
Graycar, R., Morgan, J. *The Hidden Gender of Law* (1990)
Grayling, A.C. "The Rise and Fall of the Ivory Tower" (2012) 395 *Literary Review* 50
Grey, T.C. *The Wallace Stevens Case: Law and the Practice of Poetry* (1991)
Gurney, S *British Poetry of the Nineteenth Century* (1993)
Handford, P.R. *Mullaly and Handford's Tort Liability for Psychiatric Injury* (2nd Ed 2006)
Harris, A. "Race and Existentialism in Feminist Legal Theory" (1990) 42 *Stanford LR* 581
Harris, B. *The Literature of the Law* (1998)
Harris, D.A. *Inspirations Unbidden: The "Terrible Sonnets" of Gerard*

Manley Hopkins (1982)
Harris, J.W. *Legal Philosophies* (2nd Ed. 1997)
Harris-Short, S., Miles, J. *Family Law: Text, Cases and Materials* (2007)
Hecht, A. *The Hidden Law: The Poetry of W.H. Auden (1993)*
Hedley, S. "Sado-masochism, Human Rights and the House of Lords" 1933) 52 *CLJ* 194
Heerey, P. "Truth, Lies and Stereotype: Stories of Mary and Louis" (1996) 1 (3) *Newcastle LR* 1
Hegel, G.W.F. *Outlines of the Philosophy of Right* (1821)
Henderson, P. *Swinburne: Portrait of a Poet* (1974)
Hepburn, S. "Equity and Infatuation: (1993) 18 *Alternative LJ* 208
Hepburn, S. *Principles of Equity and Trusts* (2nd Ed, 2001)
Heuston, R.F.V. "*Liversidge v Anderson* in Retrospect" (1970) 86 *LQR* 33
Hewart, G. *The New Despotism* (1928)
Higgins, R.C.A. "The Empty Eloquence of Fools' Rhetoric in Classical Greece" in *Rediscovering Rhetoric: Law, Language and the Practice of Persuasion* (2008, Ed. Gleeson and Higgins) 3
Hillman, R.A. "'Instinct with Obligation' and 'Normative Ambiguity of Rhetorical Power'" (1955) 56 *Ohio State LJ* 775
Hodges, E.P. "Writing in a Different Voice" (1988) 66 *Texas LR* 629
Hogg,R. "Prisoners and the Penal Estate in Australia" in *Prisoners as Citizens: Human Rights in Australian Prisons* (Ed Brown and Wilkie, 2002) 3
Holt, R. *Sport and the British: A Modern History* (1989)
Horace. *Epistles I, xvi,40*
Hunt, A. "The Big Fear: Law Confronts Postmodernism" (1990) 35 *McGill LJ* 507
Hunt, A. "The Critique of Law: What is 'Critical Legal Studies'?"
Hutchinson, A. "Inessentially Speaking (Is There Politics After Postmodernism?) 91 *Michigan LR* 1549
Hutchinson, A. "Initially Speaking (Is There Politics After Postmodernism?)" (1992) 89 *Michigan LR* 1549
James, C. "There You Come Home" (2011) LV (4) *Quadrant* 12
Jenkins, L.M. *Wallace Stevens: Rage for Order* (2000)
Jenkins, W.D. "Swinburne, Robert Buchanan and W.S. Gilbert: 'The Pain that is all but Pleasure'" (1972) 60 *Studies in Philology* 369
Jennings, I. *The Law and the Constitution* (5th Ed, 1959)

Johnson, H.A. "Marbury v Madison" in *The Oxford Guide to the Supreme Court of the United States* (2005 Ed. Hall) 605

Johnston, M. "Should Australia Force the Square Peg of Privacy into the Round Hole of Confidence or Look for a New Tort" (2007) 12 *Media and Arts LR* 44

Jolowicz, H.F. *Historical Introduction to the Study of Roman Law* (1939)

Keeton, G.W. "*Liversidge v Anderson*" (1942) 5 *MLR* 162

Keeton, G.W. Sheridan, L.A. *The Modern Law of Charities* (2nd Ed. 1971)

Kelson, H. *General Theory of Law and State* (1945, Tr. Wedberg)

Kempe, R.S., Kempe, C.H. *Child Abuse* (1978)

Kennedy, R. "Racial Critiques of Legal Academia" (1989) 102 *Harvard LR* 174

Kenny, A. *Arthur Hugh Clough: A Poet's Life* (2006)

Kenny, C.S. "The Evolution of the Law of Blasphemy" (1922) 1 *CLJ* 127

Kermode, F. *Wallace Stevens* (1960)

Kinkead-Weekes, M. *D.H. Lawrence: Triumph to Exile 1912-22* (1996)

Knightley, P., Kennedy, C. *An Affair of State: The Profumo Case and the Framing of Stephen Ward* (1987)

Lehman, D (Ed). *The Oxford Book of American Poetry* (2006)

Leigh, L.H. "Sado-masochism: Consent and the Reform of the Criminal Law: (1976) 39 *MLR* 130

Levy, L.W. *The Law of Commonwealth and Chief Justice Shaw: The Evolution of American Law* (1957)

Liebling, A. "Measuring Prisons and Their Moral Performance" in *Corrections Criminology* (Ed. O'Toole and Eyland 2005) 199

Lindquist, S., Cross, F.B. "Empirically Testing Dworkin's Chain Novel" (2005) *New York ULR*

Lofgren, C.A. *The Plessy Case: A Legal Historical Interpretation* (1987)

Lowe, N., Douglas, G, *Bronley's Family Law* (10th Ed, 2006)

Lynch, B. "A Victory for Pragmatism? Nervous Shock Reconsidered" (1992) 108 *LQR* 367

Lynen, J.F. *The Pastoral Art of Robert Frost* (1960)

MacBeth, G (Ed) *The Penguin Book of Victorian Poetry* (1969)

Macdonald J.H.A. *Practical Treatise on the Criminal Law of Scotland* (1867)

Malcolm. D. "A Human Rights Act for Australia" (2006) 8 *U Notre Dame Australia LJ* 19

Malkoff, K. *Theodore Roethke: An Introduction to the Poetry* (1966)
Marcus, S. *The Other Victorians: A Study of Sexuality and Pornography in Nineteenth Century England* (1966)
Martin, B.K. *Philip Larkin* (1978)
Matsuda, M. "Pragmatism Modified and the False Consciousness Problem" (1990) 63 *S California LR* 1763
McClean, J.D. "The Battered Baby and the Limits of the Law" (1978) 5 *Monash ULR* 1
McCredden, L. *James McAuley* (1992)
McKenzie, N.H. *A Reader's Guide to Gerard Manley Hopkins* (1981)
Meagher, R.P. , Gummow, W.M.C. *Jacobs' Law of Trusts in Australia* (6th Ed. 1997)
Meagher, R.P., Heydon, J.D., Leeming, M. *Equity: Doctrines and Remedies (4th Ed, 2002)*
Megarry, R.E. *A New Miscellany – At Law: Yet Another Diversion for Lawyers and Others* (2005 Ed. Garner)
Merryman, J.H. *The Civil Law Tradition* (1969)
Michael, J., Adler, M. *Crime, Law and Social Science* (1933)
Millett, P. "Villainy in Venice" in *On Villainy* (2007)
Morris, H. "A Paternalistic Theory of Punishment" (1981) 18 (4) *Am Phil Q* 263
Morris, H. "Persons and Punishment" 52 *Monist* 475
Moynihan, W.T. *The Craft and Art of Dylan Thomas (1966)*
Muir, F., ed. *Oxford Book of Humourous Verse* (1992)
Munro, C. "Prior Restraint of the Media and Human Rights Law" 2002 *Jur Rev* 1
Nasir, K.J. "Nervous Shock and *Alcock*: The Judicial Buck Stops" (1992) 55 *MLR* 705
Nehls, E.(Ed) *D.H Lawrence: A Composite Biography* Vol. 3 1925-1959
Nicholson, C.J. "The Changing Nature of Families" (1997) 11 *Aust J Fam L* 13
Norris, C. *Deconstruction: Theory and Practice* (1982)
O'Donovan, K. "Family Law and Legal Theory" in *Legal Theory and Common Law* (1986)
Olivecrona, K. *Preface* to A. Hägerstrom's, *Inquiries into the Nature of Law and Morals* (1953, Trs. Broad)
Olsen, E. *The Poetry of Dylan Thomas* (1954)

Ormerod, D. *Smith and Hogan's Crininal Law* (2nd Ed, 2008)
Otto, D. "A Barren Future? Equity's Conscience and Women's Inequality" (1991) 18 *Melbourne ULR* 808
Pearce, D.C. *Statutory Interpretation in Australia* (1974)
Perce, R.A., Stevens, J. *The Law of Trusts and Equitable Obligations* (4th Ed. , 2006)
Petch, S. *The Art of Philip Larkin* (1981)
Pliny. *Ep, VI* 33
Polenburg, R. *The World of Benjamin Cardozo: Personal Values and the Judicial Process* (1997)
Posner, R.A. *Law and Literature* (1998, Revised and Enlarged Ed.)
Posner, R.A. *Overcoming Law* (1995)
Pothier, R.J. *Traité des Obligations* (1761)
Prentice, R.A. "Supreme Court Rhetoric" (1983) 25 *Arizona LR* 85
Radan, P., Stewart, C. *Principles of Australian Equity and Trusts* (2010)
Redmount, R.S. "A Conceptual View of The Legal Education Process" (1972) 24 *J Legal ED* 129.
Robertson, A.H. *Characterisation in the Conflict of Laws* (1940)
Robinson, C. *Ted Hughes as a Shepherd of Being* (1989)
Robinson, O.F., Ferguson, T.D., Gordon, W.M. *European Legal History* (2nd Ed, 1994)
Ruoff, Theo. "Links with London" (1971) 45 *Aust LJ* 640
Sager, K. *The Art of Ted Hughes* (2nd ed 1978)
Sapideen, C., Vines, P. (Eds) *Fleming's The Law of Torts* (19th Ed, 2001)
Sarmas, L. "A Response to Justice Peter Heerey" (1998) 3 (1) *Newcastle LR* 82
Sarmas, L. "Storytelling and the Law: A Case Study of *Louth v Diprose*" (1994) 19 *Melbourne ULR* 701
Scheppele, M. "Forward: Telling Stories" (1989) 87 *Michigan LR* 2073
Schmidt, M. *The Great Modern Poets: An Anthology of the Best Poets anad Poetry Since 1990* (2006)
Scigay, L.M. *the Poetry of Ted Hughes: Form and Imagination* (1986)
Scoles, E.F., Hay P., Borchers, S.C, Symeonides, S.C. *Conflict of Laws* (4th Ed., 2000)
Scott, J. *Caught in Court: A Selection of Cases with Cricketing Connections* (1989)
Sedley, S. "In the Court of Appeal" (2007) 20(17) *London Review of Books*

Shearer, I.A. *Starke's International Law* (11th ed 1994)
Sheridan, L.A., Delany, V.T.H. *The Cy-Pres Doctrine* (1959)
Sidney, Sir Philip. *The Defense of Poesie* (11595)
Simpson, A.W.B. *In the Highest Degree Odious* (1992)
Singer, J.W. "Persuasion" (1989) 87 *Michigan LR* 2442
Smith, G.R. "A Primer of Opinion Writing for Four Judges" (1967) 21 *Arkansas LR* 197
Smith, J.C. *Liability in Negligence* (1984)
Smith, T.B. "The Contribution of Lord Cooper of Culross to the Law of Scotland" (1955) 67 *Jur Rev* 249
Smith, T.B. *British Justice: The Scottish Contribution* (1961)
Spearing, A.C. "The Canterbury Tales IV: Exemplum and Fable" in *The Cambridge Chaucer Companion* (1986)
Spencer, J.R. "Blasphermous Libel Resurrected – Gay News and Grim Tidings" [1979] *CLJ* 245
Spiegelman, J. "Access to Justice and Human Rights Treaties" (2000) 22 *Sydney LR* 141
Squires, R. "Tilbury Town Today" in *Edwin Arlington Robinson: Centenary Essays* (Ed. Barnard, 1969) 175
St. John Stevas, N. "Obscenity and the Law" [1954] *Criminal Law R* 817
Stein, P., Shand, J. *Legal Values in Western Society* (1974)
Steven, H., ed. *Letters of Wallace Stevens* (1966)
Stevens, C.J. *Lawrence at Tregerthen* (1988)
Stevick, R.D. "The Metrical Style of E A Robinson" in *Edwin Arlington Robinson: Centenary Essays* (Ed. Barnard, 1969) 554
Stone, O.M. "Family Law" in "Symposium on the Teaching of Various Subjects"(1953) 3 *JSPTL* 107
Stone, O.M. "University Teaching of Law" (1960) 5 *JSPTL* 130
Stowe, H. "The Unruly Horse Has Bolted: *Tinsley v Milligan*" (1994) 57 *MLR* 441
Stuckey. M. "A Consideration of the Emergence and Exercise of Judicial Authority in the Star Chamber" (1993) 19 *Monash ULR* 117
Taylor, A.J.P. *The Origins of the Second World War* (1961)
Teachout, P.R. "Lapse of Judgment" (1989) 77 *California LR* 120
Teff, H. "Liability for Psychiatric illness after Hillsbrough" (1992) 12 *OJLS* 440

Thomson, A. "Critical Legal Education in Britain in *Critical Legal Studies* (1987, eds. Fitzpatrick and Hunt)
Thorhton, M. "Discord in the Legal Academy: the Case of the Feminist Scholar" (1993) 3 *Aust. Feminist LJ* 53
Tindall, W Y. *Reader's Guide to Dylan Thomas* (1962)
Van Doren, M. *Edwin Arlington Robinson* (1927)
Vendler, H. *Words Chosen Out of Desire* (1986)
Von Hirsch, A. *Doing Justice: The Choice of Punishments. Report for the Study of Incarceration* (1976)
Von Hirsch, A. *Past or Future Crimes* (1985)
Wade, E.C.S. "Mistaken Identity in the Law of Contract" (1922) *LQR* 201
Wade, H.W.R. *Administrative Law* (2nd Ed, 1967)
Walker, D.M. *Oxford Companion to Law* (1980)
Walker, N. *Why Punish?* (1991)
Waller, P.L., Williams, C.R. *Criminal Law: Text and Cases* (10th Ed 2005)
Ward, C (ed) *Walt Whitman: Civil War Poetry and Prose* (1995)
Ward, I. *Law and Literature : Possibilities and Perspectives.* (1995)
Watson, A. *The Nature of Law* (1977)
Weir, T. *A Casebook on Tort* (5th Ed 1983)
Welland, D. *Wilfred Owen: A Critical Study* (1978)
Wells, W.A.N. *Evidence and Advocacy* (1988)
White, J.B. *Justice as Translation: An Essay in Cultural and Legal Criticism* (1990)
Willard, J. "Illusions of the Origin of *Cy Prés*" (1894) 8 *Harvard LR* 69
Williams, D.G.T. "The Control of Obscenity" [1965] *Criminal LR* 472
Williams, G. *The Proof of Guilt: A Study of the English Criminal Trial* (3rd Ed, 1963)
Williams, G.L. "The Definition of Crime" (1955) 8 *Current Legal Problems* 107
Wilson Knight, G. *The Mutual Flame: On Shakespeare's Sonnets and The Phoenix and the Turtle* (2nd ed. 1982)
Wilson, C. *The Misfits: A Study of Sexual Outsiders* (1988)
Wilson, P. "What Future for the Prison?" in *Corrections Criminology* (Ed. O'Toole and Eyland 2005) 230
Winter, S. "The Cognitive Dimension of the *Agon* Between Legal Power and Narrative Meaning" (1989) 22 *Harvard Civil Rights – Civil Liberties LR* 323

Winters, Y. "The Shorter Poems" in *Edwin Arlington Robinson: A Collection of Critical Essays* (Ed. Murphy 1970) 40

Worthen, J. *D.H. Lawrence: The Life of an Outsider* (2005)

"Y". *The Autobiography of An Englishman* (1975)

Young, L., Monahan, G. *Family Law* (7th Ed 2009)

Zabel, M.D. "Robinson in America" in *Edwin Arlington Robinson: Centenary Essays* (Ed. Barnard, 1969) 29

Zellick, G. "Films and the Law of Obscenity" [1971] *Criminal LR* 216

Table of Cases

A Local Authority v W, L, T and R (by the Children's Guardian) [2006] 1 FLR 1 – **452**

A v B plc [2003] QB 195 – **547-8, 556**

A-G v Guardian Newspapers (No 2) [1990] 1 AC 109 – **557**

Alcock v Chief Constable of South Yorkshire [1992] 1 AC 310 – **495, 498, 502-512**

Anderson Greenwood and Co v NLRB 604 F 2d 322 (1979). – **127-8**

Anglo-Swedish Society v IRC (1931) 47 TLR 295 – **214**

Anns v Merton London Borough [1978] AC 728 at 751 – **59**

Apted v Apted and Bliss [1930] P 246 - **557**

Arab Bank plc v Mercantile Holdings Ltd The Times Law Reports October 10th 1993 – 24

Attorney-General (NSW) v Perpetual Trustee Co Ltd (1940) 63 CLR 209 – **204-5**

Attorney-General v Corke [1933] Ch. 89 – **527-8**

Attorney-General v Wilts United Dairies (1921) 37 TLR 884 – **274-5**

Baehr v Lewin 852 P 2d 44 (1993) – **50**

Bas v Tingy 4 US 37 (1800) – **89**

Blanch v Blanch and Crawford (1999) FLC 92-837 – **399**

Blomley v Ryan (1956) 99 CLR 632 – **411**

Bolton v Stone [1975] 2 NZLR 106 – **526**

Bonar Law Memorial Trust v IRC [1929] 1 Ch. 557 – **213**

Bonnard v Perryman [1891] 2 Ch. 269 – **538**

Boughey v The Queen (1986) 161 CLR 10 – **348-358**

Bourhill v Young [1943] AC 92 – **499**

Bowditch v Balchin (1850) 5 Ex 378 – **279**

Bowmakers Ltd v Barnet Instruments [1945] 1 KB 65 – **7,9,77 n13**

Bowman v Secular Society [1917] AC 406 – **218, 338-341**

Bradley v Bradley [1973] 3 All ER 750 **452** –

Bridgewater v Leahy (1998) 194 CLR 457. – **440-1**

British Steel Corporation v Granada Television Ltd [1981] AC 1096 – **552, 565**

Brooker v Police [2007] 3 NZLR 91 – **371**

Brown v State 216 SE 2d 356 (1975) – **118**

Brusewitz v Brown [1923] NZLR 1106 – **415, 418**

Burnie Port Authority v General Jones (1994) 170 CLR 520 - **528**
Busby v Chief Manager, Human Resources, Australian Telecommunications Commission (1988) 183 ALR 67 – **79 n 95**
Buxton v IRC (1962) 41 TC 235 – **214**

Calder and Hebble Navigation Co v Pilling (1845) 14 M & W 76 – **223**
Campbell v MGM Ltd [2004] 2 AC 457 – **540-1, 545**
Cashman v Jordan [2009] TASSC112 – **373-4**
Castle v St Augustine's Golf Links Ltd (1922) 38 TLR 615 - **526**
CC v AB [2007] 2 FLR 301 – **537-556**
Chandler v DPP [1964] AC 763 – **160, 162-6, 169, 171, 202**
Chard v Chard [1956] P 259 – **183, 474** n249
Chatenay v Brazilian Submarine Telegraph Co 1891] 1 QB 79 - **152-3**
Cheng Albert v Tse Wai Chun Paul (2000) 10 BHRC 525 – **539-40**
Chester v Bateson [1920] 1 KB 829 - **274**
Cleary v Cleary [1974] 1 WLR 73 - **461**
Clements Wire and Manufacturing Co. Inc v NLRB 589 F 2d 894 (1979) – 127-**8**

Collins v Brantford Police Services Board (2001) 158 CCC (3d) 405 - **560**
Commercial Bank of Australia v Amadio (1983) 151 CLR 447 – **413, 424**
Commissioners for Special Purposes of Income Tax v Pemsel [1891] AC 531 - **203**
Commonwealth v Aves 18 Pick, (35 Mass) 193 (1939) - **27**
Cooper Brookes (Wollongong) Pty Ltd v FCT (1981) 147 CLR 297 - **22**
Cottington v Fletcher (1740) 2 Atk 155 – **77 n 16**
Craig v R (1993) 49 CLR 426 - **430**
Cream Holdings Ltd v Banerjee [2005] 1 WLR 637 - **551**
Crowe v Graham (1968) 41 ALJR 402 - **258**
Cundy v Lindsay (1878) 3 App Cas 459 – **46-7**

Dawkins v Gown Suppliers The Times, February 4th 1993 - **234**
Dennis v Dennis [1955] P 153 - **462**
Devine v Byrd 667 F. Supp 414 (1982) - **117**
Distillers Co Biochemicals (Aust) Pty Ltd v Ajax Insurance Co Ltd (1970) 130 CLR 1 – **190**
Douglas v Hello! Ltd [2001] QB 967 – **543-5**

Donoghue v Stevenson [1932] AC 563 – **59, 71, 239, 496, 500**
DPP v Knuller [1973] AC 435 – **314-9**
DPP v Withers [1975] AC 824– **312**
Duchess of Argyll v Duke of Argyll [1965] 1 All ER 611. - **350**

Fenton v J Thorley & Co Ltd [1903] AC 443 – **355, 478**
Fisher v Lowe 333 NW 2d 67 (1983) – **116-8**
Fitzgibbon v Baker, Gardner and Leader Associated Newspapers: Re Schwarzkopff (1993) FLC 92-381 – **452**
Friedrich v Friedrich 78 F3d 1060 (1996, 6th Cir) – **33**

Galletly v Laird 1953 SC (J) 16 - **265**
Gallie v Lee [1969] 2 Ch. 18 – **81 n 218**
Genish-Grant v Director General, Department of Community Services (2002) 29 Fam LR 51 - **34**
Gillick v West Norfolk and Wisbech Area Health Authority [1986] AC 112 – **60-2**
Gilmour v Coats [1949] AC 426 – **233-4, 239**

Habershon v Vardon (1851) 4 De G & Sm 467 - **214**

Hambrook v Stokes Bros [1925] 1 KB 141 – **501**
Hewer v Bryant [1970] 1 QB 357 - **62**
Hill v Baxter [158] 1 QB 277 – **486-8**
Hinz v Berry [1970] 2 QB 40 - **73**
Home Office v Dorset Yacht Co [1970] AC 1004 – **57-9, 85 n370**

In re Fouveaux (1845) 14 M & W 76 - **226**
In re Rome 542 P 2d 676 (1975) – **119, 124**
In the Marriage of Deniz 1977) FLC 90-252 – **453**
In the Marriage of Gillie (1978) FLC 90-442 – **453, 465**
In the Marriage of Paisio (1979) FLC 90-659 - **234**
In the Marriage of Schwarzkopff (1992) FLC 92 - 303 - **407**
In the Marriage of Tye (*No 2*) (1976) FLC 90-048 – **455**
In the Marriage of Tye (1976) FLC 90-028 – **455**
Ingram and Others v Little [1961] 1 QB 31 – **37-9, 73**
Insurance Commissioner v Joyce 1948) 77 CLR 39 – **482-4**
IRC v McMullen [1981] AC 1 – **248**

Jaensch v Coffey (1984) 155 CLR 549 – **499-500**
Jameel v Wall Street Journal Europe SPRL [2007] 1 AC 359 –

552

JG and BG (1994) FLC 92-515 - **401**

K v Z (1997) FLC 92-783 – **32-35**
King's Norton Metal Co Ltd v Eldridge, Merrett W Co Ltd (1897) 14 TLR 98 – **44-5**
Kinney v Police [1971] NZLR 924 – **370**

Lahey v Sanderson [1959] Tas SR 17 at 21 - **374**
Lane v Wallace 579 F 2d 1200 (1978) - **117**
Lewis v Avery [1972] 1 QB 198 – **41-44, 47, 575**
Linwood v Andrews and Moore (1888) 58 LT 612 - **557**
Liversidge v Anderson [1942] AC 206 – **276-81**
Lochner v New York 198 US 45 (1905) - **26**
Louth v Diprose (1992) 175 CLR 162 – **410-439**
M v M (2000) FLC 93-006 - **403**
Mackensworth v American Trading Transport Co 367 F. Supp 373 (1973). – **113-118**
Marbury v Madison 5 US 137 (1803) - **89**
McGovern v Attorney-General [1981] 3 All ER 493 – **214-5, 218**
McGowan v Langsmuir 1931 SLT 94 – **255-8, 261**
McLoughlin v O'Brien [1983] 1 AC 410 – **497-507**

Melser v Police [1967] NZLR 437 – **366, 369-72**
Minckleston v Brown (1801) 6 Ves 53 – 77 n 16
Miller v Jackson [1977] QB 966 – **98-102, 105, 131, 133-5, 578**
Mozes v Mozes 239 F 3d 1067 (2001) – **129**

National Anti-Vivisection Society v Inland Revenue Commissioners [1948] AC 31 – **208-12, 217, 225-6, 248**
Nelson v Nelson (1995) 184 CLR 538 – **6-8, 11, 15-6, 18**
Nettleship v Weston[1971] 2 QB 691 – **481, 486**
Neville Estates Ltd v Madden [1949] AC 426 - **233**
Newcastle Breweries v R [1920] 1 KB 854 - **247**
Newell v Gillingham Corporation [1941] 1 All ER 552 – **172-6**
NLRB'S v Robbins Tyre and Rubbert Co 437 US 214 (1978) – **127**

Orford v Orford (1921) 58 DLR 251 – **462**

Page v Horne (1848) 11 Beav. 227 – 272
Palsgraf v Long Island Railroad Co 248 N.Y. 339 (1928) – **478**
Pell v Trustees of National Gallery [1998] 2 VR 391.720 – 225

People v Defoe 150 NE 585 (1926) – **72**
Perre v Anand Pty Ltd (1999) 198 CLR 180 – **508**
Phillips v Brooks Ltd [1919] 2 KB 243 – 22
Phillips v Eyre (1870) 6 LR QB 1 – **35, 63**
Phillips v Phillips (2002) FLC 93-104 – **455**
Plessy v Ferguson 163 US 537 (1896) – **28**
Polanski v Condé Nast Publications Ltd [2005] 1 WLR 637 – 357
Proprietary Articles Trade Association v Attorney-General of Canada [1931] AC 310 – **309**

R (at the prosecution of Zadig) v Halliday [1917] AC 260 – **280**
R v Bond (1990) 48 A Crim R 1 – **375**
R v Brown [1994] 1 AC 212 – **287, 319,**
R v Central Independent Television plc. [1994] Fam. 192 – **544-5**
R v Chief Metropolitan Magistrate; Ex parte Chowdhury [1991] 1 QB 429 – **343**
R v Clarence (1888) 22 QBD 23 – **54**
R v Clarke [1949] 2 All ER 448 – **54**
R v Coyer (1988) 20 OAC 105 – **561**

R v Donovan [1997] QB 47 – **295**
R v Gosney [1971] 2 QB 691 - **488**
R v Hicklin (1868) LR 3 QB 360 – **257**
R v Lemon and Gay News [1979] AC 617 – **336**
R v Llewellyn-Jones (1967) 51 Cr. App Rep 204 - **322**
R v Martin Secker and Warburg [1954] 2 All ER 683 – **260**
R v Mayling [1963] 2 QB 717 – 169, 206
R v Miller [1954] 2 QB 282 – **53**
R v Perez Varges (1986) 8 NSWLR 559 – 246
R v R [1992] 1 AC 599 – **55-6**
R v Sargeant (1967) 51 Cr. App Rep 204. – 213
R v Somerset County Council, ex parte Fewings 1 All ER 513. – 144
R v Spurge [1961] 2 QB 205. – 319
R v Stanley [1965] 2 QB 327 – **264-5**
R v Wilson [1996] 2 Cr App Rep. 214 – **294**
R v Whitehead [1929] 1 KB 99 at 102 – 68
Re Blunn v Cleaver: Re Section 48 of the Administrative Appeals Tribunal Act 197 (1993) 119 ALR 65 – **20-22, 48**
Re Bushnell [1975] 1 WLR 1596 – **214**
Re Caus [1934] 1 Ch. 162 – **233**

Re Hopkins. [1965] Ch. 669 – 164-165
Re Hopkinson [1949] 1 All ER 346 – **214**
Re Shaw [1957] 1 WLR 729 – **248-50, 317-8**
Red Food Stores v NLRB 604 F 2d 324 (1979) - **128**
Repatriation Commission v Law (1980) 31 ALR 140 – **189, 195**
Repatriation Commission v O'Brien (1984) 58 ALR 119 - **195**
Ridge v Baldwin [1964] AC 40 – **281**
Roberts v City of Boston 5 Cush. (Mass) 198 (1849) - **27**
Roberts v Ramsbottom 248 N.Y. 339 (1928) – **480-1, 486-8**
Robinson v *Pioche, Bayerque & Co* 5 Cal. 460 (1855) – **140 n157**
Roper v Roper [1972] 1 WLR 1314 – **461**
Ruka v Department of Social Welfare [1996] NZFLR 913 – **56**
Rylands v Fletcher (1866) LR 1 Ex 265; (1868) LR 3 HL 230 – **524-6**

S.C.M (United Kingdom) Ltd v W.J. Whitall and Sons Ltd (1971) 1 QB 337 - 19
Schaefer v Schuhmann [1972] AC 572 – **558**
Sedleigh-Denfeld v O'Callaghan [1940] AC 880 at 903 – **131-2**
Shaw v DPP [1962] AC 220 – **309**

Solle v Butcher [1950] 1 KB 671 – **81 n218**
Sowler v Potter [1940] 1 KB 271 – **45-6**
Spartan Steel and Alloys Ltd v Martin Co (Contractors) Ltd [1973] QB 27 – **28-31**
Stack v Boyle 342 US 1 (1951) - **382**
State of Kansas ex rel Commission on Judicial Qualifications v Richard J. Jones 623 P 2d 1307 (1981) – **124**
Stephens v Avery [1988] 1 Ch. 449 – **546, 548**
Stuart v Laird 5 US 299 (1803) - **89**
Sturges v Bridgman 1897) 11 Ch. D. 852 – **134-5**
Sullivan v Sullivan(1818) 2 Hag Con 238 – **453**

T and N (2003) FLC 93-172 - 267
Tammer v *Estonia* (2001) 29 EHRR CD 257 - **572**
The Church of the New Faith v Commissioner for Payroll Tax (Victoria) (1983) 154 CLR 120 – **235-9**
The Observer and The Guardian v United Kingdom 2006] 1 FLR 1 - **543**
The Zomora [1916] 2 AC 77 – **162**
Theakston v MGN Ltd [2002] EMLR 398 – **546**

Thomas v Times Book Co [1965] Ch. 669 – **251-3**
Thornton v Howe (1979) FLC 90-659 – 156
Tinsley v Milligan [1994] AC 340 – **8-11, 15-18**

US v Batson 782 F 2d 1307 (1986) - **126**
US v Ven-Fuel Inc. 602 F 2d 747 (1979) – **125**

Victoria Park Racing and Recreation Grounds Co v Taylor (1937) 58 CLR 479 – **533**
Vita Food Products Inc v Unus Shipping Co [1939] AC 277 - **152**

Von Hannover v Germany (2005) 40 EHRR 24 – **546, 553**

Watmore v *Jenkins* [1962] 2 QB 57 – 319
Weatherall v Canada (Attorney-General) [1993] 2 SCR 872 – **562**
Weisz, ex p Hector McDonald Ltd [2007] 2 FLR 301- **557**
Weller v Foot and Mouth Disease Research Institute (1979) FLC 90-659 - **239**
Wheat v Fraker. 130 SE 2d 251 (1963) – **115, 118**
Wilton v Farnworth (1948) 76 CLR 646 – **418, 425**
Wingrove v United Kingdom (1996) 24 EHHR 1 - **543**

Index

Abraham and Isaac (Biblical story) - 147
Accident- definition - 28-9
Accidents, Automobile - 29
Adultery – 461-2, 464-6, 539, 548-9
Advancement, Presumption of – 6-8, 16
Advocacy - 12-13, 564
Affray - 323
Aftermath doctrine – 497, 502-9, 537, 581
American Civil War - 200
Analogy - 28, 30, 33, 72, 103, 2270, 295, 321-2, 405, 414, 484, 497, 529
Anderson, Doug, "Infantry Assault" – 171-2
Annulment thesis – 321-2
Apollinaire, Guillaume "Les Onze Mille Vierges" - 346
Apprehend violence orders - 399
Apprenticeship – 172-5
Aristotle - 48, 72, 103-4
 - *The Art of Rhetoric* - 104
Armstrong, Thomas (1848-1920)
 -"The Trimdon Grange Explosion"- 493-5
 - "Wor Nannie's a Maisor" - 495
Assault - 55, 287-290, 293-4, 321-2, 339, 352, 375, 399, 405-8, 465, 498, 500, 502, 508, 560
Auden, W.H. "September 1, 1939" – 155-16

Audience – 13, 74, 87, 96, 106-111, 169, 219, 327, 441, 579, 589
Automatism - 481

Bacon, Francis – 249-251
Barristers- training - 110
Blake, William, "Jerusalem" -
Blasphemy – 335-340, 344-8
Bodily harm – 287-290, 294, 349-50, 356, 375
Boxing - 219
Bragg, Billy - 381
Brighton, Kate, "Anthem" – 145-6
Britain:
- Commercial dominance - 152-3
- Military decline - 152
Burke, Edmond, *Revolution in France* - 531

Capitalism - 159
Carroll, Lewis, "The Hunting of the Snark" - 130
Carter, Sydney, "Friday Morning" – 347-8
Chain novel - 28, 31-34, 40-41, 66-67
Characterisation – 62, 71, 92
Charity, Definition of - 203-4, 213
Chaucer, Geoffrey
 - *Canterbury Tales* - 325
 - "The Pardoner's Tale" – 325-335, 348, 550, 586

Cherokee nation - 180
Child
- Best interests of - 33
- Custody – 57, 62, 234-5, 407. 409, 465, 528

Children
- Emotional Damage/ Abuse – 403-4, 406
- Rights - 541

Church of the New Faith – 235, 239
Civil disobedience – 161, 165
Civil law – judge's role - 13-14
Class – 149, 154, 210-1
Clough, Arthur Hugh, "The Latest Decalogue"-
Cold War - 166
Commercial Law - 152
Common Law – 6, 9, 13-14, 27, 34-35, 41, 46, 53, 55, 60, 91, 98, 111-5, 164-5, 183, 248, 257-8, 270, 278, 310, 317-8, 338, 340-9, 350, 352, 379, 398, 409, 429, 431, 500, 535-6, 544, 559
Compensation payments – 17, 20-23, 275, 483, 499-500, 505
Competence - 62
Competing rights - 551
Confidentiality – 61, 534, 540, 542, 546-7, 557
Conflict of laws – 35, 63, 116
Conscientious objectors – 173-6
Consensual behaviour – 288, 290
Contemplative orders - 232
Contempt – 251, 338, 340, 374-5, 452, 555-557
Contraception – 60-61

Contract, Unconscionable -
Contracts - 6, 8, 17-18, 35-47, 52-3, 63
Convention - 48, 107, 109, 157, 171, 256, 583
Coprophobia - 261
Crabbe, George, *The Borough* - 117
Cricket – 99-102, 526, 555, 578
Crime, Nature of - 308
Criminal Conspiracy – 310-2
Criminal Law – 55, 290-1, 308-19, 337, 340-1, 351, 368, 376, 407-8
Critical Legal Studies – 49-53, 63-66
Cross-examination – 12, 161
Cruelty to animals – 209-213, 225

Daniel, Samuel, "Love" – 396-7
Davidson, John, "The Runnable Stag" – 219-222
Death, Presumption of - 18, 183
Death penalty *see* Execution
Deconstruction - 51
Defence of the Realm Acts 1914-1915 – 270-9, 296
Dehumanisation – 170-1, 176, 178, 184, 187, 195, 198-9, 205, 358
Demonstrations - 161
Denning, Lord – Style – 29-31, 42-44, 62, 99-102, 105, 428, 461
Dialogue – 105-7, 182,
Dickens, Charles - 5
Domestic violence *see* Family violence

Doubt, Reasonable - 125, 189, 192-4
Douglas, Keith, "Vergissmeinnicht" – 186-8
Drivers - duty of care – 483-4
Duffy, Carol Ann
- "Adultery" – 464-5
- "Passing Bells" - 75-76
- "Words, Wide Night" - 396

Duty of Care – 29-31
Dylan, Bob
- "As I Went out one Morning" – 530-1, 535, 559, 564
- *Highway 61 Revisited* - 109
- "Walls of Red Wing" – 372-3

Economic loss – 29,
Eliot, T. S., "Burnt Norton" - 450
Emphasis (in rhetoric) - 100, 108-9
Equitable relief - 7
Equity - 7-18, 112, 411-3, 425, 532, 537, 555
Erinyes, The *see* Furies, The
Erhardt, W. D., "Finding My Old Battalion Command Post"
European Convention on Human Rights – 56, 217, 5414, 559-60
Evidence - 10, 13-4, 24, 33, 40, 42-43, 45, 60, 72, 87, 123-4, 153, 161-5, 173-4, 182, 193-4, 197, 216, 233, 249-253, 258-91, 260, 273, 277-8, 288-9, 294, 296, 337-8, 341-3, 367, 370-1, 337-8, 398, 400-2, 405, 411, 414-20, 422, 425, 430-7, 585

Execution – 321, 327, 356-62, 531, 587
Exegesis - 34

Fair trial - 119
False imprisonment - 280
False pretences - 36
Family Law – 33, 47, 53, 91, 262, 397-8, 400, 407, 409-10, 449, 461, 465, 545, 549-50, 588-9
Family violence – 408, 452, 548
Faulkner, William - 5
Fear – 148, 150, 155, 208, 401, 403, 306, 445-53
Fiction in law v legal fiction - 50
Flogging – 286-88, 296
Foreseeability – 30, 479-80, 496-509, 529
Fox hunting - 292
Fraud – 7-16, 36-47, 125-6, 318, 325, 415-19,, 453
Freedom of speech – 534, 538, 540, 544, 551, 560, 565
Frisk searching – 562-3
Frost, Robert, "Mending Wall" – 518-22, 530
Fry, Stephen - 206, 511-2
Furies, The - 69

Gender – 420, 423-4, 428-9, 432, 434-9, 589
Geneva Red Cross Convention – 166-7
Gift, Presumption of - 10
Gifts – 10, 16-7, 205, 211-3, 218, 226-7, 233-4, 239, 248-52, 411-425, 435

Gilbert, W. S. *Patience* - 298
Grainger, Percy – 299-300
Greco-Roman litigation - 109
Greed versus need - 15
Grief – 33, 129, 282, 444, 491, 505

Habitual residence - 130
Hague Convention III
Hague Convention on Civil Aspects of International Child Abduction - 33
Hall, Donald , "When the Young Husband"
Harassment, Sexual – 427-8, 433-5, 437
Hard cases – 28-31, 67
Hardy, Thomas
- "Men Who March Away" – 144-8, 151
- "The Convergence of the Twain" - 512
- "The Man He Killed" – 184-5

Herbert, George,
- "Antiphon" - 235
- "The Elixir" – 227-8

Hermeneutics – 48,52, 60, 86,
Homosexuality – 51, 287, 314-6, 319, 336-8, 546-8
Hopkins, Gerard Manley,
- "Heaven-Haven: A Nun Takes the Veil" - 232
- "I Wake and Feel the Fell Dark, Not Day" – 229-230
- "The Wreck of the Deutchland" - 512

Horace, *Epistles I* - 110

Hostile intent - 352
Howe, Julia Ward, "The Battle Hymn of the Republic" – 180-1
Hughes, Ted , *Cave Birds*
Hugo, Richard, "On Hearing a New Escalation" - 149
Human interest – 70
Human rights – 530-1
Hunting - 219-222

Illegal transaction - 7, 9-10
Imagination – 86-7,89, 92, 96, 98, 154, 250, 286, 467, 578-9, 588
Impartiality (Portia) – 12-13
Imprisonment, 'Preventative' – 324, 333
Indulgences, Selling of - 235-6
Injury, Physical – 478-485
Injury, Psychological – 507, 513
Inquisitorial versus adversary system - 13
Intention – 6, 17-8, 21, 39, 55, 123, 152, 153, 205, 214, 225, 252, 260, 274, 322, 3336-344. 348-9, 350, 352, 356, 420, 454, 486-9, 594
International law – 143, 144, 159-6, 166-7
International law, Public - 398
Intimidation – 104, 371

Jarrell, Randall, "The Death of the Ball Turret Gunner" – 169-170
Judges – Freedom of speech – 120, 340
Judgements as literary text – 28, 33

Judicial conduct – 120-4
Judicial decision – 6, 34, 46, 64-66, 342
Judicial humour - 122
Judicial rhetoric – 176, 404, 579
Jurisprudence – 53, 543
Jurors - Eligibility - 50

Kipling, Rudyard,
- "Mesopotamia 1917" - 185
- "My Boy Jack" – 182-4
- "The Mother's Son" – 513-5

Koch, Kenneth, "Permanently" – 575-7

Langland, William, *The Vision of Piers Plowman*
Language – 19, 22-25, 49, 51-52, 74, 86, 102, 108, 114, 118, 169, 184, 188, 192, 206, 214, 222, 224, 272, 279, 317, 340, 345, 351, 444-5, 461, 509, 517, 557, 577-8, 586, 590
Larkin, Phillip, "MCMXIV" – 150-1, 153-5, 167-9
Law and literature - justification for study – 6, 14, 18-9,25-8, 47-7
Law and literature - study of – 50, 64, 68, 73-4
Lawful correction – 292-3, 296
Lawrence, D. H.
- expulsion from Cornwall - 268
- *Kangaroo* - 276, 296-7
- *Lady Chatterley's Lover* – 253, 260
- "Liberty's Old Old Story" - 297
- "Neptune's Little Affair with Freedom" - 253-4
- "New Brooms" - 297
- *Pansies* – 260-65, 297
- "Jeune Fille", "Be a Demon"," Demon Justice","Innocent England" - 263
- *The Rainbow* - 253, 267
- *Women in Love* - 253

Lee, Harper, *To Kill a Mockingbird* - 5
Legal decision process – 60,
Legal education - Teaching Methodology – 47-9, 63-5
Legal judgment - Teaching of – 5-6, 18, 63
Legal judgment - Written in verse – 113-125
Legal process – 313, 66, 160, 166, 439, 583-4, 589
Legal realism - 64
Legal reasoning – 22, 34, 57, 62, 64, 66, 152
Legal text, the – 28, 48-52, 60
Legislative intention - 22
Libel – 340-1, 538
Libel, Blasphemous – 336-7, 342-5, 543, 586
Love – 396, 403-4, 410, 412-3, 419, 420, 422, 425, 442, 451-2, 454, 458-63, 491, 500, 503, 506

Manslaughter - 375
Marriage – 32, 50-1. 54-6, 234, 236, 399-401, 497-8, 410, 414, 422, 444, 449, 451, 453-4, 457-63

McAuley, James, "Because" – 458-61
McDonnell, A. E., *England, Their England* - 101
McGonagall, William Topaz, "The Tay Bridge Disaster" – 510-2
Melville, Herman
- *Billy Budd* - 27
- "Shiloh: A Requiem" – 200-1
- "The College Colonel" - 179

Metaphor – 26, 51, 67, 71-5, 88, 97-8, 148, 150, 160, 168-9, 188, 281-2, 321-2, 431, 450, 457, 492
Millay, Edna St. Vincent
- "The Fawn" – 207-8
- "Time /does Not Bring Relief"

Mistaken identity – 37-46, 52, 67, 90
Morality – 5, 29, 104, 212, 224-6, 285, 309, 311, 319, 369, 398, 537, 548, 582, 582, 585
Motive – 15-8, 89, 162, 164-6, 237, 273, 338, 340, 342, 443, 449, 454, 539-49, 550, 590
Mourning – 75, 492
Murder – 234, 321, 333-347, 348, 349-350, 354, 356, 360, 587

Narrative in legal analysis
Negligence – 30, 59, 134, 152, 239, 479, 481-8, 490, 497-500, 503, 506, 524
Neighbours, Disputes between - 518-20, 592

Nemerov, Howard, "Redeployment" – 198-200
Nemesis - 320
Nervous shock – 30, 496-506, 545
Nicholson, Norman, "The Field" - 100
Non-payment of wages
Nostalgia - 155
Nuclear disarmament – 160-1
Nuisance – 131-3
Nuisance, Private – 133, 525

Obscenity – 254-267, 336, 340, 583
Obscure meaning – 19, 51, 98, 108, 151, 331, 335, 445, 451
Official Secrets Act 1911 – offences against – 161-2
Outcomes approach - 63
Owen, Wilfred –
- "Anthem for a Doomed Youth" – 75,
- "Dulce et Decorum Est" – 149, 167-9
- "Strange Meeting" - 185
- "The Parable of the Old man and the Young" – 147-9, 154, 166

Ownership, Joint – 9-10

Paine, Tom (1737-1809)
- *The Age of Reason* - 531
- *The Rights of Man* – 531, 536, 559

Paradox - 158-8, 170, 182, 207, 347-8, 378, 396-7, 429, 452, 516, 578, 581, 588

Parental rights - 61
Past, The idea of – 99-102
Patmore, Coventry, "A London Fete" - 357-61
Persuasion, Means of - 103-4, 108, 111, 215, 565, 579, 583-4
Plain English – 23, 52
Pliny *Ep VI* – 11
Policy – 7, 16, 29-31, 66
Pope, Alexander - 117
Portia (Shakespeare character) – 11-14
Possibility – 8, 17, 31, 193-4, 197, 202, 211, 264, 276, 332-3, 339, 351, 354-5, 413, 420, 425, 428, 443, 464, 457, 462, 483, 486, 497,-8, 501, 511,523, 528, 556, 587, 587
Presumption – 6-11, 16-8, 38-43, 46, 90, 164, 182, 341-2, 381, 415-6, 433
Presumption of death – 18, 183, 442
Primogeniture - 4424
Prison officers – 372
Prisoners – 380-5
Prisoners of conscience - 214
Privacy – 133, 158, 264, 290, 295, 313, 364, 408, 584, 593-4
Probability – 341-2, 350, 462, 587
Professional discourse – 18-9
Profits, Loss – 28-30
Property gifts/sales - undue influence – 411-25, 435
Property damage - 29
Property interest /right - 10
Provocation – 401-2, 465

Proximity – 134, 213, 482, 496-506, 592
Psychological disability
Psychological injury - 592
Public benefit – 208, 212, 215, 218, 226-7, 233, 239,
Public conscience test – 9-10
Public interest – 133, 163, 275, 295, 374, 538, 544-5, 552-3, 556, 561
Public mischief – 279, 310-3
Public scorn and ridicule – 117-124
Public v private interest – 133, 275, 295
Punishment, Function of - 215-7, 257, 270-1, 310, 318-320

Rape in marriage – 54-6, 67
Rationalisation, ex post facto – 22, 67
Religion - legal definition – 233-9
Religious faith – 229, 331, 512, 522, 531, 549
Repatriation cases – 189-197
Representation – 36-7, 46
Research – 143-5, 148-9, 169, 173, 175-6, 181, 184, 197, 203,208, 211, 213, 218-9, 220, 226, 237-40, 248-9, 313, 406, 438, 583, 587
Retribution - 320-4, 331, 334-6, 359, 364, 383, 385-7
Rhetoric – 53, 64, 86-7, 100, 103-113, 131, 135, 248, 253, 255, 266, 273, 279, 296, 4101, 493-4, 410,

420, 441, 458, 493, 509, 518, 527, 535, 536, 564-5, 575-596
Rhetoric, Classical – 109-112
Rhetoric, Literary – 86-88, 91, 95, 106, 108, 117
Rhetoric, Tendentious – 110, 105
Rich, Adrienne - 597
Right wing - 296
Robinson, Edwin Arlington
- "Eros, Turanos" – 444, 446-58
- "Miniver Cheevey" - 445
- "Richard Corey" - 445
- "The Clerks" - 445
- "The Sheaves" - 446
- "The Unforgiven" - 451
- "Tristram" – 595-6
Roethke, Theodore
- "Elegy for Jane" – 490-1
- "In a Dark Time" – 515-7
Rushdie, Salman ,*The Satanic Verses*
Rylands v Flecher, Rule in - 524-30

Sado-masochism – 285-88
Sandburg, Carl, "Grass"
Satire - 101
Scientology *see* Church of the New Faith
Scott, Margaret – 467-8
Segregation - 28
Semantics - 587
Sentence structure
Sentencing – 321-2
Sentimentality - 220
Shakespeare, William
- "Sonnet LXV" - 68
- *Much Ado About Nothing*
- *The Merchant of Venice* see Portia
Shaw, Lemuel (1781-1861) – 27-8
Sin – 330, 333, 586
Slavery - 27
Smith, Iain Crichton, "The Bouquet [15]" in *Poems for SJ* - 445
Smollett, Tobias, *Tristram Shandy* - 67
Social class – 420-3
Social security payments – 9. 11, 15
Speech – 86, 103, 105-110, 175, 545, 552-3, 565, 577, 579, 593
Sport – 100, 150, 219, 223, 291-2, 481-4, 488
Standard of care
Stereotypes - 55
Stevens Wallace,
- "Cy est Pourtraicte, Madame Ste Ursule.." – 345-6
- Harmonium
- "The Idea of Order at Key West" – 91-7
- "The Motive for Metaphor" – 97-8, 130
Storytelling , Legal – 420-42
Style(s) – 98, 102-5, 107-9, 380
Swift, Jonathon, "Celia" - 261
Swinburne, Algernon
- *Atalanta in Calydon* - 281
- "Faustine" - 285
- "Itylus" 281, 286
- *Lesbia Brandon* - 287

- "Our Lady of Pain" - 285
- *Poems and Ballads* – 284-5, 298
- "Rococo" – 282-3
- *The Flogging Block* - 286

Tasmanian *Criminal Code* - 351-5
Taxation – 15, 218
Tennyson, Alfred, Lord
  - "Enoch Arden" – 18, 442
  - "The Charge of the Light Brigade" - 512
The Pearl (Magazine) - 287
The Whippingham Papers - 286
Thomas Dylan
  -"Ears in the Turrets Hear" -
  - "If I Were Tickled by the Rub of Love" - 85
  - *Holy Sonnets* - 69
  - "Lament" – 252, 386-7
  - "Refusal to Mourn the Death by Fire, of a Child in London" – 492-3
  - *Under Milk Wood* - 252-3
Thompson, Francis, "The Hound of Heaven"- 230-2
Tort damage - 115
Treaty of Versailles - 156
Trespass – 45, 524-530
Trusts – 6, 13, 16, 18, 52, 203-4, 214, 217, 227, 234, 248-9
Trusts, Charitable – Tax exemption – 203-4
Trusts, Resulting - 6-8, 16-7, 110

Universal Declaration of Human Rights - 214

Verse as a vehicle for judgement – 113-125
Vietnam War – 149, 171-2, 198, 367
Vivisection – 208-216, 248

War – aftermath – 176-7, 118, 201-3
War – conventions of – 143-4, 166
War – declaration of - 143
War - dehumanisation/depersonalisation – 170-2, 176, 178, 184, 187-9, 203
War – rules of – 143-4, 166
War and class - 149, 154
War and elites - 158
War service – Incapacity claims – 189-19, 195
War service – Widow's pension – 189-191
War, 1914-1918 – 144-8, 150-1, 154, 270-9, 296
War, 1914-1918 – Soldier's innocence/ignorance – 151-5, 169
War, Afghanistan - 145
Whitman, Walt
  - "The Singer in the Prison" – 383-5
  - "The Wound Dresser" - 385
Wilbur, Richard "The Winter" - 450
Wilde, Oscar, *The Importance of Being Ernest* - 15

Wolfenden Committee on Homosexuality and Prostitution
Wordsworth, William
- "Michael: A Pastoral Poem" - 442
- "Nuns Fret not at their Convent's Narrow Rooms" - 430

Young offenders – 366, 371, 588

i want morebooks!

Buy your books fast and straightforward online - at one of world's fastest growing online book stores! Environmentally sound due to Print-on-Demand technologies.

Buy your books online at
www.get-morebooks.com

Kaufen Sie Ihre Bücher schnell und unkompliziert online – auf einer der am schnellsten wachsenden Buchhandelsplattformen weltweit! Dank Print-On-Demand umwelt- und ressourcenschonend produziert.

Bücher schneller online kaufen
www.morebooks.de

VDM Verlagsservicegesellschaft mbH
Heinrich-Böcking-Str. 6-8   Telefon: +49 681 3720 174   info@vdm-vsg.de
D - 66121 Saarbrücken   Telefax: +49 681 3720 1749   www.vdm-vsg.de

Printed in Great Britain
by Amazon